Essentials of Human Communication

Essentials of Human Communication

NINTH EDITION

Joseph A. DeVito
Hunter College of the City University of New York

Boston   Columbus   Indianapolis   New York   San Francisco   Amsterdam
Cape Town   Dubai   London   Madrid   Milan   Munich   Paris   Montréal   Toronto   Delhi
Mexico City   São Paulo   Sydney   Hong Kong   Seoul   Singapore   Taipei   Tokyo

Publisher, Communication: Karon Bowers
Editorial Assistant: Nikki Toner
Director of Development: Brita Nordin
Program Team Lead: Maureen Richardson
Program Manager: Anne Ricigliano
Project Team Lead: Melissa Feimer
Project Manager: Raegan Heerema
Product Marketer: Becky Rowland
Project Coordination, Text Design, and Electronic Page Makeup: Integra
Cover Creative Director: Maria Lange
Cover Credit: Kenneth Munzlinger/Getty Images

Text Permissions Specialist: Peggy Davis
Text Permissions Project Manager: Tom Wilcox, Lumina Datamatics, Inc.
Photo Research: Jen Simmons, Lumina Datamatics, Inc.
Digital Project Lead: Peggy Bliss
Digital Media Project Manager: Sean Silver
Operations Manager: Mary Fischer
Manufacturing Buyer: Mary Ann Gloriande
Printer/Binder: LSC Communications
Cover Printer: LSC Communications

Credits and acknowledgments borrowed from other sources and reproduced, with permission, in this text-book appear on pages 343–346.

Library of Congress Cataloging-in-Publication Data

DeVito, Joseph A.,
    Essentials of human communication / Joseph A. DeVito. — Nineth Edition.
        pages cm
    Includes bibliographical references and index.
    ISBN 978-0-13-418495-1 — ISBN 0-13-418495-5
    1. Communication.   I. Title.
    P90.D483 2017
    302.2—dc23

                                                    2015030617

Student Edition:
ISBN-13: 978-0-13-418495-1
ISBN-10:   0-13-418495-5

Instructor's Review Copy:
ISBN-13: 978-0-13-420244-0
ISBN-10:   0-13-420244-9

À la Carte:
ISBN-13: 978-0-13-420245-7
ISBN-10:   0-13-420245-7

PEARSON

www.pearsonhighered.com

Contents

Specialized Contents

SKILL DEVELOPMENT EXPERIENCES

These exercises are designed to help you work actively with the skills and applications discussed in the text and to help you make these skills a part of your everyday communication behavior.

Welcome to Essentials of Human Communication, Ninth Edition

It's a pleasure to write a preface to this ninth edition of *Essentials of Human Communication*. This book continues to be responsive to the need for a brief, interesting, but serious text that emphasizes the *essential* theories, research, and especially the skills of human communication, including interpersonal communication, small group communication, and public speaking. I continue to try my best to follow Einstein's directive that "things should be made as simple as possible, but not simpler." This new, ninth edition remains true to that central purpose. The overriding theme and goal of this textbook is to help you build greater competence in interpersonal, group, and public communication. You should emerge from this course a more effective interpersonal communicator, group member and leader, and public speaker.

This ninth edition of *Essentials of Human Communication* is divided into three parts: Part One, Foundations of Human Communication, includes five chapters that cover the concepts and principles of human communication: the communication process, perception of self and others, listening, verbal messages, and nonverbal messages. Part Two, Interpersonal and Small Group Communication, also includes five chapters. Chapters 6, 7, and 8 cover the concepts and skills of interpersonal communication and conversation, interpersonal relationships, and managing interpersonal conflict; Chapters 9 and 10 focus on small group interaction, the types of small groups, and the principles of effective group membership and leadership. Part Three, Public Speaking (Chapters 11–14), explains the nature of public speaking and the principles and skills for preparing and presenting effective informative and persuasive speeches.

What's New in the Ninth Edition?

REVEL™

Educational technology designed for the way today's students read, think, and learn

The most noticeable change in this new edition is the incorporation of REVEL, a new educational technology designed for the way today's students read, think, and learn. When students are engaged deeply, they learn more effectively and perform better in their courses. This simple fact inspired the creation of REVEL: an immersive learning experience designed for the way today's students read, think, and learn. Built in collaboration with educators and students nationwide, REVEL is the newest, fully digital way to deliver respected Pearson content.

REVEL enlivens course content with media interactives and assessments—integrated directly within the authors' narrative—that provide opportunities for students to read about and practice course material in tandem. This immersive educational technology boosts student engagement, which leads to better understanding of concepts and improved performance throughout the course.

Learn more about REVEL

http://www.pearsonhighered.com/REVEL/

Rather than simply offering opportunities to read about and study communication, REVEL facilitates deep, engaging interactions with the concepts that matter most. For example, when learning about small group communication, students are presented with a self-assessment that scores their level of apprehension when participating in group discussions. The results of the assessment prompt students to examine their level of anxiety in groups and consider how they could reduce their apprehension in these situations. By providing opportunities to read about and practice communication in tandem, REVEL engages students directly and immediately, which leads to a greater mastery of course material. A wealth of student and instructor resources and interactive materials can be found within REVEL, such as:

- **Test Yourself Self-Assessments** Interactive self-assessments allow students to analyze their own communication styles, enabling them to learn and grow over the duration of the course. A variety of self-assessment styles are offered, including fill-in-the-blank, True or False, and numerical ratings.

- **Dialogue and Speech Examples** In-line audio examples of effective and ineffective communication approaches are enhanced with audio demonstrations, adding dimension and reinforcing learning in a way that a printed text cannot. Dialogue examples range from effective communication between two people to individual communication strategies.

- **Videos and Video Quizzes** Video examples of interpersonal and group role-plays located throughout the narrative and speech samples located in the last four chapters boost mastery of the concepts, and many videos are bundled with correlating self-checks, enabling students to test their knowledge.

- **Interactive Figures** Interactive figures (such as Figure 2.3: Climbing to Higher Self-Esteem and Figure 8.2: The Process of Conflict Resolution) give students a hands-on experience, increasing their ability to grasp difficult concepts. By allowing students to examine specific parts of a model and offering accompanying real-life examples, broad and theoretical concepts suddenly become easier to understand.

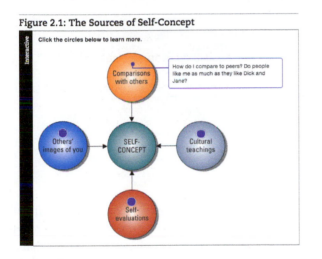

- **Interactive Cultural Maps** recall the major cultural differences (such as ambiguity tolerance, masculine and feminine orientation, and power distance) and illustrate how the impact on communication differs around the world. In REVEL, readers are given the opportunity to manipulate and interact with the maps.

- **Integrated Writing Opportunities** To help students connect chapter content with their own personal and social lives, each chapter offers two varieties of writing prompts: the journal prompt, eliciting a free-form, topic-specific response addressing topics at the module level, and the shared writing prompt, eliciting a focused, brief response addressing topics at the chapter level, which students can share with each other.

To access your own REVEL account and get more information about the tools and resources in REVEL, go to www.pearsonhighered.com/REVEL.

Text Features

In addition to the interactive enhancements of REVEL, this new edition fully integrates the latest research as well as updated examples, photos, and cartoons to keep the text current and pedagogically effective. Throughout the book, readers will find new instances of the following features.

- **Learning Objectives** Learning objectives appear at the beginning of the chapter, in the text proper (with each major heading), and in the summary at the end of the chapter. These objectives highlight the major concepts and skills of the chapter. The learning objectives system used here—and there are a variety of these—identifies three major levels of thinking, each of which is included throughout the text (Bloom, 1956; Teacher & Educational Development, 2005; Eggen & Kauchak, 2013):

  - **Knowledge** (recalling, remembering, and comprehending), introduced by such specific verbs as *define*, *paraphrase*, *describe*, and *differentiate*.

  - **Application** (applying a concept to a new situation), introduced by such specific verbs as *diagram*, *illustrate*, *use*, and *give examples*.

  - **Problem solving** (analyzing/breaking a concept into its parts, synthesizing/combining elements into a new whole, and evaluating/making value or appropriateness judgments), introduced by such specific verbs as *assess*, *construct*, *organize*, and *evaluate*.

- **Skill Development Experiences** appear at the ends of chapters and ask students to work actively with the concepts discussed in the text and cover a wide variety of essential communication skills. Completing these experiences will help readers apply the material in the chapter to specific situations and thereby increase and perfect their own communication skills. In REVEL, the Experiences are often interactive or short-answer writing opportunities.

Skill Development Experience

5.1 Selecting a Seat at the Company Meeting

Nonverbal choices influence your communication effectiveness and your image as a communicator.

The accompanying graphic represents a table with 12 chairs, one of which is occupied by the "boss." For each of the following messages, indicate (a) where you would sit to communicate each message and (b) any other possible messages that your choice of seat will probably communicate.

A. You want to ingratiate yourself with your boss. _____
B. You aren't prepared and want to be ignored. _____
C. You want to challenge the boss's proposal that is scheduled to come up for a vote. _____
D. You want to get to know better the person at seat number 7. _____

objectives. In REVEL, the Choice Points are available as interactive writing opportunities.

Communicating Ethically

THE ETHICS OF IMPRESSION MANAGEMENT

Impression management strategies may sometimes be used unethically and for less than noble purposes. For example, people may use affinity-seeking strategies to get you to like them so that they can then extract favors from you. Politicians frequently portray themselves as credible in order to win votes. The same could be said of the stereotypical used-car salesperson or insurance agent trying to make a sale. Some people use self-handicapping or self-deprecating strategies to get you to see their behavior from a perspective that benefits them rather than you. Self-monitoring strategies are often deceptive, designed to present a more polished image than what might surface without self-monitoring. And, of course, influencing strategies have been used throughout history in deception as well as in truth. Even image-confirming strategies can be used to deceive, as when people exaggerate their positive qualities (or make them up) and hide their negative ones.

ETHICAL CHOICE POINT

You're ready to join one (perhaps several) of the online dating services. You need to write your profile and are wondering if everyone (or nearly everyone) exaggerates, you shouldn't also. Specifically, you're considering saying that you earn a very good salary (actually, it's not so great but you're hoping for a promotion), that you're twenty pounds lighter (actually, you intend to lose weight), and that you own a condo (actually, that's a goal once you get the promotion and save a down payment). If you don't exaggerate, you reason, you'll disadvantage yourself and not meet the people you want to meet. Also, you figure that people expect you to exaggerate and assume that you're probably a lot less ideal than your profile would indicate. *Would this be ethical?*

- **New summary tables** and bulleted lists throughout the text summarize major sections, making it easier for students to review section content and fix it more firmly in memory.

JOURNAL
COMMUNICATION CHOICE POINT
Face-to-Face

You've been communicating with Pat over the Internet for the past seven months and you finally have decided to meet for coffee. You really want Pat to like you. *What are some impression-management strategies you might use to get Pat to like you? What messages would you be sure not to communicate?*

Table 7.2 In a Nutshell Movement among the Stages as Predicted by Relationship Theories		
You move toward intimacy when:	**Relationship Stages**	**You move away from intimacy when:**
Attraction Theory Attraction increases; you're attracted to those who are similar, nearby, who reinforce you, and who you think are attractive	Contact	**Attraction Theory** Attraction decreases
Rules Theory Rules are followed comfortably and willingly.	Involvement	**Rules Theory** Rules are broken, disregarded, or disrespected.
Social Exchange Theory Rewards increase, costs decrease, profits increase. Relationships develop and are maintained when the rewards exceed the costs.	Intimacy	**Social Exchange Theory** Rewards decrease, costs increase, profits decrease
Equity Theory Equity prevails; each derives rewards in proportion to the costs paid. Relationships are satisfying when each person's rewards are proportional to their costs.	Deterioration	**Equity Theory** Inequities exist and grow greater; one person is under-benefited and one person is over-benefited
	Dissolution	

- **Viewpoints Photos and Captions** ask readers to consider a variety of communication issues, many of which are research based and/or focus on the themes of social media, the workplace, and culture.

- New and revised **figures** and **models** help illustrate such concepts as self-concept, self-esteem, perception, impression management, the power of nonverbal communication, and conflict management. In REVEL, many of the figures and models are interactive.

- **Essential terms** in boldface and a glossary at the end of the text help students learn and review essential terms. In REVEL, key terms appear in boldface with pop-up definitions and each chapter concludes with a flashcard deck for study and review.

- **The Public Speaking Sample Assistant** feature in each of the four public speaking chapters provide sample annotated speeches and outlines. New examples and speeches are included with accompanying videos.

VIEWPOINTS: Importance of Communication

Both men and women want partners who know how to communicate and listen. *How important, compared to all the other factors you might take into consideration in choosing a partner, is the ability to communicate and listen? What specific communication skills would you consider "extremely important" in a life partner?*

- Through Journal: **Communication Choice Points** and **Ethical Choice Points,** students are encouraged to identify, consider, and evaluate their communication choices in different contexts. In this edition, the choice points are more closely aligned with the chapter learning

Public Speaking Sample Assistant
THE PREPARATION OUTLINE

Here is a relatively detailed preparation outline similar to the outline you might prepare when constructing your speech. The side notes should clarify both the content and the format of a preparation outline.

Have you Ever Been Culture Shocked?

General Purpose:	To inform	The title, purposes, and thesis of the speech appear
Specific Purpose:	To inform my audience of the four phases of culture shock.	before the outline.
Thesis:	Culture shock can be described in four stages.	

INTRODUCTION

I. How many of you have experienced culture shock?

Chapter Updates

Here, briefly are some of the chapter-by-chapter changes. In addition to these changes, all chapters have been revised for greater clarity and less redundancy and the incorporation of new research, examples, photos, and cartoons. Structural changes include the placement of the skill development experiences at the ends of the chapters and the sample speeches at the end of the relevant chapters. The purpose here was to avoid interrupting the text flow and also to enable these experiences and speeches to be assigned as appropriate to the specific course goals. In addition, a variety of periodic summaries are used to recall the essential concepts of various sections of the text.

Chapter 1, The Essentials of Human Communication, includes expanded coverage on the benefits derived from studying human communication; making reasoned choices; and being an effective code switcher. New coverage includes the section titled "Communication Takes Place in Varied Forms," which addresses the importance of understanding both online and offline environments and a Cultural Map on ambiguity tolerance.

Chapter 2, Perception of Self and Others, contains three new figures that illustrate the sources of self-concept, how to climb to higher self-esteem, and impression management goals and strategies, as well as a new Cultural Map on masculine and feminine orientations. This chapter also includes new and revised coverage on comparison with others on social media sites, how to attack self-destructive beliefs, the advantages of preventing inaccurate perceptions, and guidelines for resisting pressure to self-disclose. The chapter ends with a new Skill Development Experience that deals with applying impression management strategies.

Chapter 3, Listening in Human Communication, features an expanded section on critical listening and a reorganized section on listening styles, now presented in a four-part model consisting of empathic, critical, polite, and active listening. The essential material from the table on communication between those with and those without hearing impairments (Table 3.1 in the previous edition) is now integrated into the basal text.

Chapter 4, Verbal Messages, now contains a new figure that illustrates disconfirmation with -isms (for example, racism, ageism, or sexism); an expansion of the exercise on confirming, rejecting, and disconfirming responses; and a reduction in certain sections that were thought too long.

Chapter 5, Nonverbal Messages, includes expanded coverage and updated research about the benefits of developing one's nonverbal communication competence and a new figure on the power of nonverbal messages. The section on temporal communication has been significantly expanded to include coverage of psychological time (with an integrated Self Test and Cultural Map on long- and short-term orientation), interpersonal time, and cultural time. The table on communication between people with and those without visual impairment (Table 5.4 in the previous edition) is now part of the basal text. A new summary table on channels of communication concludes the section.

Chapter 6, Interpersonal Communication and Conversation, opens with new headings that clarify and highlight the definition and process of interpersonal communication; the section on conversation includes the principle of cooperation; and the coverage on communication between people with and without speech disorders (Table 6.2 in the previous edition) is now part of the basal text. The chapter concludes with three new Skill Development Experiences on making small talk, making apologies, and giving or receiving compliments.

Chapter 7, Interpersonal Relationships, remains essentially as in the previous edition with the addition of a new figure summarizing the relationship theories and relationship movement and a variety of stylistic changes and tightening.

Chapter 8, Managing Interpersonal Conflict, introduces new coverage on social allergens and includes a new Cultural Map on success and a new figure on the process of conflict resolution.

Chapter 9, Small Group Communication, contains new coverage on the advantages and disadvantages of groups, specifically about the concepts of social facilitation and social loafing. This chapter also includes a new Cultural Map on high- and low-context cultures and concludes with a new Skill Development Experience on listening to new ideas.

Chapter 10, Members and Leaders in Small Group Communication, includes a new Cultural Map on high- and low-power distance.

Chapter 11, Public Speaking Preparation (Steps 1–6), contains new excerpts from a 2015 speech about Alzheimer's disease and a new Public Speaking Sample Assistant shows readers what *not* to do in a speech about biases. Audio and video excerpts of the sample speeches are available in REVEL.

Chapter 12, Public Speaking Preparation and Delivery (Steps 7–10), also includes several new speech excerpts, new tables on body motions and the functions of transitions, and updated research on how to thank audiences. Audio and video excerpts of the speech examples are available in REVEL.

Chapter 13, The Informative Speech, has been reorganized to present the three types of informative speeches directly after the first section on guidelines of informative speaking. The chapter also includes a new annotated informative speech on decellularization with accompanying video of the speech's delivery available in REVEL.

Chapter 14, The Persuasive Speech, has been reorganized to present the three types of persuasive speeches before supporting materials. The chapter also includes a new annotated persuasive speech on FBI entrapment with accompanying video of the speech's delivery available in REVEL.

Essential Content and Themes

Essentials of Human Communication highlights several interwoven themes in the study of human communication and—taken together—they define the uniqueness of this text: social media, culture, the workplace, choice, politeness, and ethics.

Social Media

All communication forms—interpersonal, small group, and public—incorporate the varied **social media** that are now an essential part of our everyday lives. And so, to take just one example, the definition of listening—long defined as the reception of auditory signals—is redefined to include the reading of social media messages. The reasoning is simply that if posting on Facebook and tweeting are examples of communication (which they surely are) then the reading of these messages must also be part of communication and seems to fit most logically with listening.

Culture

In *Essentials of Human Communication*, the crucial role that **culture** plays in your communication experiences is a recurring theme. You're living in a world defined by cultural diversity, where you interact with people differing in affectional orientation, socioeconomic position, race, religion, and nationality. Culture and cultural differences are always influential in communication. For this reason, this text fully integrates culture into every chapter, and it includes a new Cultural Maps feature that illustrates major cultural differences around the world in selected chapters where relevant. Topics covered include the following.

- Culture and communication, the importance of culture, the dimensions of cultural differences, the aim of a cultural perspective, ethnic identity and ethnocentrism, and a cultural map on ambiguity tolerance (Chapter 1).
- Cultural teachings in self-concept formation, increasing cultural sensitivity, stereotyping, self-disclosure and

culture, and a cultural map on masculine–feminine orientations (Chapter 2).
- The influences of culture and gender on listening (Chapter 3).
- Gender and cultural differences in directness and politeness; cultural rules in verbal communication; sexism, heterosexism, racism, and ageism; and cultural identifiers (Chapter 4).
- Cultural differences in nonverbal communication, most notably facial expressions, colors, touch, silence, and time orientation, and a cultural map on long and short-term orientation (Chapter 5).
- The role and influence of culture and gender in conversation (Chapter 6).
- Cultural and gender differences in friendship, love, and family relationships (Chapter 7).
- Gender and cultural influences on conflict and conflict management, cultural differences in face-enhancing and face-attacking strategies, and a cultural map on success (Chapter 8).
- Small group culture and the nature and importance of group and cultural norms in small group communication, high- and low-context cultures, and a cultural map of this orientation (Chapter 9).
- The role of culture in small group membership and leadership; cultural differences between individual and collective orientations and high- and low-power distances; and a cultural map of this orientation (Chapter 10).
- The role of culture in speech topics; guidelines to help public speakers avoid taboo topics when addressing culturally varied audiences; and cultural factors in audience analysis (Chapter 11).
- Cultural considerations in the language of public speaking, culture shock, and cultural sensitivity in speech criticism (Chapter 12).
- Cultural sensitivity in selecting supporting materials (Chapter 13).
- Adapting to the culture (collectivist, high-power distance, uncertainty avoidance, and long-term orientation) of the audience; and the impact of cultural differences on credibility appeals (Chapter 14).

The Workplace

Effective human communication is as important in the **workplace** as it is in any part of your life. Workplace material includes frequent examples, illustrations, and photo ViewPoints and discussions of a variety of clearly workplace-related topics such as workplace messages, values in the workplace as seen by long- and short-term-oriented executives, emotions at work, romantic relationships in the workplace, and workplace conflict. A separate booklet, *The Interviewing Guidebook*, focusing on informative and employment interviews, is available for packaging with this book or for purchase separately.

Choices

Throughout your communication interactions, you'll need to make **choices** between saying one thing or another, between sending an e-mail or calling on the phone, between being supportive or critical, and so on. Because of the central importance of choice, Journal: Communication Choice Points invite you to identify and evaluate your choices for communicating.

Ethics

Because the messages you use have effects on others, they also have ethical implications. As such, **ethics** receives focused attention throughout the text. Chapter 1 introduces ethics as a foundation concept in all forms of communication, an essential part of communication competence. In all remaining chapters, *Communicating Ethically* boxes highlight varied communication situations and ask you to apply ethical principles to various scenarios. For example, here are considered such ethical issues as cultural practices, lying, and ways to engage in interpersonal conflict ethically. These boxes will serve as frequent reminders that ethical considerations are an integral part of all the communication choices/decisions you make. A list of these Communicating Ethically boxes appears in the Specialized Contents.

Pearson MediaShare

Pearson's comprehensive media upload tool allows students to post video, images, audio, or documents for instructor and peer viewing, time-stamped commenting, and assessment. MediaShare is an easy, mobile way for students and professors to interact and engage with speeches, presentation aids, group projects, and other files. MediaShare gives professors the tools to provide contextual feedback to demonstrate how students can improve their skills.

Structured like a social networking site, MediaShare helps promote a sense of community among students. In face- to-face and online course settings, MediaShare saves instructors valuable time and enriches the student learning experience by providing contextual feedback.

- Use MediaShare to assign or view speeches, outlines, presentation aids, video-based assignments, role-plays, group projects, and more in a variety of formats including video, Word, PowerPoint, and Excel.
- Assess students using customizable, Pearson-provided rubrics or create your own around classroom goals, learning outcomes, or department initiatives.
- Set up assignments for students with options for full-class viewing and commenting, private comments between you and the student, peer groups for reviewing, or as collaborative group assignments.

- Record video directly from a tablet, phone, or other webcam (including a batch upload option for instructors) and tag submissions to a specific student or assignment.
- Set up Learning Objectives tied to specific assignments, rubrics, or quiz questions to track student progress.
- Embed video from YouTube to incorporate current events into the classroom experience.
- Set up quiz questions on video assignments to ensure students master concepts and interact and engage with the media.
- Sync slides to media submissions for more robust presentation options.
- Import grades into most learning management systems.
- Ensure a secure learning environment for instructors and students through robust privacy settings.
- Upload videos, comment on submissions, and grade directly from our new MediaShare app, available free from the iTunes store and GooglePlay; search for Pearson MediaShare.

Pearson MediaShare is available as a standalone product, as part of MyCommunicationLab, or in a package with REVEL.

Instructor and Student Resources

Key instructor resources include an Instructor's Manual (ISBN 0-13-420243-0), TestBank, (ISBN 0-13-420242-2), and PowerPoint Presentation Package (ISBN 0-13-420240-6). These supplements are available at www.pearsonhighered.com/irc (instructor login required). MyTest online test-generating software (ISBN 0-13-420239-2) is available at www.pearsonmytest.com (instructor login required). For a complete list of the instructor and student resources available with the text, please visit the Pearson Communication catalog, at www.pearsonhighered.com/communication.

Acknowledgments

I want to thank those who reviewed the text at the various stages of revision; they gave generously of their time and expertise and I am, as always, in their debt.

Diana Cooley: Lone Star College–North Harris
Charlotte Toguchi: Kapiolani Community College
Anna Maheshwari: Schoolcraft College
Norman Earls Jr: Valdosta State University
Shannon Proctor: Highline Community College
Ellen Bremen: Highline Community College
Willis Watt: Methodist University
Victoria Butler: Darton State College
Nader Chaaban: Montgomery College
Thomas Jewell: Bergen Community College

I also want to thank the many people who worked so hard to turn a manuscript into this book. I'm especially grateful to the people at Pearson who make revisions so enjoyable, especially communication editor Karon Bowers for her wise counsel and patience; Angela Kao for her developmental work and for turning printed material into the new REVEL system; Stephanie Laird for managing the book's assessment questions; Anne Ricigliano, program manager; Raegan Heerema, project manager; Nikki Tonner, editorial assistant; Blair Tuckman, senior field manager; Becky Rowland, product marketing manager; Margaret McConnell, Integra–Chicago project editor; and the photo researchers at Lumina.

Joseph A. DeVito
jadevito@earthlink.net
http://tcbdevito.blogspot.com

Chapter 1
The Essentials of Human Communication

The need for communication began at the beginning.

CHAPTER OUTLINE	Learning Objectives
Forms, Benefits, and Myths of Human Communication	**1.1** Identify the forms, benefits, and myths of human communication.
Communication Models and Concepts	**1.2** Draw a model of communication that includes sources–receivers, messages, context, channel, noise, and effects; and define each of these elements.
Principles of Communication	**1.3** Paraphrase the major principles of human communication.
Culture and Human Communication	**1.4** Explain the role of culture in human communication, the seven ways in which cultures differ from one another, the aim of a cultural perspective; and define *ethnic identity* and *ethnocentrism*.
Communication Competence	**1.5** Define *communication competence* and explain the qualities identified as part of competence.

Fair questions to ask at the beginning of this text and this course are "What will I get out of this?" and "Why should I study human communication?" One very clear answer is given by the importance of communication: It's a major part of human existence that every educated person needs to understand. Much as you need to understand history, science, geography, and mathematics, for example, you need to understand how people exchange thoughts and feelings, how they communicate interpersonally, in groups, on social media, and in public. But, as you'll see in the section on "Benefits of Studying Human Communication" and throughout this text's fourteen chapters, there are numerous practical benefits that you'll derive.

Forms, Benefits, and Myths of Human Communication

1.1 **Identify the forms, benefits, and myths of human communication.**

Human communication consists of the sending and receiving of verbal and nonverbal messages between two or more people. This seemingly simple (but in reality quite complex) process is the subject of this book, to which this chapter provides a foundation. Here we begin the study of human communication by looking first at the forms of human communication, the benefits you'll derive and the skills you'll learn, and some of the myths about communication (to get rid of them).

Forms of Human Communication

You'll accomplish these objectives and acquire these skills as you engage in and master a variety of human communication forms. **Intrapersonal communication** is the communication you have with yourself—when you talk with, learn about, and judge yourself. You persuade yourself of this or that, reason about possible decisions to make, and rehearse messages that you plan to send to others.

Interpersonal communication occurs when you interact with a person with whom you have some kind of relationship. Through interpersonal communication you interact with others, learn about them and yourself, and reveal yourself to others. Whether with new acquaintances, old friends, lovers, family members, or colleagues at work, it's through interpersonal communication that you establish, maintain, sometimes destroy, and sometimes repair personal relationships.

Interviewing is a form of interpersonal communication that proceeds by question and answer. Through interviewing you learn about others and what they know, counsel or get counseling from others, and get or don't get the job you want. Today, much interviewing (especially initial interviews) takes place through e-mail, phone conferencing, or video conferencing with Skype, for example.

Small-group communication or team communication is communication among groups of, say five to ten people and may take place face-to-face or, increasingly, in virtual space. Through small-group communication you interact with others, solve problems, develop new ideas, and share knowledge and experiences.

Public communication is communication between a speaker and an audience. Through public communication a speaker will inform and persuade you. And you, in turn, inform and persuade others—to act, to buy, or to think in a particular way. Much as you can address large audiences face-to-face, you also can address such audiences electronically. Through social networks, newsgroups, or

"I'd like to see you do this online."

blogs, for example, you can post your "speech" for anyone to read and then read their reactions to your message.

Computer-mediated communication is a general term that includes all forms of communication between people that take place through some kind of computer, whether it's on your smartphone or via a standard Internet connection as in social media such as Twitter and Facebook. Examples include e-mail, blogging, instant messaging, or posting or chatting on social network sites. Throughout this text, we'll make frequent reference to the similarities and differences between face-to-face and computer-mediated communication.

Mass communication refers to communication from one source to many receivers who may be scattered throughout the world. Newspapers, magazines, radio, television, and film are the major mass media. Though referred to in illustrations and examples throughout the text, this topic is beyond the scope of this book and this course.

This text focuses on all these forms of communication—and on you as both message sender and message receiver. It has two major purposes.

- **To explain the concepts and principles, the theory and research in human communication,** so that you'll have a firm understanding of what communication is and how it works.
- **To provide you with skills of human communication** that will help you increase your communication competence and effectiveness in your personal and professional lives.

Benefits of Studying Human Communication

Of all the knowledge and skills you have, those concerning communication are among your most important and useful. Your communication ability will influence how effectively you live your personal and professional life; it will influence your effectiveness as a friend and lover. It will often make the difference between getting a job and not getting it. Your communication skills will determine your influence and effectiveness as a group member and your emergence as group leader. Your communication skills will increase your ability to communicate information and influence the attitudes and behaviors of others in a variety of public speaking situations.

Let's identify more clearly the skills that you'll learn—and the corresponding benefits that you'll reap—through your study of human communication.

- **Critical and creative thinking skills,** emphasized throughout this book, help you approach new situations mindfully—with full conscious awareness, increase your ability to distinguish between a sound and valid argument and one that is filled with logical fallacies, and your ability to use language to reflect reality more accurately.
- **Interaction skills** help you improve your communication in a wide range of forms, from the seemingly simple small talk to the employment interview for the job of a lifetime. Interaction skills will enable you to communicate with greater ease, comfort, and effectiveness whether you're proposing a life-long relationship or apologizing for some transgression.
- **Relationship skills** enable you to build friendships, enter into love relationships, work with colleagues, and interact with family members. These are the interpersonal and relationship skills for initiating, maintaining, repairing, and sometimes dissolving relationships of all kinds. And unless you're going to be living totally alone, these are skills you'll use every day, in every encounter. These are the skills that businesses of all kinds have on their lists of most important competencies for organizational success; they are an essential part of business competence (Bassellier & Benbasat, 2004).

The Essentials of Human Communication

JOURNAL
COMMUNICATION CHOICE POINT
Choices and Human Communication

Throughout this book you'll find marginal items labeled Communication Choice Points. These items are designed to encourage you to apply the material discussed in the text to specific communication situations by first analyzing your available choices and then making a communication decision.

- **Leadership skills** enable you to communicate information effectively in small groups or with large audiences and your ability to influence others in these same situations are among your most important leadership skills. In a workplace world that operates largely on group interaction, these skills are increasingly essential if you are to be an effective organizational member and will help you rise in the organization. After all, people in power will often come to know you best through your communications. As you rise in the hierarchy, you'll need leadership skills to enable you to lead groups and teams in informative, problem-solving, and brainstorming sessions.

- **Presentation skills** enable you to present yourself as a confident, likable, approachable, and credible person. Your effectiveness in just about any endeavor depends heavily on your self-presentation—your ability to present yourself in a positive light, through your verbal and nonverbal messages. Incidentally, it is also largely through your skills of self-presentation (or lack of them) that you display negative qualities as well.

Myths about Human Communication

A good way to begin your study of human communication is to examine just a few of the popular but erroneous beliefs about communication, many of which are contradicted by research and theory. Understanding these myths and why they are false will help eliminate potential barriers and pave the way for more effective and efficient learning about communication.

- **The more you communicate, the better your communication will be.** Although this proposition seems logical—the same idea lies behind the popular belief that practice makes perfect—it actually is at the heart of much faulty learning. Practice may help make your communication perfect if you practice the right habits. But if you practice bad habits, you're likely to grow less, rather than more, effective. Consequently, it's important to learn and practice the principles of effectiveness.

- **When two people are in a close relationship, neither person should have to communicate needs and wants explicitly; the other person should know what these are.** This assumption is at the heart of many communication difficulties. People aren't mind readers, and to expect them to be sets up barriers to open and honest communication.

  - **Interpersonal or group conflict is a reliable sign that the relationship or group is in trouble.** Conflict is inevitable in relationships and in groups. If the conflict is managed effectively, it may actually benefit the individuals and the relationship.

  - **Like good communicators, leaders are born, not made.** Although some people are better suited to leadership than others, leadership, like communication and listening, is a learned skill. You'll develop leadership abilities as you learn the principles of human communication and those unique to group communication and group leadership.

  - **Fear of speaking in public is detrimental and must be eliminated.** Most speakers are nervous—and, to be perfectly honest, you're probably not going to learn from this book or this course to eliminate what is commonly called stage fright or communication apprehension. But you can learn to *manage* your fear, making it work for you rather than against you; you can learn, and this is crucial, to become a more effective speaker regardless of your current level of anxiety.

VIEWPOINTS: Importance of Communication

Both men and women want partners who know how to communicate and listen. *How important, compared to all the other factors you might take into consideration in choosing a partner, is the ability to communicate and listen? What specific communication skills would you consider "extremely important" in a life partner?*

Communication Models and Concepts

1.2 **Draw a model of communication that includes sources-receivers, messages, context, channel, noise, and effects; and define each of these elements.**

Figure 1.1 The Linear View of Human Communication

The speaker speaks and the listener listens.

In early **models** (representations) or theories, the communication process was thought to be linear. According to this *linear* view, the speaker spoke and the listener listened. Communication was seen as proceeding in a relatively straight line. Speaking and listening were seen as taking place at different times; when you spoke, you didn't listen, and when you listened, you didn't speak (Figure 1.1).

A more satisfying view, the one held currently, sees communication as a transactional process in which each person serves as both speaker and listener, sending and receiving messages (Watzlawick, Beavin, & Jackson, 1967; Watzlawick, 1977, 1978; Barnlund, 1970). In face-to-face communication, while you send messages you're also receiving messages from your own communications and from the reactions of the other person. This is also true in phone communication, in instant messaging, and in chatting. Other online communications, such as posting on Facebook or e-mail, more closely resemble the linear model of communication where sending and receiving occur at different times.

The transactional view also sees the elements of communication as interdependent (never independent). This means that each element exists in relation to the others. A change in any one element of the process produces changes in the other elements. For example, if you're having a meeting with a group of your coworkers and your boss enters the room, this change in "audience" will lead to other changes. Perhaps you'll change what you're saying or how you're saying it. Regardless of what change is introduced, other changes will occur as a result.

Communication occurs when you send or receive messages and when you assign meaning to another person's signals. All human communication occurs within a context, is transmitted via one or more channels, is distorted by noise, and has some effect. We can expand the basic transactional model of communication by adding these essential elements, as shown in Figure 1.2.

Sources–Receivers

According to the transactional model, each person involved in communication is both a **source** (speaker) and a **receiver** (listener); hence the term *sources–receivers*. You send messages when you speak, write, gesture, or smile. You receive messages in listening, reading, seeing, smelling, and so on. At the same time that you send messages, you're also receiving messages: You're receiving your own messages (you hear yourself, feel your own movements, see many of your own gestures), and, at least in face-to-face communication, you're receiving the messages of the other person—visually, auditorily, or even through touch or smell. As you speak, you look at the person for responses—for approval, understanding, sympathy, agreement, and so on. As you decipher these nonverbal signals, you're performing receiver functions. When you write to or text someone with video; the situation is very similar to the face-to-face situation. Without video, you might visualize the responses you expect/want the person to give.

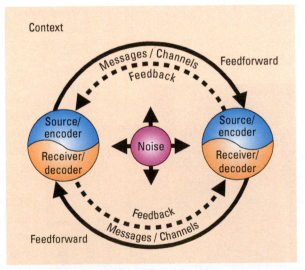

Figure 1.2 The Essentials of Human Communication

This is a general model of communication between two people and most accurately depicts communication as a transactional process. It puts into visual form the various elements of the communication process. *How would you revise this model to depict small-group interaction or public speaking?*

When you put your ideas into speech, you're putting them into a code; hence you're **encoding**. When you translate the sound waves (the speech signals) that impinge on your ears or read the words on a screen, into ideas, you take them out of the code they're in; hence you're **decoding**. Thus, speakers or writers are often referred to as **encoders**, and listeners or readers as **decoders**. The linked term *encoding–decoding* emphasizes the fact that you perform these functions simultaneously.

Usually, you encode an idea into a code that the other person understands—for example, English, Spanish, or Indonesian, depending on the shared knowledge that you and your listener possess. At times, however, you may want to exclude others by speaking in a language that only one of your listeners knows or by using jargon. The use of abbreviations and jargon in text messaging is another example of how people communicate in a code that only certain people will understand.

Messages

Communication **messages** take many forms and are transmitted or received through one or more sensory organs or a combination of them. You communicate verbally (with words) and nonverbally (without words). Your meanings or intentions are conveyed with words (Chapter 4) and with the clothes you wear, the way you walk, and the way you smile (Chapter 5). Everything about you communicates a message. Three specific types of messages need to be identified here: feedforward, feedback, and metamessages.

FEEDFORWARD MESSAGES   **Feedforward** is information you provide before sending your primary messages (Richards, 1951). It reveals something about the messages to come and includes, for example, the preface or table of contents of a book, the opening paragraph of a chapter, a Facebook profile, movie previews, magazine covers, and introductions in public speeches. In e-mail, feedforward is given in the header, where the name of the sender, the date, and the subject of the message are identified. Caller ID is also an example of feedforward.

Feedforward may be verbal ("Wait until you hear this one") or nonverbal (a prolonged pause or hands motioning for silence to signal that an important message is about to be spoken). Or, as is most often the case, it is some combination of verbal and nonverbal.

Another type of feedforward is **phatic communication**—"small talk" that opens the way for "big talk." It includes the "How are you?" and "Nice weather" greetings that are designed to maintain rapport and friendly relationships (Placencia, 2004; Burnard, 2003). Similarly, listeners' short comments that are unrelated to the content of the conversation but indicate interest and attention also may be considered phatic communication (McCarthy, 2003).

FEEDBACK MESSAGES   When you send a message—say, in speaking to another person—you also hear yourself. That is, you get **feedback** from your own messages; you hear what you say, you feel the way you move, you see what you write. In addition to this self-feedback, you also get feedback from others. This feedback can take many forms. A frown or a smile, a yea or a nay, a returned poke or a retweet, a pat on the back or a punch in the mouth are all types of feedback.

Feedback tells the speaker what effect he or she is having on listeners. On the basis of feedback, the speaker may adjust, modify, strengthen, de-emphasize, or change the content or form of the messages. For example, if someone laughs at your joke (giving you positive feedback), it may

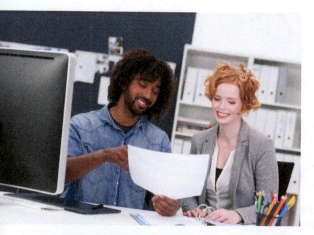

VIEWPOINTS: Feedback

Based on your own experiences, how would you distinguish between people who accurately read and respond to feedback and those who don't read feedback as accurately?

encourage you to tell another one. If the feedback is negative—no laughing, just blank stares—then you may resist relaying another "humorous" story.

METAMESSAGES   A **metamessage** is a message that refers to another message; it is communication about communication. For example, remarks such as "This statement is false" or "Do you understand what I am trying to tell you?" refer to communication and are therefore "metacommunicational."

Nonverbal behavior may also be metacommunicational. Obvious examples include crossing your fingers behind your back or winking when telling a lie. On a less obvious level, consider the blind date. As you say, "I had a really nice time," your nonverbal messages—the lack of a smile, failure to maintain eye contact—metacommunicate and contradict the verbal "really nice time," suggesting that you did not enjoy the evening. Nonverbal messages may also metacommunicate about other nonverbal messages. The individual who, on meeting a stranger, both smiles and extends a totally lifeless hand shows how one nonverbal behavior may contradict another.

Communication Context

Communication exists in a **context** that determines, to a large extent, the meaning of any verbal or nonverbal message. The same words or behaviors may have totally different meanings when they occur in different contexts. For example, the greeting "How are you?" means "Hello" to someone you pass regularly on the street but "Is your health improving?" to a friend in the hospital. A wink to an attractive person on a bus means something completely different from a wink that signifies a put-on or a lie. Divorced from the context, it's impossible to tell what meaning was intended from just examining the signals.

The context will also influence what you say and how you say it. You communicate differently depending on the specific context you're in. Contexts have at least four aspects: **physical context**, **cultural context**, **social-psychological context**, and **temporal context**.

- The **physical context** is the tangible or concrete environment, the room, park, or auditorium; you don't talk the same way at a noisy football game as you do at a quiet funeral.
- The **cultural context** involves the lifestyles, beliefs, values, behavior, and communication of a group; it is the rules of a group of people for considering something right or wrong.
- The **social-psychological context** has to do with the status relationships among speakers, the formality of the situation, the norms of a group or organization; you don't talk the same way in the cafeteria as you would at a formal dinner at your boss's house.
- The **temporal context** is a message's position within a sequence of events; you don't talk the same way after someone tells you about the death of a close relative as you do after someone reveals they've won the lottery.

These four contexts interact—each influences and is influenced by the others. For example, arriving late for a date (temporal context) may lead to changes in the degree of friendliness (social-psychological context), which would depend on the cultures of you and your date (cultural context), and may lead to changes in where you go on the date (physical context).

Channel

The communication **channel** is the vehicle or medium through which messages pass. Communication rarely takes place over only one channel. Rather, two, three, or four channels may be used simultaneously. In face-to-face conversations, for example, you speak and listen (vocal channel), but you also gesture and receive signals visually (visual channel). You also emit and smell odors (olfactory channel) and often touch one another; this tactile channel, too, is communication.

Another way to classify channels is by the means of communication. Thus, face-to-face contact, telephones, e-mail, movies, television, smoke signals, Facebook, Twitter, Pinterest, and telegraph all are types of channels.

Noise

Noise is anything that interferes with your receiving a message. At one extreme, noise may prevent a message from getting from source to receiver. A roaring noise or line static can prevent entire messages from getting through to your phone receiver. At the other extreme, with virtually no noise interference, the message of the source and the message received are almost identical. Most often, however, noise distorts some portion of the message a source sends as it travels to a receiver. Just as messages may be auditory or visual, noise comes in both auditory and visual forms. Four types of noise are especially relevant: **physical noise, physiological noise, psychological noise,** and **semantic noise**.

- **Physical noise** is interference that is external to both speaker and listener; it interferes with the physical transmission of the signal or message and would include the screeching of passing cars, the hum of a computer, sunglasses, blurred type or fonts that are too small or difficult to read, misspellings and poor grammar, and pop-up ads.

- **Physiological noise** is created by barriers within the sender or receiver and would include visual impairments, hearing loss, articulation problems, and memory loss.

- **Psychological noise** refers to mental interference in the speaker or listener and includes preconceived ideas, wandering thoughts, biases and prejudices, close-mindedness, and extreme emotionalism. You're likely to run into psychological noise when you talk with someone who is close-minded or who refuses to listen to anything he or she doesn't already believe.

- **Semantic noise** is interference that occurs when the speaker and listener have different meaning systems; it would include language or dialectical differences, the use of jargon or overly complex terms, and ambiguous or overly abstract terms whose meanings can be easily misinterpreted. You see this type of noise regularly in the medical doctor who uses "medicalese" without explanation or in the insurance salesperson who speaks in the jargon of the insurance industry.

As you can see from these examples, noise is anything that distorts your receiving the messages of others or their receiving your messages.

A useful concept in understanding noise and its importance in communication is **signal-to-noise ratio**. In this term the word *signal* refers to information that you'd find useful, and *noise* refers to information that is useless (to you). So, for example, a post or feed that contains lots of useful information is high on signal and low on noise; one that contains lots of useless information is high on noise and low on signal.

All communications contain noise. Noise can't be totally eliminated, but its effects can be reduced. Making your language more precise, sharpening your skills for sending and receiving nonverbal messages, adjusting your camera for greater clarity, and improving your listening and feedback skills are some ways to combat the influence of noise.

Effects

Communication always has some **effect** on those involved in the communication act. For every communication act, there is some consequence. For example, you may gain knowledge or learn how to analyze, synthesize, or evaluate something. These are intellectual or cognitive effects. You may acquire new feelings, attitudes, or beliefs or change existing ones (affective effects). You may learn new bodily movements, such as how to throw a curve ball, paint a picture, give a compliment, or express surprise (psychomotor effects).

Principles of Communication

1.3 **Paraphrase the major principles of human communication.**

Several principles are essential to an understanding of human communication in all its forms. These principles, as you'll see throughout the text, also have numerous practical implications to help you increase your own communication effectiveness.

Communication Is Purposeful

You communicate for a purpose; some motivation leads you to communicate. When you speak or write, you're trying to send some message and to accomplish some goal. Although different cultures emphasize different purposes and motives (Rubin, Fernandez-Collado, & Hernandez-Sampieri, 1992), five general purposes seem relatively common to most, if not all, forms of communication.

- **to learn:** to acquire knowledge of others, the world, and yourself
- **to relate:** to form relationships with others, to interact with others as individuals
- **to help:** to assist others by listening, offering solutions
- **to influence:** to strengthen or change the attitudes or behaviors of others
- **to play:** to enjoy the experience of the moment

In research on the motivations/purposes for using social networking sites, it's the relationship purpose that dominates. One research study, for example, finds the following motivations/purposes, in order of frequency mentioned: staying in touch with friends, staying in touch with family, connecting with friends with whom you've lost contact, connecting with those who share your interests, making new friends, reading comments by celebrities, and finding romantic partners (Smith, 2011). As you can see, the reasons are mostly to relate but the other purposes are likely served in the process.

Popular belief and research findings both agree that men and women use communication for different purposes. Generally, men seem to communicate more for information and women more for relationship purposes (Gamble & Gamble, 2003; Stewart, Cooper, & Stewart, 2003; Helgeson, 2009). Gender differences also occur in electronic communication. For example, women chat more for relationship reasons; men chat more to play and to relax (Leung, 2001).

Communication Takes Place in Varied Forms

Communication often takes place face-to-face, as when we talk with other students before class, interact with family or friends over dinner, or trade secrets with intimates. But, of course, communication also takes place over some kind of computer network, through texting, e-mailing, posting to Facebook, phoning, pinning to Pinterest, and tweeting. In this text, face-to-face communication and online/social media communication are integrated for a number of important reasons:

1. It's the way we communicate; we interact face-to-face and online. Some interactions are likely exclusively face-to-face, while others are exclusively online. Increasingly, our interactions are with people with whom we communicate both online and offline.

2. Contemporary communication can only be understood as a combination of online and offline interaction. The research and theory discussed here on face-to-face and on online communication inform each other. Most of the communication

VIEWPOINTS: **Mixed-Media Communication**
How would you describe the similarities and the differences in the ways you communicate face-to-face and on a phone or tablet?

theories discussed here were developed for face-to-face interaction but have much to say about online relationships as well.

3. It's part of the skill set that employers expect potential employees to have. As already noted, the ability to communicate orally and in writing (and of course that includes online and offline) is consistently ranked among the most important qualities employers are looking for.

4. Both forms of communication are vital to developing, maintaining, and even dissolving relationships. More and more relationships are started and maintained online with many of them moving to face-to-face interactions if the online interaction proves satisfying.

5. Both forms of communication are important to your achieving your goals. For example, your employability will depend, in great part, on how effectively you communicate in your e-mails, in your phone conferences, in your Skype interviews, and in your in-person interviews. Social networking recruiting is perhaps the major means used to hire new employees (Bersin, 2013).

Communication Is Ambiguous

Ambiguity is the condition in which something can be interpreted in more than one way. The first type, *language ambiguity*, is created by words that can be interpreted differently. Informal time terms offer good examples; *soon, right away, in a minute, early, late*, and similar terms can be understood differently by different people. The terms are ambiguous. A more interesting type of ambiguity is grammatical ambiguity. You can get a feel for this type of ambiguity by trying to paraphrase—rephrase in your own words—the sentence: Flying planes can be dangerous. Notice that it can be interpreted as meaning "to fly planes is dangerous" but also "planes that fly can be dangerous."

Although this is a particularly dramatic example and is a widely used linguistic example, some degree of ambiguity exists in all communication. When you express an idea, you never communicate your meaning exactly and totally; rather, you communicate your meaning with some reasonable accuracy—enough to give the other person a reasonably clear idea of what you mean.

The second type of ambiguity is *relationship ambiguity*. All relationships are ambiguous to some extent. Consider your own close relationships and ask yourself the following questions. Answer using a six-point scale on which 1 = completely or almost completely uncertain, and 6 = completely or almost completely certain. How certain are you about:

1. What can you say or not say to each other in this relationship?
2. Do you and your partner feel the same way about each other?
3. How would you and your partner describe this relationship?
4. How do you see the future of this relationship?

You probably were not able to respond with 6s for all four questions, and it is equally likely that your relationship partner would not respond with all 6s to these questions, adapted from a relationship uncertainty scale (Knobloch & Solomon, 1999).

You can look at the skills of human communication presented throughout this text as a means for appropriately reducing ambiguity and making the meanings you send and the meanings you receive as unambiguous as possible.

JOURNAL
COMMUNICATION CHOICE POINT
Relationship Ambiguity

You've been dating Jessie on and off for the past six months. Today Jessie asks you to come to dinner and meet Mom and Dad and the grandparents. You're not sure what this means, what message Jessie's trying to send. *What options do you have for disambiguating this dinner invitation message? What would you say?*

Communication Involves Content and Relationship Dimensions

Communication exists on at least two levels: a message referring to something external to both speaker and listener (e.g., the weather) or to the relationship between speaker and listener (e.g., who is in charge). These two aspects are referred to as **content and relationship dimensions** of communication (Watzlawick, Beavin, & Jackson, 1967). In the cartoon shown here, the father is explicitly teaching his son the difference between content and relationship messages. In real life this distinction is rarely discussed (outside of textbooks and counseling sessions).

Some research shows that women send more **relationship messages** than men; they talk more about relationships in general and about the present relationship in particular. Men use more **content messages**; they talk more about things external to the relationship (Wood, 1994; Pearson, West, & Turner, 1995; Helgeson, 2009).

Problems often result from a failure to distinguish between the content and the relationship levels of communication. Consider a couple, Pat and Chris. Pat made plans to attend a rally with friends during the weekend without first asking Chris, and an argument has ensued. Both would probably have agreed that attending the rally was the right choice to make. Thus, the argument is not centered on the content level. The argument, instead, centers on the relationship level. Chris expected to be consulted about plans for the weekend. Pat, in not doing so, rejected this definition of the relationship.

"It's not about the story. It's about Daddy taking time out of his busy day to read you the story."
Peter C. Vey/The New Yorker Collection/The Cartoon Bank

Communication Is Punctuated

Communication events are continuous transactions that have no clear-cut beginning or ending. As a participant in or an observer of communication, you divide this continuous, circular process into causes and effects, or stimuli and responses. The **punctuation of communication** is the segmenting of the continuous stream of communication into smaller pieces (Watzlawick, Beavin, & Jackson, 1967). Some of these pieces you label causes (or stimuli) and others effects (or responses).

Consider this example: The manager of a local supermarket lacks interest in the employees, seldom offering any suggestions for improvement or any praise for jobs well done. The employees are apathetic and morale is low. Each action (the manager's lack of involvement and the employees' low morale) stimulates the other. Each serves as the stimulus for the other, but there is no identifiable initial starting point. Each event may be seen as a stimulus or as a response.

To understand what the other person in an interaction means from his or her point of view, try to see the sequence of events as punctuated by the other person. The manager, for example, needs to see the problem from the point of view of the employees; and the employees need to see it from the viewpoint of the manager. Further, recognize that neither person's punctuation reflects what exists in reality. Rather, it reflects the subjective and fallible perception of each individual (the other person as well as you).

Communication Is Inevitable, Irreversible, and Unrepeatable

INEVITABILITY Communication is inevitable; that is, in interactional situations it is always taking place, even when a person may not intend or want to communicate. To understand the **inevitability** of communication, think about a student sitting in the back of a classroom with an expressionless face, perhaps staring out the window.

Although the student might claim not to be communicating with the instructor, the instructor may derive a variety of messages from this behavior. Perhaps the instructor assumes that the student lacks interest, is bored, or is worried about something. In any event, the teacher is receiving messages even though the student may not intentionally be sending any (Watzlawick, Beavin, & Jackson, 1967; Motley, 1990a, 1990b; Bavelas, 1990). This does not mean that all behavior is communication. For instance, if the student looked out the window and the teacher didn't notice, no communication would have taken place. The two people must be in an interactional situation and the behavior must be perceived for the principle of inevitability to operate.

Notice, too, that when you're in an interactional situation, you cannot *not* respond to the messages of others. For example, if you notice someone winking at you, you must respond in some way. Even if you don't respond actively or openly, your lack of response is itself a response: It communicates.

IRREVERSIBILITY   Another all-important attribute of communication is its **irreversibility**. Once you say something or click "send" on your e-mail, you cannot uncommunicate the message. You can, of course, try to reduce its effects. You can say, for example, "I really didn't mean what I said." But regardless of how hard you try to negate or reduce the effects of a message, the message itself, once it has been received, cannot be taken back. In a public speaking situation in which the speech is recorded or broadcast, inappropriate messages may have national or even international effects. Here, attempts to reverse what someone has said (e.g., efforts to offer clarification) often have the effect of further publicizing the original statement.

In face-to-face communication, the actual signals (nonverbal messages and sound waves in the air) are evanescent; they fade almost as they are uttered. Some written messages, especially computer-mediated messages (such as those sent through e-mail or posted on social network sites) are unerasable. E-mails among employees in large corporations or even at colleges are often stored on disk or tape and may not be considered private by managers and administrators (Sethna et al., 1999). Much litigation has involved evidence of racist or sexist e-mails that senders thought had been erased but were not. E-mails and entire hard drives are finding their way into divorce proceedings. As a result of the permanency of computer-mediated communication, you may wish to be especially cautious in these messages.

In all forms of communication, because of irreversibility (and unerasability), be careful not to say things you may be sorry for later, especially in conflict situations, when tempers run high. Commitment messages—"I love you" messages and their variants—also need to be monitored. Messages that you considered private but that might be interpreted as sexist, racist, or homophobic may later be retrieved by others and create all sorts of problems for you and your organization. Interestingly enough, only 55 percent of online teens say they do not post content that might reflect negatively on them in the future (Lenhart et al., 2011). In group and public communication situations, when the messages are received by many people, it's especially crucial to recognize the irreversibility of communication.

UNREPEATABILITY   Communication also possesses the characteristics of **unrepeatability**. A communication act can never be duplicated. The reason is simple: Everyone and everything is constantly changing. As a result, you can never recapture the exact same situation, frame of mind, or relationship dynamics that defined a previous communication act. For example, you can never repeat meeting someone for the first time, comforting a grieving friend, leading a small group for the first time, or giving a public speech. You can never replace an initial impression; you can only try to counteract this initial (and perhaps negative) impression by making subsequent impressions more positive.

A summary of these principles appears in Table 1.1.

Table 1.1 In a Nutshell: Some Principles of Human Communication

Here, in brief, are the six principles of human communication, their basic ideas and implications.

Principles	Basic Ideas	Skill Implications
Communication is purposeful.	Communication may serve a variety of purposes—for example, to learn, to relate, to help, to influence, to play.	Use your purposes to guide your verbal and nonverbal messages. Identify the purposes in the messages of others.
Communication takes place in varied forms.	Communication today takes place through a mixture of forms.	Phrase your messages so that they are appropriate to the form of communication you're using.
Communication is ambiguous.	All messages and all relationships are potentially ambiguous.	Use clear and specific terms, ask if you're being understood, and paraphrase complex ideas.
Communication involves content and relationship dimensions.	Messages may refer to the real world, to something external to both speaker and listener (the content) *and* to the relationships between the parties.	Distinguish between content and relationship messages and deal with relationship issues as relationship issues.
Communication is punctuated.	Communication events are continuous transactions, punctuated into causes and effects for convenience.	See alternative punctuations when trying to understand another's point of view.
Communication is inevitable, irreversible, and unrepeatable.	Messages are (almost) always being sent, can't be uncommunicated, and are always unique, one-time occurrences.	Be careful of what you say; you won't be able to take it back.

Culture and Human Communication

1.4 **Explain the role of culture in human communication, the seven ways in which cultures differ from one another, the aim of a cultural perspective; and define** *ethnic identity* **and** *ethnocentrism*.

Culture consists of the beliefs, ways of behaving, and artifacts of a group. By definition, culture is transmitted through communication and learning rather than through genes.

A walk through any large city, many small towns, or just about any college campus will convince you that the United States is a collection of many different cultures. These cultures coexist somewhat separately but all influence one another. This coexistence has led some researchers to refer to these cultures as *cocultures* (Shuter, 1990; Samovar & Porter, 1991; Jandt, 2010).

Gender is considered a cultural variable largely because cultures teach boys and girls different attitudes, beliefs, values, and ways of communicating and relating to one another. This means that you act like a man or a woman in part because of what your culture has taught you about how men and women should act. This is not to deny that biological differences also play a role in the differences between male and female behavior. In fact, research continues to uncover the biological roots of behavior we once thought was entirely learned—acting happy or shy, for example (McCroskey, 1997).

Yet we're living in a time of changing gender roles. Many men, for example, are doing more housekeeping chores and caring for their children. More obvious perhaps is that women are becoming more visible in career fields once occupied exclusively by men—politics, law enforcement, the military, and the clergy are just some examples. And, of course, women are increasingly present in the corporate executive ranks; the glass ceiling may not have disappeared, but it has cracked.

Because your communication is heavily influenced by the culture in which you were raised, culture is highly relevant to communication, and a cultural perspective serves numerous important purposes.

The Importance of Culture

Culture is important for a variety of reasons. Here are a few.

- **Demographic changes**: Whereas at one time the United States was a country largely populated by Europeans, it's now greatly influenced by the enormous number of new citizens from Latin America, South America, Africa, and Asia.

With these changes have come different customs and the need to understand and adapt to new ways of looking at communication.

- **Sensitivity to cultural differences**: As a people, we've become increasingly sensitive to cultural differences. U.S. society has moved from an *assimilationist perspective* (the idea that people should leave their native culture behind and adapt to their new culture) to a view that values *cultural diversity* (people should retain their native cultural ways). At the same time, the ability to interact effectively with members of other cultures often translates into financial gain and increased employment opportunities and advancement prospects.

- **Economic interdependence**: Today most countries are economically dependent on one another. Our economic lives depend on our ability to communicate effectively across cultures. Similarly, our political well-being depends in great part on that of other cultures. Political unrest or financial problems in any part of the world—Africa, Europe, or the Middle East, to take a few examples—affects our own security. Intercultural communication and understanding now seem more crucial than ever.

- **Communication technology**: Technology has made intercultural interaction easy, practical, and inevitable. It's common to have social network friends from different cultures, and these relationships require a new way of looking at communication and culture.

- **Culture-specific nature of communication**: Still another reason culture is so important is that communication competence is culture specific. As we'll see throughout this text, what proves effective in one culture may prove ineffective (even offensive) in another.

The Dimensions of Culture

Because of its importance in all forms of human communication, culture is given a prominent place in this text; and theories and research findings that bear on culture and communication are discussed throughout this chapter. Prominent among these discussions are the seven major dimensions of culture, which we briefly preview here: **uncertainty avoidance, masculinity–femininity, power distance, individualism–collectivism, high and low context, indulgence and restraint**, and **long- and short-term orientation.**

- **Uncertainty avoidance**: The degree to which a culture values predictability. In high-uncertainty-avoidance cultures, predictability and order are extremely important; in low-uncertainty-avoidance cultures, risk-taking and ambiguity are tolerated more easily. (See the Cultural Map in this chapter.)

- **Masculinity–femininity**: The extent to which cultures embrace traditionally masculine characteristics, such as ambition and assertiveness, or embrace traditionally feminine characteristics, such as caring and nurturing others.

- **Power distance**: The way power is distributed throughout the society. In high-power-distance cultures, there is a great power difference between those in authority and others. In low-power-distance cultures, power is distributed more evenly.

- **Individualism–collectivism**: A culture's emphasis on the importance of the individual or of the group. Individualist cultures value qualities such as self-reliance, independence, and individual achievement; collectivist cultures emphasize social bonds, the primacy of the group, and conformity to the larger social group.

- **High and low context**: The extent to which information is seen as embedded in the context or tacitly known among members. In high-context cultures information is part of the context and does not have to be verbalized explicitly. In low-context cultures information is made explicit and little is taken for granted.

- **Indulgence and restraint**: The relative emphasis a culture places on the gratification of desires, on having fun, and on enjoying life (indulgent cultures)

The Cultural Map

AMBIGUITY TOLERANCE

Ambiguity tolerance refers to the degree to which members of a culture are accepting of uncertainty; high-ambiguity tolerant cultures are comfortable with not knowing exactly what will happen next, whereas low-ambiguity tolerant cultures resist uncertainty and, in many cases, are stressed out by it.

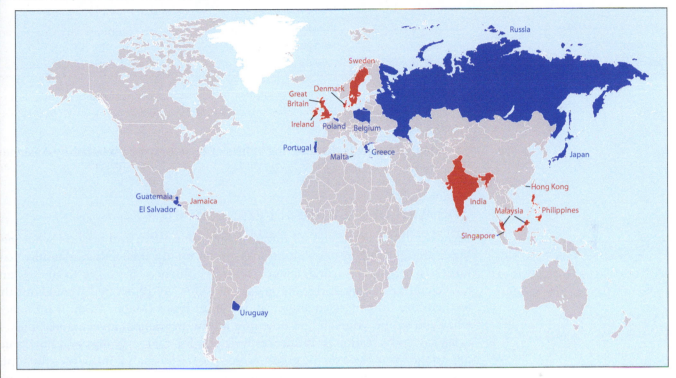

In these high-ambiguity tolerant cultures (generally, the top 10 countries are highlighted in these cultural maps), uncertainty is considered normal and expected. High ambiguity tolerant people are comfortable in uncertain situations and with unfamiliar tasks and assignments. They are also tolerant of ethnic differences and diversity and are generally positive to foreigners.

In these low-ambiguity tolerant cultures, members try to avoid uncertainty, because uncertainty is typically uncomfortable and anxiety provoking for them. Members of these cultures are also more prejudiced toward other ethnic groups and would not be welcoming to immigrants.

How do you feel when an instructor gives an ambiguous assignment? Do you see the lack of specific direction as stressful or as an opportunity to get creative and think of different ways you might approach the assignment?

as opposed to cultures that emphasize the curbing of these desires (restraint cultures).

- **Long- and short-term orientation**: The degree to which a culture teaches an orientation that promotes the importance of future rewards (long-term orientation) versus cultures that emphasize the importance of immediate rewards. These cultures also differ in their view of the workplace. Organizations in long-term-oriented cultures look to profits in the future. Managers or owners and workers in such cultures share the same values and work together to achieve a common good. Organizations in short-term-oriented cultures, on the other hand, look to more immediate rewards. Managers and workers are very different in their thinking and in their attitudes about work.

Table 1.2 Values of the Workplace

Asian (long-term culture) and American (short-term culture) executives were asked to rank those values they considered most important in the workplace. The top six responses are presented here (in order of perceived importance) and show a dramatic difference between the two cultural groups (Hofstede, Hofstede, & Minkov, 2010). Notice that "hard work" makes both lists but in very different positions.

Values Selected by Asian (Long-Term Orientation) Executives	Values Selected by American (Short-Term Orientation) Executives
Hard work	Freedom of expression
Respect for learning	Personal freedom
Honesty	Self-reliance
Openness to new ideas	Individual rights
Accountability	Hard work
Self-discipline	Personal achievement

Table 1.2 presents the differing values of the workplace selected by Asian and American executives.

The Aim of a Cultural Perspective

Because culture permeates all forms of communication, and because what messages are effective in one culture may prove totally ineffective in another culture, it's necessary to understand cultural influences if you're to understand how communication works and master its skills. As illustrated throughout this text, culture influences communications of all types (Moon, 1996). It influences what you say to yourself and how you talk with friends, lovers, and family in everyday conversation. It influences how you interact in groups and how much importance you place on the group versus the individual. It influences the topics you talk about and the strategies you use in communicating information or in persuading.

Cultural differences exist across the communication spectrum—from the way you use eye contact to the way you develop or dissolve a relationship (Chang & Holt, 1996). But these differences should not blind you to the great number of similarities among even the most widely separated cultures. Close interpersonal relationships, for example, are common in all cultures, although they may be entered into for very different reasons by members of different cultures. Further, when reading about cultural differences, remember that they are usually matters of degree. For example, most cultures value honesty, but not all value it to the same extent. The advances in media and technology and the widespread use of the Internet, among other factors, are influencing cultures and cultural change and are perhaps homogenizing cultures, lessening intercultural differences, and increasing similarities. They're also Americanizing various cultures—because the dominant values and customs evidenced in the media and on the Internet are in large part American.

This focus on cultural understanding does not imply that you should accept all cultural practices or that all cultural practices must be evaluated as equally good. For example, cockfighting, foxhunting, and bullfighting are parts of the cultures of some Latin American countries, England, and Spain, respectively; but you need not find these activities acceptable or equal to cultural practices in which animals are treated kindly. Similarly, you can reject your own culture's values and beliefs;

VIEWPOINTS: **Campus Culture**
How would you describe the level of cultural awareness and cultural sensitivity on your campus?

its religion or political system; or its attitudes toward the homeless, the disabled, or the culturally different. Of course, going against your culture's traditions and values is often very difficult. Still, it's important to realize that culture *influences* but does not *determine* your values or behavior. Often, factors such as personality (your degree of assertiveness, extroversion, or optimism, for example) will prove more influential than culture (Hatfield & Rapson, 1996).

Ethnic Identity and Ethnocentrism

As you learn your culture's ways, you develop an **ethnic identity**—for example, you self-identity as a member of the group, you embrace (largely) the attitudes and beliefs of the group, and behave as a member of the group (perhaps celebrating ethnic holidays or preparing ethnic foods).

A healthy ethnic identity is generally regarded as a positive trait. It helps to preserve the ethnic culture, build group cohesiveness, and enable it to make its unique contributions to the culture as a whole. On the other hand, **ethnocentrism** is an extreme ethnic identity; it's the tendency to see others and their behaviors through your own cultural filters, often as distortions of your own behaviors. It's the tendency to evaluate the values, beliefs, and behaviors of your own culture as superior and as more positive, logical, and natural than those of other cultures. Although ethnocentrism may give you pride in your own culture and its achievements and encourage you to sacrifice for the culture, it also may lead you to see other cultures as inferior and may make you unwilling to profit from the contributions of other cultures. For example, there's a "substantial relationship" between ethnocentrism and homophobia (Wrench & McCroskey, 2003).

Ethnocentrism exists on a continuum (Table 1.3). People are not either ethnocentric or nonethnocentric; most are somewhere between these polar opposites. And, of course, your degree of ethnocentrism often varies depending on the group on which you focus. For example, if you're Greek American, you may have a low degree of ethnocentrism when dealing with Italian Americans but a high degree when dealing with Turkish Americans or Japanese Americans. Your degree of ethnocentrism will influence your communication in all its forms, as we'll see throughout this text.

JOURNAL
COMMUNICATION CHOICE POINT
Conflicting Cultural Beliefs

You're talking with new work colleagues, and one of the cultural practices you find unethical is discussed with approval; your colleagues argue that each culture has a right to its own practices and beliefs. *Given your own beliefs about this issue and about cultural diversity and cultural sensitivity, what are some of the things you can say to be honest with yourself and yet not jeopardize your new position?*

Table 1.3 **The Ethnocentrism Continuum**

This table summarizes some of the interconnections between ethnocentrism and communication (Gudykunst & Kim, 1992; Gudykunst, 1991). Five degrees of ethnocentrism are identified; in reality, there are as many degrees as there are people. The "communication distances" are general terms that highlight the attitude that dominates that level of ethnocentrism. Under "communications" are some of the major ways people might interact given their particular degree of ethnocentrism.

Degree of Ethnocentrism	Communication Distance	Communications
Low	Equality	You treat others as equals; you view different customs and ways of behaving as equal to your own.
	Sensitivity	You want to decrease the distance between yourself and others.
	Indifference	You lack concern for others; you prefer to interact in a world of similar others.
	Avoidance	You avoid and limit interactions, especially intimate communication with interculturally different others.
High	Disparagement	You engage in hostile behavior and belittle others; you view different cultures and ways of behaving as inferior to your own.

Communication Competence

1.5 **Define** *communication competence* **and explain the qualities identified as part of competence.**

Your ability to communicate effectively is your **communication competence** (Spitzberg & Cupach, 1989; Wilson & Sabee, 2003). A major goal of this text (and of your course) is to expand and enlarge your competence so you'll have a greater arsenal of communication options at your disposal. The greater your competence, the more options you'll have for communicating interpersonally, in small groups, and in public communication settings. The greater your competence, the greater your own power to accomplish successfully what you want to accomplish—to ask for a raise or a date; establish temporary work relationships, long-term friendships, or romantic relationships; participate in and lead small groups; or inform or persuade an audience.

In short, communication competence includes knowing how communication works and how to best achieve your purposes by adjusting your messages according to the context of the interaction, the person with whom you're interacting, and a host of other factors discussed throughout this text. Let's spell out more clearly a few major traits of a competent communicator.

The Competent Communicator Thinks Critically and Mindfully

Without critical thinking, there can be no competent exchange of ideas. Critical thinking is logical thinking; it's thinking that is well reasoned, unbiased, and clear. It involves thinking intelligently, carefully, and with as much clarity as possible. It's the opposite of what you'd call sloppy, illogical, or careless thinking. And, not surprisingly, according to one study of corporate executives, critical thinking is one of the stepping stones to effective management (Miller, 1997).

A special kind of critical thinking is mindfulness. **Mindfulness** is a state of awareness in which you're conscious of your reasons for thinking or behaving. In its opposite, **mindlessness**, you lack conscious awareness of what or how you're thinking (Langer, 1989; Beard, 2014; Grierson, 2014). To apply communication skills effectively in conversation, you need to be mindful of the unique communication situation you're in, of your available communication options, and of the reasons why one option is likely to be better than the others (Burgoon, Berger, & Waldron, 2000; Elmes & Gemmill, 1990).

To increase mindfulness, try the following suggestions (Langer, 1989).

- **Create and re-create categories.** Group things in different ways; remember that people are constantly changing, so the categories into which you may group them also should change. Learn to see objects, events, and people as belonging to a wide variety of categories. Try to see, for example, your prospective romantic partner in a variety of roles—child, parent, employee, neighbor, friend, financial contributor, and so on.

- **Be open to new information and points of view, even when these contradict your most firmly held beliefs.** New information forces you to reconsider what might be outmoded ways of thinking and can help you challenge long-held but now inappropriate beliefs and attitudes.

- **Beware of relying too heavily on first impressions (Chanowitz & Langer, 1981; Langer, 1989).** Treat first impressions as tentative, as hypotheses that need further investigation. Be prepared to revise, reject, or accept these initial impressions.

- **Think before you act.** Especially in delicate situations such as anger or commitment messages, it's wise to pause and think over the situation mindfully (DeVito, 2003). In this way, you'll stand a better chance of acting and reacting appropriately.

The Competent Communicator Makes Reasoned Choices

Throughout your communication life and in each communication interaction you're presented with **choice points**—moments when you have to make a choice as to whom you communicate, what you say, what you don't say, how you phrase what you want to say, and so on. Competence in communication choice making can be viewed as a series of four interrelated characteristics.

VIEWPOINTS: **Communication Choices**
What are some of the important communication choices you've made this week? Did you make any choices you regret? Any choices that you are particularly pleased with?

1. The competent communication choice maker realizes that each communication situation can be approached in different ways. For example, there are lots of ways to offer an apology; there are lots of ways to lead a group; there are lots of ways to introduce a speech.

2. The competent communication choice maker has a large arsenal of available choices. For example, the competent communicator would know the characteristics of an effective apology, the varied leadership styles, and the numerous ways in which a speech can be introduced.

3. Because each communication situation is different from every other communication situation, the competent choice maker can effectively evaluate the available choices based on knowledge of the research and theory in human communication. The competent choice maker can make reasonable predictions as to what choices will work and what choices won't. For example, the competent communicator would have the knowledge of human communication that would enable him or her to evaluate the type of apology, the style of leadership, or the specific introduction that would work best for this unique communication situation.

4. The competent communication choice maker has the interpersonal, small-group, and public speaking skills for executing these choices effectively.

This course and this text aim to enlarge your communication options; regardless of your present level of competence, you should emerge from this course with a greater number of communication options under your control. In addition, this course and text provide you with the background—the theory and research bearing on these choices—to help you make more effective communication predictions and decisions.

The Competent Communicator Is an Effective Code Switcher

Technically, **code switching** refers to using more than one language in a conversation, often in the same sentence (Bullock & Toribio, 2012). And so a native Spanish speaker might speak most of a sentence in English and then insert a Spanish term or phrase. More popularly, however, **code switching** refers to using different language styles depending on the situation. For example, you probably talk differently to a child than to an adult—in the topics you talk about and in the language you use. Similarly, when you text or tweet, you use a specialized language consisting of lots of abbreviations and acronyms that you discard when you write a college term paper or when you're interviewing for a job.

The ability to code-switch serves at least two very important purposes. First, it identifies you as one of the group; you are not an outsider. It's a way of bonding with the group. Second, it often helps in terms of making your meaning clearer; some things seem better expressed in one language or code than in another.

Code switching can create problems, however. When used to ingratiate yourself or make yourself seem one of the group when you really aren't—and that attempt is obvious to the group members—code switching is likely to work against you. You risk being seen as an interloper, as one who tries to gain entrance to a group to which one really doesn't belong. The other case where code switching creates problems is when you use the code appropriate to one type of communication in another where it isn't appropriate, for example, when you use your Facebook or Twitter grammar during a job interview. Communication competence, then, involves the ability to code-switch when it's appropriate—when it makes your message clearer and when it's genuine (rather than an attempt to make yourself one of the group).

The Competent Communicator Is Culturally Aware and Sensitive

The term *culture* refers to the lifestyle of a group of people. A group's culture consists of its values, beliefs, artifacts, ways of behaving, and ways of communicating. Culture includes all that members of a social group have produced and developed—their language, ways of thinking, art, laws, and religion. Culture is transmitted from one generation to another not through genes but through communication and learning, especially through the teachings of parents, peer groups, schools, religious institutions, and government agencies. Because most cultures teach women and men different attitudes and ways of communicating, many of the gender differences we observe may be considered cultural. So, while not minimizing the biological differences between men and women, most people agree that gender differences are, in part, cultural.

Competence is sometimes culture specific; communications that prove effective in one culture will not necessarily prove effective in another. For example, giving a birthday gift to a close friend would be appreciated by members of many cultures and in some cases would be expected. But Jehovah's Witnesses frown on this practice because they don't celebrate birthdays (Dresser, 1999, 2005). Because of the vast range of cultural differences that affect human communication, every chapter discusses the role of culture, and Chapter 2 focuses exclusively on culture and intercultural communication.

The Competent Communicator Is Ethical

Human communication also involves questions of **ethics**, the study of good and bad, of right and wrong, of moral and immoral. Ethics is concerned with actions, with behaviors; it's concerned with distinguishing between behaviors that are moral (ethical, good, right) and those that are immoral (unethical, bad, wrong). Not surprisingly, there's an ethical dimension to any communication act (Bok, 1978; Neher & Sandin, 2007).

Some people take an **objective view** of ethics and argue that the rightness or wrongness of an act is absolute and exists apart from the values or beliefs of any individual or culture. With this view, you'd hold that there are standards that apply to all people in all situations at all times. If lying, false advertising, using illegally obtained evidence, or revealing secrets

JOURNAL
COMMUNICATION CHOICE POINT
Cultural Insensitivity

You post a remark on your friend's Facebook wall that you now realize can be seen as culturally insensitive. You don't want anyone to see you as prejudiced and you want to remain friends. You need to say something. *What are your options for communicating your feelings? What would you do?*

you've promised to keep were considered unethical, then they would be unethical regardless of circumstances or of cultural values and beliefs. In an objective view the end can never justify the means; an unethical act is never justified regardless of how good or beneficial its results (or ends) might be.

Others take a **subjective view** of ethics and argue that absolute statements about right and wrong are too rigid and that the ethics of a message depends on the culture's values and beliefs as well as on the particular circumstances. Thus, a subjective position would claim that lying might be wrong to win votes or sell cigarettes, but that it might be quite ethical if good would result from it—as when we try to make friends feel better by telling them that they look great or that they'll get well soon. In a subjective view a good end would often justify the use of means that would in other situations be considered unethical.

Consider your own beliefs about ethics by responding to these few questions with True if you feel the statement accurately explains what ethical behavior is and with False if you feel the statement does not accurately explain what ethical behavior is.

_____ 1. My behavior is ethical when I feel (in my heart) that I'm doing the right thing.

_____ 2. My behavior is ethical when it is consistent with my religious beliefs.

_____ 3. My behavior is ethical when it is legal.

_____ 4. My behavior is ethical when the majority of reasonable people would consider it ethical.

_____ 5. My behavior is ethical when the effect of the behavior benefits more people than it harms.

These statements are based on responses given to the question, What does ethics mean to you? (www.scu.edu/ethics/practicing/decision/whatisethics.html) and are presented here to stimulate thinking and discussion about what is and what is not a useful ethical theory. All five of these statements are false; none of them state a useful explanation of what is and what is not ethical.

1. Statement 1 is false simply because people often do unethical things they feel are morally justified. Jack the Ripper killing prostitutes is a good historical example but there are many current ones such as stalking (*I'm so in love I need to be with this person*) or insurance scams (*My family needs the money more than the insurance company*). Even though Jack, the stalker, and the scam artist may feel justified in their own minds, it doesn't make their behavior moral or ethical.

2. Statement 2 must be false when you realize that different religions advocate very different kinds of behavior, often behaviors that contradict one another. Examples abound in almost every issue of a daily newspaper.

3. Statement 3 must be false when you realize so much discrimination against certain people is perfectly legal in many parts of the world, and, in many countries, war (even preemptive war) is legal.

4. Statement 4 is false because the thinking of the majority changes with the times and has often proven to be extremely immoral. The burning of people supposed to be witches or of those who spoke out against majority opinion (as in the Inquisition) are good examples.

5. Statement 5 is false because immoral acts frequently benefit the majority and harm the minority. The burning of witches, for example, was in the interest of the majority as was slavery and discrimination against gay men and lesbians, certain religions, or different races. But, despite this majority interest, we'd readily recognize these actions as immoral.

In addition to this introductory discussion, ethical dimensions of human communication are presented in each of the remaining chapters in Ethical Messages boxes.

Summary of Concepts and Skills

This chapter considered the nature of human communication, its major elements and principles, the role of culture in human communication, and communication competence.

Forms, Benefits, and Myths of Human Communication

1.1   **Identify the forms, benefits, and myths of human communication.**

1. Human communication exists in varied forms: interpersonal, interviewing, small-group communication, public communication, computer-mediated communication, and mass communication.

2. Among the benefits you'll derive from this course are improvements and enhancements to your self-presentation skills, relationship skills, interviewing skills, group and leadership skills, and presentation or public speaking skills.

3. Among the myths of human communication are that the more you communicate, the more effective you'll become and that fear of public speaking is detrimental and must be eliminated before you can be successful.

Communication Models and Concepts

1.2   **Draw a model of communication that includes sources–receivers, messages, context, channel, noise, and effects; and define each of these elements.**

4. Human communication is the act, by one or more persons, of sending and receiving messages that are distorted by noise, occur within a context, have some effect (and some ethical dimension), and provide some opportunity for feedback.

5. Communication is transactional. It is a process of interrelated parts in which a change in one element produces changes in other elements.

6. The essentials of communication—the elements present in every communication act—are sources–receivers; messages (feedforward, feedback, and metamessages); context (physical, cultural, social-psychological, and temporal); channel; noise (physical, physiological, psychological, and semantic); and effects.

Principles of Communication

1.3   **Paraphrase the major principles of human communication.**

7. Communication is purposeful. Through communication, you learn, relate, help, influence, and play.

8. Communication involves choices and those choices will determine effectiveness or ineffectiveness.

9. Communication and relationships are always—in part—ambiguous.

10. Communication involves both content and relationship dimensions.

11. Communication and relationships invariably involve issues of power.

12. Communication sequences are punctuated for processing. Individuals divide the communication sequence into stimuli and responses in different ways.

13. In any interactional situation, communication is inevitable (you cannot not communicate, nor can you not respond to communication), irreversible (you cannot take back messages), and unrepeatable (you cannot exactly repeat messages).

Culture and Human Communication

1.4   **Explain the role of culture in human communication, the seven ways in which cultures differ from one another, the aim of a cultural perspective; and define** *ethnic identity* **and** *ethnocentrism.*

14. Culture permeates all forms of communication, and intercultural communication is becoming more and more frequent as the United States becomes home to a variety of cultures and does business around the world.

15. Significant dimensions along which cultures may differ are uncertainty avoidance, masculinity–femininity, power distance, individualism–collectivism, high and low context, indulgence and restraint, and long- and short-term orientation.

16. Ethnocentrism, existing on a continuum, is the tendency to evaluate the beliefs, attitudes, and values of our own culture positively and those of other cultures negatively.

Communication Competence

1.5   **Define** *communication competence* **and explain the qualities identified as part of competence.**

17. Communication competence refers to your knowledge of how communication works and your ability to use communication effectively. Communication competence includes, for example:

- thinking critically and mindfully
- making reasoned choices
- effective code switching
- being culturally aware and sensitive
- communicating ethically

Several important communication skills emphasized in this chapter are presented here in summary form (as they are in every chapter). These skill checklists don't include all the skills covered in the chapter but rather are representative of the most important skills. Place a check mark next to those skills that you feel you need to work on most.

_____ 1. I'm sensitive to contexts of communication. I recognize that changes in physical, cultural, social-psychological, and temporal contexts will alter meaning.

_____ 2. I assess my channel options and evaluate whether my message will be more effective if delivered face-to-face, through e-mail, or by some third party, for example.

_____ 3. I look for meaning not only in words but also in nonverbal behaviors.

_____ 4. I am sensitive to the feedback and feedforward that I give to others and that others give to me.

_____ 5. I combat the effects of the various types of physical, psychological, and semantic noise that distort messages.

_____ 6. I listen not only to the more obvious content messages but also to the relational messages that I (and others) send, and I respond to the relational messages of others to increase meaningful interaction.

_____ 7. Instead of looking only at the punctuation patterns, I also look at the patterns that others might be using in order to understand better the meanings communicated.

_____ 8. Because communication is transactional, I recognize that all elements influence every other element in the communication process and that each person communicating is simultaneously a speaker/listener.

_____ 9. Because communication is purposeful, I look carefully at both the speaker's and the listener's purposes.

_____ 10. Because communication is inevitable, irreversible, and unrepeatable, I look carefully for hidden meanings, am cautious in communicating messages that I may later wish to withdraw, and am aware that any communication act occurs but once.

_____ 11. I can effectively switch codes depending on the unique communication situation.

_____ 12. I am sensitive to cultural variation and differences, and I see my own culture's teachings and those of other cultures without undue bias.

Key Terms

ambiguity
channel
choice points
code switching
communication competence
computer-mediated communication
content and relationship
   dimensions
context
cultural context
culture
decoders
decoding
effect
encoders
encoding
ethics
ethnic identity
ethnocentrism

feedback
feedforward
high and low context
individualism–collectivism
indulgence and restraint
inevitability
interpersonal communication
interviewing
irreversibility
long- and short-term
   orientation
masculinity–femininity
mass communication
messages
metamessage
mindfulness
mindlessness
models
noise

objective view
phatic communication
physical context
physical noise
physiological noise
power distance
psychological noise
public communication
punctuation of communication
relationship messages
semantic noise
signal-to-noise ratio
small-group communication
social-psychological context
subjective view
temporal context
uncertainty avoidance
unrepeatability

Skill Development Experiences

1.1 Communicating Content and Relationship Messages

Content and relationship messages serve different communication functions. Being able to distinguish between them is a prerequisite to using and responding to them effectively.

How would you communicate both the content and the relationship messages in the following situations?

1. After a date that you didn't enjoy and don't want to repeat ever again, you want to express your sincere thanks; but you don't want to be misinterpreted

as communicating any indication that you would go on another date with this person.

2. You're tutoring a high school freshman in algebra, but your tutee is really terrible and isn't paying attention or doing the homework you assign. You need to change this behavior and motivate a great change, yet at the same time you don't want to discourage or demoralize the young student.

3. You're interested in dating a friend on Facebook who also attends the college you do and with whom you've been chatting for a few weeks. But you don't know if the feeling is mutual. You want to ask for the date but to do so in a way that, if you're turned down, you won't be horribly embarrassed.

1.2 Writing Your Social Network Profile

Heightened awareness of how messages help create meanings should increase your awareness of the varied choices you have for communicating and ultimately your own communication effectiveness.

Examine your own social network profile (or that of a friend) in terms of the principles of communication discussed in this chapter:

1. What purposes does your profile serve? In what ways might it serve the five purposes of communication identified here (to learn, relate, influence, play, and help)?

2. In what way is your profile page a package of signals? In what ways do the varied words and pictures combine to communicate meaning?

3. Can you identify and distinguish between content from relational messages?

4. In what ways, if any, have you adjusted your profile as a response to the ways in which others have fashioned their profiles?

5. In what ways does your profile exhibit power? In what ways, if any, have you incorporated into your profile the six types of power discussed in this chapter (legitimate, referent, reward, coercive, expert, or information)?

6. What messages on your profile are ambiguous? Bumper stickers and photos should provide a useful starting point.

7. What are the implications of inevitability, irreversibility, and unrepeatability for publishing a profile on and communicating via social network sites?

Chapter 2
Perception of Self and Others

We are (almost) always self-presenting.

This chapter looks at the ways in which you perceive yourself, the ways others perceive you, and the ways you perceive others. First, we explore the nature of the self and a special form of communication known as self-disclosure and the nature of perception. With this as a background, we then explain how we perceive or form impressions of others, how they do the same of us, and how we manage the impressions that we communicate to others.

The Self in Human Communication

2.1   Define *self-concept*, *self-awareness*, and *self-esteem* and explain the ways in which self-awareness and self-esteem may be increased.

Who you are and how you see yourself influence not only the way you communicate but also how you respond to the communications of others. This first section explores the self: the self-concept and how it develops; self-awareness and ways to increase it; self-esteem and ways to enhance it; and self-disclosure, or communication that reveals who you are.

Self-Concept

Your **self-concept** is your image of who you are. It's how you perceive yourself: your feelings and thoughts about your strengths and weaknesses, your abilities and limitations. Self-concept develops from the image that others have of you, comparisons between yourself and others, your cultural experiences, and your evaluation of your own thoughts and behaviors (Figure 2.1).

OTHERS' IMAGES OF YOU   If you want to see how your hair looks, you'll probably look in a mirror. But what if you want to see how friendly or how assertive you are? According to the concept of the **looking-glass self** (Cooley, 1922), you'd look at the image of yourself that others reveal to you through the way they communicate with you.

Of course, you would not look to just anyone. Rather, you would look to those who are most significant in your life, such as your friends, family members, and romantic partners. If these significant persons think highly of you, you will see a positive self-image reflected in their behaviors; if they think little of you, you will see a more negative image.

COMPARISONS WITH OTHERS   Another way you develop self-concept is by comparing yourself with others, most often with your peers (Festinger, 1954). For example, after an exam, you probably want to know how you performed relative to the other students in your class. This gives you a clearer idea of how effectively you performed. If you play on a baseball team, it's important to know your batting average in comparison to those of your teammates. You gain a different perspective when you see yourself in comparison to your peers.

For good or ill, social media have provided us with the tools (all very easy to use) to compare ourselves to others, perhaps to estimate our individual worth or make us feel superior. Here are several ways social media enable you to find out how you stand in comparison with others.

- **Search engine reports**   Type in your name or a colleague's name on Google, Bing, or Yahoo, for example, and you'll see the number of websites on which your names appear.

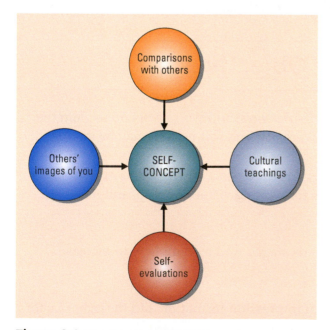

Figure 2.1 The Sources of Self-Concept

The four contributors to how you see yourself. As you read about self-concept, consider the influence of each factor throughout your life. *Which factor influenced you most as a preteen? Which influences you most now? Which will influence you most in 25 or 30 years?*

- **Network spread** The number of friends on Facebook or the number of contacts on LinkedIn or Plaxo is in some ways a measure of potential influence.

- **Online influence** Network sites such as Klout and PeerIndex provide a score (from 0 to 100) of online influence. Your Klout score, for example, is a combination of your "true reach"—the number of people you influence, "amplification"—the degree to which you influence them, and "network"—the influence of your network.

- **Twitter activities** The number of times you tweet might be one point of comparison but, more important, is the number of times you are tweeted about or your tweets are repeated (retweeted).

- **Blog presence** Your blog presence is readily available from your "stats" tab where you can see how many people visited your blog since inception or over the past year, month, week, or day.

The Cultural Map

MASCULINE AND FEMININE ORIENTATION

Online and face-to-face friendships, romantic relationships, family, and workplace relationships dominate our lives. These relationships are influenced by the masculine-feminine cultural differences. The aggressive, ambitious, and competitive masculine cultural orientation will encourage relationships that are different from what the modest, tender, relationship-focused feminine culture will encourage.

These countries are among the most strongly affiliated with masculine qualities. Masculine cultures emphasize aggressiveness, strength, and success and socialize their members to be assertive, competitive, and ambitious.

These countries are among the most strongly affiliated with feminine qualities. Feminine cultures emphasize modesty, quality of life rather than material success, and a concern for relationships.

Look at your own relationships (friendship and romantic). *Are they mainly with those who have a masculine orientation or mainly with those who have a feminine orientation? If there is a difference, to what do you attribute it?*

CULTURAL TEACHINGS   Your culture instills in you a variety of beliefs, values, and attitudes about such things as success (how you define it and how you should achieve it); the relevance of religion, race, or nationality; and the ethical principles you should follow in business and in your personal life. These teachings provide benchmarks against which you can measure yourself. Your ability, for example, to achieve what your culture defines as success contributes to a positive self-concept; your failure to achieve what your culture values contributes to a negative self-concept.

Especially important in self-concept are cultural teachings about gender roles—how a man or woman should act (see the Cultural Map in this chapter). A popular classification of cultures is in terms of their masculinity and femininity (Hofstede, 1997). [Some intercultural theorists note that equivalent terms would be cultures based on "achievement" and "nurturance," but because research is conducted under the terms *masculine* and *feminine* and these are the terms you'd use to search electronic databases, we use them here (Lustig & Koester, 2013).] Masculine cultures socialize people to be assertive, ambitious, and competitive. For example, members of masculine cultures are more likely to confront conflicts directly and to fight out any differences. Feminine cultures socialize people to be modest and to value close interpersonal relationships. For example, they are more likely to emphasize compromise and negotiation in resolving conflicts.

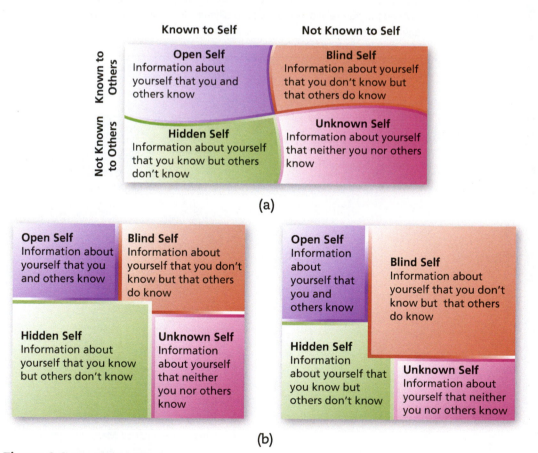

Figure 2.2 The Johari Window

The top window (a) presents a commonly used tool for examining what we know and don't know about ourselves. It can also help explain the nature of self-disclosure, covered later in this chapter. The window gets its name from its originators, *Joseph* Luft and *Harry* Ingham. The two windows at the bottom (b) illustrate Johari windows of different structures. Notice that as one self grows, one or more of the other selves shrink. *How would you describe the type of communication (especially self-disclosure) that might characterize the two people represented by these two windows?*

SOURCE: Joseph Luft, *Group Process: An Introduction to Group Dynamics*, 3rd ed. Copyright © 1984. New York: McGraw-Hill. Reprinted by permission.

When you display the traits prized by your culture—whether they be masculine or feminine—you're likely to be rewarded and complimented, and this feedback contributes to a positive self-concept. Displaying contrary traits is likely to result in criticism, which, in turn, will contribute to a more negative self-concept.

SELF-INTERPRETATIONS AND SELF-EVALUATIONS   Your self-interpretations (the reconstruction of your behavior in a given event and your understanding of it) and self-evaluations (the value—good or bad—that you place on that behavior) also contribute to your self-concept. For example, let's say you believe that lying is wrong. If you then lie and view what you said as a lie (rather than as, say, a polite way of avoiding an issue), you will probably evaluate this behavior in terms of your internalized beliefs about lying and will react negatively to your own behavior. You may, for example, experience guilt about violating your own beliefs. On the other hand, let's say that you pull someone out of a burning building at great personal risk. You will probably evaluate this behavior positively; you'll feel good about your behavior and, as a result, about yourself.

Self-Awareness

Self-awareness is basic to all communication and is achieved when you examine several aspects of yourself as they might appear to others as well as to you. One commonly used tool for this examination is the **Johari window**, a metaphoric division of the self into four areas, as shown in Figure 2.2(a).

YOUR FOUR SELVES   The four areas or "panes" in the Johari window show different aspects or versions of the self: the open self, the blind self, the hidden self, and the unknown self. These areas are not separate from one another: They are interdependent. As one dominates, the others recede to a greater or lesser degree; or, to stay with our metaphor, as one windowpane becomes larger, one or more others become smaller.

- The **open self** represents all the information, behaviors, attitudes, and feelings about yourself that you, and also others, know. The size of the open self varies according to your personality and the people to whom you're relating. For example, you may have a large open self about your romantic life with your friends (you tell them everything) but a very small open self about the same issues with, say, your parents.

- The **blind self** represents knowledge about you that others have but you don't. This might include your habit of finishing other people's sentences or your way of rubbing your nose when you become anxious. A large blind self indicates low self-awareness and interferes with accurate communication. To reduce your blind self, you can follow the suggestions offered below, in "Growing in Self-Awareness."

- The **unknown self** represents those parts of yourself that neither you nor others know. This is information buried in your subconscious. You may, for example, learn of your obsession with money, your fear of criticism, or the kind of lover you are through hypnosis, dreams, psychological tests, or psychotherapy.

- The **hidden self** represents all the knowledge you have of yourself but keep secret from others. This windowpane includes all your successfully kept secrets, such as your fantasies, embarrassing experiences, and any attitudes or beliefs you want to keep private.

Each person's Johari window will be different, and each individual's window will vary from one time to another and from one communication situation to another. You probably have a very different configuration of window panes depending on whether you're talking face-to-face with a parent or on Facebook with a close friend. Figure 2.2(b) illustrates two possible configurations.

GROWING IN SELF-AWARENESS Because self-awareness is so important in communication, try to increase awareness of your own needs, desires, habits, beliefs, and attitudes. You can do this in various ways.

- **Listen to others** Conveniently, others are constantly giving you the very feedback you need to increase self-awareness. In every interaction, people comment on you in some way—on what you do, what you say, how you look. Sometimes these comments are explicit: "Loosen up" or "Don't take things so hard." Often they're "hidden" in the way others look at you or in what they talk about. Pay close attention to this kind of information.

- **Increase your open self** Revealing yourself to others will help increase your self-awareness. As you talk about yourself, you may see connections that you had previously missed. With feedback from others, you may gain still more insight. Also, by increasing your open self, you increase the chances that others will reveal what they know about you.

- **Seek information about yourself** Encourage people to reveal what they know about you. Use situations that arise every day to gain self-information: "Do you think I came down too hard on the kids today?" "Do you think I was assertive enough when asking for the raise?" But seek this self-awareness in moderation. If you do it too often, your friends may soon perceive you as insecure or self-centered and look for someone else with whom to talk.

- **Dialogue with yourself** No one knows you better than you know yourself. Ask yourself self-awareness questions: What motivates me to act as I do? What are my short- and long-term goals? How do I plan to achieve them? What are my strengths and weaknesses?

Self-Esteem

Self-esteem is a measure of how valuable you think you are. If you have high self-esteem, you think highly of yourself; if you have low self-esteem, you tend to view yourself negatively. Self-esteem includes cognitive or thinking, affective or emotional, and behavioral components (Reasoner, 2010).

- **Cognitive self-esteem** refers to your thinking about your strengths and weaknesses, about who you are versus who you'd like to be. What is your ideal self? How close are you to achieving this ideal self?

- **Affective self-esteem** refers to your analysis of your own strengths and weaknesses. For example, do you feel pleased with yourself? Does your analysis lead you to feel dissatisfied and perhaps depressed?

- **Behavioral self-esteem** refers to verbal and nonverbal behaviors such as your disclosures, your assertiveness, your conflict strategies, your gestures. Do you assert yourself in group situations? Do you allow others to take advantage of you? Are you confident to disclose who you really are?

Before reading further about this topic, consider your own self-esteem by taking the accompanying self-test, How's Your Self-Esteem?

The basic idea behind self-esteem is that when you feel good about yourself—about who you are and what you're capable of doing—you will perform better. When you think you're a success, you're more likely to act like you're a success. Conversely, when you think you're a failure, you're more likely to act like you're a failure. When you reach for the phone to ask the most popular student in the school for a date and you visualize yourself being successful and effective, you're more likely to give a good impression. If, on the other hand, you think you're going to forget what you want to say or stutter or say something totally stupid, you're less likely to be successful.

Low self-esteem is learned (Lancer, 2013). Somewhere, somehow you learned that your feelings are not justified or that you aren't capable of doing this or that. And because it's learned behavior, it's possible to change this, although it's not an easy process (Gross, 2013).

Test Yourself

HOW'S YOUR SELF-ESTEEM?

Respond to each of the following statements with **T** (for true) if the statement describes you at least a significant part of the time and **F** (for false) if the statement describes you rarely or never.

_____ **1.** Generally, I feel I have to be successful in all things.

_____ **2.** Despite outward signs of success, I still feel unsuccessful.

_____ **3.** A number of my acquaintances are often critical or negative of what I do and how I think.

_____ **4.** I often tackle projects that I know are impossible to complete to my satisfaction.

_____ **5.** When I focus on the past, I more often focus on my failures than on my successes and on my negative rather than my positive qualities.

_____ **6.** I make little effort to improve my personal and social skills.

"True" responses to the questions generally are seen as getting in the way of building positive self-esteem. "False" responses indicate that you think much like a self-esteem coach would want you to think. The discussion that follows elaborates on these issues and illustrates why each of them creates problems for the development of healthy self-esteem.

Here are six suggestions for increasing self-esteem that parallel the statements in the self-test (Figure 2.3).

Figure 2.3 Climbing to higher self-esteem
Here are just a few things you can do to increase your self-esteem.

ATTACK SELF-DESTRUCTIVE BELIEFS Challenge **self-destructive beliefs**—ideas you have about yourself that are unproductive or that make it more difficult for you to achieve your goals (Einhorn, 2006; Butler, 1981; Gross, 2006). Often, these self-destructive beliefs tell you that you *should* be able to achieve unrealistic goals. Here, for example, are some beliefs that are likely to prove self-destructive:

- I *should* be liked by everyone.
- I *should* be successful in everything I do.
- I *should* always win.
- I *should* be totally in control of my life.
- I *should* always be productive.

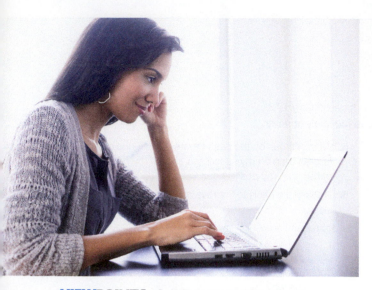

VIEWPOINTS: **Self-Esteem and Facebook**
The difference between those with high and those with low self-esteem is even shown in how they post on social media (Nie & Sundar, 2013). Those with high self-esteem post information about their family, work, and education. Those with low self-esteem do this less and spend their social media time monitoring their wall and deleting any posts or photos that may reflect on them negatively. *How do you see the relationship between self-esteem and posting to social media?*

These beliefs set unrealistically high standards, and therefore almost always end in failure. As a result, you may develop a negative self-image, seeing yourself as someone who constantly fails. So replace these self-destructive beliefs with more productive ones, such as these:

- It would be nice to be liked by everyone, but it isn't necessary to my happiness.
- Being successful is great but it's impossible to be successful at everything.
- Winning makes me feel powerful but no one can win all the time. Learning to deal with losing also builds strength.
- I can't possibly control everything that has an impact on my life. Life is full of surprises.
- There is a limit on what one person can do; it's okay if I do what I can do and leave the rest for another day.

BEWARE THE IMPOSTOR PHENOMENON   The **impostor phenomenon** refers to the to disregard outward signs of success and to consider yourself an "impostor," a fake, a fraud, one who doesn't really deserve to be considered successful (Clance, 1985; Harvey & Katz, 1985). Even though others may believe you are a success, you "know" that they are wrong. One of the dangers of this belief is that it may prevent you from seeking advancement in your profession, believing you won't be up to the task. Becoming aware that such beliefs are not uncommon and that they are not necessarily permanent should help relieve some of these misperceptions. Another useful aid is to develop a relationship with an honest and knowledgeable mentor who will not only teach you the ropes but will let you know that you are successful.

SEEK OUT NOURISHING PEOPLE   Psychologist Carl Rogers (1970) drew a distinction between *noxious* and *nourishing* people. Noxious people criticize and find fault with just about everything. Nourishing people, on the other hand, are positive and optimistic, and make us feel good about ourselves. To enhance your self-esteem, seek out nourishing people and avoid noxious people. At the same time, seek to become more nourishing yourself so that you can build others' self-esteem while improving your own.

WORK ON PROJECTS THAT WILL RESULT IN SUCCESS   Some people want to fail, or so it seems. Often they select projects that will result in failure simply because they are impossible to complete. Avoid this trap and choose projects that will result in success. Each success will help build self-esteem and make the next success a little easier. If a project does fail, recognize that this does not mean you're a failure. Everyone fails somewhere along the line. Failure is something that happens to you; it's not something you've created, and it's not something inside you.

REMIND YOURSELF OF YOUR SUCCESSES   Some people have a tendency to focus, sometimes too much, on their failures, their missed opportunities, their social mistakes. To counteract this tendency to dwell on failures, remind yourself of your successes. Recall these successes both intellectually and emotionally. Realize why they were successes, and relive the emotional experience when you sank the winning basket or helped your friend overcome personal problems.

SECURE AFFIRMATION   It's frequently recommended that you remind yourself of your successes with affirmations—that you focus on your good deeds; on your positive qualities, strengths, and virtues; and on your productive and meaningful relationships with friends, loved ones, and relatives (Aronson, Wilson, & Akert, 2013). The idea behind this advice is that the way you talk to yourself will influence what you think of yourself. If you *affirm* yourself—if you tell yourself that you're a success, that others like you, that you will succeed on the next test, and that you will be welcomed when asking for a date—you will soon come to feel more positive about yourself. Self-affirmations include statements like: "I'm a worthy person," "I'm responsible and can be depended upon," and "I'm capable of loving and being loved."

Some researchers argue, however, that such affirmations—although extremely popular in self-help books—may not be very helpful. These critics contend that if you have low self-esteem, you're not going to believe yourself (Paul, 2001). They propose that the alternative to self-affirmation is affirmation secured from others. You'd obtain this, for example, by becoming more competent in communication and interacting with more positive people. In this way you'd get more positive feedback from others—which, these researchers argue, is more helpful than self-talk in raising self-esteem.

Self-Disclosure

2.2 Define *self-disclosure*, its rewards and dangers, and explain the suggested guidelines for making, responding to, and resisting self-disclosure.

Self-disclosure means communicating information about yourself to another person. Although we often limit the term to revealing information that you normally keep hidden, it can also refer to information that you would share with just about anyone: your likes and dislikes (as you do on Facebook); your brief tweets that say something about what you like or don't like; simply what you're thinking about; or your preferences for foods, books, or music that you reveal when you post a photo on Pinterest or Instagram (Greene, Derlega, & Mathews, 2006). It may involve information about (1) your values, beliefs, and desires ("I believe in reincarnation"); (2) your behavior ("I shoplifted but was never caught"); or (3) your self-qualities or characteristics ("I'm dyslexic"). Overt and carefully planned statements about yourself as well as slips of the tongue would be classified as self-disclosing communications. Similarly, you could self-disclose nonverbally by, for example, wearing gang colors; a wedding ring; a shirt with slogans that reveal your political or social concerns, such as "Pro-Choice" or "Go Green;" or photos on Facebook. Self-disclosure also may involve your reactions to the feelings of others, for example, when you tell your friend that you're sorry she was fired.

Self-disclosure occurs in all forms of communication, not just interpersonal. It frequently occurs in small-group settings, in public speeches, on television talk shows such as *Maury* and *Jerry Springer*, and even on *Jimmy Fallon* or *Live! with Kelly & Michael*. And self-disclosure can occur not only in face-to-face settings but also through the Internet. On social network sites such as Twitter or Facebook, for example, a great deal of self-disclosure goes on, as it does when people reveal themselves in personal e-mails, newsgroups, and blog posts. In fact, research finds that reciprocal self-disclosure occurs more quickly and at higher levels online than it does in face-to-face interactions (Joinson, 2001; Levine, 2000).

Some researchers have pointed to a **disinhibition effect** that occurs in online communication. We seem less inhibited in communicating in e-mail or in social media, for example, than we do face-to-face. Among the reasons for this seems to be the fact that, in online communication, there is a certain degree of anonymity and invisibility (Suler, 2004). Other research, however, finds the opposite. In an examination of blog posts, the research showed that those posts that were accompanied by a photograph of the author

"You'd know that about me if you followed me on Twitter."
William Haefeli/The New Yorker Collection/The Cartoon Bank

actually disclosed more than those posts that did not so identify the author (Hollenbaugh & Everett, 2013).

You probably self-disclose for a variety of reasons. Perhaps you feel the need for catharsis—a need to get rid of feelings of guilt or to confess some wrongdoing. You may also disclose to help the listener, for example, to show the listener how you dealt with an addiction or succeeded in getting a promotion. Of course, you may self-disclose to encourage relationship growth, or to maintain or repair a relationship, or even as a strategy for ending a relationship.

Although self-disclosure may occur as a single message—for example, you tell a stranger on a train that you're thinking about getting a divorce—it's best viewed as a developing process in which information is exchanged between people over the period of their relationship (Spencer, 1993, 1994). If we view it as a developing process, we can then appreciate how self-disclosure changes as the relationship changes; for example, as a relationship progresses from initial contact through involvement to intimacy, the self-disclosures increase. If the relationship deteriorates and perhaps dissolves, the disclosures decrease. We can also appreciate how self-disclosure differs depending on the type of relationship, on whether the other person is your friend, lover, parent, child, or counselor.

Self-disclosure involves at least one other individual; it cannot be an intrapersonal communication act. To qualify as self-disclosure, the information must be received and understood by another person. As you can appreciate, self-disclosure can vary from the relatively insignificant ("I'm a Sagittarius") to the highly revealing and deeply personal ("I'm currently in an abusive relationship" or "I'm almost always depressed"). It can occur face-to-face and it can occur over the Internet. It can be limited to one person or to a network of thousands on Twitter or Facebook.

The remaining discussion of this concept will be more meaningful if you first consider your own willingness to self-disclose by responding to the accompanying self-test.

Self-disclosure often brings rewards, but it can also create problems. Whether or not you self-disclose will depend on your assessment of the possible rewards and dangers.

Self-Disclosure Rewards

There are many rewards related to self-disclosure:

- **Self-knowledge** Self-disclosure helps you gain a new perspective on yourself and a deeper understanding of your own behavior. As you talk about yourself and listen to the reactions of others, you're likely to learn a great deal about yourself.

- **Improved coping abilities** Self-disclosure may help you deal with a variety of problems. By verbalizing any problem or perceived failure, you'll likely see it more objectively and dispassionately. And, assuming you receive support rather than rejection from the other person, you'll likely be better able to cope with these and future problems or failures.

- **Communication enhancement** Self-disclosure often improves communication. You understand the messages of others largely to the extent that you understand the individuals. You can tell what certain nuances mean, whether a person is serious or joking, and whether the person is being sarcastic out of fear or resentment.

- **More meaningful relationships** By self-disclosing you tell others that you trust, respect, and care enough about them and your relationship to reveal yourself. This, in turn, is likely to lead the other individual to self-disclose and forms at least the start of a relationship that is honest and open and allows for more complete communication. Even in public speaking, self-disclosure—if it's relevant to the issue—is often helpful in building a bond between the speaker and the audience.

Test Yourself

HOW WILLING TO SELF-DISCLOSE ARE YOU?

Respond to each of the following statements by indicating the likelihood that you would disclose such items of information to, say, other members of this class in a one-on-one face-to-face situation, on Facebook (either posting or commenting) and on the phone.

Use the following scale to fill in all three columns: **1** = would definitely self-disclose; **2** = would probably self-disclose; **3** = don't know; **4** = would probably not self-disclose; and **5** = would definitely not self-disclose.

Information	Face-to-Face Communication	On a Social Media Site	On the Phone
My attitudes toward other religions, nationalities, and races	_____	_____	_____
My financial status: how much money I earn, how much I owe, how much I have saved	_____	_____	_____
My feelings about my parents	_____	_____	_____
My sexual fantasies	_____	_____	_____
My physical and mental health	_____	_____	_____
My ideal romantic partner	_____	_____	_____
My drinking and/or drug behavior	_____	_____	_____
My most embarrassing moment	_____	_____	_____
My unfulfilled desires	_____	_____	_____
My self-concept	_____	_____	_____

There are, of course, no right or wrong answers to this self-test. The higher your scores, the more apt to disclose you are in this channel. In addition, people will self-disclose most in interpersonal communication situations, least in public communication situations, and somewhere in between in group communication. Taking this test should get you started thinking about your own self-disclosing behavior and especially the factors that influence it. How does your personality influence the topics and the channels of your self-disclosures? Are there certain topics on which you are less willing to disclose than others? Will you disclose some topics over one channel but not another? Are you more likely to disclose positive secrets than negative ones? Is this true in all channels? Are there topics about which you wish you had the opportunity to self-disclose but somehow can't find the right situation?

- **Preventing inaccurate perceptions** One further advantage of self-disclosure is that in its absence, people may wonder about this or that and construct inaccurate explanations that may be worse than any secret (say, 2014). In some cases, romantic partners, friends, or family will snoop to discover information that you've kept hidden. According to some research, approximately 44 percent of couples have at least one partner who snoops and 37 percent of the couples snooped on each other (Helsper & Whitty, 2010). In another study, over 60 percent of college students admitted to using Facebook to keep tabs on romantic partners and others (Stern & Willis, 2007). Snooping is so prevalent that dating websites such as eHarmony provide advice on whether or not to snoop.

Self-Disclosure Dangers

There are also, however, some dangers related to self-disclosure:

- **Personal risks** The more you reveal about yourself to others, the more areas of your life you expose to possible attack. Especially in the competitive context of

VIEWPOINTS: Self-Disclosure and Culture
Different cultures view self-disclosure differently. Some cultures view disclosing inner feelings as weakness. Among some groups, for example, it would be considered "out of place" for a man to cry at a happy occasion such as a wedding, whereas in some Latin cultures that same display of emotion would go unnoticed. Similarly, it's considered undesirable in Japan for workplace colleagues to reveal personal information, whereas in much of the United States it's expected (Barnlund, 1989; Hall & Hall, 1987). *How would you describe your own culture's unwritten rules for appropriate self-disclosure?*

work (or even romance), the more that others know about you, the more they'll be able to use against you.

- **Relationship risks** Even in close and long-lasting relationships, self-disclosure can cause problems. For example, parents, normally the most supportive people in most individuals' lives, frequently reject children who self-disclose their homosexuality or their plans to marry someone of a different race, or their belief in another faith.

- **Professional risks** Sometimes self-disclosure may result in professional or material losses. Students who disclose their alcohol or drug behavior in Facebook photos or posts may discover that jobs are more difficult to find or they may even be fired from an existing position. In an organization, disclosures that go against organizational norms—for example, the disclosures are too personal or not job-related—carry additional risks (Rosh & Offermann, 2013).

Remember that self-disclosure, like any other communication, is irreversible. You cannot self-disclose and then take it back. Nor can you erase the inferences listeners make on the basis of your disclosures. Remember, too, to examine the rewards and dangers of self-disclosure in light of cultural rules. As with all cultural rules, following rules about self-disclosure brings approval, and violating them brings disapproval.

Guidelines for Making Self-Disclosures

In addition to weighing the potential rewards and dangers of self-disclosure, consider the following suggestions, which should help you raise the right questions before you make what must be your own decision. Additional suggestions that apply especially to the workplace are identified in Table 2.1.

- **Consider the motivation for the self-disclosure.** Self-disclosure should be motivated by a concern for the relationship, for the others involved, and for yourself. Self-disclosure should serve a useful and productive function for all persons involved. Self-disclosing past indiscretions because you want to clear the air and be honest may be worthwhile; disclosing the same indiscretions to hurt your partner, however, is likely to damage the relationship.

- **Consider the appropriateness of the self-disclosure.** Self-disclosure should be appropriate to the context and to the relationship between you and your

Table 2.1 Self-Disclosure Cautions in the Workplace

Self-disclosure in the workplace involves somewhat different considerations from face-to-face disclosure with a friend, for example. Here are a few suggested cautions and comments.

Cautions	Comments
Assume that your disclosure will be repeated—especially if they may be interpreted as sexist or racist, for example.	Although it may not be, assuming it will be, will give you a useful "what if" perspective.
Realize that your disclosure may be used against you.	This seems especially true if you're in a highly competitive organization; includes the relatively innocent office joking to the more serious issues of promotion and bonuses.
Realize that disclosure very often leads to a loss of power.	Assess whether you're willing to give up some of the power you have when people are not quite sure about you.
Understand that disclosure of a disability is your decision.	Whether or not you disclose a disability is entirely your decision, according to the U.S. Department of Labor's Office of Disability Employment Policy.
Realize that one colleague's disclosure does not obligate you to disclose.	Although reciprocating is a natural tendency, you are not required to also self-disclose—but you may be missing a great opportunity to connect with a colleague.

listener. Before making any significant self-disclosure, ask whether this is the right time (Do you both have the time to discuss this at the length it requires?) and place (Is the place free of distractions? Is it private?). Generally, the more intimate the disclosure, the closer the relationship should be. It's probably best to resist making intimate disclosures (especially negative ones) with casual acquaintances, or in the early stages of a relationship.

JOURNAL
COMMUNICATION CHOICE POINT
Corrective Self-Disclosure

When you met your current partner—with whom you want to spend the rest of your life—you minimized the extent of your romantic history. You now want to come clean and disclose your "sordid" past and need to preface this in some way. *What kinds of feedforward might you use? Through what channels? What would you say?*

- **Consider the disclosures of the other person.** During your disclosures, give the other person a chance to reciprocate with his or her own disclosures. If the other person does not reciprocate, reassess how much more you need to reveal. It may be that for this person at this time and in this context, your disclosures are not welcome or appropriate. For example, if you reveal your romantic mistakes to a friend and your friend says nothing or reveals only the most minor details, it may be a cue to stop disclosing. Generally, it's best to disclose gradually and in small increments so you can monitor your listener's responses and retreat if they're not positive enough.

- **Consider the possible burdens self-disclosure might entail.** Carefully weigh the potential problems that you may incur as a result of your disclosure. Can you afford to lose your job if you disclose your prison record? Are you willing to risk relational difficulties if you disclose your infidelities? Are you willing to post on Facebook those images of you partying that a graduate school admissions officer or a prospective employer is likely to see?

Guidelines for Facilitating and Responding to Others' Disclosures

When someone discloses to you in person or through a social media site, it's usually a sign of trust and affection. In carrying out this most important receiver function, keep the following guidelines in mind:

- **Support and reinforce the discloser.** Express support for the person during and after the disclosures. Make your supportiveness clear through your verbal and nonverbal responses: Maintain eye contact, lean toward the speaker, ask relevant questions, and echo the speaker's thoughts and feelings. In social media, *like*, *thumbs up*, and *+1* serve similar supportive functions. Try to refrain from judgment. Concentrate on understanding and empathizing with the discloser.

- **Be willing to reciprocate (generally).** When you make relevant and appropriate disclosures of your own in response to another's disclosures, you're demonstrating your understanding of that person's meanings and at the same time your willingness to communicate on a meaningful level—although you have no obligation to do so.

- **Keep the disclosures confidential.** If you reveal confidential disclosures, negative effects are inevitable. But most important, betraying a confidence is unfair; it debases what could be and should be a meaningful experience. Generally, the netiquette rule to not pass on e-mails to a third party without permission is a useful one for self-disclosure generally.

- **Don't use the disclosures against the person.** Many self-disclosures expose some kind of vulnerability. If you later turn around and use a disclosure against someone, you betray the confidence and trust invested in you. Regardless of how angry you may get, resist the temptation to use the disclosures of others as weapons.

Guidelines for Resisting Pressure to Self-Disclose

You may, on occasion, find yourself in a position where a friend, colleague, or romantic partner pressures you to self-disclose. In such situations, you may wish to weigh the pros and cons of self-disclosure and then make your decision about whether and what you'll disclose. Keep in mind that one of the consequences of social media and the Internet generally is that more information easily accessible. Therefore, although you may resist, say, revealing your age in your office, it can probably be found online. Nevertheless, there are occasions when you do not want to disclose and you're still being pressured, and you need to say something. Here are a few suggestions:

- **Don't be pushed.** Although there may be certain legal or ethical reasons for disclosing, generally, if you don't want to disclose, you don't have to. Don't be pushed into disclosing because others are doing it or because you're asked to.

- **Be assertive in your refusal to disclose.** Say, very directly, "I'd rather not talk about that now" or "Now is not the time for this type of discussion."

- **Delay a decision.** If you don't want to say no directly but still don't want to disclose, delay the decision. Say something like, "That's pretty personal; let me think about that before I say too much" or "This isn't really a good time (or place) to talk about this; I'll get back to you and we'll talk."

- **Move to another topic.** Avoid the question by changing the subject. This is a polite way of saying, "I'm not talking about it," and may be the preferred choice in certain situations. Most often people will get the hint and understand your refusal to disclose.

With an understanding of the self in human communication, we can explore perception—the processes by which you come to understand yourself and others and, of course, the processes by which others come to understand you.

Perception

2.3 Define *perception* and its stages, and explain how to increase perceptual accuracy.

Perception is your way of understanding the world; it helps you make sense of what psychologist William James called the "booming buzzing confusion." More technically, perception is the process by which you become aware of objects, events, and especially people through your senses of sight, smell, taste, touch, and hearing. Your perceptions result both from what exists in the outside world *and* from your own experiences, desires, needs and wants, loves and hatreds. Perception is important in communication because it influences your communication choices. The messages you send and listen to, the photos and messages you post and view will depend on how you see the world, how you see yourself, how you size up a specific situation, or what you think of the people with whom you interact.

Perception is a continuous series of processes that blend into one another. For convenience of discussion we can separate these processes into five stages (which may occur in a split second): (1) You sense or pick up some kind of stimulation; (2) you organize the stimuli in some way; (3) you interpret and evaluate what you perceive; (4) you store your perception in memory; and (5) you retrieve it when needed. See Figure 2.4.

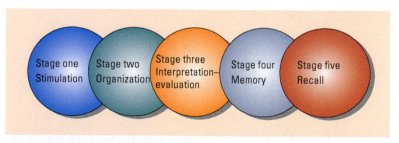

Figure 2.4 The Five Stages of Perception

Perception occurs in five stages: stimulation, organization, interpretation–evaluation, memory, and recall. Understanding how perception works will help make your own perceptions (of yourself and of others) more accurate.

Stimulation (Stage 1)

At the first stage of perception, your sense organs are *stimulated*—you hear new music, you smell someone's perfume, you taste an orange, you feel another's sweaty palm. Naturally, you don't perceive everything; rather, you engage in **selective perception**, which includes selective attention and selective exposure.

- In **selective attention** you attend to those things that you anticipate will fulfill your needs or will prove enjoyable. For instance, when daydreaming in class, you don't hear what the instructor is saying until he or she calls your name. Your selective attention mechanism focuses your senses on the sound of your name.
- In **selective exposure** you tend to expose yourself to information that will confirm your existing beliefs, will contribute to your objectives, or will prove satisfying in some way. At the same time, you avoid information that would tell you that you made the wrong decision.

You're also more likely to perceive stimuli that are greater in intensity than surrounding stimuli. For example, television commercials normally play at a greater intensity than regular programming to ensure that you take special notice. And you're more likely to perceive stimuli that have novelty value; for example, you're more likely to notice the coworker who dresses in a unique way than the one who dresses like everyone else.

Organization (Stage 2)

At the second stage, you organize the information your senses pick up. One of the major ways you organize information is by rules. One frequently used rule of perception is that of **proximity**, or physical closeness: Things that are physically close to each other are perceived as a unit. Thus, using this rule, you would perceive people who are often together, or messages spoken one immediately after the other, as units, as belonging together.

Another rule is **similarity**: Things that are physically similar (they look alike) are perceived to belong together and to form a unit. This principle of similarity would lead you to see people who dress alike as belonging together. Similarly, you might assume that people who work at the same jobs, who are of the same religion, who live in the same building, or who talk with the same accent belong together.

The rule of **contrast** is the opposite of similarity: When items (people or messages, for example) are very different from each other, you conclude that they don't belong together; they're too different from each other to be part of the same unit. If you're the only one who shows up at an informal gathering in a tuxedo, you'd be seen as not belonging to the group because you contrast too much with other group members.

Interpretation–Evaluation (Stage 3)

The third stage involves interpretation–evaluation (a combined term because the two processes cannot be separated)—and it is greatly influenced by your experiences, needs, wants, values, beliefs about the way things are or should be, expectations, physical and emotional state, and so on. Your interpretation–evaluation will be influenced by your gender; for example, women have been found to view others more positively than men (Winquist, Mohr, & Kenny, 1998).

Judgments about members of other cultures are often ethnocentric; because of your stereotypes, you can easily (but inappropriately) apply these to members of other cultures. And so it's easy to infer that when members of other cultures do things that conform to your ways of doing things, they're right, and when they do things that contradict your ways, they're wrong—a classic example of ethnocentric thinking. This tendency can easily contribute to intercultural misunderstandings.

JOURNAL
COMMUNICATION CHOICE POINT
Relationship Uncertainty

You've been dating someone casually over the past six months. You want to move to a more exclusive relationship in which you date only each other, but you've been getting mixed signals. *In what ways might you go about discovering how your partner feels?*

Memory (Stage 4)

Your perceptions and their interpretations–evaluations are put into memory; they're stored so that you may ultimately retrieve them at some later time. For example, you have in memory your stereotype for college athletes and the fact that Ben Williams is a football player. Ben Williams is then stored in memory with "cognitive tags" that tell you that he's strong, ambitious, academically weak, and egocentric. Despite the fact that you've not witnessed Ben's strength or ambitions and have no idea of his academic record or his psychological profile, you still may store your memory of Ben along with the qualities that make up your stereotype for college athletes.

Recall (Stage 5)

At some later date, you may want to recall or access the information you have stored in memory. Let's say you want to retrieve your information about Ben because he's the topic of discussion among you and a few friends. As we'll see in our discussion of listening in the next chapter, memory isn't reproductive; you don't simply reproduce what you've heard or seen. Rather, you reconstruct what you've heard or seen into a whole that is meaningful to you. It's this reconstruction that you store in memory. When you want to retrieve this information, you may recall it with a variety of inaccuracies.

Impression Formation

2.4 **Describe the nature of impression formation and the major factors that influence it.**

With an understanding of the self and how perception works, we can look at the ways they are intimately connected: first in impression formation and then in impression management—academic terms for what you do every day.

Impression formation (sometimes referred to as *person perception*) refers to the processes you go through in forming an impression of another person—whether it's the student sitting next to you in class or looking at a person's Facebook page. **Impression management** refers to the processes you use to give others the impression you want them to have.

Impression Formation Processes

How you perceive another person and ultimately come to some kind of evaluation or interpretation of him or her is influenced by a variety of processes. Here, we consider some of the more significant: the self-fulfilling prophecy, primacy–recency, stereotyping, and attribution.

SELF-FULFILLING PROPHECY   A **self-fulfilling prophecy** is a prediction that comes true because you act on it as if it were true. Self-fulfilling prophecies occur in such widely different situations as parent–child relationships, educational settings, and business (Merton, 1957; Rosenthal, 2002; Madon, Guyll, & Spoth, 2004; Tierney & Farmer, 2004). There are four basic steps in the self-fulfilling prophecy:

1. You make a prediction or formulate a belief about a person or a situation. For example, you predict that Pat is friendly in social situations.

2. You act toward that person or situation as if such a prediction or belief were true. For example, you act as if Pat were a friendly person.

3. Because you act as if the belief were true, it becomes true. For example, because of the way you act, Pat becomes comfortable and friendly.

4. You observe your effect on the person or the resulting situation, and what you see strengthens your beliefs. For example, you observe Pat's friendliness, and this reinforces your belief that Pat is, in fact, friendly.

The self-fulfilling prophecy also can be seen when you make predictions about yourself and fulfill them. For example, suppose you enter a group situation convinced that the other members will dislike you. Almost invariably you'll be proved right; to you, the other members will appear to dislike you. What you may be doing is acting in a way that encourages the group to respond to you negatively. In this way, you fulfill your prophecies about yourself.

A widely known example of the self-fulfilling prophecy is the **Pygmalion effect** (Rosenthal & Jacobson, 1992). In this classic research study, experimenters told teachers that certain pupils were expected to do exceptionally well—that they were late bloomers. And although the experimenters selected the "late bloomers" at random, the students who were labeled "late bloomers" performed at higher levels than their classmates. These students became what their teachers thought they were. The expectations of the teachers may have caused them to pay extra attention to the students, and this may have positively affected the students' performance. The Pygmalion effect has also been studied in such varied contexts as the courtroom, the clinic, the work cubicle, management and leadership practices, athletic coaching, and stepfamilies (Eden, 1992; Solomon et al., 1996; Einstein, 1995; McNatt, 2001; Rosenthal, 2002).

VIEWPOINTS: **Your Public Messages**
Many college and graduate admissions offices and employers examine your social media messages. *Does knowing this influence your postings? If so, in what way?*

PRIMACY–RECENCY Assume for a moment that you're enrolled in a course in which half the classes are extremely dull and half extremely exciting. At the end of the semester, you evaluate the course and the instructor. Would your evaluation be more favorable if the dull classes occurred in the first half of the semester and the exciting classes in the second? Or would it be more favorable if the order were reversed? If what comes first exerts the most influence, you have a **primacy effect**. If what comes last (or most recently) exerts the most influence, you have a **recency effect**.

In the classic study on the effects of **primacy–recency** in perception, college students perceived a person who was described as "intelligent, industrious, impulsive, critical, stubborn, and envious" more positively than a person described as "envious, stubborn, critical, impulsive, industrious, and intelligent" (Asch, 1946). Notice that the descriptions are identical; only the order was changed. Clearly, there's a tendency to use early information to get a general idea about a person and to use later information to make this impression more specific.

Often, of course, first impressions are incorrect. For example, if you judged a job applicant as generally nervous and ill-at-ease when he or she may simply be showing normal nervousness in an interview for a much-needed job, you will have misperceived this individual. Similarly, this tendency can lead you to distort subsequent perceptions so as not to upset your original impression. For example, you may fail to see signs of deceit in someone you like because of your early impressions that this person is a good and honest individual.

STEREOTYPING One of the most common shortcuts in perception is stereotyping. A **stereotype** is a fixed impression of a group of people. We all have attitudinal stereotypes—of national, religious, sexual, or racial groups, or perhaps of criminals, prostitutes, teachers, or plumbers. If you have these fixed impressions, you will, on meeting a member of a particular group, often see that person primarily as a member of that group and apply to him or her all the characteristics you assign to the group. If you meet someone who is a prostitute, for example, there are a host of characteristics for prostitutes that you may apply to this one person. To complicate matters further, you will often "see" in this person's behavior the manifestation of characteristics that you would not "see" if you didn't know what the person did for a living.

JOURNAL
COMMUNICATION CHOICE POINT
First Impression Correction
You made a bad impression at work—you drank too much at an office party and played the clown. This is an impression you want to change fast. Although you can't erase such an impression, you need to counteract it in some way. *What might you say and do to help lessen the negative effects?*

"Fred always makes a poor first impression — he says it saves a lot of time."

Baloo-Rex May/CartoonStock.com

Stereotypes can easily distort accurate perception and prevent you from seeing an individual purely as an individual. Stereotypes can be especially prevalent in online communication; because there are few visual and auditory cues, it's not surprising that people often rely heavily on stereotypes in forming impressions of online partners (Jacobson, 1999).

The tendency to group people and to respond to individuals primarily as members of groups can lead you to perceive an individual as possessing those qualities (usually negative) that you believe characterize his or her group (e.g., "All Mexicans are …"). As a result, you may fail to appreciate the multifaceted nature of all individuals and groups. Stereotyping also can lead you to ignore each person's unique characteristics so that you fail to benefit from the special contributions each individual might bring to an encounter.

ATTRIBUTION OF CONTROL Another way in which you form impressions is through the **attribution of control**, a process by which you focus on explaining why someone behaved as he or she did. For example, suppose you invite your friend Desmond to dinner at 7 p.m. and he arrives at 9. Consider how you would respond to each of these reasons:

Reason 1: "I just couldn't tear myself away from the beach. I really wanted to get a great tan."

Reason 2: "I was driving here when I saw some guys mugging an older couple. I broke it up, took the couple home, and stayed with them until their children arrived. The storm knocked out all the cell towers and electricity, so I had no way of calling to tell you I'd be late."

Reason 3: "I got in a car accident and was taken to the hospital."

Depending on the reason, you would probably attribute very different motives to Desmond's behavior. With reasons 1 and 2, you'd conclude that Desmond was in control of his behavior; with reason 3, that he was not. Further, you would probably respond negatively to reason 1 (Desmond was selfish and inconsiderate) and positively to reason 2 (Desmond was a good Samaritan). Because Desmond was not in control of his behavior in reason 3, you would probably not attribute either positive or negative motivation to it. Instead, you would probably feel sorry that he got into an accident.

In perceiving and especially in evaluating other people's behavior, you frequently ask if they were in control of their behavior. Generally, research shows that if you feel a person was in control of negative behaviors, you'll come to dislike him or her. If you believe the person was not in control of negative behaviors, you'll come to feel sorry for, and not blame, him or her.

In your attribution of controllability—or in attributing motives on the basis of any other reasons (e.g., hearsay or observations of the person's behavior), beware of three potential errors:

- **Self-serving bias** You commit the **self-serving bias** when you take credit for the positive and deny responsibility for the negative. For example, you're more likely to attribute your positive outcomes (say, you get an A on an exam) to internal and controllable factors—to your personality, intelligence, or hard work. And you're more likely to attribute your negative outcomes (say, you get a D) to external and uncontrollable factors—to the exam's being exceptionally difficult or to your roommate's party the night before (Bernstein, Stephan, & Davis, 1979; Duval & Silva, 2002).

- **Overattribution** The tendency to single out one or two obvious characteristics of a person and attribute everything that person does to these characteristics is known as **overattribution**. For example, if a person is blind or was born into great wealth, there's often a tendency to attribute everything that person does to such factors. So you might say, "Alex overeats because he's blind," or "Lillian is irresponsible because she never has had to work for her money." To prevent overattribution, recognize that most behaviors and personality characteristics result from many factors. You almost always make a mistake when you select one factor and attribute everything to it.

- **Fundamental attribution error** The **fundamental attribution error** occurs when you overvalue the contribution of internal factors (e.g., your supervisor's personality) and undervalue the influence of external factors (e.g., the context or situation the person is in). This type of error leads you to conclude that people do what they do because that's how they are, not because of the situation they're in. When Pat is late for an appointment, you're more likely to conclude that Pat is inconsiderate or irresponsible than to attribute the lateness to a possible bus breakdown or traffic accident.

Table 2.2 presents a summary of the various impression formation processes and some of the cautions to observe.

Table 2.2 Impression Formation

Impression Formation Processes	Cautions to Observe
Self-Fulfilling Prophecy: you act on your prediction as if it were true, and it become true.	Beware of your predictions that come true; you may be influencing them in that direction.
Primacy–Recency: you are most influenced by what occurs first and by what occurs last.	Basing your impressions on the basis of early or late information may bias your perceptions.
Stereotyping: you form an impression of someone based on your racial, religious, or other stereotype.	Beware of stereotypes; often they were learned without conscious awareness and are often misleading.
Attribution of control: you evaluate what a person did on the basis of the control you perceive this person to have had on his or her behavior.	Beware of the self-serving bias, overattribution, and the fundamental attribution error.

Increasing Accuracy in Impression Formation

Successful communication depends largely on the accuracy of the impressions you form of others. We've already identified the potential barriers that can arise with each of the perceptual processes—for example, the self-serving bias or overattribution. In addition to avoiding these barriers, here are other ways to increase your accuracy in impression formation.

ANALYZE YOUR IMPRESSIONS Subject your perceptions to logical analysis, to critical thinking. Here are a few suggestions:

- **Recognize your own role in perception.** Your emotional and physiological state will influence the meaning you give to your perceptions. A movie may seem hysterically funny when you're in a good mood but just plain stupid when you're in a bad mood. Understand your own biases. For example, do you tend to perceive only the positive in people you like and only the negative in people you don't like?

- **Avoid early conclusions.** On the basis of your observations of behaviors, formulate hypotheses to test against additional information and evidence; avoid drawing conclusions that you then look to confirm.

- **Look for a variety of cues.** When a variety of cues point in the same direction, the more likely your conclusion will be correct. Be especially alert to contradictory cues that seem to refute your initial hypotheses.

- **Seek validation.** It's often helpful to seek validation from others. Do others see things the same way you do? If not, ask yourself if your perceptions may be distorted in some way.

- **Beware of the just world hypothesis.** Many people believe in what is called the **just world hypothesis**, the belief that the world is just: Good things happen to good people (because they're good) and bad things happen to bad people (because they're bad) (Aronson, Wilson, & Akert, 2013; Hunt, 2000). Even when you mindfully dismiss this assumption, you may use it mindlessly when perceiving and evaluating other people. Consider a particularly vivid example: In certain cultures (e.g., in Bangladesh or Yemen), a rape victim is often considered a disgrace to her family and deserving of severe punishment—in some cases, death. While you may assert that this is wrong and unfair, research shows that many in the United States also blame the rape victim and not the perpetrator, especially if the victim is male (Adams-Price, Dalton, & Sumrall, 2004; Anderson, 2004).

CHECK YOUR PERCEPTIONS   The process of **perception checking** is another way to reduce uncertainty and to ensure that your initial impressions are more accurate. The goal of perception checking is to further explore the thoughts and feelings of the other person, not to prove that your initial perception is correct. With this simple technique, you lessen your chances of misinterpreting another's feelings. At the same time, you give the other person an opportunity to elaborate on his or her thoughts and feelings. Let's take an example: Dolly and Jane have been Facebook friends for several years and have been very supportive of each other. Recently however, Dolly's messages have become more critical, often negative. Jane wonders if she did something wrong that offended Dolly or if something is wrong with Dolly. In using perception checking, Jane would seek to clarify the reasons for Dolly's behavior, rather than simply assume that her initial impression was correct. In its most basic form, perception checking consists of two parts:

- **Description/interpretation.** The first step is to describe what you see or hear or read and how you interpret the behavior. The descriptive part of this is that Jane sees that Dolly's messages have been unnecessarily negative. The interpretation part of this is that Jane's initial impressions are that she did something to offend Dolly or that something is wrong with Dolly.

- **Clarification.** At this second step Jane would seek clarification. Jane would ask Dolly, in one form or another, what's going on. For example, Jane may simply say "What's up? Your posts seem different" or "You didn't seem to like my last ten photos; did I do something wrong?" The objective here is simply to find out what was going on with Dolly. Be careful that your request for clarification does not sound as though you already know the answer.

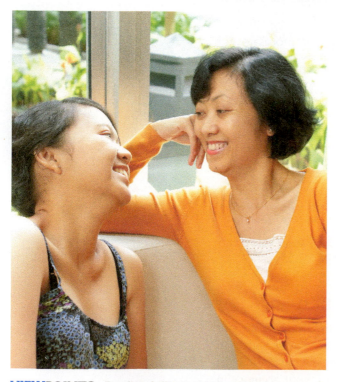

VIEWPOINTS: **Predictability and Uncertainty**

As you and another person develop a closer and more intimate relationship, you generally reduce your uncertainty about each other; you become more predictable to each other. *What level of predictability do you want in a romantic partner? Are there certain things about your partner (best friend, lover, or family member) that you'd simply rather not know?*

- **Set up a mental "ghost-thinking team,"** much as corporations and research institutes maintain think tanks (DeVito, 1996). Select a team of four to eight people. These can be people you admire and know or historical figures such as Galileo or Steve Jobs, fictional figures such as Wonder Woman or Sherlock Holmes, public figures such as Hillary Clinton or Ralph Nader, or persons from other cultures or of a different sex or affectional orientation. You then pose a question or problem and then imagine how this team of ghosts would respond to your problem. Of course, you're really listening to yourself, but you are putting your perspectives aside and attempting to think like these other people. The technique forces you to step outside your normal role and to consider the perceptions of someone totally different from you.

REDUCE YOUR UNCERTAINTY   In every communication situation, there is some degree of ambiguity. A variety of strategies can help reduce uncertainty about another person (Berger & Bradac, 1982; Gudykunst, 1993; Brashers, 2007).

- **Observe.** Observing another person while he or she is engaged in an active task—preferably interacting with others in an informal social situation—will often reveal a great deal about the person, as people are less apt to monitor their behaviors and more likely to reveal their true selves in informal situations.

- **Construct situations.** You can sometimes manipulate situations so as to observe the person in more specific and revealing contexts. Employment interviews, theatrical auditions, and student teaching are good examples of situations arranged to give you an accurate view of the person in action.

- **Get the lay of the land.** When you log on to an Internet group, reduce uncertainty by reading the exchanges between the other group members before you say anything yourself. By doing so, you learn about the people in the group and about the group itself. When uncertainty is reduced, you're more likely to make contributions that will be appropriate to the group and less likely to violate the group's norms.

- **Ask.** Learn about a person through asking others. You might inquire of a colleague if a third person finds you interesting and might like to have dinner with you.

- **Interact.** Interacting with the individual will of course give you considerable information. For example, you can ask questions: "Do you enjoy sports?" "What would you do if you got fired?" You also gain knowledge of another by disclosing information about yourself. These disclosures help to create an environment that encourages disclosures from the person about whom you wish to learn more.

INCREASE YOUR CULTURAL SENSITIVITY   Recognizing and being sensitive to cultural differences will help increase your accuracy in perception. For example, Russian or Chinese artists, such as ballet dancers, will often applaud their audience by clapping. Americans seeing this may easily interpret it as egotistical. Similarly, a German man will enter a restaurant before a woman in order to see if the place is respectable enough for the woman to enter. This simple custom can easily be interpreted as rude by people from cultures in which it's considered courteous for the woman to enter first (Axtell, 2007).

Cultural sensitivity will help counteract the difficulty many people have in understanding the nonverbal messages of people from other cultures. For example, it's easier to interpret the facial expressions of members of your own culture than those of another culture (Weathers, Frank, & Spell, 2002). This "in-group advantage" will assist your perceptional accuracy for members of your own culture but will often hinder your accuracy for members of other cultures (Elfenbein & Ambady, 2002).

Within every cultural group there are wide and important differences. As all Americans are not alike, neither are all Indonesians, Greeks, or Mexicans. When you make assumptions that all people of a certain culture are alike, you're thinking in stereotypes. Recognizing differences between another culture and your own, and among members of the same culture, will help you perceive people and situations more accurately.

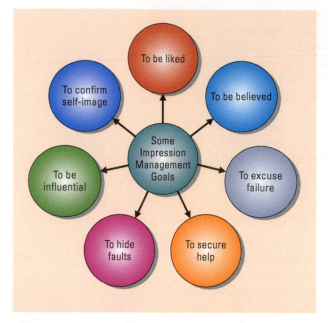

Figure 2.5 Impression Management Goals and Strategies

Impression Management: Goals and Strategies

2.5 **Explain and give examples of the strategies of impression management.**

Impression management (some writers use the term *self-presentation* or *identity management*) refers to the processes you go through to communicate the impression you want other people to have of you.

Impression management is largely the result of the messages communicated. In the same way that you form impressions of others largely on the basis of how they communicate, verbally and nonverbally, they also form impressions of you based on what you say (your verbal messages) and how you act and dress (your nonverbal messages). Communication messages, however, are not the only means for impression formation and management. For example, you also communicate your self-image and judge others by the people with whom they associate; if you associate with VIPs, then surely you must be a VIP yourself, the conventional wisdom goes. Or you might form an impression of someone on the basis of that person's age or gender or ethnic origin. Or you might rely on what others have said about the person and form impressions that are consistent with these comments. And, of course, they might well do the same in forming impressions of you. See Figure 2.5.

Part of the art and skill of communication is to understand and be able to manage the impressions you give to others. Mastering the art of impression management will enable you to present yourself as you want others to see you, at least to some extent.

The strategies you use to achieve this desired impression will depend on your specific goal. The sections that follow focus on seven major communication goals and strategies. Note that although they may help you communicate the impression you want to convey, each of these strategies may also backfire and communicate exactly the opposite of your intended purpose.

To be Liked: Affinity-Seeking and Politeness Strategies

If you're new at school or on the job and you want to be well liked, included in the activities of others, and thought of highly, you'd likely use affinity-seeking strategiesand politeness strategies.

AFFINITY-SEEKING STRATEGIES   Using the **affinity-seeking strategies** outlined here will probably increase your chances of being liked (Bell & Daly, 1984). Such strategies are especially important in initial interactions, and their use by teachers has even been found to increase student motivation (Martin & Rubin, 1998; Myers & Zhong, 2004; Wrench, McCroskey, & Richmond, 2008).

- Appear active, enthusiastic, and dynamic.
- Follow the cultural rules for polite, cooperative, respectful conversation.
- Communicate interest in the other person and include him or her in your social activities and groupings.
- Present yourself as comfortable and relaxed.
- Stimulate and encourage the other person to talk about him- or herself; reinforce his or her disclosures and contributions. Self-disclose yourself.
- Appear optimistic and positive rather than pessimistic and negative.

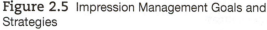

JOURNAL
COMMUNICATION CHOICE POINT
Face-to-Face

You've been communicating with Pat over the Internet for the past seven months and you finally have decided to meet for coffee. You really want Pat to like you. *What are some impression–management strategies you might use to get Pat to like you? What messages would you be sure not to communicate?*

- Appear honest, reliable, and interesting.
- Arrange circumstances so that you and the other person come into frequent contact.
- Communicate warmth, supportiveness, and empathy.
- Demonstrate that you share significant attitudes and values with the other person.

Although this research was conducted before the advent of social media, you can easily see how the same strategies could be used in online communication. For example, you can post photos to show that you're active and enthusiastic; you can follow the rules for polite interaction by giving "likes" and "+1s" to others; and you can communicate interest in the other person by inviting him or her to hang out, by joining a group, by commenting on a post, or by retweeting. Not surprisingly, plain old flattery also goes a long way toward improving your likability. Flattery can increase your chances for success in a job interview, the tip a customer is likely to leave, and even your credibility (Varma, Toh, & Pichler, 2006; Seiter, 2007; Vonk, 2002).

There is, however, a potential negative effect that can result from affinity-seeking strategies. Using them too often or in ways that might appear insincere may lead people to see you as attempting to ingratiate yourself for your own advantage and not really meaning "to be nice."

POLITENESS STRATEGIES **Politeness strategies**, another set of strategies people often use to appear likable, may be viewed in terms of negative and positive face (Goffman, 1967; Brown & Levinson, 1987; Holmes 1995; Goldsmith, 2007). Both are responsive to two needs that each individual has:

- **Positive face:** the desire to be viewed positively by others, to be thought of favorably.
- **Negative face:** the desire to be autonomous, to have the right to do as you wish.

Politeness in communication, then, refers to behavior that allows others to maintain both positive and negative face; and impoliteness refers to behaviors that attack either positive face (e.g., you criticize someone) or negative face (e.g., you make demands on someone).

To help another person maintain *positive face*, you speak respectfully to and about that person, you give him or her your full attention, you say "excuse me" when appropriate. In short you treat the person as you would want to be treated. In this way you allow the person to maintain positive face through what is called *positive politeness*. You *attack* the person's positive face when you speak disrespectfully about that individual, ignore the person or his or her comments, and fail to use the appropriate expressions of politeness such as *thank you* and *please*.

To help another person maintain *negative face*, you respect the person's right to be autonomous and so you request rather than demand that he or she do something; you say, "Would you mind opening a window" rather than "Open that window, damn it!" You might also give the person an "out" when making a request, allowing the person to reject your request if that is not what he or she wants. So you say, "If this is a bad time, please tell me, but I'm really strapped and could use a loan of $100" rather than "You have to lend me $100." If you want a recommendation, you might ask, "Would it be possible for you to write me a recommendation for graduate school?" rather than say, "You have to write me a recommendation for graduate school." In this way you enable the person to maintain negative face through what is called *negative politeness*.

Of course, we do this almost automatically and asking for a favor without any consideration for a person's negative face needs would seem totally insensitive. In most situations, however, this type of attack on negative face often appears in more subtle forms. For example, your mother saying "Are you going to wear that?"—to use Deborah Tannen's (2006) example—attacks negative face by criticizing or challenging your autonomy. This comment also attacks positive face by questioning your ability to dress properly.

As with all the strategies discussed here, politeness, too, may have negative consequences. Overpoliteness, for example, is likely to be seen as phony and be resented. Overpoliteness will also be resented if it's seen as a persuasive strategy.

To Be Believed: Credibility Strategies

If you were posting a how-to video on YouTube and wanted people to believe you knew what you were demonstrating, at least part of your strategy would involve the use of **credibility strategies**, attempts to establish a perception by others of your competence, character, and charisma. For example, to establish your competence, you might mention your long experience with the product or courses you took that qualify you as an expert. Or you can post a list of testimonials or reviews. To establish that you're of good character, you might mention how fair and honest you are, and that you would never recommend a product that didn't perform as advertised. And to establish your charisma—your take-charge, positive personality—you might demonstrate this quality in your facial expressions and vocal variation.

If you stress your competence, character, and charisma too much, however, you risk being seen as someone who lacks the very qualities that you seem too eager to present to others. Generally, people who are truly competent need say little directly about their own competence; their actions and their success will reveal it.

To Excuse Failure: Self-Handicapping Strategies

If you were about to tackle a difficult task and were concerned that you might fail, you might use what are called **self-handicapping strategies**. In the more extreme form of this strategy, you actually set up barriers or obstacles to make the task impossible. That way, when you fail, you won't be blamed or thought ineffective—after all, the task was impossible. Let's say you aren't prepared for your human communication exam and you believe you're going to fail. Using this self-handicapping strategy, you might stay out late at a party the night before so that when you do poorly on the exam, you can blame it on the party rather than on your intelligence or knowledge. In a less extreme form, you might manufacture excuses for failure and have them ready if you do fail. For example, you might prepare to blame a poorly cooked dinner on your defective stove.

On the negative side, using self-handicapping strategies too often may lead people to see you as generally incompetent or foolish. After all, a person who parties the night before an exam for which he or she is already unprepared is clearly demonstrating poor judgment.

To Secure Help: Self-Deprecating Strategies

If you want to be taken care of and protected, or if you simply want someone to come to your aid, you might use **self-deprecating strategies**. Confessions of incompetence and inability often bring assistance from others. And so you might say, "I just can't fix that drain and it drives me crazy; I just don't know anything about plumbing" with the hope that another person will offer to help.

But be careful: Your self-deprecating strategies may convince people that you are, in fact, just as incompetent as you say you are. Or people may see you as someone who doesn't want to do something and so pretends to be incompetent to get others to do it. This strategy is not likely to benefit you in the long run.

To Hide Faults: Self-Monitoring Strategies

Much impression management is devoted not merely to presenting a positive image, but to suppressing the negative, to **self-monitoring strategies** in which you censor what you say or do. You avoid your normal slang to make your colleagues think more highly of you; you avoid chewing gum so you don't look juvenile or unprofessional and you avoid posting the photos from the last party. While you readily disclose favorable parts of your experience, you actively hide the unfavorable parts.

But if you self-monitor too often or too obviously, you risk being seen as someone unwilling to reveal himself or herself, and perhaps not trusting enough of others. In more extreme cases, you may be viewed as dishonest, as hiding your true self or trying to fool other people.

To Be Followed: Influencing Strategies

In many instances you'll want to get people to see you as a leader. Here, you can use a variety of **influencing strategies**. One set of such strategies are those normally grouped under power—your knowledge (information power), your expertise (expert power), your right to lead by virtue of your position as, say, a doctor, judge, or accountant (legitimate power). You might also use leadership strategies that stress your prior experience, broad knowledge, or previous successes.

Influencing strategies can also backfire. If you try to influence someone and fail, you'll be perceived as having less power than before your unsuccessful attempt. And, of course, if you're seen as someone who is influencing others for self-gain, your attempts to influence might be resented or rejected.

To Confirm Self-Image: Image-Confirming Strategies

You may sometimes use **image-confirming strategies** to reinforce your positive perceptions about yourself. If you see yourself as the life of the party, you'll tell jokes, post photos in which you are in fact the life of the party, and just try to amuse

Communicating Ethically
THE ETHICS OF IMPRESSION MANAGEMENT

Impression management strategies may sometimes be used unethically and for less than noble purposes. For example, people may use affinity-seeking strategies to get you to like them so that they can then extract favors from you. Politicians frequently portray themselves as credible in order to win votes. The same could be said of the stereotypical used-car salesperson or insurance agent trying to make a sale. Some people use self-handicapping or self-deprecating strategies to get you to see their behavior from a perspective that benefits them rather than you. Self-monitoring strategies are often deceptive, designed to present a more polished image than what might surface without self-monitoring. And, of course, influencing strategies have been used throughout history in deception as well as in truth. Even image-confirming strategies can be used to deceive, as when people exaggerate their positive qualities (or make them up) and hide their negative ones.

ETHICAL CHOICE POINT

You're ready to join one (perhaps several) of the online dating services. You need to write your profile and are wondering if everyone (or nearly everyone) exaggerates, you shouldn't also. Specifically, you're considering saying that you earn a very good salary (actually, it's not so great but you're hoping for a promotion), that you're twenty pounds lighter (actually, you intend to lose weight), and that you own a condo (actually, that's a goal once you get the promotion and save a down payment). If you don't exaggerate, you reason, you'll disadvantage yourself and not meet the people you want to meet. Also, you figure that people expect you to exaggerate and assume that you're probably a lot less ideal than your profile would indicate. *Would this be ethical?*

people. This behavior confirms your own self-image and also lets others know that this is who you are and how you want to be seen. At the same time that you reveal aspects of yourself that confirm your desired image, you actively suppress other aspects of yourself that would disconfirm this image. Unfavorable wall postings, for example, are quickly removed.

If you use image-confirming strategies too frequently, you risk being seen as too perfect to be genuine. If you try to project an exclusively positive image, it's likely to turn others off—people want to see their friends and associates as real with some faults and imperfections. Also recognize that image-confirming strategies invariably involve your focusing on yourself, and with that comes the risk of appearing self-absorbed.

A knowledge of these impression management strategies and the ways in which they are effective and ineffective will give you a greater number of choices for achieving such widely diverse goals as being liked, being believed, excusing failure, securing help, hiding faults, being followed, and confirming your self-image.

Summary of Concepts and Skills

This chapter explored the self—the ways you perceive yourself, and perception—the way you perceive others and others perceive you.

The Self in Human Communication

2.1 Define *self-concept, self-awareness,* **and** *self-esteem* **and explain the ways in which self-awareness and self-esteem may be increased.**

1. Self-concept, the image that you have of yourself, is composed of feelings and thoughts about both your abilities and your limitations. Self-concept develops from the image that others have of you, the comparisons you make between yourself and others, the teachings of your culture, and your own interpretations and evaluations of your thoughts and behaviors.

2. The Johari window model of the self is one way to view self-awareness. In this model there are four major areas: the open self, the blind self, the hidden self, and the unknown self. To increase self-awareness, analyze yourself, listen to others to see yourself as they do, actively seek information from others about yourself, see yourself from different perspectives, and increase your open self.

3. Self-esteem is the value you place on yourself and may be enhanced by attacking self-destructive beliefs, seeking out nourishing others, working on projects that will result in success, and securing affirmation.

Self-Disclosure

2.2 Define *self-disclosure,* **its rewards and dangers, and explain the suggested guidelines for making, responding to, and resisting self-disclosure.**

4. Self-disclosure is a form of communication in which information about the self that is normally kept hidden is communicated to one or more others.

5. Self-disclosure is more likely to occur when the potential discloser (a) feels competent, is sociable and extroverted, and is not apprehensive about communication; (b) comes from a culture that encourages self-disclosure; (c) is a woman; (d) is talking to supportive listeners who also disclose; and (e) talks about impersonal rather than personal topics and reveals positive rather than negative information.

6. The rewards of self-disclosure include increased self-knowledge, the ability to cope with difficult situations and guilt, communication efficiency, and chances for more meaningful relationships. The dangers of self-disclosure include personal and social rejection and material loss.

7. Before self-disclosing, consider the motivation for the self-disclosure, the possible burdens you might impose on your listener or yourself, the appropriateness of the self-disclosure, and the disclosures of the other person.

8. When listening to others' disclosures, try to understand what the discloser is feeling, support the discloser, be willing to reciprocate, keep the disclosures confidential, and don't use the disclosures against the person.

9. When you don't want to disclose, try being firm, being indirect and changing the topic, or assertively stating your unwillingness to disclose.

Perception

2.3 Define *perception* **and its stages, and explain how to increase perceptual accuracy.**

10. Perception is the process by which you become aware of the many stimuli impinging on your senses. It occurs in five stages: (a) sensory stimulation, (b) organization, (c) interpretation–evaluation, (d) memory, and (e) recall.

Impression Formation

2.4 Describe the nature of impression formation and the major factors that influence it.

11. Four important processes influence the way you form impressions: self-fulfilling prophecies, primacy–recency, stereotyping, and attributions of controllability.

12. To increase your accuracy in impression formation, analyze your impressions and recognize your role in perception; check your impressions; reduce uncertainty; and become culturally sensitive by recognizing the differences between you and others and also the differences among people from other cultures.

Impression Management: Goals and Strategies

2.5 Explain and give examples of the strategies of impression management.

13. Impression management includes these goals and strategies: to be liked (affinity-seeking and politeness strategies); to be believed (credibility strategies that establish your competence, character, and charisma); to excuse failure (self-handicapping strategies); to secure help (self-deprecating strategies); to hide faults (self-monitoring strategies); to be followed (influencing strategies); and to confirm one's self-image (image-confirming strategies).

14. Each of these impression management strategies can backfire and give others negative impressions of you. And each of these strategies may be used to reveal your true self or to present a false self and deceive others in the process.

Throughout this discussion of the self and perception, a variety of skills were identified. Place a check mark next to those skills that you feel you need to work on most.

_____ 1. I seek to understand my self-concept and to be realistic about my strengths and weaknesses.

_____ 2. I actively seek to increase self-awareness by talking with myself, listening to others, reducing my blind self, seeing myself from different perspectives, and increasing my open self.

_____ 3. I seek to enhance my self-esteem by attacking self-destructive beliefs, seeking out nourishing others, working on projects that will result in success, and securing affirmation.

_____ 4. I regulate my disclosures on the basis of the unique communication situation.

_____ 5. When deciding whether or not to self-disclose, I take into consideration my motivation, the possible burdens on my listener and on me, the disclosure's appropriateness to the other person and its context, and the other person's disclosures.

_____ 6. I respond to the disclosures of others by trying to feel what the other person is feeling, using effective and active listening skills, expressing supportiveness, refraining from criticism and evaluation, and keeping the disclosures confidential.

_____ 7. I resist disclosing when I don't want to by being firm, by trying indirectness and changing the topic, and/or by stating assertively my refusal to disclose.

_____ 8. I think mindfully when I use perceptual shortcuts so that they don't mislead me and result in inaccurate perceptions.

_____ 9. I guard against ethnocentric thinking by regarding the behavior and customs of others from a multicultural viewpoint rather than from just my cultural perspective.

_____ 10. To guard against the self-fulfilling prophecy, I take a second look at my perceptions when they conform too closely to my expectations.

_____ 11. Recognizing how primacy–recency works, I actively guard against first impressions that might prevent accurate perceptions of future events; I formulate hypotheses rather than conclusions.

_____ 12. I recognize stereotyping in the messages of others and avoid it in my own.

_____ 13. I am aware of and careful to avoid the self-serving bias, overattribution, and the fundamental attribution error when trying to account for another person's behavior.

_____ 14. I think critically about perception, analyzing my perceptions, checking my perceptions for accuracy, using uncertainty reduction strategies, and acting with cultural sensitivity.

_____ 15. I can use the strategies of impression management (to be liked, to be believed, to excuse failure, to secure help, to hide faults, to be followed, and to confirm my self-image) effectively and ethically.

Key Terms

affinity-seeking strategies
attribution of control
contrast
credibility strategies
disinhibition effect
fundamental attribution error
image-confirming strategies
impostor phenomenon
impression formation
impression management
influencing strategies
Johari window
just world hypothesis
looking-glass self

negative face
overattribution
perception
perception checking
politeness strategies
positive face
primacy effect
primacy–recency
proximity
Pygmalion effect
recency effect
selective attention
selective exposure
selective perception

self-awareness
self-concept
self-deprecating strategies
self-destructive beliefs
self-disclosure
self-esteem
self-fulfilling prophecy
self-handicapping strategies
self-monitoring strategies
self-serving bias
similarity
stereotype

Skill Development Experiences

2.1 Checking Your Perceptions

Perception checking is best thought of as a state of mind to seek clarification before forming conclusions.

Respond to the following incidents by 1) providing a description of how you perceive the incident and 2) explaining how you'd go about seeking confirmation of your initial impressions.

1. You've extended an invitation to a classmate to be a Facebook friend but have heard nothing back.

2. Your manager at work seems to spend a lot of time with your peers but very little time with you. You're concerned about the impression you're making.

3. The person you've been dating for the last several months has stopped calling for a date. The messages have become fewer and less personal.

2.2 Using Impression Management Strategies

Practicing with these strategies will help you understand the ways in which people (including yourself) manage the impressions they give to others.

Try formulating impression management strategies for each of the following situations. In your responses focus on one or two things you would say or do to achieve the stated goals.

- **To be liked:** You're new at work and want your colleagues to like you.

- **To be believed:** You're giving a speech on something you feel deeply about; you want others to believe you.

- **To excuse failure:** You know you're going to fail that midterm and you need a good excuse.

- **To secure help:** You need help doing something on your computer that would take you hours to do on your own; you can't bear doing it alone.

- **To hide faults:** You don't have as many computer skills as your résumé might suggest and you need to appear to know a great deal.

- **To be followed:** You want members of the group to see you as the leader and, in fact, to elect you group leader.

- **To confirm self-image:** You want your colleagues to see you as a fun (but dedicated) worker.

2.3 Applying Impression Management Strategies

Everyone uses impression management strategies; using them effectively and ethically is not always easy but almost always an available choice.

Here are a few interpersonal situations in which you might want to use impression management strategies. Identify at least two impression management strategies you could use to achieve your goals in each of these situations.

1. You're interviewing for a job; you want to be seen as credible and as a good team player.
2. Your term paper is not up to par; you don't want your instructor to think this is the level at which you normally function.
3. You want to ask a former instructor to be a friend on a social network site.
4. You've just started at a new school and you want to be careful not to make a fool of yourself—as you had at your previous school.
5. You're a police officer assigned to a neighborhood patrol; you want to be seen as firm but approachable.

Chapter 3
Listening in Human Communication

Without listening, there is no communication.

CHAPTER OUTLINE	Learning Objectives
Stages of Listening	**3.1** Define *listening* and its five stages and describe the ways you can increase listening accuracy at each of these stages.
Listening Barriers	**3.2** Describe the four major barriers to effective listening and describe how you can improve effectiveness in your own listening.
Four Listening Styles	**3.3** Define the four styles of listening and explain how each may be used effectively.
Listening Differences: Culture and Gender	**3.4** Explain the major cultural and gender differences found in listening and their influence on listening.

In light of Facebook, Twitter, wikis, and blogs, we need to expand the traditional definition of listening as the receiving and processing of auditory signals. If posting messages on social media sites is part of human communication (which it surely is), then reading these messages must also be part of human communication and most logically a part of listening. **Listening**, then, may now be defined as the process of receiving, understanding, remembering, evaluating, and responding to verbal and/or nonverbal messages.

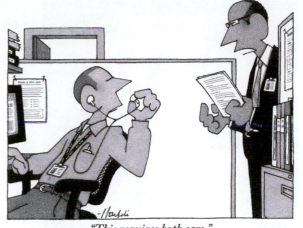

"This requires both ears."

William Haefeli/The New Yorker Collection/The Cartoon Bank

The skills of listening will prove crucial to you in both your professional and personal lives (Brownell, 2013; Worthington & Fitch-Hauser, 2012). In today's workplace listening is regarded as a crucial skill. Employees' communication skills are especially significant in this era of technological transformation; workers' advancement will depend on their ability to speak and write effectively, to display proper etiquette, and *to listen attentively*. In a survey of 40 CEOs of Asian and Western multinational companies, respondents cited a lack of listening skills as *the major shortcoming* of top executives (Witcher, 1999).

There can be little doubt that listening skills play a crucial role in developing and maintaining a variety of relationships (Brownell, 2013). When asked what they want in a partner, women overwhelmingly reply, "a partner who listens." And most men would agree that they too want a partner who listens. Among friends, listening skills rank consistently high; in fact, it would be hard to think of a person as a friend if that person were not a good listener.

The effective listener is more likely to emerge as group leader and a more effective salesperson, healthcare worker, and manager (Johnson & Bechler, 1998; Lauer, 2003; Stein & Bowen, 2003; Levine, 2004; Pelham & Kravitz, 2008; Brownell, 2013). Medical educators, claiming that doctors are not trained to listen to their patients, have introduced what they call "narrative medicine" to teach doctors how to listen to their patients and to recognize how their perceptions of their patients are influenced by their own emotions.

Here we look at the importance of listening, the nature of the listening process, the major barriers to listening effectiveness, varied styles of listening for different situations, and some cultural and gender differences in listening.

Stages of Listening

3.1 Define *listening* and its five stages and describe the ways you can increase listening accuracy at each of these stages.

According to our contemporary definition, listening is a collection of skills involving (1) attention and concentration (*receiving*), (2) learning (*understanding*), (3) memory (*remembering*), (4) critical thinking (*evaluation*), and (5) feedback (*responding*). You can enhance your listening ability by strengthening these skills, which make up the five steps of the listening process (Figure 3.1).

Note that the process of listening is circular: The response of person A stimulates a response from person B, which stimulates a response from person A, and so on. All five stages overlap. When you listen, you're

Figure 3.1 A Five-Stage Model of the Listening Process

This model, which depicts the various stages involved in listening, draws on a variety of previous models that listening researchers have developed (e.g., Alessandra, 1986; Barker, 1990; Brownell, 2013; Steil, Barker, & Watson, 1983). *In what other ways might you visualize the listening process?*

performing all five processes at essentially the same time. For example, when listening in conversation, you're not only paying attention to what other people are saying but also critically evaluating what they just said and perhaps giving feedback. Let's take a look at each stage separately.

Receiving

Hearing (which is not the same as *listening*) begins and ends with the first stage of the listening process, receiving. Hearing happens when you get within range of some auditory stimulus. Listening, on the other hand, begins only when the messages the speaker sends are received, or heard.

That hearing and listening are the same and that listening, like hearing, just happens is one of the great myths of listening. See Table 3.1 for some popular myths about listening.

At the *receiving* stage, you note not only what is said (verbally and nonverbally) but also what is omitted. For example, you receive not only the politician's summary of accomplishments in education but also his or her omission of failures in health care or pollution control. This receiving stage of listening can be made more effective if you follow these suggestions:

- Focus attention on the speaker's verbal and nonverbal messages, on what is said and what is not said—not on what you'll say next.
- Maintain your role as listener by not interrupting the speaker.
- Avoid assuming you understand what the speaker is going to say before he or she actually says it.

In this brief discussion of receiving, and in fact throughout this chapter on listening, the unstated assumption is that both individuals can receive auditory signals without difficulty. But for many people who have hearing impairments, listening presents a variety of problems. Here are a few suggestions for communication between people with and without hearing disorders.

- **Set up a comfortable context.** Lessen the distance between yourself and the person with a hearing impairment, and reduce background noise. Make sure the lighting is adequate so you can see each other's lips.
- **Avoid overlapping speech.** In group situations, only one person should speak at a time. Similarly, direct your comments to the person with hearing loss; don't relay your message to the person through a third party.

VIEWPOINTS: Who Deserves Your Listening Attention?

What types of people or situations engage your listening attention? Would you spend more time listening to someone's whoops of joy over winning the lottery or the sadness of a friend overcome by the death of a loved one?

Table 3.1 6 Myths of Listening

Myths	Realities
Hearing and listening are the same.	Hearing is just the first step in the listening process; it is not the entire process.
Listening just happens; it's a natural, passive process.	Listening takes effort; it's an active rather than a passive process.
Listening is an objective process; you receive what is said.	As you listen you process the message along with all your preconceptions, knowledge, and attitudes, for example.
Listening is powerless.	Listening can also communicate power, though it is often perceived as less powerful than speaking.
Listening is the same regardless of the situation.	Listening should be situational; you don't listen the same way at a class lecture and on a date.
Listening can't be learned or improved and anyway I'm already a good listener.	Listening can be improved; it involves skills just like public speaking or leadership.

- **Don't avoid common terms.** Use terms like *hear, listen, music,* or *deaf* when they're relevant to the conversation. Trying to avoid these common terms will make your speech sound artificial.

Understanding

Understanding occurs when you decode the speaker's signals and grasp both the thoughts that are expressed and the emotional tone that accompanies them—for example, the urgency, joy, or sorrow expressed in the message. The understanding phase of listening can be made more effective if you follow these suggestions.

- **Relate** the speaker's new information to what you already know.
- **See the speaker's messages from the speaker's point of view**, in part by not judging the message until it's fully understood as the speaker intended it.
- **Rephrase/paraphrase** the speaker's ideas, a simple process that's especially important when listening to complicated instructions.

Remembering

Effective listening depends on *remembering*. When Joe says his mother is ill, the effective listener remembers this and inquires about her health later in the week.

Perhaps the most important point to understand about memory is that what you remember is not what was said but what you remember was said. Memory for speech is not reproductive; you don't simply reproduce in your memory what the speaker said. Rather, memory is reconstructive; you actually reconstruct the messages you hear into a system that makes sense to you.

If you want to remember what someone says or the names of various people, this information needs to pass from your **short-term memory** (the memory you use, say, to remember a phone number just long enough to dial it) into **long-term memory**. Short-term memory is very limited in capacity— you can hold only a small amount of information there. Long-term memory is unlimited. Here are FOUR suggestions for facilitating the passage of information from short-term to long-term memory.

- **Focus** your attention on the central ideas. Even in the most casual of conversations, there are central ideas. Fix these in your mind. Repeat these ideas to yourself as you continue to listen. Avoid focusing on minor details that often lead to detours in listening and in conversation.
- **Organize** what you hear; summarize the message in a more easily retained form, but take care not to ignore crucial details or qualifications. If you chunk the material into categories, you'll be able to remember more information. For example, if you want to remember 15 or 20 items to buy in the supermarket, you'll remember more if you group them into chunks—say, produce, canned goods, and meats.
- **Unite** the new with the old; relate new information to what you already know. Avoid treating new information as totally apart from all else you know. There's probably some relationship and if you identify it, you're more like to remember the new material.
- **Repeat** names and key concepts to yourself or, if appropriate, aloud. By repeating the names or key concepts, you in effect rehearse these names and concepts, and as a result

VIEWPOINTS: **False Memories**

The term *false memory syndrome* refers to a phenomenon in which you "remember" past experiences that never actually occurred (Loftus, 2004), a situation depicted here from the 1995 movie *Indictment: The McMartin Trial*. Most of the studies on false memory syndrome have centered on erroneous recollections of abuse and other traumatic experiences. Often these false memories are implanted by therapists and interviewers, whose persistent questioning over a period of time can create such a realistic scenario that you come to believe these things actually occurred (Porter, Brit, Yuille, & Lehman, 2000). *In what other ways can false memory syndrome occur and create problems?*

they'll be easier to learn and remember. If you're introduced to Alice, you'll stand a better chance of remembering her name if you say "Hi, Alice" than if you say just "Hi."

Evaluating

Evaluating consists of judging the messages you hear. At times you may try to evaluate the speaker's underlying intent, often without much conscious awareness. For example, Elaine tells you she is up for a promotion and is really excited about it. You may then try to judge her intention. Does she want you to use your influence with the company president? Is she preoccupied with the possible promotion and therefore telling everyone? Is she looking for a pat on the back? Generally, if you know a person well, you will be able to identify his or her intention and respond appropriately.

In other situations, your evaluation may be more like critical analysis. For example, in a business meeting on upgrading office equipment, you would evaluate the office manager's proposals while listening to them. As you listen, you'd be asking yourself, "Are the proposals practical? Will they increase productivity? What is the evidence? Are there more practical alternatives?" Follow these three steps to make the evaluation stage of listening more effective.

- **Resist evaluating** until you fully understand the speaker's point of view.
- **Assume that the speaker is a person of goodwill** and give the speaker the benefit of any doubt by asking for clarification on issues you object to (e.g., are there any other reasons for accepting this new proposal?).
- **Distinguish facts from opinions** and personal interpretations and identify any biases, self-interests, or prejudices that may lead the speaker to slant unfairly what is presented.

Responding

Responding occurs in two forms: (1) responses you make while the speaker is talking and (2) responses you make after the speaker has stopped talking. Responses made while the speaker is talking should be supportive and should acknowledge that you're listening. These responses are called **backchanneling cues**—messages (words and gestures) that let the speaker know you're paying attention, as when you nod in agreement or say, "I see" or "Uh-huh."

Responses after the speaker has stopped talking are generally more elaborate and might include empathy ("I know how you must feel"); requests for clarification ("Do you mean this new health plan will replace the old plan, or will it only be a supplement?"); challenges ("I think your evidence is weak"); and/or agreement ("You're absolutely right, and I'll support your proposal when it comes up for a vote"). You can improve this responding phase of listening by following these suggestions.

- **Express support** and understanding for the speaker throughout the conversation.
- **Use varied backchanneling cues** (for example, nodding, using appropriate facial expressions, or saying "I see") that tell the speaker that you're listening.
- **Own your own responses;** that is, state your thoughts and feelings as your own, using **I-messages**—for example, saying, "I don't agree" rather than "No one will agree with that."
- **Avoid the common problem-causing listening responses,** such as being static or overly expressive, giving feedback that is monotonous and not responsive to the messages, avoiding eye contact, or appearing preoccupied with, say, a cell phone.

JOURNAL
COMMUNICATION CHOICE POINT
Listening Cues

Friends have told you that people don't direct comments to you because you often give the impression that you either aren't listening or aren't interested. *What are some of the things you can do to help change this perception?*

Communicating Ethically
ETHICAL LISTENING

As a listener you have at least two ethical obligations (generally).

- You owe the other person an honest hearing, without prejudgment, putting aside prejudices and preconceptions as best you can. At the same time, you owe the person your best effort at understanding emotionally as well as intellectually what he or she means. This does not mean, however, that there are not situations when you don't owe the speaker a fair hearing.
- You owe the other person honest responses. Just as you should be honest with the listener when speaking, you should be honest with the speaker when listening. This means giving open and honest feedback and also reflecting honestly on the questions that the speaker raises. Again, this does not mean that there are not situations in which you would not owe the speaker an honest response.

These obligations, as you might have guessed, will vary with the relationship between yourself and the other person. If this "other person" is a life partner, then your obligations are considerable. If this "other person" is a stranger, your obligations are less. Generally, as the intimacy of a relationship increases, so do your obligations to serve as a supportive and honest listener.

ETHICAL CHOICE POINT
Your partner of ten years has decided to come clean about a sordid past, essentially the ten years before you met. You really don't want to hear this (it just depresses you) but your partner insists on self-disclosing. *What is your ethical obligation to both your partner and to yourself?*

Table 3.2 provides a summary of the stages of listening and the guides to effective listening.

Table 3.2 In a Nutshell: Listening Stages and Effective Listening

Listening Stage	Effective Listening
At the **receiving** stage, you note not only what is said (verbally and nonverbally) but also what is omitted.	• Focus on the speaker. • Ignore distractions. • Do not interrupt. • Consider what is omitted.
Understanding is the stage at which you learn what the speaker means, the stage at which you grasp both the thoughts and the emotions expressed.	• Do not assume you know what the speaker is going to say before he or she actually says it. • See the speaker's messages from the speaker's point of view. • Ask questions for clarification. • Rephrase (paraphrase) the speaker's ideas in your own words.
Remembering is not reproductive, but rather reconstructive in that you recall what makes sense to you.	• Focus your attention on the central ideas. • Organize what you hear. • Relate new information with the old. • Repeat names and key concepts to yourself or even aloud.
Evaluating consists of judging the messages in some way.	• Resist evaluation until you fully understand the speaker's point of view. • Distinguish facts from the speaker's personal opinions. • Identify the speaker's possible biases, self-interests, or prejudices. • Recognize some popular but fallacious forms of "reasoning" speakers may employ, such as name-calling, testimonial, and bandwagon.
Responding occurs in two phases: responses you make while the speaker is talking and responses you make after the speaker has stopped talking.	• Support the speaker. • Own your responses. • Resist "responding to another's feelings" with "solving the person's problems." • Focus on the other person. • Avoid being a thought-completing listener.

Table 3.3 Listening in the Classroom

In addition to following the general guidelines for listening noted throughout this chapter, here are a few additional suggestions for making your listening for understanding in the classroom more effective.

General Suggestions	Specifically
Prepare yourself to listen.	Sit where you can clearly and comfortably see your instructor and any visual aids. Remember that you listen with your eyes as well as your ears.
Avoid distractions.	Avoid mental daydreaming, and put away physical distractions like your laptop, smartphone, or newspaper.
Pay special attention to the introduction.	Listen for orienting remarks and for key words and phrases (often written on the board or on PowerPoint slides), such as "another reason," "three major causes," and "first." Using these cues will help you outline the lecture.
Take notes in outline form.	Avoid writing in paragraph form. Listen for headings and then use these as major headings in your outline. When the instructor says, for example, "there are four kinds of noise," you have your heading and you will have a numbered list of four kinds of noise.
Assume relevance.	A piece of information may eventually prove irrelevant (unfortunately), but if you listen with the assumption of irrelevancy, you'll never hear anything relevant.
Listen for understanding.	Avoid taking issue with what is said until you understand fully and then, of course, take issue if you wish. But, generally, don't rehearse in your own mind your arguments against a particular position. When you do this, you run the risk of missing additional explanation or qualification.

Listening Barriers

3.2 Describe the four major barriers to effective listening and describe how you can improve effectiveness in your own listening.

In addition to practicing the various skills for each stage of listening, consider some of the common barriers to listening. Here are four such barriers and some suggestions for dealing with them as both listener and speaker, because both speaker and listener are responsible for effective listening. As you read this, consider the barriers that arise in listening in the classroom, a topic discussed in Table 3.3.

Distractions: Physical and Mental

Physical barriers might include hearing impairment, a noisy environment, or loud music. Multitasking (for example, trying to watch TV and listen to someone at the same time) with the aim of being supportive simply doesn't work. As both listener and speaker, try to remove whatever physical barriers can be removed; for those that you can't remove, adjust your listening and speaking to lessen the effects as much as possible. As a listener, focus on the speaker; you can attend to the room and the other people later.

Mental distractions too get in the way of focused listening. These barriers may take the form of thinking about your upcoming Saturday night date or becoming too emotional to think (and listen) clearly. When listening, recognize that you can think about your date or other distracting thoughts later. In speaking, make what you say compelling and relevant to the listener.

JOURNAL
COMMUNICATION CHOICE POINT
Hate Speech

Your work colleagues in neighboring cubicles regularly use derogatory racial terms. You really don't want to listen to this and want to protest this kind of talk. At the same time, however, you don't want to alienate people you're going to have to work with for some time. *What are some of the things you can say to register your protest (cooperatively)?*

Biases and Prejudices

In biased and prejudiced listening, you hear what the speaker is saying through stereotypes. This type of listening occurs when you listen differently to a person because of his or her race, affectional orientation, age, or gender when these characteristics are irrelevant to the message.

Such listening can occur in a wide variety of situations. For example, when you dismiss a valid argument or attribute validity to an invalid argument because the speaker is of a particular race, affectional orientation, age, or gender, you're listening with prejudice.

However, there are many instances in which these characteristics are pertinent to your evaluation of the message. For example, the sex of a speaker talking about pregnancy, fathering a child, birth control, or surrogate motherhood probably is, most would agree, relevant to the message. So, in these cases it is not sexist listening to take the gender of the speaker into consideration. It is, however, sexist listening to assume that only one gender can be an authority on a particular topic or that one gender's opinions are without value. The same is true when listening through the filter of a person's race, affectional orientation, or age.

Lack of Appropriate Focus

Focusing on what a person is saying is necessary for effective listening—yet there are many influences that can lead you astray. For example, listeners often get lost because they focus on irrelevancies, such as an especially vivid example that conjures up old memories. Try not to get detoured from the main idea. Try to repeat the idea to yourself and see the details in relation to this main concept. As a speaker, try to avoid language or examples that may divert attention from your main idea.

Another misplaced focus is often on the responses a listener is going to make while the speaker is still speaking. Anticipating how you're going to respond or what you're going to say (and even interrupting the speaker) prevents you from hearing the message in full. Instead, make a mental note of something and then get back to listening. As a speaker, when you feel someone is preparing to argue with you, ask him or her to hear you out: "I know you disagree with this, but let me finish and we'll get back to that."

Premature Judgment

Perhaps the most obvious form of premature judgment is assuming you know what the speaker is going to say and that there's no need to really listen. Let the speaker say what he or she is going to say before you decide that you already know it. As a speaker, it's often wise to assume that listeners will do exactly this, so make clear that what you're saying will be unexpected.

A common listener reaction is to draw conclusions or judgments on incomplete evidence. Sometimes, listeners will stop listening after hearing, for example, an attitude they disagree with or some sexist or culturally insensitive remark. Instead, this is a situation that calls for especially concentrated listening so that you don't rush to judgment. Wait for the evidence or argument; avoid making judgments before you gather all the information. Listen first, judge second. As a speaker, be aware of this tendency and, when you feel this is happening, ask for a suspension of judgment. A simple "Hear me out" is often sufficient.

Four Listening styles

3.3 Define the four styles of listening and explain how each may be used effectively.

Listening is situational (Brownell, 2013). The way you listen should depend on the situation you are in. For example, you don't listen to a State of the Union address in the same way that you listen to Jimmy Fallon's monologue. At the least, you need to adjust your listening on the basis of (1) your purposes (for example, are you listening to learn? to give comfort? to judge?) and (2) your knowledge of and relationship to the other person (is this person prone to exaggeration? or does this person need support?). The following discussion identifies four styles of listening that will cover most listening situations. Select the style (or combination of styles) that best fit your specific situation. The four styles are

"Empathy? Yeah, I can see how that could be useful."

Charles Barsotti/The New Yorker Collection/The Cartoon Bank

empathic, polite, critical, and active. Before doing so, take the following self-test to examine our own listening style.

Empathic Listening

If you're going to understand what a person means and what a person is feeling, you need to listen with some degree of **empathy** (Rogers, 1970; Rogers & Farson, 1981). To empathize with others is to see the world as they see it, to feel what they feel. When you listen empathically as a neighbor tells of having her apartment burgled and all her prized possessions taken, you can share on some level the loss and emptiness she feels. Only when you achieve empathy can you fully understand another person's meaning. Empathic listening will also help you enhance your relationships (Barrett & Godfrey, 1988; Snyder, 1992). In this connection also see Table 3.4.

There is some evidence to show that empathy also has a negative side. For example, the more empathy you feel toward people who are similar to you racially and ethnically, the less empathy you feel toward those who are different. The same empathy that increases your understanding of your own group decreases your understanding of other groups. So although empathy may encourage understanding, it also can create dividing lines between your group and "them" (Angier, 1995).

Still another potential danger is over-empathizing with another's feelings that you lose control over your own feelings (Stern, 2015). It's important to remember that with effective empathy, you feel what the other is feeling but don't lose your own feelings.

In empathic listening, keep the following recommendations in mind.

- **See from the speaker's point of view.** See the sequence of events as the speaker does, and try to figure out how this perspective can influence what the speaker says and does.
- **Engage in equal, two-way conversation.** To encourage openness and empathy, try to eliminate any physical or psychological barriers to equality. For example, step from behind the large desk separating you from your employees. Avoid interrupting the speaker—a sign that you think what you have to say is more important.

Test Yourself

HOW DO YOU LISTEN?

Respond to each statement using the following scale:
1 = always, **2** = frequently, **3** = sometimes, **4** = seldom, and **5** = never.

_____ **1.** I listen actively, communicate acceptance of the speaker, and prompt the speaker to further explore his or her thoughts.

_____ **2.** I listen to what the speaker is saying and feeling; I try to feel what the speaker feels.

_____ **3.** I listen without judging the speaker.

_____ **4.** I listen to the literal meanings that a speaker communicates; I don't look too deeply into hidden meanings.

_____ **5.** I listen without active involvement; I generally remain silent and take in what the other person is saying.

_____ **6.** I listen objectively; I focus on the logic of the ideas rather than on the emotional meaning of the message.

_____ **7.** I listen politely even to messages that contradict my attitudes and beliefs.

_____ **8.** I'll interrupt a speaker when I have something really relevant to say.

_____ **9.** I listen critically, evaluating the speaker and what the speaker is saying.

_____ **10.** I look for the hidden meanings, the meanings that are revealed by subtle verbal or nonverbal cues.

These statements focus on the ways of listening discussed in this chapter. All of these ways are appropriate at some times but not at other times. It depends. So the only responses that are really inappropriate are "always" and "never." Effective listening is listening that is tailored to the specific communication situation.

Table 3.4 Listening to Emotions (Ten Ways)

Listening to the emotions of others is difficult but essential. Here are a few guidelines for making it a little easier and a lot more effective.

Generally...	Specifically...
Confirm the other person and his or her emotions.	A simple "You must be worried about finding another position" confirms the feelings of a person who has just lost a job.
Show interest by encouraging the person to explore his or her feelings.	Use simple encouragers like "I see" or "I understand." Or ask questions to let the speaker know that you're listening/interested.
Give the person permission to express feelings.	Let the person know that it's acceptable and okay with you if she or he expresses feelings in the ways that feel most comfortable—for example, by crying or talking about old times.
Don't try to force the person to talk about experiences or feelings she or he may not be willing to share.	A simple "Would you like to talk about it?" will cue the person that you're listening but not forcing him or her to talk.
Be especially sensitive to leave-taking cues. Don't overstay your welcome.	Notice especially comments like "It's getting late" or a glance at the clock, or a polite yawn.
Empathize.	See the situation from the point of view of the speaker. Avoid comments such as "Don't cry; it wasn't worth it," which can be interpreted as a rejection of the person's feelings.
Focus on the other person; don't refocus the conversation on yourself.	Instead, provide a supportive atmosphere that encourages the person to express her or his feelings.
Don't try to solve the other person's problems.	Listening to another's emotions comes first; offer solutions only when asked.
Avoid trying to focus on the bright side.	Avoid expressions such as "You're lucky you have some vision left" or "It is better this way; Pat was suffering so much."
Avoid interrupting.	Emotional expression frequently involves extra-long pauses, so wait before jumping in.

- **Seek to understand both thoughts and feelings.** Don't consider your listening task finished until you've understood what the speaker is feeling as well as what he or she is thinking.

Polite Listening

Politeness is often thought of as the exclusive function of the speaker, as solely an encoding or sending function. But politeness (or impoliteness) may also be signaled through listening (Fukushima, 2000).

Of course, there are times when you would not want to listen politely (for example, if someone is being verbally abusive or condescending or using racist or sexist language). In these cases, you might want to show your disapproval by showing that you're not even listening. But most often you'll want to listen politely, and you'll want to express this politeness through your listening behavior.

Here are a few suggestions for demonstrating that you are in fact listening politely. As you read these strategies, you'll notice that they are designed to be supportive of the speaker's positive and negative face needs.

- **Avoid interrupting the speaker.** Avoid trying to take over the speaker's turn. Avoid changing the topic. If you must say something in response to something the speaker said and can't wait until he or she finishes, then say it as briefly as possible and pass the speaker's turn back to the speaker.

- **Give supportive listening cues.** These might include nodding your head, giving minimal verbal responses such as "I see" or "yes, it's true," or moving closer to the speaker. Listen in a way that demonstrates that what the speaker is saying is important. In some cultures, polite listening cues must be cues of agreement (Japanese culture is often used as an example); in other cultures, polite listening cues are attentiveness and support rather than cues of agreement (much of United States culture is an example).

- **Show empathy with the speaker.** Demonstrate that you understand and feel the speaker's thoughts and feelings by giving responses that show this level of understanding—smiling or cringing or otherwise echoing the feelings of the speaker. If you echo the speaker's nonverbal expressions, your behavior is likely to be seen as empathic.

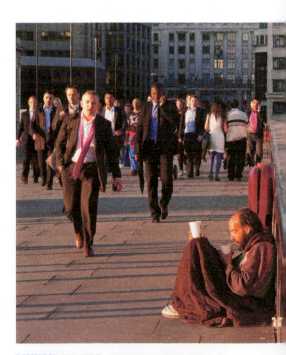

VIEWPOINTS: Negative Empathy
While empathy may encourage strong group identity and cohesion with those who are racially or ethnically or socially similar, it also can create dividing lines between your group and "others" (Angier, 1995). *Have you ever experienced or witnessed these negative effects of empathy?*

VIEWPOINTS: **Listening and Politeness**
Much of the thinking and research on listening and politeness has focused on them as face-to-face communication skills. *How would you describe listening politeness on the phone or on social network sites? Are the same principles applicable or do we need an entirely different set to describe social networking listening politeness?*

- **Maintain eye contact.** In much of the United States, this is perhaps the single most important rule. If you don't maintain eye contact when someone is talking to you, then you'll appear to be not listening and definitely not listening politely. This rule, however, does not hold true in all cultures. In some Latin and Asian cultures, polite listening would consist of looking down and avoiding direct eye contact when, for example, listening to a superior or much older person.

- **Give positive feedback.** Throughout the listening encounter and perhaps especially after the speaker's turn (when you continue the conversation as you respond to what the speaker has said), positive feedback will be seen as polite and negative feedback as impolite. If you must give negative feedback, then do so in a way that does not attack the person's negative face, for example, first mention areas of agreement or what you liked about what the person said and stress your good intentions. And, most important, do it in private. Public criticism is especially threatening and will surely be seen as a personal attack.

A somewhat different slant on politeness and listening can be seen in "forcing" people to listen when they don't want to. Generally, the polite advice is to be sensitive when the other person wants to leave and to stop asking the person to continue listening. And closely related to this is the "forced" listening that many cell phone users impose on others (or the forced waiting while someone reads and responds to texts), a topic addressed in Table 3.5.

Critical Listening

In many listening situations you'll need to exercise critical evaluation or judgment. In **critical listening**, you think logically and dispassionately about, for example, the stories your friends tell you or the sales pitch of the car dealer. Listening with an open mind will help you understand the messages better; listening with a critical mind will help you analyze and evaluate the messages. In listening critically, focus on the following guidelines.

JOURNAL
COMMUNICATION CHOICE POINT
Responding Politely

You're working as a manager at a restaurant, and a regular customer complains about the server: "I don't like the way she treated me, and I'm not coming back here." *What are some of the things you might say without losing the customer or your server (who is usually excellent)? Are there things you'd be sure not to say?*

Table 3.5 **Politeness and the Mobile Device**

The ubiquity of the cell phone and texting has led to enormous increases in communication, but it has also created problems, many of which are problems of politeness. Because much use occurs in public spaces, people often are forced to listen to conversations that don't involve them or to lose your attention when you send or respond to a text message.

General Rule	Specifics	Adjustments
Avoid using cell phones where inappropriate.	Especially avoid calling in restaurants, hospitals, theaters, museums, commuter buses or trains, and the classroom.	If you must make or take a call when in these various situations, try to move to a less public area.
Avoid texting when in a group.	Unless the text message concerns everyone and will be shared, avoid making everyone wait until you're finished.	If the text is especially important, excuse yourself and apologize for the inconvenience.
Silence your cell.	Put your phone on vibrate mode, or let your voicemail answer and take a message when your call might interfere with others.	When you can't avoid taking a call, speak as quietly as possible and as briefly as possible.
Avoid unwanted photo taking.	Don't take pictures of people who aren't posing for you, and delete photos if the person you photographed requests it.	Of course, if there's an accident or a robbery, you may want to photograph the events.
Avoid extended talking when your reception is weak.	Talking on your cell phone on a crowded street will probably result in poor reception, which is annoying to the other person.	In an emergency, caution trumps politeness.
Consider the other person.	It's easy to assume that when you have nothing better to do, the person you're calling also has nothing better to do.	As with any phone call, it's wise to ask if this is a good time to call—a strategy that helps maintain the autonomy (negative face) of the person you're calling.

- **Keep an open mind.** Avoid prejudging. Delay your judgments until you fully understand both the content and the intention the speaker is communicating. Avoid either positive or negative evaluation until you have a reasonably complete understanding. Even when a friend tells you he or she did something you disapprove of, nonjudgmental listening requires that you withhold making value judgments (in your mind as well as in your responses) that can get in the way of your understanding your friend.

- **Avoid filtering out or oversimplifying complex messages.** Similarly, avoid filtering out undesirable messages. Clearly, you don't want to hear that something you believe is untrue, that people you care for are unkind, or that ideals you hold are self-destructive. Yet it's important that you reexamine your beliefs by listening to these messages.

- **Recognize your own biases.** These may interfere with accurate listening and cause you to distort message reception through a process of assimilation—the tendency to integrate and interpret what you hear or think you hear according to your own biases, prejudices, and expectations.

- **Combat the tendency to sharpen**—to highlight, emphasize, and perhaps embellish one or two aspects of a message. Often the concepts that we tend to *sharpen* are incidental remarks that somehow stand out from the rest of the message. Be careful, therefore, about sharpening your blind date's "Thank you, I had a nice time" and assuming that the date was a big success—while ignoring the signs that it was just so-so, such as the lack of eye contact, the awkward silences, and the cell phone interruptions.

- **Focus on both verbal and nonverbal messages.** Recognize both consistent and inconsistent "packages" of messages, and use these as guides for drawing inferences about the speaker's meaning. Ask questions when in doubt. Listen also to what is omitted. Remember that speakers communicate by what they leave out as well as by what they include. When Harry says things will be okay now that his relationship is finally over but says it with downcast eyes, deep breathing, and clenched hands, consider the possibility that Harry is really hurting and that things are not okay.

Active Listening

One of the most important communication skills you can learn is that of **active listening** (Gordon, 1975). Consider the following interaction. You're disappointed that you have to redo your entire budget report, and you say, "I can't believe I have to redo this entire report. I really worked hard on this project, and now I have to do it all over again." To this you get three different responses:

> APOLLO: That's not so bad; most people find they have to redo their first reports. That's the norm here.
>
> ATHENA: You should be pleased that all you have to do is a simple rewrite. Peggy and Michael both had to completely redo their entire projects.
>
> DIANA: You have to rewrite that report you've worked on for the past three weeks? You sound really angry and frustrated.

All three listeners are probably trying to make you feel better. But they go about it in very different ways and, we can be sure, with very different results. Apollo tries to lessen the significance of the rewrite. This type of well-intended response is extremely common but does little to promote meaningful communication and understanding. Athena tries to give the situation a positive spin. With these responses, however, both these listeners are also suggesting that you should not be feeling the way you do. They're also implying that your feelings are not legitimate and should be replaced with more logical feelings.

Diana's response, however, is different from the others. Diana uses active listening. Active listening owes its development to Thomas Gordon (1975), who made it a cornerstone of his P-E-T (Parent Effectiveness Training) technique; it is a process of sending back to the speaker what you as a listener think the speaker meant—both in content and in feelings. Active listening, then, is not merely repeating the speaker's exact words but rather putting together into some meaningful whole your understanding of the speaker's total message.

FUNCTIONS OF ACTIVE LISTENING Active listening serves several important functions.

Perhaps most obvious is that active listening enables you to *check understanding*. It helps you as a listener check your understanding of what the speaker said and, more important, what he or she meant.

Reflecting back perceived meanings to the speaker gives the speaker an opportunity to offer clarification and correct any misunderstandings.

Second, through active listening you let the speaker know that you *acknowledge and accept his or her feelings*. In the sample responses given, the first two listeners challenged your feelings. Diana, the active listener, who reflected back to you what she thought you meant, accepted what you were feeling. In addition, she also explicitly identified your emotions; she commented that you sounded "angry and frustrated," allowing you an opportunity to correct her interpretation if necessary. Do be careful, however, to avoid sending what Gordon (1975) calls "solution messages." Solution messages tell the person how he or she *should* feel or what he or she *should* do. The four types of messages that send solutions and that you'll want to avoid in your active listening are (1) ordering messages—*Do this . . . , Don't touch that . . . ;* (2) warning and threatening messages—*If you don't do this, you'll . . . , If you do this, you'll . . . ;* (3) preaching and moralizing messages—*People should all . . . , We all have responsibilities . . . ;* and (4) advising messages—*Why don't you . . . , What I think you should do is . . . .*

Third, active listening *stimulates the speaker to explore his or her feelings and thoughts*. For example, Diana's response encourages you to elaborate on your feelings. This opportunity to elaborate also helps you deal with your feelings by talking them through.

TECHNIQUES OF ACTIVE LISTENING Three simple techniques may help you succeed in active listening.

- **Paraphrase the speaker's meaning.** Restating what you think the speaker means and feels in your own words can help ensure understanding and shows your interest in the speaker. Paraphrasing also gives the speaker a chance to extend what was originally said. Thus, when Diana echoes your thoughts, you're given the opportunity to elaborate on why rewriting the budget report is so daunting to you. Be especially careful not to lead the speaker in the direction you think he or she should go. Also, be careful that you don't overdo it; only a very small percentage of statements need paraphrasing. Paraphrase when you feel there's a chance for misunderstanding or when you want to express support for the other person and keep the conversation going.

- **Express understanding of the speaker's feelings.** In addition to paraphrasing the content, echo the feelings the speaker expressed or implied ("You must have felt horrible"). This expression of feelings will help you further check your perception of the speaker's feelings. This also will allow the speaker to see his or her feelings more objectively—especially helpful when they're feelings of anger, hurt, or depression—and to elaborate on these feelings.

- **Ask questions.** Asking questions strengthens your own understanding of the speaker's thoughts and feelings and elicits additional information ("How did you feel when you read your job appraisal report?"). Ask questions to provide just enough stimulation and support so the speaker will feel he or she can elaborate on these thoughts and feelings. These questions should further confirm your interest and concern for the speaker but not pry into unrelated areas or challenge the speaker in any way.

Consider this dialogue and note the active listening techniques used throughout.

PAT: That jerk demoted me. He told me I wasn't an effective manager. I can't believe he did that, after all I've done for this place.

CHRIS: I'm with you. You've been manager for three or four months now, haven't you?

PAT: A little over three months. I know it was probationary, but I thought I was doing a good job.

CHRIS: Can you get another chance?

PAT: Yes, he said I could try again in a few months. But I feel like a failure.

CHRIS: I know what you mean. It sucks. What else did he say?

PAT: He said I had trouble getting the paperwork done on time.

CHRIS: You've been late filing the reports?

PAT: A few times.

CHRIS: Is there a way to delegate the paperwork?

PAT: No, but I think I know now what needs to be done.

CHRIS: You sound as though you're ready to give that manager's position another try.

PAT: Yes, I think I am, and I'm going to let him know that I intend to apply in the next few months.

Even in this brief interaction, Pat has moved from unproductive anger and feelings of failure to a determination to correct an unpleasant situation. Note, too, that Chris didn't offer solutions but "simply" listened actively.

In communicating your understanding back to the speaker, be especially careful to avoid sending what are called "solution messages" (Gordon, 1975)—messages that tell the person how he or she *should* feel or what he or she *should* do. You'll want to avoid solution messages such as these.

- **Ordering messages:** "Do this." "Don't touch that."
- **Warning and threatening messages:** "If you don't do this, you'll…" "If you do that, you'll…"
- **Preaching and moralizing messages:** "People should all…" "You have responsibilities…"
- **Advising messages:** "Why don't you…" "I think you should…"

Listening Differences: Culture and Gender

3.4   **Explain the major cultural and gender differences found in listening and their influence on listening.**

Listening is difficult in part because of the inevitable differences in the communication systems between speakers and listeners. Because each person has had a unique set of experiences, each person's communication and meaning system is going to be unique. When speaker and listener come from different cultures or are of different genders, the differences and their effects are, naturally, much greater.

Culture and Listening

In today's multicultural world, where people from very different cultures live and work together, it's especially important to understand the ways in which cultural differences can influence listening. Three of these cultural influences on listening are (1) language and speech, (2) nonverbal behaviors, and (3) feedback.

LANGUAGE AND SPEECH   Even when a speaker and a listener speak the same language, they speak it with different meanings and different accents. Speakers of the same language will, at the very least, have different meanings for the same terms because they have had different experiences. For example, the word "parents" to someone brought up in a series of foster homes will be drastically different from someone who grew up in a "traditional" family.

Speakers and listeners who have different native languages and who may have learned English as a second language will have even greater differences in meaning. If you learned your meaning for *house* in a culture in which everyone lives in his or her own house with lots of land around it, then communicating with someone whose meaning of house was learned in a neighborhood of high-rise tenements is going to be difficult. Although each of you will hear the word *house*, the meanings you'll develop will be drastically different. In adjusting your listening—especially in an intercultural setting—understand that the speaker's meanings may be very different from yours even though you're speaking the same language.

In many classrooms throughout the United States, there will be a wide range of accents. Those whose native language is tonal, such as Chinese (in which differences in pitch signal important meaning differences), may speak English with variations in pitch that may be puzzling to others. Those whose native language is Japanese may have trouble distinguishing *l* from *r*, because Japanese does not include this distinction. The native language acts as a filter and influences the accent given to the second language.

NONVERBAL BEHAVIORS Speakers from different cultures have different *display rules*, cultural rules that govern which nonverbal behaviors are appropriate and which are inappropriate in a public setting. As you listen to other people, you also "listen" to their nonverbals. If nonverbal signals are drastically different from what you would expect on the basis of the verbal message, you may see them as a kind of noise or interference or even as a contradictory message. If a colleague at work, for example, consistently averts her eyes when talking with you, you may interpret this as an indication of shyness or dishonesty (which are often associated with averted eyes), but it may be merely a sign that your colleague's culture discourages direct eye contact. (Some, often collectivist, cultures consider direct eye contact overly forward, impolite, or inappropriate (Axtell, 2007). Other, often individualist, cultures consider direct eye contact a sign of honesty and forthrightness.) To complicate matters further, different cultures often have very different meanings for the same nonverbal gesture. For example, the thumb and forefinger forming a circle means "OK" in most of the United States, but it means "money" in Japan, "zero" in some Mediterranean countries, and "I'll kill you" in Tunisia.

FEEDBACK Members of some cultures give very direct and very honest feedback. Speakers from these largely individualist cultures—the United States is a good example—expect feedback to be an honest reflection of what their listeners are feeling. In other largely collectivist cultures—Japan and Korea are good examples—it's more important to be positive (and to respect the other person's need for positive face) than to be truthful. As a result, people may respond with positive feedback (say, in commenting on a business colleague's proposal) even if it doesn't reflect their true opinion. Listen to feedback, as you would to all messages, with a full recognition that various cultures view feedback very differently.

Gender and Listening

Men and women learn different styles of listening, just as they learn different styles for using verbal and nonverbal messages. Not surprisingly, these different styles can create difficulties in opposite-sex communication.

RAPPORT AND REPORT TALK According to linguistic scholar and popular writer Deborah Tannen (1990) in her best-selling *You Just Don't Understand: Women and Men in Conversation*, women seek to share feelings, build rapport, and

JOURNAL
COMMUNICATION CHOICE POINT
Support Not Solutions

You need to make some major decisions in your life, and you need to bounce your ideas off someone, just to clarify them in your own mind. Your romantic partner almost always tries to solve your problems rather than just be a supportive listener. *What are some of the things you might say to help secure support rather than the offering of solutions?*

establish closer relationships, and they use listening to achieve these ends. Men, on the other hand, play up their expertise, emphasize it, and use it to dominate the interaction. Their focus is on reporting information. Tannen argues that in conversation a woman seeks to be liked, so she expresses agreement. The goal of a man, on the other hand, is to be given respect, so he seeks to show his knowledge and expertise.

LISTENING CUES   Men and women give different types of listening cues and, consequently, show that they're listening in different ways. In conversation, a woman is more apt to give lots of listening cues— interjecting "Yeah" or "Uh-huh," nodding in agreement, and smiling. A man is more likely to listen quietly, without giving lots of listening cues as feedback. Women also make more eye contact when listening than do men, who are more apt to look around and often away from the speaker (Brownell, 2013). As a result of these differences, women seem to be more engaged in listening than do men.

AMOUNT AND PURPOSES OF LISTENING   Tannen (1990, 1994a) argues that men listen less to women than women listen to men. The reason, says Tannen, is that listening places the person in an inferior position, but speaking places the person in a superior position. Men may seem to assume a more confrontational posture while listening and to ask questions that are argumentative or seek to puncture holes in the speaker's position as a way to play up their own expertise. Women are more likely than men to ask supportive questions and offer constructive criticism. Men and women act this way both to members of the same and of the opposite sex; their usual ways of speaking and listening don't seem to change depending on whether the person they're communicating with is male or female.

It's important to note that not all researchers agree that there is sufficient evidence to support the claims of Tannen and others about gender differences (Goldsmith & Fulfs, 1999). Gender differences are changing drastically and quickly; it's best to take generalizations about gender as starting points for investigation and not as airtight conclusions (Gamble & Gamble, 2003). Further, be mindful that, as you no doubt have observed from your own experiences, gender differences—although significant—are far outnumbered by similarities.

VIEWPOINTS: Gender and Listening Differences

The popular belief is that men listen in the way they do to prove themselves superior and that women listen as they do to ingratiate themselves. Although there is no evidence to show that these images are valid, they persist in the assumptions that people make about the opposite sex. *What do you believe accounts for the differences in the way men and women listen?*

Summary of Concepts and Skills

This chapter discussed the ways you listen and how you can listen more effectively.

Stages of Listening

3.1   **Define** *listening* **and its five stages and describe the ways you can increase listening accuracy at each of these stages.**

1. Listening is crucial to success in a wide range of professions and in personal relationships.

2. Listening may be defined as "the process of receiving, constructing meaning from, and responding to spoken and/or nonverbal messages."

3. Listening serves a variety of purposes: You listen to learn; to relate to others; to influence the attitudes,

beliefs, and behaviors of others; to play; and to help. Listening is a five-step process consisting of receiving, understanding, remembering, evaluating, and responding.

4. Both listener and speaker share in the responsibility for effective listening.

Listening Barriers

3.2   **Describe the four major barriers to effective listening and describe how you can improve effectiveness in your own listening.**

5. Among the obstacles to effective listening are physical and mental distractions, biases and prejudices, lack of appropriate focus, and premature judgment.

Four Listening Styles

3.3 **Define the four styles of listening and explain how each may be used effectively.**

6. Effective listening involves a process of making adjustments, depending on the situation. Among the useful styles are empathic listening, polite listening, critical listening, and active listening.

Listening Differences: Culture and Gender

3.4 **Explain the major cultural and gender differences found in listening and their influence on listening.**

7. Culture influences listening in a variety of ways. Contributing to listening difficulties are cultural differences in language and speech, nonverbal behaviors, and feedback.

8. Men and women listen differently and perhaps for different reasons. For example, women give more messages that say "I'm listening" than men. According to some theorists, women use listening to show empathy and to build rapport, and men minimize listening because it puts them in a subordinate position.

Throughout this discussion of listening, a variety of skills were identified. Place a check mark next to those skills that you feel you need to work on most.

_____ 1. I recognize that listening serves a variety of purposes, and I adjust my listening on the basis of my purposes: for example, to learn, relate, influence, play, or help.

_____ 2. I realize that listening is a multistage process, and I regulate my listening behavior as appropriate in receiving, understanding, remembering, evaluating, and responding.

_____ 3. When receiving messages, I seek to increase my chances of effective listening by, for example, paying attention to the speaker's verbal and nonverbal messages; avoiding distractions; and focusing on what the speaker is saying, not on what I'm going to say next.

_____ 4. I facilitate understanding in listening by relating new information to what I already know and trying to see the messages from the speaker's point of view.

_____ 5. In remembering the speaker's messages, I try to identify the central ideas and the major supporting materials, summarize the main ideas, and repeat important concepts to etch them more firmly in my mind.

_____ 6. In evaluating messages, I first make sure I understand the speaker's point of view and seek to identify any sources of bias or self-interest.

_____ 7. In responding, I am supportive of the speaker and own my own thoughts and feelings.

_____ 8. I am mindful of the common listening obstacles (i.e., distractions, biases, lack of focus, and premature judgment) and try to reduce their effects.

_____ 9. I am aware of and able to adjust my listening in terms of empathic, polite, critical, and active listening.

_____ 10. I practice active listening when appropriate by paraphrasing the speaker's meaning, expressing my understanding of the speaker's feelings, and asking questions.

_____ 11. I recognize the influence of culture on listening and cultural differences in listening and take these into consideration when listening in intercultural situations.

_____ 12. I recognize gender differences in listening and take these into consideration when communicating with members of the opposite sex.

Key Terms

listening	false memory syndrome	negative empathy
short-term memory	backchanneling cues	critical listening
long-term memory	empathy	active listening

Skill Development Experiences

3.1 Using Active Listening Strategies

Active listening allows you to connect with another person by demonstrating your understanding and support.

Here are three situations that might require active listening. For each situation, compose an active listening response in which you (a) paraphrase the speaker's meaning, (b) express understanding of the speaker's meaning, and (c) ask questions to clarify any potential misunderstandings.

1. Your friend has just broken up a love affair and is telling you about it: I can't seem to get Chris out of my head. All I do is think about what we used to do and all the fun we used to have.

2. A young nephew tells you that he cannot talk with his parents. No matter how hard he tries, they just don't listen. I tried to tell them that I can't play baseball and I don't want to play baseball. But they ignore me and tell me that all I need is practice.

3. Your mother has been having a difficult time at work. She was recently passed up for a promotion and received one of the lowest merit raises given in the company. I'm not sure what I did wrong. I do my work, mind my own business, don't take my sick days like everyone else. How could they give that promotion to Helen who's only been with the company for two years? Maybe I should just quit.

3.2 Responding with Empathy

Almost invariably, empathy will help you understand and relate more effective to others.

Here are ten possible responses to the "simple" statement, "I guess I'm feeling a little depressed." Assume that Apple and Orange are close friends—not best friends but more than acquaintances. You may assume that Apple and Orange are two women, two men, or a woman and a man—select the genders as you wish.

For this exercise:

- Identify why each of the ten responses is (probably) inappropriate and not empathic. You may also want to consider the motivating factors that contribute to the varied responses. That is, why does someone respond as these Oranges did?
- Write what you'd consider an appropriate and empathic response. Consider too why your response is empathic. What does your response communicate that the varied responses from Orange did not communicate?

> APPLE: I guess I'm just feeling a little depressed.
>
> ORANGE 1: I've been reading about depression and it's all in your head. This research—it was done at NYU—showed that the ....
>
> ORANGE 2: You depressed? Have you talked to Pat? Now that's depression.
>
> ORANGE 3: You're not depressed; you're just a bit sad. After all, that breakup could not have been easy.
>
> ORANGE 4: Well, then, you need to get out more; let's go and have some fun.
>
> ORANGE 5: What else is happening? Have you talked to Chris?
>
> ORANGE 6: Me too. I don't know what it is but I woke up this morning and felt so depressed. I thought it was from a dream but I'm still feeling that way. Do you think I should see a counselor?

ORANGE 7: Are you? That's really serious; it's often a sign of suicide. Remember Pat? Got depressed after the breakup and jumped off the roof.

ORANGE 8: Reminds me of that movie—what's the name? You know, the one with Meryl Streep?

ORANGE 9: Yeah, lots of people tell me the same thing.

ORANGE 10: Not you. I can't believe that. I'd believe it about anybody but you.

Chapter 4
Verbal Messages

Verbal messages come in varied forms.

CHAPTER OUTLINE	Learning Objectives
Principles of Verbal Messages	**4.1** Paraphrase the principles of verbal messages.
Disconfirmation and Confirmation	**4.2** Define and distinguish between *disconfirmation* and *confirmation* and provide examples of appropriate cultural identifiers.
Principles for Using Verbal Messages Effectively	**4.3** Explain the ways in which language can distort thinking and identify the suggestions for communicating more logically.

Your messages normally occur in "packages" consisting of both verbal and nonverbal signals (Pittenger, Hockett, & Danehy, 1960). Usually, verbal and nonverbal behaviors reinforce, or support, each other. For example, you don't usually express fear with words while the rest of your body relaxes. You don't normally express anger with your face while your words are warm and cheerful. Your entire being works as a whole—verbally and nonverbally—to express your thoughts and feelings. At other times, the verbal and nonverbal messages contradict each other; you say you enjoyed the meal but eat very little, or you say you're happy to meet someone but avoid eye contact. Regardless of whether verbal and nonverbal messages support or contradict each other, they occur together.

This chapter focuses on the verbal message system: the system's key principles, the concepts of confirmation and disconfirmation, and the ways you can use verbal messages most effectively. The next chapter will examine the nonverbal message system.

Principles of Verbal Messages

4.1   **Paraphrase the principles of verbal messages.**

Your verbal messages, of course, rely on the rules of grammar; you can't just make up sounds or words or string words together at random and expect to be understood. But following the rules of grammar is not enough to achieve effective communication. Here we look at seven principles to help you understand how verbal messages work.

Message Meanings Are in People

To discover the meaning a person is trying to communicate, it's necessary to look into the person as well as the words. The word *cancer*, for example, will mean something very different to a mother whose child has just been diagnosed with cancer than it does to an oncologist.

Also recognize that, as you change, you also change the meanings you created out of past messages; although the message sent may not have changed, the meanings you created from it yesterday and the meanings you create today may be quite different. Yesterday, when a special someone said, "I love you," you created certain meanings. But today, when you learn that the same "I love you" was said to three other people, you drastically change the meaning you derive from those three words.

Messages Are Denotative and Connotative

When you speak, you use verbal messages both denotatively and connotatively. **Denotation** has to do with the objective meaning of a term, the meaning you would find in a dictionary. It's the meaning that people who share a common language assign to a word. **Connotation** is the subjective or emotional meaning that specific speakers or listeners give to a word. Take as an example the word *migrants* (used to designate Mexicans coming into the United States to better their economic condition) with the word *settlers* (meaning Europeans who came to the United States for the same reason) (Koppelman, 2005). Though both terms describe essentially the same activity (and are essentially the same denotatively), they differ widely in their connotations, with the former often negatively evaluated and the latter often positively valued.

"It's not what you say, John, it's how you say it."

Semanticist S. I. Hayakawa (Hayakawa & Hayakawa, 1989) coined the terms **snarl words** and **purr words** to clarify further the distinction between denotation and connotation. Snarl words are highly negative: "She's an idiot," "He's a pig," "They're a bunch of losers." Purr words are highly positive: "She's a real sweetheart," "He's a dream," "They're the greatest." Snarl and purr words, although they may sometimes seem to have denotative meaning and to refer to the "real world," are actually connotative in meaning. These terms do not describe objective realities but rather express the speaker's feelings about people or events.

Messages Vary in Abstraction

Consider the following terms:

- Entertainment
- Film
- American film
- Classic American films
- *Casablanca*

At the top is an **abstraction**, or general concept—*entertainment*. Note that *entertainment* includes all the other items on the list plus various other items—*television, novels, drama, comics*, and so on. *Film* is more specific and concrete. It includes all of the items below on the list as well as various other items such as *Indian film* or *Russian film*. It excludes, however, all entertainment that is not film. *American film* is again more specific than *film* and excludes all films that are not American. *Classic American films* further limits *American film* to those considered to be timeless. *Casablanca* specifies concretely the one item to which reference is made.

A verbal message that uses the most general term—in this case, entertainment—will conjure up many different images in listeners' minds. One person may focus on television, another on music, another on comic books, and still another on radio. To some listeners, the word *film* may bring to mind the early silent films; to others it may connote high-tech special effects; to still others it will recall Disney's animated cartoons. *Casablanca* guides listeners still further—in this case, to one film. So, as you get more specific—less abstract—you more effectively guide the images that come to your listeners' minds.

Effective verbal messages include words that range widely in abstractness. At times a general term may suit your needs best; at other times a more specific term may serve better. The widely accepted recommendation for effective communication is to use abstractions sparingly and to express your meanings explicitly with words that are low in abstraction.

Messages Can Deceive

Although we operate on the assumption that people tell the truth, it should come as no surprise to learn that some people do lie. Lying also begets more lying; when one person lies, the likelihood of the other person lying increases (Tyler, Feldman, & Reichert, 2006). **Lying** refers to the act of sending messages with the intention of giving another person information you believe to be false.

Large cultural differences exist in the way lying is defined and in the way lying is treated. For example, as children get older, Chinese and Taiwanese (but not Canadians) see lying about the good deeds that they do as positive (as you'd expect for cultures that emphasize modesty), and taking credit for these same good deeds is seen negatively (Lee et al., 2002). Some cultures consider lying to be more important than others—in one study, for example, European Americans viewed lies less negatively than did Ecuadorians. Both, however, felt that lying to an out-group member was more acceptable than lying to an in-group member (Mealy, Stephan, & Urrutia, 2007).

One of the more interesting questions about lying is how liars behave. Do they act differently from those telling the truth? And, if they do act differently, how can we tell when someone is lying? These questions are not easy to answer, and we are far from having complete answers to them. But we have learned a great deal.

For example, after an examination of 120 research studies, the following behaviors were found to most often accompany lying (DePaulo et al., 2003; Knapp, 2008).

- **Liars hold back.** They speak more slowly (perhaps to monitor what they're saying), take longer to respond to questions (again, perhaps monitoring their messages), and generally give less information and elaboration.
- **Liars make less sense.** Liars' messages contain more discrepancies, more inconsistencies.
- **Liars give a more negative impression.** Generally, liars are seen as less willing to be cooperative, smile less than truth-tellers, and are more defensive.
- **Liars are tense.** The tension may be revealed by their higher pitched voices and their excessive body movements.

It is very difficult to detect when a person is lying and when a person is telling the truth. The hundreds of research studies conducted on this topic find that in most instances people judge lying accurately in less than 60 percent of the cases, only slightly better than chance (Knapp, 2008).

Lie detection is even more difficult (that is, less accurate) in long-standing romantic relationships—the very relationships in which the most significant lying occurs (Guerrero, Andersen, & Afifi, 2007). One important reason for this is the **truth bias**: We assume that the person is telling the truth. This truth bias is especially strong in long-term relationships where it's simply expected that each person tells the truth (Knapp, 2008).

Messages Vary in Politeness

It will come as no surprise that messages vary greatly in politeness. Polite messages (such as compliments or pats on the back) reflect positively on the other person (contributing to positive face). They also respect the other person's right to be independent and autonomous, as when you ask permission or acknowledge the person's right to refuse (contributing to negative face needs). Impolite messages (criticism or negative facial expressions) attack our needs to be seen positively and to be autonomous.

POLITENESS AND DIRECTNESS   Direct messages are usually less polite than indirect messages; consider how "Write me a recommendation" compares to " Do you think you could write a recommendation for me?" Indirect messages sound more polite because they allow receivers to maintain autonomy and provide an acceptable way for the person to refuse your request.

Indirect messages allow you to express a desire without insulting or offending anyone; they allow you to observe the rules of polite interaction. So instead of saying, "I'm bored with this group," you say, "It's getting late and I have to get up early tomorrow." Instead of saying, "This food tastes like cardboard," you say, "I just started my diet." In each instance you're stating a preference but are saying it indirectly so as to avoid offending someone.

The differences between direct and indirect messages may easily create misunderstandings. For example, a person who uses an indirect style of speech may be doing so to be polite and may have been taught this style by his or her culture. If you assume, instead, that the person is using indirectness to be manipulative, because your culture regards it so, then miscommunication is inevitable.

POLITENESS AND GENDER   There are considerable gender differences in politeness (Tannen, 1994b; Holmes, 1995; Kapoor et al., 2003; Dindia & Canary, 2006). Among the research findings are, for example, that women are more polite and more indirect in giving orders than are men; they are more likely to say, for example, "It would be great if these letters could go out today" than "Have these letters out by three." Men are more likely to be indirect when they express weakness, reveal a problem, or admit an error. Generally, men will speak indirectly when expressing meanings that violate the masculine stereotype (e.g., messages of weakness or doubt or incompetence). Women's greater politeness is also seen in the finding that women express empathy, sympathy, and supportiveness more than men. Women also apologize more than men, and both women and men make most of their apologies to women.

POLITENESS ONLINE   Internet communication has very specific rules for politeness, called **netiquette** (Kallos, 2005). Much as the rules of etiquette provide guidance in communicating in social situations, the rules of netiquette provide guidance in communicating online, and they concern everyone using computer-mediated communication (CMC). These rules are helpful for making Internet communication more pleasant and easier and also for achieving greater personal efficiency. As you review these guidelines, think of how you might apply them to specific online communication, say, e-mailing your instructor or inquiring about a job.

VIEWPOINTS: Gender Speech Patterns
When asked what they would like to change about the communication patterns of the opposite sex, men said they wanted women to be more direct, and women said they wanted men to stop interrupting and offering advice (Noble, 1994). *What one change would you like to see in the communication system of the opposite sex? Of your own sex?*

- *Familiarize yourself with the site or rules for communicating before contributing.* Before asking questions about the system, read the Frequently Asked Questions (FAQs). "Lurk" before speaking. Lurking (which, in CMC, is good) will help you learn the rules.

Communicating Ethically
LYING

Lying occurs when you try to make others believe something is true that you believe is untrue (Ekman, 2009; Knapp, 2008; Burgoon & Hoobler, 2002). You can lie by commission (i.e., by making explicitly false statements) or by omission (i.e., by omitting relevant information, thus allowing others to draw incorrect inferences). Similarly, you can lie verbally (e.g., in speech or writing) or nonverbally (e.g., wearing an innocent facial expression instead of acknowledging the commission of some wrong, or nodding knowingly instead of expressing honest ignorance) (O'Hair, Cody, & McLaughlin, 1981). Lies range from "white lies" and truth stretching to lies that form the basis of relationship infidelity, libel, and perjury. Not surprisingly, lies have ethical implications.

Some lies may be considered ethical lies, lies that are commonly accepted by society as harmless, right, and even as having some good effects (e.g., lying to a child to protect a fantasy belief in Santa Claus or the tooth fairy, or publicly agreeing with someone to enable the person to save face). Some ethical lies may even be considered to be required (e.g., lying to protect someone from harm or telling the proud parents that their child is beautiful). Other lies are clearly unethical, for example, lying to defraud investors, to falsely accuse someone of a crime, or to slander someone.

ETHICAL CHOICE POINT
Of course, not all lies are easy to classify as ethical or unethical. *For example, would it be ethical for you to lie to get what you deserve but couldn't get any other way? For example, would it be ethical to lie to get a well-earned promotion or a raise?*

- **Be brief.** Communicate only the information that is needed clearly, briefly, and in an organized way.
- **Don't shout.** WRITING IN CAPS IS PERCEIVED AS SHOUTING. It's okay to use capital letters occasionally to achieve emphasis. If you wish to give emphasis, however, it's better to highlight like _this_ or *this*.
- **Don't spam or "flame."** Don't send unsolicited mail, repeatedly send the same mail, or post the same message (or irrelevant messages) to lots of people or groups. As in face-to-face conflicts, don't make personal attacks on other users.
- **Avoid offensive language.** Refrain from expressions that would be considered offensive to others, such as sexist or racist terms.
- **Be polite.** Follow the same rules of behavior online that you would in a face-to-face encounter.

A special case of online politeness concerns the ever popular social networking sites, which have developed their own rules of netiquette, some of which are noted in Table 4.1.

Messages Can Be Onymous or Anonymous

Some messages are **onymous messages** or "signed"; that is, the author of the message is clearly identified, as it is in your textbooks, news-related editorials, feature articles, and of course when you communicate face-to-face and, usually, by phone or chat. In many cases, you have the opportunity to respond directly to the speaker/writer and voice your opinions, your agreement or disagreement, for example. Other messages are anonymous: the author is not identified. For example, on faculty evaluation questionnaires and on online ratings websites, the ratings and the comments are published anonymously.

The Internet has made anonymity extremely easy and there are currently a variety of websites that offer to send your e-mails to your boss, your ex-partner, your secret crush, your noisy neighbors, or your inadequate lawyer—all anonymously. Thus, your message gets sent but you are not identified with it. For good or ill, you don't have to deal with the consequences of your message.

One obvious advantage of anonymity is that it allows people to voice opinions that may be unpopular and may thus encourage greater honesty. In the case of ratings websites, for example, anonymity ensures that the student writing negative comments about an instructor will not be penalized. An anonymous e-mail to a sexual partner informing him or her about your having an STD and suggesting testing and treatment might never get said in a face-to-face or phone conversation. The presumption is that anonymity encourages honesty and openness.

Anonymity also enables people to disclose their inner feelings, fears, hopes, and dreams with a depth of feeling that they may be otherwise reluctant to do. A variety of websites that enable you to maintain anonymity are available for these purposes. And in these cases, not only are you anonymous but the people who read your messages

---

Table 4.1 Social Networking Politeness

The social networking sites such as Facebook and Twitter have developed their own rules of politeness. Here are five such rules.

Rules of Politeness	The Rule in Operation
Engage in networking feedforward before requesting friendship.	Send a message complimenting the person's latest post; doing so provides some background and eases the way for a friendship request.
Avoid negativity.	Refrain from writing embarrassing messages and don't post unflattering photos that may generate conflict.
Keep networking information confidential.	Don't relay information on social media about others who are not direct friends. Doing so is considered inappropriate and impolite.
Be gentle in refusals.	Don't refuse friend requests immediately; wait a few days or simply ignore it. If someone refuses your friend request, don't ask for reasons; it merely prolongs an awkward exchange.
Avoid making potentially embarrassing requests.	Consider that bosses or teachers may not accept a friend request because they want to keep their private lives separate from their work lives.

are also anonymous, a situation that is likely to encourage a greater willingness to disclose and to make disclosures at a deeper level than otherwise.

An obvious disadvantage is that anonymity might encourage people to go to extremes—since there are no consequences to the message—to voice opinions that are outrageous. This in turn can easily spark conflict that is likely to prove largely unproductive. With **anonymous messages**, you can't evaluate the credibility of the source. Advice on depression, for example, may come from someone who knows nothing about depression and may make useless recommendations.

Messages Vary in Assertiveness

Assertiveness refers to a willingness to stand up for your rights but with respect for the rights of others. Before reading any further, take the accompanying self-test, "How Assertive Are Your Messages?" Assertive people operate with an "I win, you win" philosophy; they assume that both parties can gain something from an interaction, even from a confrontation. Assertive people are more positive and score lower on measures of hopelessness than do nonassertive people (Velting, 1999). Assertive people are willing to assert their own rights, but unlike their aggressive counterparts, they don't hurt others in the process. Assertive people speak their minds and welcome others' doing likewise.

Realize that, as with many other aspects of communication, there will be wide cultural differences when it comes to assertiveness. For example, the values of assertiveness are more likely to be extolled in individualist cultures than in collectivist cultures. Assertiveness will be valued more by those cultures that stress competition, individual success, and independence. It will be valued much less by those cultures that stress cooperation, group success, and interdependence of all members. U.S. students, for example, are found to be significantly more assertive than Japanese and Korean students (Thompson, Klopf, & Ishii, 1991; Thompson & Klopf, 1991). Thus, for a given situation, assertiveness may be an effective strategy in one culture but would create problems in another. Assertiveness with an elder in many Asian and Hispanic cultures may be seen as insulting and disrespectful.

Most people are nonassertive in particular situations. If you're one of these people, and if you wish to modify your behavior, here are some suggestions for

Test Yourself

HOW ASSERTIVE ARE YOUR MESSAGES?

Indicate how true each of the following statements is about your own communication. Respond instinctively rather than in the way you feel you should respond.

Use a scale on which **5** = always or almost always true; **4** = usually true; **3** = sometimes true, sometimes false; **2** = usually false; and **1** = always or almost always false.

_____ **1.** I would express my opinion in a group even if it contradicted the opinions of others.

_____ **2.** When asked to do something that I really don't want to do, I can say no without feeling guilty.

_____ **3.** I can express my opinion to my superiors on the job.

_____ **4.** I can start up a conversation with a stranger on a bus or at a business gathering without fear.

_____ **5.** I voice objection to people's behavior if I feel it infringes on my rights.

All five items in this test identify characteristics of assertive communication. So high scores (say about 20 and above) would indicate a high level of assertiveness. Low scores (say about 10 and below) would indicate a low level of assertiveness.

The remaining discussion in this section clarifies the nature of assertive communication and offers guidelines for increasing your own assertiveness. These suggestions can help you not only to increase your assertiveness but also, when appropriate, to reduce your aggressive tendencies.

communicating assertiveness (Windy & Constantinou, 2005; Bower & Bower, 2005). (If you are always nonassertive and are unhappy about this, then you may need to work with a therapist to change your behavior.)

- **Describe the problem; don't evaluate or judge it.** *We're all working on this advertising project together. You've missed half our meetings and you still haven't produced your first report.* Be sure to use I-messages and to avoid messages that accuse or blame the other person.
- **State how this problem affects you; tell the person how you feel.** *My job depends on the success of this project, and I don't think it's fair that I have to do extra work to make up for what you're not doing.*
- **Propose solutions that are workable and that allow the person to save face.** Describe or visualize the situation if your solution were put into effect. *If you can get your report to the group by Tuesday, we'll still be able to meet our deadline. I could give you a call on Monday to remind you.*
- **Confirm understanding.** Query the other person to make sure you both understand where you stand. *It's clear that we can't produce this project if you're not going to pull your own weight. Will you have the report to us by Tuesday?*

Keep in mind that assertiveness is not always the most desirable response. Effectively assertive people are assertive when they want to be, but they can back down if the situation calls for it—for example, when they risk emotionally hurting another person. Let's say that an older relative wishes you to do something for her or him. You could assert your rights and say no, but because this would probably hurt this person's feelings, it might be better simply to do as asked.

A note of caution should be added to this discussion. It's easy to visualize a situation such as this one: People are talking behind you in a movie theater, and you—drawing from your newfound enthusiasm for assertiveness—tell them to be quiet. It's also easy to see yourself getting smashed in the teeth as a result. In applying the principles of assertive communication, be careful that you don't go beyond what you can handle effectively.

Table 4.2 provides a summary of these seven principles of verbal messages.

Disconfirmation and Confirmation

4.2 Define and distinguish between *disconfirmation* and *confirmation* and provide examples of appropriate cultural identifiers.

The terms *confirmation* and *disconfirmation* refer to the extent to which you acknowledge another person. Consider this situation. You've been living with someone for the last six months and you arrive home late one night. Your partner, let's say Pat, is angry and complains about your being so late. Which of the following is most likely to be your response?

Table 4.2 In a Nutshell: The Principles of Verbal Messages

Principle	Verbal Message Strategies
Meanings are in people, not in words.	Look not only to the words used but to the person using the words.
Meanings are both denotative and connotative.	Look at both the objective meaning and the subjective meaning expressed.
Messages vary in abstraction.	Use both general and specific terms.
Message meanings can deceive.	Acting with a truth bias is usually appropriate, but realize that in some situations, messages may be false and may be purposely designed to mislead you.
Messages (in all forms of communication) vary in politeness.	Use messages that reflect positively on others and allow them to be autonomous.
Messages may be onymous or anonymous.	Use ownership of a message as one factor in evaluating messages.
Meanings vary in assertiveness.	Act assertively in most cases, but realize that attitudes toward assertiveness vary greatly with culture.

- *Stop screaming. I'm not interested in what you're babbling about. I'll do what I want, when I want. I'm going to bed.*
- *What are you so angry about? Didn't you get in three hours late last Thursday when you went to that office party? So knock it off.*
- *You have a right to be angry. I should have called to tell you I was going to be late, but I got involved in an argument at work, and I couldn't leave until it was resolved.*

In the first response, you dismiss Pat's anger and even indicate dismissal of Pat as a person. In the second response, you reject the validity of Pat's reasons for being angry but do not dismiss either Pat's feelings of anger or Pat as a person. In the third response, you acknowledge Pat's anger and the reasons for it. In addition, you provide some kind of explanation and, in doing so, show that both Pat's feelings and Pat as a person are important and that Pat has the right to know what happened. The first response is an example of disconfirmation, the second of rejection, and the third of confirmation.

Disconfirmation is a communication pattern in which we ignore someone's presence as well as that person's communications. We say, in effect, that this person and what this person has to say are not worth serious attention or effort. The Amish community practices an extreme form of disconfirmation called "shunning," in which the community members totally ignore a person who has violated one or more of their rules. The specific aim of shunning is to get the person to repent and to reenter the community of the faithful. All cultures practice some form of exclusion for those who violate important cultural rules.

Note that **rejection** is not the same as disconfirmation. In rejection, you disagree with the person; you indicate your unwillingness to accept something the other person says or does. However, you do not deny that person's significance.

Confirmation is the opposite of disconfirmation. In confirmation you not only acknowledge the presence of the other person but also indicate your acceptance of this person, of this person's self-definition, and of your relationship as defined or viewed by this other person. Disconfirmation and confirmation may be communicated in a wide variety of ways. Table 4.3 shows a few examples.

You can gain insight into a wide variety of offensive language practices by viewing them as types of disconfirmation—as language that alienates and separates. Four obvious disconfirming practices are racism, heterosexism, ageism, and sexism; we'll look at these practices next (Figure 4.1).

Table 4.3 Disconfirmation and Confirmation

This table identifies some specific confirming and disconfirming messages. As you review this information, try to imagine a specific illustration for each of the ways you might communicate disconfirmation and confirmation (Pearson, 1993; Galvin, Braithwaite, & Bylund, 2015).

Disconfirmation	Confirmation
Ignore the presence or contributions of the other person; express indifference to what the other person says.	**Acknowledge** the presence and the contributions of the other person by interacting with what he or she says.
Make no nonverbal contact; avoid direct eye contact; avoid touching and general nonverbal closeness.	**Make nonverbal contact** by maintaining direct eye contact and, when appropriate, touching, hugging, kissing, and otherwise demonstrating acknowledgment of the other person.
Monologue; engage in communication in which one person speaks and one person listens; there is no real interaction; there is no real concern or respect for each other.	**Dialogue**; engage in communication in which both persons are speakers and listeners; both are involved; both are concerned with and have respect for each other.
Jump to interpretation or evaluation rather than working at understanding what the other person means.	**Demonstrate understanding** of what the other person says and means and reflect your understanding in what you say, or when in doubt ask questions.
Discourage, interrupt, or otherwise make it difficult for the other person to express himself or herself.	**Encourage** the other person to express his or her thoughts and feelings by showing interest and asking questions.
Avoid responding, or respond tangentially by acknowledging the other person's comment but shifting the focus of the message in another direction.	**Respond directly** and exclusively to what the other person says.

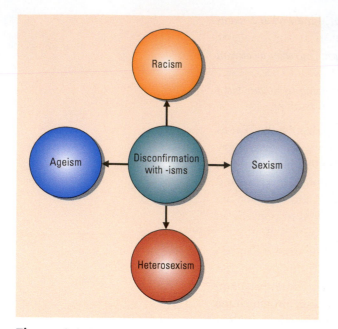

Figure 4.1 Disconfirmation with -isms

Racist Speech

Racist speech is speech that puts down, minimizes, and marginalizes a person or group because of their race. Not only does racist speech express racist attitudes, it also contributes to the development of racist attitudes in those who use or hear the language. Even when racism is subtle, unintentional, or even unconscious, its effects are systematically damaging (Dovidio et al., 2002).

Racism exists on both individual and institutional levels (Koppelman, 2005). *Individual racism* takes the form of negative attitudes and beliefs held about specific races. Assumptions that certain races are intellectually inferior to others or incapable of particular types of achievements are clear examples of individual racism. Prejudices against American Indians, African Americans, Hispanics, and Arabs, in particular, have been with us throughout U.S. history and are still a part of many people's lives today. Such racism can be seen, for example, in the negative terminology that some people use to refer to members of other races and to disparage their customs and accomplishments.

Institutional racism takes forms such as communities' *de facto* school segregation, companies' reluctance to hire members of minority groups, and banks' unwillingness to extend loans to members of some ethnic groups or readiness to charge these groups higher interest rates. Here are some "obvious" suggestions for avoiding racist speech:

- Avoid using derogatory terms for members of a particular race.
- Avoid basing your interactions with members of other races on stereotypes perpetuated by the media.
- Avoid mentioning race when it's irrelevant, as in references to "the African American surgeon" or "the Asian athlete."
- Avoid attributing individuals' economic or social problems to the race of the individuals rather than to their actual sources: for example, institutionalized racism or general economic problems that affect everyone.

Heterosexist Speech

Heterosexist speech also exists on both individual and institutional levels. *Individual heterosexism* refers to attitudes, behaviors, and language that disparage gay men and lesbians and includes the belief that all sexual behavior that is not heterosexual is unnatural and deserving of criticism and condemnation. Such beliefs are at the heart of antigay violence and "gay bashing." Individual heterosexism also includes the idea that homosexuals are more likely than heterosexuals to commit crimes (actually, they are neither more nor less likely) or to molest children (actually, child molesters are overwhelmingly heterosexual married men) (Abel & Harlow, 2001; Koppelman, 2005). It also includes the belief that homosexuals cannot maintain stable relationships or effectively raise children, a belief that contradicts research evidence (Fitzpatrick et al., 1994; Johnson & O'Connor, 2002).

Institutional heterosexism is easy to identify. The ban on gay marriage in many states and the fact that at this time only a handful of states allow gay marriage is a good example of institutional heterosexism. In some cultures homosexual relations are illegal (for example, in Pakistan, Yemen, and Iran, with sentences that can range from years in prison to death).

And, interestingly enough, in some cultures homosexual relationships are illegal for men but legal for women (for example, in Palau, Cook Islands, Tonga, and Guyana).

Heterosexist speech includes derogatory terms used for lesbians and gay men. For example, surveys in the military showed that 80 percent of those surveyed had heard "offensive speech, derogatory names, jokes or remarks about gays" and that 85 percent believed that such derogatory speech was "tolerated" (*New York Times*, March 25, 2000, p. A12). You also see heterosexism in more subtle forms of language usage; for example, someone who qualifies a person's profession with "gay" or "lesbian"—as in "gay athlete" or "lesbian doctor"—says in effect that athletes and doctors are not normally gay or lesbian.

Still another instance of heterosexism is the presumption of heterosexuality. Usually, people assume the person they're talking to or about is heterosexual. And usually they're correct, because most people are heterosexual. At the same time, however, this presumption denies the legitimacy of a lesbian or gay identity. This practice is very similar to the social presumptions of whiteness and maleness that we have taken significant steps toward eliminating. Here are a few additional suggestions for avoiding heterosexist (or what some call *homophobic*) speech:

- Avoid offensive nonverbal mannerisms that parody stereotypes when talking about gay men and lesbians. Avoid the "startle eyeblink" with which some people react to gay couples (Mahaffey, Bryan, & Hutchison, 2005).

- Avoid "complimenting" gay men and lesbians by saying that they "don't look it." This is not a compliment.

- Avoid making the assumption that every gay or lesbian knows what every other gay or lesbian is thinking. As one comic put it, it is very similar to asking an African American, "What do you think Jesse Jackson meant by that last speech?"

- Avoid denying individual differences. Comments such as "Lesbians are so loyal" or "Gay men are so open with their feelings" ignore the reality of wide differences within any group and are potentially insulting to all groups.

- Avoid overattribution—the tendency to attribute almost everything a person does, says, and believes to the fact that the person is gay or lesbian. This tendency helps to activate and perpetuate stereotypes.

- Remember that relationship milestones are important to all people. Ignoring anniversaries or, say, the birthday of a relative's partner is bound to cause resentment.

Ageist Speech

Although used mainly to refer to prejudice against older people, the term **ageism** can refer to prejudice against people of other age groups also. For example, if you describe all teenagers as selfish and undependable, you're discriminating against a group purely because of their age and thus are ageist in your statements. In some cultures—some Asian and African cultures, for example—the old are revered and respected. Younger people seek out elders for advice on economic, ethical, and relationship issues.

Individual ageism can be seen, for example, in the general disrespect many people exhibit toward older people and in negative age-based stereotypes. *Institutional ageism* can be seen in mandatory retirement laws and age restrictions in certain occupations (rather than restrictions based on demonstrated competence). In less obvious forms ageism emerges in the media's portrayal of old people as incompetent, complaining, and, as evidenced perhaps most clearly in both television and films, lacking romantic feelings. Rarely, for example, do television shows or films show older people working productively, being cooperative and pleasant, and engaging in romantic and sexual relationships.

Popular language is replete with examples of linguistic ageism; expressions such as "little old lady," "old hag," "old-timer,"

Peter Steiner/the New Yorker Collection/The Cartoon Bank

"over the hill," "old coot," and "old fogy" are some examples. As with sexism, qualifying a description of someone in terms of his or her age demonstrates ageism. For
example, if you refer to "a quick-witted 75-year-old" or "an agile 65-year-old" or "a responsible teenager," you're implying that these qualities are unusual in people of these
ages and thus need special mention. One of the problems with this kind of stereotyping
is that it's simply wrong. There are, for example, many 75-year-olds who are extremely
quick-witted (and, for that matter, many 30-year-olds who aren't).

One useful way to avoid ageism is to recognize and avoid the illogical stereotypes
that ageist language is based on:

- Avoid talking down to a person because he or she is older. Most older people
  remain mentally alert.
- Don't assume that older people don't know pop culture or technology.
- Refrain from refreshing an older person's memory each time you see the person.
  Assume that older people remember things.
- Avoid implying that relationships are no longer important. Older people continue
  to be interested in relationships.
- Speak at a normal volume and maintain a normal physical distance. Being older
  does not necessarily mean being hard of hearing or being unable to see.
- Engage older people in conversation as you would wish to be engaged. Older
  people are interested in the world around them.

Sexist Speech

Sexist speech also exists on both an individual and an institutional level. *Individual
sexism* involves prejudicial attitudes about men or women based on rigid beliefs
about gender roles. These beliefs may include, for example, the notion that all women
should be caretakers, should be sensitive at all times, and should acquiesce to men's
decisions concerning political or financial matters. Other sexist beliefs imply that all
men are insensitive, interested only in sex, and incapable of communicating feelings.

Institutional sexism involved customs and practices that discriminate against
people because of their gender. Clear examples come from the world of business: the
widespread practice of paying women less than men for the same job and the frequent
discrimination against women in the upper levels of management. Another clear
example of institutionalized sexism is the divorce courts' practice of automatically, or
almost automatically, granting child custody to the mother rather than the father.

Of particular interest here is **sexist language**—language that disparages someone
because of his or her gender (but usually language derogatory toward women). The
National Council of Teachers of English (NCTE) has proposed guidelines for nonsexist
(gender-free, gender-neutral, or sex-fair) language. These guidelines concern the use of the
generic word *man*, the use of generic *he* and *his*, and sex role stereotyping (Penfield, 1987).

- **Avoid using *man* generically.** Using the term to refer to both men and women
  emphasizes maleness at the expense of femaleness. Gender-neutral terms can easily be substituted. Instead of "mankind," say "humanity," "people," or "human
  beings." Similarly, terms such as *policeman* or *fireman* and other terms that pre-
  sume maleness as the norm—and femaleness as a deviation from this norm—are
  clear and common examples of sexist language.
- **Avoid using *he* and *his* as generic.** Instead, you can alternate pronouns or restructure your sentences to eliminate any reference to gender. For example, the NCTE
  guidelines (Penfield, 1987) suggest that instead of saying, "The average student is
  worried about his grades," you say, "The average student is worried about grades."
- **Avoid sex role stereotyping.** When you make the hypothetical elementary school
  teacher female and the college professor male or refer to doctors as male and
  nurses as female, you're sex role stereotyping, as you are when you mention the
  sex of a professional in terms such as "female doctor" or "male nurse."

Cultural Identifiers

One way to develop nonracist, nonheterosexist, nonageist, and nonsexist speech is to examine the preferred cultural identifiers to use in talking to and about members of different groups. Keep in mind, however, that preferred terms frequently change over time, so keep in touch with the most current preferences (Schwartz & Task Force, 1995; Faigley, 2009).

One general guideline is to *include* rather than *exclude*; excluding is a form of talk in which you use the terms of your own cultural group as universal, as applying to everyone. For example, *church* refers to the place of worship for some religions, not all religions. Similarly, *Bible* refers to the Christian religious scriptures and is not a general term for religious scriptures. Nor does the *Judeo-Christian tradition* include the religious traditions of everyone. Similarly, the terms *marriage, husband,* and *wife* refer to some heterosexual relationships and exclude others; in most of the world they also exclude gay and lesbian relationships.

Consider the vast array of alternative terms that are inclusive rather than exclusive. For example, the Association of American University Presses (Schwartz & Task Force, 1995) recommends using *place of worship* instead of *church* when you wish to include the religious houses of worship of all people. Similarly, *committed relationship* is more inclusive than *marriage, couples therapy* is more inclusive than *marriage counseling,* and *life partner* is more inclusive than *husband* or *wife. Religious scriptures* is more inclusive than *Bible.* Of course, if you're referring to, say, a specific Baptist church or married heterosexual couples, then the terms *church* and *marriage* are perfectly appropriate.

RACE AND NATIONALITY Some research finds that the term *African American* is preferred over *black* in referring to Americans of African descent (Hecht, Jackson, & Ribeau, 2003). Other research, however, concludes that "a majority of blacks in America today do not have a preference (Newport, 2007). *Black* is often used with *white*, as well as in a variety of other contexts (for example, Department of Black and Puerto Rican Studies, the *Journal of Black Studies,* and Black History Month)." The American Psychological Association recommends that both terms—*White* and *Black*—be capitalized, but *The Chicago Manual of Style* recommends using lowercase. The terms *Negro* and *colored,* although used in the names of some organizations (e.g., the United Negro College Fund and the National Association for the Advancement of Colored People), are not used outside these contexts.

White is generally used to refer to those whose roots are in European cultures and usually does not include Hispanics. Analogous to *African American* (which itself is based on a long tradition of terms such as *Irish American* and *Italian American*) is the phrase *European American.* Few European Americans, however, call themselves that; most prefer to emphasize their national origins, as in, for example, *German American* or *Greek American. People of color*—a more literary-sounding term appropriate perhaps to public speaking but may sound awkward in many conversations—is preferred to *non-white,* which implies that whiteness is the norm and non-whiteness is a deviation from that norm. The same is true of the term *non-Christian*: It implies that people who have other beliefs deviate from the norm.

Generally, *Hispanic* refers to anyone who identifies himself or herself as belonging to a Spanish-speaking culture. *Latina* (female) and *Latino* (male) refer to persons whose roots are in one of the Latin American countries, such as Cuba or Guatemala. *Hispanic American* refers to U.S. residents whose ancestry is in a Spanish culture; the term includes Mexican, Caribbean, and Central and South Americans. In emphasizing Spanish heritage, however, the term is really inaccurate; it leaves out the large numbers of people in the Caribbean and in South America whose origins are African, Native American, French, or Portuguese.

VIEWPOINTS: **-Isms on Campus**
How would you rate the state of racism, heterosexism, ageism, and sexism in today's society? Use a 10-point scale with 1 being "totally absent" to 10 "extremely prevalent."

Chicana (female) and *Chicano* (male) refer to persons with roots in Mexico, although it often connotes a nationalist attitude (Jandt, 2016). *Mexican American* is generally preferred.

Inuk (plural, *Inuit*), also spelled with two *n*'s (*Innuk* and *Innuit*), is preferred to *Eskimo* (a term the U.S. Census Bureau uses), a term applied to the indigenous peoples of Alaska and Canada by Europeans and that literally means "raw meat eaters."

The word *Indian* technically refers only to someone from India, not to members of other Asian countries or to the indigenous peoples of North America. *American Indian* or *Native American* is preferred, even though many Native Americans do refer to themselves as Indians and Indian people. The word *squaw*, used to refer to a Native American woman and still used in some U.S. place names and textbooks, is clearly a term to be avoided; its usage is almost always negative and insulting.

In Canada indigenous people are called *first people* or *first nations*. The term *native American* (with a lowercase *n*) is most often used to refer to persons born in the United States. Although technically the term could refer to anyone born in North or South America, people outside the United States generally prefer more specific designations such as *Argentinean, Cuban,* or *Canadian.* The term *native* describes an indigenous inhabitant; it is not used to indicate "someone having a less developed culture."

Muslim (rather than the older *Moslem*) is the preferred form to refer to a person who adheres to the religious teachings of Islam. *Quran* (rather than *Koran*) is the preferred term for the scriptures of Islam. *Jewish people* is often preferred to *Jews*, and *Jewess* (a Jewish female) is considered derogatory.

When English-language history books were being written exclusively from a European perspective, Europe was taken as the focal point and the rest of the world was defined in terms of its location relative to that continent. Thus, Asia became "the East" or "the Orient," and Asians became "Orientals"—a term that is today considered inappropriate or "Eurocentric." It is preferable simply to refer to people from Asia as *Asians*, just as people from Africa are *Africans* and people from Europe are *Europeans*.

AFFECTIONAL ORIENTATION   Generally, *gay* is the preferred term to refer to a man who has an affectional preference for other men, and *lesbian* is the preferred term for a woman who has an affectional preference for other women. (*Lesbian* means "homosexual woman," so the term *lesbian woman* is redundant.) *Homosexual* refers to both gays and lesbians, but more often to a sexual orientation to members of one's own sex. *Gay* and *lesbian* refer to a gay and lesbian identification and not only to sexual behavior. *Gay* as a noun, although widely used, may prove offensive in some contexts, as in "We have gays in our office." Because most scientific thinking holds that sexuality is largely biologically determined, the terms *sexual orientation* and *affectional orientation* are preferred to *sexual preference* or *sexual status* (which also is vague). In the case of same-sex marriages—there are two husbands or two wives. In a male-male marriage, each person is referred to as *husband* and in the case of female-female marriage, each person is referred to as *wife*. Some same-sex couples—especially those who are not married—prefer the term "partner" or "lover."

AGE   *Older person* is generally preferred to *elder, elderly, senior,* or *senior citizen* (which technically refers to someone older than 65). Terms designating age are rarely necessary. There are times, of course, when you need to refer to a person's age group, but most of the time you don't—in much the same way that gender, race, and affectional orientation terms are usually irrelevant.

SEX Generally, the term *girl* should be used only to refer to very young females and is equivalent to boy. Neither term should be used for people older than 13 or 14. *Girl* is never used to refer to a grown woman, nor is *boy* used to refer to people in blue-collar positions, as it once was. *Lady* is negatively evaluated by many because it connotes the stereotype of the prim and proper woman. *Woman* or *young woman* is preferred.

The term *ma'am*, originally an honorific used to show respect, is probably best avoided since today it's often used as a verbal tag to comment (indirectly) on the woman's age or marital status (Angier, 2010).

Transgendered people (people who identify themselves as members of the sex opposite to the one they were assigned at birth and who may be gay or straight, male or female) are addressed according to their self-identified sex. Thus, if the person identifies herself as a woman, then the feminine name and pronouns are used—regardless of the person's biological sex. If the person identifies himself as a man, then the masculine name and pronouns are used.

Transvestites (people who prefer at times to dress in the clothing of the sex other than the one they were assigned at birth and who may be gay or straight, male or female) are addressed on the basis of their clothing. If the person is dressed as a woman—regardless of the birth-assigned sex—she is referred to and addressed with feminine pronouns and feminine name. If the person is dressed as a man—regardless of the birth-assigned sex—he is referred to and addressed with masculine pronouns and masculine name.

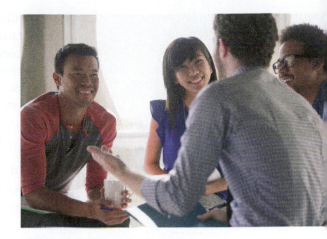

VIEWPOINTS: Negative terms

Many people feel that it's permissible for members of a particular culture to refer to themselves in terms that if said by outsiders would be considered racist, sexist, or heterosexist. Some researchers suggest a possible problem with this—the idea that these terms may actually reinforce negative stereotypes that the larger society has already assigned to the group (Guerin, 2003). Others would argue that, by using such labels, groups weaken the terms' negative impact. *Do you refer to yourself using terms that would be considered offensive or politically incorrect if said by "outsiders"? What effects, if any, do you think such self-talk has?*

Principles for Using Verbal Messages Effectively

4.3 Explain the ways in which language can distort thinking and identify the suggestions for communicating more logically.

The principles governing the verbal messages system suggest a variety of practices for using language more effectively. Here are six additional guidelines for making your verbal messages more effective and a more accurate reflection of the world in which we live: (1) extensionalize—avoid intensional orientation, (2) see the individual—avoid allness, (3) distinguish between facts and inferences—avoid fact–inference confusion, (4) discriminate among—avoid indiscrimination, (5) talk about the middle—avoid polarization, and (6) update messages—avoid static evaluation.

Extensionalize: Avoid Intensional Orientation

Intensional orientation refers to the tendency to view people, objects, and events in terms of how they're talked about or labeled rather than in terms of how they actually exist. **Extensional orientation** is the opposite: the tendency to look first at the actual people, objects, and events and then at the labels—to be guided by what you see happening rather than by the way something or someone is talked about.

Intensional orientation occurs when you act as if the words and labels were more important than the things they represent—as if the map were more important than the territory. In its extreme form, intensional orientation is seen in the person who is afraid of dogs and who begins to sweat when shown a picture of a dog or when hearing people talk about dogs. Here the person is responding to a label as if it were the actual thing. In its more common form, intensional orientation occurs when you see people through your schemata instead of on the basis of their specific behaviors. For example, it occurs when you think of a professor as an unworldly egghead before getting to know the specific professor.

The corrective to intensional orientation is to focus first on the specific object, person, or event and then on the way in which the object, person, or event is talked about. Labels are certainly helpful guides, but don't allow them to obscure what they're meant to symbolize.

See the Individual: Avoid Allness

The world is infinitely complex, and because of this you can never say all there is to say about anything—at least not logically. This is particularly true when you are dealing with people. You may think you know all there is to know about certain individuals or about why they do what they do, but you don't know everything.

You may, for example, go on a first date with someone who, at least during the first hour or so, turns out to be less interesting than you would have liked. Because of this initial impression, you may infer that this person is generally dull. Yet, it could be that this person is simply ill-at-ease or shy during first meetings. The problem is that you run the risk of judging a person on the basis of a very short acquaintanceship. Further, if you then define this person as dull, you're likely to treat the person as dull and create a self-fulfilling prophecy.

A useful extensional device that can help you avoid allness is to end each statement, sometimes verbally but always mentally, with an *et cetera* (etc.)—a reminder that there is more to learn, know, and say; that every statement is inevitably incomplete. To be sure, some people overuse "et cetera." They use it as a substitute for being specific, which defeats its purpose. Instead, it should be used to mentally remind yourself that there is more to know and more to say.

Distinguish Between Facts and Inferences: Avoid Fact–Inference Confusion

Language enables you to form statements of facts and inferences without making any linguistic distinction between the two. Similarly, when you listen to such statements, you often don't make a clear distinction between statements of facts and statements of inference. Yet there are great differences between the two. Barriers to clear thinking can result when inferences are treated as facts, a tendency called **fact–inference confusion**.

For example, you can make statements about things that you observe, and you can make statements about things that you have not observed. In form or structure these statements are similar; they cannot be distinguished from each other by any grammatical analysis. You can say, "She is wearing a blue jacket" as well as "She is harboring an illogical hatred." If you were to diagram these sentences, they would yield identical structures, and yet you know that they're different types of statements. In the first sentence, you can observe the jacket and the blue color; the sentence constitutes a factual statement. But how do you observe "illogical hatred"? This is an inferential rather than a descriptive statement, made not on the basis solely of what you observe but on the basis this plus your own conclusions.

Making inferential statements is necessary if you're to talk about much that is meaningful. However, a problem arises when you act as though those inferential statements are factual statements. You may wish to test your ability to distinguish facts from inferences by taking the accompanying self-test "Can You Distinguish Facts from Inferences?"

Distinguishing between facts and inferences does not imply that one type is better than the other. Both types of statements are useful and important. The

Test Yourself

CAN YOU DISTINGUISH FACTS FROM INFERENCES?

Carefully read the following report and the observations based on it, modeled on a test developed by William Haney (1973). Write T if the observation is definitely true, F if the observation is definitely false, and **?** if the observation may be either true or false. Judge each observation in order. Do not reread the observations after you have indicated your judgment, and do not change any of your answers.

A well-liked college teacher had just completed making up the final examinations and had turned off the lights in the office. Just then a tall, broad figure with dark glasses appeared and demanded the examination. The professor opened the drawer. Everything in the drawer was picked up and the individual ran down the corridor. The dean was notified immediately.

_____ 1. The thief was tall, broad, and wore dark glasses.

_____ 2. The professor turned off the lights.

_____ 3. A tall figure demanded the examination.

_____ 4. The examination was picked up by someone.

_____ 5. The examination was picked up by the professor.

_____ 6. A tall, broad figure appeared after the professor turned off the lights in the office.

_____ 7. The man who opened the drawer was the professor.

_____ 8. The professor ran down the corridor.

_____ 9. The drawer was never actually opened.

_____ 10. Three persons are referred to in this report.

For each statement, ask yourself, "How can I be absolutely certain that the statement is true or false?" You should find that only one statement can be clearly identified as true and only one as false; eight should be marked "?". This brief experience was designed to trap you into making inferences and thinking of them as facts. Statement 3 is true (it's in the report) and statement 9 is false (the drawer was opened). But, all other statements are inferences and should have been marked "?". Review the remaining eight statements to see why you cannot be certain that any of them are either true or false.

problem arises when you treat an inferential statement as if it were fact. Phrase your inferential statements as tentative. Recognize that such statements may be wrong. Leave open the possibility of other alternatives.

Discriminate Among: Avoid Indiscrimination

Everything is unique. Language, however, provides common nouns, such as teacher, student, friend, enemy, war, politician, liberal, and the like, that may lead you to focus on similarities within the group rather than individuals' differences.

Indiscrimination, a form of stereotyping, can be seen in such statements as these:

- He's just like the rest of them: lazy, stupid, a real slob.
- I really don't want another ethnic on the board of directors. One is enough for me.
- Read a romance novel? I read one when I was 16. That was enough to convince me.

A useful antidote to indiscrimination is the extensional device called the **index**, a spoken or mental subscript that identifies each individual in a group as an individual even though all members of the group may be covered by the same label. For example, when you think and talk of an individual politician as only a "politician," you may fail to see the uniqueness in this politician and the differences between this particular politician and other politicians. However, when you think with the index—when you think not of politician but of politician1 or politician2 or politician3—you're less likely to fall into the trap of indiscrimination and more likely to focus on the differences among politicians. The same is true with members of cultural, national, or religious groups; when you think and even talk of Iraqi1 and Iraqi2, you'll be reminded that not all Iraqis are the same. The more you discriminate among individuals covered by the same label, the less likely you are to discriminate against any group.

Talk About the Middle: Avoid Polarization

Polarization, often referred to as the fallacy of "either/or," is the tendency to look at the world and to describe it in terms of extremes—good or bad, positive or negative, healthy or sick, brilliant or stupid, rich or poor, and so on. Polarized statements come in many forms. Here are some examples:

- After listening to the evidence, I'm still not clear who the good guys are and who the bad guys are.
- Well, are you for us or against us?
- College had better get me a good job. Otherwise, this has been a big waste of time.

Most people and situations exist somewhere between the extremes of good and bad, healthy and sick, brilliant and stupid, rich and poor. Yet there seems to be a strong tendency to view only the extremes and to categorize people, objects, and events in terms of these polar opposites (Gamson, 1998).

You can easily demonstrate this tendency by filling in the opposites for each of the following words:

		Opposite
tall	__:___:___:___:___:___:___:	_____
heavy	__:___:___:___:___:___:___:	_____
strong	__:___:___:___:___:___:___:	_____
happy	__:___:___:___:___:___:___:	_____
legal	__:___:___:___:___:___:___:	_____

Filling in the opposites should have been relatively easy and quick. The words should also have been fairly short. Even if various people were to supply their own opposites, there would be a high degree of agreement among them.

Now try to fill in the middle positions with words meaning, for example, "midway between tall and short," "midway between heavy and light," and so on. Do this before continuing to read.

These midway responses (compared to the opposites) were probably more difficult to think of and took you more time. The responses should also have been long words or phrases of several words. In addition, different people would probably agree less on these midway responses than on the opposites.

This exercise illustrates the ease with which you can think and talk in opposites and the difficulty you have in thinking and talking about the middle. But recognize that the vast majority of cases exist between extremes. Don't allow the ready availability of extreme terms to obscure the reality of what lies in between (Read, 2004).

In some cases, of course, it's legitimate to talk in terms of two values. For example, this thing you're holding either is or is not a book. Clearly, the classes "book" and "not-book" include all possibilities. There is no problem with this kind of statement. Similarly, you may say that a student either will pass this course or will not, as these two categories include all the possibilities.

You create problems when you use this either/or form in situations in which it's inappropriate: for example, "The supervisor is either for us or against us." The two choices simply don't include all possibilities: The supervisor may be for us in some things and against us in others, or he or she may be neutral. Right now there is a tendency to group people into categories of pro- and antiwar; similarly, you see examples of polarization in opinions about the Middle East, with some people entirely and totally supportive of one side and others entirely and totally supportive of the other side. However, polarizing categories are created for almost every important political or social issue: "pro" and "anti" positions on abortion and taxes, for example. These extremes do not include all possibilities and prevent us from entertaining the vast middle ground that exists on all such issues and in most people's minds.

Update Messages: Avoid Static Evaluation

Language changes very slowly, especially when compared to the rapid pace at which people and things change. When you retain a judgment of a person, despite the inevitable changes in the person, you're engaging in **static evaluation**.

Although you would probably agree that everything is in a constant state of flux, the relevant question is whether you *act* as if you know this. Do you treat your little sister as if she were 10 years old, or do you treat her like the 20-year-old woman she has become? Your evaluations of yourself and others need to keep pace with the rapidly changing real world. Otherwise you'll be left with attitudes and beliefs—static evaluations—about a world that no longer exists.

To guard against static evaluation, use a device called the **date**, a mental subscript that enables you to look at your statement in the context of time. Dating your statement is especially important when your statements are evaluative. Remember that Gerry Smith$_{2002}$ is not Gerry Smith$_{2010}$, that academic abilities$_{2006}$ are not academic abilities$_{2010}$.

At the same time, recognize that each of these six guidelines can be used to deceive you. For example, when people treat individuals as they're labeled or influence you to respond to people in terms of their labels (often racist, sexist, or homophobic), they are using intensional orientation unethically. Similarly, when people present themselves as knowing everything about something (gossip is often a good example), they are exploiting the natural tendency for people to think in allness terms to achieve their own ends. When people present inferences as if they are facts (again, gossip provides a good example) to secure your belief or when they stereotype, they are relying on your tendency to confuse facts and inferences and to fail to discriminate. And, when people talk in terms of opposites (polarize) or as if things and people don't change (static evaluation) in order to influence you, they are again assuming you won't talk about the middle ground or ask for updated information.

Table 4.4 presents a brief summary of these important guides to effective messages.

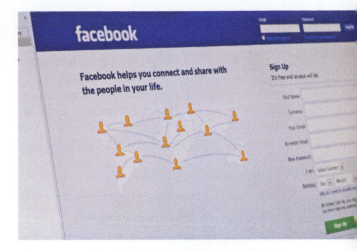

VIEWPOINTS: Social Networks and Language
How would you describe intensional orientation, allness, fact–inference distinction, indiscrimination, polarization, and static evaluation in social networking sites? Can you provide examples of problems created when the guidelines suggested here are violated?

Table 4.4 In a Nutshell: Essential Verbal Message Guidelines

Here is a brief summary of the guidelines for using verbal messages. As you review these principles, try recalling examples and the consequences of the failure to follow these principles from your own recent interactions.

Effective	Ineffective
Extensionalize: distinguish between the way people, objects, and events are talked about and what exists in reality; the word is not the thing.	**Intensionalize:** treat words and things as the same; respond to things as they are talked about rather than as they exist.
Avoid allness: no one can know or say everything about anything; always assume there is more to be said, more to learn.	**Commit allness:** assume you know everything that needs to be known or that all that can be said has been said.
Distinguish between facts and inferences and respond to them differently.	**Confuse facts and inferences:** respond to inferences as if they were facts.
Discriminate among items covered by the same label.	**Indiscriminately treat** all items (people, objects, and events) covered by the same label similarly.
Talk about the middle, where the vast majority of cases exist.	**Polarize:** view and talk about only the extremes; ignore the middle.
Recognize change: regularly update your messages, meanings, evaluations, and beliefs.	**Statically evaluate:** fail to recognize the inevitable change in things and people.

Summary of Concepts and Skills

Focusing on verbal messages, this chapter first looked at the nature of language and identified several major ways in which language works. The next section examined disconfirmation and confirmation and the related topics of racist, heterosexist, ageist, and sexist speech. The final section presented ways to make verbal communication more accurate and effective.

Principles of Verbal Messages

4.1   Paraphrase the principles of verbal messages.

1. Message meanings are in people.

2. Messages are denotative (i.e., objective and generally easily agreed on) and connotative (i.e., subjective and generally highly individual in meaning).

3. Messages vary in abstraction; they can range from extremely general to extremely specific.

4. Messages can deceive.

5. Messages vary in politeness.

6. Messages can be onymous or anonymous.

7. Messages vary in assertiveness.

Disconfirmation and Confirmation

4.2   Define and distinguish between *disconfirmation* and *confirmation* and provide examples of appropriate cultural identifiers.

8. Disconfirmation is the process of ignoring the presence and the communications of others. Confirmation means accepting, supporting, and acknowledging the importance of other people.

9. Racist, heterosexist, ageist, and sexist language disconfirms, puts down, and negatively evaluates various groups.

Principles for Using Verbal Messages Effectively

4.3   Explain the ways in which language can distort thinking and identify the suggestions for communicating more logically.

10. Avoid intensional orientation; remember that language symbolizes reality and is not the reality itself.

11. Avoid allness; you can never know all or say all about anything.

12. Avoid confusing facts with inferences; remember that language doesn't indicate this distinction grammatically.

13. Avoid indiscrimination; everything is unique.

14. Avoid polarization; avoid focusing solely on extremes.

15. Avoid static evaluation; language tends to be static, whereas people and events are forever changing.

The study of verbal messages and of how meaning is communicated from one person to another has important implications for the skills of effective communication. Place a check mark next to those skills that you feel you need to work on most.

_____ 1. Because communication is a package of signals, I ensure my verbal and nonverbal messages reinforce rather than contradict each other.

_____ 2. I try to understand not only objective, denotative meanings but also the speaker's subjective, connotative meanings.

_____ 3. I recognize that snarl and purr words describe the speaker's feelings and not objective reality.

_____ 4. I use terms varying in abstraction to best communicate my meanings.

_____ 5. I vary my directness depending on the situation and my communication goal.

_____ 6. I take special care to make spoken messages clear and unambiguous, especially when using terms for which people will have very different connotative meanings.

_____ 7. I focus attention not only on words but also on the person communicating, recognizing that meanings are largely in the person.

_____ 8. I avoid disconfirmation and instead use messages that confirm the other person.

_____ 9. I avoid racist, heterosexist, ageist, and sexist language and, in general, language that puts down other groups.

_____ 10. I use the cultural identifiers that facilitate communication and avoid those that set up barriers to effective interaction.

_____ 11. I avoid responding intensionally to labels as if they are objects; instead, I respond extensionally and look first at the reality and then at the words.

_____ 12. To avoid allness, I end my statements with an implicit "et cetera" in recognition that there is always more to be known or said.

_____ 13. I distinguish facts from inferences and respond to inferences with tentativeness.

_____ 14. I avoid indiscrimination by viewing the uniqueness in each person and situation.

_____ 15. I avoid polarization by using "middle ground" terms and qualifiers in describing the world, especially people.

_____ 16. I mentally date my statements and thus avoid static evaluation.

Key Terms

abstraction	extensional orientation	purr words
ageism	fact–inference confusion	racist speech
anonymous messages	heterosexist speech	rejection
assertiveness	index	sexist language
confirmation	indiscrimination	snarl words
connotation	intensional orientation	static evaluation
date	netiquette	truth bias
denotation	onymous messages	
disconfirmation	polarization	

Skill Development Experiences

4.1 Using Assertiveness Strategies

Assertiveness is the most direct and honest response in situations such as these. Usually it's also the most effective.

For any one of the following situations, compose (a) an aggressive, (b) a nonassertive, and (c) an assertive response. Then, in one sentence, explain why your message of assertiveness will be more effective than the aggressive or nonassertive message.

1. You've just redecorated your apartment, making it exactly as you want it. A good friend of yours brings you a house gift—the ugliest poster you've ever seen—and insists that you hang it over your fireplace, the focal point of your living room.

2. Your friend borrows $30 and promises to pay you back tomorrow. But tomorrow passes, as do 20 subsequent tomorrows. You know that your friend has not forgotten about the debt, and you also know that your friend has more than enough money to pay you back.

3. Your next-door neighbor repeatedly asks you to take care of her four-year-old while she runs some errand or another. You don't mind helping out in an emergency, but this occurs almost every day.

4.2 Constructing Confirming, Rejecting, and Disconfirming Responses

Although each type of response serves a different purpose, confirming responses seem most likely to promote communication satisfaction.

For each situation below (a) write a confirming, a rejecting, and a disconfirming response, and (b) indicate what effects each type of response is likely to generate.

1. Angel receives this semester's grades in the mail; they're a lot better than previous semesters' grades but are still not great. After opening the letter, Angel says: I really tried hard to get my grades up this semester. Angel's parents respond:

   With confirmation:
   With rejection:
   With disconfirmation:

2. Carrie's boyfriend of seven years left her and married another woman. Carrie confides this to Samantha, who responds:

   With confirmation:
   With rejection:
   With disconfirmation:

3. Pat, who has been out of work for the past several weeks, says: "I feel like such a failure; I just can't seem to find a job. I've been pounding the pavement for the past five weeks and still nothing." Pat's friend responds:

   With confirmation:
   With rejection:
   With disconfirmation:

4. Judy's colleague at work comes to her, overjoyed, and tells her that she has just been promoted to vice president of marketing, skipping three steps in the hierarchy and tripling her salary. Judy responds:

   With confirmation:
   With rejection:
   With disconfirmation:

Chapter 5
Nonverbal Messages

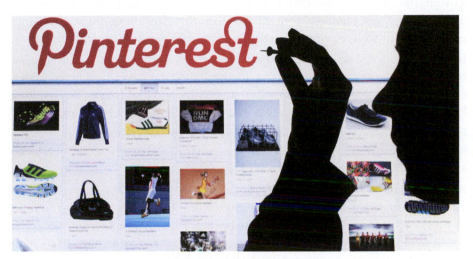

We communicate a large part of who we are without words.

CHAPTER OUTLINE	Learning Objectives
Principles of Nonverbal Communication	**5.1** Explain the principles that identify the ways in which nonverbal communication functions.
The Channels of Nonverbal Communication	**5.2** Describe the channels of nonverbal messages and give examples of messages in each channel.
Nonverbal Communication Competence	**5.3** Paraphrase the guidelines for improving your skills in decoding and encoding nonverbal messages.

Nonverbal communication is communication without words. You communicate nonverbally when you gesture, smile or frown, widen your eyes, move your chair closer to someone else's, wear jewelry, touch someone, raise your vocal volume, or even say nothing. The crucial aspect is that the message you send is in some way received by one or more other people. If you gesture while you are alone in your room and no one is there to see you, then, most theorists would argue, communication has not taken place.

Studying nonverbal communication and developing your nonverbal competence will yield a variety of benefits.

- It improves your accuracy in understanding people, both those from your own as well other cultures. Increased accuracy in understanding others—from understanding the coy smile of romantic interest to the meaning of a supervisor's gestures—will yield obvious benefits in social and workplace situations.

- It increases your effectiveness in a variety of interpersonal situations, including close relationships, workplace relationships, teacher–student relationships, intercultural communication, courtroom communication, politics, and health care (DeVito, 2014; Knapp, 2008; Richmond, McCroskey, & Hickson, 2012; Riggio & Feldman, 2005).

- It increases your own perceived attractiveness; the greater your ability to send and receive nonverbal signals, the higher your popularity and psychosocial well-being are likely to be (Burgoon, Guerrero, & Floyd, 2010).

- It enables you to make a more effective self-presentation. For example, when you meet someone for the first time at least in face-to-face situations—you form impressions of the person largely on the basis of his or her nonverbal messages. Being able to more effectively understand and manage your nonverbal messages will enable you to present yourself in the way you want to be perceived.

Perhaps the best way to begin the study of nonverbal communication is to look at your own beliefs. Which of the following statements do you think are true?

1. Nonverbal communication conveys more meaning than verbal communication.
2. Liars avoid eye contact.
3. Studying nonverbal communication will enable you to detect lying.
4. Unlike verbal communication, nonverbal communication is universal throughout the world.
5. When verbal and nonverbal messages contradict each other, it's wise to believe the nonverbal.

Actually, all of these statements are popular myths about nonverbal communication. Briefly: (1) In some instances, nonverbal messages may communicate more meaning than verbal messages, but, in most cases, it depends on the situation. You won't get very far discussing science and mathematics nonverbally, for example. (2) This is an impossible task; you may get ideas about what someone is thinking, but you really can't be certain on the basis of nonverbal behaviors alone. (3) Lie detection is a far more difficult process than any chapter or even series of courses could accomplish. (4) Although some nonverbal behaviors may be universal in meaning, many signals communicate different meanings in different cultures. (5) People can be deceptive verbally as well as nonverbally; it's best to look at the entire group of signals before making a judgment.

Principles of Nonverbal Communication

5.1   Explain the principles that identify the ways in which nonverbal communication functions.

Let's begin our study of nonverbal communication by examining several principles that, as you'll see, also identify the different functions that nonverbal messages serve

(Burgoon & Hoobler, 2002; Burgoon & Bacue, 2003; Afifi, 2007). These functions make nonverbal messages of crucial importance in all communication interactions (see Figure 5.1).

Nonverbal Messages Interact with Verbal Messages

Verbal and nonverbal messages interact with each other in six major ways: to accent, to complement, to contradict, to control, to repeat, and to substitute for each other.

- **Accent** Nonverbal communication is often used to accent or emphasize some part of the verbal message. You might, for example, raise your voice to underscore a particular word or phrase, bang your fist on the desk to stress your commitment, or look longingly into someone's eyes when saying "I love you."

- **Complement** Nonverbal communication may be used to complement, to add nuances of meaning not communicated by your verbal message. Thus, you might smile when telling a story (to suggest that you find it humorous) or frown and shake your head when recounting someone's deceit (to suggest your disapproval).

- **Contradict** You may deliberately contradict your verbal messages with nonverbal movements; for example, by crossing your fingers or winking to indicate that you're lying.

- **Control** Nonverbal movements may be used to control, or to indicate your desire to control, the flow of verbal messages, as when you purse your lips, lean forward, or make hand movements to indicate that you want to speak. You might also put up your hand or vocalize your pauses (for example, with "um") to indicate that you have not finished and aren't ready to relinquish the floor to the next speaker.

- **Repeat** You can repeat or restate the verbal message nonverbally. You can, for example, follow your verbal "Is that all right?" with raised eyebrows and a questioning look, or you can motion with your head or hand to repeat your verbal "Let's go."

- **Substitute** You may also use nonverbal communication to substitute for verbal messages. You can, for example, signal "OK" with a hand gesture. You can nod your head to indicate yes or shake your head to indicate no.

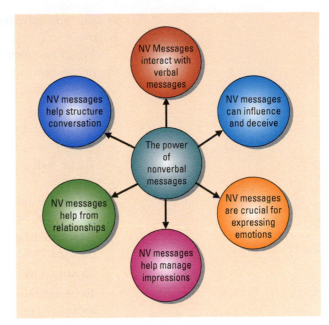

Figure 5.1 The Power of Nonverbal Messages
Nonverbal messages influence just about every aspect of communication you might name.

When you communicate electronically, of course, your message is **transmitted** by means of typed letters without facial expressions or gestures that normally accompany face-to-face communication and without the changes in rate and volume that are a part of normal spoken communication. To compensate for this lack of nonverbal behavior, the **emoticon**, and its more sophisticated counterpart, the emoji, was created. The absence of the nonverbal channel through which you can clarify your message—for example, smiling or winking to communicate sarcasm or humor—make such symbols extremely helpful. And of course you can post photos, book and music album covers, and audio clips, for example, to further communicate your emotional meaning.

Nonverbal Messages Help Manage Impressions

It is largely through the nonverbal communications of others that you form impressions of them. Based on a person's body size, skin color, and dress, as well as on the way the person smiles, maintains eye contact, and expresses himself or herself facially, you form impressions—you judge who the person is and what the person is like.

When you form impressions of others, you use a variety of strategies to manage the impressions they form of you. And, of course, many of these strategies involve nonverbal messages. Here are some examples.

- **To be liked**, you might smile, pat another on the back, and shake hands warmly. See Table 5.1 for some additional ways in which nonverbal communication may make you seem more attractive and more likeable.
- **To be believed**, you might use focused eye contact, a firm stance, and open gestures.
- **To excuse failure**, you might look sad, cover your face with your hands, and shake your head.
- **To secure help by indicating helplessness**, you might use open hand gestures, a puzzled look, and inept movements.
- **To hide faults**, you might wear flattering clothing or makeup.
- **To be followed**, you might dress the part of a leader or display your diploma or awards where others can see them.
- **To confirm self-image and to communicate it to others**, you might dress in certain ways or decorate your apartment with things that reflect your personality.

JOURNAL
COMMUNICATION CHOICE POINT
Communicating Closeness

Consider how you go about increasing the intimacy of a relationship nonverbally in face-to-face communication? *Lacking the face-to-face nonverbal signals, how would you do it on a social network site such as Google+ or Facebook?*

Nonverbal Messages Help Form Relationships

Much of your relationship life is lived nonverbally. You communicate affection, support, and love, in part at least, nonverbally (Floyd & Mikkelson, 2005). At the same time, you also communicate displeasure, anger, and animosity through nonverbal signals.

You also use nonverbal signals to communicate the nature of your relationship to another person, and you and that person communicate nonverbally with each other. These signals that communicate your relationship status are known as **tie signs**: They indicate the ways in which your relationship is

Table 5.1 Ten Nonverbal Messages and Attractiveness

Here are ten nonverbal messages that help communicate your attractiveness and ten that will probably do the opposite (Andersen, 2004; Riggio & Feldman, 2005). As you'll see, these are specific examples of general encoding skills considered later in this chapter.

Do	But Don't
Gesture to show liveliness and animation in ways that are appropriate to the situation and to the message.	Gesture for the sake of gesturing or gesture in ways that may prove offensive to members of other cultures.
Nod and lean forward to signal that you're listening and are interested.	Go on automatic pilot, nodding without any coordination with what is being said or lean so forward that you intrude on the other's space.
Smile and otherwise show your interest, attention, and positiveness facially.	Overdo it; inappropriate smiling is likely to be perceived negatively.
Make eye contact in moderation.	Stare, ogle, glare, or otherwise make the person feel that he or she is under scrutiny.
Touch in moderation when appropriate.	Touch excessively or too intimately. When in doubt, avoid touching.
Use vocal variation in rate, rhythm, pitch, and volume to communicate your enthusiasm and involvement in what you're saying.	Fall into the pattern in which, for example, your voice goes up and down, up and down, up and down without any relationship to what you're saying.
Use silence to listen at least the same amount of time as you speak. Show that you're listening with appropriate facial reactions, posture, and back-channeling cues, for example.	Listen motionlessly or in ways that suggest you're only listening half-heartedly.
Stand reasonably close to show connectedness.	Exceed the other person's comfort zone.
Present a pleasant smell and be careful to camouflage the onions, garlic, or smoke that you may be so used to you don't notice.	Overdo the cologne or perfume.
Dress appropriately to the situation.	Wear clothing that is uncomfortable or that calls attention to itself and hence away from your message.

tied together (Goffman, 1967; Afifi & Johnson, 2005; Knapp, Hall, & Horgan, 2013). Tie signs are also used to confirm the level of the relationship; for example, you might hold hands to see if this is responded to positively. And of course tie signs are often used to let others know that the two of you are tied together.

Tie signs vary in intimacy and may extend from the relatively informal handshake through more intimate forms, such as hand holding and arm linking, to very intimate contact, such as full mouth kissing (Andersen, 2004).

Nonverbal Messages Structure Conversation

When you're in conversation, you give and receive cues—signals that you're ready to speak, to listen, to comment on what the speaker just said. These cues regulate and structure the interaction. These **turn-taking cues** may be verbal (as when you say, "What do you think?" and thereby give the speaking turn over to the listener). Most often, however, they're nonverbal; a nod of the head in the direction of someone else, for example, signals that you're ready to give up your speaking turn and want this other person to say something. You also show that you're listening and that you want the conversation to continue (or that you're not listening and want the conversation to end) largely through nonverbal signals of posture and eye contact (or the lack thereof).

VIEWPOINTS: **The Divorce Ring**
An especially interesting nonverbal message is the Divorce Ring, which some women, wear on their right hand (Fried, 2013). The ring communicates a variety of messages: *I'm divorced. I'm not ashamed of being divorced; there is no stigma. I want others to know I'm divorced. I'm available for a possible relationship. What do you think of this type of nonverbal message? What do you see as its advantages and its disadvantages?*

Nonverbal Messages Can Influence and Deceive

You can influence others not only through what you say but also through your nonverbal signals. A focused glance that says you're committed; gestures that further explain what you're saying; appropriate dress that says, "I'll easily fit in with this organization"—these are just a few examples of ways in which you can exert nonverbal influence.

And with the ability to influence, of course, comes the ability to deceive—to mislead another person into thinking something is true when it's false or that something is false when it's true. One common example of nonverbal deception is using your eyes and facial expressions to communicate a liking for other people when you're really interested only in gaining their support in some endeavor. Not surprisingly, you also use nonverbal signals to detect deception in others. For example, you may well suspect a person of lying if he or she avoids eye contact, fidgets, and conveys inconsistent verbal and nonverbal messages.

But be careful. Research shows that it is much more difficult to tell when someone is lying than you probably think it is. So, use caution in judging deception (Knapp, 2008).

Nonverbal Messages Are Crucial for Expressing Emotions

Although people often explain and reveal emotions verbally, nonverbal signals communicate a great part of their emotional experience. For example, you reveal your level of happiness or sadness or confusion largely through facial expressions. Of course, you also reveal your feelings by posture (for example, whether tense or relaxed), gestures, eye movements, and even the dilation of your pupils. Nonverbal messages often help people communicate unpleasant messages that they might feel uncomfortable putting into words (Infante, Rancer, & Womack, 2003). For example, you might avoid eye contact and maintain large distances between yourself and someone with whom you didn't want to interact or with whom you wanted to decrease the intensity of your relationship.

At the same time, you also use nonverbal messages to hide your emotions. You might, for example, smile even though you feel sad so as not to dampen the party spirit. Or you might laugh at someone's joke even though you think it silly.

The Channels of Nonverbal Communication

5.2 Describe the channels of nonverbal messages and give examples of messages in each channel.

You communicate nonverbally through a wide range of channels: the body, the face, the eyes, space, artifacts, touch, paralanguage and silence, and time.

Body Communication

The body communicates with movements and gestures and just by its general appearance, an area of nonverbal communication referred to as **kinesics**.

BODY GESTURES Nonverbal researchers identify five major types of kinesic movements: emblems, illustrators, affect displays, regulators, and adaptors (Ekman & Friesen, 1969; Knapp, Hall, & Horgan 2013).

Emblems are body gestures that translate directly into words or phrases: for example, the OK sign, the thumbs-up for "good job," and the V for "victory." You use these consciously and purposely to communicate the same meaning as the words. But emblems are culture specific, so be careful when using your culture's emblems in other cultures.

As shown in Figure 5.2, there is much variation in gestures and their meanings among different cultures (Axtell, 1993). Consider a few common gestures that you might use without thinking but that could get you into trouble if you were to use them in another culture:

- Folding your arms over your chest would be considered disrespectful in Fiji.
- Waving your hand would be insulting in Nigeria and Greece.
- Gesturing the "thumbs-up" would be rude in Australia.
- Tapping your two index fingers together would be considered an invitation to sleep together in Egypt.
- Pointing with your index finger would be impolite in many Middle Eastern countries.
- Bowing to a lesser degree than your host would be considered a statement of your superiority in Japan.
- Inserting your thumb between your index and middle finger in a clenched fist would be viewed in certain African countries as a wish that evil befall someone.
- Resting your feet on a table or chair would be insulting in some Middle Eastern cultures.

Illustrators enhance (literally "illustrate") the verbal messages they accompany. For example, when referring to something to the left, you might gesture toward the left. Most often you illustrate with your hands, but you can also illustrate with head and general body movements. You might, for example, turn your head or your entire body toward the left. You might also use illustrators to communicate the shape or size of objects you're talking about. Recent research points to an interesting advantage of illustrators—namely, that they increase your ability to remember. In this research people who illustrated their verbal messages with gestures remembered 20 percent more than those who didn't gesture (Goldin-Meadow et al., 2001).

Affect displays are movements of the face (smiling or frowning, for example) but also of the hands and general body (body tenseness or relaxed posture, for example) that communicate emotional meaning. You use affect displays to accompany and

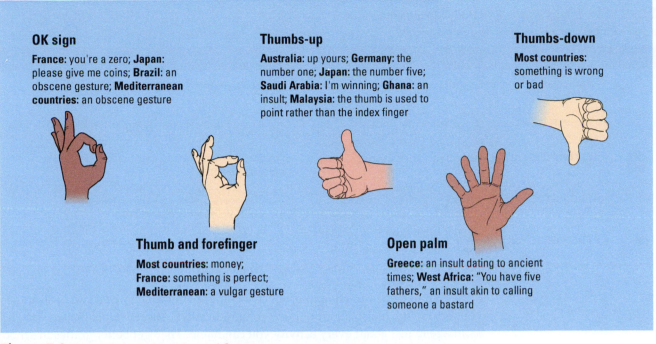

OK sign

France: you're a zero; **Japan:** please give me coins; **Brazil:** an obscene gesture; **Mediterranean countries:** an obscene gesture

Thumbs-up

Australia: up yours; **Germany:** the number one; **Japan:** the number five; **Saudi Arabia:** I'm winning; **Ghana:** an insult; **Malaysia:** the thumb is used to point rather than the index finger

Thumbs-down

Most countries: something is wrong or bad

Thumb and forefinger

Most countries: money; **France:** something is perfect; **Mediterranean:** a vulgar gesture

Open palm

Greece: an insult dating to ancient times; **West Africa:** "You have five fathers," an insult akin to calling someone a bastard

Figure 5.2 Some Cultural Meanings of Gestures

Cultural differences in the meanings of nonverbal gestures are often significant. The over-the-head clasped hands that signify victory to an American may signify friendship to a Russian. To a North American, holding up two fingers to make a V signifies victory or peace. To certain South Americans, however, it is an obscene gesture that corresponds to an extended middle finger in the United States. This figure highlights some additional nonverbal differences. Can you identify others?

reinforce your verbal messages and also as substitutes for words. For example, you might smile while saying how happy you are to see your friend, or you might simply smile. (Affect displays, being primarily centered in the facial area, are covered in more detail in the next section.)

Regulators are behaviors that monitor, control, coordinate, or maintain the speech of another individual. When you nod your head, for example, you tell the speaker to keep on speaking; when you lean forward and open your mouth, you tell the speaker that you would like to say something.

Adaptors are gestures that satisfy some personal need, such as scratching to relieve an itch or moving your hair out of your eyes. **Self-adaptors** are self-touching movements (e.g., rubbing your nose). **Alter-adaptors** are movements directed at the person with whom you're speaking: for example, removing lint from a person's jacket or straightening his or her tie, or folding your arms in front of you to keep others at a comfortable distance. **Object-adaptors** are gestures focused on objects (e.g., doodling on or shredding a Styrofoam coffee cup). Table 5.2 summarizes these five types of body movements.

BODY APPEARANCE   Your general body appearance also communicates. Height, for example, has been shown to be significant in a wide variety of situations. Tall presidential candidates have a much better record of winning elections than do their shorter opponents. Tall people seem to be paid more and are favored by personnel interviewers over shorter job applicants (Keyes, 1980; Knapp, Hall, & Horgan 2013). Taller people also have higher self-esteem and greater career success than do shorter people (Judge & Cable, 2004).

Your body also reveals your race, through skin color and tone, and may even give clues as to your nationality. Your weight in proportion to your height also will communicate messages to others, as will the length, color, and style of your hair.

Table 5.2 In a Nutshell: Five Body Movements

What other examples can you think of for these five movements?

Name and Function	Examples
EMBLEMS directly translate words or phrases; they are especially culture specific.	"OK" sign, "come here" wave, hitchhiker's sign
ILLUSTRATORS accompany and literally "illustrate" verbal messages.	Circular hand movements when talking of a circle; hands far apart when talking of something large
AFFECT DISPLAYS communicate emotional meaning.	Expressions of happiness, surprise, fear, anger, sadness, disgust/contempt
REGULATORS monitor, maintain, or control the speech of another.	Facial expressions and hand gestures indicating "keep going," "slow down," or "what else happened?"
ADAPTORS satisfy some need.	Scratching your head or frequently adjusting your hair or glasses

Your general **attractiveness**, which includes both visual appeal and pleasantness of personality, is also a part of body communication. Attractive people have the advantage in just about every activity you can name. They get better grades in school, are more valued as friends and lovers, and are preferred as coworkers (Burgoon, Guerrero, & Floyd, 2010). Not surprisingly, positive facial expressions contribute to the perception of attractiveness for both men and women (Koscriski, 2007).

Facial Communication

Throughout your communication interactions, your face communicates many things, especially your emotions. In fact, facial movements alone seem to communicate the degree of pleasantness, agreement, and sympathy felt; the rest of the body doesn't provide any additional information in those realms. But for other aspects—for example, the intensity with which an emotion is felt—both facial and bodily cues enter in (Graham, Bitti, & Argyle, 1975; Graham & Argyle, 1975). These cues are so important in communicating your full meaning that graphic representations are now commonly used in electronic communication. On the Internet, emoticon buttons to help you encode your emotions graphically are now common.

Some nonverbal research claims that facial movements may communicate at least the following eight emotions: happiness, surprise, fear, anger, sadness, disgust, contempt, and interest (Ekman, Friesen, & Ellsworth, 1972). Try to communicate surprise using only facial movements. Do this in front of a mirror and try to describe in as much detail as possible the specific movements of the face that make up a look of surprise. If you signal surprise like most people, you probably use raised and curved eyebrows, horizontal forehead wrinkles, wide-open eyes, a dropped-open mouth, and lips parted with no tension.

FACIAL MANAGEMENT As you grew up, you learned your culture's system of nonverbal communication. You also learned certain **facial management techniques** that enable you to express feelings while achieving certain desired effects—for example, to hide certain emotions and to emphasize others. Consider your own use of such facial management techniques. As you do so, think about the types of situations in which you would use facial management techniques for each of the following purposes (Malandro, Barker, & Barker, 1989; Metts & Planalp, 2002).

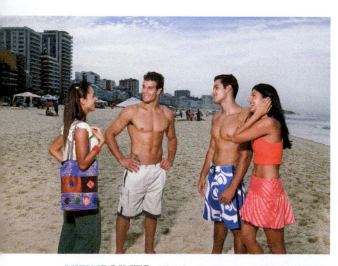

VIEW POINTS: The Importance of Appearance

On a 10-point scale, with 1 indicating "not at all important" and 10 indicating "extremely important," how important is body appearance to your own romantic interest in another person? Do the men and women you know conform to the stereotypes that say males are more concerned with the physical and females more concerned with personality?

- **to intensify**—for example, to exaggerate your astonishment at a surprise party to make your friends feel better.
- **to deintensify**—for example, to cover up your own joy about good news in the presence of a friend who didn't receive any such news.
- **to neutralize**—for example, to cover up your sadness so as not to depress others.
- **to mask**—for example, to express happiness in order to cover up your disappointment at the set of luggage you received, rather than the car you expected.
- **to simulate**—to express an emotion you don't feel.

Facial management techniques help you display emotions in socially acceptable ways. For example, if someone gets bad news in which you secretly take pleasure, the social display rule dictates that you frown and otherwise nonverbally signal sorrow. If you place first in a race and your best friend barely finishes, the display rule requires that you minimize your expression of happiness—and certainly avoid any signs of gloating. If you violate these display rules, you'll appear insensitive. So, although facial management techniques may be deceptive, they're expected and even required by the rules for polite interaction.

FACIAL FEEDBACK The **facial feedback hypothesis** claims that your facial expressions influence physiological arousal (Cappella, 1993). In one study, for example, participants held a pen in their teeth to simulate a sad expression and then rated a series of photographs. Results showed that mimicking sad expressions actually increased the degree of sadness the subjects reported feeling when viewing the photographs (Larsen, Kasimatis, & Frey, 1992). Generally, research finds that facial expressions can produce or heighten feelings of sadness, fear, disgust, and anger. But this effect does not occur with all emotions; smiling, for example, doesn't seem to make us feel happier. Further, it has not been demonstrated that facial expressions can eliminate one feeling and replace it with another. So if you're feeling sad, smiling will not eliminate the sadness and replace it with gladness. A reasonable conclusion seems to be that your facial expressions can influence some feelings, but not all (Burgoon, Guerrero, & Floyd, 2010).

CULTURE AND FACIAL EXPRESSION The wide variations in facial communication that we observe in different cultures seem to reflect which reactions are publicly permissible, rather than a difference in the way emotions are facially expressed. For example, when Japanese and American students watched a film of a surgical operation (Ekman, 2003), they were videotaped both while being interviewed about the film and alone while watching the film. When alone, the students showed very similar reactions. In the interview, however, the American students displayed facial expressions indicating displeasure, whereas the Japanese students did not show any great emotion.

Similarly, cultural differences exist in decoding the meaning of a facial expression. In one study, for example, American and Japanese students judged the meaning of a smiling and a neutral facial expression. The Americans rated the smiling face as more attractive, more intelligent, and more sociable than the neutral face. The Japanese, however, rated the smiling face as more sociable but not as more attractive—and they rated the neutral face as more intelligent (Matsumoto & Kudoh, 1993).

Eye Communication

Research on communication via the eyes (a study known technically as **oculesics**) shows that the duration, direction, and quality of the eye movements communicate different messages. For example, in every culture there are strict, though unstated, rules for the proper duration for eye contact. In our culture,

"Well, how did he react? Was it that scowling-grunt of no way, or that raised-eyebrows-grunt of just maybe?"

Chris Wildt/CartoonStock.com

the average length of gaze is 2.95 seconds. The average length of mutual gaze (two persons gazing at each other) is 1.18 seconds (Argyle & Ingham, 1972; Argyle, 1988). When eye contact falls short of this duration, you may think the person is uninterested, shy, or preoccupied. When the appropriate amount of time is exceeded, you may perceive the person as showing unusually high interest.

The direction of the eye glance also communicates. In much of the United States, you're expected to glance alternately at the other person's face, then away, then again at the face, and so on. The rule for the public speaker is to scan the entire audience, not focusing for too long on or ignoring any one area of the audience. When you break these directional rules, you communicate different meanings—abnormally high or low interest, self-consciousness, nervousness over the interaction, and so on. The quality of eye behavior—how wide or how narrow your eyes get during interaction—also communicates meaning, especially interest level and emotions such as surprise, fear, and disgust.

In thinking about eye communication, realize that not all people are sighted. Some are only partially sighted, some are blind, and some have unimpaired vision. Ninety percent of people who are "legally blind" have some vision. All people, however, have the same need for communication and information. Here are some tips for making communication better between those who have visual impairments and those without such difficulties for both the sighted and the visually impaired.

- Identify yourself. Don't assume that the visually impaired person will recognize your voice. And if you're visually impaired, don't hesitate to ask the person to identify himself or herself.
- Encode into speech all the meanings you wish to communicate. Remember that your gestures, eye movements, and facial expressions cannot be seen by the visually impaired.
- Help the sighted person meet your special communication needs. If you want your surroundings described, ask. If you want the person to read the road signs, ask.
- Be patient with the sighted person. Many people are nervous talking with people who are visually impaired for fear of offending. Put them at ease in a way that also makes you more comfortable.

EYE AVOIDANCE The eyes are "great intruders," observed sociologist Erving Goffman (1967). When you avoid eye contact or avert your glance, you help others to maintain their privacy. You may do this when you see a couple arguing in public: You turn your eyes away (though your eyes may be wide open) as if to say, "I don't mean to intrude; I respect your privacy." Goffman refers to this behavior as **civil inattention**.

Eye avoidance can also signal lack of interest—in a person, a conversation, or some visual stimulus. At times you may hide your eyes to block off unpleasant stimuli (a particularly gory or violent scene in a movie, for example) or close your eyes to block out visual stimuli and thus heighten other senses. For example, you may listen to music with your eyes closed. Lovers often close their eyes while kissing, and many prefer to make love in a dark or dimly lit room.

CULTURE, GENDER, AND EYE MESSAGES Not surprisingly, eye messages vary with both culture and gender. Americans, for example, consider direct eye contact an expression of honesty and forthrightness, but the Japanese often view this as a lack of respect. A Japanese person will glance at the other person's face rarely, and then only for very short periods (Axtell, 1990). Interpreting another's eye contact messages with your own cultural rules is a risky undertaking; eye movements that you may interpret as insulting may have been intended to show respect.

Women make eye contact more and maintain it longer (both in speaking and in listening) than men. This holds true whether women are interacting with other women or with men. This difference in eye behavior may result from women's greater tendency to display their emotions (Wood, 1994). When women interact with other women, they display affiliative and supportive eye contact, whereas when men interact with other men, they avert their gaze (Gamble & Gamble, 2003).

Spatial Communication

Space is an especially important factor in nonverbal communication, although we seldom think about it. Edward T. Hall (1959, 1963, 1966), who pioneered the study of spatial communication, called this study **proxemics**. We can sample this broad area by looking at proxemic distances and territoriality.

PROXEMIC DISTANCES   Hall (1959, 1966) distinguishes four types of proxemic distances that define types of relationships between people: (1) intimate distance, (2) personal distance, (3) social distance, and (4) public distance. Each distance communicates specific kinds of messages.

At an **intimate distance**, ranging from touching to 18 inches apart, the presence of the other individual is unmistakable. Each person experiences the sound, smell, and feel of the other's breath. You use intimate distance for lovemaking and wrestling, for comforting and protecting. This distance is so short that most people do not consider it proper in public.

Personal distance constitutes the protective "bubble" that defines your personal space, which measures from 18 inches to 4 feet. This imaginary bubble keeps you protected and untouched by others. You can still hold or grasp another person at this distance—but only by extending your arms—allowing you to take certain individuals such as loved ones into your protective bubble. At the outer limit of personal distance, you can touch another person only if both of you extend your arms.

At a **social distance**, ranging from 4 to 12 feet, you lose the visual detail you have at personal distance. You conduct impersonal business and interact at a social gathering at this social distance. The more distance you maintain in your interactions, the more formal they appear. Many people in executive and management positions place their desks so that they are assured of at least this distance from employees.

Public distance, measuring from 12 to 25 feet or more, protects you. At this distance you could take defensive action if threatened. On a public bus or train, for example, you might keep at least this distance from a menacing or intoxicated fellow passenger. Although you lose fine details of the face and eyes at this distance, you are still close enough to see what is happening. These four distances are summarized in Table 5.3.

TERRITORIALITY   Another type of communication having to do with space is **territoriality**, a possessive reaction to an area or to particular objects. You interact basically

---

Table 5.3 In a Nutshell: Relationships and Proxemic Distances

Note that the four proxemic distances can be further divided into close and far phases, and that the far phase of one level (say, the personal level) blends into the close phase of the next level (social). Do your relationships also blend into one another, or are your personal relationships totally separate from your social relationships?

Relationship	Distance		Relationship	Distance	
Intimate Relationship	Intimate Distance 0 _____ 18 inches Close phase / Far phase		Social Relationship	Social Distance 4 _____ 12 feet Close phase / Far phase	
Personal Relationship	Personal Distance 1½ _____ 4 feet Close phase / Far phase		Public Relationship	Public Distance 12 _____ 25 feet Close phase / Far phase	

in three types of territories: **primary territories, secondary territories,** and **public territories** (Altman, 1975).

- **Primary territories**: Areas that you might call your own; these areas are your exclusive preserve. Primary territories might include your room, your desk, or your office.
- **Secondary territories**: Areas that don't belong to you but that you have occupied and with which you're associated. They might include your usual table in the cafeteria, your regular seat in the classroom, or your neighborhood turf.
- **Public territories**: Areas that are open to all people; they may be owned by some person or organization, but they are used by everyone. They are places such as movie theaters, restaurants, and shopping malls.

When you operate in your own primary territory, you have an advantage, often called the **home field advantage**. In their own home or office, people take on a kind of leadership role: They initiate conversations, fill in silences, assume relaxed and comfortable postures, and maintain their positions with greater conviction. Because the territorial owner is dominant, you stand a better chance of getting your raise approved, your point accepted, or a contract resolved in your favor if you're in your own territory (e.g., your office or your home) rather than in someone else's (e.g., your supervisor's office) (Marsh, 1988).

Like many animals, humans mark both their primary and secondary territories to signal ownership. Humans use three types of **markers**: central, boundary, and earmarkers (Goffman, 1971). **Central markers** are items you place in a territory to reserve it for you—for example, a drink at the bar, books on your desk, or a sweater over a library chair. Some people, perhaps because they can't own territories, might use markers to indicate a kind of pseudo-ownership or to appropriate someone else's turf or a public territory for their own use (Childress, 2004). Examples include graffiti and the markings of gang boundaries.

Boundary markers serve to divide your territory from that of others. In the supermarket checkout line, the bar placed between your groceries and those of the person behind you is a boundary marker, as are fences, armrests that separate your seat from those on either side, and the contours of the molded plastic seats on a bus.

Earmarkers—a term taken from the practice of branding animals on their ears—are identifying marks that indicate your possession of a territory or object. Trademarks, nameplates, and initials on a shirt or attaché case are all examples of earmarkers.

Markers are also important in giving you a feeling of belonging. For example, one study found that students who marked their college dorm rooms by displaying personal items stayed in school longer than did those who didn't personalize their spaces (Marsh, 1988).

Artifactual Communication

Artifactual messages are messages conveyed through objects or arrangements made by human hands. The colors you prefer, the clothing or jewelry you wear, the way you decorate your space, and even bodily scents communicate a wide variety of meanings.

COLOR COMMUNICATION There is some evidence for what might be called **color communication**, the idea that the colors with which people surround themselves affect them physiologically and influence perceptions of people and things. For example, respiration rates increase in the presence of red light and decrease in the presence of blue light. Similarly, eye blinks increase in frequency when eyes are exposed to red light and decrease when exposed to blue. These findings seem consistent with our

VIEWPOINTS: **Status Signals**

One signal of status is an unwritten "law" granting the right of invasion. Higher-status individuals have more of a right to invade the territory of others than vice versa. The boss, for example, can invade the territory of junior executives by barging into their offices, but the reverse would be unacceptable. *In what ways do you notice this "right" of territorial invasion in your workplace (or your dorm room)?*

intuitive feelings that blue is more soothing and red more provocative. After the administration at one school changed the classroom walls from orange and white to blue, the students' blood pressure levels decreased and their academic performance improved (Ketcham, 1958; Malandro, Barker, & Barker, 1989).

Colors also influence our perceptions and behaviors (Kanner, 1989). People's acceptance of a product, for example, is strongly influenced by its packaging. In one experiment consumers in the United States described the very same coffee taken from a yellow can as weak, from a dark brown can as too strong, from a red can as rich, and from a blue can as mild. Color seems also to influence the expectation of taste sensation (Srivastava & More, 2011). For example, people expect pink pills to be sweeter than red pills, yellow pills to be salty, white and blue pills to be bitter, and orange pills to be sour.

Colors vary greatly in their meanings from one culture to another. To illustrate this cultural variation, here are some of the many meanings that popular colors communicate in a variety of different cultures (Dreyfuss, 1971; Hoft, 1995; Dresser, 1996; Singh & Pereira, 2005). As you read this section, you may want to consider your own meanings for these colors and where your meanings came from.

- **Red** In China, red signifies prosperity and rebirth and is used for festive and joyous occasions; in France and the United Kingdom, it indicates masculinity; in many African countries, blasphemy or death; and in Japan, anger and danger. Red ink, especially among Korean Buddhists, is used only to write a person's name at the time of death or on the anniversary of the person's death; this can create problems when U.S. teachers use red ink to mark homework.
- **Green** In the United States, green signifies capitalism, go ahead, and envy; in Ireland, patriotism; among some Native American cultures, femininity; to the Egyptians, fertility and strength; and to the Japanese, youth and energy.
- **Black** In Thailand, black signifies old age; in parts of Malaysia, courage; and in much of Europe, death.
- **White** In Thailand, white signifies purity; in many Muslim and Hindu cultures, purity and peace; and in Japan and other Asian countries, death and mourning.
- **Blue** In Iran, blue signifies something negative; in Ghana, joy; among the Cherokee, it signifies defeat; for the Egyptians, virtue and truth; and for the Greeks, national pride.
- **Yellow** In China, yellow signifies wealth and authority; in the United States, caution and cowardice; in Egypt, happiness and prosperity; and in many countries throughout the world, femininity.
- **Purple** In Latin America, purple signifies death; in Europe, royalty; in Egypt, virtue and faith; in Japan, grace and nobility; in China, barbarism; and in the United States, nobility and bravery.

CLOTHING AND BODY ADORNMENT   People make inferences about who you are partly on the basis of how you dress. Whether accurate or not, these inferences will affect what people think of you and how they react to you. Your social class, your seriousness, your attitudes, your concern for convention, your sense of style, and perhaps even your creativity will all be judged—in part at least—by the way you dress. In the business world, what you wear may communicate your position within the hierarchy and your willingness and desire to conform to the clothing norms of the organization. It also may communicate your level of professionalism, which seems to be the reason some organizations favor dress codes (Smith, 2003).

Your jewelry also communicates messages about you. Wedding and engagement rings are obvious examples. If you wear a Rolex watch or large precious stones, others are likely to infer that you are rich. Men who wear earrings will be judged differently from men who do not.

The way you wear your hair says something about who you are—from a concern about being up to date to a desire to shock to, perhaps, a lack of interest in

VIEWPOINTS: **Blaming Clothing**
A popular defense tactic in sex crimes against women, gay men, and lesbians is to blame the victim by referring to the way the victim was dressed and implying that the victim, by wearing certain clothing, provoked the attack. *What do you think of this tactic? Is it likely to be effective? Is it ethical?*

appearances. Men with long hair, to take only one example, will generally be judged as less conservative than those with shorter hair. And in a study of male baldness, participants rated a man with a full head of hair as younger and more dominant, masculine, and dynamic than the same man without hair (Butler, Pryor, & Grieder, 1998).

Body piercings and tattoos communicate too. Although people wearing, for example, nose rings or belly button jewelry may wish to communicate positive meanings, those interpreting the messages of body piercings seem to infer that wearers are communicating an unwillingness to conform to social norms and a willingness to take greater risks than those without such piercings (Forbes, 2001). In a study of employers' perceptions, employers rated and ranked job applicants with eyebrow piercings significantly lower than those without such piercings (Acor, 2001).

Nose-pierced job candidates received lower scores on measures of credibility, such as ratings of character and trustworthiness, as well as on sociability and hirability (Seiter & Sandry, 2003).

Tattoos—whether temporary or permanent—likewise communicate a variety of messages, often the name of a loved one or some symbol of allegiance or affiliation. Tattoos also communicate to the wearers themselves. For example, tattooed students see themselves (and perhaps others do as well) as more adventurous, creative, individualistic, and risk prone than those without tattoos (Drews, Allison, & Probst, 2000). Tattoos and piercings on healthcare professionals have been found to communicate such undesirable traits as impulsiveness, unpredictability, and a tendency toward being reckless or violent (Rapsa & Cusack, 1990; Smith, 2003).

SPACE DECORATION   The decoration of your workplace tells a lot about you. The office with the mahogany desk and bookcase and oriental rugs communicates importance and status within an organization, just as a metal desk and bare floor indicate an entry-level employee much farther down in the company hierarchy.

Similarly, people will make inferences about you based on the way you decorate your home. The expensiveness of the furnishings may communicate your status and wealth; their coordination, your sense of style. The magazines on your coffee table may reflect your interests, and the arrangement of chairs around a television set may reveal how important watching television is to you. The contents of bookcases lining the walls reveal the importance of reading in your life. In fact, there is probably little in your home that does not send messages from which others will make inferences about you. At the same time, the lack of certain items will communicate something about you. Consider what messages you would get from a home where no television, phone, or books could be seen.

People also will make judgments about your personality on the basis of room decorations—for example, your openness to new experiences (distinctive decorating usually communicates openness, as would travel souvenirs), conscientiousness, emotional stability, degree of extroversion, and agreeableness.

SMELL COMMUNICATION   Smell, or **olfactory communication**, is extremely important in a wide variety of situations and is now big business. There is some evidence (though it is clearly not very conclusive) that the smell of lemon contributes to a perception of health; the smells of lavender and eucalyptus seem to increase alertness; and the smell of rose oil seems to reduce blood pressure. The smell of chocolate seems to reduce theta brain waves and thus produces a sense of relaxation and a reduced level of attention (Martin, 1998). Findings such as these have contributed to the growth of aromatherapy and to a new profession of aromatherapists. Because humans possess so many scent glands, it has been argued that it only remains for us to discover how we use scent to communicate a wide variety of messages (Furlow, 1996, p. 41). Two particularly important messages that scent communicates are those of attraction and identification.

- **Attraction Messages**   People use perfumes, colognes, aftershave lotions, powders, and the like in an effort to enhance attractiveness. You also use scents to make yourself feel better. When you smell pleasant, you feel better about yourself; when you smell unpleasant, you feel less good about yourself—and probably shower and perhaps put on some cologne.

- **Identification Messages**   Smell is often used to create an image or an identity for a product (Spence, 2008). Advertisers and manufacturers spend millions of dollars each year creating scents for cleaning products and toothpastes, for example, which have nothing to do with products' cleaning power; instead, they function solely to create an image for the products. There is also evidence that we can identify specific significant others by smell. For example, young children were able to identify the T-shirts of their brothers and sisters solely by smell (Porter & Moore, 1981).

Touch Communication

Touch communication, or tactile communication, is perhaps the most primitive form of nonverbal communication (Montagu, 1971). Touch develops before the other senses; a child is stimulated by touch even in the womb. Soon after birth, the child is fondled, caressed, patted, and stroked. In turn, the child explores its world through touch and quickly learns to communicate a variety of meanings through touch.

Touching varies greatly from one culture to another. For example, African Americans touch each other more than European Americans; and touching declines from kindergarten to the sixth grade for European Americans but not for African American children (Burgoon, Guerrero, & Floyd, 2010). Japanese people touch each other much less than Anglo-Saxons, who in turn touch much less than southern Europeans (Morris, 1977; Burgoon, Guerrero, & Floyd, 2010).

Not surprisingly, touch also varies with your relationship stage. In the early stages of acquaintance, you touch little; in intermediate stages of relationship development (i.e., involvement and intimacy), you touch a great deal; and at stable or deteriorating stages of a relationship, you again touch little (Guerrero & Andersen, 1991).

THE MEANINGS OF TOUCH   Researchers in the field of **haptics**, or the study of touch communication, have identified the major meanings of touch (Jones, 2005; Jones & Yarbrough, 1985). Here are five of the most important.

- **Emotions**   Touch often communicates emotions, mainly between intimates or others who have a relatively close relationship. Among the most important of these positive emotions are support, appreciation, inclusion, sexual interest or intent, and affection.

- **Playfulness**   Touch often communicates the desire to play, sometimes affectionately, sometimes aggressively.

- **Control**   Touch may control or direct the behaviors, attitudes, or feelings of the other person. To get attention, for example, you may touch a person as if to say, "Look at me" or "Look over here."

- **Ritual**   Touching may also serve a ritual function, for example, shaking hands to say hello or putting your arm around another's shoulder when saying farewell.

- **Task-related**   Touching often occurs while you're performing some function, such as removing a speck of dust from another person's face or helping someone out of a car.

As you can imagine, touching may also get you into trouble. For example, touching that is too positive (or too intimate) too early in a relationship may send the wrong signals. Similarly playing that is too rough or holding someone's arm to control their movements may be resented. Using ritualistic touching incorrectly or in ways that may be culturally insensitive may likewise get you into difficulty.

TOUCH AVOIDANCE   Much as we have a tendency to touch and be touched, we also have a tendency to avoid touch from certain people or in certain circumstances. Researchers in nonverbal communication have found some interesting relationships between **touch avoidance** and other significant communication variables (Andersen & Leibowitz, 1978).

Touch avoidance is positively related to communication apprehension: Those who fear oral communication also score high on touch avoidance. Touch avoidance is also high in those who self-disclose little. Both touch and self-disclosure are intimate forms of communication; people who are reluctant to get close to another person by self-disclosing also seem reluctant to get close by touching.

Touch avoidance is also affected by age and gender (Guerrero & Andersen, 1994; Crawford, 1994). Older people have higher touch-avoidance scores for opposite-sex persons than do younger people. Males score higher on same-sex touch avoidance than do females, which matches our stereotypes (Martin & Anderson, 1993). That is, men avoid touching other men, but women may and do touch other women. On the other hand, women have higher touch-avoidance scores for opposite-sex touching than do men (Andersen, Andersen, & Lustig, 1987).

TOUCH AND CULTURE   The functions and examples of touching discussed earlier were based on studies in North America; in other cultures these functions are not served in the same way. In some cultures, for example, some task-related touching is viewed negatively and is to be avoided. Among Koreans, it is considered disrespectful for a store owner to touch a customer in, say, handing back change; doing so is considered too intimate a gesture. Members of other cultures who are used to such touching may consider the Koreans' behavior cold and aloof. Muslim children in many countries are socialized to refrain from touching members of the opposite sex, a practice that can easily be interpreted as unfriendly by American children, who are used to touching one another (Dresser, 1996).

Students from the United States reported being touched twice as much as did the Japanese students. In Japan there is a strong taboo against strangers' touching, and the Japanese are therefore especially careful to maintain sufficient distance (Barnlund, 1975).

Some cultures, such as those of southern Europe and the Middle East, are contact cultures. Others, such as those of northern Europe and Japan, are noncontact cultures. Members of contact cultures maintain close distances, touch each other in conversation, face each other more directly, and maintain longer and more focused eye contact. Members of noncontact cultures maintain greater distance in their interactions, touch each other rarely if at all, avoid facing each other directly, and maintain much less direct eye contact. As a result, northern Europeans and Japanese may be perceived as cold, distant, and uninvolved by southern Europeans—who may in turn be perceived as pushy, aggressive, and inappropriately intimate.

Paralanguage and Silence

Paralanguage is the vocal but nonverbal dimension of speech. It has to do with *how* you say something rather than what you say. **Silence**, on the other hand, is the absence of sound but not of communication.

PARALANGUAGE   An old exercise that teachers used to increase students' ability to express different emotions, feelings, and attitudes was to have the students repeat a sentence while accenting or stressing different words each time. Placing the stress on different words easily communicates significant differences in meaning. Consider the following variations of the sentence "Is this the face that launched a thousand ships?"

1. Is *this* the face that launched a thousand ships?

JOURNAL
COMMUNICATION CHOICE POINT
Touch Boundaries

A colleague at work continually touches you in passing—your arm, your shoulder, your waist. These touches are becoming more frequent and more intimate. You want this touching to stop. *What are some of your options for stopping this behavior? To whom would you speak/write? What would you say?*

2. Is this the *face* that launched a thousand ships?

3. Is this the face that *launched* a thousand ships?

4. Is this the face that launched *a thousand ships?*

Each sentence communicates something different—in fact, each asks a different question, even though the words are the same. All that varies among the sentences is which words are stressed, one aspect of paralanguage.

In addition to stress, paralanguage includes such vocal characteristics as rate, volume, and rhythm. It also includes the vocalizations you make when crying, whispering, moaning, belching, yawning, and yelling (Trager, 1958, 1961; Argyle, 1988). A variation in any of these vocal features communicates. When you speak quickly, for example, you communicate something different from when you speak slowly. Even though the words are the same, if the speed (or volume, rhythm, or pitch) differs, the meanings people receive also differ.

Judgments about People Many people make judgments about people's personalities on the basis of their paralinguistic cues. For example, they might conclude that your colleague who speaks softly when presenting ideas at a meeting isn't sure of the ideas' usefulness and believes that no one really wants to listen to them. Or they might assume that people who speak loudly have overinflated egos, or those who speak in a monotone are uninterested in what they are saying and perhaps in life in general. All such judgments are based on little evidence, yet they persist in much popular talk.

Research has found that people can accurately judge the socioeconomic status (whether high, middle, or low) of speakers from 60-second voice samples (Davitz, 1964). Participants also rated people whom they judged to be of high status as more credible than speakers judged to be of middle and low status.

Listeners also can accurately judge the emotional states of speakers from vocal expression alone. In these studies, speakers recite the alphabet or numbers while expressing emotions. Some emotions are easier to identify than others; it is easy to distinguish between hate and sympathy but more difficult to distinguish between fear and anxiety (Scherer, 1986).

Judgments about Communication Effectiveness Speech rate is an important component of paralanguage. In one-way communication (when one person is doing all or most of the speaking and the other person is doing all or most of the listening), those who talk fast (about 50 percent faster than normal) are more persuasive. That is, people agree more with a fast speaker than with a slow speaker and find the fast speaker more intelligent and objective (MacLachlan, 1979).

Although, generally, research finds that a faster-than-normal speech rate lowers listener comprehension, a rapid rate may still have the advantage in communicating information (MacLachlan, 1979; Jones, Berry, & Stevens, 2007). For example, when speaking rate increases by 50 percent, comprehension level drops by only 5 percent. When the rate doubles, the comprehension level drops only 10 percent. If, however, the speeds are more than twice that of normal speech, comprehension level falls dramatically.

Exercise caution in applying this research to all forms of communication (MacLachlan, 1979). While the speaker is speaking, the listener is generating, or framing, a reply. If the speaker talks too rapidly, the listener may not have enough time to compose a reply and may become resentful. Furthermore, the increased rate may seem so unnatural that the listener may focus on the speed rather than on the message being communicated.

Paralanguage and Culture Cultural differences need to be taken into consideration also in evaluating the results of studies on speech rate. In one study, for example, Korean male speakers who spoke rapidly were given unfavorable credibility ratings,

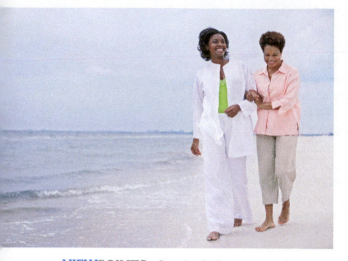

VIEWPOINTS: **Gender Differences and Nonverbal Communication**

Here is a brief summary of findings from research on gender differences in nonverbal expression (Burgoon, Guerrero, & Floyd, 2010; Guerrero & Hecht, 2006; Pearson, West, & Turner, 1995): (1) Women smile more than men; (2) women stand closer to one another than do men and are generally approached more closely than men; (3) both men and women, when speaking, look at men more than at women; (4) women both touch and are touched more than men; (5) men extend their bodies, taking up greater areas of space, more than women. *What problems might these differences create when men and women communicate with each other?*

in contrast to the positive ratings received by Americans who spoke rapidly (Lee & Boster, 1992). Researchers have suggested that in individualistic societies a rapid-rate speaker is seen as more competent than a slow-rate speaker, but in collectivist cultures a speaker who uses a slower rate is judged more competent.

SILENCE Just as words and gestures communicate meaning, so does silence (see Jaworski, 1993). Here we look at some functions of silence and at a theory of silence that has important implications for society as a whole.

Functions of Silence Silence allows the speaker and the listener *time to think,* time to formulate and organize the meaning of the message. For example, a lawyer may have many sophisticated points to make during closing arguments to the jury. A skilled lawyer will use silence, not only to give herself or himself time to present these issues in an organized way, but also to give the jury time to digest the information presented.

Silence may also signal *the importance or solemnity of the message.* Before and after messages of intense conflict or those confessing undying love, there is often silence. Similarly, there would be silence during a prayer or flag-raising service. Similarly, you might use silence to communicate your interest and respect for what someone is saying.

Some people use silence as a *weapon* to hurt others. We often speak of giving someone "the silent treatment." After a conflict, for example, one or both individuals may remain silent as a kind of punishment. Silence used to hurt others may also take the form of refusal to acknowledge the presence of another person, as in disconfirmation (see Chapter 4); in this case, silence is a dramatic demonstration of the total indifference one person feels toward the other.

People sometimes use silence because of *personal anxiety* or shyness, or in response to threats. You may feel anxious or shy among new people and prefer to remain silent. By remaining silent, you preclude the chance of rejection. Only when you break your silence and attempt to communicate with another person do you risk rejection.

Like the eyes, face, or hands, silence can also *communicate emotional responses* (Ehrenhaus, 1988). Sometimes silence communicates a determination to be uncooperative or defiant: By refusing to engage in verbal communication, you defy the authority or the legitimacy of the other person's position. Silence often communicates annoyance; in this case, it is usually accompanied by a pouting expression, arms crossed in front of the chest, and flared nostrils. Silence also may express affection or love, especially when coupled with longing gazes into another's eyes.

Of course, you also may use silence when you simply have *nothing to say,* when nothing occurs to you or you do not want to say anything.

Not all cultures view silence in the same way (Vainiomaki, 2004). In the United States, for example, silence is often interpreted negatively. At a business meeting or even in informal social groups, the silent member may be seen as not listening or as having nothing interesting to add, not understanding the issues, being insensitive, or being too self-absorbed to focus on the messages of others. Other cultures, however, view silence more positively. In many situations in Japan, for example, silence is a response that is considered more appropriate than speech (Haga, 1988).

The traditional Apache, to take another example, regard silence very differently than do European Americans (Basso, 1972). Among the Apache, mutual friends do not feel the need to introduce strangers who may be working in the same area or on the same project. The strangers may remain silent for several days. This period enables them to observe and evaluate each other. Once this assessment is made, the individuals talk. When courting, especially during the initial stages, the Apache remain silent for hours; if they do talk, they generally talk very little. Only after a couple has been dating for several months will they have lengthy conversations. These periods of silence are often erroneously attributed to shyness or self-consciousness. But the use of silence is explicitly taught to Apache women, who are especially discouraged from engaging in long discussions with their dates. Silence during courtship is a sign of modesty to many Apache.

The Spiral of Silence   The "spiral of silence" theory offers a somewhat different perspective on silence. This theory, originally developed to explain the media's influence on opinion, argues that you're more likely to voice agreement than disagreement (Noelle-Neumann, 1991; Severin & Tankard, 2001; Scheufele & Moy, 2000). The theory claims that when a controversial issue arises, you estimate the opinions of others and figure out which views are popular and which are not. You also estimate the rewards and the punishments you'd probably get from expressing popular or unpopular positions. You then use these estimates to determine which opinions you'll express and which you won't.

Generally, you're more likely to voice your opinions when you agree with the majority than when you disagree. You may do this to avoid being isolated from the majority or for fear of being proved wrong or being disliked. Or you may simply assume that the majority, because they're a majority, must be right.

As people with minority views remain silent, the majority position gets stronger (because those who agree with it are the only ones speaking); so, as the majority position becomes stronger and the minority position becomes weaker, the silence becomes an ever-widening spiral. The Internet (blogs and social network sites, especially) may in some ways act as a counteragent to the spiral of silence, because it provides so many opportunities to express minority viewpoints (anonymously if you wish) and to quickly find like-minded others (McDevitt, Kiousis, & Wahl-Jorgensen, 2003).

Communicating Ethically
COMMUNICATION SILENCE

In the U.S. legal system, although people have the right to remain silent so as not to incriminate themselves, they are obliged to reveal information about, for example, the criminal activities of others that they may have witnessed. However, rightly or wrongly (and this in itself is an ethical issue), psychiatrists, lawyers, and some clergy are often exempt from this general rule. Similarly, a wife can't be forced to testify against her husband, nor a husband against his wife.

Unlike the legal system, however, most day-by-day communication situations lack written rules, so it's not always clear whether or when silence is ethical. For example, most people (though not all) would agree that you have the right to withhold information that has no bearing on the matter at hand. Consider, for example, in what situations would it be ethical to remain silent about your previous relationship history, affectional orientation, or religion, and in what situations silence would be unethical.

ETHICAL CHOICE POINT
With all this discussion of ethics in communication, you now wonder if you should come clean to your steady dating partner of two years about previous relationships and a brief incarceration for robbery. *Would it be ethical to remain silent about these past behaviors?*

Temporal Communication

The study of **temporal communication**, known technically as **chronemics**, concerns the use of time—how you organize it, react to it, and communicate messages through it (Bruneau, 1985, 1990, 2009/2010). Here we'll look at psychological, interpersonal, and cultural time.

PSYCHOLOGICAL TIME   Before reading about **psychological time**, consider your time orientation. For each of the following statements, indicate which is TRUE and which is FALSE in terms of your general attitude and behavior.

_____ 1. I often turn to the past for guidance in the present.

_____ 2. Old people have wisdom that I can learn from.

_____ 3. I enjoy learning about and from the past.

_____ 4. Knowing about the past helps me in the present.

_____ 5. I enjoy life as it comes.

_____ 6. I avoid looking too far ahead.

_____ 7. I frequently put off work to enjoy the moment.

_____ 8. I look for immediate payoffs/rewards.

_____ 9. I work hard today basically because of tomorrow's expected rewards.

_____ 10. I enjoy planning for tomorrow and the future generally.

_____ 11. I'm willing to endure difficulties if there's a payoff/reward at the end.

_____ 12. I prepare "to do" lists fairly regularly.

These statements were designed to raise the issue of time orientation, whether you focus more on the past, the present, or the future. [The idea for this test and the insights on psychological time owe their formulation to Gonzales and Zimbardo (1985).]

- In a *past orientation*, you have special reverence for the past. You relive old times and regard the old methods as the best. You see events as circular and recurring, so the wisdom of yesterday is applicable also to today and tomorrow. Past-oriented individuals would (as you can tell from the questions) respond with TRUE to statements 1–4 and with either TRUE or FALSE for the remaining statements.

- In a *present orientation* you live in the present: for now, not tomorrow. Present-oriented individuals would response with TRUE to statements 5–8, FALSE to statements 9–12, and either TRUE or FALSE for statements 1–4.

- In a *future orientation*, you live for the future. You save today, work hard in college, and deny yourself luxuries because you're preparing for the future. Future-oriented individuals would respond with TRUE to statements 9–12, FALSE for statements 5–8, and either TRUE or FALSE for statements 1–4.

As you can see from the statements in the self-test above, your time orientation has important implications for both your college and your professional career.

The time orientation you develop depends to a great extent on your socio-economic class and your personal experiences (Gonzalez & Zimbardo, 1985). For example, parents with unskilled and semiskilled occupations are likely to teach their children a present-orientated fatalism and a belief that enjoying yourself is more important than planning for the future. Parents who are teachers, managers, or other professionals tend to teach their children the importance of planning and preparing for the future, along with other strategies for success. In the United States, not surprisingly, future income is positively related to future orientation; the more future oriented you are, the greater your income is likely to be.

The Cultural Map

LONG-TERM VERSUS SHORT-TERM ORIENTATION

Long-term-oriented cultures teach the importance of future rewards, whereas short-term-oriented cultures teach their members to appreciate the rewards of the past and the present.

These countries are associated with long-term orientation and emphasize the importance of future rewards. Work now to benefit later is a shared belief. A good education and planning for the future are strongly valued in these countries.

These countries are associated with short-term orientation and emphasize the importance of present rewards. Benefit now because you may not benefit later. Spending resources now and getting quick results are strongly valued in these countries.

How might the differences between long- and short-term orientation influence interpersonal communication? Do you think long- and short-term oriented cultural members would use social media in the same way? For example, would their posted photos be similar? Different?

As you read more about time and nonverbal communication generally, consider how these time orientations work for or against you. For example, will your time orientation help you achieve your social and professional goals? If not, what might you do about changing these attitudes and behaviors?

INTERPERSONAL TIME   **Interpersonal time** refers to a wide variety of time re-lated elements that figure into interpersonal interaction. Here are several of the more important (Burgoon, Guerrero, & Floyd, 2010; Andersen & Bowman, 1999; DeVito, 2014).

- **Punctuality** refers to being on time for a variety of occasions—for company meetings, for class, for teacher-student appointments, for a ball game, for a movie or television show, and for completing assignments, to take just a few examples.

- **Wait time** refers to the amount of time it's considered appropriate to wait for someone. Generally, the rule is that you'd wait longer for higher status people than for lower status people. You'd wait long if your supervisor is late but may wait only a few minutes for a colleague.

- **Talk time** refers to, for example, who initiates and who terminates a conversation, who talks more, who selects and directs the topics for discussion. As with so many such factors, status plays an important role here. It's the higher status person who makes the decisions. But, perhaps the best example of high status and talk time is the privilege to interrupt.

- **Relationship time** refers to the time you give or should give to the various people with whom you have a relationship. In our culture, committed romantic couples normally spend a considerable amount of time together and when that time is abbreviated (and considered too little by one of the partners), the relationship may be headed for trouble. Even long-distance relationships normally have relationship time—whether on the phone, through periodic visits, or via Skype.

- **Response time** refers to the time it takes you to respond. Response time is observed in both synchronous and asynchronous communication. For example, in face-to-face communication, the response time to some statements and questions must be immediate. There should be very little response lag between one's person's "Will you marry me?" and the other's "Yes." When the response time is inappropriately long, you may sense some kind of disagreement or lack of certainty.

CULTURAL TIME   Here we look at three types of **cultural time**: formal and informal time, monochronism and polychronism, and the social clock.

Formal and Informal Time   Formal time divisions in the United States and in most of the world include seconds, minutes, hours, days, weeks, months, and years. Some cultures, however, may use seasons or phases of the moon to demarcate their most important time periods. In the United States, if your college is on the semester system, your courses are divided into 50- or 75-minute periods that meet two or three times a week for 14-week periods. Eight semesters of 15 or 16 periods per week equal a college education. As these examples illustrate, formal time units are arbitrary. The culture establishes them for convenience.

Informal time divisions are more general, more ambiguous, and involve such informal time terms as "forever," "immediately," "soon," "right away," "as soon as possible." This type of time communication creates the most problems, because informal terms have different meanings for different people. This is especially true when these terms are used interculturally. For example, what does "late" mean when applied to a commuter train that is not on time? Apparently, it depends on your culture. In the United States (the New York area specifically), "late" means arriving six minutes or more after the scheduled time; in Britain, it means five minutes or more. But in Japan, it means one minute (LeVine & Bartlett, 1984).

Monochronism and Polychronism   Another important distinction is that between **monochronic time orientation** and **polychronic time orientation** (Hall, 1959, 1976; Hall & Hall, 1987). Monochronic people or cultures—such as those of the United States, Germany, Scandinavia, and Switzerland—schedule one thing at a time. In these cultures

"This concludes my lecture on non-verbal communication. Any comments or questions?"

Chris Wildt/CartoonStock.com

Table 5.4 In a Nutshell: Eight Channels of Nonverbal Communication

Channel	Key Concepts
Body Gestures and Body Appearance (AKA kinesics)	Five types of gestures: emblems, illustrators, affect displays, regulators, adaptors. General body build, height, and weight.
Facial Communication	Facial management, facial feedback
Eye Communication (AKA occulesis)	Eye contact, eye avoidance, pupil dilation
Spatial Messages and Territoriality (AKA proxemics)	Proxemic distances (intimate, personal, social, public) and territories (primary, secondary, public)
Artifactual Communication	Items made or arranged by the person, for example, space decoration, colors, clothing and body adornment, and scent
Touch Communication (AKA tactile communication, haptics)	Touch communicates a variety of emotions as does touch avoidance.
Paralanguage and Silence	The rate, pitch, and volume of your speech. Silence too communicates; spiral of silence
Temporal Communication (AKA chronemics)	Psychological, interpersonal, cultural, and biological time

time is compartmentalized and there is a time for everything. On the other hand, polychronic people or cultures—such as those of Latin Americans, Mediterranean peoples, and Arabs—schedule multiple things at the same time. Eating, conducting business with several different people, and taking care of family matters all may occur at the same time. No culture, of course, is entirely monochronic or polychronic; rather, these are general tendencies that are found across a large part of the culture. Some cultures combine both time orientations; for example, both orientations are found in Japan and in parts of American culture.

It's interesting to note that social network sites enable you to do (or at least appear to do) more things at one time by enabling you to schedule your tweets or the sending of birthday cards. So, you can be skiing down the slopes at the same time your tweets are posted or your cards are sent.

The Social Clock   Your culture maintains a **social clock**—a time schedule for the right time to do various important things, such as starting dating, finishing college, buying your own home, or having a child. The social clock tells you if you're keeping pace with your peers, are ahead of them, or are falling behind (Greene, 2003; Neugarten, 1979). On the basis of this social clock, which you learned as you grew up, you evaluate your own social and professional development. If you're keeping pace with the rest of your peers (for example, you started dating at the "appropriate" age or you're finishing college at the "appropriate" age), you'll feel well-adjusted, competent, and a part of the group. If you're late, you'll probably experience feelings of dissatisfaction. Although today the social clock is becoming more flexible and more tolerant of deviations from the acceptable timetable than it was in past decades, it still exerts pressure on each of us to keep pace with our peers (Peterson, 1996).

Table 5.4 summarizes the eight channels of communication discussed here.

Nonverbal Communication Competence

5.3   **Paraphrase the guidelines for improving your skills in decoding and encoding nonverbal messages.**

Throughout the discussion of nonverbal communication, you've probably deduced a number of suggestions for improving your own nonverbal communication. Here, we bring together some suggestions for both receiving and sending nonverbal messages.

Perhaps the most general skill that applies to both receiving and sending is to become mindful of nonverbal messages—those of others as well as your own. Observe those whose nonverbal behavior you find particularly effective and those you find ineffective and try to identify exactly what makes one effective and one ineffective. Consider this chapter a brief introduction to a lifelong study.

In addition to mindfulness, general suggestions can be offered under two headings: decoding (or interpreting) nonverbal messages and encoding (or sending) nonverbal messages. Putting these skills into practice will help you improve your nonverbal communication.

Decoding Skills

When making judgments about another person's nonverbal messages, one of the most important of skills is to resist leaping to conclusions. Instead, develop hypotheses (or educated guesses) about what is going on, and test the validity of your hypotheses on the basis of other evidence. This is especially true when you make judgments about another person's intentions because of a photo they posted or a response that you expected didn't come soon enough.

When making judgments, mindfully seek alternative explanations. Your first judgment may be in error, and one good way to test it is to consider possible alternatives. When your romantic partner creates a greater than normal distance in relation to you, it may signal an annoyance with you; but it can also signal that your partner needs some space to think something out. This is especially true with social media where a comment meant to be humorous is interpreted as sarcastic or condescending.

Consider the possibility that you are incorrect. This is especially true when you make a judgment that another person is lying, based on, say, eye avoidance or long pauses. These nonverbal signals may mean many things (as well as the possibility of lying). Remember that communication is irreversible and that accusations (such as that of lying) will have long-lasting consequences.

Messages come from many different channels and reasonably accurate judgments can only be made when multiple channels are taken into consideration. Although textbooks (like this one) must present the areas of nonverbal communication separately, the various elements all work together in actual communication situations.

Measure behaviors against a baseline. In judging the meaning of another's behavior, you need to know how this person behaves ordinarily so you can tell what's a deviation and what's normal for this person. For example, if Pat is normally shy and reticent to talk and you observe Pat being the life of the party, it's more meaningful than if you observed Pat being shy and reticent. Nonverbal behavior is most revealing when it deviates from the baseline.

Interpret your judgments and conclusions against a cultural context. For example, think about whether you are interpreting the nonverbal behavior of someone through its meaning only in your own culture. So, if you interpret someone's "overly close" talking distance as intrusive or pushy because that's your culture's interpretation, you may miss the possibility that this distance is simply standard in the other person's culture; or it's a way of signaling closeness and friendliness.

JOURNAL
COMMUNICATION CHOICE POINT
Demonstrating Credibility

At work people don't attribute any credibility to you, although you're probably as competent as anyone else. You need to increase the nonverbal credibility cues you give off. *What nonverbal cues can you use to communicate your competence and ability? How might you begin to integrate these into your everyday interactions?*

Consider the multitude of factors that can influence the way a person behaves nonverbally; for example, a person's physical condition, personality, or particular situation may all influence a person's nonverbal communication. An upset stomach may be more influential in unpleasant expressions than any communication factor. A low grade in an exam may make your normally pleasant roommate scowl and grumble. Without knowing these factors, it's difficult to make an accurate judgment.

Encoding Skills

Nonverbal communication involves choices just as verbal communication does. So, think about your choices for your nonverbal communication just as carefully and mindfully as you do for your verbal messages. Realize that when you post a photo on Facebook, you are telling others something about yourself. So, it's important to ask yourself if this is the message you want this post to communicate.

Monitor your own nonverbal messages with the same care that you monitor your verbal messages. If it's not appropriate to say "this meal is terrible," then it's not appropriate to have a negative expression when you're asked if you want seconds.

Keep your nonverbal messages consistent with your verbal messages; avoid sending verbal messages that say one thing and nonverbal messages that say something else—at least not when you want to be believed.

Take the situation into consideration. Effective nonverbal communication is situational; to be effective adapt your nonverbal messages to the specific situation. Nonverbal behavior appropriate to one situation may be totally inappropriate in another.

Maintain eye contact with the speaker—whether at a meeting, in the hallway, or on an elevator; it communicates politeness and says that you are giving the person the consideration of your full attention. Eye contact that is too focused and too prolonged is likely to be seen as invasive and impolite. Similarly, most situations, whether business or social, seem to appreciate a positive countenance so smile and otherwise express your interest.

Be careful with touching; it may or may not be considered appropriate or polite depending on the relationship you have with the other person and on the context in which you find yourselves. The best advice to give here is to avoid touching unless it's part of the culture of the group or organization.

At the same time that you want to use certain nonverbals in certain ways, you'll also want to avoid a variety of nonverbal behaviors. One example that you'd want to avoid is extremes and monotony. Too little nonverbal communication or too much are likely to be responded to negatively. Smiling too broadly and laughing at every remark are sure to leave a negative impression. Similarly, always giving the same nonverbal message—say, continually smiling and nodding your head when listening to a friend's long story—is likely to be seen as insincere.

You'd also want to avoid certain nonverbal adaptors, for example, combing your hair, picking your teeth, or putting your pinky in your ear; these will be seen as impolite. And, not surprisingly, the greater the formality of the situation, the greater the perception of impoliteness is likely to be. So, for example, combing your hair while sitting with two or three friends would probably not be considered impolite (or perhaps only mildly so); but in a classroom or at a company meeting, it would be considered inappropriate.

Avoid strong cologne or perfume or any scent that may prove overwhelming or unpleasant to others. While you may enjoy the scent, those around you may find it unpleasant and intrusive. Much like others do not want to hear your cell messages, they probably don't want to have their sense of smell invaded either.

Summary of Concepts and Skills

This chapter explored nonverbal communication—communication without words—and looked at the functions nonverbal messages serve, the channels of nonverbal communication, and some of the cultural and gender-related influences on and differences in nonverbal communication.

Principles of Nonverbal Communication

5.1 **Explain the principles that identify the ways in which nonverbal communication functions.**

1. Nonverbal messages often interact with verbal messages to accent, complement, contradict, regulate, repeat, or substitute.
2. Nonverbal messages help manage impressions. We present ourselves nonverbally to give people the desired impression.
3. Nonverbal messages help form relationships.
4. Nonverbal messages structure conversation.
5. Nonverbal messages can influence and deceive.
6. Nonverbal messages are crucial for expressing emotions.

The Channels of Nonverbal Communication

5.2 **Describe the channels of nonverbal messages and give examples of messages in each channel.**

7. Body messages are communicated through gestures and appearance. Body gestures are classified into five categories: emblems (which rather directly translate words or phrases); illustrators (which accompany and literally "illustrate" verbal messages); affect displays (which communicate emotional meaning); regulators (which coordinate, monitor, maintain, or control the speaking of another individual); and adaptors (which usually are unconscious and serve some kind of need, as in scratching an itch). Body appearance (for example, height and general attractiveness) also communicates a variety of messages.
8. Facial movements may communicate a variety of emotions. The most frequently studied are happiness, surprise, fear, anger, sadness, and disgust/contempt. Facial management techniques enable you to control your facial expression of emotions. The facial feedback hypothesis claims that facial display of an emotion can lead to physiological and psychological changes.
9. Eye movements may seek feedback, invite others to speak, signal the nature of a relationship, or compensate for physical distance.
10. The study of proxemics investigates the communicative functions of space and spatial relationships. Four major proxemic distances are: (1) intimate distance, ranging from actual touching to 18 inches; (2) personal distance, ranging from 18 inches to 4 feet; (3) social

distance, ranging from 4 to 12 feet; and (4) public distance, ranging from 12 to 25 or more feet. Your treatment of space is influenced by such factors as status, culture, context, subject matter, sex, age, and positive or negative evaluation of the other person. Territoriality involves people's possessive reactions to particular spaces or objects.
11. Artifactual communication consists of messages conveyed by objects or arrangements created by humans; for example, by the use of color, clothing, body adornment, space decoration, and scents.
12. Touch communication, or haptics, may communicate a variety of meanings, the most important being positive affect, playfulness, control, ritual, and task-relatedness. Touch avoidance is the desire to avoid touching and being touched by others.
13. Paralanguage and silence have to do with the vocal (or, in the case of silence, its absence) but nonverbal dimension of speech. It includes rate, pitch, volume, resonance, and vocal quality as well as pauses and hesitations. Based on paralanguage, we make judgments about people, sense conversational turns, and assess believability. Silence communicates a variety of meanings, from anger (as in the "silent treatment") to deep emotional responses.
14. Time communication, or chronemics, consists of messages communicated by our treatment of time.
15. Cultural variations in nonverbal communication are great. Different cultures, for example, assign different meanings to gestures, facial expressions, and colors; have different spatial rules; and treat time very differently.

Nonverbal Communication Competence

5.3 **Paraphrase the guidelines for improving your skills in decoding and encoding nonverbal messages.**

16. Decoding skills (being conscious of the several nonverbal channels sending messages simultaneously, interpreting messages in a cultural context) will enable you to more effectively understand the meanings being communicated with nonverbal signals.
17. Encoding skills (maintaining eye contact, avoiding intrusive touching) will enable you to communicate more effectively with nonverbal messages.

This chapter has covered a wide variety of nonverbal communication skills. Place a check mark next to those skills that you feel you want to work on most.

_____ 1. I recognize the varied functions that nonverbal messages (my own and those of others) serve: for example, to form and manage impressions,

_____ to define relationships, and to structure conversations.

_____ 2. I use body and gesture messages to help communicate my desired meanings, and I recognize these messages in others.

_____ 3. I use my eyes to seek feedback, to inform others to speak, to signal the nature of my relationship with others, and to compensate for physical distance.

_____ 4. I give others the space they need: for example, I give extra space to those who are angry or disturbed.

_____ 5. I am sensitive to the markers (i.e., central, boundary, and earmarkers) of others and use these markers to define my own territories.

_____ 6. I use artifacts thoughtfully to communicate desired messages.

_____ 7. I am sensitive to the touching behaviors of others and distinguish among touches that communicate positive emotion, playfulness, control, and ritual or task-related messages.

_____ 8. I recognize and respect each person's touch-avoidance tendency. I am especially sensitive to cultural and gender differences in touching preferences and in touch-avoidance tendencies.

_____ 9. I vary paralinguistic features (e.g., rate, emphasis, pauses, tempo, volume) to communicate my intended meanings.

_____ 10. I use silence to communicate varied meanings (e.g., disappointment or the need for time to think), and I examine the silence of others for meanings just as I would eye movements or body gestures.

_____ 11. I interpret time cues with an awareness of the cultural perspective of the person with whom I am interacting.

_____ 12. I balance my time orientation and don't ignore the past, present, or future.

_____ 13. In decoding nonverbal messages, I draw conclusions tentatively, consider alternative judgments, take into consideration the varied nonverbal channels, consider the possibility of being incorrect, interpret the judgments in a cultural context, and consider influences from other factors.

_____ 14. In encoding my own nonverbal messages, I aim for consistency between verbal and nonverbal messages, monitor my nonverbal messages, avoid extremes, and take the situation into consideration.

Key Terms

adaptors	home field advantage	public distance
affect displays	illustrators	public territories
alter-adaptors	interpersonal time	regulators
artifactual messages	intimate distance	secondary territories
attractiveness	kinesics	self-adaptors
boundary markers	markers	silence
central markers	monochronic time orientation	social clock
chronemics	nonverbal communication	social distance
civil inattention	object-adaptors	temporal communication
color communication	oculesics	territoriality
cultural time	olfactory communication	tie signs
earmarkers	paralanguage	touch avoidance
emblems	personal distance	touch communication
emoticon	polychronic time orientation	transmitted
facial feedback hypothesis	primary territories	turn-taking cues
facial management techniques	proxemics	
haptics	psychological time	

Skill Development Experiences

5.1 Selecting a Seat at the Company Meeting

Nonverbal choices influence your communication effectiveness and your image as a communicator.

The accompanying graphic represents a table with 12 chairs, one of which is occupied by the "boss." For each of the following messages, indicate (a) where you would sit to communicate each message and (b) any other possible messages that your choice of seat will probably communicate.

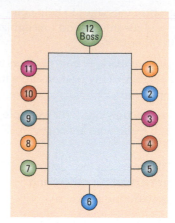

A. You want to ingratiate yourself with your boss. _____

B. You aren't prepared and want to be ignored. _____

C. You want to challenge the boss's proposal that is scheduled to come up for a vote. _____

D. You want to get to know better the person at seat number 7. _____

5.2 Height

Your height sends important messages about who you are.

Try estimating the heights of the following famous people (some historical, some contemporary) whom you've probably read about or heard about (but probably not seen in person) by circling the guessed height. In each of these examples, one of the heights given is correct.

1. Baby Face Nelson (bank robber and murderer in the 1930s): 5′5″, 5′11″, 6′2″

2. Ludwig Van Beethoven (influential German composer): 5′6″, 6′0″, 6′5″

3. Kim Kardashian (media personality): 5′2″, 5′5″, 5′8″

4. Buckminster Fuller (scientist, credited with inventing the geodesic dome): 5′2″, 5′10″, 6′3″

5. Bruno Mars (singer): 5′5″, 5′8″, 5′10″

6. Mahatma Gandhi (Indian political leader whose civil disobedience led to India's independence from British rule): 5′3″, 5′8″, 6′0″

7. Jada Pinkett Smith (actor): 5′0″, 5′6″, 5′9″

8. Joan of Arc (military leader, burned for heresy at age 19, and declared a saint): 4′11″, 5′4″, 5′10″:

9. T. E. Lawrence of Arabia (adventurer and British army officer): 5′5″, 6′0″, 6′5″

10. Salma Hayek (actor): 5′2″, 5′5″, 5′8″.

This exercise was designed to see if you would overestimate the heights of a number of these people. Fame seems to be associated with height, and so most people would think these people were/are taller than they really were/are. The specific heights for all are the shortest heights given above: Baby Face Nelson, 5′5″; Ludwig Van Beethoven, 5′6″; Kim Kardashian, 5′2″; Buckminster Fuller, 5′2″; Bruno Mars, 5′5″; Mahatma Gandhi, 5′3″; Jada Pinkett Smith, 5′0″; Joan of Arc, 4′11″; T. E. Lawrence, 5′5″; and Salma Hayek, 5′2″. How important is height to your self-image? How important is height in a romantic partner?

5.3 Using Nonverbal Impression Management Strategies

Messages are a combination of verbal and nonverbal signals; even subtle variations in, say, eye movements or intonation can drastically change the impression communicated.

Now that you've read about how nonverbal messages may help you manage impressions, consider how you would manage yourself nonverbally in the following situations. For each of these situations, indicate (a) the impressions you'd want to create (e.g., an image as a hardworking self-starter); (b) the nonverbal cues you'd use to create these impressions; and (c) the nonverbal cues you'd be especially careful to avoid.

1. You want a job at a conservative, prestigious law firm and are meeting your prospective boss for your first face-to-face interview.
2. You want a part in a movie in which you'd play a homeless drug addict.
3. You're single and you're applying to adopt a child.
4. You want to ask another student to go out with you.
5. You want to convince your romantic partner that you did not see your ex last night; you were working.

5.4 Identifying Connections between Verbal and Nonverbal Messages

You cannot speak a sentence without using nonverbal signals, and these signals influence the meaning you send to the receiver.

To demonstrate that the way you say something influences the meanings you communicate, try reading each of the sentences below aloud—first to communicate a positive meaning and then to communicate a negative meaning. As you communicate these meanings, try to identify the nonverbal differences between the ways you express positive meanings and the ways you express negative meanings. Look specifically at (a) how you read the statements in terms of rate, pauses, and volume and (b) how your facial and eye expressions differ.

1. Oh, yeah, I have the relationship of a lifetime.
2. I can't wait to receive my test results.
3. Did you see her Facebook profile and the new photos?
4. I had some fantastic date last night.
5. Did you see him pitch that great game last night?

5.5 Using Nonverbal Messages

Bringing to consciousness your automatic nonverbal behaviors will enable you to control your nonverbal messages when you want to.

You use nonverbal messages to accomplish a variety of goals almost without thinking about what you're doing. You smile or gesture or change the distance between you without giving any real conscious thought to what you're doing; it all seems so natural. To bring some of these nonverbal behaviors to consciousness, consider the three or four or five nonverbal behaviors you would use to:

1. Communicate intimacy or connection or liking for another person.
2. Communicate to a group that you are a confidence and totally in control leader.
3. Show yourself to be approachable and friendly.
4. Sell a used car.
5. Apologize for a significant indiscretion to a long-term romantic partner.

Chapter 6

Interpersonal Communication and Conversation

Conversation—increasingly less often—takes place face-to-face.

CHAPTER OUTLINE	Learning Objectives
Preliminaries to Interpersonal Communication and Conversation	**6.1** Define *interpersonal communication* and explain the interpersonal continuum and the stages of conversation.
The Principles of Conversation	**6.2** Explain the principles of cooperation, politeness, turn-taking, dialogue, and immediacy in conversation.
Everyday Conversations	**6.3** Paraphrase the suggestions for making small talk, apologizing, and complimenting.

In this chapter we introduce interpersonal communication and, perhaps the essence of interpersonal communication, "simple" conversation.

Preliminaries to Interpersonal Communication and Conversation

6.1 Define *interpersonal communication* and explain the interpersonal continuum and the stages of conversation.

Here we look at the definition of interpersonal communication and its essential processes.

Definition of Interpersonal Communication

Interpersonal communication is communication that occurs between two people who have a relationship and who are thus influenced by each other's communication messages. It includes what takes place between a server and a customer, a son and his father, two people in an interview, and so on. This definition makes it almost impossible for communication between two people not to be considered interpersonal—inevitably, some relationship exists. Even a stranger asking directions from a local resident has established a clearly defined relationship as soon as the first message is sent. Sometimes this relational, or "dyadic," definition of interpersonal communication is extended to include small groups of people, such as family members, groups of three or four friends, or work colleagues.

Social media have somewhat blurred this distinction. For example, when you write on someone's Facebook wall, it is interpersonal because it's between you and a friend but it is also sent to others in the group (making it small-group communication). And in many ways it's public since the audience can be extremely large; not only is the wall message available to those with access to your page, but it's also available to anyone who is sent the posting by others in your group.

The Interpersonal Continuum

Another way to look at interpersonal communication is along a continuum ranging from relatively impersonal to highly personal (Miller, 1978, 1990). At the impersonal end of the spectrum there is simple conversation between people who really don't know each other: the server and the customer, for example. At the highly personal end is the communication that takes place between people who are intimately interconnected, such as a father and son (see Figure 6.1).

A few characteristics distinguish these two extremes. First, in the impersonal example, the individuals are likely to respond to each other according to the roles

Figure 6.1 An Interpersonal Continuum
Here is one possible interpersonal continuum. Other people would position the relationships differently. You may want to try constructing an interpersonal continuum of your own relationships.

they are currently playing: The server treats the customer not as a unique individual but as one of many customers; and the customer, in turn, acts toward the server not as if he or she were a unique individual but as he or she would act toward any server. The father and the son, however, react to each other as unique individuals.

Notice too that the server and the customer interact according to the rules of society governing the server–customer interaction. The father and the son, on the other hand, interact on the basis of personally established rules. The way they address each other, their touching behavior, and their degree of physical closeness, for example, are unique to them and are established by them rather than by society.

Still another difference is that the messages that the server and customer exchange are themselves impersonal; there is little self-disclosure and little emotional content, for example. In the father–son example, the messages may run the entire range and may at times be highly personal with considerable disclosure and emotion.

There are, of course, many gradations between these extremes. Some friendships, for example, are casual; others are highly intimate. Romantic pairs vary in their levels of intimacy, and so do families.

Communicating Ethically
YOUR OBLIGATION TO REVEAL YOURSELF

If you're in a close interpersonal relationship, you may have an ethical obligation to reveal certain things about yourself. Conversely, you may feel that the other person—because he or she is so close to you—has an ethical obligation to reveal certain information to you. Consider at what point in a relationship, if any, you feel you would have an ethical obligation to reveal each of the 10 items of information listed here. Visualize your relationship as existing on a continuum from initial contact at 1 to extreme intimacy at 10, and use the numbers from 1 to 10 to indicate at what point you would feel an ethical obligation to reveal these items of information. If you feel you would never have the obligation to reveal this information, use 0.

At what point do you have an ethical obligation to reveal your true:	To a Romantic Partner of 1 year	To a Friend you've known for 3 years
Age	_____	_____
History of family genetic disorders	_____	_____
HIV status	_____	_____
Past sexual experiences	_____	_____
Marital history	_____	_____
Annual salary and net financial worth	_____	_____
Affectional orientation	_____	_____
Attitudes toward other races and nationalities	_____	_____
Religious beliefs	_____	_____
Past criminal activity or incarceration	_____	_____

ETHICAL CHOICE POINT

You've been communicating with someone online for the last year and lied about your age, income, and previous relationship history when you first started communicating. You've confessed your love for each other and are now planning to meet for the first time. *Aside from any potential relationship advantages or disadvantages of revealing the truth, would you consider yourself to have an ethical obligation to reveal the truth?*

The Interpersonal Process

Interpersonal communication and conversation generally is best viewed as a process rather than as an act. It's convenient to divide up this process into chunks or stages and to view each stage as requiring a choice as to what you'll say and how you'll say it. Here we divide the sequence into five steps: (1) opening, (2) feedforward, (3) business, (4) feedback, and (5) closing (see Figure 6.2). These stages and the way people follow them will vary depending on the personalities of the communicators, their culture, the context in which the conversation occurs, the purpose of the conversation, and the entire host of factors considered throughout this text.

Figure 6.2 A Five-Stage Model of Conversation
This model of the stages of conversation is best seen as a way of talking about conversation and not as a hard-and-fast depiction of stages all conversations follow. As you review the model, consider how accurately it depicts conversation as you experience it. *Can you develop a more accurate and more revealing model?*

- **Opening** The first step is to open the conversation, usually with some kind of greeting: "Hi. How are you?" "Hello, this is Joe." The greeting is a good example of phatic communication—a message that establishes a connection between two people and opens up the channels for more meaningful interaction. Openings, of course, may be nonverbal as well as verbal. A smile or kiss may be as clear an opening as "Hello." Greetings are so common that they often go unnoticed. But when they're omitted—as when a doctor begins a conversation by saying, "What's wrong?"—you may feel uncomfortable and thrown off guard.

- **Feedforward** At the second step, you (usually) provide some kind of **feedforward**, which gives the other person a general idea of the conversation's focus: "I've got to tell you about Jack," "Did you hear what happened in class yesterday?" or "We need to talk about our vacation plans." Feedforward also may identify the tone of the conversation ("I'm really depressed and need to talk with you") or the time required ("This will just take a minute") (Frentz, 1976; Reardon, 1987). Conversational awkwardness often occurs when feedforwards are used inappropriately—for example, using overly long feedforwards or omitting feedforward before a truly shocking message.

- **Business** The third step is the "business," the substance or focus of the conversation. The term *business* is used to emphasize that most conversations are goal directed. That is, you converse to fulfill one or several of the general purposes of interpersonal communication: to learn, relate, influence, play, or help (see Chapter 1). The term is also sufficiently general to incorporate all kinds of interactions. In general, the business is conducted through an exchange of speaker and listener roles. Brief, rather than long, speaking turns characterize most satisfying conversations. In the business stage, you talk about Jack, what happened in class, or your vacation plans. This is obviously the longest part of the conversation and the reason for the opening and the feedforward.

- **Feedback** The fourth step is **feedback**, the reverse of the second step. Here you (usually) reflect back on the conversation to signal that, as far as you're concerned, the business is completed: "So you want to send Jack a get-well card," "Wasn't that the craziest class you ever heard of?" or "OK, so I'll call for reservations, and you'll shop for what we need."

- **Closing** The fifth and last step, the opposite of the first step, is the closing, the goodbye, which often reveals how satisfied the persons were with the conversation: "I hope you'll call soon" or "Don't call us, we'll call you." The closing also may be used to schedule future conversations: "Give me a call tomorrow night" or "Let's meet for lunch at 12." When closings are indefinite or vague, conversation often becomes awkward; you're not quite sure if you should say goodbye or if you should wait for something else to be said.

JOURNAL
COMMUNICATION CHOICE POINT
Feedforward

You want to break up your relationship with someone you've been dating rather steadily over the last eight months. You want to remain friends but end the romance, something your partner has no idea about. *What might you say as a preface (as feedforward) to your breakup speech?*

VIEWPOINTS: Shake Hands or Kiss?
It's sometimes difficult to tell when you should shake hands and when you should hug or air kiss or actually kiss the other person. *How do you tell which form of greeting will be most appropriate?*

The Principles of Conversation

6.2   Explain the principles of cooperation, politeness, turn-taking, dialogue, and immediacy in conversation.

Although conversation is an everyday process and one we seldom think about, it is, like most forms of communication, governed by several principles. Especially important are the principles of (1) cooperation, (2) politeness, (3) turn-taking, (4) dialogue, and (5) immediacy. These principles express our general expectations about the way in which conversation should work. We expect people in conversation to, for example, cooperate in understanding each other.

The Principle of Cooperation

When you communicate interpersonally, you probably follow the general **principle of cooperation**, the mutually agreed-upon assumption that two people will try to understand each other (Grice, 1975). You cooperate largely by adhering to four maxims—rules that speakers and listeners in the United States and in many other cultures follow in conversation. As you'll see, following these maxims (the **quantity principle,** the **quality principle,** the **relation principle,** and the **manner principle**) will help ensure efficient interpersonal communication.

- The **quantity principle** requires that you be only as informative as necessary to communicate your intended meaning. Thus, you include information that makes the meaning clear but omit what does not. The maxim of quantity requires that you give neither too little nor too much information. Spam is the perfect example of messages that violate this principle; spam messages are unwanted noise and intrude on your own communication.

- The **quality principle** states that you should say what you know or believe to be true and not say what you know to be false. When you're communicating, you assume that the other person's information is true—at least as far as he or she knows. For example, when a friend tells you what happened on a trip, you assume that it's true. The **relation principle** asks that you talk about what is relevant to the conversation. Speakers who digress widely and frequently interject irrelevant comments violate the maxim of relation.

- The **manner principle** requires that you be clear, avoid ambiguities, be relatively brief, and organize your thoughts into a meaningful sequence. Thus, you use terms that the listener will understand and omit or clarify terms that you suspect the listener will not understand. When you talk to a young child, for example, you normally use familiar words and short sentences. You can also see this principle operating in computer-mediated communication's reliance on acronyms (for example, *BTW* for *by the way*, *IMHO* for *in my humble opinion*, and *TTYL* for *talk to you later*). This is an extremely efficient method of communicating (when sender and receiver both know the meanings), much like macros and autocorrect features in word processors.

The Principle of Politeness: Conversation Is (Usually) Polite

Not surprisingly, conversation is expected (at least in most cases) to follow the principle of politeness. Six general rules of politeness have been identified by linguist Geoffrey Leech (1983) and seem to encompass a great deal of what we commonly think of as conversational politeness. Before reading about these maxims, take the self-test to help you personalize the material that follows.

Now that you've considered your own level of politeness, here are six general rules that make conversations better: the **maxim of tact,** the **maxim of generosity,**

Test Yourself

HOW POLITE ARE YOU?

Try estimating your own level of politeness. For each of the statements below, indicate how closely they describe your typical communication. Avoid giving responses that you feel might be considered "socially acceptable"; instead, give responses that accurately represent your typical communication behavior. Use a 10-point scale, with 10 being "very accurate description of my typical conversation" and 1 being "very inaccurate description of my typical conversation."

_____ **1.** I tend not to ask others to do something or to otherwise impose on others.

_____ **2.** I tend to put others first, before myself.

_____ **3.** I maximize the expression of approval of others and minimize any disapproval.

_____ **4.** I seldom praise myself but often praise others.

_____ **5.** I maximize the expression of agreement and minimize disagreement.

_____ **6.** I maximize my sympathy for another and minimize any feelings of antipathy.

All six statements would characterize politeness, so high numbers, say 8–10, would indicate politeness, whereas low numbers, say 1–4, would indicate impoliteness.

As you read this material, personalize it with examples from your own interpersonal interactions, and try to identify specific examples and situations in which increased politeness might have been more effective.

the **maxim of approbation**, the **maxim of modesty**, the **maxim of agreement**, and the **maxim of sympathy**.

- The **maxim of tact** (statement 1 in the self-test) helps to maintain the other person's autonomy (what we referred to earlier in the book as negative face). Tact in your conversation would mean that you do not impose on others or challenge their right to do as they wish. For example, if you wanted to ask someone a favor, using the maxim of tact, you might say something like, "I know you're very busy but …" Not using the maxim of tact, you might say something like, "You have to lend me your car this weekend."

- The **maxim of generosity** (statement 2) helps to confirm the other person's importance—for example, the importance of the person's time, insight, or talent. Using the maxim of generosity, you might say, "I see you're busy; I'll walk the dog." Violating the maxim, you might say, "I'm really busy, why don't you walk the dog since you're not doing anything important."

- The **maxim of approbation** (statement 3) refers to praising someone or complimenting the person in some way (for example, "I was really moved by your poem") and minimizing any expression of criticism or disapproval (for example, "For a first effort, that poem wasn't half bad").

- The **maxim of modesty** (statement 4) minimizes any praise or compliments _you_ might receive. At the same time, you might praise and compliment the other person. For example, using this maxim you might say something like, "Well, thank you, but I couldn't have done this without your input; that was the crucial element." Violating this maxim, you might say, "Yes, thank you, it was one of my best efforts, I have to admit."

- The **maxim of agreement** (statement 5) refers to your seeking out areas of agreement and expressing them ("That color you selected was just right; it makes the room exciting") and at the same time avoiding and not expressing (or at least minimizing) disagreements ("It's an interesting choice, very different"). Violating this maxim, you might say "That color—how can you stand it?"

- The **maxim of sympathy** (statement 6) refers to the expression of understanding, sympathy, empathy, supportiveness, and the like for the other person. Using this

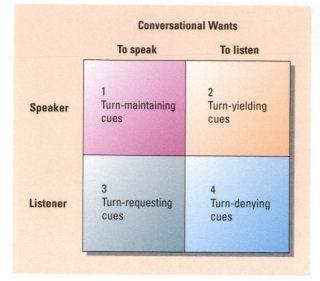

Conversational Wants

	To speak	To listen
Speaker	1 Turn-maintaining cues	2 Turn-yielding cues
Listener	3 Turn-requesting cues	4 Turn-denying cues

Figure 6.3 Turn-Taking and Conversational Wants
Quadrant 1 represents the speaker who wants to speak (continue to speak) and uses turn-maintaining cues; quadrant 2, the speaker who wants to listen and uses turn-yielding cues; quadrant 3, the listener who wants to speak and uses turn-requesting cues; and quadrant 4, the listener who wants to listen (i.e., continue listening) and uses turn-denying cues. Back-channeling cues would appear in quadrant 4, because they are cues that listeners use while they continue to listen.

maxim, you might say, "I understand your feelings; I'm so sorry." Violating this maxim, you might say, "You're making a fuss over nothing" or "You get upset over the least little thing. What is it this time?"

The Principle of Turn-Taking

Throughout the speaking–listening process, both speaker and listener exchange cues for what are called **conversational turns** (Burgoon, Buller, & Woodall, 1996; Duncan, 1972; Pearson & Spitzberg, 1990). These cues enable the speaker and listener to communicate about the exchange in which they're currently engaged; that is, a form of **metacommunication** takes place through the exchange of these often subtle cues. The use of turn-taking cues—like almost every aspect of human communication—will naturally vary from one culture to another. The description that follows here is valid largely for the United States and many Western cultures (Iizuka, 1993; Lee, 1984; Grossin, 1987; Ng, Loong, He, Liu, & Weatherall, 2000). As you read the following discussion, take a look at Figure 6.3; it provides a visual guide to the various turn signals.

SPEAKER CUES Speakers regulate the conversation through two major types of cues: turn-maintaining cues and turn-yielding cues. Using these cues effectively not only ensures communication efficiency but also increases likeability (Place & Becker, 1991; Heap, 1992).

Turn-Maintaining Cues Through **turn-maintaining cues** you communicate your wish to maintain the role of speaker by, for example, audibly inhale breath to show that you have more to say, continue a gesture to show that you've not yet completed your thought, avoid eye contact with the listener in order to indicate that you are not passing along your speaking turn, or use a vocalized pause ("er," "umm") to prevent the listener from speaking and to show that you're still talking.

In most conversations we expect the speaker to maintain relatively brief speaking turns and to turn over the speaking role to the listener willingly (when so signaled by the listener). People who don't follow those unwritten rules are likely to be evaluated negatively.

Turn-Yielding Cues. **Turn-yielding cues** tell the listener that the speaker is finished and wishes to exchange the role of speaker for the role of listener. They tell the listener to take over the role of speaker. For example, at the end of a statement you may add some cue such as "okay?" or "right?" to ask one of the listeners to assume the role of speaker. You also can indicate that you've finished speaking by dropping your intonation or pausing at length (Wennerstrom & Siegel, 2003), by making direct eye contact with a listener, by asking a question, or by nodding in the direction of a particular listener.

LISTENER CUES As a listener you can regulate the conversation by using three types of cues: turn-requesting cues, turn-denying cues, and back-channeling cues and interruptions.

Turn-Requesting Cues. **Turn-requesting cues** let the speaker know that you would like to say something and take a turn as speaker. Sometimes you can do this simply by saying, "I'd like to say something," but often it's done more subtly through some vocalized "er" or "um" that tells the speaker that you would like to speak. The request to speak is also often made with facial and mouth gestures.

Turn-Denying Cues You can use **turn-denying cues** to indicate your reluctance to assume the role of speaker—for example, by intoning a slurred "I don't know" or by giving some brief grunt that signals you have nothing to say. Often people accomplish turn-denying by avoiding eye contact with the speaker or by engaging in some behavior that is incompatible with speaking, such as coughing or blowing their nose.

Back-Channeling Cues and Interruptions Back-channeling cues are used to communicate various types of information back to the speaker without assuming the role of speaker. Some researchers call brief utterances—such as "mm-hm," "uh-huh," and "yeah"—that tell the speaker you're listening *acknowledgment tokens* (Schegloff, 1982; Drummond & Hopper, 1993). Other researchers call them *overlaps* to distinguish them from those interruptions that are aimed at taking over the speaker's turn (Tannen, 1994 a, b).

Interruptions, in contrast to back-channeling cues, are attempts to take over the role of the speaker. These are not supportive and are often disconfirming. Interruptions are often interpreted as attempts to change the topic to one that the person knows more about or to emphasize one's authority. Interruptions may also be seen as attempts to assert power and to maintain control. Not surprisingly, research finds that superiors (bosses and supervisors) and those in positions of authority (police officers and interviewers) interrupt those in inferior positions more than the other way around (Carroll, 1994; Ashcraft, 1998).

The Principle of Dialogue

Often the term *dialogue* is used as a synonym for *conversation*. But dialogue is more than simple conversation; it's conversation in which there is genuine two-way interaction (Buber, 1958; Yau-fair Ho, Chan, Peng, & Ng, 2001; McNamee & Gergen, 1999). It's useful to distinguish the ideal dialogic communicator from his or her opposite, the totally monologic communicator. Of course, no one engages in dialogue at all times, and no one is totally monologic. These descriptions represent extremes, intended only to clarify the differences between these types of communication.

During a **dialogue** each person is both speaker and listener, sender and receiver. It's conversation in which there is deep concern for the other person and for the relationship between the two. The objective of dialogue is mutual understanding and empathy. There is respect for the other person, not because of what this person can do or give but simply because this person is a human being and therefore deserves to be treated honestly and sincerely.

In a dialogic interaction you respect the other person enough to allow that person the right to make his or her own choices without coercion, without the threat of punishment, without fear or social pressure. A dialogic communicator believes that other people can make decisions that are right for them and implicitly or explicitly lets them know that, whatever choices they make, they will still be respected.

The dialogic communicator avoids negative criticism and negative personal judgments and instead practices using positive criticism ("I liked those first two explanations best; they were really well reasoned"). This person avoids dysfunctional communication patterns and keeps the channels of communication open by displaying a willingness to listen. While listening, this person indicates involvement by giving cues (e.g., nonverbal nods, brief verbal expressions of agreement, paraphrasing) that show he or she is paying attention. When in doubt the dialogic communicator asks for clarification—asks for your point of view, your perspective—and thus signals a

VIEWPOINTS: Gender Stereotypes
One of the stereotypes about gender differences in communication and widely reported in the popular writings on gender is that women talk more than men. But a recent study of 396 college students finds that women and men talk about the same number of words per day, about 16,000; more precisely women spoke an average of 16,215 words while men spoke an average of 15,669 words, a difference that was statistically insignificant (Mehl, Vazire, Ramirez-Esparza, Slatcher, & Pennebaker, 2007). *Do your own experiences support these research findings?*

real interest in you and in what you have to say. This person does not manipulate the conversation so as to get positive comments.

Monologic communication—the **monologue**—is the opposite: One person speaks and the other listens, and there is no real interaction between participants. The monologic communicator is focused only on his or her own goals and has no real concern for the listener's feelings or attitudes; this speaker is interested in the other person only insofar as that person can serve his or her purposes.

The monologic communicator frequently uses negative criticism ("I didn't like that explanation") and negative judgments ("You're not a very good listener, are you?"). This communicator also often uses dysfunctional communication patterns, such as expressing an unwillingness to talk or to listen to what the other person has to say. The monologic communicator rarely demonstrates that he or she understands you; this person gives no cues that he or she is listening (cues such as paraphrasing or expressing agreement with what you say). Nor would this person request clarification of your ideas, because he or she is less interested in you than in representing himself or herself. Still another characteristic of the monologic communicator is a tendency to request that you say positive things about him or her ("How did you like the way I handled that?").

The Principle of Immediacy

Of all the characteristics of effective communication, the one that most clearly defines effective conversation is **immediacy**—the creation of closeness, a sense of togetherness, of oneness, between speaker and listener. When you communicate immediacy, you convey a sense of interest and attention, a liking for and an attraction to the other person. As noted in our discussion of impression management strategies in Chapter 2, immediacy strategies are often used to make someone like us.

Not surprisingly, people respond to communication that is immediate more favorably than to communication that is not. You can increase your interpersonal attractiveness—the degree to which others like you and respond positively toward you—by using immediacy behaviors. In addition there is considerable evidence to show that immediacy behaviors are effective in teaching and in health care (Richmond, Smith, Heisel, & McCroskey, 2001; Richmond, McCroskey, & Hickson, 2012).

You can communicate immediacy with both verbal and nonverbal messages (Mottet & Richmond, 1998; Richmond, McCroskey, & Hickson, 2012):

- Self-disclose: reveal something significant about yourself.
- Refer to the other person's good qualities, say, dependability, intelligence, character: for example, "You're always so reliable."
- Express your positive view of the other person and of your relationship: for example, "I'm sure glad you're my roommate; you know everyone."
- Talk about commonalities, things you and the other person have done together or share.
- Demonstrate your responsiveness by giving feedback cues that indicate you want to listen more and that you're interested: for example, "And what else happened?"
- Express psychological closeness and openness by, for example, maintaining physical closeness and arranging your body to exclude third parties.
- Maintain appropriate eye contact and limit looking around at others.
- Smile and express your interest in the other person.
- Focus on the other person's remarks. Make the speaker know that you heard and understood what was said, and give the speaker appropriate verbal and nonverbal feedback.

At the same time that you'll want to demonstrate these immediacy messages, try also to avoid non-immediacy messages such as interrupting the other person, avoiding small talk, making potentially offensive or condescending comments, closing off the channels of communication ("I don't have the time to chat"), or talking about things for which the other person has no reference or experience. Nonverbally, avoid speaking in a monotone, looking away from the person you're talking to, frowning while talking, having a tense body posture, and avoiding gestures.

Not all cultures or all people respond in the same way to immediacy messages. For example, in the United States (and in individualist and low-power-distance cultures generally), immediacy behaviors are seen as friendly and appropriate. In other cultures (e.g., many collectivist and high-power-distance cultures), however, the same immediacy behaviors may be viewed as overly familiar—as presuming that a relationship is close when it is only an acquaintanceship (Axtell, 2007).

In addition, recognize that some people may interpret immediacy behaviors as indicating a desire for increased intimacy in the relationship. So, if you're trying to signal a friendly closeness, the other person may perceive a romantic invitation. Recognize too that because immediacy behaviors prolong and encourage in-depth communication, they may not be responded to favorably by persons who are fearful about communication and who want to get the interaction over with as soon as possible (Richmond, McCroskey, & Hickson, 2012).

Everyday Conversations

6.3   **Paraphrase the suggestions for making small talk, apologizing, and complimenting.**

Having covered the basic principles of conversation, we can now explore a variety of everyday conversation situations: making small talk, apologizing, and complimenting. In reviewing the everyday conversations included here, do realize that not everyone speaks with the fluency and ease that textbooks often assume. Speech and language disorders, for example, can seriously disrupt the conversation process if some elementary guidelines aren't followed. Here are a few suggestions for communication between people with and without speech and language disorders:

- Avoid finishing another's sentences. Finishing the person's sentences may communicate the idea that you're impatient and don't want to spend the extra time necessary to interact effectively. At the same time, if you're the one who stutters, say, have patience with those who try to finish your sentences; they're likely just trying to be helpful.

- Ask for clarification as needed. If you don't understand what the person said, ask him or her to repeat it. Don't pretend that you understand when you don't.

- Don't treat people who have language problems like children. A person with aphasia, say, who has difficulty with names or nouns generally, is in no way childlike. Similarly, a person who stutters is not a slow thinker; in fact, stutterers differ from non-stutterers only in their oral fluency.

- Let the other person know what your special needs are. If you stutter, you might tell others that you have difficulty with certain sounds and so they need to be patient.

Small Talk

Before reading about small talk, examine your own small talk behavior by taking the accompanying self-test.

All of us engage in **small talk**, whether it occurs on an elevator, in a hallway, on Twitter, or on some other social media site. Sometimes, we use it as a preface to big talk. For example, before a conference with your boss or even a job interview, you're likely to engage in some preliminary small talk. "How are you doing?" "I'm pleased this weather has finally cleared up." The purpose here is to ease into the major topic, or the "big talk."

Test Yourself

HOW DO YOU SMALL TALK?

Examine your small talk communication by responding to the following questions.

_____ **1** When on an elevator with three or four strangers,
   a. I try to avoid conversation.
   b. I politely respond to others but do not initiate interaction.
   c. I am the first to talk.

_____ **2** When I'm with a friend and a second friend approaches,
   a. I acknowledge the second person but continue my conversation with the first without introducing the two to each other.
   b. I wait until they introduce themselves.
   c. I immediately introduce my two friends to each other.

_____ **3** At a party with people I've never met before, I'm most likely to
   a. observe the scene and wait for someone to talk to me.
   b. smile and indicate that I'm open to a good conversation.
   c. initiate interaction with others nonverbally and verbally.

_____ **4** When confronted with someone who doesn't want to end the conversation,
   a. I just stick it out and listen.
   b. I tune out the person and hope time goes by quickly.
   c. I make an excuse to get away and end it myself.

A majority of _a_ responses would indicate some level of dissatisfaction and discomfort with the experience of small talk; _b_ responses indicate that you probably experience both satisfaction and dissatisfaction with small talk; _c_ responses indicate comfort and satisfaction with small talk.

Sometimes, small talk is a politeness strategy and a more extensive way of saying hello as you pass someone in the hallway or meet a neighbor at the post office. You might say, "Good seeing you, Jack. You're looking ready for the big meeting," or "See you in Geology at 1."

Sometimes, your relationship with another person revolves totally around small talk, perhaps with your barber or hairdresser, a colleague at work, your next-door neighbor, or a fellow student you sit next to in class. In these relationships, neither person makes an effort to deepen the relationship, and it remains on a small talk level.

Despite its name, small talk serves important purposes. One is simply to pass the time more pleasantly than you might in silence. Small talk also demonstrates that the normal rules of politeness are operating. In the United States, for example, you would be expected to smile and at least say hello to people in an elevator in your apartment building, and perhaps at your place of work. Furthermore, small talk confirms to others that all is well with you. Should you scowl and avoid eye contact with someone in your apartment building elevator, you'd signal that something is wrong.

TOPICS AND CONTEXTS OF SMALL TALK Small talk topics must be noncontroversial in the sense that they are something about which you and the other person are unlikely to disagree. If a topic is likely to arouse deep emotions or different points of view, then it is probably not a suitable topic for small talk.

Small talk is also relatively short in duration. The context in which small talk occurs allows for only a brief interaction. Waiting in line to get into a movie, riding in an elevator, or stopping briefly in the hallway of a school on the way to class are the kinds of occasions that create small talk opportunities. The cocktail party, at which guests are meant to mingle and exchange pleasantries, is perhaps the classic example.

Another popular occasion, which is an exception to this short duration characteristic, is sitting next to someone on a long plane flight. Here, the small talk—assuming you keep it to small talk—can last for hours. Sometimes, as explained in the discussion of self-disclosure in Chapter 2, this situation produces a kind of "in-flight intimacy" in

JOURNAL
COMMUNICATION CHOICE POINT
Making Small Talk

You're on an elevator with three other people from your office building. The elevator gets stuck without any indication of when power will go back on. You figure now is the time for small talk. _What are some things you might say to make the situation more comfortable?_

which you engage in significant self-disclosure, revealing secrets you normally keep hidden, largely because you know you'll never see this person again.

GUIDELINES FOR EFFECTIVE SMALL TALK Although "small," this talk still requires the application of the communication skills for "big" talk. As already noted, remember that the best topics are noncontroversial and that most small talk is relatively brief. Here are a few additional guidelines for more effective small talk.

- **Be positive.** No one likes a negative doomsayer. So, comment on the weather when it's nice; move to another topic when it isn't.

- **Be sensitive to leave taking cues.** Small talk is necessarily brief, but at times one person may want it to be a preliminary to big talk and another person may see it as the sum of the interaction.

- **Stress similarities rather than differences.** This is a good way to ensure that the small talk stays noncontroversial.

- **Answer questions with enough elaboration to give the other person information to use to interact with you.** The more elaborate answer also signals your willingness to engage in small talk, whereas the simple "yes" response can be interpreted as indicating you don't want to interact.

- **Avoid monologuing.** Listen and be responsive to the other person. Even small talk is two-way and requires each person to talk and each person to listen. Remember the principles of turn-taking and dialogue.

- **Remember that you will be associated with the topics you frequently select to talk about.** If all your small talk concerns celebrity relationships, for example, then you might become defined as someone who is only interested in shallow gossip.

"**This is the nicest conversation we've had in weeks. Let's not spoil it by talking.**"

Copyright 2004 by Randy Glasbergen www.glasbergen.com.

Apologies

Despite your best efforts, there are times when you'll say or do the wrong thing and it may be necessary to offer an **apology**—an expression of regret or sorrow for having done what you did or for what happened, a statement that says you're sorry. And so, the most basic of all apologies is simply to say "I'm sorry." In popular usage, the apology includes some admission of wrongdoing on the part of the person making the apology. Sometimes the wrongdoing is acknowledged explicitly ("I'm sorry I lied") and sometimes only by implication ("I'm sorry you're so upset"). In many cases the apology also includes a request for forgiveness ("Please excuse me for being late") and some assurance that this won't happen again ("Please forgive my lateness; it won't happen again").

An effective apology must be crafted for the specific situation. An effective apology to a longtime lover, to a parent, or to a new supervisor are likely to be very different because the individuals are different and your relationships are different. And so the first rule of an effective apology is to take into consideration the uniqueness of the situation—the people, the context, the cultural rules, the relationship, the specific wrongdoing—for which you might want to apologize. Each situation will call for a somewhat different message of apology. Nevertheless, we can offer some general recommendations.

- **Admit wrongdoing** (if indeed wrongdoing occurred). Accept responsibility. Take ownership of your actions; don't try to pass

VIEWPOINTS: Social Media Apologizing
What kinds of apologies do you see on social media sites? In what ways are apologies online different from face-to-face apologies?

them off as the work of someone else. Instead of "Smith drives so slow, it's a wonder I'm only 30 minutes late," say "I should have taken traffic into consideration."

- **Be apologetic.** Say (and mean) the words *I'm sorry*. Don't justify your behavior by mentioning that everyone does it. For example, don't say "Everyone leaves work early on Friday." And don't justify your behavior by saying that the other person has done something equally wrong: "So I play poker; you play the lottery."

- **Be specific.** State, in specific rather than general terms, what you've done. Instead of "I'm sorry for what I did," say "I'm sorry for flirting at the party."

- **Empathize.** Express understanding of how the other person feels and acknowledge the legitimacy of these feelings: "You have every right to be angry; I should have called." Express your regret that this has created a problem for the other person: "I'm sorry I made you miss your appointment." Don't minimize the problem that this may have caused. Avoid comments such as "So the figures arrived a little late. What's the big deal?"

- **Give assurance that this will not happen again.** Say, quite simply, "It won't happen again" or, better and more specifically, "I won't be late again." And, whenever possible, offer to correct the problem: "I'm sorry I didn't clean up the mess I made; I'll do it now."

- **Avoid excuses.** Be wary of including excuses with your apology: "I'm sorry the figures are late, but I had so much other work to do." An excuse often takes back the apology and says, in effect, I'm really not sorry because there was good reason for what I did, but I'm saying "I'm sorry" to cover all my bases and to make this uncomfortable situation go away.

- **Choose the appropriate channel.** Don't take the easy way out and apologize through e-mail (unless the wrongdoing was committed in e-mail or if e-mail is your only or main form of communication). Generally, it's more effective to use a more personal mode of communication—face-to-face or phone, for example. It's harder but it's more effective.

Compliments

A **compliment** is a message of praise, flattery, or congratulations. It can be expressed in face-to-face interaction or on social media sites when, for example, you retweet someone's post or indicate "like" or "+1" or when you comment on a blog post. The compliment functions like a kind of interpersonal glue; it's a way of relating to another person with positiveness and immediacy. It's also a conversation starter: "I like your watch; may I ask where you got it?" Another purpose the compliment serves is to encourage the other person to compliment you—even if not immediately (which often seems inappropriate).

Compliments can be unqualified or qualified. The unqualified compliment is a message that is purely positive: "Your paper was just great, an A." The qualified message is not entirely positive: "Your paper was great, an A; if not for a few problems, it would have been an A+." You might also give a qualified compliment by qualifying your own competence: "That song you wrote sounded great, but I really don't know anything about music."

Compliments are sometimes difficult to give and even more difficult to respond to without discomfort or embarrassment. Here are some guidelines.

GIVING A COMPLIMENT   Here are a few suggestions for giving a compliment:

- **Be real and honest.** Say what you mean and refrain from giving compliments you don't believe in. They'll probably sound insincere.

- **Compliment in moderation.** A compliment that is too extreme (for example, "That's the best decorated apartment I've ever seen in my life")

VIEWPOINTS: What Do You Compliment?
Some interpersonal watchers recommend that you compliment people for their accomplishments rather than for who they are or for things over which they have no control. *With this recommendation in mind, what are some of the things that might be appropriately complimented in the home? In the workplace? What would be some of the things that would be inappropriate to compliment at home or at the workplace?*

may be viewed as dishonest. Similarly, don't compliment at every possible occasion; if you do, your compliments will seem too easy to win and not really meaningful.

- **Be totally complimentary; avoid qualifying your compliments.** If you hear yourself giving a compliment and then adding *but* or *however*, stop and rethink what you are going to say. Many people will remember the qualification rather than the compliment, and it will instead feel like a criticism.
- **Be specific.** Direct your compliment at something specific rather than something general. Instead of saying, "I liked your story," you might say, "I liked your story—it made me realize something I had forgotten. …"
- **Be personal in your own feelings**—"Your song really moved me; it made me recall so many good times." But don't be personal about the other person: "Your hair looks so natural; is that a weave or a toupee?"

RECEIVING A COMPLIMENT   In receiving a compliment, people generally take either one of two options: denial or acceptance. Many people deny the compliment ("It's nice of you to say, but I know I was terrible"), minimize it ("It isn't like I wrote the great American novel; it was just an article that no one will read"), change the subject ("So, where should we go for dinner?"), or say nothing. Each of these responses denies the legitimacy of the compliment. Accepting the compliment is a much better alternative. An acceptance might be communicated in three ways: (1) just smile, with eye contact—avoid looking at the floor, (2) simply say "thank you," and (3) offer a personal reflection in which you explain (very briefly) why the compliment is important to you ("I really appreciate your comments; I worked hard on the project and it's great to hear it was effective").

Summary of Concepts and Skills

This chapter explored interpersonal communication and the principles of conversation and some common everyday conversations.

Preliminaries to Interpersonal Communication and conversation

6.1   Define *interpersonal communication* and explain the interpersonal continuum and the stages of conversation.

1. Interpersonal communication is communication that occurs between two people who have a relationship and who are thus influenced by each other's communication messages.
2. Interpersonal communication is along a continuum ranging from relatively impersonal to highly personal
3. The process of conversation consists of five general stages: opening, feedforward, business, feedback, and closing.

The Principles of Conversation

6.2   Explain the principles of cooperation, politeness, turn-taking, dialogue, and immediacy in conversation.

4. The principle of cooperation expects both speaker and listener to try to understand each other.

5. We expect conversation to follow the general rules of politeness.
6. Speakers regulate the conversation through two major types of cues: turn-maintaining cues and turn-yielding cues. Listeners regulate the conversation by using three types of cues: turn-requesting cues, turn-denying cues, and back-channeling cues and interruptions.
7. Dialogue is conversation in which there is genuine two-way interaction; each person is both speaker and listener, sender and receiver. Monologue communication is the opposite: One person speaks and the other listens—there's no real interaction between participants.
8. Immediacy is the creation of closeness, a sense of togetherness, between speaker and listener.

Everyday Conversations

6.3   Paraphrase the suggestions for making small talk, apologizing, and complimenting.

9. Small talk is pervasive, noncontroversial, and often serves as a polite way of introducing yourself or a topic.
10. Apologies are expressions of regret or sorrow for having done what you did or for what happened.

11. A compliment is a message of praise, flattery, or congratulations and often enables you to interact with positiveness and immediacy.

Consider your competence in using the skills of effective interpersonal communication and conversation. Place a check mark next to those skills you want to work on most.

_____ 1. I understand that conversation occurs in stages and that each stage serves a different function.

_____ 2. I follow the principles of turn-taking in conversation, giving appropriate speaker and listener cues and responding to the cues of others.

_____ 3. I engage in dialogic rather than monologic conversation.

_____ 4. I adjust my immediacy cues as appropriate to the conversation and the relationship.

_____ 5. I can engage in small talk in a variety of situations with comfort and ease.

_____ 6. I can formulate effective apologies and can use them appropriately in interpersonal interactions.

_____ 7. I can extend and receive a compliment graciously.

Key Terms

apology
back-channeling cues
compliment
conversational turns
dialogue
feedback
feedforward
immediacy
interpersonal communication
interruptions

manner principle
maxim of agreement
maxim of approbation
maxim of generosity
maxim of modesty
maxim of sympathy
maxim of tact
metacommunication
monologue
principle of cooperation

quality principle
quantity principle
relation principle
small talk
turn-denying cues
turn-maintaining cues
turn-requesting cues
turn-yielding cues

Skill Development Experiences

6.1 Opening and Closing a Conversation

Opening and closing conversations can be difficult; the way you handle these steps will help to create a lasting impression.

Consider, first, a few situations in which you might want to open a conversation. For each situation develop a possible opening message in which you seek to accomplish one or more of the following: (a) telling others that you're accessible and open to communication, (b) showing that you're friendly, or (c) showing that you like the other person.

1. You're one of the first guests to arrive at a friend's party and are now there with several other people to whom you've only just been introduced. Your friend, the host, is busy with other matters.

2. In surfing through your Facebook photos you decide that you want to get to know better someone for a possible romantic relationship. This friend-of-a-friend-of-a-friend who friended you a while back and to whom you paid no attention, now seems just the right potential partner. You've never communicated directly before.

Here are two situations in which you might want to bring a conversation to a close. For each situation, develop a possible closing message in which you seek to accomplish one or more of the following: (a) end the conversation without much more talk, (b) leave the other person with a favorable impression of you, or (c) keep the channels of communication open for future interaction.

1. You and a friend have been talking on the phone for the past hour, but not much new is being said. You have a great deal of work to do and want to wrap it up. Your friend just doesn't seem to hear your subtle cues.

2. You're at a party and are anxious to meet a person with whom you've exchanged eye contact for the past ten minutes. The problem is that a friendly and talkative older relative of yours is demanding all your attention. You don't want to insult your relative, but at the same time you want to make contact with this other person.

6.2 Making Small Talk

Small talk comes easy to some but is very difficult for others.

Here are a few occasions for small talk. What do you say (if anything)?

1. You're on a cross-continental flight and feel it would be nice to talk with the person you'll be sitting next to for the next five hours.

2. You're on the elevator with someone who works for the same company but with whom you've never talked.

3. You arrive early for class and three other students are in the room. No one is talking.

4. You're in a coffee shop where people sit at long communal tables and stare at their smartphones and tablets.

5. You're online at a supermarket and the cashier's computer goes down; it will be a three or four minute wait.

6.3 Making Apologies

Apologies will not reverse your errors, but they may help repair—at least to some extent— conversational or relationship damage.

Like excuses, apologies are an inevitable part of relationships—friendships, romantic, and family. In making an apology, consider, for example, How important is the other person to you? How important was your error? Will you have to do something as well as say something?

1. You posted an unflattering/revealing photo of your friend on your Facebook wall.

2. You revealed a friend's secret that you had promised to keep confidential.

3. You turned down a date saying you didn't feel well and later that evening, on a date with another person, you run into the person you told you were ill.

6.4 Giving and Receiving Compliments

Compliments are powerful relationship builders.

How would you express a compliment in each of these situations? How would you respond to the compliment you just gave someone else if the compliment was addressed to you?

1. Your blind date shows up and is a lot more attractive than you ever expected.

2. You had a great dinner at a colleague's home.

3. Your friend just lost weight and looks great.

Chapter 7
Interpersonal Relationships

Relationships are a universal need.

CHAPTER OUTLINE	Learning Objectives
Advantages and Disadvantages of Interpersonal Relationships	**7.1** Explain the advantages and disadvantages of interpersonal relationships.
The Stages of Interpersonal Relationships	**7.2** Explain the stages of interpersonal relationships and provide examples of the types of messages that occur at each stage.
Interpersonal Relationship Types	**7.3** Define *friendship, love, family, workplace,* and *online-only relationships.*
Theories of Interpersonal Communication and Relationships	**7.4** Explain the theories of attraction, rules, social exchange, and equity.

Contact with other human beings is so important that when you're deprived of it for long periods, depression sets in, self-doubt surfaces, and you may find it difficult to manage even the basics of daily life. Research shows clearly that the most important contributor to happiness—outranking money, job, and sex—is a close relationship with one other person (Freedman, 1978; Laroche & deGrace, 1997; Lu & Shih, 1997). The desire for relationships is universal; interpersonal relationships are important to men and to women, to homosexuals and to heterosexuals, to young and to old (Huston & Schwartz, 1995). Not surprisingly, this seems the principal motivation for much of social media communication.

This chapter looks at some of the advantages and disadvantages of interpersonal relationships, the stages of relationships, the varied types of relationships, theories that explain why we enter and exit relationships, and the influence of culture, technology, and work on our relationships.

Advantages and Disadvantages of Interpersonal Relationships

7.1   **Explain the advantages and disadvantages of interpersonal relationships.**

A good way to begin the study of interpersonal relationships is to examine your own relationships (past, present, or those you look forward to) by asking yourself what your relationships do for you. What are the advantages and the disadvantages? Visualize a 10-point scale on which 1 indicates that your relationship(s) never serves this function, 10 indicates that your relationship(s) always serves this function, and the numbers in between indicate levels between these extremes. You may wish to do this twice—once for your face-to-face relationships and once for your online relationships.

_____ **1.** My relationships help to lessen my loneliness.
_____ **2.** My relationships help me gain in self-knowledge and in self-esteem.
_____ **3.** My relationships help enhance my physical and emotional health.
_____ **4.** My relationships maximize my pleasures and minimize my pains.
_____ **5.** My relationships help me to secure stimulation (intellectual, physical, and emotional).

Let's elaborate just a bit on each of these commonly accepted advantages of interpersonal communication:

1. One of the major benefits of relationships is that they help to lessen loneliness (Rokach, 1998; Rokach & Brock, 1995). They make you feel that someone cares, that someone likes you, that someone will protect you, that someone ultimately will love you.

2. Through contact with others you learn about yourself and see yourself from different perspectives and in different roles, as a child or parent, as a coworker, as a manager, as a best friend. Healthy interpersonal relationships help enhance self-esteem and self-worth. Simply having a friend or romantic partner (at least most of the time) makes you feel desirable and worthy.

3. Research consistently shows that interpersonal relationships contribute significantly to physical and emotional health (Goleman, 1995; Pennebacker, 1991; Rosen, 1998; Rosengren, 1993) and to personal happiness (Berscheid & Reis, 1998). Without close interpersonal relationships you're more likely to become depressed—and this depression, in turn, contributes significantly to physical

VIEWPOINTS: **Parasocial Relationships**

Parasocial relationships are relationships that audience members perceive themselves to have with media personalities (Rubin & McHugh, 1987; Giles, 2001; Giles & Maltby, 2004). At times viewers develop these relationships with real media personalities and at other times the relationship is with a fictional character in a television drama or novel. *What's your view of parasocial relationships? Are there advantages to these relationships? Disadvantages?*

JOURNAL
COMMUNICATION CHOICE POINT
Advantages and Disadvantages

In addition to relationships having general advantages and disadvantages, your own individual relationships will have specific advantages and disadvantages. *What are the "must haves" (the essential advantages you'd require in a long-lasting relationship) and what are the deal breakers (the disadvantages that you just couldn't put up with)?*

---

illness. Isolation, in fact, contributes as much to mortality as high blood pressure, high cholesterol, obesity, smoking, or lack of physical exercise (Goleman, 1995).

4. The most general function served by interpersonal relationships, and the function that encompasses all the others, is that of maximizing pleasure and minimizing pain. Your good friends, for example, will make you feel even better about your good fortune and less hurt when you're confronted with hardships.

5. As plants are heliotropic and orient themselves to light, humans are stimulotropic and orient themselves to sources of stimulation (Davis, 1973). Human contact is one of the best ways to secure this stimulation—intellectual, physical, and emotional. Even an imagined relationship seems better than none.

Now, respond to these sentences as you did to the above.

_____ 6. My relationships put uncomfortable pressure on me to expose my vulnerabilities.
_____ 7. My relationships increase my obligations.
_____ 8. My relationships prevent me from developing other relationships.
_____ 9. My relationships scare me because they may be difficult to dissolve.
_____ 10. My relationships hurt me.

These statements express what most people would consider disadvantages of interpersonal relationships.

6. Close relationships put pressure on you to reveal yourself and to expose your vulnerabilities. Although this is generally worthwhile in the context of a supporting and caring relationship, it may backfire if the relationship deteriorates and these weaknesses are used against you.

7. Close relationships increase your obligations to other people, sometimes to a great extent. Your time is no longer entirely your own. And although you enter relationships to spend more time with these special people, you also incur time (and perhaps financial) obligations with which you may not be happy.

8. Close relationships can lead you to abandon other relationships. Sometimes the other relationship involves someone you like, but your partner can't stand. More often, however, it's simply a matter of time and energy; relationships take a lot of both and you have less to give to these other and less intimate relationships.

9. The closer your relationships, the more emotionally difficult they are to dissolve, a feeling that may be uncomfortable for some people. If a relationship is deteriorating, you may feel distress or depression. In some cultures, for example, religious pressures may prevent married couples from separating. And if considerable money is involved, dissolving a relationship can often mean giving up the fortune you've spent your life accumulating.

10. And, of course, your partner may break your heart. Your partner may leave you—against all your pleading and promises. Your hurt will be in proportion to how much you care and need your partner. If you care a great deal, you're likely to experience great hurt; if you care less, the hurt will be less—it's one of life's little ironies.

The Stages of Interpersonal Relationships

7.2   **Explain the stages of interpersonal relationships and provide examples of the types of messages that occur at each stage.**

As a preface to this discussion, realize that different cultures will view relationships very differently. What is presented here is generally derived from research conducted in the United States, and so, for example, the assumption made is that you voluntarily choose your relationship partners—that you consciously choose to pursue certain relationships and not others. In some cultures, however, your parents choose your romantic partner for you. In some cases your husband or wife is chosen to unite two families or to bring some financial advantage to your family or village.

In the United States, researchers study and textbook authors write about dissolving relationships and how to survive relationship breakups. It's generally assumed that you have the right to exit an undesirable relationship. However, in some cultures you simply cannot dissolve a relationship once it has been formed or once there are children. More important to such cultures may be issues such as how to maintain a relationship that has problems, what to do to survive in an unpleasant relationship, and how to repair a troubled relationship (Moghaddam, Taylor, & Wright, 1993).

You and another person don't become intimate friends immediately on meeting. Rather, you build an intimate relationship gradually, through a series of steps or stages. The same is true of most relationships.

The model in Figure 7.1 describes the six main stages in relationships: contact, involvement, intimacy, deterioration, repair, and dissolution, each of which has an early and a late phase. These stages describe relationships as they are; they don't evaluate or prescribe how relationships should be. For a particular relationship, you might wish to modify the basic model, but as a general description the stages seem fairly standard. They are also applicable generally to face-to-face as well as to online relationships. As you read about these stages, keep in mind that both partners may not perceive their relationship in the same way; one person, for example, may see the relationship as having reached the intimate stage and the other may not.

Social network sites seem to recognize this stage nature of relationships by enabling you to treat your online "friends" differently. For example, the circles on Google+ and the "friends lists" on Facebook enable you to group people on the basis of the information that you want them to be able to access. This makes it very easy to distinguish acquaintances from intimate friends, for example, as well as family from friends from workplace colleagues.

Contact

At the initial phase of the **contact** stage, there is some kind of *perceptual contact*—you see, hear, and perhaps smell the person. From this you get a physical picture: gender, approximate age, height, and so on. Or you might browse a group of photos and profiles from an online dating site. After this perception there is usually *interactional contact*, which is superficial and relatively impersonal. This is the stage at which you exchange basic information that is preliminary to any more intense involvement ("Hello, my name is Joe."); you initiate interaction ("May I join you?") and engage in invitational communication ("May I buy you coffee?"). With online relationships, each of you will have read the other's profile and so will know quite a lot about each other before you even begin to talk. According to some researchers, it's at this stage— within the first four minutes of initial interaction—that you decide whether you want to pursue the relationship (Zunin & Zunin, 1972). At the contact stage, physical appearance is especially important, because it's the characteristic most readily seen. Yet, through verbal and nonverbal behaviors, personal qualities such as friendliness,

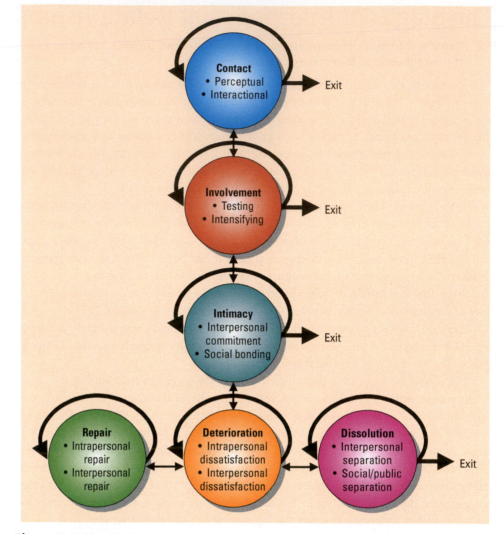

Figure 7.1 The Six Stages of Relationships

Because relationships differ so widely, it's best to think of this or any relationship model as a tool for talking about relationships rather than as a specific map that indicates how you move from one relationship position to another. What happens when the two people in a relationship experience the stages differently? Can you provide an example from literature or from your own experience?

warmth, openness, and dynamism are also revealed. With online relations people may profile themselves as warm or open or dynamic and, as a result, you may actually see the person's messages confirming this labeling.

Involvement

At the **involvement** stage a sense of mutuality, of being connected, develops. Here you experiment and try to learn more about the other person. At the initial phase of involvement, a kind of *testing* goes on. You want to see whether your initial judgment proves reasonable. You may ask questions: "Where do you work?" "What are you majoring in?" If you want to get to know the person even better, you might continue your involvement by intensifying your interaction and by beginning to reveal yourself, though in a preliminary way. In a dating relationship, you might, for example, use a variety of strategies to help you move to the next stage and perhaps to intimacy.

Here, you're committed to getting to know someone even better and so you might follow that person on Twitter or read the postings, photos, and causes, for example, on Facebook. And at this stage you continue your involvement by intensifying your interaction; the texting becomes more frequent, the Facebook postings become more complimentary and more frequent, and the photos exchanged become increasingly more personal and revealing.

For example, you might increase contact with your partner; give your partner tokens of affection, such as gifts, cards, or flowers; write affectionate messages on a person's Facebook wall; increase your own personal attractiveness; do things that suggest intensifying the relationship, such as flirting or making your partner jealous; and become more physically intimate (Tolhuizen, 1989).

Intimacy

The contact and involvement stages make up **relationship development**—a movement toward intimacy. At the **intimacy** stage you commit yourself still further to the other person and establish a relationship in which this individual becomes your best or closest friend, lover, or companion. Because intimacy is essentially an emotional/communication connection, it can occur in face-to-face and in online relationships equally. You also come to share each other's social networks, a practice followed by members of widely different cultures (Gao & Gudykunst, 1995). This is seen most clearly on social network sites where the site itself identifies people with whom you might want to become "friends" based on mutual friends or interests. Both the quantity and the quality of your interpersonal exchanges increase (Emmers-Sommer, 2004), and of course you also talk more and in greater detail about the relationship (Knobloch, Haunani, & Theiss, 2006). Not surprisingly, your relationship satisfaction also increases with the move to this stage (Siavelis & Lamke, 1992). One research study defined intimacy as the feeling that you can be honest and open when talking about yourself, sharing thoughts and feelings that you don't reveal in other relationships (Mackey, Diemer, & O'Brien, 2000).

The intimacy stage usually divides itself into two phases. In the *interpersonal commitment phase*, the two people commit themselves to each other in a private way. In the *social bonding phase*, the commitment is made public—perhaps to family and friends, perhaps to the public at large, perhaps with a simple "married to" on Facebook. Here you and your partner become a unit, an identifiable pair.

> **JOURNAL**
> **COMMUNICATION CHOICE POINT**
> Moving through Relationship Stages
>
> Your current romantic partner seems to be moving too fast for your liking. You want to take things a lot slower, yet you don't want to turn this person off; this may be The One. *What might you say (and where and through what channel might you say it) to get your partner to proceed more slowly?*

Deterioration

The relationship deterioration stage is characterized by a weakening of the bonds between the friends or lovers. The first phase of **deterioration** is usually *intrapersonal dissatisfaction*: You begin to experience personal dissatisfaction with everyday interactions and begin to view the future with your partner more negatively. If this dissatisfaction grows, you pass to the second phase, *interpersonal deterioration*. You withdraw and grow further and further apart. You share less of your free time. You exchange fewer messages. When you're together, there are awkward silences, fewer disclosures, less physical contact, and a lack of psychological closeness. Conflicts become more common and their resolution more difficult.

Relationship deterioration involves unique communication patterns. During the deterioration stage you may, for example, increase withdrawal, communicate less, respond to Facebook pokes and requests for "likes" less often; texting becomes infrequent, and face-to-face meetings are fewer. In communication, each person reduces his or her level of self-disclosure. These patterns are in part a response to the deterioration; you communicate the way you do because you feel that your relationship is in trouble. However, these patterns are also causative: The communication patterns you use largely determine the fate of your relationship.

Repair

At this stage of a relationship, some partners may pause during deterioration and try to seek **repair**. Others, however, may progress without stopping to dissolution.

At the first repair phase, *intrapersonal repair*, you analyze what went wrong and consider ways of solving your relational difficulties. You might at this stage consider changing your behaviors or perhaps changing your expectations of your partner. You might also evaluate the rewards of your relationship as it is now and the rewards to be gained if your relationship ended.

Should you decide that you want to repair your relationship, you might move to the *interpersonal repair phase*—you might discuss with your partner the problems in the relationship, the changes you want to see, and perhaps what you'd be willing to do and what you'd want your partner to do. This is the stage of negotiating new agreements and new behaviors. You and your partner might try to repair your relationship by yourselves, or you might seek the advice of friends, family, or relationship therapists.

Fortunately, social media sites offer considerable help in making relationship repair by providing ready access to cards and virtual gifts, for example, to help you express your desire to repair the relationship.

Dissolution

Dissolution—the last stage in the relationship model—involves cutting the bonds that tie you together. In the beginning it usually takes the form of *interpersonal separation*: If it's an online friendship, you might de-friend or uncircle or perhaps, most often, just cut off communication. You might move into your own apartments and begin to lead separate lives. If the separation works better than the original relationship, you enter the phase of *social* or *public separation*. Avoidance of each other and a return to a "single" status are among the primary characteristics of the dissolution of a relationship.

Interpersonal Relationship Types

7.3   **Define** *friendship, love, family, workplace,* **and** *online-only relationships.*

Each relationship, whether friendship or love, for example, is unique. Yet there are general types that research has identified—and these categories will offer considerable insight into your own interpersonal relationships. Here we consider friendship, love, family, work, and online-only relationships.

Friendship

One theory of **friendship** identifies three major types that we can easily see in our own face-to-face and online relationships: (1) friendship of reciprocity, (2) friendship of receptivity, and (3) friendship of association (Reisman 1979, 1981).

- The **friendship of reciprocity**, the ideal type, is characterized by loyalty, self-sacrifice, mutual affection, and generosity. This type of friendship is based on equality, where each individual shares equally in giving and receiving the benefits and rewards of the relationship.

- In the **friendship of receptivity**, in contrast, there is an imbalance in giving and receiving; one person is the primary giver and the other the primary receiver. This is a positive imbalance, however, because each

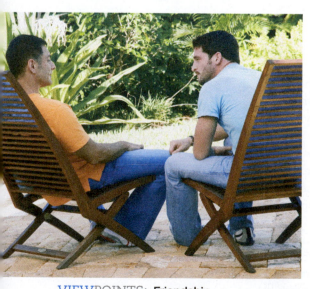

VIEWPOINTS: Friendship

How would you classify your friendships? Can you identify three or four different types of friends that you have?

person gains something from the relationship. The different needs of both the person who receives affection and the person who gives it are satisfied. This is the friendship that may develop between a teacher and a student or between a doctor and a patient. In fact, a difference in status is essential for the friendship of receptivity to develop.

- The **friendship of association** is transitory; it might be described as a friendly relationship rather than a true friendship. Associative friendships are the kind you have with classmates, neighbors, or coworkers. There is no great loyalty, no great trust, no great giving or receiving. The association is cordial but not intense.

"We broke up, Stuart—don't you read your e-mail?"

David Sipress/The New Yorker Collection/The Cartoon Bank

Love

Like friendships, **love** (an interpersonal relationship in which you feel closeness, caring, warmth, and excitement) comes in different styles as well. Six primary love styles have been identified: **eros, ludic, storge, pragma, manic,** and **agapic** (Lee, 1976; Hendrick & Hendrick, 1990).

- **Eros love** seeks beauty and sensuality and focuses on physical attractiveness, sometimes to the exclusion of qualities others might consider more important and more lasting. The erotic lover has an idealized image of beauty that is unattainable in reality. Consequently, the erotic lover often feels unfulfilled.

- **Ludic love** seeks entertainment and excitement and sees love as fun, a game. To the ludic lover, love is not to be taken too seriously; emotions are to be held in check lest they get out of hand and make trouble. The ludic lover retains a partner only so long as the partner is interesting and amusing. When the partner is no longer interesting enough, it's time to change.

- **Storge love** is a peaceful and tranquil love. Like ludic love, storge lacks passion and intensity. Storgic lovers set out not to find a lover but to establish a companionable relationship with someone they know and with whom they can share interests and activities. Storgic love is a gradual process of unfolding thoughts and feelings and is sometimes difficult to distinguish from friendship.

- **Pragma love** is practical and traditional and seeks compatibility and a relationship in which important needs and desires will be satisfied. The pragma lover is concerned with the social qualifications of a potential mate even more than with personal qualities; family and background are extremely important to the pragma lover, who relies not so much on feelings as on logic.

- **Manic love** is an obsessive love that needs to give and receive constant attention and affection. When attention and affection are not constant, or when an expression of increased commitment is not returned, reactions such as depression, jealousy, and self-doubt can lead to extreme lows.

- **Agapic love** is compassionate and selfless. The agapic lover loves both the stranger on the road and the annoying neighbor. Jesus, Buddha, and Gandhi practiced and preached this unqualified spiritual love—a love that is offered without concern for personal reward or gain and without any expectation that the love will be reciprocated.

Men and women differ in the types of love they prefer (Hendrick, Hendrick, Foote, & Slapion-Foote, 1984). For example, men indicate a preference for erotic and ludic love, whereas women indicate a preference for manic, pragmatic, and storgic love. No difference was found for agapic love. Women and men seem to experience love to a similar degree (Rubin, 1973). However, women indicate greater love than men do for their same-sex friends. This may reflect a real difference between the sexes, or it may be a function of the greater social restrictions on men. A man is not supposed to admit his love for another man, but women are permitted to communicate their love for other women.

Family Relationships

Families are central to contemporary life. It will come as no surprise to note that families come in various configurations and are undergoing major changes. Table 7.1 provides a few findings from the U.S. Census to illustrate some of the major changes.

The communication principles that apply to the traditional nuclear family (i.e., the mother-father-child family) also apply to all family configurations. In the discussion that follows, the term *primary relationship* denotes the relationship between two principal parties—husband and wife, husband-husband, wife-wife, lovers, or domestic partners, for example—and the term *family* may denote a broader constellation that includes children, relatives, and assorted significant others.

A **primary relationship** is a relationship between two people that the partners see as their most important interpersonal relationship. An interesting typology of primary relationships (based on more than 1,000 couples' responses to questions concerning their degree of sharing, their space needs, their conflicts, and the time they spend together) identifies three basic types: **traditional couples, independents**, and **separates** (Fitzpatrick, 1983, 1988, 1991; Noller & Fitzpatrick, 1993).

- **Traditional couples** share a basic belief system and philosophy of life. They see themselves as a blending of two persons into a single couple rather than as two separate individuals. They're interdependent and believe that each individual's independence must be sacrificed for the good of the relationship. In their communications, traditionals are highly responsive to each other. They lean toward each other, smile, talk a lot, interrupt each other, and finish each other's sentences.

- **Independents** stress their individuality. The relationship is important, but never more important than each person's individual identity. Although independents spend a great deal of time together, they don't ritualize it, for example, with schedules. Each individual spends time with outside friends. The communication between independents is responsive. They engage in conflict openly and without fear. Their disclosures are quite extensive and include high-risk and negative disclosures that are typically absent among traditionals.

- **Separates** live together, but they view their relationship more as a matter of convenience than a result of their mutual love or closeness. They seem to have little desire to be together and, in fact, usually are together only at ritual occasions such as mealtime or holiday get-togethers. It's important to these separates that each has his or her own physical as well as psychological space. The most significant characteristic of this type is that each person sees himself or herself as a separate individual and not as a part of a "we."

Table 7.1 The American Family in 2010–2011

Here are several findings on the American family from the U.S. Census. For each finding, indicate what you think the reasons for these changes might be and the possible trends they indicate. In one sentence of not more than 140 characters, summarize the changes you see happening in the American family.

- The percentage of one-person households was 27% (from 25% in 1990).
- The percentage of multigenerational households was 16% (from 14% in 1990).
- The percentage of births by unmarried women was 41% (from 26% in 1990).
- Fifty percent of women who marry did so at age 26 (up from age 24 in 1990).
- Two percent of people indicated being mixed race (up from 1.6% in 2000).
- In 2011, 59% of men and 50% of women between the ages of 18 and 24 live with their parents (compared to 53% of men and 46% of women of the same ages in 2005).
- In 2010, 51% of all adults were married (compared to 57% of all adults in 2000).
- In 2010, the average size of a family was 2.59; in 2000, it was 2.62.

Like couples, families can also be classified in any number of ways—for example, according to the number of people in the family, their affectional orientation, the presence or absence of children or of extended family members. In a communication-oriented typology (Koerner & Fitzpatrick, 1997, 2004) family types are looked at in terms of conformity and conversation.

Conformity-orientation refers to the degree to which family members express similar or dissimilar attitudes, values, and beliefs. So, we can speak of high-conformity families as those who express highly similar attitudes, beliefs, and values and try to avoid conflict, and low-conformity families as those whose members express highly divergent attitudes, beliefs, and values and may frequently engage in conflict interactions. As you can appreciate, families high in conformity are likely to be harmonious with children who are expected to obey their parents, largely without question. Families low in conformity are likely to be less harmonious with children who are given greater freedom to say or do as they wish.

Conversation-orientation refers to the degree to which family members can speak their mind. A family high on conversation orientation encourages members to discuss a variety of issues and the voicing of members' opinions. A family low on conversation orientation discourages discussion and the voicing of opinions.

With these two dimensions in mind, we can identify four types of families:

- **Consensual families**: high in conversation and high in conformity. These families encourage open communication and agreement.
- **Protective families**: high in conformity and low in conversation. These families stress agreement and strive to avoid conflict but with little communication.
- **Pluralistic families**: low in conformity and high in conversation. These family members are encouraged to express different attitudes and points of view and to engage in open communication while being supportive of each other.
- **Laissez-faire families**: low in confirmation and low in conversation. These families avoid interaction and communication, encourage privacy, and a "do what you want" attitude.

These family types are simply descriptions and are not meant to be evaluation; no assumption is made that one family type is better or more productive than another. What works for some people will not work for others.

Work Relationships

Workplace relationships come in a variety of types. Here we'll consider just four: we'll begin with the more positive relationships (networking, mentoring, and romance) and conclude with the negative bullying.

NETWORKING RELATIONSHIPS **Networking** can be viewed as a process of using other people to help you solve your problems, or at least to offer insights that bear on any number of problems or decisions you need to make. The most popular image that probably comes to mind is networking for a possible job. But networking is much broader and would include, for example, how to set up a blog, where to look for low-cost auto insurance, how to find an affordable apartment, or how to politely refuse an invitation to become a friend on Facebook. The great value of networking, of course, is that it provides you with access to a wealth of specialized information. At the same time, it often makes accessing that information a lot easier than if you had to find it all by yourself.

In networking it's often recommended that you try to establish relationships that are mutually beneficial. After all, much as others

"Well it doesn't look like networking to me!"

John Morris/CartoonsStock.com

are useful sources of information for you, you're likely to be a useful source of information for others. If you can provide others with helpful information, it's more likely that they will provide helpful information for you. In this way, a mutually satisfying and productive network is established.

MENTORING RELATIONSHIPS **Mentoring** is a partnership in which an experienced individual (the mentor) helps someone who is less experienced (the protégé) learn how to achieve his or her goals (Mullen, 2005; Caproni, 2012). Having a mentor, some organizational experts argue, is crucial for rising in a hierarchy and for developing your skills (Dahle, 2004). An accomplished teacher, for example, might mentor a younger teacher who has newly arrived or who has never taught before (Nelson, Pearson, & Kurylo, 2008). The mentor guides the new person through the organizational maze, teaches the strategies and techniques for success, and otherwise communicates his or her accumulated knowledge and experience to the protégé.

Not surprisingly, mentoring is frequently conducted online. One great advantage of e-mentoring is the flexibility it allows for communication. E-mail messages, for example, can be sent and received at times that are convenient for the individuals involved Stewart, 2006). Further, because the individuals may be separated geographically, it's possible to have mentor-protégé relationships with people in foreign countries and in widely differing cultures—relationships that would be impossible without online communication. Still another advantage is that persons with disabilities (whether mentor or protégé) who cannot easily travel can still enjoy and profit from e-mentoring relationships (Burgstahler, 2007).

Social networking sites, designed originally as places where people could make new friends and stay in touch with old ones, are increasingly being used for both mentoring and networking. Some sites are "by invitation only" and have been compared to gated communities or exclusive country clubs. These sites seem designed not for friendships but solely for mentoring and networking (MacMillan & Lehman, 2007). For example, Reuters Space is a private online community specifically for hedge fund managers to network, and INmobile is designed for executives in the wireless industry.

WORKPLACE ROMANCE Opinions vary widely concerning workplace romances. On the positive side, the work environment seems a perfect place to meet a potential romantic partner. After all, by virtue of the fact that you're working in the same office, you're probably both interested in the same field, have similar training and ambitions, and spend considerable time together—all factors that foster the development of a successful interpersonal relationship. Another advantage is that office romances can lead to greater work satisfaction. If you're romantically attracted to another worker, it can make going to work, working together, and even working added hours more enjoyable and more satisfying.

Office relationships, however, may cause problems for management when, for example, a promotion is to be made or relocation decisions are necessary. When an office romance goes bad or when it's one-sided, it can be especially difficult. One obvious problem is that it can be stressful for the former partners to see each other regularly

JOURNAL
COMMUNICATION CHOICE POINT
Awkward Gift

A coworker with whom you're becoming friendly gives you a very intimate gift, much too intimate for the relationship as you see it. *What are some things you might say to refuse the gift but not close off the possibility of dating?*

and to continue to work together. Other workers may feel they have to take sides, being supportive of one partner and critical of the other, which can cause friction throughout the organization. Another, perhaps more serious, issue is the potential for charges of sexual harassment, especially if the romance was between a supervisor and a worker.

The generally negative attitude of management (as well as explicit policies, rules, and regulations) toward workplace relationships and the problems inherent in dealing with the normal stresses of both work and romance seem to outweigh the positive benefits that may be derived from such relationships. Therefore, workers are generally advised not to romance their colleagues. Friendship seems the much safer course.

BULLYING   **Bullying**, especially prominent in the workplace (but also occurs in close relationships, the playground, or even the family), consists of abusive acts repeatedly committed by one person (or a group) against another. Bullying is behavior that has become a pattern; it's repeated frequently rather than being an isolated instance. On the playground, bullying often involves physical abuse; in the workplace (at least in most civilized countries), bullying is generally verbal. Bullying may take a variety of forms: gossiping about other employees, making them the butt of jokes, treating them as inferior—for example, frequently interrupting them or otherwise not giving their ideas due attention—excluding someone from social functions, verbal insults, name calling, negative facial expressions, sneering, avoiding eye contact, excessive blaming, being supervised (watched, monitored) more closely than others, being unnecessarily criticized, often with shouting and in public. From an ethical point of view, bullying destroys a person's right to personal dignity and a workplace free from intimidation and is therefore unethical. And yet, bullying is not illegal in the United States, unless it involves harassment based on a person's gender or race, for example.

A special type of bullying is cyberbullying, which can take place through any electronic communication system—Facebook, Twitter, e-mail, instant messages, blog posts—and can take the form of sending threatening messages or images, posting negative comments, revealing secrets, or lying about another person. Among the reasons why cyberbullying is so important is that it can occur at any time; the messages, photos, and videos can be distributed quickly and widely; the bully can hide behind false names or anonymity; and attacks—because they occur electronically—are often more cruel than those made in face-to-face attacks (Hinduja & Patchin, 2008).

Online-Only Relationships

In addition to the friendships, romantic, family, and workplace relationships—which will probably involve both face-to-face and online experiences—there is another group of what might be called **online-only relationships**. These are the relationships that exist between a Tweeter and a follower, a blogger and a reader, a friend or contact on Facebook or LinkedIn, for example. The suggestions for more effective relationships are the same as are the suggestions for more effective communication. In all of these relationships, it is dialogue (rather than monologue) that is emphasized. In fact, the defining characteristics of Web 2.0 is to move the online experience from monologue (for example, reading newspapers online) to dialogue (where commenting/reviewing/liking/+1ing) are essential parts of the communication experience.

TWEETING   Unlike other social network sites, people can follow you on Twitter whether you like it or not. But, assuming that you want some kind of relationships between yourself and those who follow you, consider these suggestions. In all of these lists of suggestions, the recommendations are generally applicable to all social networks and yet some seem more logically placed with one medium rather than another.

- Leave room for retweets (if you want retweets). Keep your tweet to 120 characters.
- Avoid "fast following" tools. These will likely create problems for you.
- Tweet items of interest to yourself but also keep in mind your readers.
- Treat criticism as the start of a dialogue rather than a personal attack.
- Tweet in moderation. Not everything that happens deserves a tweet.
- Tweet positively; avoid angry tweets.
- Create a complete profile; revealing what you want and keeping hidden what you don't want revealed.

VIEWPOINTS: Cyberbullying
According to the StopBullying website for the U.S. Department of Health and Human Service, a 2009 survey of 13- to 18-year-olds reported that 15 percent of respondents said they had been cyberbullied; in another study of 12- to 17-year-olds, 33 percent said they were threatened or embarrassed by things said about them online. *What has been your experience with cyberbullying? In what ways is this behavior encouraged? In what ways might it be discouraged?*

- Limit promotional materials; Twitter is personal.
- Retweet if you wish to be retweeted.

BLOGGING   Although many people view blogs as monologic, they are best viewed as dialogic. Their great value is in creating dialogue and so a blog post, at least for the traditional blog, is ideally one that provides information with a personal slant for a specific audience that creates some measure of discussion. Assuming that this is your aim or close to it, here are a few suggestions for making this a more effective interaction.

- Offer syndication. RSS feeds will greatly help in spreading the word.
- Be both informational and personal; blog posts are more personal in nature than are articles or websites that are more purely informational.
- Be consistent in style and format. It will help brand your blog as unique—not unlike McDonald's; readers will know what to expect.
- Build your blog and your posts around a theme. Posts unrelated to the theme are generally perceived as noise and are likely to lose you readers.
- Reply to comments. Dialogue.
- Track statistics so you can get insight into the posts that are read often and those that aren't.
- Create attractive titles and relevant identifying labels. Make it as easy as possible for others to retrieve your materials.

SOCIAL/WORKPLACE NETWORKING   Perhaps the social media that comes first to mind is Facebook, by far the largest of the social networking sites. But, Google+ and Myspace serve similar purposes as do numerous others. LinkedIn and Plaxo, on the other hand, serve mainly business purposes—for example, getting a job or promotion, finding likely candidates for a job, networking, or mentoring. Despite these differences, some similar suggestions govern effective relationships and communication in these types of sites.

- Be careful of uploading photos that will reflect on you negatively, especially with alcohol or drugs. Interesting enough, one research student found that 85 percent of 225 profiles examined (average age 19.9 years) made alcohol references (Egan & Moreno, 2011).
- Be positive about your current position. Complaining about your job online for all to see is likely to make management less positive toward you and also to lead prospective employers to see you as a complainer and someone who would be critical of the new organization as well.
- Avoid revealing any negative work habits or discussing inappropriate workplace behavior—even if (especially if) you think it's funny.
- Use the Friends List or the Google+ Circles to distinguish the people you want to see certain information and those you wouldn't. But, remember, again, that anyone who receives your message can post it to anyone, even those you'd rather not see it.
- Give your social network profile even more attention than you give to dressing up for a long-anticipated face-to-face date. After all, your online profile has more staying power than your outfit on any given night out.
- Keep your posts (at least on Facebook and Google+) personal and informative. Avoid promoting any commercial enterprise.
- Poke and tag in moderation. Learn first the norms of the group with which you're communicating.
- Avoid asking to be friends with anyone you think may have difficulty with your seeing their more personal side.

Theories of Interpersonal Communication and Relationships

7.4 **Explain the theories of attraction, rules, social exchange, and equity.**

Several theories offer insight into why and how people develop and dissolve relationships. Here we'll examine three such theories: attraction, relationship rules, and social exchange and equity.

Attraction Theory

Attraction theory holds that people form relationships on the basis of **attraction**. You are no doubt drawn, or attracted, to some people and not attracted to others. In a similar way, some people are attracted to you and some are not. If you're like most people, you're attracted to others on the basis of five major factors: **attractiveness, similarity, proximity, reinforcement**, and **reciprocity of liking**.

- **Physical attractiveness and personality:** It's easily appreciated that people like physically attractive people more than they like physically unattractive people. What isn't so obvious is that we also feel a greater sense of familiarity with more attractive people than with less attractive people; that is, we're more likely to think we've met a person before if that person is attractive (Monin, 2003). Additionally, you probably tend to like people who have a pleasant rather than an unpleasant personality, although people differ on what is an attractive personality to them and what isn't. The fact that different people find different personality characteristics attractive, that there does seem to be someone for everyone, may be a comforting thought.

- **Similarity:** According to the principle of **similarity**, if you could construct your mate, it's likely that your mate would look, act, and think very much like you (Burleson, Samter, & Luccetti, 1992; Burleson, Kunkel, & Birch, 1994). Generally, people like those who are similar to them in nationality, race, abilities, physical characteristics, intelligence, and attitudes (Pornpitakpan, 2003). Sometimes people are attracted to their opposites, in a pattern called **complementarity**: For example, a dominant person might be attracted to someone who is more submissive. Generally, however, people prefer those who are similar.

- **Proximity:** If you look around at people you find attractive, you will probably find that they are the people who live or work close to you. People who become friends are the people who have had the greatest opportunity to interact with each other.

- **Reinforcement:** You're attracted to people who give rewards or reinforcements, which can range from a simple compliment to an expensive cruise. You're also attracted to people you reward (Jecker & Landy, 1969; Aronson, Wilson, & Akert, 2013). That is, you come to like people for whom you do favors.

- **Reciprocity of liking:** You tend to be attracted to people you think are attracted to you; you come to like those who appear to like you. We initiate potential friendships and romantic relationships with people who we think like us, certainly not with those we think dislike us. We even like people who smile more than people who don't largely because the smile tells us that this person likes us. There is even evidence to show that people like "likers"—people who like others generally—more than they like people who don't express such liking (Eastwick & Finkel, 2009).

Relationship Rules Theory

You can gain an interesting perspective on interpersonal relationships by looking at them in terms of the rules that govern them (Shimanoff, 1980). The general assumption of **rules theory** is that relationships—friendship,

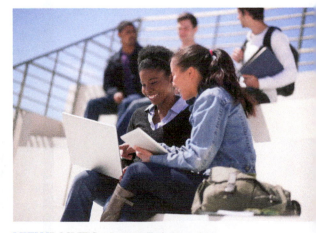

VIEWPOINTS: Online Relationships
Among the advantages of online relationships is that they reduce the importance of physical characteristics and instead emphasize such factors as rapport, similarity, and self-disclosure and in the process promote relationships that are based on emotional intimacy rather than physical attraction (Cooper & Sportolari, 1997). *What do you see as the main advantages of online relationships?*

love, family, and work—are held together by adherence to certain rules. When those rules are broken, the relationship may deteriorate and even dissolve.

Relationship rules theory helps to clarify several aspects of relationships. First, these rules help you identify successful versus destructive relationship behavior. By looking at the rules of a relationship, you can better identify the reasons a relationship is in trouble (i.e., what rules were broken) and how it may be repaired (i.e., what rules need to be reinforced and honored). Second, if you know what the rules are, you will be better able to master the social skills involved in developing and maintaining relationships.

FRIENDSHIP RULES   According to friendship rules theory, maintaining a friendship depends on your knowing the rules and having the ability to apply the appropriate interpersonal skills that friendships require (Trower, 1981; Blieszner & Adams, 1992). Friendship rules include such behaviors as standing up for your friend in his or her absence, sharing information and feelings about successes, demonstrating emotional support for your friend, trusting and offering to help your friend when in need, and trying to make your friend happy when you're together (Argyle & Henderson, 1984; Argyle, 1986). When these and other rules are followed, the friendship is strong and mutually satisfying. When the rules are broken, the friendship suffers and may die.

ROMANTIC RULES   Romantic relationships may also be viewed from a rules perspective. For example, one research study identified some of the rules that romantic relationships establish and follow (Baxter, 1986). These rules keep the relationship together—or, when broken, lead to deterioration and eventually dissolution. The general assumption here is that if people are in a close romantic relationship, then they should follow these rules.

- Acknowledge each other's individual identities and lives beyond the relationship.
- Express similar attitudes, beliefs, values, and interests.

Communicating Ethically
RELATIONSHIP ETHICS

A starting place for considering the ethical issues and guidelines that operate within a friendship or romantic, family, or workplace relationship can be identified with the acronym ETHICS: empathy (Cheney & Tompkins, 1987), talk (rather than force), honesty (Krebs, 1989), interaction management, confidentiality, and supportiveness (Johannesen, 2001).

- **Empathy:** People in relationships have an ethical obligation to empathize with their relationship partners.
- **Talk:** Decisions in a relationship should be arrived at by talk rather than by force—by persuasion, not coercion.
- **Honesty:** Relationship communication should be honest and truthful.
- **Interaction management:** Relationship communication should be satisfying and comfortable and is the responsibility of all individuals.
- **Confidentiality:** People have a right to expect that what they say in close relationships will not be revealed to others.
- **Supportiveness:** A supportive and cooperative climate should characterize the interpersonal interactions of people in relationships.

ETHICAL CHOICE POINT

A neighbor, with whom you're generally friendly, repeatedly wants you to listen to everything she did during the day—a kind of Twitter monologue. You just don't want to do this anymore. *What is your ethical obligation in this case—to your neighbor as well as to yourself?*

- Enhance each other's self-worth and self-esteem.
- Be open, genuine, and authentic with each other.
- Remain loyal and faithful to each other.
- Have substantial shared time together.
- Reap rewards commensurate with their investments relative to the other party.
- Experience a mysterious and inexplicable "magic" in each other's presence.

FAMILY RULES Family communication research also points to the importance of rules in defining and maintaining the family (Galvin, Braithwaite, & Bylund, 2015). Like the rules of friends and lovers, family rules tell you which behaviors will be rewarded (and therefore what you should do) and which will be punished (what you should not do). Rules also provide a kind of structure that defines the family as a cohesive unit and that distinguishes it from other similar families. Family rules encompass three main interpersonal communication issues (Satir, 1983):

- What can you talk about? Can you talk about the family finances? Grandpa's drinking? Your sister's lifestyle?
- How can you talk about something? Can you joke about your brother's lack of athletic ability? Can you address directly questions of family history and family skeletons?
- To whom can you talk? Can you talk openly to extended family members such as cousins and aunts and uncles? Can you talk to close neighbors about family health issues?

WORKPLACE RULES Rules also govern your workplace relationships. These rules are usually a part of the corporate culture that an employee would learn from observing other employees (especially those who move up the hierarchy) as well as from official memos on dress, sexual harassment, and the like. Of course, each organization will have different rules, so it's important to see what rules are operating in any given situation. These are among the rules that you might find:

- Work very hard.
- Be cooperative in teams; the good of the company comes first.
- Don't reveal company policies and plans to workers at competing firms.
- Don't form romantic relationships with other workers.
- Avoid even the hint of sexual harassment.

Social Exchange and Equity Theory

Social exchange theory claims that you develop relationships that will enable you to maximize your profits (Thibaut & Kelley, 1986; Stafford, 2008)—a theory based on an economic model of profits and losses. And, although the theory was formulated before social media, you'll see that it applies equally well to Facebook and Google+ relationships, for example. The theory begins with a simple equation: Profits = Rewards – Costs. Rewards are anything that you would incur costs to obtain. Research has identified six types of rewards in a relationship: money, status, love, information, goods, and services (Baron, Branscombe, & Byrne, 2009). For example, to get the reward of money, you might have to work rather than play. To earn (the status of) an A in an interpersonal communication course, you might have to write a term paper or study more than you want to.

Costs are things that you normally try to avoid, that you consider unpleasant or difficult. Examples might include working overtime, washing dishes and ironing

JOURNAL
COMMUNICATION CHOICE POINT
Virtual Infidelity

Although you've been in a monogamous relationship for the past 15 years, you have established romantic relationships online and suspect your partner has as well. You want to come clean now, but not give up these online affairs. *In your ideal world, what are some of the rules you would like to see you and your partner establish for online relationships?*

clothes, watching your partner's favorite television show that you find boring, or doing favors for those you dislike.

Equity theory uses the ideas of social exchange but goes a step farther and claims that you develop and maintain relationships in which the ratio of your rewards relative to your costs is approximately equal to your partner's (Walster, Walster, & Berscheid, 1978; Messick & Cook, 1983; Stafford, 2008). For example, if you and a friend start a business and you put up two-thirds of the money and your friend puts up one-third, equity would demand that you get two-thirds of the profits and your friend get one-third. An equitable relationship, then, is simply one in which each party derives rewards that are proportional to their costs. If you contribute more to the relationship than your partner, then equity requires that you should get greater rewards. If you both work equally hard, then equity demands that you should get approximately equal rewards. You also see the demand for equity in online relationships; if you indicate "like" or "+1" to a friend's photos or posts, you expect reciprocity; you expect equity. In fact social media have rather strict, though unwritten, equity expectations.

Equity theory puts into clear focus the sources of relational dissatisfaction seen every day. For example, in a relationship both partners may have full-time jobs, but one partner may also be expected to do the major share of the household chores. Thus, although both may be deriving equal rewards—they have equally good cars, they live in the same three-bedroom house, and so on—one partner is paying more of the costs. According to equity theory, this partner will be dissatisfied.

Equity theory claims that you will develop, maintain, and be satisfied with relationships that are equitable. You will not develop, will be dissatisfied with, and will eventually terminate relationships that are inequitable. The greater the inequity, the greater the dissatisfaction and the greater the likelihood that the relationship will end.

Table 7.2 presents a brief summary of these four theories of interpersonal relationships and the predictions they make about relationship development and deterioration.

Table 7.2 In a Nutshell Movement among the Stages as Predicted by Relationship Theories

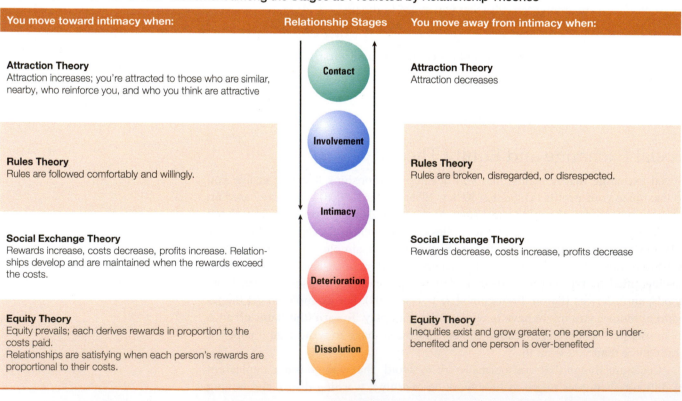

You move toward intimacy when:	Relationship Stages	You move away from intimacy when:
Attraction Theory Attraction increases; you're attracted to those who are similar, nearby, who reinforce you, and who you think are attractive	Contact	**Attraction Theory** Attraction decreases
Rules Theory Rules are followed comfortably and willingly.	Involvement	**Rules Theory** Rules are broken, disregarded, or disrespected.
Social Exchange Theory Rewards increase, costs decrease, profits increase. Relationships develop and are maintained when the rewards exceed the costs.	Intimacy / Deterioration	**Social Exchange Theory** Rewards decrease, costs increase, profits decrease
Equity Theory Equity prevails; each derives rewards in proportion to the costs paid. Relationships are satisfying when each person's rewards are proportional to their costs.	Dissolution	**Equity Theory** Inequities exist and grow greater; one person is under-benefited and one person is over-benefited

Summary of Concepts and Skills

This chapter explored interpersonal relationships—their stages and types; the reasons they are formed; and the influence of culture, technology, and work on relationships.

Advantages and Disadvantages of Interpersonal Relationships

7.1 Explain the advantages and disadvantages of interpersonal relationships.

1. Among the advantages are that relationships lessen loneliness and raise self-esteem.

2. Among the disadvantages are that relationships put pressure on you to expose weakness and increase your obligations.

The Stages of Interpersonal Relationships

7.2 Explain the stages of interpersonal relationships and provide examples of the types of messages that occur at each stage.

3. Relationships may be viewed in terms of six stages: contact, involvement, intimacy, deterioration, repair, and dissolution. Each of these stages can be further broken down into an early and a late phase.

4. Among the major causes of relationship deterioration are a lessening of the reasons for establishing the relationship, changes in the people involved, sexual difficulties, and work and financial problems.

Interpersonal Relationship Types

7.3 Define *friendship, love, family, workplace,* **and** *online-only relationships.*

5. Friendships may be classified as those of reciprocity, receptivity, and association.

6. Six primary love styles have been identified: eros, ludus, storge, pragma, mania, and agape.

7. Primary relationships may be classified into traditionals, independents, and separates; families as consensual, protective, pluralistic, and laissez-faire.

8. Work relationships can be productive (networking and mentoring), destructive (bullying), and both positive and negative (office romance).

9. Online-only relationships have their own sets of rules to promote more effective interaction.

Theories of Interpersonal Communication and Relationships

7.4 Explain the theories of attraction, rules, social exchange, and equity.

10. Attraction depends on such factors as physical and personality attractiveness, similarity (especially attitudinal), reinforcement, proximity, and reciprocity of liking.

11. The relationship rules theory views relationships as held together through adherence to an agreed on set of rules.

12. Social exchange theory holds that you develop relationships that yield the greatest profits. You seek relationships in which the rewards exceed the costs and are likely to dissolve relationships when the costs exceed the rewards.

13. Equity theory claims that you develop and maintain relationships in which the rewards are distributed in proportion to costs. When your share of the rewards is less than would be demanded by equity, you are likely to experience dissatisfaction and exit the relationship.

Throughout this discussion of interpersonal relationships, a variety of relationship skills were discussed. Place a check mark next to those skills that you feel you want to work on most.

_____ 1. I adjust my communication patterns on the basis of the relationship's intimacy.

_____ 2. I can identify changes in communication patterns that may signal deterioration.

_____ 3. I can use the accepted repair strategies to heal an ailing relationship: for example, reversing negative communication patterns, using cherishing behaviors, and adopting a positive action program.

_____ 4. I can deal with relationship dissolution and apply such skills as breaking the loneliness-depression cycle, bolstering self-esteem, and seeking support.

_____ 5. I understand the different types of friendships and can identify the goals that each type serves.

_____ 6. I understand the different types of love and can appreciate the varied ways in which people can love.

_____ 7. I understand the varied types of primary relationships and families and can see the similarities and differences among them.

_____ 8. I can communicate effectively in the workplace.

_____ 9. I follow the rules for effective communication in online communication.

_____ 10. I can effectively manage physical proximity, reinforcement, and emphasizing similarities as ways to increase interpersonal attractiveness.

_____ 11. I can apply the rules of friendship, romantic relationships, family relationships, and work relationships as appropriate.

_____ 12. I can identify, and to some extent control, the rewards and costs of my relationships.

_____ 13. I can appreciate the other person's perception of relationship equity and can modify my own behavior to make the relationship more productive and satisfying.

_____ **14.** I understand the differences between face-to-face and online relationships and can modify my behavior accordingly.

_____ **15.** I take into consideration the advantages and disadvantages of workplace romantic relationships.

Key Terms

agapic love
attraction
attraction theory
bullying
complementarity
conformity-orientation
contact
conversation-orientation
deterioration
dissolution
equity theory

eros love
friendship
intimacy
involvement
love
ludic love
manic love
mentoring
networking
online-only relationships
parasocial relationships

pragma love
primary relationship
proximity
reciprocity of liking
reinforcement
relationship development
repair
rules theory
similarity
social exchange theory
storge love

Skill Development Experiences

7.1 Exchanging Cherishing Messages

Lists of cherishing behaviors will also give you insight into your own relationship needs and the kind of communicating partner you want.

Cherishing behaviors are an especially insightful way to affirm another person and to increase favor exchange, a concept that comes from the work of William Lederer (1984). Cherishing behaviors are those small gestures you enjoy receiving from your partner (e.g., a smile, a wink, a squeeze, a kiss, a phone call, an "I love you").
Prepare a list of ten cherishing behaviors that you would like to receive from your real or imagined relationship partner. Identify these cherishing behaviors according to the following categories:

1. Specific and positive—nothing overly general or negative
2. Focused on the present and future rather than on issues about which you've argued in the past
3. Capable of being performed daily
4. Easily executed—nothing that you have to go out of your way to accomplish

If you have a relationship partner, ask him or her also to prepare a list, and exchange lists, and begin exchanging cherishing behaviors. Ideally, you and your partner will begin to perform these cherishing behaviors for one another. In time these behaviors should become a normal part of your interaction, which is exactly what you'd hope to achieve.

7.2 Analyzing Interpersonal Relationships in the Media

Becoming mindful of what the media teach and how they do it will help you to avoid internalizing relationship values before examining them critically.

Interpersonal relationships, as they're expressed in the popular media, provide an interesting perspective on the ways in which our culture views relationships and on the principles of relationship communication it teaches. Think of all the media you're exposed to throughout an average day and consider the messages you are receiving about relationships. Look at the media in any form—television (in dramas, sitcoms, commercials, talk shows, reality shows), newspapers, magazines, blogs, websites, music, and film—and try to identify the values and attitudes they communicate about interpersonal relationships. Think about these examples:

- Do the popular media approve of certain types of relationships and not others?
- How do the media "define" friendship, love, and family?
- What do the media say about the rules for relationships?
- How do the media deal with the dark side of interpersonal relationships, such as relationship violence and spousal abuse?

Chapter 8
Managing Interpersonal Conflict

Online conflicts are often difficult to resolve online.

	Learning Objectives
Preliminaries to Interpersonal Conflict	**8.1** Define *interpersonal conflict*, identify the major conflict issues, and explain the myths about interpersonal conflict.
Principles of Interpersonal Conflict	**8.2** Explain the three principles of conflict and give examples of each.
Conflict Management Strategies	**8.3** Describe and distinguish between the effective and ineffective conflict management strategies.

Of all your interpersonal interactions, those involving conflict are among your most important. Interpersonal conflict often creates ill will, anxiety, and problems for relationships. But as you'll soon see, conflict can also create opportunities for improving and strengthening relationships.

Preliminaries to Interpersonal Conflict

8.1   Define *interpersonal conflict*, identify the major conflict issues, and explain the myths about interpersonal conflict.

Before considering the stages and strategies of conflict management, it's necessary to define exactly what is meant by *interpersonal conflict*, the issues around which interpersonal conflict often centers, and some of the myths surrounding conflict.

Definition of Interpersonal Conflict

You want to go to the movies with your partner. Your partner wants to stay home. Your insisting on going to the movies interferes with your partner's staying home, and your partner's determination to stay home interferes with your going to the movies. You can't both achieve your goals, so there will be conflict.

As this example illustrates, **interpersonal conflict** is disagreement between or among connected individuals (e.g., close friends, lovers, family members) who perceive their goals as incompatible (Hocker & Wilmot, 2007; Folger, Poole, & Stutman, 2013; Cahn & Abigail, 2007). More specifically, interpersonal conflict occurs when people:

- **are interdependent (they're connected in some significant way);** what one person does has an impact or an effect on the other person.

- **are mutually aware that their goals are incompatible;** if one person's goal is achieved, then the other person's goal cannot be achieved. For example, if one person wants to buy a new car and the other person wants to pay down the mortgage, and there is not enough money to do both, there is conflict.

- **perceive each other as interfering with the attainment of their own goals.** For example, you may want to study but your roommate may want to party; the attainment of either goal would interfere with the attainment of the other goal.

An important implication of this concept of interdependency is that, the greater the interdependency, the greater (1) the number of issues around which conflict can center and (2) the impact of the conflict and the conflict management interaction on the individuals and on the relationship (see Figure 8.1). Looked at in this way, it's easy to appreciate the importance to your relationships of understanding interpersonal conflict and learning strategies for effective conflict management.

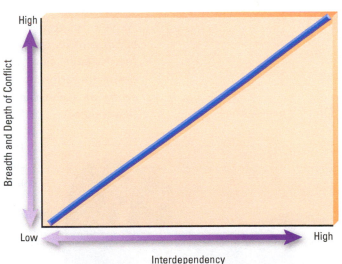

Figure 8.1 Conflict and Interdependency

Conflict with those who are especially important in our lives—close friends, family members, romantic partners, work colleagues—is more important than conflict with those who are more distant. This figure illustrates this commonly observed situation: As interdependency and closeness increase, so do the potential for and the importance of conflict. *Can you give a specific example from your own experience to illustrate this relationship?*

Interpersonal Conflict Issues

According to the eHarmony.com website, nine issues are at the heart of couple conflicts: free time, money, household responsibilities, politics, sex, children and pets, religion, jealousy, and stress. And, in a study on the issues argued about by gay, lesbian, and heterosexual couples, researchers found that respondents identified

JOURNAL
COMMUNICATION CHOICE POINT
Escalating to Relationship Conflict
Your own interpersonal conflicts often
start out as content conflicts but quickly
degenerate into relationship conflicts, and
that's when things get ugly. *What types of
things might you say or do to keep conflicts
and their resolution focused on content and
not on the relationship?*

six major issues that were virtually identical for all couples (Kurdek, 1994). These issues are arranged here in order, with the first being the most often mentioned. As you read this list, ask yourself how many of these issues lead into interpersonal conflict.

- **intimacy issues**, such as affection and sex
- **power issues**, such as excessive demands or possessiveness, lack of equality in the relationship, friends, and leisure time
- **personal flaws issues,** such as drinking or smoking, personal grooming, and driving style
- **personal distance issues,** such as frequent absence and heavy school or job commitments
- **social issues**, such as politics and social policies, parents, and personal values
- **distrust issues**, such as lying about previous lovers or finances

Another class of issues that create conflict is that of the **social allergen**, a personal habit of a friend or romantic partner that you find annoying or inconsiderate. Each person has his or her own list of what constitutes an annoyance, but common allergens between men and women include use of the silent treatment, being too critical, forgetting important dates such as birthdays or anniversaries, or a wandering eye (Cunningham, 2009; Eccles, 2009). More specific allergens mentioned on the many websites that discuss this issue include leaving wet towels on the bathroom floor or the toothpaste tube uncapped, blowing one's nose at the dinner table, leaving toe nail clippings on the floor, smoking too much, drinking too much, being on Facebook too much, or talking on the phone too much.

Depending on how these conflicts play out, they may focus largely on content issues (on the budget or the vacation plans) or on relationship issues (on who is in charge and who makes the final decision). And sometimes, it's a combination of content and relationship issues. Often a conflict starts out as a content conflict (say, the budget) but escalates into a relationship conflict (who has the right to make financial decisions).

In the workplace, conflicts also center on both content and relationship issues. As you can appreciate, conflict is an especially important issue in the workplace because of its many potential negative effects such as personnel leaving the job (necessitating new recruitment and retraining), low morale, and lessening of the desire to perform at top efficiency. Workplace conflicts, according to one study, center on such issues as these, a clear mix of both content and relationship issues (Psychometrics, 2010):

- personality differences and resulting clashes, 86 percent
- ineffective leadership, 73 percent
- lack of openness, 67 percent
- physical and emotional stress, 64 percent
- differences in values and resulting clashes, 59 percent

Of course, content and relationship dimensions are always easier to separate in a textbook than they are in real life, where many conflicts contain elements of both. For example, you can probably imagine both content and relationship dimensions in each of the "content" issues mentioned. Yet certain issues seem oriented more toward one dimension than the other. For example, disagreements on political and social issues are largely content focused, whereas intimacy and power issues are largely relational.

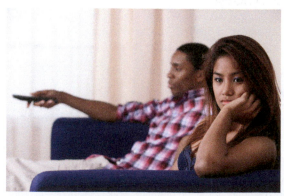

VIEWPOINTS: Conflict Issues
What issues do you fight about? Are the issues you fight over similar to those you read about or see in the lives of friends and relatives? In what ways are your conflicts unique? In what ways are they similar?

Myths about Interpersonal Conflict

Many people have problems dealing with conflict because they hold false assumptions about what conflict is and what it means. Think about your own assumptions about interpersonal and small-group conflict, which were probably shaped by the communications you witnessed in your family and in your social interactions. For example, do you think the following statements are true or false?

- Conflict is best avoided. Time will solve the problem; it will all blow over.

- If two people experience relationship conflict, it means their relationship is in trouble.

- Conflict damages an interpersonal relationship.

- Conflict is destructive because it reveals our negative selves—our pettiness, our need to be in control, our unreasonable expectations.

- In any conflict, there has to be a winner and a loser. Because goals are incompatible, someone has to win and someone has to lose.

- These are myths and, as we'll see in this chapter, they can interfere with your ability to deal with conflict effectively.

"I can't remember what we're arguing about, either. Let's keep yelling, and maybe it will come back to us."

David Sipress/The New Yorker Collection/The Cartoon Bank

Principles of Interpersonal Conflict

8.2   **Explain the three principles of conflict and give examples of each.**

You can increase your understanding of interpersonal conflict by looking at some general principles: (1) conflict can be positive or negative, (2) conflict is influenced by culture and gender, and (3) conflict styles have consequences.

Conflict Can Be Negative or Positive

Although interpersonal conflict is always stressful, it's important to recognize that it has both negative and positive aspects.

NEGATIVE ASPECTS   Conflict often leads to increased negative regard for the opponent. One reason for this is that many conflicts involve unfair fighting methods (which we'll examine shortly) and are focused largely on hurting the other person. When one person hurts the other, increased negative feelings are inevitable; even the strongest relationship has limits.

At times, conflict may lead you to close yourself off from the other person. When you hide your true self from an intimate, you prevent meaningful communication from taking place. Because the need for intimacy is so strong, one or both parties may then seek intimacy elsewhere. This often leads to further conflict, mutual hurt, and resentment—qualities that add heavily to the costs carried by the relationship. Meanwhile, rewards may become difficult to exchange. In this situation, the overall costs increase and the rewards decrease, which often leads to relationship deterioration and eventual dissolution.

POSITIVE ASPECTS   The major value of interpersonal conflict is that it forces you to examine a problem and work toward a potential solution. If both you and your opponent use productive conflict strategies (which will be described in this chapter), the relationship may well emerge from the encounter stronger, healthier, and more satisfying than before. And you may emerge stronger, more confident, and better able to stand up for yourself (Bedford, 1996).

Through conflict and its resolution, you also can stop resentment from increasing and let your needs be known. For example, suppose your partner needs lots of attention after coming home from work but you need to review and get closure on the day's work. If you both can appreciate the legitimacy of these needs, then you can find solutions. Perhaps you can make your important phone call after your partner's attention needs are met, or perhaps your partner can delay the need for attention until you get closure about work. Or perhaps together you can find a way for your closure needs and your partner's attention needs to be met simultaneously through, for example, talking while cuddling at the end of the day. This situation would be considered a *win–win*.

Consider, too, that when you try to resolve conflict within an interpersonal relationship, you're saying in effect that the relationship is worth the effort. Usually, confronting a conflict indicates commitment and a desire to preserve the relationship.

Conflict Is Influenced by Culture and Gender

As in other areas of interpersonal communication, it helps to consider conflict in light of the influences of culture and gender. Both exert powerful influences on how people view and resolve conflicts.

CONFLICT AND CULTURE Culture influences both the issues that people fight about and the ways of dealing with conflict that people consider appropriate and inappropriate. Cohabiting teens, for example, are more likely to experience conflict with their parents about their living style if they live in the United States than if they live in Sweden, where cohabitation is more accepted and more prevalent. Similarly, male infidelity is more likely to cause conflict between U.S. spouses than in cultures in which such behavior is more common. Students from the United States are more likely to engage in conflict with another U.S. student than with someone from another culture; Chinese students, on the other hand, are more likely to engage in a conflict with a non-Chinese student than with another Chinese (Leung, 1988).

The types of interpersonal conflicts that tend to arise depend on the cultural orientation of the individuals involved. For example, in **collectivist cultures** (such as those of Ecuador, Indonesia, and Korea), conflicts most often involve violations of larger group norms and values, such as failing in your role, for example, as family provider or overstepping your social status by publicly disagreeing with a superior. Conversely, in **individualistic cultures** (such as those of the United States, Canada, and Western Europe), conflicts are more likely to occur when people violate expected norms—for example, not defending a position in the face of disagreement (Ting-Toomey, 1985).

CONFLICT AND GENDER Do men and women engage in interpersonal conflict differently? One of the few stereotypes that are supported by research is that of the withdrawing and sometimes aggressive male. Men are more apt to withdraw from a conflict situation than are women. It has been argued that this may happen because men become more psychologically and physiologically aroused during conflict (and retain this heightened level of arousal much longer than do women) and so may try to distance themselves and withdraw from the conflict to prevent further arousal. Another explanation for the male tendency to withdraw is that the culture has taught men to avoid conflict. Still another explanation is that withdrawal is an expression of power (Gottman & Carrere, 1994; Canary, Cupach, & Messman, 1995; Goleman, 1995; Noller, 1993).

Women, on the other hand, want to get closer to the conflict; they want to talk about it and resolve it. Even adolescents reveal these differences; in a study of boys and girls aged 11 to 17, boys withdrew more than girls but were more aggressive when they didn't withdraw (Lindeman, Harakka, & Keltikangas-Jarvinen, 1997). Similarly, a study of offensive language found that girls were

VIEWPOINTS: Conflict and Culture

What does your own culture teach about conflict and its management? For example: What strategies does it prohibit? Are some strategies prohibited in conflicts with certain people (say, your parents) but not in conflicts with others (say, your friends)? Does your culture prescribe certain ways of dealing with conflict? Does it have different expectations for men and for women? Do these teachings influence your actual conflict behaviors?

The Cultural Map

SUCCESS

One of the major differences between individualistic and collectivist cultures is the way in which *success* is defined. In individualistic cultures, success is winning, beating the others, and coming out on top. In collectivist cultures, success is contributing to the group's goals, and being an effective member of a team.

These countries are among the most strongly affiliated with individualism. In high individualist cultures, the individual's goals are given the highest priority, and success is measured by the extent to which you surpass other members of your group.

These countries are among the most strongly affiliated with collectivism. In high collectivist cultures, the group's goals are given the highest priority, and success is measured by your contributions to the group as a whole.

What is success to you right now? What qualities or achievements would contribute most to your definition of success? In visualizing your successful self, are you more likely to behave as would an individualist or as a collectivist?

more easily offended by language than boys, but boys were more apt to fight when they were offended by the words used (Heasley, Babbitt, & Burbach, 1995a, 1995b). Another study showed that young girls used more prosocial strategies (i.e., behaviors designed to help others rather than oneself) than boys (Rose & Asher, 1999).

It should be mentioned that some research fails to support these gender differences in conflict style—the differences that cartoons, situation comedies, and films portray so readily and so clearly. For example, several studies dealing with both college students and men and women in business found no significant differences in the ways men and women engage in conflict (Wilkins & Andersen, 1991; Canary & Hause, 1993; Gottman & Levenson, 1999).

Conflict Styles Have Consequences

The way in which you engage in conflict has consequences for who wins and who loses, if and when the conflict is resolved, and ultimately for the relationship as a whole. As you read through these styles (Blake & Mouton, 1984), try to identify your

Table 8.1 Five Conflict Styles and Their Consequences

Here are the five conflict styles and their likely consequences or outcomes (Blake & Mouton, 1984).

	You	Other
Competing: great concern for your needs; little concern for other's	Win ☺	Lose ☹
Avoiding: little concern for your own or other's needs	Lose ☹	Lose ☹
Compromising: some concern for your own and other's needs	Win and lose ☺ ☹	Win and lose ☺ ☹
Accommodating: great concern for other's needs; little concern for your own	Lose ☹	Win ☺
Collaborating: great concern for your own and other's needs	Win ☺	Win ☺

own conflict style as well as the styles of those with whom you have close relationships. A summary of these five styles appears in Table 8.1.

COMPETING: I WIN, YOU LOSE   The **competing style** involves great concern for your own needs and desires and little for those of others. As long as your needs are met, you think the conflict has been dealt with successfully. In conflict motivated by competitiveness, you'd be likely to be verbally aggressive and to blame the other person.

This style represents an "I win, you lose" philosophy. This is the conflict style of a person who simply imposes his or her will on the other: "I make the money, and we'll vacation at the beach or not at all." But this philosophy often leads to resentment on the part of the person who loses, which can cause additional conflicts. Further, the fact that you win and the other person loses probably means that the conflict hasn't really been resolved but has only concluded (for now).

JOURNAL
COMMUNICATION CHOICE POINT
Avoiding Conflict

Your team members at work all seem to have the same conflict style: avoidance. When there is disagreement, they refuse to argue for one alternative or the other or even to participate in the discussion. You need spirited discussion and honest debate if your team is going to come up with appropriate solutions. *What options do you have for dealing with this problem? What would you say?*

AVOIDING: I LOSE, YOU LOSE   In the **avoiding style**, the individuals are relatively unconcerned with their own or with their opponents' needs or desires. They avoid any real communication about the problem, change topics when the problem is brought up, and generally withdraw both psychologically and physically.

As you can appreciate, the avoiding style does little to resolve any conflicts and may be viewed as an "I lose, you lose" philosophy. If a couple can't agree about where to spend their vacation, but each person refuses to negotiate a resolution to the disagreement, the pair may not take any vacation at all; both sides lose. Interpersonal problems rarely go away of their own accord; rather, if they exist, they need to be faced and dealt with effectively. Avoidance merely allows the conflict to fester and probably grow, only to resurface in another guise.

COMPROMISING: I WIN AND LOSE, YOU WIN AND LOSE   The **compromising style** is the kind of strategy you might refer to as "meeting each other halfway," "horse trading," or "give and take." There's some concern for your own needs and some concern for the other's needs. This strategy is likely to result in maintaining peace, but there will be a residue of dissatisfaction over the inevitable losses that each side has to endure.

Compromise represents an "I win and lose, you win and lose" philosophy. So, if you and your partner can't vacation at both the beach and the mountains, then you might settle for weekend trips or use the money to have a hot tub installed instead. These may not be your first choices, but they're not bad and may satisfy (to some degree at least) each of your vacation wants.

ACCOMMODATING: I LOSE, YOU WIN   In the **accommodating style**, you sacrifice your own needs for the needs of the other person(s). Your primary goal is to maintain harmony and peace in the relationship or group. This style may help maintain peace and may satisfy the opposition, but it does little to meet your own needs, which are unlikely to go away.

Accommodation represents an "I lose, you win" philosophy. If your partner wants to vacation in the mountains and you want to vacation at the beach, and you, instead of negotiating an agreement acceptable to both, give in and accommodate, then you lose and your partner wins. Although this style may make your partner happy (at least on this occasion), it's not likely to provide a lasting resolution to an interpersonal conflict. You'll eventually sense unfairness and inequality and may easily come to resent your partner, and perhaps even yourself.

COLLABORATING: I WIN, YOU WIN   In the **collaborating style**, you address both your own and the other person's needs. This style, often considered the ideal, takes time and a willingness to communicate—especially to listen to the perspectives and needs of the other person.

Collaboration enables each person's needs to be met, an "I win, you win" situation. For example, you might both agree to split the vacation—one week in the mountains and one week at the beach. Or you might agree to spend this year's vacation at the beach and next year's in the mountains. This is obviously the style that, in an ideal world, most people would choose for interpersonal conflict.

Stu's Views, www.stus.com

Conflict Management Strategies

8.3   **Describe and distinguish between the effective and ineffective conflict management strategies.**

When managing conflict, you can choose from a variety of productive or unproductive strategies, which we'll investigate here. Realize that the strategies you choose will be influenced by numerous factors. Understanding these factors may help you select more appropriate and more effective conflict strategies (Koerner & Fitzpatrick, 2002).

- **Goals**   The goals (short-term and long-term) you wish to achieve will influence your choice of conflict strategies. If you only want to salvage today's date, you may want to simply "give in" and ignore the difficulty. If you want to build a long-term relationship, on the other hand, you may want to fully analyze the cause of the problem and look for strategies that will enable both parties to win.

- **Emotional state**   You're unlikely to select the same strategies when you're sad as when you're angry. You will tend to use different strategies if you're seeking to apologize than if you're looking for revenge.

- **Assessment of the situation**   For example, your attitudes and beliefs about what is fair and equitable will influence your readiness to acknowledge the fairness in the other person's position. Your own assessment of who (if anyone) is the cause of the problem will also influence your conflict style. You may also assess the likely effects of various possible strategies. For example, do you risk alienating your teenager if you use force?

- **Personality and communication competence**   If you're shy and unassertive, you may tend to avoid conflict rather than fight actively. If you're extroverted and have a strong desire to state your position, then you may be more likely to fight actively and to argue forcefully.

- **Family history**   If, for example, your parents argued aggressively about religious differences, you might tend to be aggressive when your partner expresses different religious beliefs. If you haven't *un*learned family conflict patterns, you're likely to repeat them.

Before examining these various strategies, take the self-test on conflict management strategies included here, and examine your own patterns of conflict management.

Test Yourself

CONFLICT MANAGEMENT STRATEGIES

The following statements refer to ways in which people engage in interpersonal conflict.

Respond to each statement with True if this is a generally accurate description of your interpersonal conflict behavior and False if the statement is a generally inaccurate description of your behavior.

_____ **1.** I strive to seek solutions that will benefit both of us.

_____ **2.** I look for solutions that will give me what I want.

_____ **3.** I confront conflict situations as they arrive.

_____ **4.** I avoid conflict situations as best I can.

_____ **5.** My messages are basically descriptive of the events leading up to the conflict.

_____ **6.** My messages are often judgmental.

_____ **7.** I take into consideration the face needs of the other person.

_____ **8.** I advance the strongest arguments I can find even if these attack the other person.

_____ **9.** I center my arguments on issues rather than on personalities.

_____ **10.** I use messages that may attack a person's self-image if this will help me win the argument.

This test on conflict management strategies was designed to make you sensitive to some of the conflict strategies discussed in this section of the chapter. It is not intended to give you a specific score. Generally, however, you'd be following the principles of effective interpersonal conflict management if you answered True to the odd-numbered statements (1, 3, 5, 7, and 9) and False to the even-numbered statements (2, 4, 6, 8, and 10). As you think about your responses and read the text discussion, ask yourself what you can do to improve your own conflict management skills.

Avoidance and Fighting Actively

Conflict **avoidance** may involve actual physical flight. You may leave the scene of the conflict (e.g., walk out of the apartment or go to another part of the office), fall asleep, or blast the stereo to drown out all conversation. Avoidance also may take the form of emotional or intellectual avoidance, in which you may leave the conflict psychologically by not dealing with any of the arguments or problems raised.

Sometimes avoidance is a response to demands—a conflict pattern known as _demand-withdrawal_. Here one person makes demands (e.g., _You will go out again tonight_) and the other person, unwilling to accede to the demands, withdraws from the interaction (Canary, Cupach, & Messman, 1995; Sagrestano, Heavey & Christensen, 2006; Guerrero, Andersen & Afifi, 2007). This pattern is obviously unproductive, but it can be easily broken by either individual—either by not making demands or by not withdrawing and instead participating actively in the conflict management.

Nonnegotiation is a special type of avoidance. Here you refuse to discuss the conflict or to listen to the other person's argument. At times nonnegotiation takes the form of hammering away at your own point of view until the other person gives in—a technique known as "steamrolling."

Instead of avoiding the issues, take an active role in your interpersonal conflicts.

- **Involve yourself on both sides of the communication exchange.** Be an active participant; voice your own feelings and listen carefully to your opponent's feelings. This is not to say that periodic moratoriums are not helpful; sometimes they are. But in general, be willing to communicate.

- **Take ownership of your thoughts and feelings.** When you disagree with your partner or find fault with her or his behavior, take responsibility for these feelings. Say, for example, "I disagree with …" or "I don't like it when you. …" Avoid statements that deny your responsibility: "Everybody thinks you're wrong about ..." or "Chris thinks you shouldn't. ..."

- **Focus on the present.** Concentrate your attention on the here and now, rather than on issues that occurred two months ago. Similarly, focus your conflict on the person with whom you're fighting, not on the person's parents, child, or friends.
- **Listen carefully.** Act and think as a listener. Turn off the television, stereo, or computer; face the other person. Devote your total attention to the other person. Make sure you understand what the person is saying and feeling. Use perception checking (Chapter 2) and active listening techniques (Chapter 3). And, get ready to listen to the other person's responses to your statements.

Force and Talk

When confronted with conflict, many people prefer to force their position on the other person, not to deal with the issues. **Force** is an unproductive conflict strategy that may be emotional or physical. In either case, however, the issues are avoided and the "winner" is the combatant who exerts the most force. This is the technique of warring nations, quarreling children, and even some normally sensible and mature adults.

In one study more than 50 percent of both single people and married couples reported that they had experienced physical violence in their relationships. If symbolic violence was included (e.g., threatening to hit the other person or throwing something), the percentages rose above 60 percent for singles and above 70 percent for married couples (Marshall & Rose, 1987). In another study, 47 percent of a sample of 410 college students reported some experience with violence in a dating relationship (Deal & Wampler, 1986). In most cases the violence was reciprocal—each person in the relationship used violence. In cases in which only one person was violent, the research results are conflicting. For example, some surveys (Deal & Wampler, 1986; Cate, Henton, Koval, Christopher, & Lloyd, 1982) have found that in such cases the aggressor was significantly more often the female partner. Other research, however,

Communicating Ethically
ETHICAL LISTENING

Because communication strategies also have an ethical dimension, it's important to look at the ethical implications of conflict management strategies. Here are a few questions to consider as you reflect on the conflict strategies discussed in this chapter:

- Does conflict avoidance have an ethical dimension? For example, is it unethical for one relationship partner to refuse to discuss disagreements or to walk out of an argument?
- Can the use of physical force to influence another person ever be ethical? Can you identify a situation in which it would be appropriate for someone with greater physical strength to overpower another person to compel that person to accept his or her point of view?
- Are face-attacking strategies inherently unethical, or might it be appropriate to use them in certain situations? Can you identify such situations?
- Is verbal aggressiveness necessarily unethical?

ETHICAL CHOICE POINT
Mary spent the night gambling (and losing a considerable amount of money), but she knows that revealing this will cause conflict and hurt her partner. *Would it be ethical for Mary to say she had to work late to avoid the conflict and hurt?*

has tended to confirm the widespread view that men are more likely to use force than women (DeTurck, 1987).

Instead of resorting to force, consider the value of talking and listening.

- Explain what you think the problem is about and listen to what the other person says about the problem.
- Talk about what you want and listen to what the other person wants.
- Talk over possible solutions and listen to the proposed solutions of the other person.
- Talk the conflict through a logical sequence from understanding the nature and causes of the conflict through putting a solution into operation. Figure 8.2 explains one possible pattern you might follow, and owes much of its formulation to John Dewey's (1910) problem-solving sequence.

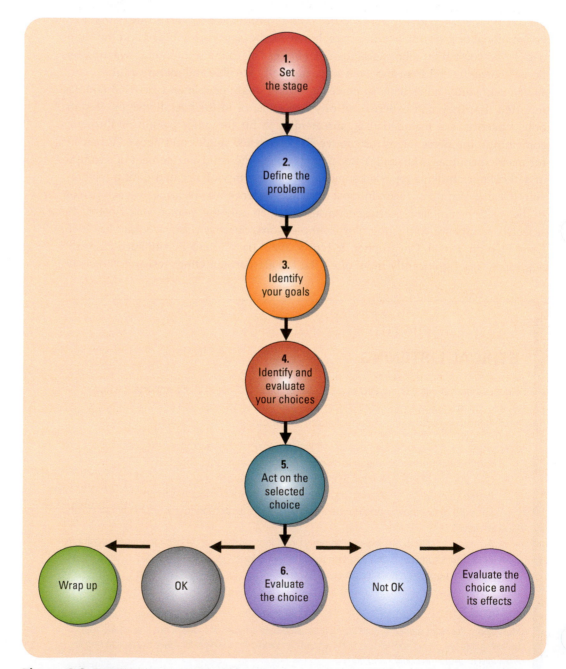

Figure 8.2 The Process of Conflict Resolution

One way to view conflict resolution is as a series of steps from defining the sources of the conflict to accepting a solution, as illustrated here.

Defensiveness and Supportiveness

Although talking is preferred to using force, not all talk is equally productive in conflict resolution. One of the best ways to look at destructive versus productive talk is to look at how the style of your communications can create unproductive **defensiveness** or a productive sense of **supportiveness**, a system developed by Jack Gibb (1961). The type of talk that generally proves destructive and sets up defensive reactions in the listener is talk that is evaluative, controlling, strategic, indifferent or neutral, superior, and certain.

EVALUATION   When you evaluate or judge another person or what that person has done, that person is likely to become resentful and defensive and perhaps at the same time to become equally evaluative and judgmental. In contrast, when you describe what happened or what you want, it creates no such defensiveness and is generally seen as supportive. The distinction between evaluation and description can be seen in the differences between **you-messages** and **I-messages**.

Evaluative You-Messages	Descriptive I-Messages
You never reveal your feelings.	I sure would like hearing how you feel about this.
You just don't plan ahead.	I need to know what our schedule for the next few days will be.
You never call me.	I'd enjoy hearing from you more often.

If you put yourself in the role of the listener hearing these statements, you probably can feel the resentment or defensiveness that the evaluative messages (you-messages) would create and the supportiveness from the descriptive messages (I-messages).

CONTROL   When you try to control the behavior of another person, when you order that person to do this or that, or when you make decisions without mutual discussion and agreement, defensiveness is a likely response. Control messages deny the legitimacy of the person's contributions and in fact deny his or her importance. On the other hand, when you focus on the problem at hand—not on controlling the situation or getting your own way—defensiveness is much less likely. This problem orientation invites mutual participation and recognizes the significance of each person's contributions.

STRATEGY   When you use strategy and try to get around other people or situations through **manipulation**—especially when you conceal your true purposes—others are likely to resent it and to respond defensively. But when you act openly and with **spontaneity**, you're more likely to create an atmosphere that is equal and honest.

NEUTRALITY   When you demonstrate **neutrality**—in the sense of indifference or a lack of caring for the other person—it's likely to create defensiveness. Neutrality seems to show a lack of empathy or interest in the thoughts and feelings of the other person; it is especially damaging when intimates are in conflict. This kind of talk says, in effect, "You're not important or deserving of attention and caring." When, on the other hand, you demonstrate empathy, defensiveness is unlikely to occur. Although it can be especially difficult in conflict situations, try to show that you can understand what the other person is going through and that you accept these feelings.

SUPERIORITY   When you present yourself as superior to another person, you put the other person in an inferior position, and this is likely to be resented. Such superiority messages say in effect that the other person is inadequate or somehow second class. A superior attitude is a violation of the implicit equality contract that people in a close relationship have. The other person may then begin to attack your superiority; the conflict can quickly degenerate into a conflict over who's the boss, with personal attacks being the mode of interaction.

CERTAINTY The person who reflects an attitude of **certainty**—who appears to know it all—is likely to be resented and often sets up a defensive climate. After all, there is little room for negotiation or mutual problem solving when one person already has the answer. An attitude of **provisionalism**—"Let's explore this issue together and try to find a solution"—is likely to be much more productive than an attitude of **closed-mindedness**.

The following suggestions will help you foster supportiveness rather than defensiveness.

- Talk descriptively rather than evaluatively.
- Focus on the problem rather than on personalities.
- Act and react honestly and spontaneously, rather than strategically.
- Empathize with the other person.
- Approach the conflict resolution process as an equal and treat the other person as an equal.
- Be provisional; suggest rather than demand.

Face-Attacking and Face-Enhancing Strategies

In the discussion of politeness in Chapter 2, the concepts of face and face-threatening acts were introduced. The concepts of face and face-threatening acts have special relevance to interpersonal conflict. **Face-attacking conflict strategies** are strategies that attack a person's positive face (e.g., making comments that criticize the person's contribution to a relationship or the person's ability) or a person's negative face (e.g., making demands on a person's time or resources that attack the person's autonomy). **Face-enhancing conflict strategies**, on the other hand, are those that support and confirm a person's positive face (e.g., praise, a pat on the back, a sincere smile) or negative face (e.g., giving the person space and asking rather than demanding).

One popular but destructive face-attacking strategy is **beltlining** (Bach & Wyden, 1968). Much like fighters in a ring, each of us has an emotional "beltline." When you hit below it, you can inflict serious injury. When you hit above the belt, however, the person is able to absorb the blow. With most interpersonal relationships, especially those of long standing, you know where the beltline is. You know, for example, that to hit Pat with the inability to have children is to hit below the belt. You know that to hit Chris with the failure to get a permanent job is to hit below the belt. This type of face-attacking strategy doesn't help move a conflict toward resolution, and often has the opposite effect of intensifying it. Keep blows to areas your opponent can absorb and handle.

Another such face-attacking strategy is **blame**. Instead of focusing on a solution to a problem, some people try to affix blame to the other person. Whether true or not, blaming is generally unproductive for at least two reasons. First, it diverts attention away from the problem and from its potential solution. Second, it creates resentment that is likely to be responded to with resentment. The conflict then spirals into personal attacks, leaving the individuals and the relationship worse off than before the conflict was ever addressed.

Strategies that enhance positive face involve helping the other person to maintain a positive image, an image as competent and trustworthy, able and good. Even when you get what you want, say by bargaining, it's wise to help the other person retain positive face; this makes it less likely that future conflicts will arise and increases the likelihood that the relationship can be repaired (Donahue, 1992).

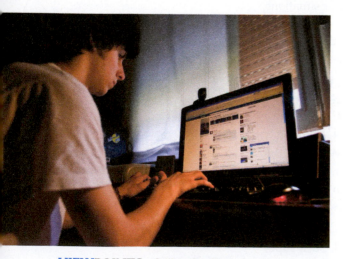

VIEWPOINTS: Online Conflict

One study found that, generally at least, people are more positive in dealing with conflict in face-to-face situations than in computer-mediated communication (Zornoza, Ripoll, & Peiró, 2002). *Do you notice this in your own interactions? If so, why do you think it's true?*

Instead of using face-attacking strategies, consider face-saving strategies.

- Confirm the other person's self-image.
- Listen supportively and actively. Express your support or empathy: *I can understand how you feel. I can appreciate that my handling the check book could create a feeling of inequality.*
- Use I-messages that avoid blaming the other person.
- Use excuses and apologies as appropriate.
- Respect the other person's negative face needs by making few (if any) demands; also respect the other person's time, space (especially in times of stress), and point of view.

Silencers and Facilitating Open Expression

Silencers are a wide variety of unproductive fighting techniques that literally silence another person. One frequently used silencer is crying. When a person is unable to deal with a conflict or when winning seems unlikely, the person may cry, and thus silence the other person.

Another silencer is to feign extreme emotionalism—to yell and scream and pretend to be losing control. Still another is to develop some "physical" reaction—headaches and shortness of breath are probably the most popular. One of the major problems with such silencers is that as an opponent you can never be certain that they are mere tactics; they may be real physical reactions that you should pay attention to. Regardless of what you do, the conflict remains unexamined and unresolved.

In addition to avoiding silencers, avoid power tactics (e.g., raising your voice or threatening physical force) that suppress or inhibit freedom of expression. Such tactics are designed to put the other person down and to subvert real interpersonal equality.

Instead of using silencers, try to facilitate open expression.

- Listen actively and give appropriate and positive feedback.
- Verbalize your appreciation for how the other person sees the conflict (say, by punctuating the conflict episode differently).
- Create or increase **immediacy**—a sense of interest in and liking for the other person in an interchange (discussed in Chapter 6).
- Give the other person permission to express himself or herself openly and honestly.

Gunnysacking and Present Focus

The process of **gunnysacking** is the unproductive conflict strategy of storing up grievances—as if in a gunnysack—and then unloading them when an argument arises (Bach & Wyden, 1968). The immediate occasion for unloading stored-up grievances may be relatively simple (or so it may seem at first); for example, say you come home late one night without calling. Instead of arguing about this, the gunnysacker pours out a mass of unrelated past grievances. As you probably know from experience, gunnysacking does nothing to help resolve conflict and often begets further gunnysacking. Frequently, the trigger problem never gets addressed. Instead, resentment and hostility escalate.

Instead of gunnysacking, focus on the present.

- Concentrate on the here and now, rather than on issues that occurred two months ago.
- Focus your conflict on the person with whom you're fighting, not on the person's mother, child, or friends.

Verbal Aggressiveness and Argumentativeness

An especially interesting perspective on conflict has emerged from work on verbal aggressiveness and argumentativeness, concepts that were isolated by communication researchers but quickly interested people in other disciplines such as psychology,

Table 8.2 Differences between Verbal Aggressiveness and Argumentativeness

Here are just a few differences between being verbally aggressive and arguing (Atvgis & Rancer, 2010; Infante & Rancer, 1995; Rancer & Atvgis, 2006). As you read this table, consider your own conflict tendencies.

Verbal Aggressiveness	Argumentativeness
Is **destructive;** the outcomes are negative in a variety of communication situations.	Is **constructive;** the outcomes are positive in a variety of communication situations.
Leads to relationship **dissatisfaction,** not surprising for a strategy that aims to attack another's self-concept.	Leads to relationship **satisfaction.**
May lead to **relationship violence.**	May **prevent relationship violence,** especially in domestic relationships.
Damages organizational life and demoralizes workers on varied levels.	**Enhances organizational life;** for example, subordinates prefer supervisors who encourage argumentativeness.
Prevents meaningful parent–child communication and makes corporal punishment more likely.	**Enhances parent–child communication** and enables parents to gain greater compliance.
Decreases the user's credibility, in part because it's seen as a tactic to discredit the person rather than address the argument.	**Increases the user's credibility;** argumentatives are seen as trustworthy, committed, and dynamic.
Decreases the user's power of persuasion.	**Increases the user's power of persuasion;** argumentatives are more likely to be seen as leaders.

education, and management, among others (Infante, 1988; Rancer, 1998; Wigley, 1998; Rancer & Avtgis, 2006). Understanding these two concepts will help you understand some of the reasons why things go wrong and some of the ways in which you can use conflict to improve rather than damage your relationships (see Table 8.2).

Verbal aggressiveness is a method of winning an argument by inflicting psychological pain, by attacking the other person's self-concept. The technique is a type of disconfirmation in that it seeks to discredit the individual's view of self. **Argumentativeness**, a quality to be cultivated rather than avoided, refers to your willingness to argue for a point of view, your tendency to speak your mind on significant issues. It's the mode of dealing with disagreements that is the preferable alternative to verbal aggressiveness (Infante & Rancer, 1995).

Argumentativeness differs greatly from verbal aggressiveness (Rancer & Avtgis, 2006). Argumentativeness is constructive in a variety of communication situations and leads to relationship satisfaction. In organizations, it enhances relationships between subordinates and supervisors. Verbal aggressiveness is destructive and leads to relationship dissatisfaction. In organizations, it demoralizes workers.

Argumentative individuals are generally seen as having greater credibility; they're seen as more trustworthy, committed, and dynamic than their aggressive counterparts. In addition, argumentativeness is likely to increase your power of persuasion and will also increase the likelihood that you'll be seen as a leader. Aggressiveness tactics, on the other hand, decrease your power and your likelihood of being seen as a leader.

Instead of being verbally aggressive, try to practice argumentativeness (Infante, 1988; Rancer & Avtgis, 2006).

- **Treat disagreements as objectively as possible.** Avoid assuming that, because someone takes issue with your position or your interpretation, they're attacking you as a person.

- **Center your arguments on issues rather than personalities.** Avoid attacking a person (rather than a person's arguments), even if this would give you a tactical advantage—it will probably backfire at some later time and make your relationship or group participation more difficult.

JOURNAL
COMMUNICATION CHOICE POINT
Verbal Aggressiveness

Your partner engages in verbal aggression whenever you have an argument. Regardless of what the conflict is about, you feel that your self-concept is attacked. *What are some of the things you might say or do to stop these attacks? What channel(s) would you use?*

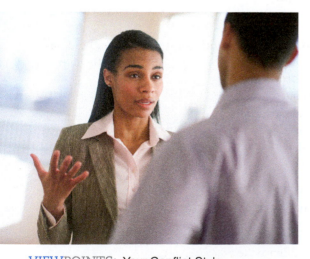

VIEWPOINTS: Your Conflict Style
How would you describe your conflict style in your own close relationships in terms of competing-avoiding-compromising-accommodating-collaborating? Is it the same at work?

- **Reaffirm the other person's sense of competence.** Compliment the other person as appropriate.

- **Allow the other person to state her or his position fully.** Do this before you respond and, of course, avoid interrupting.

- **Stress equality.** Stress the similarities that you have with the other person or persons; stress your areas of agreement before attacking with disagreements.

- **Express interest in the other person's position, attitude, and point of view.**

- **Avoid getting overemotional.** Avoid using an overly loud voice or interjecting vulgar expressions that will prove offensive and eventually ineffective.

- **Allow people to save face.** Never humiliate another person.

Summary of Concepts and Skills

This chapter looked at the nature of interpersonal conflict and at how best to manage conflict.

Preliminaries to Interpersonal Conflict

8.1   **Define *interpersonal conflict*, identify the major conflict issues, and explain the myths about interpersonal conflict.**

1. Interpersonal conflict (in face-to-face situations and in cyberspace) is a disagreement between or among connected individuals whose positions are to some degree both interrelated and incompatible.

2. Conflict can center on intimacy, power, and social issues, for example.

3. The popular myths about conflict can seriously delay effective conflict management.

Principles of Interpersonal Conflict

8.2   **Explain the three principles of conflict and give examples of each.**

4. Conflict can have both negative and positive effects.

5. Conflict is heavily influenced by both culture and gender, and any effective management of conflict needs to consider these influences.

6. Conflict styles (competing or win–lose, avoiding or lose–lose, accommodating or lose–win, collaborating or win–win, and compromising or win–lose/win–lose) have consequences.

Conflict Management Strategies

8.3   **Describe and distinguish between the effective and ineffective conflict management strategies.**

7. Conflict management strategies are influenced by the goals you seek, your emotional state, your cognitive assessment of the situation, your personality and communication competence, and your family history.

8. Conflict management strategies include making decisions between avoidance and active fighting, force and talk, defensiveness and supportiveness, face-attacking and face-enhancing strategies, silencers and facilitating open expression, gunnysacking and present focus, and verbal aggressiveness and argumentativeness.

The skills covered in this chapter are vital to managing interpersonal conflict. Place a check mark next to those skills you want to work on most.

_____ 1. I seek to derive positive benefits from interpersonal conflict and to avoid conflict's possible negative outcomes.

_____ 2. I engage in conflict with an understanding of the cultural and gender influences present.

_____ 3. I understand the consequences of different conflict styles and adjust my style of conflict depending on the specific circumstances.

_____ 4. I look for win–win rather than win–lose strategies.

_____ 5. I engage in conflict actively rather than avoid the problem.

_____ 6. I talk conflict differences through rather than try to force my way of thinking on the other person.

_____ 7. I express support rather than encourage defensiveness.

_____ 8. I use I-messages (rather than you-messages) and assume responsibility for my thoughts and feelings.

_____ 9. I use face-enhancing rather than face-attacking tactics.

_____ 10. I express empathy rather than try to blame the other person.

_____ 11. I facilitate open expression rather than try to silence the other person.

_____ 12. I focus on the present rather than gunnysack.

_____ 13. I use the skills of argumentativeness rather than verbal aggressiveness.

Key Terms

accommodating style
argumentativeness
avoidance
avoiding style
beltlining
blame
certainty
closed-mindedness
collaborating style
collectivist cultures

competing style
compromising style
defensiveness
face-attacking conflict strategies
face-enhancing conflict strategies
force
gunnysacking
I-messages
immediacy
individualistic cultures

interpersonal conflict
manipulation
neutrality
nonnegotiation
provisionalism
social allergen
spontaneity
supportiveness
verbal aggressiveness
you-messages

Skill Development Experiences

8.1 Generating Win–Win Solutions

Win–win solutions exist for most interpersonal conflict situations if the people involved are willing to put in a little effort to find them.

For any one of the situations listed, (a) generate as many win–lose solutions as you can—solutions in which one person wins and the other loses; (b) generate as many possible win–win solutions as you feel the individuals involved in the conflict could reasonably accept; and (c) explain in one sentence the difference between win–lose and win–win solutions.

1. Jessie and Johnnie have decided to get a pet. Jessie wants a cat; Johnnie wants a dog.
2. Casey, who has been in a 12-year relationship with Devon, recently received a $10,000 bonus and has already used the whole amount for a down payment on a new car. Devon was expecting to share the bonus.
3. Pat smokes and stinks up the apartment. Chris hates this, and they argue about it almost daily.

8.2 Constructing I-Messages

Generally and perhaps especially in conflict situations, I-messages are less likely to aggravate conflict than are you-messages.

Recognizing a conflict starter early—some incident that signals that this is the beginning of an interpersonal conflict—can often diffuse a later and more extensive conflict. Here, for example, are accusatory comments using you-messages. Turn each of these into an I-message. What do you see as the major differences between you-messages and I-messages?

1. You're late again. You're always late. Your lateness is so inconsiderate!
2. Well, there goes another anniversary that you forgot.
3. You never want to do what I want. We always have to do what you want.

Chapter 9
Small Group Communication

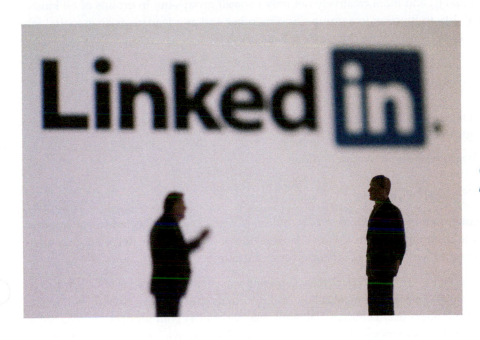

Online groups are as diverse as the world itself.

CHAPTER OUTLINE	Learning Objectives
The Nature of Small Groups and Teams	**9.1** Define *small group* and *team* and the advantages and disadvantages of small groups.
Small Group Stages, Formats, and Culture	**9.2** Explain the stages of small group communication, small group formats, and small group culture.
Idea Generating and Sharing Groups	**9.3** Define *brainstorming* and *focus groups* and describe how each operates.
Problem-Solving Groups	**9.4** Describe the problem-solving sequence, decision-making methods, nominal group, and the Delphi method.

Consider the number of groups to which you belong. Your family is the most obvious example, but you might also be a member of a team, a class, a club, an organization, a sorority or fraternity, a collection of friends on Facebook or Google+, a work group at your job, professional groups on LinkedIn, or perhaps a band or theater group. Some of your most important and satisfying communications probably take place in groups and teams like these.

In this and the next chapter we concentrate on what is called "small group communication," identifying the types of groups and the skills needed for effective participation and leadership. These skills will enable you to function more effectively, more productively, and more creatively not only in *small* groups but in groups of all kinds. Your ability to function in a group—as a member and as a leader—is an essential job skill in today's workplace (Morreale & Pearson, 2008).

The Nature of Small Groups and Teams

9.1 Define *small group* and *team* and the advantages and disadvantages of small groups.

Let's begin with some basic definitions.

The Small Group

A **small group** is (1) a collection of individuals who (2) are connected to one another by some common purpose, (3) are interdependent, (4) have some degree of organization among them, and (5) see themselves as a group.

COLLECTION OF INDIVIDUALS   Generally, a small group consists of approximately 3 to 12 people. The collection of individuals must be few enough in number that all members may communicate with relative ease as both senders and receivers. In face-to-face situations, there are also limits that the available space imposes; in online groups, no such spatial barrier exists. If the group gets much larger than 12, however, even online group communication becomes difficult. On Facebook and similar social networking sites, the number of individuals in a group may number in the hundreds of friends.

COMMON PURPOSE   The members of a group must be connected to one another through some common purpose. People on a bus normally do not constitute a group, because they're not working toward a common goal. However, if the bus were to get stuck in a ditch, the riders may quickly become a group and work together to get the bus back on the road. This does not mean that all members of a group must have exactly the same purpose, but generally there must be some similarity in the individuals' reasons for interacting. Social media groups—whether professional as on LinkedIn or more purely social such as Facebook or a mixture as on Google+—enable you to form groups on just about any topic you'd like. If you're interested in something, there are probably others out there who are interested in the same thing and who would like to get together in virtual space.

VIEWPOINTS: Uses and Gratifications
One study identified seven gratifications you derive from online communication: being in a virtual community, seeking information, aesthetic experience, financial compensation, diversion, personal status, and maintaining relationships (Song, LaRose, Eastin, & Lin, 2004). *How would you describe the gratifications you receive from online groups? Which are the most important?*

INTERDEPENDENCE   In a small group, members are interdependent, meaning that the behavior of one member is significant to and has an impact on all other members. When one member attacks or supports the ideas of another member, that behavior influences the other members and the group as a whole. When one member proposes a great idea or posts a clever quotation or photo, that behavior has an effect on all group members.

ORGANIZING RULES Members of small groups must be connected by some organizing rules, or structure. At times the structure is rigid, as in groups operating under parliamentary procedure, in which each comment must follow prescribed rules. At other times, as in a social gathering, especially online groups, the structure is very loose; however, there's some organization and some structure—for example, comments or questions by one member are responded to by others rather than ignored, and so on.

SELF-PERCEPTION AS A GROUP Members of small groups feel they are, in fact, members of a larger whole. This doesn't mean that individuality is ignored or that members do not see themselves as individuals; it simply means that each member thinks, feels, and acts as a part of the group. The more members see themselves as part of the group, the greater the group cohesion (or sense of "groupness"); the more they see themselves as individuals, separate from the group, the less the group cohesion. Members in highly cohesive groups are usually more satisfied and more productive than members of low-cohesiveness groups.

The Team

A **team** is a particular kind of small group. As such it possesses all of the characteristics of the small group, as well as some additional qualities. Drawing on a number of small group researchers in communication and organizational theory, the team can be defined as a small group (1) constructed for a specific task, (2) whose members have clearly defined roles and (3) are committed to achieving the same goal, and (4) which is content focused (Beebe & Masterson, 2012; Kelly, 2006; Hofstrand, 2006).

- **Specific Purpose** A team is often constructed for a specific purpose or task. After it is completed, the members of the group may be assigned to other teams or go their separate ways. Players on a baseball team, for example, come together for practice and for the actual game; but after the game, they each go their separate ways.

- **Clearly Defined Roles** In a team, member's roles are rather clearly defined. A sports team is a good example. Each player has a unique function: The shortstop's functions are very different from the pitcher's or the catcher's, for example.

- **Goal Directed** In a team all members are committed to achieving the same, clearly identified goal. Again, a sports team is a good example: All members are committed to winning the game.

- **Content Focused** Teams are generally content focused. Teams communicate largely through the exchange of content messages—on winning the game—and much less through relationship messages about the interpersonal relationships of its members.

Virtual Groups and Teams

Small groups and teams use a wide variety of channels. Often, interactions take place face-to-face and increasing often takes place online, among geographically separated members who communicate as a group via computer or phone connections—with Skype, LinkedIn, or Facebook, for example. These **virtual groups** and teams serve both relationship and social purposes on the one hand and business and professional purposes on the other.

Perhaps the best example of virtual groups serving relationship purposes are social networking sites, where friends interact in groups but may be separated by classrooms or by oceans. And, of course, these social networking sites are being used to perform business tasks as well—for finding jobs, conducting business, solving organizational problems, and conducting just about any kind of function that a face-to-face group would serve.

"If I put mustaches on all of us, we look more like a team."

Peter C. Vey/The New Yorker Colection/The Cartoon Bank

Business and professional purposes often are served by virtual teams. Some of these team members may be working at home; but increasingly, virtual teams consist of people who are in different work spaces, perhaps in different parts of an office building, perhaps in different countries.

The same principles of effective group communication apply to all kinds of groups and teams, whether social or business, face-to-face or virtual (we'll use the most inclusive term "small group" to refer to all types of groups). Whether you're working on a team project with colleagues in different countries, communicating with new friends on Facebook, or interacting face-to-face with your extended family, the principles discussed here will prove useful.

Advantages and Disadvantages of Groups

Groups have both advantages and disadvantages. Some problems and issues can profit greatly from small group interaction, especially if the members are knowledgeable and interact effectively. In fact, some projects are simply too big for only one person and so group work is essential. Other problems and issues are best tackled alone; often, one expert is able to make a better decision than a group or several groups of nonexperts.

Perhaps the most important advantage is that a group brings different perspectives, resources, and knowledge to an issue. In this regard groups are perfect learning environments; we teach others and we learn from others. In a problem-solving group, members will feel they're a part of the solution. In business situations, worker commitment to, say, a new company policy is often crucial in determining whether the solution works or not.

Among the disadvantages, groups can be time-consuming when even phone or Skype conferences are often difficult to arrange. It's not always easy to find the right time for all six or more people to interact. Another potential disadvantage is that members may feel the pressure to agree with the majority or with the supervisor or senior member of the group and not to voice any disagreements or alternatives. And it's easy for perspective overload to occur; sometimes too many choices work against effective decisions (Iyengar, 2010).

Small Group Stages, Formats, and Culture

9.2 **Explain the stages of small group communication, small group formats, and small group culture.**

With the nature of the small group and team in mind, we can examine the stages of the small group process, some formats, and some cultural dimensions important in small group communication.

Small Group Stages

With knowledge of the various kinds of small groups, we can now look at how groups interact in the real world. Small group interaction develops in much the same way as a conversation; there are five stages: opening, feedforward, business, feedback, and closing.

- **Opening** The opening period is usually a getting-acquainted time during which members introduce themselves and engage in small talk (e.g., "How was your weekend?" "Does anyone want coffee?"). Your objective here is to get comfortable with the group members.

- **Feedforward** After this preliminary get-together, there is usually some feedforward—some attempt to identify what needs to be done, who will do it, and so on. In a more formal group, the agenda (which is a perfect example of feedforward) may be reviewed and the tasks of the group identified. This is much like making a "to do" list.

- **Business** The business portion is the actual discussion of the tasks—the problem solving, the sharing of information, or whatever else the group needs to achieve.

- **Feedback** At the feedback stage, the group may reflect on what it has done and perhaps on what remains to be done. Some groups may even evaluate their performance at this stage: for example, *We need to focus more on the financial aspects* or *We need to consider additional alternatives.*

- **Closing** At the closing stage, the group members return to their focus on individuals and will perhaps exchange closing comments ("Good seeing you again," "See you next time").

Note that the group focus shifts from members to task and then back again to members. A typical pattern would look like Figure 9.1. Different groups will naturally follow different patterns. For example, a work group that has gathered to solve a problem is likely to spend a great deal more time focused on the task than on each other; whereas an informal social group, say two or three couples who get together for dinner, will spend most of their time focused on the concerns of individuals. Similarly, the amount of time spent on the opening or closing, for example, will vary with the type and purpose of the group.

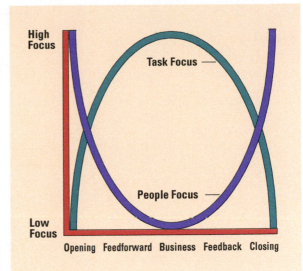

Figure 9.1 Small Group Stages and the Focus on Task and People

Do the groups to which you belong follow these five stages when interacting? Do face-to-face groups and online groups follow the same general pattern? In what ways do they differ?

Small Group Formats

Small groups serve their functions in a variety of formats. Among the most popular small group formats for relatively formal functions are the round table, the panel, the symposium, and the symposium-forum (Figure 9.2).

- In the **roundtable**, group members arrange themselves physically (usually in chairs) in a circular or semicircular pattern. They share information or solve a problem without any set pattern of who speaks when. Group interaction is informal, and members contribute as they see fit. A leader or moderator may be present; he or she may, for example, try to keep the discussion on the topic or encourage more reticent members to speak up.

- In the **panel**, group members are "experts" but participate informally and without any set pattern of who speaks when, as in a roundtable. The difference is that they are sitting, often side-by-side, in front of an audience, whose members may interject comments or ask questions.

- In the **symposium**, each member delivers a prepared presentation much like a public speech. All speeches address different aspects of a single topic. A symposium leader introduces the speakers, provides transitions from one speaker to another, and may provide periodic summaries.

- The symposium-forum consists of two parts: a symposium with prepared speeches (as explained above) and a **forum**, a period of questions from the audience and responses by the speakers. The leader introduces the speakers and moderates the question-and-answer session.

These four formats are *general* patterns that describe a wide variety of groups. Within each type, there will naturally be variation. For example, in the symposium-forum, there is no set pattern for how much time will be spent on the symposium part and how much on the forum part. Combinations may also be used. Thus, for example, group members may each present a position paper (basically a symposium) and then participate in a roundtable discussion.

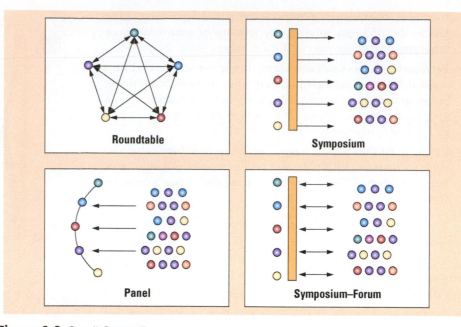

Figure 9.2 Small Group Formats

With how many of these group formats have you had experience?

Small Group Culture

Many groups—especially those of long standing—develop cultural norms and are greatly influenced by their own high-context or low-context orientation. Each of these cultural dimensions influences the group, its members, and its communication.

GROUP NORMS Rules or standards, known as **group norms**, identify which behaviors are considered appropriate (such as being willing to take on added tasks or directing conflict toward issues rather than toward people) and which are considered inappropriate (such as arriving late or failing to contribute actively). These rules for appropriate behavior are sometimes explicitly stated in a company contract or policy: *All members must attend department meetings* or *No cell phones during meetings.* Sometimes they are unstated: *Group members should be well groomed* or *No sexually explicit photos on social media.*

Online groups vary a great deal in terms of norms and, as with all groups, it's wise to familiarize yourself with the norms of the group before actively participating. For example, social media groups will vary greatly in their tolerance for self-promotion and commercializing. LinkedIn groups and other sites frown upon self-promotion and may monitor or remove your posts for doing so. And even if you don't get thrown off Facebook, you're likely to incur considerable negative reaction. Sometimes, a group will tolerate self-promotion officially, while individual members may look on the posts very negatively.

Norms may apply to individual members as well as to the group as a whole and, of course, will differ from one cultural group to another (Axtell, 1990, 1993). For example, although business associates from the United States might prefer to get right down to business, those from Japan might prefer rather elaborate socializing before addressing the business at hand. In the United States, men and women in business are expected to interact when making business decisions as well as when socializing. In Muslim and Buddhist societies, however, religious restrictions prevent mixing between the sexes. In some cultures (e.g., those of the United States, Bangladesh, Australia, Germany, Finland, and Hong Kong), punctuality for business meetings is very important. But in others (e.g., those of Morocco, Italy, Brazil, Zambia, Ireland, and Panama), punctuality is less important; being late is no great insult and in some situations is even expected. In the United States and in much of Asia and Europe, meetings are held between two parties. In many Persian Gulf states, however, a business executive is likely to conduct meetings with several different groups—sometimes dealing with totally different issues—at the same time. In the United States very little interpersonal touching goes on during business meetings, but in Arab countries touching such as hand holding is common and is a gesture of friendship.

HIGH-CONTEXT AND LOW-CONTEXT CULTURES A cultural distinction that has special relevance to small group communication is that between high-context and low-context cultures (Hall, 1976; Singh & Pereira, 2005). In a **high-context culture** (for example, Japan, China, Korea, Malaysia, and Indonesia) much of the information conveyed is communicated by the context, or in the person, rather than explicitly coded in verbal messages. In such cultures, individuals have a great deal of information in common, and this shared knowledge does not have to be made explicit. In a **low-context culture** (for example, Denmark, Germany, the United States, Canada, Australia, and New Zealand), most information is communicated through explicitly stated verbal messages. In such cultures, people do not assume that they share certain information and so must make all crucial details explicit.

Members of high-context cultures spend a lot of time getting to know each other before engaging in any small group interaction. Because of this prior personal knowledge, a great deal of information is already shared and therefore does not have to be explicitly stated. Members of low-context cultures, on the other hand, spend less time getting to know each other and therefore do not have that shared knowledge. As a result, everything has to be stated explicitly. When this simple difference is not taken into account, misunderstandings can result. For example, the directness and explicitness characteristic of the low-context culture may prove insulting, insensitive, or unnecessary to members of a high-context culture. Conversely, to someone from a low-context culture, members from a high-context culture may appear vague, underhanded, and even dishonest in their reluctance to be explicit or to engage in what a low-context culture would consider to be open and direct communication. See also the Cultural Map in this chapter.

VIEWPOINTS: Group Norms

What norms govern your class in human communication? What norms govern your family? What norms govern your place of work? Do you have any difficulty with these norms?

JOURNAL
COMMUNICATION CHOICE POINT
Violating Team Norms?

You're working with a team off-site, all expenses paid. Your coworkers all pad their expense accounts. You don't want to do this and yet you don't want to not do it for fear that your expense account will reveal your coworkers' padding, thus violating an important group norm. *What might you do?*

Idea Generating and Sharing Groups

9.3 Define *brainstorming* and *focus groups* and describe how each operates.

A number of important small groups are concerned with generating ideas and with sharing information. Two such groups are the brainstorming group and the focus group.

Brainstorming Groups

Many small groups exist solely to generate ideas through **brainstorming**— a technique for analyzing a problem by presenting as many ideas as possible (Osborn, 1957; Beebe & Masterson, 2012). Although brainstorming also can be useful when you're trying to come up with ideas by yourself—ideas for speeches or term papers, ideas for a fun vacation, or ways to make money—it is more typical in small group settings. Organizations have come to embrace brainstorming, because it

Harley Schwadron/Jantoo Cartoons/CartoonStock Ltd

The Cultural Map

HIGH- AND LOW-CONTEXT CULTURES

Context refers to the extent to which information is made explicit or left implicit (since it's known from past experiences or just assumed). In low-context cultures information is made explicit (as in contracts and signed agreements); the communication is direct. In high-context cultures, much of the information is in the context or in what each person already knows from previous experiences; the communication is often indirect.

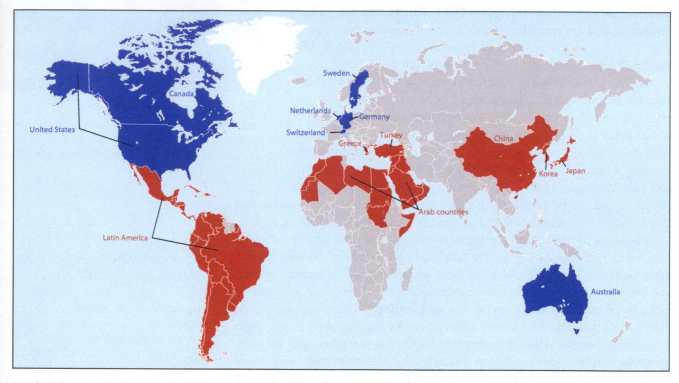

■ In high-context cultures such as these, much meaning is encoded through facial, eye, and other nonverbal movements. The context is more important than the actual words.

■ In low-context cultures such as these, meaning is encoded largely in verbal form; little is left to chance. The words are more important than the context.

Using the concepts of high and low context how would you compare your posts on Facebook or Twitter to writing an e-mail to your instructor?

lessens group members' inhibitions and encourages all participants to exercise their creativity. It also fosters cooperative teamwork; members soon learn that their own ideas and creativity are sparked by the contributions of others. The technique builds member pride and ownership in the final solution (or product or service), because all members contribute to it.

Brainstorming occurs in two phases: (1) the brainstorming period itself and (2) the evaluation period. The procedures are simple. First, a problem is selected. The "problem" may be almost anything that is amenable to many possible solutions or ideas—for example, how to recruit new members to the organization or how to market a new product. Before the actual session, group members are informed of the problem so they can think about the topic. When the group meets, each person contributes as many ideas as he or she can think of. Companies often use chalkboards, whiteboards, or easels to record all the ideas. A brainstorming group may appoint one person to be the scribe; that person keys the group's notes into a laptop for instant circulation via e-mail to other group members after the group has concluded its business. During the initial idea-generating session, members follow four rules.

- **Rule 1: No evaluations are permitted at this stage.** All ideas are recorded for the group to see (or hear later). Prohibiting both verbal and nonverbal evaluation encourages group members to participate freely.

    This first rule is perhaps the most difficult for members to follow, so you might want to practice responding to what are called "idea killers." For example, what might you say if someone were to criticize an idea with the following comments?

We tried it before and it didn't work.	It would cost too much.
No one would vote for it.	We don't have the facilities.
It's too complex.	What we have is good enough.
It's too simple.	It just doesn't fit us.
It would take too long.	It's not possible.

- **Rule 2: Quantity of ideas is the goal.** The more ideas generated, the more likely it is that a useful solution will be found.

- **Rule 3: Combinations and extensions of ideas are encouraged.** Although members may not criticize a particular idea, they may extend or combine it. The value of a particular idea may be that it stimulates another idea.

- **Rule 4: Freewheeling (i.e., developing as wild an idea as possible) is desirable.** A wild idea can be tempered easily, but it's not so easy to elaborate on a simple or conservative idea.

After all the ideas are generated—a period that lasts about 15 or 20 minutes—the group evaluates the entire list. Unworkable ideas are crossed off the list; those showing promise are retained and evaluated. During this phase, criticism is allowed.

Focus Groups

A different type of information-sharing group is the **focus group**, a small group that is assembled and subjected to a kind of in-depth interview, often for market research. The aim of conducting a focus group is to discover through a sample of individuals what it is that people in general think about an issue or product; for example, what do men between 18 and 25 think of a particular brand of aftershave lotion and its packaging? In the focus group, a leader/interviewer tries to discover the members' beliefs, attitudes, thoughts, and feelings to use as a guide for decisions on, for example, changing the scent or redesigning the packaging. It is the leader's task to prod members of the focus group to analyze their thoughts and feelings on a deeper level and to use the thoughts of one member to stimulate the thoughts of others.

Generally, a focus group leader, who is usually a professional facilitator rather than a member of the hosting organization itself, assembles approximately 12 people who represent the general population. The leader explains the process, the time limits, and the general goal of the group— let's say, to discover why these 12 individuals requested information on the XYZ health plan but purchased a plan from another company. The leader then asks a variety of questions. In our example the questions might be, "How did you hear about the XYZ health plan? What other health plans did you consider before making your actual purchase? What influenced you to buy the plan you eventually bought? Were any other people influential in helping you make your decision?" Through the exploration of these and similar questions, the facilitator and the relevant organizational members (who may be seated behind a one-way mirror, watching

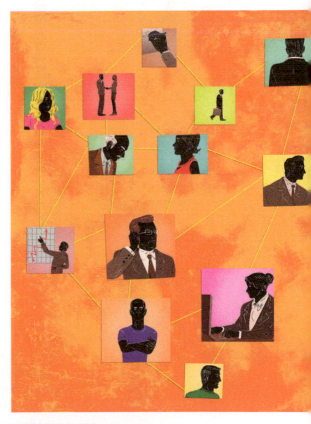

VIEWPOINTS: Chatting

In research of online messages, it was found that people were more likely to comment on a message when that message was negative than when it was positive (Rollman, Krug, & Parente, 2000). *Do you find this to be true in your social network messages? If so, why do you think this occurs? Would it be fair to say, from your own experience, that the reverse would be true in face-to-face communication?*

Communicating Ethically
THE ETHICS OF GOSSIP

Gossip is social talk that involves making evaluations about persons who are not present during the conversation; and it can occur between only two people or in a small group, as in office gossip at the cafeteria, for example (Eder & Enke, 1991; Wert & Salovey, 2004). One study estimates that approximately two-thirds of people's conversation time is devoted to social topics, and that most of these topics can be considered gossip (Dunbar, 2004). Gossip bonds people together and solidifies their relationship; it creates a sense of camaraderie (Greengard, 2001; Hafen, 2004). At the same time, of course, it helps to create an in-group (i.e., those doing the gossiping) and an out-group (i.e., those being gossiped about).

As you might expect, in many instances gossip would be considered unethical. Some instances generally identified as unethical include the following (Bok, 1983):

- When gossip is used to unfairly hurt another person—for example, spreading gossip about an office romance or an instructor's past indiscretions
- When you know that what you're saying is not true—for example, lying to make another person look bad or spreading false rumors
- When no one has the right to such personal information—for example, revealing the income of neighbors to others or revealing another student's poor grades to your friends
- When you've promised secrecy—for example, revealing something that you promised not to repeat to others

ETHICAL CHOICE POINT

You're supervising a new group of interns and you're wondering if you should tell them about the supervisor who has made romantic overtures to several former interns. *Would this just be unethical gossip or would it be ethical and well within your mission to warn them?*

JOURNAL
COMMUNICATION CHOICE POINT
Stimulating Contributions

You're in charge of a focus group in which members will discuss what they like and dislike about the websites they visit. The problem you anticipate, based on past experience, is that a few members will do all the talking and the rest will hardly talk at all. *What are some of the ways you can confront this problem?*

---

the discussion) may put together a more effective health plan or more effective advertising strategies.

Problem-Solving Groups

9.4   Describe the problem-solving sequence, decision-making methods, nominal group, and the Delphi method.

A **problem-solving group** meets to solve a particular problem or to reach a decision on some issue. In a sense, this is the most demanding kind of group. It requires not only a knowledge of small group communication techniques but also a thorough knowledge of the particular problem on the part of all group members. Also, for the most successful outcome, it usually demands faithful adherence to a set of procedural rules.

The Problem-Solving Sequence

The **problem-solving sequence** identifies six steps and owes its formulation to philosopher John Dewey's (1910) insights into how people think (see Figure 9.3). These steps are designed to make problem solving more efficient and effective.

STEP 1: DEFINE AND ANALYZE THE PROBLEM   In some instances, the nature of the problem is clearly specified. For example, a work team might discuss how to package new tablets or smart phones for Valentine's Day. In other instances, however, the problem may be vague, and it may be up to the group to define it—for example, the general topic of poor campus communications. In this case, the topic has to be more clearly defined and limited—for example, how the college website can be improved. Define the problem as an open-ended question ("How can we improve the college website?") rather than as a statement ("The website needs to be improved") or as a yes/no question ("Does the website need improvement?").

STEP 2: ESTABLISH CRITERIA FOR EVALUATING SOLUTIONS Decide how you'll evaluate the solutions before proposing them. Identify the standards or criteria you'll use in evaluating solutions or in preferring one solution over another. For example, you might decide that a solution must lead to a 10 percent increase in website visits, that the solutions must not increase the budget, that the website information must not violate anyone's right to privacy, or that the website must provide a forum for all members of the college community. Set up criteria that are realistic and that can, in fact, be attained; otherwise, no solution is going to prove acceptable.

STEP 3: IDENTIFY POSSIBLE SOLUTIONS Identify as many solutions as possible. Focus on quantity rather than quality. Brainstorming may be particularly useful at this point. Solutions to the website improvement problem might include incorporating reviews of faculty publications, student evaluations of specific courses, reviews of restaurants in the campus area, outlines for new courses, and employment information.

STEP 4: EVALUATE SOLUTIONS After all solutions have been proposed, evaluate each one. For example, does incorporating reviews of area restaurants meet the criteria? Would it increase the budget, for example? Would posting grades violate students' rights to privacy? Each potential solution should be matched against the evaluating criteria.

STEP 5: SELECT THE BEST SOLUTION(S) Select the best solution and put it into operation. Let's assume that reviews of faculty publications and outlines for new courses best meet the evaluating criteria for solutions. The group might then incorporate these two new items into the website.

Groups use different decision-making methods when deciding, for example, which solution to accept. The method to be used should, naturally, be stated at the outset of the group discussion. Three main decision-making methods can be followed:

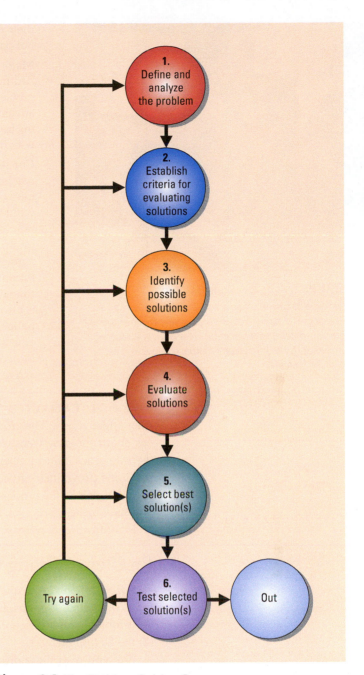

Figure 9.3 The Problem-Solving Sequence

Although most small group theorists would advise you to follow the problem-solving pattern as presented here, others would alter it somewhat. For example, some would advise you to reverse steps 2 and 3: to identify possible solutions first and then consider the criteria for evaluating them. The advantage of this approach is that you're likely to generate more creative solutions, because you will not be restricted by standards of evaluation. The disadvantage is that you may spend a great deal of time generating impractical solutions that will never meet the standards you will eventually propose.

- **Authority** In decision making by authority, group members voice their feelings and opinions, but the leader or boss makes the final decision. This method has the advantages of being efficient and of giving greater importance to the suggestions of more experienced members. The disadvantage is that members may feel that

VIEWPOINTS: Developing Criteria

What type of criteria would an advertising agency use in evaluating a campaign to sell soap? A university, in evaluating a new multicultural curriculum? Parents, in evaluating a preschool for their children? A group of people creating a sign for protest?

their contributions have too little influence and therefore may not participate with real enthusiasm.

- **Majority rule** The group agrees to abide by the majority decision and may vote on various issues as the group searches to solve its problem. Like decision by authority, this method is efficient. A disadvantage is that it may lead the group to limit discussion by calling for a vote once a majority has agreed. Also, members not voting with the majority may feel disenfranchised and left out.

- **Consensus** In small group decision making, consensus means reaching agreement. The agreement does not have to be unanimous; it is, rather, something that the group members can live with; they agree that they can do whatever the group's solution requires (Kelly, 1994). It does not imply that each individual group member agrees with the solution, but only that members agree that at this time (for this situation, for this group) this solution should be adopted and followed. Consensus is the most time-consuming of the decision-making methods. However, it is also the method that best secures the cooperation and participation of all members in implementing the group's decisions. If you want members of the group to be satisfied with and committed to the decision, consensus seems to be the best way to arrive at a solution (Beebe & Masterson, 2012).

STEP 6: TEST SELECTED SOLUTIONS After putting solutions into operation, test their effectiveness. The group might, for example, poll the students or college employees about the new website. Or the group might analyze the number of visits to the website to see if the number of visits increases by the desired 10 percent. If the selected solutions prove ineffective, the group will need to return to a previous stage and repeat that part of the process. This often involves selecting other solutions to test. But it also may mean going even farther back in the process—to a reanalysis of the problem, an identification of other solutions, or a restatement of criteria, for example.

Problem-Solving Groups at Work

The problem-solving sequence discussed here is used widely in a variety of different types of business groups. Let's examine two popular approaches that rely largely on the problem-solving techniques just discussed: (1) the nominal group technique and (2) the Delphi method.

As you read these discussions, realize that the available technology will dictate some of the ways in which these groups operate. If the members only have a whiteboard, then much will be recorded on the board. If all members have computers connected to the company website, then much of the record keeping will go onto the website and at the same time into each laptop or tablet.

THE NOMINAL GROUP TECHNIQUE The **nominal group** technique is a method of problem solving that uses limited discussion and confidential voting to obtain a group decision. It's especially helpful when some members may be reluctant to voice their opinions in a regular problem-solving group or when the issue is controversial or sensitive. According to the Department of Health and Human Services (2006), the nominal group technique can be divided into four main steps:

1. The problem is presented to the group members who each write down their ideas independently.

2. Each idea is recorded without any discussion or debate.

3. Each recorded idea is discussed so that it is clear to all members.

4. Members then vote to prioritize the ideas, which are then listed in order; those ideas ranking the highest are put into operation.

THE DELPHI METHOD   In the **Delphi method**, a group of "experts" is established, but there's no interaction among them; instead, they communicate by repeatedly responding to questionnaires (Kelly, 1994; Tersine & Riggs, 1980; Hsu & Sanford, 2007). The Delphi method is especially useful when you want to involve people who are geographically distant from one another, when you want all members to become part of the solution and to uphold it, or when you want to minimize the effects of dominant members or even of peer pressure (Yousuf, 2007; Linstone & Turoff, 1975/2002). The method is best explained as a series of eight steps (Kelly, 1994).

1. The problem is defined (for example, "We need to improve intradepartmental communication"). What each member is expected to do is specified (for example, each member should contribute five ideas on this specific question).

2. Each member then anonymously contributes five ideas in writing.

3. The ideas of all members are combined, written up, and distributed to all members.

4. Members then select the three or four best ideas from this composite list and submit these.

5. From these responses another list is produced and distributed to all members.

6. Members then select the one or two best ideas from the new list and submit these.

7. From these responses another list is produced and distributed to all members. The process may be repeated any number of times, but usually three rounds are sufficient for achieving a fair degree of agreement.

8. The "final" solutions are identified and are communicated to all members.

JOURNAL
COMMUNICATION CHOICE POINT
Critical Thinking

You're on a team (all equal in your organizational position) charged with designing the packaging for a new cell phone, and you need to establish how a decision will be made. *What are some of your decision-making options? What are the advantages and disadvantages of each decision-making option?*

Summary of Concepts and Skills

This chapter provided an overview of the nature of the small group and of small group communication and some of the major types of groups.

The Nature of Small Groups and Teams

9.1 Define *small group* and *team* and the advantages and disadvantages of small groups.

1. A small group is a collection of individuals who share a common purpose, are interdependent, operate with organizing rules, and see themselves as a group. A team is also a small group, but it is usually established for a specific task in which the members' roles are specifically defined; members are committed to accomplishing the task; and their messages are largely content focused.

2. Virtual groups and teams are increasing dramatically in businesses and social networking.

3. Groups provide added opportunities for learning different perspectives on an issue but can also pose problems for effective decision making.

Small Group Stages, Formats, and Culture

9.2 Explain the stages of small group communication, small group formats, and small group culture.

4. Small group interactions generally follow the five stages of conversation: opening, feedforward, business, feedback, closing.

5. Four popular small group formats are the roundtable, the panel, the symposium, and the symposium-forum.

6. Small groups develop norms (i.e., rules or standards of behavior) and are heavily influenced by the larger culture of which the groups are a part.

Idea Generating and Sharing Groups

9.3 **Define *brainstorming* and *focus groups* and describe how each operates.**

7. The brainstorming group attempts to generate as many ideas as possible by avoiding critical evaluation and encouraging quantity of ideas, combinations and extensions of ideas, and freewheeling.

8. The focus group tries to understand what people want in a product or service through a mutual sharing of knowledge or insight.

Problem-Solving Groups

9.4 **Describe the problem-solving sequence, decision-making methods, nominal group, and the Delphi method.**

9. The problem-solving group attempts to solve a particular problem, or at least to reach a decision that may be a preface to solving the problem, and may do so through decision by authority, majority rule, or consensus.

10. The steps in the problem-solving approach are (1) define and analyze the problem, (2) establish criteria for evaluating solutions, (3) identify possible solutions, (4) evaluate solutions, (5) select the best solution(s), and (6) test selected solution(s).

11. Small group approaches that are widely used in business today include the nominal group and the Delphi method.

The skills covered in this chapter focus on your ability to function effectively in a variety of small groups. Place a check mark next to those skills you want to work on most.

_____ 1. I actively seek to discover the norms of the groups in which I function and take these norms into consideration when interacting in the group.

_____ 2. I can communicate in virtual groups, such as social networking groups.

_____ 3. I can adjust my messages and listening in light of differences between high-context and low-context cultures.

_____ 4. I follow the general rules when brainstorming: I avoid negative criticism, strive for quantity, combine and extend the contributions of others, and contribute as wild an idea as I can.

_____ 5. I appropriately restimulate a brainstorming group that has lost its steam.

_____ 6. I follow the six steps when in group problem-solving situations: define and analyze the problem, establish the criteria for evaluating solutions, identify possible solutions, evaluate solutions, select the best solution(s), and test selected solution(s).

_____ 7. I can make use of techniques such as the nominal group or the Delphi method.

Key Terms

brainstorming	group norms	roundtable
consensus	high-context culture	small group
Delphi method	low-context culture	symposium
focus group	nominal group	team
forum	panel	virtual group
gossip	problem-solving group	

Skill Development Experiences

9.1 Small Group Apprehension

Fear of speaking in small groups can be managed.

Just as you may have apprehension about public speaking (a topic discussed in Chapter 11), you probably experience apprehension to some degree in group discussions. Because small groups vary so widely, you're likely to experience different degrees of apprehension depending on the nature of the specific group. Work groups, for example, may cause greater apprehension than groups of friends. And interacting with superiors is likely to generate greater anxiety than meeting with peers or subordinates. Similarly, the degree of familiarity you have with the group members and the extent to which you see yourself as a part of the group (as opposed to an outsider) also will influence your level of apprehension.

Test Yourself

HOW APPREHENSIVE ARE YOU IN GROUP DISCUSSIONS?

This brief test is designed to measure your apprehension in small group communication situations. The questionnaire consists of six statements concerning your feelings about participating in group discussions.

Indicate the degree to which each statement applies to you by marking whether you **1** = strongly agree, **2** = agree, **3** = are undecided, **4** = disagree, or **5** = strongly disagree. (Each of these answers then becomes the "score" for each item.) There are no right or wrong answers. Do not be concerned that some of the statements are similar. Work quickly; just record your first impression.

____ **1.** I dislike participating in group discussions.

____ **2.** Generally, I am comfortable while participating in group discussions.

____ **3.** I am tense and nervous while participating in group discussions.

____ **4.** I like to get involved in group discussions.

____ **5.** Engaging in a group discussion with new people makes me tense and nervous.

____ **6.** I am calm and relaxed while participating in group discussions.

To obtain your score, use the following formula:

Start with 18; add the scores for items 2, 4, and 6; then subtract the scores for items 1, 3, and 5. A score of over 18 shows some degree of apprehension.

Think about the kinds of groups that generate the most anxiety for you. Can you identify the major characteristics of these high-apprehension groups? How do these differ from groups generating little apprehension? What other factors might influence your small group apprehension? When you read suggestions for reducing public speaking anxiety given in Chapter 10, consider how you might use them in the various types of groups in which you participate.

SOURCE: From James C. McCroskey, *An Introduction to Rhetorical Communication*, 9/e. Copyright © 2005 by Allyn & Bacon. Printed and electronically reproduced by permission of Pearson Education, Inc., Englewood Cliffs, New Jersey.

9.2 Using Brainstorming Techniques

Brainstorming is useful even if you do it by yourself. Follow the same rules.

Together with a small group or with the class as a whole, sit in a circle and brainstorm on one of the topics identified in the Skill Development Experience "Solving Problems in Groups" presented below. Be sure to appoint someone to write down all the contributions, or record the discussion. After this brainstorming session, consider these questions:

1. Did any members give negative criticism (even nonverbally)?
2. Did any members hesitate to contribute really wild ideas? Why?
3. Was it necessary to re-stimulate the group members at any point? Did this help?
4. Did possible solutions emerge that would not have been thought of without the group stimulation?

9.3 Listening to New Ideas

It's often easier to analyze an idea when you follow specific steps; in this way there's less likelihood that you'll omit some crucial element in the process.

A useful skill for listening to new ideas is PIP'N, a technique that derives from Carl Rogers's (1970) emphasis on paraphrasing as a means for ensuring understanding and Edward deBono's (1976) PMI (*plus, minus,* and *interesting*) technique. PIP'N involves four steps.

P = Paraphrase. State in your own words what you think the other person is saying. This will ensure that you and the person proposing the idea are talking about the same thing. Your paraphrase also will provide the other person with the opportunity to elaborate or clarify his or her ideas.

I = Interesting. State something interesting that you find in the idea. Say why you think this idea might be interesting to you, to others, to the organization.

P = Positive. Say something positive about the idea. What is good about it? How might it solve a problem or make a situation better?

N = Negative. State any negatives that you think the idea might entail. Might it prove expensive? Difficult to implement? Is it directed at insignificant issues?

Try using PIP'N the next time you hear about a new idea; say, in conversation or in a small group. For practice, try PIP'N on the PIP'N technique itself: (1) Paraphrase the PIP'N technique; (2) Say why the technique is interesting; (3) Say something positive about it; and (4) Say something negative about it.

9.4 Solving Problems in Groups

Following patterns like this helps you move a discussion along without unnecessary detours, and it ensures that you'll cover all essential steps.

Together with four, five, or six other group members—online or face-to-face—problem-solve one of the following questions:

a. What should we do about the homeless?
b. What should we do to improve the college's website?
c. What should we do to better prepare ourselves for the job market?
d. How can social networking sites be used more effectively?
e. How can we improve student–faculty communication?

Before beginning discussion of the topic, prepare a discussion outline, answering the following questions.

1. What is the problem? What are its causes? What are its effects?
2. What criteria should a solution have to satisfy?
3. What are some possible solutions?
4. What are the advantages and disadvantages of each of these solutions?
5. What solution seems best (in light of the advantages and disadvantages)?
6. How might this solution be tested?

Chapter 10

Members and Leaders in Small Group Communication

Leadership means different things to different people.

CHAPTER OUTLINE	Learning Objectives
Members in Small Group Communication	**10.1** Describe and give examples of the three major types of group members and identify the important membership skills.
Leaders in Small Group Communication	**10.2** Define *leadership*, the theories of leadership, and identify the important leadership skills.
Membership, Leadership, and Culture	**10.3** Explain the role of culture in small group communication and define and distinguish between individual and collective orientations and high- and low-power distances.

As you saw in Chapter 9, you're a part of many different groups, and you serve a wide variety of roles and functions in these groups. This chapter focuses on both membership and leadership in small groups but with clear application to all kinds and sizes of groups. By gaining insight into these roles and functions, you'll increase your own effectiveness as a group member and leader.

Members in Small Group Communication

10.1   Describe and give examples of the three major types of group members and identify the important membership skills.

Much like actors play roles in a film, group members play various roles as they interact in their groups. Often these roles become patterns of behavior and so, for example, Pat will usually try to be encouraging to others and Chris will always try to seek compromises. The role you play in any group (or in many groups) will depend on such factors as the nature of the group, your position among group members, your personality, and your perception of what others expect of you. Before reading about these roles, take the accompanying self-test, "What Kind of Group Member Are You?"

Member Roles

Group member roles fall into three general classes—group task roles, group building and maintenance roles, and individual roles—a classification introduced in early research (Benne & Sheats, 1948) and still widely used today (Lumsden & Lumsden, 1996; Beebe & Masterson, 2012). These roles are frequently served by leaders as well.

GROUP TASK ROLES   **Group task roles** help the group focus on achieving its goals. Effective group members serve several roles. Some people lock into a few specific

---

Test Yourself

WHAT KIND OF GROUP MEMBER ARE YOU?

For each statement below, respond with **T** (for True) if the statement is often true of your group behavior or **F** (for False) if the statement generally does not apply to your group behavior.

_____ **1.** I present new ideas and suggest new strategies.

_____ **2.** I ask for facts and opinions.

_____ **3.** I stimulate the group.

_____ **4.** I give examples and try to look for positive solutions.

_____ **5.** I positively reinforce group members.

_____ **6.** I try to reconcile differences.

_____ **7.** I go along with the other members.

_____ **8.** I offer compromises as ways of resolving conflict.

_____ **9.** I express negative evaluation of the actions and feelings of the group members.

_____ **10.** I try to run the group.

_____ **11.** I express personal perspectives and feelings.

_____ **12.** I express confusion or deprecate myself.

As you'll see as you read further, these behaviors are characteristic of the three general types of group member roles. The first four statements refer to your taking on group task roles, and the next four refer to your taking on group building and maintenance roles. Both of these types of roles are productive. The final four refer to your taking an individual rather than a group focus; these are the behaviors that often work against the group achieving its goals. As you read the sections in the text on member roles, try to relate these roles to your own behavior or to group behavior you've witnessed. Then ask yourself what worked and what didn't work. Which roles were productive, and which ones were unproductive?

roles, but this single focus is usually counterproductive—it's better for the roles to be spread more evenly among the members and for the roles to be alternated frequently. Here are some examples of group task roles.

- **The information seeker or giver or the opinion seeker or giver** asks for or gives facts or opinions, seeks clarification of issues being discussed, and presents facts or opinions to group members: "Sales for May were up 10 percent. Do we have the sales figures for June?"

- **The initiator-contributor** presents new ideas or new perspectives on old ideas, suggests new goals, or proposes new procedures or organizational strategies: "We need to also look at the amount of time visitors spend on our new site."

- **The elaborator** gives examples and tries to work out possible solutions, trying to build on what others have said: "That three-part division worked at ABC and should work here as well."

- **The evaluator-critic** evaluates the group's decisions, questions the logic or practicality of the suggestions, and provides the group with both positive and negative feedback: "That's a great idea, but it sounds expensive."

- **The procedural technician** or recorder takes care of various mechanical duties, such as distributing group materials and arranging the seating; writing down the group's activities, suggestions, and decisions; and/or serving as the group's memory: "We have another meeting scheduled to discuss just this issue, so perhaps we can skip it for today."

GROUP BUILDING AND MAINTENANCE ROLES   No group can be task oriented at all times. Group members have varied interpersonal relationships, and these need to be nourished if the group is to function effectively. Group members need to be satisfied if they are to be productive. **Group building and maintenance roles** serve these relationship needs. Here are some examples of these roles.

- **The encourager** or **harmonizer** provides members with positive reinforcement through social approval or praise for their ideas and mediates the various differences between group members: "Pat, another great idea."

- **The compromiser** tries to resolve conflict between his or her ideas and those of others and offers compromises: "This looks like it could work if each department cut back at least 10 percent."

- **The gatekeeper-expediter** keeps the channels of communication open by reinforcing the efforts of others: "Those were really good ideas; we're on a roll."

- **The standard setter** proposes standards for the functions of the group or for its solutions: "We need to be able to increase the number of visits by several thousand a day."

- **The follower** goes along with members, passively accepts the ideas of others, and functions more as an audience than as an active member: "If you all agree, that's fine with me."

INDIVIDUAL ROLES   Whereas group task and group building and maintenance roles are productive and help the group achieve its goal, **individual roles** hinder the group from achieving its goal and are individual rather than group oriented. Such roles, often termed dysfunctional, hinder the group's effectiveness in terms of both productivity and personal satisfaction. Here are some examples of individual roles.

- **The aggressor** expresses negative evaluation of members and attacks the group: "That's a terrible idea. It doesn't make any sense."

- **The recognition seekers and self-confessors** try to focus attention on themselves, boast about their accomplishments rather

VIEWPOINTS: Group Roles in Interpersonal Relationships

Can you identify roles that you habitually or frequently serve in certain groups? Do you serve these roles in your close interpersonal relationships as you do in your workplace relationships?

than the task at hand, and express their own feelings rather than focus on the group: "The system I devised at B&B was a great success; everyone loved it. We should just go with that."

- **The blocker** provides negative feedback, is disagreeable, and opposes other members or suggestions regardless of their merit: "You're dreaming if you think that will work."

  - **The special interest pleader** disregards the goals of the group and pleads the case of some special group: "This solution isn't adequate; it doesn't address the needs of XYZ."

  - **The dominator** tries to run the group or members by pulling rank, flattering members, or acting the role of boss: "I've been here the longest; I know what works and what doesn't work."

A popular individual role born on the Internet is *trolling*, the practice of posting messages that you know are false or outrageous just so you can watch the group members correct you or get emotionally upset by your message. As in any group, behavior such as trolling or flaming wastes time and energy and diverts the group from its primary objective.

JOURNAL
COMMUNICATION CHOICE POINT
Individual Roles

In a group of workers, one member consistently plays the role of blocker, objecting to everything anyone says. Another member plays the role of self-confessor, revealing feelings no one wants to hear. *What are some of the options that members have for dealing with individual role players like these?*

Member Skills

Here are several guidelines to help make your participation in small group communication more effective and enjoyable.

BE GROUP ORIENTED When participating in a small group, you serve as a member of a team. You share common goals with the other group members, and your participation is valuable to the extent that it advances this shared goal. In a team situation, you need to pool your talents, knowledge, and insights to promote the best possible solution for the group. Although a group orientation calls for the participation and cooperation of all group members, this guideline does not suggest that you abandon your individuality, personal values, or beliefs for the group's sake. Individuality *with* a group orientation is most effective. And because the most effective and the most creative solutions often emerge from a combination of ideas, approach small group situations with flexibility; come to the group with ideas and information but without firmly formulated conclusions. The importance of a group orientation is also seen in one of the rules of netiquette, which holds that you should not protest the subject of, say, a mailing list or a chat group. If you don't wish to be group oriented and discuss what the group is discussing, you're expected to unsubscribe from the mailing list or withdraw from the group.

CENTER CONFLICT ON ISSUES Conflict in small group situations is inevitable; it's a natural part of the give and take of ideas and often promotes a better outcome. To manage conflict effectively, however, center it on issues rather than on personalities. When you disagree, make it clear that your disagreement is with the ideas expressed, not with the person who expressed them. For example, if you think that a colleague's ideas to raise funds for your social service agency are impractical and shortsighted, concentrate your criticisms on your colleague's proposed plan and suggest ways that the plan could be improved rather than attacking your colleague personally. Similarly, when someone disagrees with you, try not to take it personally or react emotionally. Rather, view the disagreement as an opportunity to discuss issues from an alternative point of view. In the language of the Internet, don't flame—don't attack the person. And don't contribute to flame wars by flame baiting, or saying things that will further incite the personal attacks.

BE CRITICALLY OPEN-MINDED When members join a group with their minds already made up, the small group process degenerates into a series of debates in

Table 10.1   Social Loafing

Here are a few factors that influence the likelihood that social loafing will occur and some correctives (Kenrick, Neuberg, & Cialdini, 2007).

When Social Loafing Is More Likely to Occur	Corrective
An individual group member's contributions cannot be easily identified.	Make contributions easily identifiable and make members aware of this.
The punishment for or cost of poor performance is insignificant.	Reward excellent performance and/or punish poor performance.
The group lacks cohesion.	Stress the importance of being part of a group or team; following the suggestions for group membership and leadership will help here.
The task has little personal importance.	Stress the personal connection between the members of the group and the task.

which each person argues for his or her position—a clear example of members taking on individual and dysfunctional roles. Group goals are neglected and the group process breaks down.

Let's say you have spent several hours developing what you think is the best, most effective advertising campaign to combat your company's low sales numbers. At the group meeting, however, members' reactions are extremely critical. Instead of becoming defensive, listen to their criticisms and try to think of ways that your plan could be modified to be as effective as possible for the company. To avoid this situation in the future, try to come to the group with ideas rather than conclusions; with suggestions rather than final decisions; and, of course, with information that will contribute to the discussion and the group goal. Be willing to accept other people's suggestions as well as to revise your own in light of the discussion. Listen openly but critically to comments of all members (including your own).

BEWARE OF SOCIAL LOAFING   Visualize yourself in a rope pulling contest—you need to successfully pull the other side into the pond or they will pull you. With this vision in mind, consider whether you would exert more effort if you were alone or if you were part of a group of five or six. The concept of **social loafing**—the theory that you exert less effort when you're part of a group than when alone—resulted from experiments such as this that measured the amount of effort people actually exerted alone versus in groups (Latané, Williams, & Harkins, 2006). Being aware of this tendency is a useful first step in combating it. It's often an unproductive group tendency that leads to less productive group interactions and decisions. And when noticed by others will hurt you professionally. Some of the factors that influence social loafing and corresponding correctives are identified in Table 10.1.

ENSURE UNDERSTANDING   Make sure all participants understand your ideas and information. If something is worth saying, it's worth making clear. When in doubt, ask questions: "Is that clear?" "Did I explain that clearly?" Make sure, too, that you fully understand other members' contributions, especially before you disagree with them. In fact, it's often wise to preface any expression of disagreement with some kind of paraphrase to ensure you really are in disagreement. For example, you might say, "If I understand you correctly, you feel that marketing should bear sole responsibility for updating the product database." After waiting for the response, you would state your thoughts.

BEWARE OF GROUPTHINK   In some groups, agreement among members becomes so important that it takes the form of **groupthink**—a tendency that shuts out realistic and logical analysis of a problem and of possible alternatives (Janis, 1983; Mullen, Tara, Salas, & Driskell, 1994).

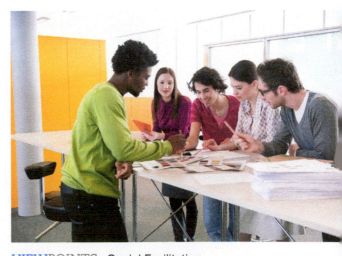

VIEWPOINTS: Social Facilitation

The opposite of social loafing is **social facilitation**, which holds that in a group you exert more effort than you would if you were alone. You might feel this way if you felt you were being watched and evaluated, for example. *Under what conditions are you likely to perform below your normal level? Under what conditions are you likely to perform above your normal level?*

"All those in favor say 'Aye.'"
"Aye."   "Aye."   "Aye."
        "Aye."   "Aye."   "Aye."

Henry Martin/The New Yorker Collection/The Cartoon Bank

In groupthink, members are extremely selective about the information they consider. They tend to ignore facts and opinions contrary to the group's position, and they readily and uncritically accept those that support the group's position. When you recognize that groupthinking is occurring, try the following.

- When too-simple solutions are offered to problems, try to illustrate (with specific examples, if possible) for the group members how the complexity of the problem is not going to yield to the solutions offered.

- When you feel that members are not expressing their doubts about the group's decisions, encourage them to voice disagreement, to play devil's advocate, to test the adequacy of the solution. If you feel there is unexpressed disagreement, ask specifically if anyone disagrees.

- To combat the group pressure toward agreement, reward members who do voice disagreement or doubt. Say, for example, "That's a good argument; we need to hear more about the potential problems of this proposal. Does anyone else see any problems?"

Leaders in Small Group Communication

10.2 Define *leadership*, the theories of leadership, and identify the important leadership skills.

Leadership is defined in two very different ways in research and theory.

- Leadership is the process of influencing the thoughts, feelings, and behaviors of group members and establishing the direction that others follow; leadership and influence are parts of the same skill.

- Leadership is the process of empowering others; the leader is the person who helps others to maximize their potential and to take control of their lives.

These two definitions are not mutually exclusive; in fact, most effective leaders do both: They influence and they empower. As you read about leadership, keep these two definitions or functions of power and empowerment in mind. Many common beliefs about leadership are erroneous. The following are three examples of myths about leadership paraphrased from small group theorists (Bennis & Nanus, 2003).

- **Myth: The skills of leadership are rare.** Actually, all of us have the potential for leadership. There are millions of people throughout the world who are serving leadership functions in government, business, education, and countless other fields.

- **Myth: Leaders are born.** Actually, the major leadership skills can be learned by just about everyone. No specific genetic endowment is necessary. We all can improve our leadership abilities.

- **Myth: Leaders are all charismatic.** Actually, only some leaders are. According to one survey of leaders they were of all heights, varied in articulateness, and dressed both well and poorly (Bennis & Nanus, 2003, p. 208).

In many small groups one person serves as leader; in other groups leadership may be shared by several persons. In some cases a person may be appointed the leader or may serve as leader because of her or his position within the company or hierarchy. In other cases the leader may emerge as the group proceeds in fulfilling its functions or instead may be elected by the group members. Two significant factors exert considerable influence on who emerges as group leader. One is the extent of active participation: The person who talks the most is more likely to emerge as leader (Mullen, Salas, & Driskell, 1989; Shaw & Gouran, 1990). The second factor is effective listening: Members who listen effectively will emerge as leaders more often than those who do not (Johnson & Bechler, 1998; Bechler & Johnson, 1995).

At this point you should find it interesting to analyze your own leadership qualities by taking the self-test, "What Kind of Leader Are You?" It will help personalize the preceding discussion on the four approaches to leadership.

Leadership Theories

Not surprisingly, leadership has been the focus of considerable research attention. Researchers have identified several views of leadership, called *approaches*. Looking at a few of these approaches will give you a better idea of the varied ways in which leadership may be viewed and a better grasp of what leadership is and how it may be achieved.

THE TRAITS APPROACH This approach views the leader as the one who possesses those characteristics or skills that contribute to leadership. The traits approach is valuable for stressing the characteristics that often (but not always) distinguish leaders from non-leaders. For example, some of the world's leading corporations seek

Test Yourself
WHAT KIND OF LEADER ARE YOU?

This self-test will help you think about yourself in the role of leader. Respond to each of the following statements with **T** (for True) if you feel the statement is often or always true of your leadership behavior or **F** (for False) if you feel the statement often or always does not apply to your leadership behavior.

_____ **1.** Popular with group members

_____ **2.** Knowledgeable about the topics discussed

_____ **3.** Dependable

_____ **4.** Effective in establishing group goals

_____ **5.** Competent in giving directions

_____ **6.** Capable of energizing group members

_____ **7.** Charismatic (i.e., dynamic, engaging, powerful)

_____ **8.** Empowering of group members

_____ **9.** Moral and honest

_____ **10.** Skilled in satisfying both task and relationship needs

_____ **11.** Flexible in adjusting leadership style on the basis of the situation

_____ **12.** Able to delegate responsibility

This test was designed to encourage you to look at yourself in terms of the four approaches to leadership to be discussed in this section of the chapter. Perceptions 1–3 refer to the *traits approach* to leadership, which defines a leader as someone who possesses certain qualities. If you answered **True** for these statements, you have the qualities normally associated with the trait theory of leadership. **False** responses would indicate that you don't see yourself possessing these traits. Perceptions 4–6 refer to the *functional approach*, which defines a leader as someone who performs certain functions. **True** responses indicate that you serve the functions normally viewed as the province of a leader. Perceptions 7–9 refer to the *transformational approach*, which defines a leader as someone who enables the group members to become the best they can be. **True** responses indicate your leadership is transformational. Perceptions 10–12 refer to the *situational approach*, which defines a leader as someone who can adjust his or her style to balance the needs of the specific situation. **True** responses indicate your flexibility to adjust to changing circumstances. As you read the remainder of this chapter, try to identify specific skills and competencies you might learn that would enable you to respond with **True** to all 12 statements.

technology project managers and leaders by looking for people who have technological skills, group-building skills, and interpersonal skills (Crowley, 1999). Research has found that the traits most frequently associated with leadership include intelligence, self-confidence, determination, integrity, and sociability (Northouse, 1997).

A shortcoming of the traits approach is that these qualities often vary according to the situations in which the leader functions, such as the group type, the personalities and roles of the other members, and the group's cultural context. Thus, for some groups (e.g., a new computer game company), a youthful, energetic, humorous leader might be most effective; for other groups (e.g., a medical diagnosis team), an older, more experienced and serious leader might be most effective.

THE FUNCTIONAL APPROACH   This approach to leadership focuses on what the leader should do in a given situation. We've already encountered some of these functions in the discussion of group roles. Other functions associated with leadership are setting group goals, giving the group members direction, and summarizing the group's progress (Schultz, 1996). Additional functions are identified in the section entitled "Leadership Skills" later in this chapter.

THE TRANSFORMATIONAL APPROACH   This approach describes a "transformational" (also called visionary or charismatic) leader who elevates the group's members, enabling them not only to accomplish the group task but also to emerge as more empowered individuals (Hersey, Blanchard, & Johnson, 2001). At the center of the transformational approach is the concept of charisma, that quality of an individual that makes us believe or want to follow him or her. Gandhi, Martin Luther King, Jr., and John F. Kennedy are often cited as examples of transformational leaders. These leaders were role models, were seen as extremely competent and able, and articulated moral goals (Northouse, 1997). We'll return to this concept of charisma and its qualities when we examine credibility in Chapter 14.

THE SITUATIONAL APPROACH   This approach holds that the effective leader shifts his or her emphasis between task accomplishment (i.e., identifying and focusing on the specific problem that the group must solve) and member satisfaction (i.e., providing for the psychological and interpersonal needs of the group members) on the basis of the specific group situation. This twofold function, you'll notice, rests on essentially the same distinction between relationship and task groups that we considered in Chapter 9. Some groups call for a high focus on task issues and need little people encouragement; this might be the case, for example, with a group of experienced scientists researching a cure for AIDS. In contrast, a group of recovering alcoholics might require leadership that stresses the members' emotional needs. The general idea of situational leadership is that there is no one style of leadership that fits all situations; each situation will call for a different ratio of emphasis on task and on member satisfaction (Fielder, 1967).

Effective leadership, according to this approach, depends on the leader's assessment of the group's ability to do the task and their willingness and commitment to do it. This theory identifies four leadership styles.

- **Telling style** The leader provides high levels of task guidance and *tells* the group members what to do, when and where to do it, and how to do it. This style is most appropriate for a group that lacks knowledge of the issues involved and needs direct guidance on how to complete the task.

- **Selling style** The leader gives the group high levels of both task guidance and relationship support. This leader not only tells people what to do but also tells them why they should do it; the leader wants to get the members' psychological support (i.e., to get them to "buy into" the task at hand).

- **Participating style** The leader gives the group high levels of relationship support but little in the way of task direction. This leadership style is appropriate for a group that knows what to do (hence little task direction is needed) but that seems to have lost the motivation or willingness to accomplish the task.

- **Delegating style** The leader gives little task direction and little emotional support. This leadership style is most appropriate for a group that knows what to do and how to do it and also has the confidence, commitment, and motivation to accomplish the task. The leader's function here is to delegate tasks for the group's goals to be accomplished.

Leadership Skills

Keeping the various views of leadership in mind, especially the situational theory with its concern for both task and people, we can look at some of the major functions leaders serve and their corresponding skills, the skills of leadership. These functions/skills are not exclusively the leader's; they are often shared or served wholly by group members. But when there's a specific leader, she or he is expected to perform these functions and exhibit the skills for accomplishing these goals.

PREPARE MEMBERS AND START INTERACTION Groups form gradually and often need to be eased into meaningful discussion. As the leader, you need to prepare members for the small group interaction as well as for the discussion of a specific issue or problem. Don't expect diverse members to work together cohesively to solve a problem without first becoming familiar with one another. Similarly, if members are to discuss a specific problem, a proper briefing may be necessary. If materials need to be distributed before the actual discussion, consider e-mailing them to members. Or perhaps members need to view a particular film or television show. Whatever the preparations, you need to organize and coordinate them. Once the group is assembled, you may need to stimulate the members to interact.

BUILD GROUP COHESIVENESS Groups vary greatly in **cohesiveness**—the members' closeness to and liking for each other. In general, cohesiveness is a positive quality, and cohesive groups seem to be more effective. For example, cohesive group members enjoy the interaction more and consequently come to meetings on time and stay until the end. They are more likely to be satisfied with the time spent in the group and to develop a "we-ness," seeing the group as a unit. Because members are comfortable with one another, they will be more willing to offer suggestions and ideas that may at first seem impossible, which may help the group eventually find a workable solution.

In a group that is excessively cohesive, however, members may be less apt to disagree with one another, which may hinder the group's critical analysis of any proposed idea. Still, a cohesive group is more likely to be successful. Cohesiveness is built by leaders who stress the positives, reward members frequently, and make the entire group experience as pleasant and personally rewarding as possible. Simple compliments and expressions of fondness will help build a cohesive group. Group accomplishments also build cohesiveness.

MAINTAIN EFFECTIVE INTERACTION Even after the group has begun to interact, you'll need to monitor the members' effective interaction. When the discussion begins to drag, you may need to step in and motivate the group: "Do we have any additional comments on the proposal to eliminate required courses?" "What do you, as members of the college curriculum committee, think about the proposal?" You'll also want to ensure that all members have an opportunity to express themselves.

Communicating Ethically

THE LEADER'S ETHICAL RESPONSIBILITIES

In addition to mastering the skills of effective and efficient leadership, as a leader you also need to consider the ethical issues involved in leading a group. Because the leader is often called a "chair," CHAIR seems an appropriate acronym to help identify at least some of the characteristics of the ethical leader. As you reflect on these qualities, you'll probably think of other ethical qualities that a leader should possess.

- **C is for Concern for the welfare of group members:** Leaders who are more concerned with their own personal interests, rather than with the group task or the interpersonal needs of the members, are acting unethically.
- **H is for Honesty:** Leaders should be honest with the group members by, for example, revealing any hidden agendas and presenting information fairly.
- **A is for Accountability:** Leaders should take responsibility for their actions and decisions, admit making mistakes, and take corrective action when necessary.
- **I is for Integrity:** Leaders have integrity; they take the high road. They don't lie or deceive. And they avoid actions that would violate the rights of others.
- **R is for Responsiveness:** The leader must be responsive to all members of the group.

ETHICAL CHOICE POINT

You're leading a discussion among a group of high school freshmen whom you're mentoring. The topic turns to marijuana, and the students ask you directly if you smoke pot. The truth is that on occasion you do—but it's a very controlled use, and you feel that it would only destroy your credibility and lead the students to experiment with or continue smoking pot if they knew you did (something you do not want to do). At the same time, you wonder if you can ethically lie to them and tell them that you do not smoke. *What is your ethical obligation in this situation? What would you do?*

JOURNAL
COMMUNICATION CHOICE POINT
Leader Guidance

Members of your group are not participating equally. Of the eight members, three monopolize the discussion; the other five say as little as possible. *What are some of the things you might say to get the group into better balance?*

GUIDE MEMBERS THROUGH THE AGREED-ON AGENDA   As the leader, you need to keep the discussion on track by asking relevant questions, summarizing the group discussions periodically, or offering a transition from one issue to the next. This involves following the list of tasks to be accomplished by the group as outlined in the meeting agenda and efficiently managing the amount of time allotted for each event.

ENSURE MEMBER SATISFACTION   Members have different psychological needs and wants, and many people enter groups because of them. Even though a group may, for example, deal with political issues, members may have come together for psychological as well as for political reasons. If a group is to be effective, it must achieve the group goal (in this case, a political one) without denying the psychological purposes or goals that motivate many of the members to come together. One way to meet these needs is for you as leader to allow digressions and personal comments, assuming they are not too frequent or overly long. Another way is to be supportive and reinforcing.

EMPOWER GROUP MEMBERS   An important function of a leader is to empower other group members—to help them gain increased power over themselves and their environment. Empowerment will occur when you follow these guidelines as a leader.

- Raise members' self-esteem; compliment, reinforce; resist fault finding.
- Share skills and decision-making power and authority.
- Be constructively critical. Be willing to offer your perspective and to react honestly to suggestions from all group members, not only those in high positions.
- Listen willingly and eagerly. Acknowledge your understanding by appropriately nodding or using such minimal responses as *I see* or *I understand*, ask

questions if something isn't clear, maintain eye contact, and lean forward as appropriate.

- Avoid interrupting to change the topic or to shift the focus to something else. When you interrupt, you say, in effect, that what the other group member is saying is less important than what you're saying.
- React supportively. Let other group members know that you appreciate what they are saying.

ENCOURAGE ONGOING EVALUATION AND IMPROVEMENT All groups encounter obstacles as they try to solve a problem, reach a decision, or generate ideas. No group is totally effective. All groups have room for improvement. To improve, the group must focus on itself. Along with trying to solve some external problem, it must try to solve its own internal problems—for example, personal conflicts, failure of members to meet on time, or members who come unprepared. When you notice some serious group failing, address it, perhaps suggesting that a particular issue (say, member tardiness) is a problem to be solved.

MANAGE CONFLICT   As in interpersonal relationships, conflict is a part of small group interaction. And it's a leader's responsibility to deal with it effectively. The conflict management techniques that are useful in small groups are the same techniques discussed in the context of interpersonal communication (see Chapter 8). You may wish to think of them as small group conflict management strategies.

MENTOR   Another function of leadership that is especially applicable to the small group but is used extensively in the workplace and in business and personal relationships generally is that of **mentoring**—a process that occurs when an experienced individual helps to train less experienced group members. An accomplished teacher, for example, might mentor younger teachers who are newly arrived or who have never taught before. A group leader might be the group members' supervisor and may mentor those supervised. The mentor guides new people through the ropes, teaches strategies and techniques for success, and otherwise communicates his or her accumulated knowledge and experience to the "mentee" or protégé. At the same time, the mentor benefits from clarifying his or her thoughts, from seeing the job from the perspective of a newcomer, and from considering and formulating answers to a variety of questions. Just as a member learns from the leader, the leader learns from the members.

Membership, Leadership, and Culture

10.3 Explain the role of culture in small group communication and define and distinguish between individual and collective orientations and high- and low-power distances.

Because most of the research (and also the resulting theory) concerning small group communication, membership, and leadership has been conducted in universities in the United States and reflects U.S. culture, it's important that we look at both membership and leadership from the point of view of different cultures.

All cultures maintain their own belief systems, which influence group members' behavior. Members of many Asian cultures, influenced by Confucian principles, believe that "the protruding nail gets pounded down" and are therefore not likely to voice disagreement with the majority of the group. Members of U.S. culture, on the other hand, influenced by the axiom that "the squeaky wheel gets the grease," are likely to voice disagreement or to act in ways different from other group members in order to get what they want (Hofstede, Hofstede, & Minkov, 2010).

"Sage nodding got me where I am today."

William Haefeli/The New Yorker Collection/The Cartoon Bank

All cultures also have their own rules of preferred and expected leadership style. In the United States, the general and expected style for a group leader is democratic. Our political leaders are elected by a democratic process; similarly, company directors are elected by the shareholders of their corporations. In other situations, of course, leaders are chosen by those in authority. The president of a company will normally decide who will supervise and who will be supervised. Even in this situation, however, the supervisor is expected to behave democratically: to listen to the ideas of the employees; to take their views into consideration when decisions are to be made; to keep them informed of corporate developments; and not to discriminate on the basis of sex, race, or affectional orientation. In the United States people expect that organizational and other group leaders will be changed fairly regularly, much as we change political leaders on a regular basis. In some other cultures, leaders get their positions by right of birth. They are not elected, nor are they expected to behave democratically.

Business executives in different cultures also have different strengths and weaknesses as leaders (Bains, 2015). For example, leaders from China and Latin America are more "likable" and "engaging" than are leaders from India or the United States. Sub-Saharan leaders are excellent at strategic thinking but not at "commercial" thinking.

Individual and Collective Orientations

Small group cultures and cultures in general differ in the extent to which they promote individualistic values (e.g., power, achievement, hedonism, and stimulation) versus collectivist values (e.g., benevolence, tradition, and conformity).

One of the major differences between an **individual orientation** and a **collective orientation** is in the extent to which an individual's goals or the group's goals are given precedence. Individual and collective tendencies are, of course, not mutually exclusive; this is not an all-or-none orientation, but rather one of emphasis. You probably have both tendencies. Thus, you may, for example, compete with other members of your basketball team to make the most baskets; but in a game, you'd likely act in a way that will benefit the entire team (and thus emphasize group goals). In practice, both individual and collective tendencies will help both you and your team achieve your goals. Still, most people and most cultures have a dominant orientation.

In an *individualist culture* you're responsible to your own conscience; responsibility is largely an individual matter. Examples of individualist cultures include those of the United States, Australia, United Kingdom, Netherlands, Canada, New Zealand, Italy, Belgium, Denmark, and Sweden (Hofstede, Hofstede, & Minkov, 2010; Singh & Pereira, 2005). In a *collectivist culture* you're responsible to the rules of the social group; all members share responsibility for accomplishments as well as for failures. Examples include the cultures of Guatemala, Ecuador, Panama, Venezuela, Colombia, Indonesia, Pakistan, China, Costa Rica, and Peru (Hofstede, Hofstede, & Minkov, 2010). Individualistic cultures foster competition, whereas collectivist cultures promote cooperation.

One obvious consequence of this difference in orientation can be seen in how individualistic and collectivist groups treat members who commit serious errors. A group governed by individualistic norms is likely to single out, reprimand, and perhaps fire an errant member. Further, the leader or supervisor is likely to distance himself or herself from this group member for fear that the error will reflect negatively on his or her leadership. In a more collectivist culture, the error is more likely to be seen as a group mistake. The group is unlikely to single out the member—especially not in public—and the leader is likely to bear part of the blame. The same is true when one member comes up with a great idea. In individualist cultures that person is likely to be singled out for praise and rewards, even though the effort was to benefit the group. In collectivist cultures the group is recognized and rewarded for the idea.

JOURNAL
COMMUNICATION CHOICE POINT
Asserting Yourself in a Group
In your meetings at work, the supervisor consistently ignores your cues that you want to say something—and when you do manage to say something, no one reacts. You're determined to change this situation. *What are some of your options for addressing this situation?*

High- and Low-Power Distances

In **high-power-distance cultures**, power is concentrated in the hands of a few, and there is a great difference between the power held by these people and the power held by the ordinary citizen; examples include the cultures of Malaysia, Panama, Guatemala, the Philippines, Venezuela, Mexico, China, the Arab world, Indonesia, and Ecuador (Hofstede, Hofstede, & Minkov, 2010; Singh & Pereira, 2005). In **low-power-distance cultures**, power is more evenly distributed throughout the citizenry; examples include Austria, Israel, Denmark, New Zealand, Ireland, Norway, Sweden, Finland, Switzerland, and Costa Rica (Hofstede, Hofstede, & Minkov, 2010).

The power distance between groups will influence the group of friends you develop, as well as whom you might date (Andersen, 1991). For example, in India (which is high-power distance) your group of friends is expected to be chosen from those within your cultural class (as are your dating partners). In Sweden (which is low-power distance), a

The Cultural Map
HIGH- AND LOW-POWER DISTANCE

Cultures differ greatly in power distance, the degree of discrepancy between those with power and those without power.

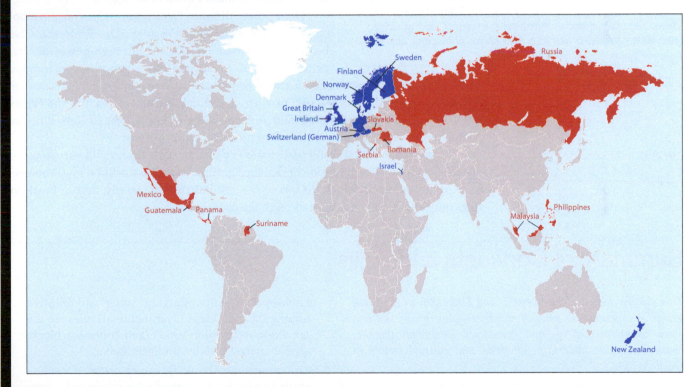

In high-power-distance countries such as these, there is great discrepancy between those with and those without power. In the workplace, managers will turn to their superiors and to formal rules in deciding what to do. There is also a very clear distinction between white- and blue-collar workers; white-collar workers are considered more important, whereas blue-collar workers are considered less important.

In low-power-distance countries such as these, there is little discrepancy between those with and those without power. Workplace managers rely on their own experiences and consult with subordinates in making decisions. There is also less distinction between blue- and white-collar workers; both are highly valued.

How would you describe the power distance in your various classes? Do your classes differ in power distance? How would you describe the power distance at your workplace? In your family?

VIEWPOINTS: Power Distances

In low-power-distance cultures, there is a general feeling of equality, which is consistent with acting assertively; so you're expected to confront a friend, partner, or supervisor assertively (Borden, 1991). In high-power-distance cultures, direct confrontation and assertiveness may be viewed negatively, especially if directed at a superior. *How would you describe the cultures of the group in which you participate—face-to-face and online?*

person is expected to form friendships (and romances) on the basis not of class or culture but of individual factors such as personality, appearance, and the like.

In high-power-distance cultures, you're taught to have great respect for authority; people in these cultures see authority as desirable and beneficial and generally do not welcome challenges to authority (Westwood, Tang, & Kirkbride, 1992; Bochner & Hesketh, 1994). In low-power-distance cultures, there's a certain distrust of authority; it's seen as a kind of necessary evil that should be limited as much as possible. This difference in attitudes toward authority can be seen in the classroom. In high-power-distance cultures, there's a great power distance between students and teachers; students are expected to be modest, polite, and totally respectful. In low-power-distance cultures, students are expected to demonstrate their knowledge and command of the subject matter, participate in discussions with the teacher, and even challenge the teacher—something many members of high-power-distance cultures wouldn't think of doing.

High-power-distance cultures rely on symbols of power. For example, titles (e.g., Dr., Professor, Chef, Inspector) are more important in high-power-distance cultures. Failure to include these honorifics in forms of address is a serious breach of etiquette. Low-power-distance cultures rely less on symbols of power, so there is less of a problem if you fail to use a respectful title (Victor, 1992). Regardless, you still may create problems if, for example, you address a medical doctor, police captain, military officer, or professor with "Ms." or "Mr."

The groups in which you'll participate as a member or a leader will vary in power distance; some will be high-power-distance groups and others will be low. You need to recognize which is which, to follow the cultural rules generally, and to break the rules only after you've thought through the consequences.

Summary of Concepts and Skills

This chapter looked at membership and leadership in the small group. It examined the roles of members—some productive and some counterproductive—and considered leadership theories, leadership styles, leadership functions, and cultural factors in small groups.

Members in Small Group Communication

10.1 Describe and give examples of the three major types of group members and identify the important membership skills.

1. A popular classification of small group member roles divides them into three types: group task roles, group building and maintenance roles, and individual roles.

2. Among the group task roles are those of information seeker or giver, opinion seeker or giver, evaluator-critic, and procedural technician or recorder. Among the group building and maintenance roles are the encourager/harmonizer, compromiser,

gatekeeper-expediter, standard setter, and follower. Among the individual (dysfunctional) roles are the aggressor, recognition seeker/self-confessor, blocker, special interest pleader, and dominator.

3. Group members should be group-oriented, center-conflict on issues, be critically open-minded, recognize social loafing, ensure understanding, and be wary of groupthink, an excessive concern with securing agreement that discourages critical thinking and the exploration of alternative ways of doing things.

Leaders in Small Group Communication

10.2 Define *leadership*, the theories of leadership, and identify the important leadership skills.

4. Several theories of leadership help to clarify aspects of leadership. The traits approach identifies characteristics, such as intelligence and self-confidence, which contribute to leadership. The functional approach

focuses on what the leaders should do. The transformational approach focuses on leaders as people who raise the performance of group members and empower them. The situational approach views leadership as varying its focus between accomplishing the task and serving the members' social and emotional needs, depending on the specific group and the unique situation.

5. Among the leader's functions and requisite skills are to prepare members for and start the group interaction, build group cohesiveness, maintain effective interaction, guide members through the agreed-on agenda, ensure member satisfaction, empower members, encourage ongoing evaluation and improvement, manage conflict, and mentor.

Membership, Leadership, and Culture

10.3 **Explain the role of culture in small group communication and define and distinguish between individual and collective orientations and high- and low-power distances.**

6. Group membership and leadership attitudes and behaviors are likely to be heavily influenced by culture, especially by the individual and collective orientations and high- and low-power distances.

The skills identified in this discussion center on increasing your ability to function more effectively as a small group member and leader. Place a check mark next to those skills you feel you should work on most.

_____ 1. I recognize and appreciate the cultural differences that people have toward group membership and leadership.

_____ 2. I avoid playing the popular but dysfunctional individual roles in a small group—those of aggressor, blocker, recognition seeker, self-confessor, and dominator.

_____ 3. When participating in a small group, I am group-oriented rather than individual-oriented, center the conflict on issues rather than on personalities, am critically open-minded, and make sure that my meanings and the meanings of others are clearly understood.

_____ 4. I recognize the symptoms of groupthink and actively counter my own groupthink tendencies as well as those evidenced in the group.

_____ 5. I adjust my leadership style according to the task at hand and the needs of group members.

_____ 6. As a small group leader, I start group interaction, maintain effective interaction throughout the discussion, keep members on track, ensure member satisfaction, encourage ongoing evaluation and improvement, and prepare members for the discussion as necessary.

Key Terms

authoritarian leader	groupthink	low-power-distance cultures
cohesiveness	high-power-distance cultures	mentoring
collective orientation	individual orientation	social facilitation
democratic leader	individual roles	social loafing
group building and maintenance roles	laissez-faire leader	
group task roles	leadership	

Skill Development Experiences

10.1 Responding to Individual Roles

One major value of small group interaction is that everyone profits from the insights of everyone else; individual roles can get in the way.

For each of the five individual roles, compose a response or two that you as a leader might make in order to deal with this dysfunctional role-playing. Be careful that your responses don't alienate the individual or the group.

Individual, Dysfunctional Roles	Responding to Individual Roles
The aggressor	_____
The recognition seeker or self-confessor	_____
The blocker	_____
The special interest pleader	_____
The dominator	_____

10.2 Empowering Group Members

Power is not a zero-sum game; empowering others often adds to, rather than subtracts from, your own power.

For each situation, indicate what you might say to help empower the other person, using such strategies as (a) raising the other person's self-esteem; (b) listening actively and supportively; (c) being open, positive, and empathic; and (d) avoiding verbal aggressiveness or any unfair conflict strategies.

1. You're managing four college interns, three men and one woman, who are working on redesigning your company's website. The men are extremely supportive of one another and regularly contribute ideas. Although equally competent, the woman doesn't contribute; she seems to lack confidence. Because the objective of this redesign is to increase the number of female visitors, you really need the woman intern's input and want to empower her.

2. You're a third-grade teacher. Most of the students are from the same ethnic-religious group; three, however, are from a different group. The problem is that these three have not been included in the social groupings of the students; they're treated as outsiders. As a result, these children stumble when they have to read in front of the class and make a lot of mistakes at the chalkboard (though they consistently do well in private). You want to empower these students.

Chapter 11
Public Speaking Preparation (Steps 1–6)

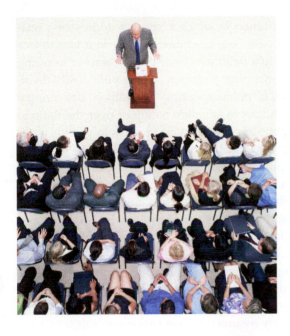

Your immediate audience is today often only a small part of those who will hear or read the speech or hear or read about the speech.

CHAPTER OUTLINE	Learning Objectives
The Nature of Public Speaking	**11.1** Explain the nature of public speaking and communication apprehension, and identify the suggestions for managing apprehension in public speaking and for overcoming procrastination.
Step 1: Select Your Topic, Purposes, and Thesis	**11.2** Describe how public speaking topics, purposes, and theses can be selected and limited.
Step 2: Analyze Your Audience	**11.3** Explain the sociological and psychological characteristics of an audience and how these might be used in audience analysis and adaptation.
Step 3: Research Your Topic	**11.4** Identify the basic principles of and sources for researching your speech topic and the criteria for evaluating research and for integrating and citing research.
Step 4: Collect Supporting Materials	**11.5** Identify the types of supporting materials in informative and persuasive speeches.
Step 5: Develop Your Main Points	**11.6** Describe how main points may be generated from your theses.
Step 6: Organize Your Speech Materials	**11.7** Describe the major patterns of speech organization.

Before getting to the steps for preparing and presenting a public speech, we'll define public speaking and consider the benefits that will reward your public speaking efforts. In addition, we'll address what is probably your number one problem: the fear that so often accompanies giving speeches.

The Nature of Public Speaking

11.1 Explain the nature of public speaking and communication apprehension, and identify the suggestions for managing apprehension in public speaking and for overcoming procrastination.

Public speaking is a form of communication in which a speaker addresses a relatively large audience with a relatively continuous discourse, usually in a face-to-face situation. A student delivering a report to a political science class, a teacher lecturing on the structure of DNA, a minister preaching a sermon, and a politician delivering a campaign speech are all examples of public speaking. In addition, delivering a speech to a television camera to be broadcast to an entire nation or over the radio to be heard by thousands or millions of people is similar in many ways to what is traditionally thought of as public speaking. One way in which it differs is in the nature of the audience feedback. In face-to-face public speaking, the audience gives the speaker immediate feedback largely through facial expressions, head nodding, and posture. In mediated public speaking, the feedback may come a while after the speech in the form of political commentary, for example. Increasingly, however, both remote and immediate audiences are communicating with both face-to-face and mediated public speaking through social media sites such as Twitter. While the speaker is speaking (and afterward as well), listeners are sending messages—communicating approval or disapproval or asking questions they hope the speaker will address—to the speaker as well as to other audience members. The simple hashtag has already brought about dramatic changes in public speaking and will surely continue to do so (Atkinson, 2010).

Benefits and Skills of Public Speaking

Public speaking draws together a wide variety of social, academic, and career skills. Although these skills are central to public speaking, they also enrich other competencies. Among these are your ability to present yourself to others with confidence and self-assurance, to conduct research efficiently and effectively, to understand human motivation, to analyze and evaluate the validity of persuasive appeals, and to use persuasion effectively.

Public speaking will also develop and refine your general communication abilities by helping you explain complex concepts; organize a variety of messages for clarity and persuasiveness; develop logical, emotional, and ethical appeals to support an argument; and improve your listening and delivery skills.

It's important to remember, however, that effective public speakers aren't born; they're made. Through instruction, exposure to different speeches, feedback, and individual learning experiences, you can become an effective speaker. Regardless of your present level of competence, you can improve your public speaking skills through proper training.

Now that you have a good idea of what public speaking is and what benefits you'll derive from studying it, we can focus on what is probably your major concern: communication apprehension/stage fright/fear of speaking in public.

Communication Apprehension

People experience **communication apprehension** in all types of situations (as illustrated throughout this text), but it is in the public speaking situation that apprehension is most common and most severe (Richmond, Wrench, & McCroskey, 2013;

Wrench, McCroskey, & Richmond, 2008). To measure your own fear of speaking in public, take the apprehension self-test that follows.

If you experience public speaking apprehension, the following 10 suggestions will help you reduce it, as well as any communication apprehension you might have in small-group and interpersonal communication situations (Beatty, 1988; Wrench, McCroskey, & Richmond, 2008).

- **Gain experience.** New situations such as public speaking are likely to make you anxious, so try to reduce their newness. The best way to do this is to get as much public speaking experience as you can. With experience, your initial fears and anxieties will give way to feelings of control, comfort, and pleasure. Experience will show you that the feelings of accomplishment in public speaking are rewarding and will outweigh any initial anxiety.

- **Think positively.** When you see yourself as inferior—for example, when you feel that others are better speakers or that they know more than you do—anxiety increases. To gain greater confidence, think positive thoughts and be especially thorough in your preparation. Visualize success; dismiss thoughts of failure.

- **Be realistic.** Unrealistically high expectations are likely to create anxiety and make you more fearful of the public speaking situation (Ayres, 1986). You do not have to be perfect; you do not have to give the best speech in the class. View your goal as giving a speech that represents the best you can do. At the same time, avoid "catastrophizing," visualizing the very worst that can happen.

- **See public speaking as conversation.** When you're the center of attention, as you are in public speaking, you feel especially conspicuous; this often increases anxiety. It may help, therefore, to think of public speaking as another type of conversation (some theorists call it "enlarged conversation").

- **Focus on your listeners.** When you focus on your listeners, you'll be less fixated on your own performance and less apprehensive. Focus on informing them about

Test Yourself

HOW APPREHENSIVE ARE YOU ABOUT PUBLIC SPEAKING?

This questionnaire consists of six statements concerning your feelings about public speaking. Indicate the degree to which each statement applies to you by marking whether you (1) strongly agree, (2) agree, (3) are undecided, (4) disagree, or (5) strongly disagree with each statement. There are no right or wrong answers. Don't be concerned that some of the statements are similar to others. Work quickly; just record your first impression.

____ **1.** I have no fear of giving a speech.

____ **2.** Certain parts of my body feel very tense and rigid when I am giving a speech.

____ **3.** I feel relaxed while giving a speech.

____ **4.** My thoughts become confused and jumbled when I am giving a speech.

____ **5.** I face the prospect of giving a speech with confidence.

____ **6.** While giving a speech, I get so nervous that I forget facts I really know.

To obtain your public speaking apprehension score, use the following formula: Start with 18 points; add the scores for items 1, 3, and 5; then subtract the scores for items 2, 4, and 6. A score above 18 shows some degree of apprehension. Most people score above 18, so if you scored relatively high, you're among the vast majority of people.

SOURCE: Adaptation of "Test Yourself: How Apprehensive Are You about Public Speaking?" from *An Introduction to Rhetorical Communication* by James C. McCroskey, 9th Ed. Copyright © 2006 by Pearson Education, Inc. Printed and Electronically reproduced by permission of Pearson Education, Inc. Upper Saddle River, New Jersey.

your topic or persuading them to think differently or do something. The more attention you place on your audience, the less you'll have for worrying about your performance.

- **Stress similarity.** When you feel similar to (rather than different from) your audience, your anxiety should lessen. With all audiences, but especially with multicultural gatherings, stress similarities in experiences, attitudes, and values; it will make you feel more at one with your listeners.

- **Project confidence.** Stand tall, and maintain direct eye contact with your listeners. Behaving confidently is likely to feed back and lead you to feel confident. Acting confidently is also likely to increase the positive reactions from the audience, which will further help to put you at ease.

- **Prepare and practice thoroughly.** Much of the fear you experience is a fear of failure. Adequate and even extra preparation will lessen the possibility of failure and the accompanying apprehension. Because apprehension is greatest during the beginning of the speech, try memorizing the first few sentences of your talk. If there are complicated facts or figures, be sure to write these out and plan to read them; this will remove from your mind any worry about forgetting them.

- **Move about and breathe deeply.** Physical activity—gross bodily movements as well as the small movements of the hands, face, and head—lessens apprehension. Using a visual aid, for example, will temporarily divert attention from you and will allow you to get rid of your excess energy. If you breathe deeply a few times before getting up to speak, you'll sense your body relax. This will help you overcome your initial fear of walking to the front of the room.

- **Avoid chemicals as tension relievers.** Unless prescribed by a physician, avoid any chemical means for reducing apprehension. Alcohol does not lessen public speaking anxiety (Himle, Abelson, & Haghightgou, 1999); and tranquilizers, marijuana, and artificial stimulants are likely to create problems rather than reduce them. They're likely to impair your ability to remember the parts of your speech, to accurately read audience feedback, and to regulate the timing of your speech.

If, as a listener, you perceive that the speaker is apprehensive, you can help in at least these three ways:

JOURNAL
COMMUNICATION CHOICE POINT
Apprehension Management

This is your first experience with public speaking, and you're very nervous; you're afraid you'll forget your speech and stumble. So you're wondering if it would be a good idea to alert your audience to your nervousness. *If you decide to say something, what would you say? What good reasons can you give for saying nothing?*

- Positively reinforce the speaker. A nod, a smile, an attentive appearance (especially maintaining eye contact) will help put the speaker at ease. Resist the temptation to check your text messages or talk with a friend or otherwise indicate that you aren't paying attention.

- If there's a question period, ask information-seeking questions rather than firing off critical challenges. And ask questions in a way that won't encourage defensiveness. Instead of saying, "Your criticism of heavy metal music is absurd," say, "Why do you find the lyrics of heavy metal harmful?"

- Don't focus on errors. If the speaker fumbles, don't put your head down, cover your eyes, or otherwise communicate your awareness of the fumble. Instead, continue listening to the content of the speech; let the speaker know that you're focused on what is being said.

Starting Early

At the most obvious level, starting early provides you with the time needed to process the information you're going to talk about and to get used to the idea of preparing for the presentation of your speech. Starting early also provides you with the time to overcome the inevitable unanticipated roadblocks: a website that you thought would be helpful is now dead, the person you wanted to interview isn't available, or your neighbor's parties make the weekends useless for working on your speech. You will also have the time to rehearse your speech to ensure that your delivery will be effective. Starting early is also likely to help reduce any fear of public speaking you might have since you'll have the time to develop mastery and with that will come increased confidence. Starting early may also enable you to avoid health problems often associated with procrastination; for example, college students who procrastinate experience more colds and flu, more gastrointestinal problems, and more insomnia (Marano, 2003).

Here are several suggestions for overcoming this tendency to delay certain tasks.

- **Make a commitment to starting early.** Create a computer file for your speech, collect information, and file it for easy retrieval.
- **Don't lie to yourself about the value of procrastination** (Marano, 2003). You don't do better under pressure, for example.
- **Beware of your tendency to seek out distractions.** You don't have to rearrange and organize your photos or redo your Facebook profile, for example. When you get the urge to do something else, become mindful of what you're really doing—making an excuse to delay the task at hand.
- **Avoid self-handicapping strategies** (for example, partying the night before as an excuse for possible ineffectiveness); these will only make it more difficult for you to prepare and present an effective speech.
- **Work in small steps.** Fortunately, this aid to overcoming procrastination is built into the 10-step public speaking system used here; each step is already a relatively small unit. Set aside 30 or 40 minutes (it's often best to start with small units of time) and see what you can do with Step 1. Then, when you're farther along in the process, increase the time you spend on each step.

The rest of this chapter looks at the first six of the 10 steps for preparing an effective public speech, as summarized in Figure 11.1. The final four steps are covered in the next chapter.

"I thought up an incredible sting of rapid-fire witticisms. Too bad they came two hours after my speech."

Chris Wildt/Cartoon Stock

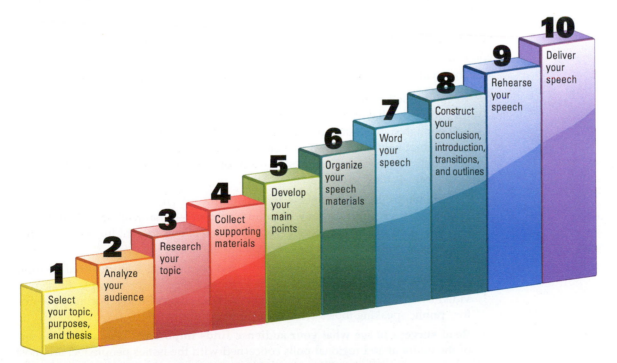

Figure 11.1   The Steps in Public Speaking Preparation and Delivery
Speakers differ in the order in which they follow these steps. Some speakers, for example, prefer to begin with audience analysis, asking themselves what the audience is interested in and then selecting the topic and purpose. Some speakers prefer to identify their main points before conducting extensive research; others prefer to allow the propositions to emerge from the research. The order presented here will prove useful to most speakers for most situations; however, vary the order when it serves your purposes. As long as you cover all the steps, you should be in good shape.

Step 1: Select Your Topic, Purposes, and Thesis

11.2 **Describe how public speaking topics, purposes, and theses can be selected and limited.**

The first step in preparing an effective public speech is to select the topic on which you'll speak, the general and specific purposes you hope to achieve, and your thesis or central idea. Since this is a learning environment, different instructors will establish different parameters to better achieve the specific goals of the course. So use what is said here in conjunction with your instructor's guidance.

Your Topic

Select a worthwhile topic that will be interesting to the audience. If your first speech is to be informative, select a topic about which your audience probably knows little but would be curious to learn more. If your first speech is persuasive, you might select a topic about which you and the audience agree, and aim to strengthen their attitudes. Or you might select a topic on which you and the audience disagree; your aim would be to persuade them to change their attitudes.

Not surprisingly, the appropriateness of a speech topic will vary with the culture of the audience. For example, each culture has its own topics that tend to cause conflict. Generally these subjects should be avoided, especially by visitors from other cultures. Although the topics that are **taboo** (culturally disapproved behavior) vary from one culture to another and from one time to another, generally it is best to avoid criticizing any deeply held belief, whether about religion or politics or child-rearing practices. If you're going to address an audience with members from cultures other than your own, find out what these taboo topics are and avoid them; or at least present them in a way that will not cause audience members to tune you out.

FINDING YOUR TOPIC   Public speaking topics are all around you. Select a topic that you're interested in and know something about. And, of course, select a topic that your audience will find interesting and worthwhile. Here are a few ways you can find topics.

- **Keep yourself in mind.** What are you interested in? What news articles or blogs do you read, what feeds do you subscribe to? What titles of articles would interest you enough so that you would open them and read them? If you plan a speech on a topic that you're interested in, your enthusiasm for your topic is likely to make your delivery more exciting, less anxiety-provoking, and more engaging to the audience.

- **Try brainstorming.** You can use the small-group technique of brainstorming to generate speech topics. Begin with your "problem"—what will I talk about?—and let your mind go, writing down every idea that comes to you. In just a few minutes, you should have a sizable list of potential topics.

- **Use topic lists.** A variety of educational and commercial websites contain topic generators where you can view a wide variety of topics—for example, those provided by WritingFix and McMaster eBusiness Research Center. For more, search for "public speaking topics +.edu".

- **Read surveys to see what your audience finds important.** Take a look at some of the national and regional polls concerned with the issues people feel are most significant. Search for polling sites with your favorite search engine or start with some of the more widely known, such as the Gallup Poll, the Marist Poll, or Pew Research Center. Or take a look at what people are talking about on social media sites. What are people tweeting about? What are they posting about? What's trending? You can also conduct a survey yourself through a variety of social media sites or classroom management systems.

- **Check news sites.** A useful starting point is your online news page, which will provide you with important international, domestic, financial, and social issues all conveniently accessible from one screen. But, of course, news items also appear on Twitter and on blogs and a variety of social media sites.

VIEWPOINTS: Taboo

What is and what is not taboo will also vary with different audiences. Consider your own classroom. *What public speaking topics would be considered taboo?*

LIMITING YOUR TOPIC   Plan to cover a limited topic in depth, rather than a broad topic superficially. The limiting process is simple: Repeatedly divide the topic into its significant parts. First, divide your general topic into its component parts, then divide one of these parts into its component parts. Continue until you arrive at a topic that seems manageable—a topic that you can reasonably cover in some depth in the allotted time.

For example, if you were to take *mass communication* as a general topic area (see Figure 11.2), without some limitation, it would take you a lifetime to cover adequately. But you could divide this general subject into subtopics, such as Internet, film, television, radio, and advertising. You could then select one of these topics and further subdivide it. For example, you could subdivide television into comedy, children's programs, educational programs, news, movies, soap operas, game shows, and sports. You might then take one of these topics, say comedy, and divide it into subtopics. You might consider comedy on a time basis and divide television comedy into its significant time periods: pre-1960, 1961–2000, and 2001 to the present. Or you might focus on situation comedies. Here you might examine a topic such as "Women in Television Comedy," "Race Relations in Situation Comedy," or "Families in Television Comedies." At this stage the topic is beginning to look manageable.

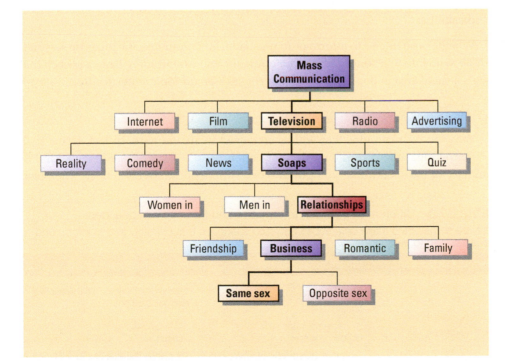

Figure 11.2   Tree Diagram for Limiting Speech Topics

Here is a tree diagram illustrating how a topic can be divided until it becomes manageable for a short speech, for example, "Same-Sex Business Relationships in Television Soaps." Construct a different tree diagram by selecting Internet, film, radio, television, or advertising as a topic and subdividing it until you reach a level that would be appropriate for a 5- to 10-minute informative or persuasive speech.

Your Purposes

In some cases you'll select your topic and purpose almost simultaneously. At other times you'll select your topic and later formulate your purpose. In preparing public speeches, you'll need to formulate both a general and a specific purpose.

YOUR GENERAL PURPOSE   The two **general purposes** (major aims or objectives) of public speeches are to inform and to persuade. The **informative speech** creates understanding; it clarifies, enlightens, corrects misunderstandings, demonstrates how something works, or explains how something is structured (see Chapter 13). The **persuasive speech**, on the other hand, influences attitudes or behaviors. It may strengthen existing attitudes or change the audience's beliefs. Or it may move the audience to act in a particular way (see Chapter 14). Table 11.1 identifies some of the major differences between informative and persuasive speeches; keep these distinctions in mind as you read the next sections.

YOUR SPECIFIC PURPOSE   Your **specific purpose** identifies the information you want to communicate (in an informative speech) or the attitude or behavior you want to change (in a persuasive speech). For example, your specific purpose in an informative speech might be:

- to inform my audience of three ways to save time using the Internet for research;
- to inform my audience about how the new interoffice e-mail system works; or
- to inform my audience of the benefits of integrated work teams.

Your specific purpose in a persuasive speech might be:

- to persuade my audience that all cigarette advertising should be abolished;
- to persuade my audience that the college should establish courses on the prevention of AIDS and other STDs; or
- to persuade my audience to contribute time to working with students with disabilities.

Whether you intend to inform or to persuade, limit your specific purpose so you'll be able to go into it in some depth. Your audience will benefit more from a speech that covers a small area in depth than one that covers a broad topic superficially.

Your Thesis

The **thesis** is the main idea that will be conveyed to an audience. In fact, terms such as "central idea" or "controlling idea" are often used instead of *thesis*. It's a kind of summary of the speech that you put into one simple declarative sentence. The thesis

---

Table 11.1   **Differences between Informative and Persuasive Speeches**

Here are some of the major differences between speeches that primarily aim to inform and those that aim to persuade.

Element of Speech	Informative Speeches	Persuasive Speeches
	Examples include classroom lectures, demonstrations of how things work	Examples include political speeches, religious sermons
Topic/subject	Significant but generally noncontroversial	Significant and controversial or debatable
Purpose	To communicate new information to listeners	To change the attitudes, beliefs, or behaviors of listeners
Thesis	States the central idea of the speech	States the debatable position to be argued
Support	Primarily examples, definitions, numerical data, and presentation aids	In addition to informative support, relies heavily on logical, emotional, and credibility support

of Lincoln's Second Inaugural Address was that northerners and southerners should work together for the good of the entire country. The thesis of many science fiction movies is that, working together, people—often from very different cultures and different walks of life—can repel any conquering force and achieve just about anything.

Let's say, for example, you're planning to present a persuasive speech in favor of the election of Senator Winters. Your thesis statement might be, "Winters is the best candidate." This is what you want your audience to believe, what you want your audience to remember even if they forget everything else.

Sometimes, you'll want to state your thesis in your speech; at other times, you may want to imply it and let the audience "discover" it. Here, for example, is how one student, Kevin King, expressed his thesis in a persuasive speech on the need to fund research on Alzheimer's disease (King, 2015):

> We have to end our collective silence about this disease and make Alzheimer's research a financial priority—before it's too late.[1]

In an informative speech, on the other hand, the thesis statement focuses on what you want your audience to learn. For example, for a speech on jealousy, a suitable thesis might be: "Two main theories of jealousy exist." Additional examples of thesis statements are given in the sample outlines later in this chapter.

The thesis and the purpose of a speech are similar in that they both guide you in selecting and organizing your materials. In two major ways, however, they are different.

- **Form of expression** Thesis and purpose differ in how they are phrased. The thesis is phrased as a complete, declarative sentence. The purpose is phrased as an infinitive phrase ("to inform …," "to persuade …").

- **Focus** The thesis focuses on the message; the purpose focuses on the audience. The thesis succinctly identifies the central idea of your speech. The purpose identifies the change you hope to bring about in your audience—for example, to learn information, to change attitudes, or to influence them to act in a certain way.

Step 2: Analyze Your Audience

11.3 Explain the sociological and psychological characteristics of an audience and how these might be used in audience analysis and adaptation.

At one time, the **audience** for a public speech was limited to the people who were actually at the speaking event. Today, the audience for a public speech

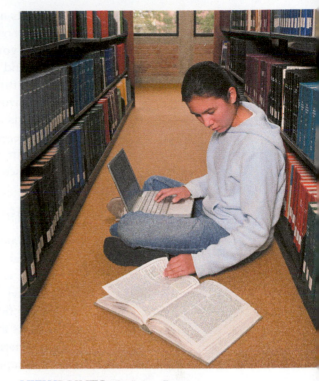

VIEWPOINTS: Defining Purpose

Izzie is considering developing her 10-minute persuasive speech around one of the following purposes that will persuade her listeners (1) to vote for the pro-life candidate in the upcoming election, (2) to contribute $250 to the college's scholarship fund, or (3) to attend a religious ceremony of a religion other than the listeners' own. *Assuming that the audience was your human communication class, what do you see as the advantages and disadvantages of each purpose?*

JOURNAL
COMMUNICATION CHOICE POINT
Unpopular Thesis

You've decided to tackle the hypocrisy you see in classmates who publicly support the values of racial equality but privately express racist attitudes. You're afraid, however, that your audience will walk out on you as soon as you state your thesis. *What are some of the things you can do to avoid any knee-jerk reaction from your listeners? What might you say (especially in your introduction) to make them listen to what essentially will be criticism?*

---

[1]The speech, titled *Funding Alzheimer's Research*, from which this excerpt was taken was constructed and delivered by Kevin King from the University of Texas at Austin. Excerpts from this excellent speech appear throughout these public speaking chapters to further illustrate the principles discussed in the text by looking at how one speaker applied these principles to accomplish a variety of goals. When asked why he became interested in the topic, Kevin said: "I've watched a number of relatives and family friends battle Alzheimer's. After doing some basic research, I uncovered a truly frustrating problem—we simply aren't doing enough to find a cure for this disease." Kevin's biggest challenge was "to construct the tightest possible structure, and one that offered my audience members very tangible solutions."

consists not only of those who witness it firsthand but also those who watch it after the fact online or who read about it through other media outlets.

If you are going to inform or persuade an audience—your immediate audience and your remote audience—you must know who they are. What are their beliefs, attitudes, and values? What are their interests? What do they already know? What would they want to know more about? Where do they stand on the issues you wish to address? We can group these various questions into two general categories: sociological and psychological characteristics. We'll then look at some of the things you can do during the speech to help you analyze and adapt to your audience.

Audience Sociology

When analyzing an audience, be careful not to assume that people covered by the same label are necessarily all alike. As soon as you begin to use a sociological characteristic with an expressed or implied "all," consider the possibility that you may be stereotyping. Don't assume that all women or all older people or all highly educated people think or believe the same things. They don't. Nevertheless, there are characteristics that seem to be more common among one group than another, and it is these characteristics that you want to explore in analyzing your audience. Some of the most important factors are considered in Table 11.2.

Audience Psychology

Focus your psychological analysis of the audience on three questions: How willing is your audience? How knowledgeable is your audience? And how favorable is your audience?

Table 11.2 Audience Sociology

No list of audience characteristics can possibly be complete, and the list presented here is no exception. These, then, are some of the audience factors you may want to consider and some questions you may want to ask, depending on your specific thesis and audience.

Audience Characteristics	Questions to Ask
Cultural factors	Are the cultural beliefs and values of the audience relevant to your topic and purpose? Might the cultural memberships of this audience influence the way they see the topic? Are there important cultural differences among your listeners?
Age	Will the ages of your audience members influence how your speech topic and purpose are viewed? Will they see what you're saying as relevant to the present and near future?
Gender	Will both genders find your topic and supporting materials interesting and relevant? Will men and women have different attitudes toward the topic or different experiences that will be relevant to your topic?
Religion and religiousness	Will the religion and religiousness of your listeners influence their responses to your speech? Might your topic or purpose be seen as an attack on the religious beliefs of any segment of your audience?
Educational levels	Does the educational level of your audience suggest any stylistic adjustment? Will technical terms have to be defined? Will the educational level suggest different persuasive strategies or supporting materials?
Occupation and income	Is your audience's level of job security and occupational pride related to your topic, purpose, or examples? Will people from different economic levels see your topic and purpose in different ways?
Relational status	Will singles be interested in hearing about the problems of selecting preschools? Will those in long-term relationships be interested in the depression many people who are not in close relationships feel?
Values	What do audience members value? What do they consider important to their current and future lives? What do they hold sacred? What do they consider profane?
Special interests	What special interests do the audience members have? What occupies their leisure time? How can you integrate these interests into your examples and illustrations or use them as you select quotations?
Political beliefs	Will audience members' political affiliations influence how they view your topic or purpose? Are they politically liberal? Conservative? Might this influence how you develop your speech?
Organizational memberships	Might audience members' affiliations give you cues as to their other beliefs and values? Might you use references to these organizations in your speech, perhaps as examples or illustrations?

HOW WILLING IS YOUR AUDIENCE?   If you face an audience that is willing (even eager) to hear your speech, you'll have an easy time relating your speech to them. If, however, your audience is listening unwillingly, consider the following suggestions.

- Secure their attention as early in your speech as possible—and maintain their interest throughout—with supporting materials that will speak to their motives, interests, and concerns.
- Relate your topic and supporting materials directly to your audience's needs and wants; show them how what you are saying will help them achieve what they want.
- Show the audience why they should listen to your speech by connecting your purpose to their purposes.
- Involve the audience directly in your speech by showing them that you understand their perspective, asking rhetorical questions, and referring to their experiences and interests.

VIEWPOINTS: Analyzing an Audience
Sophia wants to give her speech on the values of atheism. *If this speech were to be given to your class, what are some of the things Sophia would need to know about her audience?*

HOW KNOWLEDGEABLE IS YOUR AUDIENCE?   If your audience knows little about your topic, consider these suggestions.

- Don't talk down to audience members.
- Don't confuse a lack of knowledge with a lack of intelligence.

  If your audience knows a great deal about your topic, consider these suggestions.

- Let the audience know that you are aware of their knowledge and expertise and that your speech will not simply repeat what they already know but will go beyond it.
- Emphasize your competence in this general subject area.

HOW FAVORABLE IS YOUR AUDIENCE?   If you face an audience that has unfavorable attitudes toward your topic or your purpose, or even toward you, consider these suggestions:

- Build on commonalities; emphasize not the differences but the similarities between you and the audience.
- Build your speech from areas of agreement, through areas of slight disagreement, up to the major differences.
- Strive for small gains.
- Ask for a fair hearing.

Analysis and Adaptation during the Speech

In your classroom speeches, you'll face a known audience, an audience you've already analyzed and for which you've made appropriate adaptations. At other times, however, you may face an audience that you've not been able to analyze beforehand or that differs greatly from what you expected. In these cases you'll have to analyze and adapt as you speak. Here are a few suggestions.

FOCUS ON LISTENERS AS MESSAGE SENDERS   As you're speaking, look at your listeners and make adjustments as necessary. For example, if your audience shows signs of boredom, increase your volume, move closer to them, or tell them how what you're going to say will be of value to them. If your audience shows signs of disagreement or hostility, stress a similarity you have with them. If your audience looks puzzled or confused, pause a moment and rephrase your ideas, provide necessary definitions, or insert an internal summary. If your audience seems impatient, say, for example, "my last argument" instead of your originally planned "my third argument."

"I know you're angry at me—I'm angry at me, too!"

David Sipress/The New Yorker Collection/The Cartoon Bank

USE ANSWERS TO YOUR "WHAT IF" QUESTIONS   The more preparation you put into your speech, the better prepared you'll be to make on-the-spot adjustments and adaptations. For example, let's say that you're to explain the opportunities available to the nontraditional student at your college. You've been told that your audience will consist mainly of working women in their 30s and 40s who are just beginning college. As you prepare your speech with this audience in mind, ask yourself "what if" questions. Keeping such questions in mind will force you to consider possible answers as you prepare your speech: What if the audience has a large number of men? What if the audience consists of women much older than 40? What if the audience members also come with their spouses or their children?

ADDRESS AUDIENCE RESPONSES DIRECTLY   Another way of dealing with audience responses is to confront them directly. To those who are giving disagreement feedback, for example, you might say this.

> You may disagree with this position, but all I ask is that you hear me out and see if this new way of doing things will not simplify your accounting procedures.

Or, to those who seem impatient, you might offer this response.

> I know this has been a long day, but give me just a few more minutes and you'll be able to save hours recording your accounts.

By responding to your listeners' reactions and feedback, you acknowledge their needs. You let them know that you hear them, that you're with them, and that you're responding to their very real needs.

Step 3: Research Your Topic

11.4 Identify the basic principles of and sources for researching your speech topic and the criteria for evaluating research and for integrating and citing research.

Research is the systematic search for information; it's an investigation of the relevant information on a topic. It is essential in public speeches. Throughout the process of preparing your public speeches, you'll conduct research to find examples, illustrations, and definitions to help you inform your listeners; testimony, statistics, and arguments to support your major ideas; and personal anecdotes, quotations, and stories to help you bring your topics to life. Here we consider some general research principles, some major sources of information, ways to evaluate the research you find, and suggestions for integrating research into your speech.

Research Principles

Here are a few principles to help you research your speeches more effectively and more efficiently.

- **Begin your search by examining what you already know.** Write down, for example, what relevant books, articles, or websites you're familiar with or people who might know something about the topic.
- **Continue your search by getting a general overview of the topic.** An encyclopedia article, book chapter, or magazine article will serve this purpose well.

This general overview will help you see the topic as a whole and how its various parts fit together. If you search for material on any search engine, you'll find that Wikipedia comes up among the top search suggestions. This is often a useful first step but realize that the articles in Wikipedia are not necessarily written by experts and are not fact-checked as they would be in, say, the *Encyclopaedia Britannica*. However, most articles have extensive references that you can and should check, especially for controversial issues.

- **Follow up the general overview with more detailed sources.** Fortunately, many of the general articles contain references or links to specialized sources for this very purpose.
- **Gather a variety of different types of research.** Although what is and what isn't appropriate research will depend partly on your topic; a variety of different types of research will generally prove more interesting and more convincing.

Here are a few types of sources to investigate.

- **News sources** are especially useful for political speeches, financial news, or reports on natural disasters, congressional actions, international developments, or any of a host of other topics.
- **Biographical material** will help you explain the competence and background of those you mention in your speech, present their credibility to the audience, and answer audience questions about them.
- **Academic research articles** will enable you to secure the most reliable and valid research available.

Distinguish between primary and secondary sources as you research. A primary source is original information about a topic or event—for example, an original research study in an academic journal, a corporation's annual report, and an eyewitness report of an accident. In contrast, a secondary source discusses information originally presented elsewhere—for example, a summary of research appearing in a popular magazine, a television news story on a corporation's earnings, and a report by someone who talked with an eyewitness to an accident.

> **JOURNAL**
> **COMMUNICATION CHOICE POINT**
> Asking a Favor
>
> You're preparing a speech on the growth of the independent film and want to ask some directors a few questions so you can integrate their most recent thoughts (and interject a more personalized note) into your speech. *What are some of your options for accomplishing this? What would you do?*

Research Evaluation

All research materials must be evaluated. This is especially true of online materials simply because anyone can "publish" on the Internet, making it essential that you subject everything you find there to critical analysis. An article on the Internet can be written by world-renowned scientists or by elementary school students; by fair and objective reporters; or by people who would spin the issues to serve their own political, religious, or social purposes. It's not always easy to tell which is which. Table 11.3 presents five criteria you'd want to use in evaluating research from the Internet or from any other place.

Research Integration and Citation

By integrating and acknowledging your sources of information in your speech, you'll give fair credit to those whose ideas and statements you're using; and, at the same time, you'll help establish your own reputation as a responsible researcher.

Be certain to mention your sources in your speech by citing at least author names and, if helpful, the publication titles and the dates. In your written outline, you would then give the complete bibliographical reference. Here is an example of how you might cite your source orally.

> The top careers for 2016, according to this month's *U.S. News & World Report*, are in health care and technology.

> Or:

> My discussion of the ways to estimate the value of the U.S. dollar is based on the analysis provided by measuringworth.com, which I accessed earlier this week.

> Here is an example from an Alzheimer's speech (King, 2015).

Table 11.3 Evaluating Research, Especially on the Internet

This table identifies five essential criteria that need to be examined when evaluating research of all kinds but perhaps Internet research in particular. These are some of the questions you'd want to ask and the precautions that you should take.

Criteria	Questions to Ask	Precautions to Take
Qualifications	Does the author have the necessary credentials? For example, does the author have enough of a background in science or medicine to write authoritatively on health issues?	Do an Internet search to check on the writer's expertise and credentials.
Currency	When was the information published? When were the sources that are cited in the article written?	To ensure currency, check important figures in a recent almanac, in a newspaper, or at a frequently updated source, such as FedStats, which lists statistics from over 100 government agencies.
Fairness	Does the author of the material present the information fairly and objectively, or is there a bias favoring one position? Some websites, although objective on the surface, are actually arms of political, religious, or social organizations.	It's often useful to go to the home page and look for information on the nature of the organization sponsoring the website. Reviewing a range of research on the subject will help you see how other experts view the issue.
Sufficiency	Is the information presented sufficient to establish the claim or conclusion? The opinion of one dietitian is insufficient to support the usefulness of a particular diet; statistics on tuition increases at five elite private colleges are insufficient to illustrate national trends in tuition costs.	The broader your conclusion, the more information you'll need to meet the requirements for sufficiency. If you claim the usefulness of a diet for all people, then you're going to need a great deal of information from different populations—men and women, old and young, healthy and sickly, and so on.
Accuracy	Is the information presented accurate? (Although accuracy is not always easy to determine, the more you learn about your topic, the more able you'll be to judge its accuracy.) Is the information primary or secondary? If it's secondary information, you may be able to locate the primary source material (often a link in the Internet article or a reference at the end).	Check to see whether the information is consistent with information found in other sources and whether the recognized authorities in the field accept this information.

Initially, our conversations about Alzheimer's disease are ill-informed, or worse, because of stigma, nonexistent. The February 5, 2015 *Houston Chronicle* reveals many patients are so embarrassed by their diagnosis, they work to conceal the disease. That's because as a September 4, 2014 *Medical Daily* article notes, sixty percent of patients feared people would trivialize the disease or begin to exclude them socially.

Although it's possible to overdo the oral citation—giving more information than the listeners really need—it's better than leaving out useful information. Because your speeches in this course are learning experiences, it's better to err on the side of more information rather than less.

Avoid expressions such as "I have a quote here" or "I want to quote an example." Let the audience know that you're quoting by pausing before the quote, taking a step forward, or referring to your notes to read the extended quotation.

In addition to the oral citation, you'd also need a written citation, which would take the form of the references listed at the end of the typical textbook. Numerous websites—for example, bibme.com and easybib.com—will help you format your sources according to the style manual your college uses.

Step 4: Collect Supporting Materials

11.5 **Identify the types of supporting materials in informative and persuasive speeches.**

Now that you have your purpose and thesis clearly in mind and have researched your topic, you need to collect **supporting materials**—materials that will allow you to amplify and literally support your thesis. In the informative speech, your support primarily amplifies the concepts you discuss. Specifically, you might use these forms of support.

- **Examples, illustrations, and the testimony of various authorities** to breathe life into abstract or vague concepts.
- **Definitions to clarify complex terms** to provide different ways of looking at some process or event.

- **Numerical data** to explain trends in a wide variety of topics.
- **Presentation aids—charts, maps, objects, slides, films, tapes, DVDs,** and so on—to help clarify ideas.

The above forms are covered in detail in Chapter 13.

In a persuasive speech, your support is proof—material that offers evidence, argument, and motivational appeal and that establishes your credibility and reputation. You can persuade your audience with several types of support.

- **Logical support** includes reasoning from specific instances and from general principles, from causes and effects, and from signs.
- **Motivational support** includes appeals to the audience's emotions and to their desires for status, financial gain, or increased self-esteem.
- **Credibility appeals** involve establishing your own personal reputation or credibility, especially your competence, high moral character, and charisma.

These forms of support are covered in depth in Chapter 14.

> **JOURNAL**
> **COMMUNICATION CHOICE POINT**
> Supporting Materials
>
> Imagine that you're preparing an informative speech on the minimum wage throughout the world to be delivered to your class. *What are some of the supporting materials you might use?*

Communicating Ethically
PLAGIARISM

Because plagiarism is such an important issue in public speaking, this ethics box is a bit longer than other boxes in the text. It will cover the nature of plagiarism, the reasons why it is unacceptable, and what you can do to avoid this problem.

What Is Plagiarism?

Plagiarism is the process of passing off the work (e.g., ideas, words, or illustrations) of others as your own. Plagiarism is not the act of using another person's ideas—we all do that. Rather, it is the act of using someone else's ideas without acknowledging that they are the ideas of this other person; it is presenting the ideas as if they were your own. Plagiarism exists on a continuum, ranging from appropriating an entire term paper or speech written by someone else to using a quotation or research finding without citing the author.

Plagiarism also includes situations in which you get help from a friend without acknowledging this assistance. In some cultures—especially in collectivist cultures—teamwork is strongly encouraged. Students are encouraged to help other students with their work. But in the United States and in many individualist cultures, teamwork without acknowledgment is considered plagiarism.

In U.S. institutions of higher education, plagiarism is a serious violation of the rules of academic honesty and is subject to serious penalties, sometimes even expulsion. Further, as with all crimes, ignorance of the law is not an acceptable defense against charges of plagiarism. This last point is especially important, because people often commit plagiarism through ignorance about what does and does not constitute plagiarism.

Why Plagiarism Is Unacceptable

There are three key reasons why plagiarism is unacceptable.

- Plagiarism is a violation of another person's intellectual property rights. Much as it would be wrong to take someone's watch without permission, it is wrong to take another person's ideas without giving due credit.
- You're in college to develop your own ideas and ways of expressing them; plagiarism defeats this fundamental purpose.
- Evaluations (everything from grades in school to promotions in the workplace) assume that what you present as your work is in fact your work.

Avoiding Plagiarism

Let's start with the easy part. In a speech or term paper, for example, you do not have to—and should not—cite sources for information that is readily available and not likely to be disputed. For example, the population of Thailand, the amendments to the U.S. Constitution, the actions of the United Nations, and the way the heart pumps blood are all common knowledge; and you should not cite the almanac or the book from which you got such information. On the other hand, if you were talking about the attitudes of people from Thailand or the reasons the constitutional amendments were adopted, then you would need to cite your sources, because this information is not common knowledge and may well be disputed.

For information that is not common knowledge, you need to acknowledge your source. Here are four simple rules that will help you avoid even the suggestion of plagiarism (for more extended discussion, see Stern, 2007).

- Acknowledge the source of any ideas you present that are not your own. If you learned of an idea in your history course, cite the history instructor or history textbook. If you read an idea in an article, cite the article.
- Acknowledge the words of another person. When you're quoting someone exactly, you need to cite the person you're quoting. You should also cite the person even when you paraphrase her or his words, because you are still using another person's ideas.
- Acknowledge help from others. If your roommate gave you examples or ideas, or helped you style your speech, acknowledge the help.
- When in doubt, it's best to err on the side of over-referencing rather than under-referencing.

Take a look at some of the plagiarism websites established by different universities; these often include exercises and extended examples; those by Indiana University and Purdue University are especially helpful.

ETHICAL CHOICE POINT

You're really pressed to come up with a persuasive speech on a contemporary social issue, and you just don't have the time to research it. Fortunately, a friend at another school wrote a term paper for her sociology course that you could easily adapt to your required public speaking assignment. *What is your ethical obligation here? What would you do?*

Step 5: Develop Your Main Points

11.6 Describe how main points may be generated from your theses.

In this step, you use your thesis (which you created in Step 1) to generate your major points or ideas. Once you phrase the thesis statement, the main divisions of your speech will suggest themselves. Let's look at an example: You're giving a speech on the value of a college education to a group of people in their 30s and 40s who are considering returning to college. Your thesis is "A college education is valuable." To generate your main points, you'd then ask, "Why is it valuable?" These answers constitute your major points and might look something like this.

There are several reasons why a college education is valuable.

1. It helps you get a job.
2. It increases your potential to earn a good salary.
3. It gives you greater job mobility.
4. It helps you secure more creative work.
5. It helps you appreciate the arts more fully.
6. It helps you understand an increasingly complex world.
7. It helps you understand different cultures.

8. It helps you avoid taking a regular job for a few years.
9. It helps you meet lots of people and make friends.
10. It helps you increase personal effectiveness.

For purposes of illustration, let's stop here. You have 10 possible main points—too many to cover in a short speech. Further, not all are equally valuable or relevant to your audience. You need to make the list shorter and more relevant. Here are some suggestions.

Eliminate or Combine Points

You might want to eliminate, say, number 8—it's inconsistent with the positive value of college, the thesis of your speech. Furthermore, your audience is unlikely to be able to stop working to go to college full-time.

Also notice that the first four points center on jobs. You might, therefore, consider grouping them under a general heading.

A college education will help you secure a better job.

This might be one of your major propositions, which you can develop by defining what you mean by "a better job." This main point and its elaboration might look like this.

I. A college education will help you secure a better job.
   A. College graduates earn higher z.
   B. College graduates enter more creative jobs.
   C. College graduates have greater job mobility

Note that A, B, and C are all aspects or subdivisions of "a better job."

Select Points That Are Most Relevant

You might drop number 5 on the assumption that your audience will be interested in more practical outcomes. And, you might eliminate number 9 on the assumption that your audience is not looking for college to help them make friends; they probably already have friends and families that occupy most of their time. Further, you might conclude that this audience cares a lot about personal effectiveness, so you might make this your second major proposition: *A college education will help you increase your personal effectiveness.*

And, much as you developed the subordinate points in your first proposition by defining what you meant by "a good job," you would define what you mean by "personal effectiveness."

II. A college education will help you increase your personal effectiveness.
   A. A college education will help you improve your ability to communicate.
   B. A college education will help you acquire learning skills.
   C. A college education will help you acquire coping skills.

You would then follow the same procedure used to generate these subordinate points (A, B, and C) to develop the subheadings. For example, you might divide A into two major subheads.

A. A college education will improve your ability to communicate.
   1. A college education teaches writing skills.
   2. A college education teaches speech skills.

Remember, your aim is not to cover every aspect of a topic but to emphasize selected parts. Further, you want to have enough time to amplify and support the points you present. With too many propositions, this becomes impossible. Also, you don't want to present too much information, because your audience simply will not be able to remember it. Ideally you should use two, three, or four main points.

Phrase Propositions in Parallel Style

To make it easier for listeners to follow and remember your speech, use parallel grammatical structures in wording your major propositions.

Not this:

   I. Social media functions
      A. Social media entertain.
      B. The social media function to inform.
      C. Making friends and establishing relationships are major functions.

This:

   I. Social media functions
      A. Social media entertain.
      B. Social media inform.
      C. Social media help establish relationships.

> **JOURNAL**
> **COMMUNICATION CHOICE POINT**
> Generative Main Points
>
> What are three or four possible main points that you might generate from any one of these theses? (1) The minimum wage must be raised. (2) Bullying exists in lots of different forms. (3) The Freedom of Information Act is relevant to all of us.

Develop Main Points Separately and Distinctly

Don't overlap your main points. Overlapping is likely to create confusion rather than clarity.

Not this:

   I. Color and style are important in clothing selection.

This:

   I. Color is important in clothing selection.
   II. Style is important in clothing selection.

Step 6: Organize Your Speech Materials

11.7 **Describe the major patterns of speech organization.**

Organize your materials to help the audience understand and remember what you say. There are a wide variety of options to choose from. The important thing to observe is to use an organizational pattern that is appropriate to your topic and that will help the audience follow your train of thought. Here are 12 organizational patterns that should cover just about any informative or persuasive topic. Another pattern, the motivated sequence, most often associated with persuasive speaking, is covered in Chapter 14.

Time Pattern

When you organize your topic on the basis of a time, or chronological, order, you generally divide the speech into two, three, or four major parts. You might begin with the past and work up to the present or future, or begin with the present or future and work back to the past. Most historical topics lend themselves to organization by a time pattern. Topics such as events leading to the Civil War, how to plant a vegetable garden, and the history of the Internet are all candidates for temporal patterning. For example, you might organize a speech on children's development of speech and language according to a temporal pattern.

General Purpose: To inform

Specific Purpose: To inform my audience of the four stages in the child's acquisition of language

Thesis: The child goes through four stages in learning language.

    I. Babbling occurs first.

    II. Lallation occurs second.

    III. Echolalia occurs third.

    IV. Communication occurs fourth.

Spatial Pattern

Organizing the main points of a speech on the basis of its spatial patterns is similar to temporal patterning. Discussions of most physical objects fit well into spatial patterns. For example, a presentation on the structure of a hospital, a school, a skyscraper, or even a dinosaur might lend itself to this pattern. Here, a speech on places to visit in Central America uses a spatial pattern.

General Purpose: To inform

Specific Purpose: To inform my audience of a great way to visit Central America

Thesis: You can have a great visit to Central America by visiting four countries.

    I. First, visit Guatemala.

    II. Second, visit Honduras.

    III. Third, visit Nicaragua.

    IV. Fourth, visit Costa Rica.

Topical Pattern

The topical pattern divides the speech topic into subtopics or component parts. The world's major religions, great works of literature, and the problems facing the college graduate are other examples of speech topics that lend themselves to a topical organizational pattern. This pattern is an obvious choice for organizing a speech on a topic such as the branches of government.

General Purpose: To inform

Specific Purpose: To inform my audience of the ways the three branches of government work

Thesis: Three branches govern the United States.

    I. The legislative branch is controlled by Congress.

    II. The executive branch is controlled by the president.

    III. The judicial branch is controlled by the courts.

Problem–Solution Pattern

As its name indicates, the problem–solution pattern divides the main ideas into two main parts: problems and solutions. Let's say you're trying to persuade an audience that home health aides should be given higher salaries and increased benefits. In the first part of the speech, you might discuss some of the problems confronting home health aides. In the second part, you would consider the possible solutions to these problems. The speech, in outline form, might look like this.

General Purpose: To persuade

Specific Purpose: To persuade my audience of the solutions to the three main problems of the home health care industry

Thesis: The home health care industry can be improved with three changes.

   I. Three major problems confront home health care.
- A. Industry lures away the most qualified graduates.
- B. Numerous excellent health aides leave the field after a few years.
- C. Home health care is currently a low-status occupation.

  II. Three major solutions to these problems exist.
- A. Increase salaries for home health aides.
- B. Make benefits for health aides more attractive.
- C. Raise the status of the home health care profession.

In some instances you may want to use a topical pattern (for the main heads) and a problem–solution pattern (for the subheads). Here, for example, is how Kevin King (2015) used this organizational system in his speech on the need to increase funding for Alzheimer's disease. Stigma, Practical challenges, and Advocacy are in a topical pattern, but the subpoints for each are presented in a problem–solution pattern.

   I. Stigma
- A. Stigma as problem
- B. Stigma solutions

  II. Practical challenges [lack of research subjects]
- A. Practical challenges as problem
- B. Practical challenges solutions

 III. Advocacy
- A. Lack of advocacy as problem
- B. Lack of advocacy solutions

Cause–Effect/Effect–Cause Pattern

Similar to the problem–solution pattern of organization is the cause–effect, or effect–cause (sometimes referred to as a causal), pattern. Using this pattern, you divide the speech into two major sections: (1) causes and (2) effects. Highway accidents, illnesses, or low self-esteem, for example, could be explained using a cause–effect pattern. An outline of the causes and effects of low self-esteem might look something like this:

General Purpose: To inform

Specific Purpose: To inform my audience of the causes and effects of low self-esteem

Thesis: Low self-esteem is caused by a history of criticism and unrealistic goals, which lead to depression and an unwillingness to socialize.

   I. Low self-esteem often has two main causes.
- A. A history of criticism can contribute to low self-esteem.
- B. Unrealistic goals can contribute to low self-esteem.

  II. Low self-esteem often has two main effects.
- A. Depression is one frequent effect.
- B. An unwillingness to socialize with others is another frequent effect.

You can also organize your persuasive speeches around causes and effects. For example, you might organize a persuasive speech around persuading your audience that, say, a history of criticism does in fact contribute to low self-esteem as do unrealistic goals. Here you would have two major points:

    I. A history of criticism leads to low self-esteem.

        A. Double blind studies show …

        B. A recent survey …

        C. Psychologist, John Smith of Harvard University, has said …

    II. Unrealistic goals lead to low self-esteem.

        A. My own experience illustrates …

        B. A study conducted …

        C. Educational theorists have long …

Structure–Function Pattern

In this pattern there are generally two main points, one for structure and one for function. This pattern is useful in informative speeches in which you want to discuss how something is constructed (its structure) and what it does (its function). It might prove useful, for example, in a speech explaining what a business organization is and what it does, identifying the parts of a university and how they operate, or describing the nature of a living organism: its anatomy (its structures) and its physiology (its functions).

General Purpose: To inform

Specific Purpose: To inform my audience of the structure and function of the brain

Thesis: To understand the brain you need to understand its structure and its function

    I. The brain consists of two main parts [explanation of structures]

        A. The cerebrum consists of …

        B. The cerebellum consists of …

    II. The brain enables us to do a variety of things [explanations of functions]

        A. The cerebrum enables us to …

        B. The cerebellum enables us to …

Comparison-and-Contrast Pattern

In the comparison-and-contrast pattern your main points might be the main divisions of your topic. This pattern is often useful in informative speeches in which you want to analyze two different theories, proposals, departments, or products in terms of their similarities and differences. In this type of speech you would be concerned not only with explaining each theory or proposal but also with clarifying how they're similar and how they're different.

General Purpose: To inform

Specific Purpose: To inform my audience of two main differences between liberal and conservative political philosophies

Thesis: Liberal and conservative political philosophies differ in important ways.

    I. Government regulation …

        A. The liberal attitude is …

        B. The conservative attitude is …

    II. Redistribution of income …

        A. Liberals view this …

        B. Conservatives view this …

Pro-and-Con Pattern

In the **pro-and-con pattern**, sometimes called the advantages–disadvantages pattern, the speech has two main points—the advantages of Plan A and the disadvantages of Plan A (or Plan B). This pattern is useful in informative speeches in which you want to explain objectively the advantages (the pros) and the disadvantages (the cons) of a plan, method, or product. Or you can use this pattern in a persuasive speech in which you want to show the superiority of Plan A (identifying its advantages) over Plan B (identifying its disadvantages). In this example, we'll consider a persuasive speech.

General Purpose: To persuade

Specific Purpose: To persuade my audience that Plan A is better than Plan B

Thesis: The proposals of the two health plans differ in co-payments, hospital benefits, and sick leave.

   I. Co-payments …
- A. Plan A provides lower co-payments.
- B. Plan B provides higher co-payments.

  II. Hospital benefits …
- A. Plan A provides greater hospital benefits.
- B. Plan B provides fewer hospital benefits.

III. Sick leave …
- A. Plan A provides for more sick days
- B. Plan B provides for fewer sick days.

Claim-and-Proof Pattern

In the **claim-and-proof pattern** your thesis would essentially be your claim, and then each main point would be support for your claim. This pattern is especially useful in a persuasive speech in which you want to prove the truth or usefulness of a particular proposition. It's the pattern that you see frequently in trials, where the claim made by the prosecution is that the defendant is guilty and the proof is the varied evidence designed to show that the defendant had a motive, opportunity, and no alibi.

General Purpose: To persuade

Specific Purpose: To persuade my audience that the city must actively combat drug addiction

Thesis/Claim: The city must become proactive in dealing with the drug addicted.

   I. Drug usage is increasing. [Proof No. 1]
- A. A particularly vivid example …
- B. Recent statistics …

  II. Drug related crimes are increasing. [Proof No. 2]
- A. On-street crimes have increased …
- B. Business break-ins …

Multiple-Definition Pattern

In the **multiple-definition pattern** each of your main points would consist of a different type of definition. This pattern is useful for informative speeches in which you want to explain the nature of a concept.

General Purpose: To inform

Specific Purpose: To inform my audience of the meaning of creative thinking

Thesis: The nature of creative thinking is often misunderstood.

    I. Creative thinking is not … [definition by negation]

    II. According to Webster's dictionary … [dictionary definition]

    III. Edward deBono defines … [a creative thinking theorist's view]

    IV. A good example of creative thinking … [definition by example]

Who? What? Why? Where? When? Pattern

In this pattern your main points are explanations of who, what, why, where, and/or when. This is the pattern traditionally used by journalists and is useful when you wish to report or explain an event; for example, a robbery, political coup, war, or trial.

General Purpose: To inform

Specific Purpose: To inform my audience of the nature of the U.S. Constitution as a citizen's responsibility

Thesis: Understanding the Constitution is a first step toward responsible citizenship.

    I. The Constitution is a document that sets forth … [answers the question What is the Constitution?]

    II. The Constitution was needed because … [answers the question Why was it written?]

    III. The Constitution was written at a time … [answers the question When was it written?]

    IV. The Constitution was written by … [answers the question Who wrote it?]

Fiction–Fact pattern

In the **fiction–fact pattern** your main points would be the fiction, and under these would be the facts. This pattern may be useful in informative speeches when you wish to clarify misconceptions that people have about various things. In persuasive speeches this pattern might be used to defend or attack, whether a proposal, belief, or person.

General Purpose: To inform

Specific Purpose: To inform my audience of the three misconceptions people have about the flu shot

Thesis: Three main misconceptions exist about the flu shot.

    I. The first misconception is that you can get the flu from the flu shot.

        A. Studies show …

        B. The flu shot contains …

    II. The second misconception is that antibiotics will help with the flu.

        A. Actually, antibiotics ….

        B. Viruses, such as the flu, however, …

    III. The third misconception is that older people spread the flu.

        A. Actually, children …

        B. In studies done …

JOURNAL
COMMUNICATION CHOICE POINT
Organizing a Speech

Consider one of the theses noted in the previous section: (1) the minimum wage must be raised; (2) bullying exists in lots of different forms; or (3) the Freedom of Information Act is relevant to all of us. *What organizational patterns might be especially appropriate if the speech were to be delivered to your class?*

Public Speaking Sample Assistant

A POORLY CONSTRUCTED INFORMATIVE SPEECH

Here is an example of a poorly constructed informative speech. As you'll see, no one really gives a speech this bad. It was constructed to illustrate clearly and briefly some of the major faults that can occur in such speeches. The Public Speaking Sample Assistant in Chapter 13 offers an example of a truly excellent speech. Together, the negative and the positive speech examples will offer you a variety of guidelines for errors you'll want to avoid and principles you'll want to follow in your own speeches. Not surprisingly researchers have found that we learn a great deal from negative examples (Hesketh & Neal, 2006).

THE SPEECH	PROBLEMS AND CORRECTIVES
Title: Biases	The title is likely to lead listeners to think of racial or religious bias—which the speech is not about. Select a title that is interesting, attention-getting, and relevant to the speech. After reading the speech, give the speech an interesting, attention-grabbing title.
Thesis: What are confirmation, disconfirmation, in-group, and belief biases?	Stating the thesis as a question will prove confusing. Instead state the thesis as a declarative sentence, for example: Types of biases include confirmation, disconfirmation, in-group, and belief.
General Purpose: To inform	The general purpose is fine although when you read the speech, you'll see the speaker moves beyond informing.
Specific Purpose: To inform you about biases	The specific purpose is too general. It needs to be more specific: to define confirmation, disconfirmation, in-group, and belief biases.

INTRODUCTION

Whew! I'm here. This public speaking is all new to me. My major requires public speaking so I may be a bit nervous—I mean, a lot nervous.	These kinds of introductory comments are best avoided. They merely focus the listeners' attention on your weaknesses. Instead encourage listeners to focus on your strengths.
Let's see [shuffles through notes, arranging them and mumbling, "page 1, page 2"—OK, it's all here.]	Things like this reveal a decided lack of preparation. Instead, have your notes arranged and in order before getting up to speak.
I want to talk with you about bias and biases—confirmation, disconfirmation, in-group, and belief. I read an interesting article on this on the Internet and I thought, you know, since I have to give an informative speech this would be really good. It's interesting; really it is.	Getting right into the topic is not necessarily a bad idea. But, some more attention-grabbing way of gaining attention might have worked better. Perhaps a question or a dramatic illustration.
I have a lot of biases so I'm really concerned with this topic and I know you all have lots of biases so this might help you. So you should listen, like our textbook says.	Confessing to having biases—which are almost universally considered negative—is probably not a very good way to establish a connection with the audience. And, saying the audience has biases, will likely prove insulting to many listeners. Again, stress strengths rather than weaknesses. The "So you should listen…" sentence was intended to get a laugh but is likely to fall on its face. Pretest your humor; it may not be as funny to others as it is to you.
So, like I said, I mean, that I'm going to talk about biases.	This statement functions as a transition—a sentence or phrase that guides the listeners from one part of the speech to another but it is too brief. A more elaborate transition here might have identified the four biases and the reason why these are being discussed.

BODY

Confirmation bias—this means, like, you know, that you seek the kinds of information that will confirm your beliefs. And, not only this, but you also would give more importance to information that confirms your beliefs that to information that would not confirm your beliefs. I guess this could be about anything—religion or politics, maybe. I can give you a good example of this. My sister thinks that Chevrolet is the best car and only reads advertisements for Chevys.	The speaker begins here with the first bias but doesn't define bias. It needs to be defined first and then the other four biases could be introduced as types of bias. Further, you would want to answer the audience's inevitable question, Why these four biases? Some reason for selecting these biases or some unifying thread would be effective in answering the audience's question.

Another example is if you want to persuade an audience to believe X, then you're going to do your research to find information that makes you believe X. But, that may be because you just want to get the speech prepared and don't want to waste time looking at information you won't use.

This X example doesn't work; it says that the speaker didn't think hard enough about this topic. It tells listeners that the speaker hasn't thought about this sufficiently to come up with a good specific example. Generally, specific examples work better than the unidentified "X."

Disconfirmation bias—this means that people will reject information that goes against their beliefs—So, my sister would reject advertisements that claim that BMW is a better car. It's crazy but she does that. BMW is definitely the better car. That's what I want to get when I get a permanent job and make the big bucks.

The sister example is trite. And the personal asides about BMW and the car the speaker wants to get just detract from the speech and, again, make you think the speaker didn't think this out clearly. Examples are extremely important; think them out and rehearse them carefully.

Let's say, for example, that you believe X and someone gives you the information in favor of X and against X. You would believe the information in favor of your belief about X and that you will also reject information that goes against what you believe about X. This was actually shown in a research study on capital punishment.

Again, the X adds little to clarity. But, the research study cited on capital punishment would have made an excellent example and could have easily explained how those who were for capital punishment believed the studies that supported capital published more than the studies that did not support capital punishment.

Also, the study on capital punishment requires an oral citation, a more specific identification of the study cited.

In-group bias—this is also called intergroup bias—this means that people like people who are in the same groups as they are. So, if you're in the photography club and you hear that someone else is in the club, you'll probably have positive feelings for this person. I don't know about this, though; I'm in the photography club and I don't like a lot of the people. And I think some of them don't like me—actually a lot of them. This is supposed to work but I'm not sure.

Notice that the speaker is evaluating the concept rather than simply explaining it. If the speech were on evaluating these bias theories, then this personal example would not have been so inappropriate. In a speech of definition, stick to defining.

Wikipedia says that there are two theories about in-group bias: realistic conflict theory and social identity theory. I'm not sure that helps but that's what Wikipedia says.

Introducing these two theories without any explanation will confuse rather than clarify, unless the audience was very sophisticated in their knowledge of this topic. Further, some instructors may frown upon using Wikipedia as a source. So, know your audience.

Belief bias—this means that people will accept a conclusion if it fits in with the beliefs they have. And, at the same time, people will reject a conclusion if it doesn't fit in with the beliefs they have. So, what happens here is that people don't look at the evidence; they only look at the conclusion. Like my sister doesn't examine the research on BMW; she just goes with the conclusion that Chevys are the best.

By this time, the sister example is likely to seem silly to the audience. Avoid examples that might be considered silly; one laugh at the wrong time is likely to prove upsetting even to a seasoned speaker.

This is really confusing and has to do with the validity of arguments. It seems if you have belief bias you don't care about the validity of the argument. That's because you just look at the conclusion.

The term validity might have been defined though it's a complex term and would likely take up too much time. It may have been easier to not use the term and say something like "the strength or truthfulness of the arguments."

CONCLUSION

There are four biases—confirmation bias (like my sister and her car), disconfirmation bias (my sister and her car again), in-group bias (the photography club), and belief bias (my sister again).

This summary does little to help listeners remember what was discussed; they're likely to remember the example of the speaker's sister and not the four types of biases. It might also have helped to use a transitional sentence to guide the listener from the body of the speech to the conclusion, for example, "As we've seen there are four biases …"or even "In summary, we've seen there are four biases that …"

By the way, I got most of my information from a website which I can't remember.

This type of source credit is woefully inadequate. As we'll see, in the discussion of the oral citation (pp. 000-000), citing sources is an essential component of the speech. And, of course, one or two sources are hardly sufficient for such a complex topic.

If you want to read more about these, they are on the Internet.

This is much too general and more of a throw-away line. Something more specific might have helped, for example, a handout on the terms and where listeners can get more information.

Further the speaker seems almost without concern about whether or not listeners will want to learn more about these biases. Express enthusiasm about your topic, from the start of the speech to the very end. Listeners prefer speakers who are enthusiastic about their topic and really want to share their knowledge.

Summary of Concepts and Skills

This chapter explained the nature of public speaking and described the first six steps involved in preparing an effective public speech.

The Nature of Public Speaking

11.1 **Explain the nature of public speaking and communication apprehension, and identify the suggestions for managing apprehension in public speaking and for overcoming procrastination.**

1. In public speaking a speaker addresses a relatively large audience with a relatively continuous discourse, usually in a face-to-face situation.

2. Effective public speaking will yield a variety of personal, social, academic, and professional benefits.

3. Apprehension can be managed by gaining experience, thinking positively, being realistic, seeing public speaking as conversation, focusing on your listeners, stressing similarity, projecting confidence, preparing and practicing thoroughly, moving about and breathing deeply, and avoiding using chemicals as tension relievers (unless prescribed by a physician).

4. Public speaking takes place within a cultural context, and that context must be taken into consideration in preparing and delivering speeches.

5. Starting early is the best way to ensure adequate time for dealing with unexpected problems.

The preparation of a public speech involves 10 steps. The first six of these were discussed in this chapter; the remaining four are discussed in Chapter 12.

Step 1: Select Your Topic, Purposes, and Thesis

11.2 **Describe how public speaking topics, purposes, and theses can be selected and limited.**

6. Speech topics should deal with significant issues that interest the audience. Subjects and purposes should be limited in scope. The thesis should be stated as a complete sentence.

Step 2: Analyze Your Audience

11.3 **Explain the sociological and psychological characteristics of an audience and how these might be used in audience analysis and adaptation.**

7. When analyzing the audience, consider audience members' sociology: age; sex; cultural factors; occupation, income, and status; and religion and religiousness. Also consider the psychology of the audience: that is, the degree to which the audience is willing to hear your speech, their attitudes toward the topic and thesis, and the knowledge they possess of the topic.

Step 3: Research Your Topic

11.4 **Identify the basic principles of and sources for researching your speech topic and the criteria for evaluating research and for integrating and citing research.**

8. Research your topic, beginning with general sources and gradually exploring more specific and specialized sources.

9. In evaluating research material (especially material on the Internet) consider the qualifications of the author, the currency of the information, and its fairness, sufficiency, and accuracy.

Step 4: Collect Supporting Materials

11.5 **Identify the types of supporting materials in informative and persuasive speeches.**

10. Support your main points with a variety of materials that amplify and provide evidence.

Step 5: Develop Your Main Points

11.6 **Describe how main points may be generated from your theses.**

11. Formulate the thesis of your speech. Develop your main points by asking relevant questions about this thesis.

Step 6: Organize Your Information

11.7 Describe the major patterns of speech organization.

12. Organize your speech materials into a clear, easily identifiable pattern. Useful examples include the time pattern, the spatial pattern, the topical pattern, the problem–solution pattern, the cause–effect/effect–cause pattern, the structure–function pattern, the comparison-and-contrast pattern, the pro-and-con pattern, the claim-and-proof pattern, the multiple-definition pattern, the five W's (who, what, why, where, when), and the fiction–fact pattern.

These first six steps in preparing a public speech entail a variety of specific skills. Place a check mark next to those skills you most want to work on.

_____ 1. When preparing a public speech, I follow a logical progression of steps, such as the sequence outlined here.

_____ 2. I select appropriate topics, purposes, and theses and narrow them to manageable proportions.

_____ 3. I analyze my audience in terms of members' sociological and psychological characteristics, and I adapt the speech on the basis of these findings.

_____ 4. I research topics effectively and efficiently and critically evaluate the reliability of the research material.

_____ 5. I collect materials relevant to my topic, purpose, and thesis—for instance, examples, statistics, and visual aids and with logical, emotional, and ethical proofs.

_____ 6. I identify my major propositions from my thesis statement.

_____ 7. When organizing the speech's main points, I select a pattern appropriate to the subject matter, purpose, and audience.

Key Terms

audience
claim-and-proof pattern
communication apprehension
fact–fiction pattern
general purposes
informative speech

multiple-definition pattern
persuasive speech
plagiarism
pro-and-con pattern
public speaking

research
specific purpose
supporting materials
taboo
thesis

Skill Development Experiences

11.1 Using Cultural Beliefs as Assumptions

Knowing your audience's beliefs will help you identify with your listeners, avoid offending them, and adapt your speech.

How effective would it be to use each of the following cultural beliefs as a basic assumption in a speech to your public speaking class? Use the following scale: **A** = the audience would favorably accept this assumption and would welcome a speaker with this point of view; **B** = some members would listen open-mindedly, but others wouldn't; or **C** = the audience would reject this assumption and would not welcome a speaker with this point of view.

_____ 1. Religious differences are the main causes of war.

_____ 2. The group is more important than the individual.

_____ 3. The rich (countries, individuals) are morally obligated to give to the poor.

_____ 4. Men and women should each enter occupations for which they are biologically suited.

_____ 5. Pleasure is the only real goal in life.

11.2 Topic Appropriateness

The appropriateness of a topic depends largely on the audience.

Look around your classroom or assess the students in your online class and indicate why the following topics/theses would or would not be appropriate.

1. Let's get rid of fraternities and sororities.
2. Dental implants are the best solution for missing teeth.
3. Recreational marijuana should be made legal in all states.
4. Religious freedom laws encourage discrimination.
5. College athletes should get paid.

11.3 Limiting Topics

A limited topic makes your speech easier to construct and easier to understand and remember.

Think about the overly general topics listed below. Using one of the methods discussed in this chapter (or any other method you're familiar with), limit one of these topics to a subject that would be reasonable for a 5- to 10-minute informative speech.

Bullying	Nutrition
Children	Parole
Civil disobedience	Plastic surgery
Comic books	Political corruption
Drug laws	Self-driving cars
Fitness	Sports
Fraternities and sororities	Student problems
Male–female relationships	Surveillance on the Internet
MOOCs	Tattoos
Morality	Violence

Chapter 12
Public Speaking Preparation and Delivery (Steps 7–10)

The higher you go in the orga-nizational hierarchy, the more important your public speaking abilities.

CHAPTER OUTLINE	∨	Learning Objectives

Step 7: Word Your Speech

12.1 Define *clarity, vividness, appropriateness, personal style,* and *power* in wording a speech.

Step 8: Construct Your Conclusion, Introduction, Transitions, and Outlines

12.2 Explain the functions of the introduction, conclusion, and transitions and the nature of preparation and delivery outlines for your speeches.

Step 9: Rehearse Your Speech

12.3 Explain the methods of delivery and rehearsal.

Step 10: Deliver Your Speech

12.4 Explain the principles of effective voice and bodily action.

Critically Evaluating Speeches

12.5 Describe the guidelines for expressing and receiving speech criticism.

At this point, you're probably deep into your speech preparation. You've selected and limited your topic, defined your purpose, and stated your thesis. You've analyzed your audience and thought of adaptations you can make based on the nature of your specific audience. You've researched the topic. You've identified your main points. You've organized the points and selected appropriate supporting materials.

In this chapter, we continue the process of preparing a speech with suggestions on wording the speech (Step 7); constructing the conclusion, introduction, transitions, and outlines (Step 8); rehearsing the speech (Step 9); and finally delivering the completed public speech (Step 10).

Step 7: Word Your Speech

12.1 Define *clarity, vividness, appropriateness, personal style,* and *power* in wording a speech.

When you're reading, you can look up an unfamiliar word, reread difficult portions, or look up an unfamiliar word or check a reference. When you're listening, you don't have this luxury. Because of differences between reading and listening, and because your listeners will hear your speech only once, your talk must be instantly intelligible.

Researchers who have examined a great number of speeches and writings have found several important differences among them (DeVito, 1981; Akinnaso, 1982). Generally, **oral style**, the style of spoken language, consists of shorter, simpler, and more familiar words than does written language. For most speeches, this "oral style" is appropriate. The specific suggestions offered throughout this section will help you to style a speech that will retain the best of the oral style while maximizing comprehension and persuasion.

Clarity

Clarity in speaking style should be your primary goal. Here are some guidelines to help you make your meanings clear.

- **Be economical.** Don't waste words. Notice the wasted words in expressions such as "at 9 a.m. *in the morning*," "we *first* began the discussion," "I *myself personally*," and "blue *in color*." By withholding the italicized terms, you eliminate unnecessary words and move closer to a more economical and clearer style.

- **Use specific terms and numbers.** Be specific to create a clearer and more detailed picture. Don't say "dog" when you want your listeners to picture a St. Bernard. Don't say "car" when you want them to picture a limousine. The same is true of numbers. Don't say "earned a good salary" if you mean "earned $90,000 a year." Don't say "taxes will go up" when you mean "taxes will increase 7 percent."

- **Use short, familiar terms.** Generally, favor the short word over the long, the familiar over the unfamiliar, and the more commonly used over the rarely used term. Choose *harmless* instead of *innocuous, clarify* instead of *elucidate, use* instead of *utilize, find out* instead of *ascertain, expense* instead of *expenditure.*

- **Carefully assess idioms. Idioms** are expressions that are unique to a specific language and whose meaning cannot be deduced from the individual words used. Expressions such as "kick the bucket," and "doesn't have a leg to stand on" are idioms. Either you know the meaning of the expression or you don't; you can't figure it out from the definitions of the individual words. Idioms give your speech a casual and informal style, making your speech sound like speech and not like a written essay. But, idioms can create problems for audience members who are not native speakers of your language.

- **Vary the levels of abstraction.** Combining high **abstraction** (i.e., the very general) and low abstraction (i.e., the very concrete) seems to work best. Too many generalizations will be vague and difficult for your audience to comprehend, but too many specifics will leave them wondering what the big picture is.

Vividness

Select words that make your ideas vivid, words that make them come alive in your listeners' minds. Active verbs, imagery, and figures of speech such as **alliteration, hyperbole, metaphor, personification, simile** and **rhetorical questions** are invaluable tools to help you achieve this goal.

- **Use active verbs.** Favor verbs that communicate activity. Try selecting verbs that will enable listeners to visualize an action—verbs like *dance, climb,* and *run,* for example.
- **Use figures of speech.** A **figure of speech** is a stylistic device in which words are used beyond their literal meaning. One of the best ways to achieve vividness is to use figures of speech. Table 12.1 presents a few that you may find helpful.
- **Use imagery.** Inject vividness into your speech by using words that appeal to the audience's visual, auditory, and tactile senses. Help your audience envision the sweat pouring down the tired, smudged faces of coal miners, experience the deafening roar of angry protesters, or feel the surprise of a fighter's sudden punch.

Note the effective imagery in this excerpt from the Alzheimer's speech (King, 2015).

> The reality is this disease is a brutal thief that will steal your memory, speech, bladder control, and ability to feed yourself.

Appropriateness

Appropriate language is consistent in tone with your topic, your audience, and your own self-image. It's language that does not offend anyone or make anyone feel uncomfortable; it seems natural given the situation. Here are some guidelines to help you choose appropriate language:

- **Speak at the appropriate level of formality.** Although public speaking usually takes place in a somewhat formal situation, relatively informal language seems to

---

Table 12.1 Figures of Speech

These are only a few of the many figures of speech you can use in your speeches. Too many are likely to make your speech sound unnatural and overly formal, so use these sparingly. On the other hand, a good figure of speech goes a long way toward making your speech memorable. Can you think of additional examples for each of the types identified here?

Figure of Speech/Definition	Examples
Alliteration Repetition of the same initial consonant sound in two or more words close to one another	Choose from our fifty famous flavors! The basement was dirty, dingy, dark, and dank.
Hyperbole Use of extreme exaggeration	I'm so hungry I could eat a horse. She's got tons of money.
Metaphor Comparison of two unlike things	She was feeling blue and totally torn apart. His heart was broken.
Personification Attribution of human characteristics to inanimate objects	The snow blanketed the city. My car is crying for some expert attention.
Simile Comparison of two unlike objects using the words *like* or *as*	His handshake was as cold as a snow ball. They attacked each other like warriors.
Rhetorical Question A question used to make a statement or produce some desired effect rather than to secure the answer, which is obvious	Do you want to be popular? Would you like to get a raise?

work best in most situations. One way to achieve a more informal style is to use contractions: *don't* instead of *do not, wouldn't* instead of *would not.* Contractions give a public speech the sound and rhythm of conversation—a quality listeners generally like.

- **Avoid written-style expressions.** Avoid expressions that are more familiar in writing, such as "the former" or "the latter" as well as expressions such as "the argument presented above." These make listeners feel you're reading to them rather than talking with them.

- **Avoid slang and vulgar and offensive expressions.** Be careful not to offend your audience with language that embarrasses them or makes them think you have little respect for them. Although your listeners may use such expressions, they generally resent their use by public speakers. Above all, avoid terms that might be interpreted as sexist, heterosexist, ageist, or racist.

Personal Style

Audiences favor speakers who use a personal rather than an impersonal style—who speak *with* them rather than *at* them. A personal style makes the audience feel more involved with the speaker and the speech topic.

- **Use personal pronouns.** Choose I, *me, he, she,* and *you.* rather than expressions such as the impersonal *one* (as in, "One is led to believe that …"), *this speaker,* and *you, the listeners.* These expressions are overly formal and distance the audience, creating barriers rather than bridges.

- **Direct questions to the audience.** Involve the audience by asking them questions. With a small audience, you might even take brief responses. With larger audiences, you might ask the question, pause to allow the audience time to consider their responses, and then move on. When you direct questions to your listeners, you make them feel they are part of the experience.

- **Create immediacy.** Create immediacy (a closeness with your audience) by referring directly to your listeners, using you; say, "You'll enjoy reading …" instead of "Everyone will enjoy reading …." Refer to commonalities between you and the audience and to shared experiences and goals: for example, "We all need a more responsive PTA."

Power

Public speaking, perhaps even more than interpersonal or small-group communication, often requires a powerful style—a style that is certain, definite, and persuasive.

The first step toward achieving a powerful style of speech is to eliminate the powerless forms that you may use now. The following weaknesses characterize powerless speech (Molloy, 1981; Kleinke, 1986; Johnson, 1987; Dillard & Marshall, 2003; Lakoff, 1975; Timmerman, 2002).

- **Hesitations** make you sound unprepared and uncertain: "I, er, want to say that, ah, this one is, er, the best, you know?"

- **Too many intensifiers** make your speech monotonous and don't allow you to stress what you do want to emphasize: "Really, this was the greatest; it was truly awesome, phenomenal."

- **Disqualifiers** signal a lack of competence and a feeling of uncertainty: "I didn't read the entire article, but …" "I didn't actually see the accident, but …"

- **Self-critical statements** signal a lack of confidence and may make public your own inadequacies: "I'm not very good at this," "This is my first public speech."

- **Slang and vulgar language** signal low social class and hence little power: "No problem!" "@*+#?$!!"

JOURNAL
COMMUNICATION CHOICE POINT
Slang

You're preparing to speak to an audience of high school sophomores about going to Regional Community College. You wonder how you can use language to help relate to these students. For example, you wonder if you should break the general rule against using slang, thinking that slang is the language of the students and imagine that they'd be more likely to identify with you if you spoke their language. *What options do you have in choosing an appropriate style? How would you describe the style you would use?*

Table 12.2 Powerful Bodily Action

Here are some nonverbal behaviors that are likely to help you communicate power in public speaking (Burgoon, Guerrero, & Floyd, 2010; DeVito, 2014).

Suggestions for Communicating Power with Bodily Action	Reasons
Avoid self-manipulations (playing with your hair or touching your face, for example); avoid leaning backward.	These signals communicate a lack of comfort and an ill-at-ease feeling and are likely to damage your persuasiveness.
Walk slowly and deliberately to and from the podium.	To appear hurried is to appear powerless, as if you were rushing to meet the expectations of those who have power over you.
Use facial expressions and gestures as appropriate.	These help you express your concern for the audience and for the interaction and help you communicate your comfort and control of the situation.
Use consistent packaging; be careful that your verbal and nonverbal messages do not contradict each other.	Inconsistency between verbal and nonverbal messages may be seen as uncertainty and a lack of conviction.

At the same time that you'll want to make your speech powerful, you'll also want to do similarly with your bodily action. Table 12.2 provides a few suggestions.

Sentence Construction

Effective public speaking style also requires careful attention to the construction of sentences. Here are some guidelines that will help you achieve a clear, vivid, appropriate, personal, and powerful speaking style.

- **Use short rather than long sentences.** Short sentences are more forceful and economical. They are easier to understand and to remember. Listeners don't have the time or inclination to unravel long and complex sentences. Help them to listen more efficiently by using short rather than long sentences.

- **Use direct rather than indirect sentences.** Direct sentences are easier to understand. They are also more forceful. Instead of saying, "I want to tell you the three main reasons why we should not adopt the Bennett proposal," say, "We should not adopt the Bennett proposal. Let me give you three good reasons."

- **Use active rather than passive sentences.** Active sentences are easier to understand. They also make your speech livelier and more vivid. Instead of saying, "The lower court's original decision was reversed by the Supreme Court," say, "The Supreme Court reversed the lower court's decision." Instead of saying, "The change was favored by management," say, "Management favored the change."

- **Use positive rather than negative sentences.** Positive sentences are easier to comprehend and to remember (DeVito, 1976; Clark, 1974). Notice how sentences A and C are easier to understand than B and D.

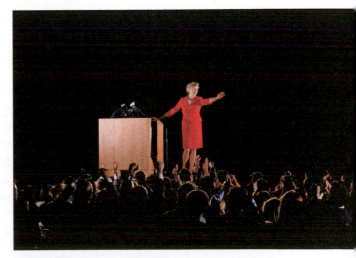

VIEWPOINTS: Wording the Speech for Different Audiences

You're scheduled to give two speeches, one to a predominantly female audience of health professionals and one to a predominantly male audience of small business owners. Your topic for both groups is the same: neighborhood violence and how it must be confronted. *In what major ways (identify two or three) would these speeches need to be different?*

Positive Sentences	Negative Sentences
A. The committee rejected the proposal.	B. The committee did not accept the proposal.
C. This committee works outside the normal company hierarchy.	D. This committee does not work within the normal company hierarchy.

© 2000 Ted Goff

"You're not allowed to use the sprinkler system to keep your audience awake."

Ted Goff

- **Vary the type and length of sentences.** The advice to use short, direct, active, and positive sentences is valid most of the time. But too many sentences of the same type or length will make your speech sound boring. Use variety but generally follow the guidelines.

Step 8: Construct Your Conclusion, Introduction, Transitions, and Outlines

12.2 Explain the functions of the introduction, conclusion, and transitions and the nature of preparation and delivery outlines for your speeches.

Your conclusion and introduction need special care, because they will determine, in large part, the effectiveness of your speech. Because you've just finished the body of the speech, and the major function of the conclusion is to summarize, it will probably be easier to work first on your conclusion and then on the introduction.

The Conclusion

Devote particular attention to this brief but crucial part of your speech. In your conclusion, summarize your main points and make closing remarks.

SUMMARIZE You may summarize your speech in a variety of ways.

- **Restate your thesis.** Present again the essential thrust of your speech—your thesis, or perhaps the purpose you hoped to achieve.
- **Restate the importance of your thesis.** Tell the audience again why your topic or thesis is so important.
- **Restate your main points.** Reiterate your two, three, or four main points.

CLOSE The conclusion's second function is to provide closure—to give the speech a crisp and definite end. Don't leave your audience wondering whether you've finished.

- **Summarize with a quotation.** A quotation that clearly and directly summarizes your thesis or provides an interesting perspective on your point of view often provides effective closure.
- **Pose a challenge or question.** You may wish to end your speech with a provocative question or challenge: "What do you intend to do about the company's refusal to increase wages?" "Go home and clean high-cholesterol foods out of your refrigerator." "Sign this petition; it will help put an experienced person in office."
- **Thank the audience.** Some speakers thank the audience and others don't. The contest speeches that appear in this text as examples do not thank the audience. TED speakers almost always thank the audience (Donovan, 2014; Gallo, 2014). The problem with saying "Thank you" is that it may prevent you from developing and presenting a really crisp closing; it may dilute the force of your conclusion. The best advice here is to find out what's the accepted practice. If you do thank the audience, you may want to relate the thanks to your thesis: "I really appreciate your attention and hope you'll join us in Sunday's protest." Or you might say, "I want to thank you for listening and for your willingness to sign the Student Senate's petition to expand the college's online website."
- **Motivate your audience to do something.** Remind your audience of what they should do now: "The next time you go online, visit one of the websites I mentioned,"

"You can sign up to volunteer at the desk in the Student Union," or "So, read the article in this handout; it could change your life."

Here Kevin King (2015) concludes his speech on Alzheimer's by briefly summarizing his talk but mainly to motivate the audience to do something about Alzheimer's funding.

> Today we explored three independent causes to the lack of research funding for Alzheimer's and provided tangible solutions for each. Last spring, my grandfather failed the clock test, an early tool for detecting Alzheimer's. He has not been fully diagnosed, but when he is I want to know I have done everything I can to help end this brutal disease. I encourage each of you, in your own circumstances, to join me.

JOURNAL
COMMUNICATION CHOICE POINT
Conclusions

You're scheduled to give a speech on careers in computer technology to high school students who are required to attend Career Day on Saturday. You're planning to focus on the enjoyment, high salary, and employment opportunities of such careers and you're wondering about your conclusion. *What are some of the ways you might conclude your speech?*

The Introduction

In your introduction, try to accomplish two goals: (1) gain your audience's attention and (2) orient the audience—tell them a little bit about what you'll talk about.

GAIN ATTENTION   In your introduction, focus the audience's attention on your topic. Then work to maintain that attention throughout your speech.

- **Ask a question.** Questions are effective because they are a change from normal statements and involve the audience. They tell the audience that you're talking directly to them and care about their responses. Questions are also useful in setting the stage for what will follow.

- **Refer to specific audience members.** Involving members directly makes them perk up and pay attention. Depending on the nature of the audience and your knowledge of specific members, you might say something like this.

   > Pat, you defended the NRA, whereas Chris, you argued against it. And Pablo, you argued for a pro-life position on abortion, but Sarah, you argued for a pro-choice position. Even in a small class such as this, there are wide differences in beliefs, values, and attitudes. And that's what I want to talk about today: differences in beliefs and how these can cause conflict in our relationships.

- **Refer to the specific context.** Instead of referring to specific people, you might note the relevance of the specific context. Here, for example, is how Secretary of State Hillary Clinton (1995) referred to the context of her remarks at the U.N. World Conference on Women.

   > By gathering in Beijing, we are focusing world attention on issues that matter most in our lives—the lives of women and their families: access to education, health care, jobs and credit, the chance to enjoy basic legal and human rights and to participate fully in the political life of our countries.

- **Use illustrations or dramatic or humorous stories.** We are all drawn to illustrations and stories about people—they make a speech vivid and concrete. Use them to secure audience attention in the introduction and to maintain it throughout. Here, for example, one speaker used a dramatic illustration in opening her speech on bullying (Bacon, 2011).

   > A typical ninth-grade female goes to her locker after a long day of classes to find a note. As she opens the note, her day goes from typical to horrendous. The note reads, "Get a new hair cut, you look like a dyke. Start wearing clothes that fit and go home and die."

Here, from the speech on Alzheimer's, is a very different type of illustration of someone with whom the audience is familiar (King, 2015).

VIEWPOINTS: **Constructing an Introduction**
What are some of the things you might include in your introduction to a pro-choice speech to a pro-life audience (or, if you prefer, a pro-life speech to a pro-choice audience)? Try constructing such an introduction.

Last Spring, comedian Seth Rogen set aside his joint and headed to the halls of Congress to testify before the Senate Committee on Appropriations. For the past 9 years, Rogen has watched his mother-in-law's health spiral out of control at the hands of Alzheimer's disease. In his February 26, 2014 testimony, Rogen called on Congress to prioritize Alzheimer's research. And his plea was heard—by 2 of the committee's 30 members.

Other ways to gain attention include using a visual aid; a short music or video clip; a dramatic, humorous, or interesting quotation; a startling statistic or series of little-known facts; or a sincere compliment.

ORIENT THE AUDIENCE   Previewing what you're going to say will help listeners follow your thoughts more closely. Here are two general ways you can orient your audience.

- **Give the audience an idea about your subject.** In a speech on Alzheimer's the speaker previewed his main points and at the same time previewed his organizational pattern (King, 2015):

  > To do so, let's discuss three causes of insufficient Alzheimer's research funding—stigma, practical challenges, and lack of advocacy—and follow each directly with a solution.

- **Identify the goal you hope to achieve.** A librarian addressing my public speaking class oriented the audience by stating goals in this way: "Pay attention for the next few minutes and you'll be able to locate anything we have in the library by using the new touch-screen computer access system." In another example, President Barack Obama (2009) combined some of these purposes in his "Call to Renewal" speech.

  > Today I'd like to talk about the connection between religion and politics and perhaps offer some thoughts about how we can sort through some of the often bitter arguments that we've been seeing over the last several years.

Avoiding Some Common Mistakes

Here are a few tips for avoiding the mistakes that beginning speakers often make in introducing and concluding their speeches.

- **Engage your listeners before speaking.** Survey your audience; make eye contact and engage their attention. Stand in front of the audience with a sense of control. Pause briefly, then begin speaking.
- **Demonstrate enthusiasm and a desire to speak.** People much prefer listening to a speaker who shows that she or he enjoys speaking to them.
- **Don't apologize.** In the United States, avoid expressions such as "I am not an expert on this topic," or "I didn't do as much reading on this topic as I should have." And never start a speech with, "I'm not very good at giving public speeches." This rule, however, does not hold in all cultures; in fact, self-deprecating comments are expected in some collectivist cultures.
- **Begin with a strong introduction.** Avoid statements such as "Before I begin my talk, I want to say …" These make it difficult for you to open your speech with a strong attention grabber.
- **Reinforce what you have already said.** Once you reach your conclusion, it's too late to introduce new material. Instead, reinforce what you have already said, summarize your essential points, or give new expression to ideas already covered.
- **After your last statement, pause, maintain audience eye contact, and then walk (don't run) to your seat.** Show no signs of relief; focus your attention on whatever activity is taking place. If a question period follows your speech and you're in

charge of this, pause after completing your conclusion and ask audience members in a direct manner if they have any questions. If there's a chairperson who will ask for questions, pause after your conclusion, then nonverbally signal to the chairperson that you're ready to take questions.

Transitions and Internal Summaries

Transitions (sometimes called "connectives") are words, phrases, or sentences that connect the various parts of a speech. Because your audience will hear your speech only once, they may not see the connections you want them to see. By using transitions, you can help your listeners see how one point leads to another or where one argument ends and another begins. Table 12.3 identifies some major transitional functions.

Closely related to the transition is the **internal summary**, a statement that summarizes what you have already discussed. Usually it summarizes some major subdivision of your speech. Incorporate several internal summaries into your speech—perhaps working them into the transitions connecting, say, the major arguments or issues. An internal summary that is also a transition might look something like this.

> The three arguments advanced here were (1) …, (2) …, (3) …. Now, what can we do about them? I think we can do two things. First, …

Outlines

Now that you have completed your speech, it's time to put it all together in the form of an outline, something you already did, for example, when you identified your main points and amplified them with illustrations and definitions. There are three kinds of speech outlines: (1) the preparation outline, (2) the template outline, and (3) the delivery outline.

Table 12.3 Transitional Functions

Here are some transitional functions and some ways you may phrase them.

To connect our introduction to the body of the speech (your first point)	• Now that I identified the 3 major causes of ABC, let's look at the first cause in more detail. • The first argument/cause/issue …
To connect one major point to another	• Not only is ABC, caused by X, it's also caused by Y. • X is only one cause; the second is even more important.
To signal that you're drawing a conclusion	• Thus … • Therefore … • So, as you can see … • It follows, then, that …
To announce the start of a main point	• First …, • A second argument … • A closely related problem … • If you want further evidence, look at … • My next point … • An even more compelling argument …
To signal a qualification or exception	• But … • However, also consider … • On the other hand …
To signal a connection with another issue	• In contrast to … • Consider also … • Not only …, but also …. • In addition to …, we also need to look at …
To signal the next part of your speech	• By way of introduction … • In conclusion … • Now, let's discuss why we are here today … • So, what's the solution? What should we do?

Public Speaking Sample Assistant
THE PREPARATION OUTLINE

Here is a relatively detailed preparation outline similar to the outline you might prepare when constructing your speech. The side notes should clarify both the content and the format of a preparation outline.

Have You Ever Been Culture Shocked?

General Purpose:	To inform
Specific Purpose:	To inform my audience of the four phases of culture shock.
Thesis:	Culture shock can be described in four stages.

The title, purposes, and thesis of the speech appear before the outline.

INTRODUCTION

I. How many of you have experienced culture shock?

   A. Many people experience culture shock, a reaction to being in a culture very different from what they were used to.

   B. By understanding culture shock, you'll be in a better position to deal with it if and when it happens.

II. Culture shock occurs in four stages (Oberg, 1960).

   A. The Honeymoon occurs first.

   B. The Crisis occurs second.

   C. The Recovery occurs third.

   D. The Adjustment occurs fourth.

   [Let's follow the order in which these four stages occur beginning with the first stage, the honeymoon.]

Note that the introduction, body, and conclusion are clearly labeled and separated visually.

Notice that references are integrated throughout the outline, just as they would be in a term paper. In the actual speech, the speaker might say, "anthropologist Kalervo Oberg, who coined the term *culture shock*, said it occurs in four stages."

This introduction serves two functions: It gains attention by involving the audience and it orients the audience to what is to follow.

The transition at the end of the introduction tells the audience to expect a four-part presentation. Also, the numbers repeated throughout the outline will further aid the audience in keeping track of where you are in the speech. Most important, the transition tells the audience that the speech will follow a temporal thought pattern.

BODY

I. The Honeymoon occurs first.

   A. The Honeymoon is the period of fascination with the new people and culture.

   B. You enjoy the people and the culture.

      1. You love the people.

         a. For example, the people in Zaire spend their time very differently from the way New Yorkers do.

         b. For example, my first 18 years living on a farm was very different from life in a college dorm.

      2. You love the culture.

         a. The great number of different religions in India fascinated me.

         b. Eating was an especially great experience.

   [But like many relationships, contact with a new culture is not all honeymoon; soon there comes a crisis.]

Observe the parallel structure throughout the outline. For example, note that I, II, III, and IV in the body are all phrased in exactly the same way. This will help your audience follow your speech more closely and will also help you structure your thoughts logically.

II. The Crisis occurs second.

    A. The Crisis is the period when you begin to experience problems.

        1. One-third of American workers abroad fail because of culture shock (Samovar, Porter, & McDaniel, 2008).

        2. The personal difficulties are also great.

    B. Life becomes difficult in the new culture.

        1. Communication is difficult.

        2. It's easy to offend people without realizing it.

[As you gain control over the various crises, you begin to recover.]

III. The Recovery occurs third.

    A. The Recovery is the period when you learn how to cope.

    B. You begin to learn intercultural competence (Jandt, 2016; Lustig & Koester, 2016).

        1. You learn how to communicate.

            a. Being able to go to the market and make my wants known was a great day for me.

            b. I was able to ask for a date.

        2. You learn the rules of the culture.

            a. The different religious ceremonies each have their own rules.

            b. Eating is a ritual experience in lots of places throughout Africa.

        [Your recovery leads naturally into the next and final stage, the adjustment.]

IV. The Adjustment occurs fourth.

    A. The adjustment is the period when you come to enjoy the new culture.

    B. You come to appreciate the people and the culture.

[Let me summarize, then, the stages you go through in experiencing culture shock.]

CONCLUSION

I. Culture shock can be described in four stages.

    A. The Honeymoon is first.

    B. The Crisis is second.

    C. The Recovery is third.

    D. The Adjustment is fourth.

II. By knowing the four stages, you can better understand the culture shock you may now be experiencing on the job, at school, or in your private life.

References

Jandt, F. E. (2016). *An introduction to intercultural communication: Identifies in a global community* (8th ed). Los Angeles, CA: Sage.

Lustig, M. W., & Koester, J. (2016). *Intercultural competence: Interpersonal communication across cultures* (8th ed.). Boston: Allyn & Bacon.

Oberg, K. (1960). Culture shock: Adjustment to new cultural environments. *Practical Anthropology, 7,* 177–182.

Samovar, L. A., Porter, R. E., & McDaniel, E. R. (2008). *Communication between cultures*, 6th ed. Belmont, CA: Cengage.

Notice that there are many examples in this speech. They are identified only briefly in the outline and would naturally be elaborated on in the speech.

Note, too, the internal organization of each major point. Each main assertion in the body contains a definition of the stage (I.A, II.A, III.A, and IV.A) and examples (I.B, II.B, III.B, and IV.B) to illustrate the stage.

Notice that each statement in the outline is a complete sentence. You can easily convert this outline into a phrase or key word outline to use in delivery. The full sentences, however, will help you see relationships among items more clearly.

Transitions are inserted between all major parts of the speech. Although they may seem too numerous in this abbreviated outline, they will be appreciated by your audience because the transitions will help them follow your speech.

Notice that these four points correspond to II.A, B, C, and D of the introduction and to I, II, III, and IV of the body. Notice how the similar wording adds clarity.

This step provides closure; it makes it clear that the speech is finished. It also serves to encourage reflection on the part of the audience as to their own experience of culture shock.

This reference list includes only those sources that appear in the completed speech.

THE PREPARATION OUTLINE A preparation outline like the one in the Public Speaking Sample Assistant box in this chapter (as well as the template and delivery outlines that are discussed next) will help you not only to organize your thoughts more coherently but also to deliver your speech more effectively.

THE TEMPLATE OUTLINE The **template outline** is another useful type of organizational tool. Much as a template in PowerPoint guides you to fill in certain information in particular places, the template outline serves a similar function; it ensures that you include all the relevant material in reasonable order. At the same time, it also helps you see your speech as a whole—and may reveal gaps that need to be filled or items that are discussed at too great a length. As you become more familiar with the public speaking process, you'll soon be able to develop your speech without any template outline.

The sample template outline in The Public Speaking Sample Assistant included here would be appropriate for a speech using a time, spatial, or topical organization pattern. Note that in this outline there are three main points (I, II, and III in the body). These correspond to items II.A, B, and C in the introduction (where you would orient the audience) and to I.A, B, and C in the conclusion (where you would summarize your major propositions). The transitions are signaled by square brackets. As you review this outline you will see how it can be adapted for use with other organization patterns, such as the problem–solution, the cause–effect, or the motivated sequence.

THE DELIVERY OUTLINE The **delivery outline** will assist you during the presentation of a speech and should be used instead of your preparation outline. Although you may feel inclined to read from your preparation outline, it is not an effective way to give a speech. Instead, write a brief delivery outline such as that presented in the next Public Speaking Sample Assistant box, which was constructed from the preparation outline on culture shock.

Some public speaking coaches and instructors recommend putting your delivery outline on a 3 × 5 or 4 × 6 index card. One advantage is that you will need to condense your delivery outline to only key words and phrases, which will prevent you from reading your speech and help you interact more freely with your audience. When notes are too extensive, speakers have a tendency to read them rather than speak to their audience. Another benefit is that the card won't bend as would an 8½ × 11 piece of paper. Additional index cards might be used for quotations or statistics that won't fit on the one card. Or you may find it helpful to use three cards, one for each of the three main parts of your speech. If you do use more than one card (but avoid using more than four), be sure to number and label them clearly; you don't want to have to fumble through the cards looking for a particular quotation or statistic.

If you're using PowerPoint (or any similar presentation software)—discussed in detail in the next chapter—then your delivery outline is going to be either the PowerPoint slides themselves or the speaker's notes that you generate along with your PowerPoint presentation (discussed in the "Using Notes" section later in this chapter). Here are some guidelines for delivery outlines.

- **Be brief.** Don't allow the outline to stand in the way of direct speaker–audience contact. Use key words to trigger in your mind the ideas you wish to discuss. Notice how brief the sample delivery outline is compared to the preparation outline, yet it's detailed enough to include all essential parts of your speech, even transitions.

- **Be delivery-minded.** Include any delivery guides you might wish to remember while you're speaking—for example, to pause or to show the visual aid.

- **Rehearse your speech with this delivery outline.** Make your rehearsal as close to the real thing as possible.

Public Speaking Sample Assistant

THE TEMPLATE OUTLINE

Thesis:
Your main assertion; the core of your speech _____

Specific Purpose:
What you hope to achieve from this speech _____

INTRODUCTION

I. Gain attention _____

II. Orient audience _____

    A. First main point; same as I in body _____

    B. Second main point; same as II in body _____

    C. Third main point; same as III in body _____

[Transition:]
Connect introduction to body _____

BODY

I. First main point _____

    A. Support for I (first main point) _____

    B. Further support for I _____

[Transition:]
Connect first main point to second _____

II. Second main point _____

    A. Support for II (second main point) _____

    B. Further support for II _____

[Transition:]
Connect second main point to third _____

III. Third main point _____

    A. Support for III _____

    B. Further support for III _____

[Transition:]
Connect third main point (or all main points) to conclusion _____

CONCLUSION

I. Summary _____

    A. First main point; same as I in body _____

    B. Second main point; same as II in body _____

    C. Third main point; same as III in body _____

II. Closure _____

Public Speaking Sample Assistant
THE DELIVERY OUTLINE

PAUSE!

LOOK OVER THE AUDIENCE!

I. Many experience CS

    A. CS: the reaction to being in a culture very different from your own

    B. By understanding CS, you'll be better able to deal with it

PAUSE—SCAN AUDIENCE

II. CS occurs in 4 stages (WRITE ON BOARD)

    A. Honeymoon

    B. Crisis

    C. Recovery

    D. Adjustment

[Let's examine these stages of CS.]

PAUSE/STEP FORWARD

I. Honeymoon

    A. Fascination w/people and culture

    B. Enjoyment of people and culture

        1. Zaire example

        2. Farm to college dorm

[But, life is not all honeymoon—the crisis.]

II. Crisis

    A. Problems arise

        1. One-third Am workers fail abroad

        2. Personal difficulties

    B. Life becomes difficult

        1. Communication

        2. Offend others

[As you gain control over the crises, you learn how to cope.]

PAUSE

III. Recovery

    A. Period of learning to cope

    B. You learn intercultural competence

        1. Communication becomes easier

        2. You learn the culture's rules

[As you recover, you adjust.]

IV. Adjustment

    A. Learn to enjoy (again) the new culture

    B. Appreciate people and culture

[These then are the 4 stages; let me summarize.]

PAUSE

CONCLUSION

I. CS occurs in 4 stages: honeymoon, crisis, recovery, and adjustment

II. By knowing the 4 stages, you can better understand the culture shock you may now be experiencing on the job, at school, or in your private life.

PAUSE

Ask for Questions

Step 9: Rehearse Your Speech

12.3 **Explain the methods of delivery and rehearsal.**

Before you begin rehearsing, you need to decide on the methods of delivery you'll use. Generally, you'll find that the extemporaneous method will suit your needs best and is likely to be the delivery method used in your course. Nevertheless, other methods of delivery have their value as well. We then consider some suggestions for making your rehearsals efficient and effective.

Methods of Delivery

Speakers vary widely in delivery methods. Some speak off-the-cuff, with no apparent preparation. Others read their speeches from a manuscript. Others construct a detailed outline and compose the speech at the moment of delivery. These approaches represent the three general methods of delivery: (1) impromptu, (2) manuscript, and (3) extemporaneous.

THE IMPROMPTU METHOD An **impromptu speech** involves speaking without preparation. On some occasions, you can't avoid impromptu speaking. In a classroom, you may be asked to comment on the speaker and speech you just heard: In effect, you give an impromptu speech of evaluation. At meetings, people are often asked for impromptu comments on various issues. Or you may have to fill in for someone who has not shown up. You can greatly improve impromptu speaking by cultivating your public speaking ability in general. The more proficient you are as a speaker, the better you will be impromptu.

THE MANUSCRIPT METHOD   When you give a **manuscript speech**, you write out the speech and read it. This is the safest method when exact timing and wording are required. For example, it could be disastrous if a political leader did not speak from manuscript on sensitive issues. An ambiguous word, phrase, or sentence that may be insulting, belligerent, or conciliatory could cause serious problems. With a manuscript speech, you can control style, content, organization, and all other elements. A variation of the manuscript method is to write out the speech and then memorize it. You then recite the entire speech from memory, much as an actor recites a part in a play. The great disadvantages of the manuscript and memorized method are that the speech doesn't sound natural, it limits eye contact, and there is little opportunity to adjust the speech on the basis of audience feedback.

THE EXTEMPORANEOUS METHOD   The **extemporaneous speech** is useful when exact timing and wording are not required. Good lecturing by college teachers is extemporaneous. They have prepared thoroughly, know what they want to say, and have the lecture's organization clearly in mind. But they are not committed to exact wording. This method allows greater flexibility for feedback. For example, when speaking extemporaneously you can clarify a point if it needs clarification. It's also easy to be natural, because you're being yourself.

The major disadvantage of this method is that you may stumble and grope for words. You can address this disadvantage by rehearsing the speech several times. Although you won't give the precise attention to style that you would in the manuscript and memorizing methods, you can memorize certain key phrases.

The extemporaneous method is recommended for most situations, especially classroom speeches, in which the objective is to learn the art of public speaking. Overall it offers the greatest advantages with the fewest disadvantages. However, speaking impromptu and speaking from manuscript are also important skills. Fortunately, the principles of extemporaneous speaking discussed here will help you in these other kinds of speeches as well. Even when you use the extemporaneous method, however, consider the advantages of memorizing certain parts of your speech.

- Memorize your opening and closing lines—perhaps the first and last two or three sentences. This will help you focus your attention on the audience at the two most important moments of your speech.
- Memorize the main points and the order in which you will present them. After all, if you expect your audience to remember these points, they will expect you to remember them as well.

Effective Rehearsing

Rehearsal should enable you to see how the speech will flow as a whole and to make any necessary changes and improvements. It will also allow you to time your speech so that you stay within the allotted time. The following procedures should help you use your rehearsal time most effectively.

- Rehearse the speech from beginning to end, rather than in parts. Be sure to include all the examples and illustrations (and audiovisual aids if any) in your rehearsal.

VIEWPOINTS: **Announcing Your Speech**
What are some of the ways in which you might announce your upcoming speech on social media sites?

JOURNAL
COMMUNICATION CHOICE POINT
Method of Delivery

You have to give a 10-minute speech to your work colleagues on the new health care options. You have considerable communication apprehension and want to minimize its effects. *What delivery method would you choose to use? How might you adapt the method to help you deal with your apprehension?*

- Time the speech during each rehearsal. Adjust your speech—both what you say and your delivery rate—on the basis of this timing.

- Rehearse the speech under conditions as close as possible to those under which you'll deliver it. If possible, rehearse in the room in which you'll present the speech and in front of a few supportive listeners.

- Rehearse the speech in front of a full-length mirror to help you see how you'll appear to the audience. As you deliver your speech (aloud, of course), practice your eye contact, your movements, and your gestures in front of the mirror.

- Don't interrupt your rehearsal to make notes or changes; do these between rehearsals. If possible, record your speech (ideally, on videotape) so you can hear and see exactly what your listeners will hear and see.

- Rehearse at least three or four times, or as long as your rehearsals continue to result in improvements.

Step 10: Deliver Your Speech

12.4 Explain the principles of effective voice and bodily action.

Voice

In public speaking it's especially important to give attention to **paralanguage**—the vocal but nonverbal aspect of speech. Using dimensions such as volume, rate, articulation and pronunciation, and pauses appropriately will help you use your voice to complement and reinforce your message.

VOLUME   **Volume** refers to the relative loudness or softness of your voice. When your voice is adequately controlled, you adjust its volume according to factors such as the distance between you and your listeners, the competing noise, and the emphasis you want to give an idea. Vary your volume to best reflect your ideas—perhaps increasing volume for key words or phrases, lowering volume when talking about something extremely serious. Be especially careful not to fade away at the ends of sentences.

RATE   The speed at which you speak is referred to as the **rate**—an average of about 140 words per minute for speaking as well as for reading aloud. If your rate is too fast, you deprive your listeners of the time they need to digest what you're saying. If it's too slow, your listeners' thoughts will wander. So speak at a pace that engages but doesn't bore and that allows listeners time for reflection.

ARTICULATION AND PRONUNCIATION   **Articulation** results from physiological movements of the speech organs as they modify and interrupt the air stream from the lungs. Different movements of the tongue, lips, teeth, palate, and vocal cords produce different sounds. **Pronunciation** is the production of syllables or words according to some accepted standard, such as that of a dictionary. The most common problems associated with faulty articulation and pronunciation are these.

JOURNAL
COMMUNICATION CHOICE POINT
Speaking Volume

After sitting through two rounds of speeches, you wonder if the class wouldn't be ready for a speech spoken at noticeably higher volume than normal—rather like television commercials, which are played louder than the regular broadcast. *What are some of your options concerning the use of volume?*

- **Errors of omission (articulation)** Omitting sounds or even syllables is a common articulation problem that you can easily overcome with concentration and practice. Some examples include saying *gov-a-ment, studyin, gonna, hafta,* or *comp-ny* instead of the correct *gov-ern-ment, study-ing, go-ing to, have to,* and *comp-a-ny.*

- **Errors of substitution (articulation)** Substituting an incorrect sound for the correct one is also easy to fix. Among the most common substitutions are *d* for *t* and *d* for *th*—for example, *wader, dese, bedder,* and *ax* for the correct: *waiter, these, better,* and *ask.* Other common substitution errors include *ekcetera, congradulations,* and *lenth* for the correct *et cetera, congratulations,* and *length.*

- **Errors of addition (articulation)** These errors involve adding sounds where they don't belong, as in saying *acrost*, *athalete*, and *Americar* instead of the correct *across*, *athlete*, and *America*.

- **Errors of accent (pronunciation)** Every word has its own accepted accent, or stress pattern. Examples of words that are often accented incorrectly include *New Orleáns*, *ínsur*ance, *compárable*, and *orátor* for the correct *New Órleans*, *insúrance*, *cómparable*, and *órator*.

- **Errors of adding sounds (pronunciation)** For some words, many people add sounds that are not part of the standard pronunciation, in many cases because they are part of the written word. Such errors would include pronouncing the *s* in *Illinois* or adding a syllable to *evening* instead of *Illinoi* and *evning*.

"Plunder, you idiot. We came to plunder."

Dave Coverly

PAUSES **Pauses** are interruptions in the flow of speech. Filled pauses are gaps that you fill with vocalizations such as *er, um,* and *ah*. Even expressions such as *well* and *you know*, when used merely to fill up silence, are *filled pauses*. These pauses are ineffective and detract from the strength of your message. They will make you appear hesitant, unprepared, and unsure.

Unfilled pauses, silences interjected into the stream of speech, can be especially effective if used correctly. Here are a few examples of places where unfilled pauses— silences of a second or two—can enhance your speech.

- **Pause at transitional points.** This will signal that you're moving from one part of the speech or from one idea to another. It will help listeners separate the main issues you're discussing.

- **Pause at the end of an important assertion.** This allows the audience to think about its significance.

- **Pause after asking a rhetorical question.** This will give the audience time to think about how they would answer.

- **Pause before an important idea.** This will help signal that what comes next is especially significant.

- **Pause before you begin your speech and after you finish it.** This will allow you to scan and assess the audience and gather your thoughts before your speech and then to let your ideas sink in after and to dispel any impression that you're anxious to escape.

Body Action

You speak with your body as well as your mouth, a point made clear in the discussion of the various nonverbal channels in Chapter 5. The four aspects of body action that are especially important in public speaking are (1) eye contact, (2) facial expression, (3) gestures and posture, and (4) movement. As you read about these types of action, be sure to follow the most important and general rule: Use consistent packaging; be careful that your verbal and your nonverbal messages do not contradict each other. So, if you say you're happy to be speaking today, your nonverbals (facial expression, general enthusiasm, posture and eye contact, for example) should echo that sentiment. You don't want to give your audience conflicting cues. Consistency among verbal and nonverbal messages will also communicate your self-confidence and conviction.

EYE CONTACT The most important single aspect of bodily communication is eye contact. The two major problems related to this body action are not enough eye contact and eye contact that does not cover the audience fairly. If you do not maintain enough eye contact, you may appear distant, unconcerned, and less trustworthy than a speaker who looks directly at an audience. And, of course, without eye contact, you will not be able to secure that all-important audience feedback. Maintain eye contact with the entire audience. Communicate equally with the audience members on the left and on the right, in both the back and the front of the room. Keep in mind, however, that cultures differ widely on the amount and intensity of eye contact they consider appropriate. In some cultures, eye contact that is too intense may be considered offensive.

FACIAL EXPRESSION   Appropriate facial expressions help you express your concern for the public speaking interaction and will help you communicate your comfort and control of the public speaking situation. Nervousness and anxiety, however, can prevent you from relaxing enough for your positive emotions to come through. Time and practice will allow you to relax, and your feelings will reveal themselves appropriately and automatically.

GESTURES AND POSTURE   Spontaneous and natural gestures will help illustrate your verbal messages. If you feel relaxed and comfortable with yourself and your audience, you'll generate natural body action without conscious or studied attention. When delivering your speech, stand straight but not stiffly. Try to communicate your command of the situation rather than any nervousness you may feel. Avoid putting your hands in your pockets or leaning on the desk or chalkboard. Avoid self-manipulation (e.g., playing with your hair or touching your face) and backward leaning, which can signal an ill-at-ease feeling.

MOVEMENT   Use movement to emphasize transitions and to introduce important assertions. For example, when making a transition, you might step forward to signal that something new is coming. Similarly, use movement to signal an important assumption, bit of evidence, or closely reasoned argument. Walk slowly and deliberately (but not too slowly, of course) to and from the podium. Avoid appearing hurried, as if you want to get your speech over with as soon as possible. Walking more slowly will help you convey an air of control.

Using Notes

Speakers who prepare their speeches around a series of slides made with one of the presentation software packages (such as PowerPoint or Corel Presentations) may use these slides as their notes. In most public speaking classes, your notes will consist of a delivery outline and your audiovisual aids. Effective delivery depends on the smooth use of notes—whether a series of slides or transparencies or an 8½ × 11 inch piece of paper or an index card or two—during the speech. A few simple guidelines may help you avoid common errors (McCroskey, 2006).

- Use only your delivery outline when presenting your speech; never use the preparation outline. One 8½ × 11 inch page or no more than four index cards should be sufficient for most speeches. This aid will relieve anxiety over forgetting your speech but not be extensive enough to prevent meaningful speaker–audience interaction.

- Know your notes intimately. Rehearse at least twice with the same notes you will take to the speaker's stand.

- Use your notes with "open subtlety." Don't make your notes more obvious than necessary, but don't try to hide them. Don't gesture with them, but don't turn your back on the audience to steal a glance at them, either. Watch the way television talk show personalities use notes; many of these media hosts provide models you'll find useful to imitate.

Critically Evaluating Speeches

12.5 Describe the guidelines for expressing and receiving speech criticism.

Part of learning about public speaking is learning to express **criticism**—to evaluate the finished, delivered speeches and to express your evaluations in a clear and constructive way. Let's look first at some of the questions you'll want to consider and then at some suggestions for expressing these evaluations.

Questions to Consider

The following questions, which come from topics covered in this chapter and Chapter 11, can serve as a beginning guide to speech evaluation. Use them to check your own speeches as well as to evaluate the speeches of others. These questions follow the steps outlined in these two chapters with the exception of rehearsal since you can't observe that step.

Subject, Purpose, and Thesis

1. Is the subject worthwhile? Relevant? Interesting to the audience and speaker?
2. Is the general purpose of the speech to inform or to persuade?
3. Is the topic narrow enough to be covered in some depth?
4. Is the specific purpose clear to the audience?
5. Is the speech's thesis clear and limited to one main idea?

Audience

6. Has the speaker considered the relevant audience variables such as culture, age, gender, occupation, income, status, and religion? How does the speaker take these factors into consideration?
7. Has the speaker considered and adapted to the willingness, favorableness, and knowledge of the audience?

Research

8. Is the speech adequately researched? Are the sources reliable and up-to-date?
9. Does the speaker seem to understand the subject thoroughly?

Supporting Materials

10. Is each major proposition adequately and appropriately supported?
11. Do the supporting materials amplify what they purport to amplify? Do they prove what they purport to prove?

Major Propositions

12. Are the speech's main points clearly related to the thesis?
13. Are there an appropriate number of main points in the speech (not too many, not too few)?

Organization

14. How is the body of the speech organized? What is the organization pattern?
15. Is the organization pattern appropriate to the speech and to the audience?
16. Does it help the audience follow the speech?

Conclusion, Introduction, and Transitions

17. Does the conclusion effectively summarize and close the speech?
18. Does the introduction gain the audience's attention and provide a clear orientation?
19. Are there adequate transitions?

Wording

20. Is the language clear, vivid, appropriate, personal, and powerful?

21. Are the sentences short, direct, active, positive, and varied?

Delivery

22. Does the speaker maintain eye contact with the audience?

23. Are the volume, rate, and pauses appropriate to the audience, occasion, and topic?

24. Does the speaker's articulation and pronunciation contribute to clarity and general effectiveness?

25. Are the body actions (i.e., gesture and eye, face, and body movement) appropriate to the speaker, subject, and audience?

Expressing and Listening to Criticism

The major purpose of classroom evaluation is to improve each class member's public speaking technique. Through constructive criticism, you will more effectively learn—as both a speaker and a listener-critic—the principles of public speaking. You will discover what you do well and what you can improve.

Despite all the benefits of evaluation, however, many people resist this process, often perceiving evaluations and suggestions for improvement as personal attacks. Before reading the specific suggestions for expressing criticism, take the self-test, "What's Wrong with These Comments?" Then consider the suggestions for offering criticism more effectively that follow the test.

EXPRESSING CRITICISM Here are a few suggestions for expressing your evaluations and criticisms.

- **Say something positive.** Start any criticism with something positive. So, instead of saying—as in the self-test—"The speech didn't do anything for me," tell the speaker what you liked first and then bring up a weakness and suggest how it might be corrected: "Your introduction really made me realize that many colleges have problems with campus violence, but I wasn't convinced early on that we have one here at Andrews. I would have preferred to hear the examples that you gave near the end of the speech—which were excellent, by the way—in the introduction."

- **Be specific.** Criticism is most effective when it's specific. Statements such as "I thought your delivery was bad" or "I thought your examples were good" (or, as in the self-test, "I loved the speech. ... Really great" and "The speech

Test Yourself

WHAT'S WRONG WITH THESE COMMENTS?

Examine each of the following critical comments. For the purposes of this exercise, assume that each comment represents the critic's complete criticism. What's wrong with each?

____ **1.** I loved the speech. It was great. Really great.

____ **2.** The introduction didn't gain my attention.

____ **3.** You weren't interested in your own topic. How do you expect us to be interested?

____ **4.** Nobody was able to understand you.

____ **5.** The speech was weak.

____ **6.** The speech didn't do anything for me.

____ **7.** Your position was unfair to those of us on athletic scholarships; we earned those scholarships.

____ **8.** I found four things wrong with your speech. First, ...

____ **9.** You needed better research.

____ **10.** I liked the speech; we need more police on campus.

Before reading the discussion that follows, try to explain why each of these statements is ineffective. To help improve your criticism, try to restate the basic meaning of each of these comments in a more constructive manner.

was weak") don't specify what the speaker might do to improve delivery or to capitalize on the examples used. Refer to specifics such as the evidence used, the language choices, the delivery style, or whatever else is of consequence.

- **Be culturally sensitive.** There are vast cultural differences in what is considered proper when it comes to criticism. People in cultures that are highly individualistic and competitive (the United States, Germany, and Sweden are examples) may see public criticism as a normal part of the learning process. Thus, they may readily criticize others and are likely to expect the same "courtesy" from other listeners. People from cultures that are more collectivist and that emphasize the group rather than the individual (Japan, Mexico, and Korea are examples) are likely to find giving and receiving public criticism uncomfortable. They may feel that it's more important to be polite and courteous than to help someone learn a skill.

- **Limit criticism.** Cataloging a speaker's weak points, as in "I found four things wrong with your speech," will overwhelm, not help, the speaker. Mentioning one or two items that you found especially good or that might have been improved is likely to be more effective in helping the speaker.

- **Be constructive.** Give the speaker the insight that you feel will help in future public speaking situations. For example, "The introduction didn't gain my attention" doesn't tell the speaker how he or she might have gained your attention. Instead, you might say, "The example about the computer crash would have more effectively gained my attention in the introduction."

- **Focus criticism on behavior.** Look at what the speaker said and did during the actual speech. Avoid mind-reading the speaker and assuming that you know *why* the speaker did one thing rather than another. Instead of saying, "You weren't interested in your topic" (a comment that attacks the speaker), say, "I would have liked to see greater variety in your delivery. It would have made me feel you were more involved."

LISTENING TO CRITICISM   At the same time that you are expressing criticism effectively, you'll also want to listen to criticism. Here are some suggestions for making listening to criticism a less difficult and more productive experience. These guidelines are appropriate in a learning environment such as a public speaking class, where criticism is used as a learning tool. In business and professional public speaking, in contrast, listeners don't offer suggestions for improvement; rather, they focus on the issues you raised.

- **Listen with an open mind.** If you've already given your first speech, you know that public speaking is highly ego-involving. Because of this, it may be tempting to block out criticism. After all, it's not easy to listen to criticism, especially in a fairly public place like a classroom filled with your peers. But if you do block out such criticism, you'll likely lose out on some useful suggestions for improvement. Encourage critics to share their insights by demonstrating your willingness to listen with an open mind. Don't take criticism too personally; view criticism as objectively as you can.

- **Accept the critic's viewpoint.** If the critic says your evidence wasn't convincing, it doesn't help to identify the 12 references that you used in your speech; this critic simply was not convinced. Instead, think about why your evidence was not convincing to this person.

- **Seek clarification.** If you don't understand the criticism, ask for clarification. If you're told that your specific purpose was too broad, but it's unclear to you how you might improve it, ask the critic how you might narrow the specific purpose.

VIEWPOINTS: **Noting an Error**
In listening to a speech, you note that the speaker misstated an important statistic. *What are some of the things you might say? What would be inappropriate to say?*

Communicating Ethically
THE ETHICAL CRITIC

Just as the speaker and the listener have ethical obligations, so does the critic. As you reflect on the suggestions that follow, consider any additional guidelines that you would like to see critics of public speaking follow (especially in the classroom).

- The ethical critic separates personal feelings about the speaker from his or her evaluation of the speech. A liking for the speaker should not lead the critic to give positive evaluations of the speech, nor should disliking the speaker lead to negative evaluations. Similarly, attitudes toward the speaker's thesis should not get in the way of fair and objective evaluation. The ethical critic recognizes the validity of an argument even if it contradicts a deeply held belief and, at the same time, recognizes the fallaciousness of an argument even if it supports a deeply held belief.
- The ethical critic takes responsibility for his or her own thoughts. The best way to express this ownership is to use I-messages rather than you-messages. Instead of saying, "You needed better research," say, "I would have been more persuaded if you had used more recent research."
- The ethical critic rejects any ethnocentric orientation and doesn't negatively evaluate customs and beliefs simply because they differ from her or his own. The ethical critic doesn't discriminate against or favor speakers simply because they're of a particular gender, race, affectional orientation, nationality, religion, or age group.

ETHICAL CHOICE POINT

You and your best friend are taking a communications course together. Your friend just gave a terrible speech, and unfortunately, the instructor has asked you to offer a critique. The wrinkle here is that the instructor's grades seem to be heavily influenced by what student critics say. So in effect your critique will largely determine your friend's grade. You'd like to give your friend a positive critique so he can earn a good grade—which he badly needs—and you figure you can always tell him the truth later and even help him to improve. *What is your ethical obligation in this situation? What would you do?*

Public Speaking Sample Assistant
A POORLY CONSTRUCTED PERSUASIVE SPEECH

This speech illustrates some really broad as well as some more subtle errors that a beginning speaker might make when constructing a persuasive speech. First, read the entire speech without reading any of the "Problems/Correctives." As you read the speech, consider what errors are being demonstrated and how you might correct them. Then, after you've read the entire speech, reread each paragraph and combine your own analysis with the "Problems/Correctives" annotations.

SPEECH	PROBLEMS AND CORRECTIVES
Title: Prenups **Topic:** Prenuptial agreements **Purpose:** Prenuptials are bad. **Thesis:** Why do we need prenuptial agreements?	This title sounds like an informative speech title and doesn't give the idea that a position will be argued. In addition, the topic, purpose, and thesis are not clearly focused or appropriately worded. A more appropriate title might be something like "Prenups Have Got to Go" or "The Dangers of Prenups." The topic would need to be narrowed by some qualification such as *The negative aspects of prenuptial agreements.* The purpose should be stated as an infinitive phrase: *To persuade my audience that prenuptial agreements should be declared illegal.* The thesis needs to be stated as a declarative sentence: *Prenuptial agreements should be declared illegal.*

SPEECH	PROBLEMS AND CORRECTIVES

INTRODUCTION

You're probably not worried about prenuptial agreements yet. But maybe you will be. At any rate, that's what my speech is on. I mean that prenuptial agreements should be made illegal.

This opening is weak and can easily turn off the audience. After all, if they're not worried about it now, why listen? The speaker could have made a case for the importance of this topic in the near future, however. It appears as if the speaker knows the topic's not important but will speak on it anyway. A more effective introduction would have (1) captured the audience's attention—perhaps by citing some widely reported celebrity prenup; (2) provided a connection among the speaker-audience-topic—perhaps by noting the consequences individuals might suffer with or without a prenup; and (3) oriented the audience as to what is to follow.

BODY

Here, a transition would help. In fact, transitions should be inserted between the introduction and the body and between the body and the conclusion. Using transitions between the main points and signposts when introducing each main point would help. The speaker might have said something like: "There are three main reasons why prenups should be banned."

Prenuptial agreements make marriage a temporary arrangement. If you have a prenuptial agreement, you can get out of a marriage real fast—and we know that's not a good thing. So if we didn't have prenups—that's short for prenuptial agreements—marriages would last longer.

This is the speaker's first argument but it isn't introduced in a way the audience will find easy to understand. Abbreviations should be introduced more smoothly. A simple signpost like, "My first argument against prenups is …." would make the audience see where the speaker is and get a visual of the outline. To introduce the abbreviation that will be used throughout the speech, the speaker might have incorporated it into the first sentence—"Prenuptial agreements—for short, prenups—make a marriage. …"

Right now, most people don't have prenups and yet somewhere around 50 percent of marriages last. That would be equivalent to a baseball player batting 500. If we had prenups that number would go up—I mean down—I mean the number of marriages that last will go up if we had prenups, I mean if we didn't.

The fact that 50 percent of the marriages fail seems to be the more telling statistic, yet the speaker treats a 50 percent success rate as good—something the audience is likely to see very differently. And the baseball analogy seems weak at best. The speaker also betrays a lack of preparation in confusing *up* with *down*.

Poor people are going to be discriminated against. Poor people won't be able to marry rich people because rich people will want a prenup and if a poor person doesn't want a prenup they wouldn't get married.

This argument just doesn't seem logical and the speaker would have been better served by omitting this entirely. For this argument to be useful in advancing the speaker's purpose, the speaker would have had to show that in fact poor people suffer in, say, divorce proceedings *because* of prenups.

These agreements are difficult to discuss. I mean, how do you tell someone you've told you love that you now want a prenup just in case the marriage gets screwed up? I guess you can say something like, "By the way, how about signing a prenup?"

This argument too doesn't seem important or logical. The fact that something is difficult to discuss doesn't mean you shouldn't discuss it; it merely means it's difficult to discuss. The speaker seems to be implying that if something is difficult to discuss, it should be abandoned—clearly a poor communication strategy.

And they're expensive. I mean you need a lawyer and all. I don't know what a lawyer charges but I'd guess it's a lot. So it's expensive and a young couple could use the money on other things.

This argument also seems weak simply because if there is enough money involved to warrant a prenup, there's probably enough money to hire a lawyer. If the speaker wanted to make this argument, specific costs should have been cited.

I had a prenup two years ago. And when we got divorced, I got nothing. If we didn't have a prenup, I'd be rich and I'd be at some private college instead of here.

Here the audience is likely thinking that there was a personal and emotional reason for arguing against prenups and not any logical reasons. And yet, the audience is probably asking itself, what were the specifics of the prenup and how much money was involved. The speaker probably should have disclosed this earlier in the speech and assured the audience that this personal experience led to a thorough study of the subject. And if a personal experience is going to be used—and there's no reason it shouldn't—then it needs to be discussed more fully and, at the least, answer the audience's obvious questions.

SPEECH	PROBLEMS AND CORRECTIVES
CONCLUSION	
My conclusions. So you can see that prenups are not a good thing. Like they're unfair to poor people. And it creates a lot of stress for the couple, especially for the one who didn't want the prenup in the first place, like myself.	Using the word "conclusion" is not a bad idea but it stands out like a heading in a textbook. This speech also needed a more detailed conclusion, reiterating the main points in the speech. This speaker also commits one of the common faults of conclusions—that is, to introduce new material. Notice that we hadn't heard of the stress factor before. The speaker might have said something like: "In conclusion, we can see there are three main arguments against prenups. First, …"
Any questions?	This seems too abrupt. A good pause should preface this request for questions and perhaps a more inviting request could be offered— something like, "If anyone has any questions, I'd be happy to respond."

Summary of Concepts and Skills

This chapter looked at the last four steps in the public speaking process: wording the speech; constructing the conclusion, introduction, transitions, and outlines; and rehearsing and delivering the speech.

Step 7: Word Your Speech

12.1 Define *clarity, vividness, appropriateness, personal style,* and *power* in wording a speech.

1. Compared with written style, oral style contains shorter, simpler, and more familiar words; greater qualification; and more self-referential terms.

2. Effective public speaking style is clear (economical and specific; uses transitions, and short, familiar, and commonly used terms); vivid (uses active verbs, strong verbs, figures of speech, and imagery); appropriate to your audience (is on a suitable level of formality; avoids written-style expressions; avoids slang, vulgar, and offensive terms); personal (uses personal pronouns, asks questions, and creates immediacy); and powerful (avoids hesitations, intensifiers, disqualifiers, self-critical statements, and slang and vulgar language).

3. Effective sentences for public speeches are generally short, direct, active, positively phrased, and varied in type and length.

Step 8: Construct Your Conclusion, Introduction, Transitions, and Outlines

12.2 Explain the functions of the introduction, conclusion, and transitions and the nature of preparation and delivery outlines for your speeches.

4. Conclusions summarize and close the speech.

5. Introductions gain the attention of the audience and orient them about what is to follow.

6. Transitions and internal summaries connect the parts of a speech and help listeners better remember the speech.

7. Preparation, template, and delivery outlines all serve different functions and will help any speaker, but especially the beginning speaker, in preparing and presenting effective public speeches.

Step 9: Rehearse Your Speech

12.3 Explain the methods of delivery and rehearsal.

8. There are three basic methods of delivering a public speech: (1) the impromptu method, which involves speaking without any specific preparation; (2) the manuscript method, which involves writing out the entire speech and reading it to the audience; and (3) the extemporaneous method, which involves thorough preparation and memorizing the main ideas and their order of appearance, but not a commitment to exact wording.

9. Use rehearsal to time and perfect your speech from beginning to end; rehearse under realistic conditions and with listeners if possible.

Step 10: Deliver Your Speech

12.4 Explain the principles of effective voice and bodily action.

10. When you deliver your speech, regulate your voice for greatest effectiveness. For example, adjust your volume on the basis of the distance between you and your audience and the emphasis you wish to give certain ideas. Adjust your rate on the basis of time constraints, the speech's content, and the listening conditions.

11. Avoid the major problems of articulation and pronunciation; errors of omission, substitution, addition, and accent.

12. Use unfilled pauses to signal a transition between the major parts of the speech, to allow the audience time to think, to allow the audience to ponder a rhetorical question, and to signal the approach of a particularly

important idea. Avoid filled pauses; they weaken your message.

13. Effective body action involves maintaining eye contact with your entire audience, allowing facial expressions to convey your feelings, using your posture to communicate command of the public speaking interaction, gesturing naturally, moving around a bit, and using notes effectively.

Critically Evaluating Speeches

12.5 Describe the guidelines for expressing and receiving speech criticism.

14. When expressing critical evaluations, try to say something positive, be specific, be culturally sensitive, limit criticism, be constructive, and focus on behavior. When receiving criticism, listen with an open mind, accept the critic's point of view, and seek clarification as needed.

This chapter stressed several significant skills for style and delivery. Place a check mark next to those skills you most want to work on.

_____ 1. I word my speech so it's clear, vivid, appropriate, and personal.

_____ 2. I construct sentences that are short, direct, active, and positive, and I vary the type and length of sentences.

_____ 3. I construct conclusions that summarize the major ideas of the speech and bring the speech to a crisp close.

_____ 4. I construct introductions that gain attention and preview what is to follow.

_____ 5. I use transitions and internal summaries to connect the parts of the speech and to help listeners remember what I say.

_____ 6. In general, I use the extemporaneous method of delivery.

_____ 7. I rehearse my speech from beginning to end, time it, rehearse under similar conditions to the actual delivery, rehearse in front of a mirror, and rehearse often.

_____ 8. I vary my vocal volume and rate to best reflect and reinforce my verbal messages and avoid the common problems with volume and rate.

_____ 9. I avoid the articulation and pronunciation errors of omission, substitution, addition, accent, and pronouncing sounds that should be silent.

_____ 10. I use pauses to signal transitions, to allow listeners time to think, and to signal the approach of a significant idea.

_____ 11. During my delivery of a speech, I maintain eye contact with the entire audience, allow my facial expressions to convey my feelings, gesture naturally, and incorporate purposeful body movements.

_____ 12. When expressing critical evaluations of the speeches of others, I try to say something positive, be specific, be culturally sensitive, limit criticism, be constructive, and focus my criticism on behavior.

Key Terms

abstraction	idiom	personification
alliteration	impromptu speech	pronunciation
articulation	internal summary	rate
criticism	manuscript speech	rhetorical question
delivery outline	metaphor	simile
extemporaneous speech	oral style	template outline
figure of speech	paralanguage	transitions
hyperbole	pauses	volume

Skill Development Experiences

12.1 Constructing Conclusions and Introductions

Because the conclusion and the introduction are often the parts that listeners remember most, give them special attention.

Prepare a conclusion and an introduction to a hypothetical speech on one of the topics listed here, making sure that in your conclusion you (1) review the speech's main points and (2) provide closure. In your introduction, make sure that you (1) gain attention and (2) orient the audience.

1. Competitive sports programs in high schools and colleges should be abolished.
2. Same-sex marriage should be legalized.
3. Properties owned by religious institutions should be taxed.
4. Assisted suicide should be legalized.
5. Gambling should be declared illegal by all states.

12.2 Checking Your Pronunciation

Mispronouncing words may significantly lessen your credibility, and your own uncertainty about pronunciation may increase your apprehension.

Here are 50 words that are often mispronounced. Consult an online audio dictionary to check on the correct pronunciations:

abdomen, accessory, across, arctic, ask, asterisk, buffet, candidate, clothes, costume, diagnosis, dilate, escape, especially, espresso, et cetera, ethnicity, February, federal, film, fiscal, herb, hierarchy, jewelry, library, miniature, mischievous, nausea, nuclear, often, phenomenon, potable, prerogative, probably, prostate, realtor, relevant, remuneration, repeat, salmon, sandwich, similar, statistics, substantive, supposedly, thesaurus, ticklish, xenophobia

Chapter 13
The Informative Speech

In informing we also reveal ourselves.

CHAPTER OUTLINE	∨ Learning Objectives
Guidelines for Informative Speaking	**13.1** Paraphrase the suggested guidelines for informative speaking.
Three Types of Informative Speeches	**13.2** Define and give examples of *speeches of description, definition*, and *demonstration*.
Supporting Materials	**13.3** Define *examples, illustrations, narratives, testimony, numerical data*, and *definitions* as supporting materials in informative speeches.
Presentation Aids	**13.4** Describe the varied types of presentation aids.

This chapter covers speeches of information, through which a speaker tells listeners something they didn't already know. Chapter 14 covers speeches of persuasion, through which a speaker changes listeners' attitudes or beliefs or gets them to do something.

Guidelines for Informative Speaking

13.1 **Paraphrase the suggested guidelines for informative speaking.**

When you communicate **information** in a speech, you tell your listeners something they don't know, something new. You can inform them about a new way of looking at old things or an old way of looking at new things. You may discuss a theory not previously heard of or a familiar concept not fully understood. You may talk about events that the audience may be unaware of or explain happenings they may have misconceptions about. Regardless of what type of informative speech you intend to give, the following guidelines should help.

Center Information on the Audience

The information you communicate in your informative speech should center around and focus on the audience's needs and interests. The audience should want to hear what you have to say. Somewhere early in your speech, answer the audience's unspoken questions: Why should I listen? Why should I care about this information? In your speech, for example, you might stress that what you have to say will save the audience money or time, will help them understand the current financial market, or will enable them to make themselves more attractive. In this way you'll capture and hold your audience's attention by showing them that the information you have is relevant and useful to their goals and interests.

Limit the Information

There's a limit to the amount of information that your listeners can take in at one time. Resist the temptation to overload them. Instead of enlarging the breadth of information you communicate, expand its depth. It's better to present two new items of information and explain these in depth, with examples, illustrations, and descriptions, than to present five items without this needed amplification. The speaker who attempts to discuss the physiological, psychological, social, and linguistic differences between men and women, for example, is clearly trying to cover too much and is going to be forced to cover each area only superficially. Instead, select one subdivision of one area—say, language development or differences in language problems—and develop that in depth. Use the techniques for limiting a topic covered in Chapter 11.

Adjust the Level of Complexity

As you know from attending college classes, information can be presented in very simple or very complex forms. The level of complexity of the information you communicate should depend on the wide variety of factors considered throughout this book: the level of knowledge your audience has, the time you have available, the purpose you hope to achieve, the topic on which you're speaking, and so on. If you simplify a topic too much, you risk boring or, even worse, insulting your audience; if your talk is too complex, you risk confusing your audience and failing to communicate your message. In your beginning speeches at least, try to keep it simple. Make sure the words you use are familiar to your audience and that you explain clearly any unfamiliar terms.

Communicating Ethically

SPEAKING ETHICALLY

One interesting approach to ethics that has particular relevance to public speaking offers four guidelines or principles (Wallace, 1955; Johannesen, Valde, & Whedbee, 2007). As you reflect on these principles, consider if there are other guidelines about speaking ethics that should be considered.

- The ethical speaker has a thorough knowledge of the topic, an ability to answer relevant questions, and an awareness of the significant facts and opinions bearing on the topic.
- The ethical speaker presents both facts and opinions fairly, without bending or spinning them to personal advantage; the listener makes the final decision.
- The ethical speaker reveals the sources of cited facts and opinions and helps listeners evaluate any biases and prejudices in the sources.
- The ethical speaker acknowledges and respects opposing arguments and evidence and avoids hiding valid opposing arguments from the audience.

ETHICAL CHOICE POINT

You're giving an informative speech to explain the new initiative for more healthy food on campus. Among the important items that should logically be covered is the cost of this change, which is going to come from an increase in student fees. Since you are in favor of this initiative, you'd like to omit discussing cost largely because the students may vote against this plan if they find out that their fees will be raised. You decide that you don't have time to include all issues, that it's really the responsibility of the audience to ask where the money is coming from, and that this initiative is really for everyone's benefit. *What is your ethical obligation in this situation? What would you do?*

Relate New Information to Old

Listeners will learn information more easily and retain it longer when you relate it to what they already know. Relate the new to the old, the unfamiliar to the familiar, the unseen to the seen, the untasted to the tasted. Here, for example, Teresa Jacob, a student from Ohio State University (Schnoor, 1997, p. 97), relates the problems of drug interactions (i.e., the new) to the dangers of mixing chemicals in the school lab (i.e., the old or familiar).

During our high school years, most of us learned in a chemistry class the danger of mixing harmless chemicals in lab. Add one drop of the wrong compound, and suddenly you've created a stink bomb, or worse, an explosion. Millions of Americans run the same risk inside their bodies each day by combining drugs that are supposed to help restore or maintain good health.

Make the Information Easy to Remember

The principles of public speaking (of language, delivery, and supporting materials, for example) will all help your listeners remember your speech. Here are a few additional suggestions.

- **Repeat or restate important points.** Help your audience to remember what you want them to remember.
- **Use guide phrases.** Direct your audience's attention to your most important points by saying, for example, "The first point to remember is that ..."
- **Use internal summary transitions.** These will remind the audience of what you have said and how it relates to what is to follow, for example, "Now that we've seen the problem, let's look at the solution."

JOURNAL
COMMUNICATION CHOICE POINT
Principles of Informative Speaking

Imagine that you're preparing a speech on the minimum wage to be delivered to your class. *What are some of the ways you can use the principles of informative speaking to make this speech meaningful?*

- **Pattern your messages.** If the audience can see the logic of the organization of your speech, they'll be better able to organize (and remember) what you say in their own minds.
- **Focus audience attention.** The best way to focus listeners' attention is to tell them to focus their attention. Simply say, "I want you to focus on three points that I'll make in this speech. First, …" or "What I want you to remember is this: …"

Three Types of Informative Speeches

13.2 Define and give examples of *speeches of description, definition, and demonstration.*

Now that you have considered the principles of informative speaking, types of supporting materials, and presentation aids, it's time to consider the three types of informative speeches: speeches of description, definition, and demonstration. In addition, see the accompanying Public Speaking Sample Assistant on Special Occasion Speeches (p. 000).

Speeches of Description

In a **speech of description**, you're concerned with explaining an object, person, event, or process. You would describe an object or person in a speech about, for example, the structure of the brain, the contributions of Thomas Edison, the parts of a telephone, the layout of Philadelphia, the hierarchy of a corporation, or the components of a computer system.

You would be describing an event or process in a speech about, for example, the process of organizing a bodybuilding contest; how to create a blog; how a child acquires language; how people purchase stocks online; or the events leading to the Arab Spring.

THESIS AND MAIN POINTS The thesis of a speech, as explained in Chapter 11, is your single most important concept, your main or central idea. The thesis of a speech of description simply states what you'll describe in your speech.

The child acquires language in four stages.

There are three steps to purchasing stock online.

Four major events led to the changing of US-Cuban relations.

The main points of a speech of description are the major subdivisions of the thesis. You derive your main points from your thesis by asking strategic questions.

What are the four stages in child language acquisition?

What are the three steps to purchasing stock online?

What events led to the changing of U.S.–Cuban relations?

SUPPORT Instead of simply listing your main points, you should instead flesh them out and make them memorable, interesting, and, most of all, clear. In a speech of description you do this by using a variety of materials that amplify and support your main ideas. Because you are giving a speech of description, give extra consideration to the variety of description you might use in your supporting materials: examples, illustrations, testimony, numerical data, and presentation aids.

ORGANIZATION Consider using a *spatial* or a *topical organization* when describing objects and people. For example, if you were to describe the layout of the center of

Philadelphia, you might start from the north and work down to the south (using a spatial pattern). If you were to describe the contributions of Steve Jobs, you might select the three or four major contributions and discuss each of these equally (using a topical pattern).

Consider using a *temporal pattern* when describing events and processes. If you were to describe the events leading up to the Arab Spring, for example, you might start with the earliest and work up to the latest. A temporal pattern would also be appropriate for describing how a hurricane develops or how a parade is put together. The "who, what, where, when, and why" pattern of organization can also be useful to describe an event or a process. For example, if you're going to describe how to purchase a house, you might want to consider the people involved (who?), the steps you have to go through (what?), the places you'll have to go (where?), the timing or sequence of the steps (when?), and the advantages and disadvantages of buying the house (why?).

Here is an example of how the bare bones of a descriptive speech might look. Notice that the speaker derives the main points from asking a question about the thesis.

> **General purpose:** To inform
>
> **Specific purpose:** To describe the way fear works in intercultural communication
>
> **Thesis:** Fear influences intercultural communication. (What fears influence intercultural communication?)
>
> I. We fear disapproval.
> II. We fear embarrassing ourselves.
> III. We fear being harmed.

In delivering such a speech, the speaker might begin with this information.

The speaker would then amplify and support this fear of disapproval, giving examples of disapproval seen in his or her own experience, the testimony of communication theorists on the importance of such fear, research findings on the effects that such fear might have on intercultural communication, and so on.

Speeches of Definition

What is leadership? What is a born-again Christian? What is the difference between sociology and psychology? What is a cultural anthropologist? What is safe sex? These are all topics suitable for the **speech of definition**.

In giving a speech of definition, you may focus on defining a term, defining a system or theory, or pinpointing the similarities and/or differences among terms or systems. For example, a speech in which you define a term might cover an endless range of topics: What is a smart card? What is machismo? What is political correctness?

A speech may also define a system or theory: What are the major beliefs in Confucianism? What is expressionism? What is the "play theory" of mass communication?

Some speech topics may involve your defining similar and dissimilar terms or systems: Football and soccer—what's the difference? What do Christians and Muslims have in common? How does Facebook differ from Twitter?

THESIS AND MAIN POINTS   The thesis in a speech of definition is a statement identifying a term or system and stating your intention to define it or to contrast it with other terms.

> Christianity and Islam have much in common.

> Text and online dictionaries are similar and different.

You derive the main points from asking questions of your thesis: What do Christianity and Islam have in common? How are text and online dictionaries similar and different?

SUPPORT Once you have each of the main points for your speech of definition, support them with examples, testimony, and the like. For example, one of your main points in the Christianity-Islam example might be that both religions believe in the value of good works. You might then quote from the New Testament and from the Quran to illustrate this belief, you might give examples of noted Christians and Muslims who exemplify this characteristic, or you might cite the testimony of religious leaders who have talked about the importance of good works.

Because this is a speech of definition, you'll want to give special attention to all your definitions, as discussed earlier.

ORGANIZATION For a speech of definition, an obvious organizational pattern is the pattern of multiple definitions (see Chapter 11). Alternatively, you might consider using a topical order, in which each main idea is treated equally. In either case, however, proceed from the known to the unknown. Start with what your audience knows and work up to what is new or unfamiliar.

Here is an example of how you might go about constructing a speech of definition. In this particular example, the speaker selects three major types of lying for discussion and arranges these in a topical pattern.

> **JOURNAL**
> **COMMUNICATION CHOICE POINT**
> Speech of Definition
>
> You want to give a speech defining the basic tenets of your religion. Most members of your audience, you suspect, have a negative view of your religion; a few may hold neutral or slightly positive views. You want to acknowledge your understanding of these attitudes. *What are some things you can say to help you get this point across? What would you say?*

General purpose: To inform

Specific purpose: To define lying by explaining the major types of lying

Thesis: There are three major kinds of lying. (What are the three major kinds of lying?)

I.   Concealment is the process of hiding the truth.

II. Falsification is the process of presenting false information as if it were true.

III. Misdirection is the process of acknowledging a feeling but misidentifying its cause.

In delivering such a speech, the speaker might begin with this.

A lie is a lie is a lie. True? Well, not exactly. Actually, there are a number of different ways we can lie. We can lie by concealing the truth. We can lie by falsification, by presenting false information as if it were true. And we can lie by misdirection, by acknowledging a feeling but misidentifying its cause. Let's look at the first type of lie—the lie of concealment. …

Speeches of Demonstration

In a **speech of demonstration**, you show the audience how to do something or how something operates. Examples of speeches in which you demonstrate how to do something might include how to give mouth-to-mouth resuscitation, how to drive defensively, how to mix colors, how to ask for a raise, how to burglarproof your house, or how to use Prezi in business meetings. Examples of speeches in which you demonstrate how something operates might include how the body maintains homeostasis, how perception works, how divorce laws work, how e-mail works, how a hurricane develops, or how a heart bypass operation is performed.

THESIS AND MAIN POINTS The thesis for a speech of demonstration identifies what you will show the audience how to do or how something operates.

E-mail works through a series of electronic connections from one computer to a server to another computer.

You can burglarproof your house in three different ways.

These guidelines will help you get that raise.

You derive the main points by asking a simple *how* or *what* question related to your thesis.

How do these electronic connections work?

What are the things you can do to burglarproof your house?

What are the guidelines for asking for a raise?

SUPPORT   To support each of the main ideas in a speech of demonstration, you can use a variety of materials. For example, you might show diagrams of houses with different burglarproofing arrangements, demonstrate how various locks work, or show how different security systems are installed.

VIEWPOINTS: Description, Definition, Demonstration

Speeches often have three general purposes—description, definition, and demonstration. *Can you identify these elements of informative speeches in class lectures, home shopping network shows, cooking shows, or social media sites?*

Presentation aids are especially helpful in speeches of demonstration. Signs in restaurants demonstrating the Heimlich maneuver, for example, demonstrate the sequence of steps with both words and pictures. The combination of verbal and graphic information makes it easy to understand this important process. In a speech on this topic, however, it would be best to use only the pictures as aids so that written words would not distract your audience from your oral explanation.

ORGANIZATION   In most cases, a temporal pattern will work best in speeches of demonstration. Demonstrate each step in the sequence in which it is to be performed. In this way, you'll avoid one of the major difficulties in demonstrating a process—backtracking. Don't skip steps even if you think they're familiar to the audience; they may not be. Connect each step to the next with appropriate transitions. For example, in explaining the Heimlich maneuver, you might say, "Now that you have your arms around the choking victim's chest, your next step is to …" Assist your listeners by labeling the steps clearly: for example, say, "The first step," "The second step," and so on.

Begin with an overview. It's often helpful when demonstrating to give a broad general picture and then present each step in turn. For example, suppose your talk were about how to prepare a wall for painting. You might begin with a general overview to give your listeners a general idea of the process, saying something like this.

> In preparing the wall for painting, you want to make sure that the wall is smoothly sanded, free of dust, and dry. Sanding a wall isn't like sanding a block of wood. So let's look first at the proper way to sand a wall.

Here is an example of a speech of demonstration using a temporal organization. In this example, the speaker identifies and demonstrates the steps of listening actively.

General purpose: To inform

Specific purpose: To demonstrate three techniques of active listening

Thesis: We can engage in active listening by following three techniques. (What are these techniques?)

   I. Paraphrase the speaker's meaning

  II. Express understanding of the speaker's feelings

III. Ask questions

In delivering the speech, the speaker might begin with this.

> Active listening is a special kind of listening. It's listening with total involvement, with a concern for the speaker. It's probably the most important type of listening you can engage in. Active listening consists of three steps: paraphrasing the speaker's meaning, expressing understanding of the speaker's feelings, and asking questions. Your first step in active listening is to paraphrase the speaker's meaning.

Public Speaking Sample Assistant

SPECIAL OCCASION SPEECHES

Largely Informative

In addition to the speeches of description, definition, and demonstration, there are special occasion speeches. These speeches are dominated by the context and occasion for the speech. Here are a few such speeches that are largely (though not exclusively) informative.

The Speech of Presentation or Acceptance

In a **presentation speech** you seek to (1) place an award or honor in some kind of context and (2) give the award an extra air of dignity or status. A speech of presentation may focus on rewarding a colleague for an important accomplishment (being named Teacher of the Year) or on recognizing a particularly impressive performance (winning an Academy Award). It may honor an employee's service to a company or a student's outstanding grades or athletic abilities.

The **acceptance speech** is the other side of this honoring ceremony. Here the recipient accepts the award and attempts to place the award in some kind of context.

In your speeches of presentation, follow these three principles.

- State the reason for the presentation. Make clear why this particular award is being given to this particular person.
- State the importance of the award.
- Be brief.

Follow these guidelines when preparing and presenting your speech of acceptance.

- Thank the people responsible for giving you the award.
- Acknowledge those who helped you achieve the award.
- Put the award into personal perspective.

The Eulogy

The **eulogy**, a speech of tribute to praise someone who has died, puts a person's life and contributions in a positive light. This type of speech is often given at a funeral or at the anniversary of the person's birth or death. This is not the time for a balanced appraisal of the individual's life. Rather, it's a time for praise. In developing the eulogy, consider the following.

- Relate the person whose life you're celebrating to yourself and to those in the audience.
- Be specific; show that you really knew the person or know a great deal about the person.
- Make the audience see this person as deserving of the praise you're bestowing.
- Show the audience what they can learn from this individual's life.

"We are gathered here today to bid farewell to the best assistant any magician could ask for."

Tom Cheney/The New Yorker Collection/The Cartoon Bank

The Toast

The **toast** is a brief speech designed to celebrate a person or an occasion. You might, for example, toast the next CEO of your company, a friend who just got admitted to a prestigious graduate program, or a colleague on the occasion of a promotion. Often toasts are given at weddings or at the start of a new venture. The toast is designed to say "congratulations" or "good luck" in a relatively formal sense. In developing your toast consider the following.

- Be brief; realize that people want to get on with the festivities.
- Focus attention on the person or persons you're toasting, not on yourself.
- Avoid inside jokes that only you and the person you're toasting understand.
- When you raise your glass in the toast—an almost obligatory part of toasting—make the audience realize that they should drink and that your speech is at an end.

Supporting Materials

13.3 Define *examples, illustrations, narratives, testimony, numerical data,* and *definitions* as supporting materials in informative speeches.

In constructing your speech you'll want to use a variety of what are called supporting materials—numerical data and illustrations, for example. These supporting materials serve a variety of functions and will help you clarify and explain ideas; make ideas vivid, interesting, and attention getting; and reinforce your ideas so that they are remembered.

In selecting appropriate supporting materials, keep in mind the nature of your audience. Select materials that are appropriate to their educational and age levels and their interests, for example. Also, select materials with cultural sensitivity. Using examples from only one religion (say, your own) when a variety of religious beliefs would be more appropriate and relevant is likely to distance your audience rather than draw them to you.

Here we look at four major material types in detail: (1) examples, illustrations, and narratives; (2) testimony; (3) numerical data; and (4) definitions. We'll also look at some additional forms in brief.

Examples, Illustrations, and Narratives

Examples, illustrations, and narratives are specific instances that help you explain your ideas. An **example** is a relatively brief specific instance:

> Pat's on the varsity and has a 4.0.

An **illustration** is a longer and more detailed example:

> Pat has always been an athlete but at the same time has always maintained an outstanding academic record, and there are many others on the varsity that have been both athletes and scholars, effectively destroying the stereotype of the dumb jock.

Here is another example of an illustration from the speech on Alzheimer's disease (King, 2015):

> Carol Harrison told the *Philadelphia Inquirer* on March 18, 2015, she thought she had seen the worst of both her mother and aunt's Alzheimer's until she visited one morning to find the two sisters sitting next to each other, neither with any sense the other was there.

A **narrative** is longer still and presented in the form of an anecdote or brief story. The parables in many religious works are good examples of narratives used to illustrate a general principle.

Examples, illustrations, and narratives may be factual or imaginary. Thus, in explaining friendship, you might tell about an actual friend's behavior, or you might formulate a composite, ideal friend and describe how this person would act in a particular situation. In using these forms of support, be sure to include only those details that are needed to help your audience understand the point you're making. Don't clutter up an otherwise pointed example with unnecessary details. Also, because it is the example, illustration, or narrative that listeners will remember most clearly, be sure to connect this very explicitly to the proposition in your speech.

Testimony

Testimony is a form of supporting material consisting of experts' opinions or of witnesses' accounts. Testimony supports your ideas by adding a note of authority. So, for example, if one of your main points was that the deficit is increasing, you might cite an economist's predictions concerning the increasing size of the deficit. Or if one of your main points was that today's prisons are inhumane, you might cite the eye-witness

Table 13.1 Guidelines for Interviewing

General Guidelines	Examples
Select the person you wish to interview.	You might, for example, look through your college catalog for an instructor teaching a course that involves your topic. Or visit blogs and look for people who have posted articles on your topic. If you want to contact a book author, you can always write to the author in care of the publisher or editor (listed on the copyright page), though many authors are now including their e-mail address.
Secure an appointment.	Phone the person or send an e-mail requesting an interview. State the purpose of your request and say that you hope to conduct a brief interview by phone or that you'd like to send this person a series of questions by e-mail.
Create a cheat sheet.	A **cheat sheet** is a list of what you want to say during the interview. If this is a phone or chat interview, you can keep the cheat sheet in front of you; if this is a face-to-face interview, review the cheat sheet immediately before the interview.
Ask open-ended questions.	Generally, ask questions that provide the interviewee with room to discuss the issues you want to raise. Avoid questions that can be answered with *yes* or *no*.
Ask for permission to tape or print the interview.	It's a good idea to keep an accurate record of the interview, so ask permission to tape the interview if it's in person or by telephone.
After closing the interview, follow up with an expression of appreciation.	Even though you thank the person at the end of the interview, it's polite to follow up with a thank you note, later that day or the next day. Or perhaps you might send the person you interviewed a copy of your speech (e-mail would work well here) with a note of thanks.

JOURNAL
COMMUNICATION CHOICE POINT
Testimony

You want to present the testimony of a retired judge to explain the problems that probation causes. *For your purposes, what would be the ideal qualifications of this judge? How might you weave these qualifications into your speech? What are some of the things you might say?*

testimony of a former inmate or prison guard. You can present testimony by paraphrasing what someone has said or by quoting them directly.

Often, you'll want to interview someone either in person or via email or phone. Table 13.1 offers a few suggestions for interviewing (DeVito, 2010).

In presenting the testimony, stress the person's credibility. When you cite an authority, make sure the person is in fact an authority. Tell the audience who the authority is, and state the basis for the individual's expertise. The testimony will be much more effective when your audience is convinced that this person is worth listening to.

Numerical Data

Numerical data are useful for supporting a wide variety of statements. For example, if you want to show that significant numbers of people now get their news from the Internet, you could give the total number of online users for each of the last 10 years and compare that with the numbers of newspaper readers and television news viewers in those same years. These data would then allow you to show that the number of people who get their news from the Internet is increasing while the number of those getting the news from papers and television is declining. Or, you might compare the percentage of a tuition increase at your school with the national average or with the rate of inflation. To illustrate the growth of instant messaging or social networking as a means of communication, you might note the percentage that usage has grown in each of the last five years.

When using numerical data of any kind, consider these suggestions.

- **Make the numbers easy to remember.** Your audience will hear the figures only once. For most purposes it's best to round off any figures so that they are more easily processed and remembered. For example, if you're trying to make the point that the population of China dwarfs many European nations, you are probably better off rounding China's population to "over 1 billion people" or perhaps "1.3 billion people" than saying China's population is 1,336,718,015.

- **Clarify your meaning for using numbers.** For example, if you state that the average home health aide makes less than $30,000 a year, you need to compare this figure to the salaries of other workers and to your proposition that these salaries need to be increased.

- **Connect numbers to something familiar.** Comparisons and analogies will prove useful in making your numbers relevant and meaningful to your specific audience. Instead of saying the new exhibition hall will be 750 × 350 feet—hard in itself to visualize—elaborate on the figures with something like, *it will be twice the size of a professional football field, forty times the size of our cafeteria.*

- **Reinforce your numerical data.** Use a presentation aid—perhaps a graph or a chart—with numbers presented as visual reinforcement.

- **Use numbers in moderation.** Most listeners' capacity for numerical data presented in a speech is limited.

- **Stress reliability.** If you want your audience to accept your figures, you need to show that they come from a trusted source.

- **Stress currency.** Most things that are described with numbers change rapidly. So, use the most recent figures you can find and stress their currency to the audience.

Definitions

Definitions, essentially explanations of terms and concepts that may not be familiar to your listeners, may be useful as a form of support in many types of speeches. Here are several ways to incorporate definitions in a speech.

- **Define by etymology or linguistic development.** For example, in defining *communication* you might note that it comes from the Latin *communis* meaning "common"; in "communicating" you seek to establish a commonness, a sameness, a similarity with another individual.

- **Define by authority.** For example, you might define "inflation" by citing the definition of a noted economist or define "metal fatigue" in the words of a respected engineer.

- **Define by negation.** For example, you might say that "A teacher isn't someone who teaches you what to learn but rather one who teaches you how to learn."

- **Define by the actual object or by a picture or model of it.** For example, a speech on magazine layout or types of fabrics might include actual layout pages or fabric samples.

- **Define by operations.** An **operational definition** describes how you would construct the object. For example, in defining a chocolate cake, you could give instructions about how to bake a cake.

Additional Forms of Support

There are several other useful forms of support you might consider.

- **Quotations** Quote the exact words of an expert or of an interesting or notable person to add spice and wit as well as authority to your speeches. Quotations work best when they're short and easily comprehended and remembered. Most important, connect the quotations directly to the point you're making and do so as smoothly as possible (avoid the too-often-used "I have a quote …").

- **Comparisons and contrasts** Focus on the major similarities and differences between two ideas, events, or concepts but avoid itemizing every possibility. Consider using a presentation aid that visualizes the most crucial information.

- **Statements of fact or a series of facts** Illustrate and support a statement for your position by linking the facts to your main points. State the connections when introducing the facts and perhaps again after you've finished identifying the list of facts.

- **Repetition and restatement** Repeat ideas in the same words at strategic places during the speech) or *restate* ideas in different words to add clarity and emphasis and to also help compensate for the audience's inevitable lapses in attention.

VIEWPOINTS: Supporting Materials

What types of supporting materials would you use in an informative speech in which your purpose is to explain the way in which a particular sport or game is played to an audience who never heard of the sport or game?

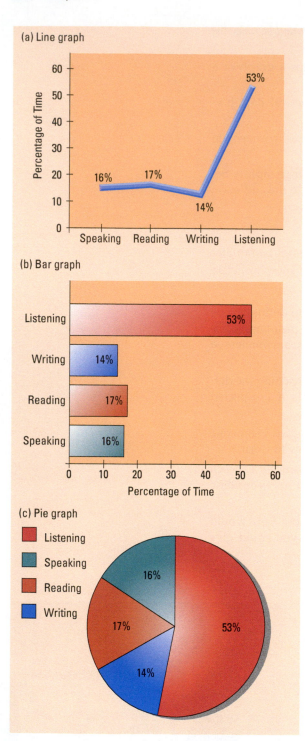

(a) Line graph

(b) Bar graph

(c) Pie graph

Figure 13.1 Three Graphs

Three graphs illustrating data from a study on the amount of time people spend on each of the four communication activities (Barker, Edwards, Gaines, Gladney, & Holley, 1980). All of these graphs are useful for illustrating comparisons. Many additional types of graphs can be easily constructed using the graphics software integrated with most word processing packages or, of course, with the more sophisticated graphics programs.

Presentation Aids

13.4 Describe the varied types of presentation aids.

Presentation aids—visual or auditory means for clarifying ideas—can also be considered a form of supporting material. But because they're so important in public speaking today, because they're so numerous and varied, and because technology has provided a wealth of alternatives and some pretty sophisticated techniques, we'll look at presentation aids separately here and will consider them in detail.

As you plan any type of speech, consider using some kind of presentation aid. Ask yourself how you can visually present what you want your audience to understand and remember. For example, if you want your audience to see the growing impact of the sales tax, consider showing them a chart of rising sales taxes over the last 10 years. Of course, you can deliver your entire speech supplemented by projected slides—using PowerPoint or Prezi, for example.

Types of Presentation Aids

You have a wealth of presentation aids that you can choose from when preparing an informative speech.

- **Object being discussed** If it's feasible, bring the object itself to your speech. Notice that infomercials sell their products not only by talking about them but by showing them to potential buyers.

- **Models** Replicas of the actual object are useful if you want to explain complex structures such as the human hearing or vocal mechanisms, the brain, or the structure of DNA. Models can clarify relative size and position and how the parts interact.

- **Graphs** Graphs are useful for illustrating differences over time, how a whole is divided into parts, and different amounts or sizes. Figure 13.1 shows three types of graphs. Keep your graphs as simple as possible, limiting the number of items to five or fewer, and be sure you add the legend, the labels, and the numerical values you wish to emphasize.

- **Word chart** You can use a word chart (which also can contain numbers and graphics) to identify the key points of one of your propositions or of your entire speech. Figure 13.2 is an example of a simple word chart that identifies the major topics discussed in a speech on culture shock. The word chart in Figure 13.3, an organizational chart, clarifies relationships among roles in an organization, and Figure 13.4, a flowchart, identifies the steps in a process.

- **Maps** You can use maps to illustrate the locations of geographic features, population densities, immigration patterns, world literacy rates, varied economic conditions, the spread of diseases, and hundreds of other issues you may wish to examine in your speeches.

- **People** If you want to demonstrate the muscles of the body, different voice patterns or hairstyles, consider using people as your aids. Their presence also helps to secure and maintain the attention and interest of the audience.

Figure 13.2 A Word Chart

The word chart is helpful when your main ideas can be clearly explained in key words or when you wish to emphasize certain concepts.

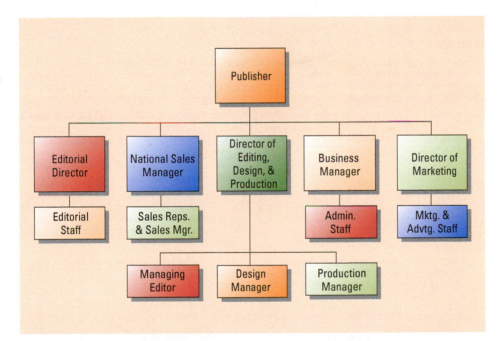

Figure 13.3 An Organizational Chart

Organizational charts can easily be constructed using the table function on most word processors and then enlarged for an entire audience to see. This figure was constructed in Illustrator.

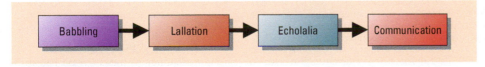

Figure 13.4 A Flowchart

This **flowchart** identifies the stages a child goes through in learning language. You can use such charts to guide your audience through an entire speech—where each section of the chart might represent a main point of your speech.

- **Photographs and illustrations** Types of trees, styles of art, kinds of exercise machines, and the horrors of war—all of these can be made more meaningful with photographs and illustrations. Be sure to project the image in a format large enough for everyone to see clearly.

Once you've decided on the type of presentation aid to use, you need to decide on the medium you'll use to present it. Acquire skill in using both low-tech (the whiteboard or flip chart) and high-tech (presentation software such as PowerPoint or Prezi) resources. A variety of media, with their major uses, and some suggestions for using them effectively are presented in Table 13.2.

Using Presentation Aids

Your presentation aids will be more effective if you follow a few simple guidelines.

- **Know your presentation aids intimately.** Be sure you know in what order your aids are to be presented and how you plan to introduce them.
- **Pretest the presentation aids.** Verify that your aids can be seen easily from all parts of the room.
- **Rehearse your speech with the presentation aids.** Do all your rehearsals with your presentation aids so that you'll be able to use them smoothly and effectively.

Table 13.2 Some Forms of Presentation Aids

Once you've decided on the type of presentation aid you'll use, you need to decide on the medium you'll use to present it. Acquire skill in using both low-tech (the chalkboard or flip chart) and high-tech (the computerized slide show) resources. In this way you'll be able to select your presentation aids from the wide array available, choosing on the basis of the message you want to communicate and the audience to whom you'll be speaking.

Type of Aid	Uses	Suggestions
Whiteboards	Used to record key terms or names, important numerical data, or even the main points of your speech (in very abbreviated form).	• Don't use whiteboards when you can present the same information with a preplanned chart or model. • Keep what you write brief; don't lose audience eye contact.
Chartboards Large semirigid boards that come in a variety of colors and sizes.	Used to present one or two relatively simple graphs, a few word charts, or diagrams that you want to display during your speech.	• Be sure you have a way of holding the boards up—for example, with masking tape or with the aid of an audience member. • Black lettering on a white background generally works best; it's easiest for people to read.
Flip Charts Large pads of paper (usually about 24 × 24 inches) mounted on a stand or easel.	Used to record a variety of information, such as key concepts or main points. Writing these out before the speech saves you the time of writing them during the speech.	• Be sure the print is legible to the back of the audience. • Keep the charts simple.
Slides and Transparencies Visuals created with many of the popular computer programs.	Helpful in showing a series of visuals that may be of very different types—from photographs and illustrations to charts and tables.	• Follow the general suggestions for using computer-assisted presentations.
Audios and Videos Basically, you have two options with videos or audios: record a scene from a film or television show or create your own.	Adds variety to your presentation and helps to maintain audience attention. A speech on advertising jingles or music styles would be greatly helped by having actual samples for the audience to hear.	• Videos are best used in small doses; in many instances just 20- or 30-second excerpts will prove sufficient to illustrate your point.
Handouts Printed materials that are distributed to the audience; a variety of handouts can be easily prepared with many of the computer presentation packages that we'll consider later in this chapter.	Used to explain complex material and to provide listeners with a permanent record of some aspect of your speech. They are also useful for presenting complex information that you want your audience to refer to throughout the speech. Handouts encourage listeners to take notes—especially if you leave enough white space on each page or even provide a specific place for notes—which keeps them actively involved in your presentation.	• Be careful: If you distribute your handouts during your speech, you run the risk of your listeners reading the handout and not concentrating on your speech. • If you distribute your handouts at the end of the speech, they may never be read. Encourage your audience to read them by including additional material (and giving your audience an idea of what you've included).

Test Yourself

USING PRESENTATION SOFTWARE

Indicate whether you think each of the following statements is **T** (true) or **F** (false).

____ 1. A good size font to use is about 16 or 18 points with about 8 or 9 lines per slide.

____ 2. Use italics for emphasis.

____ 3. Read your slides word for word.

____ 4. Use lots of color and sound effects; these will keep the audience awake.

____ 5. Blue and green or red and green are almost always appropriate colors for slides.

____ 6. As in a preparation outline, use full sentences for the slides.

____ 7. Your slides should be your main attraction.

____ 8. When you have few words on a slide, add a photo or graphic.

____ 9. A 10-minute informative speech can easily have 30 or 40 slides.

____ 10. Liven up your slides by including images from websites.

This test was designed to point out some of the misconceptions people have about computer-assisted presentations; all are false. Briefly, here's why.

1. Sixteen or 18 is too small; use at least 24 point font, although 30 point font would be even better. Four lines is best, although six is generally fine. Any more than this will work against you. See Figure 13.5.

2. Italics are difficult to read and don't give real emphasis.

3. Never do this.

4. Too much color and too many sounds will be distracting.

5. These colors do not provide sufficient contrast—as would, say, red and black. Also, many people have difficulty distinguishing red and green.

6. Use phrases for the slides; sentences take too much time to read.

7. No, you should be the main attraction. Your slides are simply aids to your presentation.

8. Only add photos or graphics when they are integral to your slide's message.

9. Any more than 10 slides is probably too much.

10. Images from websites don't translate well to slides; instead, use clip art images if you need graphics.

- **Integrate presentation aids into your speech seamlessly.** Just as a verbal example should flow naturally into the text so should a presentation aid. The aid should appear to be an essential part of the speech.

- **Avoid talking to your aids.** Know your aids so well that you can point to what you want without breaking eye contact with your audience.

- **Use your aids only when they're relevant.** Present each aid when you want the audience to concentrate on it; then remove it. If you don't, the audience's attention may remain focused on the visual when you want them to focus on your next assertion.

Presentation Software

In many instances you'll want to use presentation software to create and present your slides. Take the following self-test to see what you already know about presentation software packages.

Computer-assisted presentations possess all of the advantages of aids already noted (from maintaining interest and attention to adding clarity and reinforcing your message). They can also give your speech a professional, up-to-date look, and in the process add to your credibility. They show that you're prepared and that you care about your topic and audience.

WAYS OF USING PRESENTATION SOFTWARE   Presentation software enables you to produce a variety of aids. The easiest is to create your slides and then show them on your computer screen. If you're speaking to a very small group and you have a large monitor, it may be possible to have your listeners gather around your computer as you speak. With larger audiences, you'll need a computer projector.

Figure 13.5 A Simple Slide

Here, for example, is a simple slide identifying the four parts of a speech on culture shock, useful in introducing the topic and in summarizing the speech. Presentation software is a fact of life for public speakers. Resolve to learn to use it as effectively as you can and keep up with the new developments.

Computer presentation software also enables you to print out a variety of materials to use as handouts: slides, slides with speaker's notes, slides with room for listener notes, and outlines of your speech. You can print out your complete set of slides to distribute to your listeners, or you can print out a selection of slides from the talk or even slides that you didn't have time to cover in your speech but would like your audience to look at later.

Another useful option is to print out your slides with speaker's notes for your own use (as illustrated in Figure 13.6). That way you'll have your slides and any notes you may find useful—examples you want to use, numerical data that would be difficult to memorize, quotations that you want to read to your audience, or delivery notes. Still another option is to print out your slides with room for listeners to write their own notes (as illustrated in Figure 13.7).

REHEARSING WITH PRESENTATION PROGRAMS Presentation programs are especially helpful in enabling you to rehearse your speech and time it precisely. As you rehearse, the computer program records the time you spend on each slide and will display it under the slide; it will also record the presentation's total time. You can see these times at the bottom of each slide in a variety of views, but they won't appear in the slides the audience sees or in a printed handout. If you find in your rehearsal that your speech is too long, these times can help you see which parts could be shortened.

Another aspect of rehearsal is checking out the equipment available in the room you'll speak in and its compatibility with the presentation software you're using. If possible, rehearse with the actual equipment you'll have available on the day you're speaking. In this way you can adjust to or remedy any incompatibilities or idiosyncrasies that you come across.

VIEWPOINTS: Presentation Aids

Although presentation aids are extremely useful, speakers often use them ineffectively. *What are some of the major mistakes people make in using presentation aids?*

Have You Ever Been Culture Shocked?

PAUSE!
Scan audience.
Slide #1
Have you ever been culture shocked?
PAUSE!
I have.
And many of you have too.
If you haven't, you will be.
People all over the world (and especially bright college graduates like ourselves) are becoming increasingly mobile.
We'll all spend time in different cultures.
Understanding culture shock → better to deal with it.
Preventive medicine.

Figure 13.6 Slide with Speaker's Notes

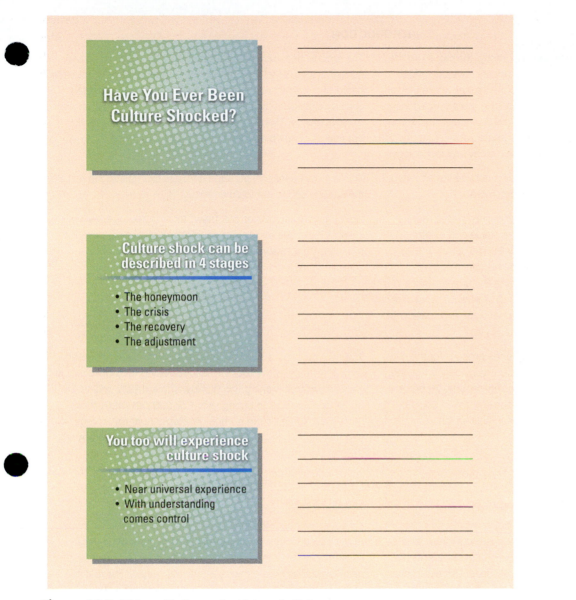

Figure 13.7 Slides with Space for Listener's Notes

Public Speaking Sample Assistant

AN EXCELLENT INFORMATIVE SPEECH

This excellent informative speech was constructed and delivered by Blake Joseph Bergeron, a student from the University of Texas at Austin. Blake explains his interest in the topic: "I have worked in healthcare for a couple of years now. So, health topics tend to interest me. I heard about decellularizing hearts, my second sub-point in my second point, and upon further research, the topic really interested me." Blake's biggest challenge "was to inform the audience, yet still keep things fun and interesting."

SPEECH	COMMENTS
A Lot of Heart	What do you think of this title? Does it make you want to listen to this speech? What expectations does this title set up?

INTRODUCTION

Art can be a feast for the eyes and apparently, the mouth. At the New York Parsons School of Design, students have decided to move away from the paint brush and to the beaker where they are taking used plant and animal tissues, soaking them in solutions, and creating something like this—it's a piece of steak. Tasty. The students, using a process known as decellularization, intended to explore humanities relationship between biology and technology.

The topic of decellularization is one that is both significant and current. It's likely that a good number of listeners would not have heard of or at least not know much about the topic. So, the speaker's task is to gain attention and make the subject relevant to his audience. This specific example not only gains attention but makes it clear that listeners will learn something new.

However, *Nature* on May 9, 2014 explains outside the art realm, this easy to use process can do so much more.

This is a neat transition from the art class example to the rest of the speech and to the topic generally.

The May 2014 *Harvard Science Journal* defines decellularization as the process of taking an organ or tissue and oxidizing it, removing all of its personalized blood cells. The January 2015 *American Journal of Transplantation* emphasizes this whole process can be done for about 50 dollars. By turning organs into blank slates, *Science Daily* on May 11, 2014 outlines, scientists can create personalized organs using a patient's stem cells, making them a perfect match for transplants.

Here the speaker defines this "new" term of decellularization (using a reputable and recent source) and shows its great potential, thus establishing the importance of the topic. It's something we feel we should know.

This technology could not only expedite the process for the over 122,000 patients on donor waiting lists but considering that the July 2014 *Greater Louisville Medical Society* reports, 28 percent of organ transplants end in rejection, decellularization could be the cure the medical community has been waiting for.

122,000 patients is surely a lot and again helps to establish the importance of the topic. Public speaking textbooks would generally advise making this number more meaningful to the audience. Saying something like: *122,000 patients—that's more than 10 times the number of students at my college—* might have helped listeners appreciate how large a number this is.

BODY

To better understand the process that went from the lab to the studio, let's first examine how decellularization works, its impact on the medical community, and finally discuss some implications. *LiveScience* on July 31, 2014 explains every day 18 patients die waiting for the transplants they desperately need. Decellularization could save the 90 lives that will be lost before this tournament even ends.

Here the speaker explains the purpose of the speech: to inform his audience about the process of decellularization. The thesis of the speech might be stated as *We can understand decellularization.* From this we might ask, *How can we understand decellularization?* We'd then get answers very similar to those of the speaker: *We can understand it by examining (1) how it works, (2) its impact, and (3) its implications.*

Once the importance of the topic is established, the speaker provides a clear orientation as to what the speech will cover. The speech clearly follows a topical organization pattern with three main points: how decellularization works, its impact on the medical community, and some implications of this process.
In outline the body of the speech would look something like this:

I. Workings of decellularization
II. Impact of decellularization
III. Implications of decellularization

The speaker cleverly emphasizes the importance of this process by connecting it to the lives that will be lost before this speaking tournament is over. Referring to the speaking tournament also encourages the audience to feel at one with the speaker—we're all in this together.

The Greeks kind of had their own form of decellularization except instead of organs, they used parchment. Because parchment was more durable than paper, fifth-century Greeks developed a process where they would essentially wash the parchment using milk and oat bran. I guess breakfast really is the most important meal of the day.

Let's explore decellularization in two key ways: how it's done in the lab and at home.

As a preface to the discussion of how decellularization works, the speaker explains with a simple example its general workings.

Here we learn that the first main point will have two subdivisions: how it's done in the lab and how it's done in the home. In outline, it would look something like this:
  I. Workings of decellularization
      A. In the lab
      B. In the home

Decellularization is the process of removing existing cells from an organ. As Dr. Doris Taylor explains in the 2014 documentary *Stem Cell Universe*, each of the cells in our body have unique chemical makeup. It's kind of like a fingerprint, but in our cells. This unique chemical makeup is what causes organ rejection because no two organs are ever the same.

Here a general description of the process is provided before explaining how it's done in the lab and then how it's done in the home.

Decellularization wipes away all of those personalized cells by soaking the organ in chemicals and leaving the extracellular matrix; basically the skeleton of the organ. Scientists have recently perfected the process and as the February 2014 book *Biocoder* explains, the main chemicals needed are sodium dodecyl sulfate, nucleic acids, and soluble cytoplasmic inclusions. With these three things, scientists can remove all of the personalized cells of an organ, leaving only a blank slate.

Here an extremely complex process is described to provide an initial or basic understanding.
With terms like these it's important that the speaker pronounce them without hesitation or stumbling. Some significant rehearsal was obviously needed.

But scientists aren't the only ones doing this anymore. As Michelle Quint explains in her February 14, 2014 Ted Talk, modern science has made this process simple and it can be done using water, OxyClean, salt, and Everclear because who said science can't be fun. I've even done it. Using OxyClean, I decellularized a sheep heart. As Nina Tandon describes in her 2014 book *Super Cells*, the chemical similar to that in OxyClean, peracetic acid, washes away all of the cells in the organ, leaving only the matrix. It's like bleaching a white shirt that got washed with the reds. The OxyClean acts like the bleach, removing all of the blood cells and leaving only the product in its most basic state.

Here we learn that the speaker has actually worked with the process, which is an effective way of establishing credibility. The speaker makes use of a wide variety of research sources that convinces us that he knows the topic and has done more than adequate research on the topic.

Now, I have no clue what someone could do with a decellularized steak. I mean, I know they definitely can't eat it.

Here is an excellent transition connecting the first major point with the second.

Thankfully, there are two clear uses for the process that got that steak there: research and transplants.

Here is an orientation to the second major point, which we learn will be divided into two parts: research and transplants. In outline, it would look something like this:
  II. Impact of decellularization
      A. On research
      B. On transplants

Initially, decellularized organs can be used to study the human body, without needing the human. As it stands, scientists have a hard time understanding how certain chemicals and conditions affect our organs directly. This is because, as the January 5, 2015 journal *Cell* points out, the government thankfully forbids testing dangerous products on humans. The National Center on Biomedical Technology on August 19, 2014, highlights that scientists are currently using decellularized human lungs in order

Here the speaker explains how decellularization can be used in research.

to figure out how smoking directly affects their structure. While we know that smoking covers our lungs in tar, little is known concerning how chemicals affect our body on a cellular level. Decellularization allows researchers to look beyond just the surface and see something more.

Second, decellularized organs could be transplanted into human bodies. At the head of this application is the Texas Heart Institute. As the Texas Heart Institute outlines in July 2014, after a heart has been decellularized, the next step is to take somatic stem cells from the person in need—these are the stem cells that are found all over our body—and attach those stem cells to the organ. Once these cells are placed on the heart, as *Transformational Technologies* details on August 8, 2014, they instantaneously take hold. After about 48 hours, the organ is covered in a layer of cells that exactly match the patient in need, meaning decellularization allows for organ transplants free from the worries of rejection.

In 2006, the FDA decided to step into the stem cell debate, when they classified any type of stem cell as a drug; thus, putting them under FDA regulation. Yet, discourse over these laws was only inside the scientific community. Outside the field of science, decellularization could have lasting implications. Let's look at two.

Initially, decellularization challenges our perceptions of stem cell regulations. When the government decided to regulate stem cells in 2006, the limited scope of the debate caused us to misunderstand what exactly was and was not regulated. This is because NPR on October 14, 2014, explains the debate focused solely on embryonic stem cells, leaving other types behind.

Decellularization challenges our perception of those laws because it uses the very stem cells that were left out of the conversation—causing us to not only question the regulations but the government's initial classification of stem cells as a drug. When the government has its hands on something our body naturally produces, it sets a dangerous legal precedent for future regulatory policies, urging us to ask: where is the line between protecting people and turning our bodies into government-regulated drug factories?

Next, decellularization could lead to the complete commercialization of organs. Currently, it is illegal to pay for an organ in any way, whether it be placing yourself higher on a waiting list or to paying someone for their organ. However, *ScienceDirect* points out on January 15, 2015, nine companies are already manufacturing decellularized organs and selling them. While most are for research, once the transplant application is fully developed, it is feasible that a major pharmaceutical company could create a system, where with the right amount of money, an individual could purchase a complete organ transplant. These types of procedures could question the technical legality of purchasing an organ. Further, insurance companies are forced to define whether these procedures cosmetic or medically necessary, subsequently allowing them to have complete control over who lives and who doesn't.

Here is the second use of decellularization: transplants. Again, the speaker succeeds in making an extremely complex process understandable by explaining the several steps involved in the process.

Here is the speaker's third main point: the implications of decellularization. Again the speaker divides this into 2 parts. In outline, this point would look something like this:
III. Implications of decellularization
    A. Government regulation
    B. Commercialization of organs

The first implication is the government's classification of decellularization as a drug.

This classification as a drug, argues the speaker, can create a dangerous legal precedent.

The second implication is the potential commercialization of organs which we might have thought of negatively may actually be a positive.

CONCLUSION

Today we have examined the background, applications, and implications to the next big wave in modern science.

Turns out artists and scientists have more in common than we thought. Artists like Michelangelo and Caravaggio were praised for their works depicting human life; turns out the next generation of artists might be creating life itself.

Here the speaker brief summarizes the three main points.

In this final sentence the speaker reconnects this summary with the opening about the artists and scientists working together and thus brings the speech to a crisp close.

WORKS CITED

Your instructor or college may have a specific reference style that is preferred. So, it's best to find out the format used early in your speech preparation process so you can record all the information you'll need.

"The 3D Bioprinting Revolution." *Harvard Science Review*. N.p., 01 May 2014. Web. 09 Apr. 2015.

"About Regenerative Medicine Research at the Texas Heart Institute." *About Regenerative Medicine Research at the Texas Heart Institute*. Texas Heart Institute, 1 July 2014. Web. 09 Apr. 2015.

"American Journal of Transplantation." *Volume 15, Issue 1*. N.p., 1 Jan. 2015. Web. 09 Apr. 2015.

"Better Tissue Healing with Disappearing Hydrogels." *ScienceDaily*. ScienceDaily, 11 May 2014. Web. 09 Apr. 2015.

Cell | Vol. 160, Iss. 1–2, Pgs 1–354 (15 January 2015) | "ScienceDirect.com." *Cell | Vol. 160, Iss. 1–2, Pgs. 1–354, (15 January 2015) | ScienceDirect.com*. Science Direct, 5 Jan. 2015. Web. 09 Apr. 2015.

"Chapter 10. Mission Possible: Ghost Heart Protocol." *BioCoder: Issue 2*. N.p., 15 Feb. 2014. Web. 09 Apr. 2015.

"Download PDFs." *An Overview of Tissue and Whole Organ Decellularization Processes*. Cell, 5 Jan. 2015. Web. 09 Apr. 2015.

"Embryonic Stem Cells Restore Vision in Preliminary Human Test." NPR. NPR, 14 Oct. 2014. Web. 09 Apr. 2015.

"Ghost Heart: Miracle in Medicine." *Guardian Liberty Voice*. Transformational Technologies, 8 Aug. 2014. Web. 09 Apr. 2015.

"Perfusion Decellularization of Whole Organs." *Nature.com*. Nature Publishing Group, 9 May 2014. Web. 09 Apr. 2015.

Price, Andrew P., Kristen A. England, Amy M. Matson, Bruce R. Blazar, and Angela Panoskaltsis-Mortari. "Development of a Decellularized Lung Bioreactor System for Bioengineering the Lung: The Matrix Reloaded." *Tissue Engineering. Part A*. Mary Ann Liebert, Inc., 28 Aug. 2014. Web. 09 Apr. 2015.

Quint, Michelle. "A Ghost Heart?" *Ideastedcom*. N.p., 13 Feb. 2015. Web. 09 Apr. 2015.

Society, Greater Louisville Medical. "Organs." *In Kentucky There's One* (n.d.): N.p. *Greater Louisville Medical Society*. Greater Louisville Medical Society, 1 July 2014. Web. 09 Apr. 2015.

Staff, By Live Science. "Transparent Organs: Images Reveal See-Through Mouse." *LiveScience*. TechMedia Network, 31 July 2014. Web. 09 Apr. 2015.

Tadon, Nina. "'Super Cells—Building with Biology'—The Hope (And Hype) of Bio-Design [Book Review]." *PlanetSave*. Np., 15 Apr. 2014. Web. 09 Apr. 2015.

Taylor, Doris. "Stem Cell Universe." *Youtube*. Youtube, 1 June 2014. Web. 9 Apr. 2015.

Summary of Concepts and Skills

This chapter covered the nature of the informative speech and the ways you can most effectively communicate information.

Guidelines for Informative Speaking

13.1 Paraphrase the suggested guidelines for informative speaking.

1. When preparing informative speeches, observe the guidelines for informative speaking: center the information on the audience, limit the amount of information, adjust the level of complexity, stress the information's relevance and usefulness, relate new information to information the audience already knows, and make the information easy to remember.

Three Types of Informative Speeches

13.2 Define and give examples of *speeches of description, definition*, and *demonstration*.

2. Speeches of description focus on or explain an object, person, event, or process.

3. Speeches of definition define important concepts and perhaps similarities and differences between concepts.

4. Speeches of demonstration explain how something operates or how to do something.

Supporting Materials

13.3 **Define *examples, illustrations, narratives, testimony, numerical data,*** **and** ***definitions*** **as supporting materials in informative speeches.**

5. To make your ideas clear to your audience, use amplifying materials such as examples, illustrations, and narratives; testimony; numerical data; definitions; and presentation aids.

Presentation Aids

13.4 **Describe the varied types of presentation aids.**

6. Presentation aids include a wide variety of audio and visual means to help you communicate your ideas and also to maintain interest and attention.

Effective public speakers need to master a variety of informing skills. Place a check mark next to those skills you most want to work on.

_____ 1. In my informative speeches I follow the principles of informative speaking: I stress the information's usefulness, relate new information to information the audience already knows, present information through several senses, adjust the level of complexity, limit the amount of information I present, and recognize cultural variations.

_____ 2. For my informative speeches I select a variety of amplifying materials; examples, illustrations, and narratives; testimony; definitions; numerical data; and visual aids.

_____ 3. When developing a speech of information, I follow the suggestions for constructing speeches of description, definition, and demonstration.

Key Terms

acceptance speech	illustration	speech of definition
cheat sheet	information	speech of demonstration
definitions	narrative	speech of description
eulogy	operational definition	testimony
example	presentation aids	toast
flowchart	presentation speech	

Skill Development Experiences
13.1 Supporting Statements

Often it's the vivid example or alarming statistic that your listeners will remember most; give your supporting materials full attention.

Select one of the following overly broad statements and support it, using at least three different types of supporting material. Because the purpose of this exercise is to provide greater insight into supporting materials, in this case you may invent facts, figures, illustrations, examples, and the like.

- Immigrants contribute significantly to the U.S. economy.
- The author of this essay is a real authority.
- People in their 80s and older have contributed greatly to society.
- Candidate Williams cares for people.

13.2 Evaluating Testimony

Testimony is likely to be more effective if you establish the person's qualifications to the audience's satisfaction.

If you were presenting someone's testimony on one of the following issues, how would you establish the person's qualifications so that your audience would accept what he or she said?

- Nutritionist, on proper diet
- Real estate agent, on the advantages and disadvantages of condos and co-ops

- Psychiatrist, on the nature of bipolar disorder
- Biologist, on how to feed your pet
- Drama teacher, on how to write a play

13.3 Preparing an Informative Speech

Working repeatedly with the process of preparing a speech will ultimately make the process easier, more efficient, and more effective.

Select a topic in which you're interested (or consult an online idea generator) and then follow these steps.

1. Formulate a thesis and a specific purpose suitable for an informative speech of approximately 10 minutes.
2. Analyze this class as your potential audience and identify ways in which you can relate this topic to their interests and needs.
3. Generate at least two main points from your thesis. Support these main points with examples, illustrations, definitions, testimony, and so on.
4. Construct a conclusion that summarizes your main ideas and brings the speech to a definite close.
5. Construct an introduction that gains attention and orients your audience.

Discuss these outlines in small groups or with the class as a whole. Try to secure feedback from other members on how you can improve your outline.

Chapter 14
The Persuasive Speech

The power of persuasive speaking is enormous, whether face-to-face or on social media.

CHAPTER OUTLINE	⌄ Learning Objectives
Goals of Persuasion	**14.1** Explain the goals of persuasive speaking.
Guidelines for Persuasive Speaking	**14.2** Explain the guidelines for persuasive speaking.
Three Types of Persuasive Speeches	**14.3** Define and give examples of persuasive speeches on questions of fact, value, and policy.
Supporting Materials	**14.4** Explain the types of and the fallacies of logical, emotional, and credibility appeals.

You'll no doubt find yourself in a wide variety of situations in which you'll have to persuade others—to urge them to accept or reject a union proposal, redesign a company's website, negotiate a business deal, or donate blood or money or time, to give only a few examples. As with having to provide information, the higher up you go in your organization's hierarchy, the more you'll find yourself having to persuade others.

Goals of Persuasion

14.1 Explain the goals of persuasive speaking.

It's useful to view **persuasion** along a continuum. Let's say that you want to give a speech in favor of paying college athletes. You might visualize your audience as existing on a continuum ranging from strongly in favor to strongly opposed, as shown in Figure 14.1. Your task is to move your audience along this continuum in the direction of your persuasive purpose, which you can do in any of three ways (corresponding to the goals of persuasion).

- **Strengthen or weaken attitudes, beliefs, or values.** Persuasion often aims to strengthen audience views. For example, religious sermons and public service announcements usually seek to strengthen the existing beliefs of the listeners. At times, however, you may want to weaken the existing beliefs of the audience—to suggest that what they currently believe may not be entirely true.

- **Change attitudes, beliefs, or values.** Sometimes you'll want to change how your audience feels. You may want to change their attitudes toward the college's no-smoking rules, their beliefs about television's influence on viewer violence, or their values about the efficacy of war.

- **Motivate your audience to take action.** Ultimately, your goal is to get people to do something—for example, to vote for one person rather than another, to donate money to a fund for the homeless, or to take a course in personal finance.

If your purpose is to persuade the audience to *oppose* paying college athletes, then any movement toward the right of the continuum in Figure 14.1 will be successful persuasion; if your purpose is to persuade listeners to *support* paying college athletes, then any movement toward the left of the continuum will be successful persuasion. Notice, however, that it's quite possible to give a speech in which you attempt to move your listeners in one direction but actually succeed in moving them in the other direction. This "negative persuasion" could occur, for example, if the audience perceives you as dishonest or self-promoting or feels that you presented biased evidence or faulty reasoning.

> **JOURNAL**
> **COMMUNICATION CHOICE POINT**
> Reasonable Goals
>
> Assume you're preparing a 10-minute persuasive speech on colleges paying athletes to be delivered in your class. *On the basis of your audience analysis of your class, what would be a reasonable goal to achieve? What goal would be unreasonable? Why?*

Figure 14.1 The Persuasion Continuum

Any movement along the continuum would be considered a result of persuasion.

Guidelines for Persuasive Speaking

14.2 **Explain the guidelines for persuasive speaking.**

You can become more successful in strengthening or changing attitudes or beliefs and in moving your listeners to action by following these guidelines for persuasive speaking.

Focus on Your Audience

Begin constructing your persuasive speech with knowledge about your specific audience. What will work with one audience will not work with another; appeals to increase salaries for teaching will probably prove effective with teachers but may not do so well with homeowners who feel overtaxed.

If you show your audience that you share with them important attitudes, beliefs, and values, you'll clearly advance your persuasive goal. For example, if you know your listeners are concerned with helping the homeless, you might share your own experiences in working at a homeless shelter. Similarities of cultural, educational, or social background may also help you identify yourself with your audience. But beware of insincere or dishonest attempts at identification: These are likely to backfire and create problems, so avoid even implying similarities between you and your audience that don't exist.

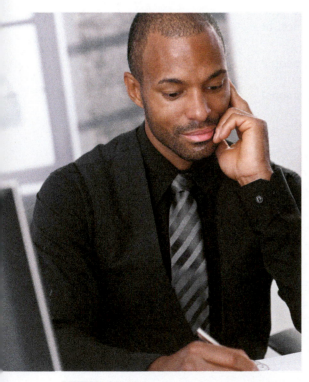

VIEWPOINTS: Gender And Persuasion
You're planning to give a speech urging more conscientious recycling to two separate audiences. One audience will be composed solely of women and the other of men. Otherwise the audience members will be similar: college-educated professionals about 30 years old. *In what ways would you make the two speeches differ? What general principles or assumptions about gender are you making as you differentiate these two speeches?*

Ask for Reasonable Amounts of Change

Persuasion is most effective when it strives for small changes and works over a period of time. Put in terms of the continuum of persuasion shown in Figure 14.1, this guideline suggests that you'll be more successful if you ask for small (rather than large) movements. The greater and more important the change you want your audience to make, the more difficult your task will be. The reason is simple: Listeners demand a greater number of reasons and a lot more evidence before making big changes such as changing careers, moving to another state, or committing to an investment strategy.

When you're addressing an audience that is opposed to your position and your goal is to change their attitudes, beliefs, or values, it is especially important that you focus on small changes. Let's say, for example, that your ultimate goal is to get a pro-life group to favor abortion on demand. Obviously, this goal is too great to achieve in one speech. Therefore, you need to strive for small changes. Here, for example, is an excerpt in which the speaker tries to get a pro-life audience to agree that at least some abortions should be legal. Notice that the speaker does not state a pro-choice position but instead focuses on one situation involving abortion and attempts to get the audience to agree that in some cases abortion should be legal.

> One of the great lessons I learned in college was that most extreme positions are wrong. Most of the important truths lie somewhere between the extreme opposites. And today I want to talk with you about one of these truths. I want to talk with you about rape and the problems faced by the mother carrying a child conceived in this most violent of all violent crimes.

Anticipate Selective Exposure

As discussed in Chapter 2, perception follows the principle of **selective exposure**, which states that (1) listeners actively seek out information that supports their opinions, beliefs, values, decisions, and behaviors; and

(2) listeners actively avoid information that contradicts their existing opinions, beliefs, attitudes, values, decisions, and behaviors.

Let's say you're giving a speech on the need to reduce spending on college athletic programs. If your audience consists largely of people who agree with you, you can lead with your thesis and show them that you're on the same side. Your introduction might go something like this.

> Our college athletic program is absorbing money that we can more profitably use for the library and computer labs. Let me explain how the excessive money now going to athletic programs could be better spent in these other areas.

But if you want to persuade an audience that holds attitudes different from those you're advocating, you'll need to anticipate selective exposure and proceed inductively; that is, hold back on your thesis until you've given your evidence and argument, then relate this evidence and argument to your thesis. If you present your listeners with your thesis first, they may tune you out without giving your position a fair hearing.

> **JOURNAL**
> **COMMUNICATION CHOICE POINT**
> Countering Selective Exposure
>
> You're planning to give a persuasive speech advocating a position you know your audience is opposed to and you know that selective exposure will be operating. *What are some of the things you might say to counteract this tendency?*

Adapt to the Culture of Your Audience

Cultural distinctions become especially important in persuasion; the appeals you would use to influence one cultural group would not be the same you would use for a different group (Singh & Pereira, 2005; Hofstede, Hofstede, & Minkov, 2010). Here are a few examples of the kinds of cultural adaptations you'll find useful to consider.

- **Collectivist cultures** If addressing members of a *collectivist* culture (such as Guatemala, Panama, Venezuela, Pakistan, and China, where the group is more important than the individual), you'll need to emphasize the importance of family, loyalty (to brand names or local organizations), and national identity and pride. On the other hand, if addressing members of individualistic cultures (such as the United States, Canada, New Zealand, Italy, and Sweden, where the individual is more important than the group), you'd emphasize such themes as independence, nonconformity, and uniqueness.

- **High-power-distance cultures** With audience members from *high-power-distance* cultures (such as Malaysia, the Philippines, Russia, Suriname, and Mexico, where there are great differences in power among groups of the population), references to important and prominent people and to what they believe and advocate will prove effective. In contrast, in a low-power-distance culture (such as Austria, Denmark, Ireland, Norway, and Great Britain, where there is little distance in power between people), these appeals will prove less effective than would, say, references to or testimonials from people much like the people you want to influence.

- **Uncertainty avoidance cultures** With audience members from cultures high in *uncertainty avoidance* (such as Greece, Portugal, Russia, Poland, and Japan, where they're uncomfortable with ambiguity and uncertainty), you would present information from experts (or supported by experts) that would explain very clearly where everyone can go for information and guidance. Because these audiences also value tradition, appeals to the past will prove effective. Audiences low in uncertainty avoidance (from countries such as Singapore, Jamaica, Denmark, Hong Kong, and India) can tolerate more ambiguity, and appeals to the new and different will be more effective.

- **Long-term orientation cultures** With audience members from cultures teaching a *long-term orientation* (such as South Korea, China, Ukraine, Germany, and Russia, where the importance of future rewards is stressed), appeals to delayed rewards (for example, the values of working hard to get a promotion) will prove more effective than they would to short-term oriented cultures (such as Puerto Rico, Ghana, Egypt, Dominican Republic, and Iran, where immediate rewards are valued).

Follow a Motivated Sequence

One time-honored principle of persuasion is the **motivated sequence**, an organizational pattern in which you do five things: (1) gain attention, (2) establish a need for a change, (3) advance a proposal to satisfy the need, (4) visualize for the audience what things would be like were they to do what you suggest, and (5) move them to action (German, Gronbeck, Ehninger, & Monroe, 2013). Let's explain each in more detail.

1. **Attention** Your first step is to persuade the audience to give you their undivided attention. If you execute this step effectively, your audience should be eager to hear what you have to say. You can gain audience attention by, for example, asking a rhetorical question, referring to specific audience members, or using a dramatic or humorous story. These and other ways of gaining attention are discussed more fully in Chapter 13.

2. **Need** Second, prove to the audience that they need to learn or do something. You can establish need in three ways.
   - State the need or problem as it exists or will exist.
   - Illustrate the need with specific examples, illustrations, statistics, testimony, and other forms of support.
   - Point to how this need affects your specific listeners—for example, their financial status, career goals, or individual happiness.

   For example, in a speech to convince people in their 60s and 70s to purchase home computers, you might say the following.

3. **Satisfaction** Third, present the "solution" that satisfies the need you demonstrated in step 2. This step should convince the audience that what you are informing them about or persuading them to do will satisfy the need. You answer the question "How will the need be satisfied by what I am asking the audience to learn, believe, or do?" This step usually contains two types of information: (1) a clear statement (with examples and illustrations if necessary) of what you want the audience to learn, believe, or do; and (2) a statement of how or why what you are asking them to learn, believe, or do will lead to satisfying the need identified in step 2. For example, you might say

   You might then show your listeners, perhaps with an actual demonstration, how this would be done.

4. **Visualization** Fourth, intensify the audience's feelings or beliefs; take them beyond the present place and time and help them imagine what it would be like if the need were satisfied (with the solution suggested in step 3). You can accomplish this by (1) demonstrating the positive benefits to be derived if this advocated proposal were put into operation or (2) demonstrating the negative consequences that will occur if your plan is not followed. You could also combine the two methods and demonstrate both the positive benefits of your plan and the negative effects of the existing situation or of a competing proposal. For example, you might say something like this.

   You might then demonstrate with a specific example how they would find this information.

5. **Action** Tell the audience what they should do to satisfy the need you have identified. Your goal is to move the audience in a particular direction. Here are a few ways to accomplish this step.
   - State exactly what audience members should do.
   - Appeal to their emotions.
   - Give them guidelines for future action.

     For example:
     Or you might suggest that they consider taking an appropriate adult education course at the local community college.

Table 14.1 In a Nutshell: The Motivated Sequence as a Persuasive Strategy

Step and Purpose	Audience Question Speaker Should Answer	Ideal Audience Response	Cautions
Attention: Focus listeners' attention on you and your message.	Why should I listen? Is this worth my time?	• This sounds interesting. • Tell me more.	Make attention relevant to speech topic.
Need: Demonstrate that there is a problem that affects them.	Why do I need to know or do anything?	• Ok, I understand; there's a problem. • Something needs to be done.	Don't overdramatize the need.
Satisfaction: Show listeners how they can satisfy the need.	How can I do anything about this?	• I can change things. • I know what I can do. • I'm empowered.	Answer any objections listeners might have to your plan.
Visualization: Show listeners what the situation will be like with the need satisfied.	How would anything be different or improved?	• *Wow!* Things look a lot better this way. • That change was really needed.	Be realistic; don't visualize the situation as perfect.
Action: Urge listeners to act.	What can I do to effect this change?	• Let me sign up. • Here's my contribution. • I'll participate.	Be specific. Ask for small changes and behaviors.

Notice that if you limit your persuasive purpose to strengthening or changing attitudes or beliefs, you must go at least as far as visualization. If you aim to get your listeners to behave in a certain way, you'll need to go all the way through the action step.

Table 14.1 provides a way of looking at the motivated sequence in terms of audience responses and some cautions to observe in using the motivated sequence.

Three Types of Persuasive Speeches

14.3 Define and give examples of persuasive speeches on questions of fact, value, and policy.

Here we examine persuasive speeches on questions of fact, value, and policy and look at how you can develop appropriate theses and main points, supporting materials, and organizational pattern for such speeches. In addition see the accompanying Public Speaking Sample Assistant: Special Occasion Speeches (Largely Persuasive) on page 000.

Persuasive Speeches on Questions of Fact

Questions of fact concern what is or is not true, what does or does not exist, what did or did not happen. Some questions of fact are easily answered. These include many academic questions you're familiar with: Who was Nostradamus? When was the first satellite launched? Questions of fact also include more mundane questions: What's on television? What's Jenny's e-mail address? You can easily find answers to these questions by finding the information online or in a book or asking someone who knows the answer.

The questions of fact that persuasive speeches deal with are a bit different. Although these questions also have answers, the answers are not that easy to find and in fact may never be found. The questions concern controversial issues for which different people have

VIEWPOINTS: Organizing a Speech

Sean wants to give a speech on how to find a date on the Internet. *How might Sean use the motivated sequence? How, in brief, would Sean accomplish each of the five steps?*

different answers. Daily news reports abound in questions of fact. For example, on August 5, 2015, the online news sites such as Google, Bing, Yahoo, and the Huffington Post had news items dealing with such questions of fact as: Will Apple stock price rise or fall? Will the Iran deal be approved? Is eating spicy food good for you? Were the Ferguson protests effective? Were Kelly Osborn's comments on Latinos offensive?

THESIS AND MAIN POINTS   For a persuasive speech on a question of fact, you'll formulate a thesis based on a factual statement.

- This company has a glass ceiling for women.
- The plaintiff was slandered [or libeled or defamed].
- The death was a case of physician-assisted suicide.
- Gay men and lesbians make competent military personnel.
- Television violence leads to violent behavior in viewers.

If you were preparing a persuasive speech on, say, the first example given above, you might phrase your thesis as "This company discriminates against women." Whether or not the company does discriminate is a question of fact; clearly the company either does or does not discriminate. Whether you can prove either option, however, is another issue and the subject of your speech.

Once you've formulated your thesis, you can generate your main points by asking the simple question "How do you know this?" or "Why would you believe this is true [or factual]?" The answers to one of these questions will enable you to develop your main points. The bare bones of your speech might then look something like this.

> **General purpose:** To persuade
>
> **Specific purpose:** To persuade my listeners that this company discriminates against women
>
> **Thesis:** This company discriminates against women. (How can we tell that this company discriminates against women?)
>
> I. Women earn less than men.
> II. Women are hired less often than men.
> III. Women occupy fewer managerial positions than men.

Make sure that you clearly connect your main points to your thesis in your introduction, when introducing each of the points, and again in your summary. Don't allow the audience to forget that when women earn lower salaries than men, it directly supports the thesis that this company discriminates against women.

SUPPORT   Once you've identified your main points you can then use the supporting materials you've collected to flesh out and develop the main points. Taking the first point, you might develop it something like this.

> I. Women earn less than men.
>
>   A. Over the past five years, the average salary for editorial assistants was $6,000 less for women than it was for men.
>
>   B. Over the past five years, the entry-level salaries for women averaged $4,500 less than the entry-level salaries for men.
>
>   C. Over the past five years, the bonuses earned by women were 20 percent below the bonuses earned by men.

In a speech on questions of fact, you'd want to emphasize logical support. Facts are your best support. The more facts you have, the more persuasive you'll be in

Public Speaking Sample Assistant

SPECIAL OCCASION SPEECHES

Largely Persuasive

Sometimes a special occasion presents an opportunity for a speaker to give a speech with a persuasive message. Here are three types of special occasion speeches, with ideas to help you make them effective. For specific examples of these and other types of special occasion speeches, search YouTube or any search engine's videos.

The Speech to Secure Goodwill

The **goodwill speech** is part information and part persuasion. On the surface, the speech informs the audience about a product, company, profession, institution, or person. Beneath this surface, however, lies a more persuasive purpose: to heighten the image of a person, product, or company—to create a more positive attitude toward this person or thing. Many speeches of goodwill have a further persuasive purpose: to get the audience ultimately to change their behavior toward the person, product, or company.

A special type of goodwill speech is the speech of self-justification, in which the speaker seeks to justify his or her actions to the audience. In securing goodwill, whether for another person or for yourself, consider the following suggestions.

- Demonstrate the contributions that deserve goodwill.
- Establish credibility.
- Don't be obvious. The effective goodwill speech looks, on the surface, very much like an objective informative speech. It will not appear to ask for goodwill, except on close analysis.

The Commencement Speech

The **commencement speech** is designed to congratulate and inspire recent graduates and is often intended to mark the transition from school to the next stage in life. When giving a commencement speech, consider the following.

- Organize the speech in a temporal pattern, beginning with the past, commenting on the present, and projecting into the future.
- Do your research. Learn SOMETHING about the school, the student body, the goals and ambitions of the graduates, and integrate these into your speech.
- Be brief. Recognize that your audience has other things on their minds.
- Congratulate the graduates, parents, and instructors.
- Offer the graduates some kind of motivational message, some guidance.
- Offer your own good wishes to the graduates.

The Speech of Inspiration

The **speech of inspiration** is designed to raise the spirits of an audience, to inspire them. Many religious speeches are of this type. Similarly, speeches that corporate leaders give to stockholders when introducing a new product or a new CEO, for example, would be designed to inspire investors. In speaking to inspire, follow these guidelines.

- Demonstrate your oneness with the audience. Try to show in some way that you and your listeners have significant similarities.
- Demonstrate your own intense involvement, the kind of intensity you want your audience to show.
- Stress emotional appeals. Inspiring an audience has to do more with emotions than with logic.
- Stress the positive—especially at the end of your speech, which should conclude on a positive note. Inspirational speeches are always positive.

dealing with questions of fact. For example, the more evidence you can find that women earn less than men, the more convincing you will be in proving that women do in fact earn less and, ultimately, that women are discriminated against.

Use the most recent materials possible. The more recent your materials, the more relevant they will be to the present time and the more persuasive they're likely to be. Note that, in this example, if you were to say that in 1980 women earned on average $13,000 less than men, it would be meaningless in proving that the company discriminates against women *now*.

ORGANIZATION Speeches on questions of fact fit clearly into a topical organizational pattern, in which each reason for your thesis is given approximately equal weight. Notice, for example, that the outline for this "discrimination" example uses a topical order: All three facts (women earn less, women are hired less often, women occupy fewer managerial positions) pointing to discrimination are treated as equal main points (I, II, and III).

Persuasive Speeches on Questions of Value

Questions of value concern what people consider good or bad, moral or immoral, just or unjust. On August 5, 2015, online news sites published items dealing with such questions of value as: Is suicide justifiable? Is President Obama's environmental initiative a good one? Is the death penalty moral? Can hunting wild animals for sport be morally justified? Should gay boy scout leaders be accepted?

Speeches on questions of value will usually seek to strengthen audiences' existing attitudes, beliefs, or values. This is true of much religious and political speaking: People who listen to religious speeches, for example, usually are already believers and are willing to listen; these speeches strive to strengthen the beliefs and values the people already hold. Speeches that seek to change audience values are much more difficult to construct, because most people resist change. When you try to get people to change their values or beliefs, you're fighting an uphill (though not necessarily impossible) battle.

Be sure that you define clearly the specific value on which you're focusing. For example, let's say that you're developing a speech to persuade high school students to attend college. You want to stress that college is of value, but what type of value do you focus on? The financial value (e.g., that college graduates earn more money than high school graduates)? The social value (e.g., that college is a lot of fun and a great place to make friends)? The intellectual value (e.g., that college will broaden your view of the world and make you a more critical and creative thinker)? Once you clarify the type of value on which you'll focus, you'll find it easier to develop the relevant points. You'll also find it easier to locate appropriate supporting materials.

THESIS AND MAIN POINTS Theses devoted to questions of value might look something like this.

- The death penalty is unjustifiable.
- Bullfighting is inhumane.
- Discrimination on the basis of affectional orientation is wrong.
- Human cloning is morally justified.
- College athletics minimize the importance of academics.

As with speeches on questions of fact, you can generate the main points for a speech on a question of value by asking a strategic question of your thesis, such as "Why is this good?" or "Why is this immoral?" For example, you can take the first thesis given above and ask, "Why is the death penalty unjustifiable?" The answers to this question will give you the speech's main points. The body of your speech might then look something like this.

General purpose: To persuade

Specific purpose: To persuade my listeners that the death penalty is unjustifiable

Thesis: The death penalty is unjustifiable. (Why is the death penalty unjustifiable?)

   I. The criminal justice system can make mistakes.

  II. The death penalty constitutes cruel and unusual punishment.

 III. No one has the moral right to take another's life.

SUPPORT   Once you've identified your main points, you can then use the supporting materials you've collected to develop the main points. For example, to show that mistakes have been made (your first main point), you might itemize three or four high-profile cases in which people were put to death and later, through DNA, found to have been innocent.

At times, and with certain topics, it may be useful to identify the standards you would use to judge something moral, justified, fair, or good. For example, in the "bullfighting is inhumane" speech, you might devote your first main point to defining when an action can be considered inhumane. In this case, your main points and subpoints might look like this.

I. An inhumane act has two qualities.
   A. It is cruel and painful.
   B. It serves no human necessity.
II. Bullfighting is inhumane.
   A. It is cruel and painful.
   B. It serves no necessary function.

Notice that in the example of capital punishment the speaker aims to strengthen or change the listeners' beliefs about the death penalty. The speaker is not asking the audience to do anything about capital punishment, but merely to believe that it's not justified. However, you might also follow up your goal of changing their beliefs by persuading them to take some action—for example, to support an anti–death-penalty politician, to vote for or against a particular proposition, or to join an organization fighting against the death penalty.

ORGANIZATION   Like speeches on questions of fact, speeches on questions of value often lend themselves to topical organization. For example, the speech on capital punishment outlined earlier uses a topical order. But within this topical order there is another level of organization that begins with those items on which there is least disagreement or opposition and that moves on to the items that your listeners are likely to see very differently. It's likely that even those in favor of the death penalty would agree that mistakes can be made; in fact, they probably would be willing to accept evidence that mistakes have been made, especially if you cite reliable statistical evidence and expert testimony. By starting with this issue, you secure initial agreement and can use that as a basis for approaching aspects on which you and the audience are more likely to disagree.

Persuasive Speeches on Questions of Policy

When you move beyond focusing on values to urging your audience to do something about an issue, you've broached **questions of policy**. For example, in a speech designed to convince your listeners that bullfighting is inhumane, you'd be focusing on a question of value. But, if you were to urge that bullfighting should therefore be declared illegal, you'd be focusing on a question of policy. Items that focused on questions of policy on the online news sites for August 5, 2015 included: What should California's laws be on the death penalty? What should government policy be toward suicide? What woman should appear on the new US currency? What should be policy of the Boy Scouts of America be in regard to gay scout leaders? Should Whole Foods have removed asparagus water from their shelves?

Questions of policy concern what should be done, what procedures should be adopted, what laws should be changed—in short, what policy should be followed. In some speeches you may want to

VIEWPOINTS: Fact, Value, and Policy in the News

Examine one issue of an online news page for the city in which you live. *What are the questions of fact, value, and policy that this news outlet features? Now, examine an online news page from a foreign country—Google will translate for you—for the same types of questions? Do they differ? If so, in what ways?*

defend a specific policy; in others you may wish to argue that a current policy should be discontinued.

THESIS AND MAIN POINTS   Persuasive speeches frequently revolve around questions of policy and may use theses such as the following.

- Smoking in municipal parks should be banned.
- Facebook's privacy settings should be changed.
- Colleges should not allow guns on campus.
- Abortion should be available on demand.
- Medical marijuana should be legalized.

As you can tell from these examples, questions of policy almost invariably involve questions of values. For example, the argument that hate speech should be banned at colleges is based on the value judgment that hate speech is wrong. To argue for a zero tolerance policy on guns in schools implies that you think it's wrong for students or faculty to carry guns to school.

You can develop your main points on a question of policy by asking a strategic question of your thesis. With policy issues, the question will be "Why should this policy be adopted?" or "Why should this policy be discontinued?" or "Why is this policy better than what we now have?" Taking our first example, we might ask, "Why should smoking be banned from municipal parks?" From the answers to this question, you would develop your main points, which might look something like this.

General purpose: To persuade

Specific purpose: To persuade my audience to support the no-smoking ban

Thesis: Smoking in municipal parks should be banned.

 I. Smoking creates dangers for park land.
 II. Smoking creates health hazards for park users.
 III. Smoking creates litter problems.

SUPPORT   Once you've identified your main points, you're ready to incorporate the supporting materials you've collected to develop these points. For example, you would further develop each main point with supporting materials that would convince your audience that smoking should be banned from municipal parks. Taking the first main point as an illustration, you might develop it something like this.

 I. Smoking creates dangers for park land.
  A. The forest fire in Montana was caused by a cigarette.
  B. Japanese cherry trees in Wisconsin were destroyed by careless smokers.
  C. Animals in numerous parks lost their homes.

JOURNAL
COMMUNICATION CHOICE POINT
Selecting Arguments

You want to prepare a persuasive speech on a question of policy, arguing that owners of psychic services should be prosecuted for fraud. *What are some of your options for persuading your audience to accept your thesis?*

In some speeches on questions of policy, you might simply want your listeners to agree that the policy you're advocating is a good one. In other cases you might want them to do something about the policy—to vote for a particular candidate, to take vitamin C, to write to their elected officials, to participate in a walkathon, to wear an AIDS awareness ribbon, or to vote against smoking in parks in the upcoming referendum.

ORGANIZATION   Speeches on questions of policy may be organized in a variety of ways. For example, if you're comparing two policies, consider the comparison-and-contrast method. If the existing policy is doing harm, consider using a cause–effect pattern. If your proposed policy is designed to solve a problem, consider the problem–solution pattern. In the smoking in parks example, a simple topical pattern was used.

Table 14.2 presents a brief summary of these questions of fact, value, and policy.

Table 14.2 In a Nutshell: Questions of Fact, Value, and Policy

Questions and Purposes	Examples	Questions Audience May Want Answered
Questions of Fact To persuade listeners that something is true or false	• Higgins is guilty (not guilty). • What he did was criminal (legal). • The stock market will go much higher (much lower).	• Is this the most likely interpretation of the issue? • Are other, more likely, explanations possible? • How do we know that this is true or that this is false?
Questions of Value To persuade listeners in the value of something, that something is good, moral, or just	• Higgins deserves the chair (to go free). • Universal health care is essential (not essential). • The war is just (unjust).	• Why is this good or just or the right thing to do? Are there alternatives that would be more just or fairer?
Questions of Policy To persuade listeners that this is the policy to adopt or not adopt	• The verdict must be guilty (not guilty). • Plan B needs to be enacted (discarded). • The war needs to be continued (discontinued).	• Might there be better courses of action to follow? • Are there downsides to this course of action?

Supporting Materials

14.4 Explain the types of and the fallacies of logical, emotional, and credibility appeals.

In addition to the supporting materials described in Chapter 13—examples, testimony, numerical data, and definitions, for example—three forms of support are of special importance in persuasive speeches: logical appeals, emotional appeals, and credibility appeals. These forms of support have been an essential part of public speaking for over 2,000 years and were known in the rhetoric of Greece and Rome as *logos*, *pathos*, and *ethos*. Each of these, unfortunately, can also be misused; such fallacies are noted for each of these three forms of support.

Logical Appeals

When you use **logical appeals**—when you argue on the basis of logic supported by reliable facts and evidence—your listeners are more likely to remain persuaded over time and to resist counterarguments that may come up in the future (Petty & Wegener, 1998). There are three main ways of using logical appeals: (1) specific instances, (2) causes and effects, and (3) sign.

REASONING FROM SPECIFIC INSTANCES AND GENERALIZATIONS When **reasoning from specific instances** (or examples), you examine several specific instances and then conclude something about the whole. This form of reasoning, known as *induction*, is useful when you want to develop a general principle or conclusion but cannot examine the whole. For example, you sample a few communication courses and conclude something about communication courses in general; you visit several Scandinavian cities and conclude something about the whole of Scandinavia. In reasoning from specific instances, be sure to examine a sufficient number of instances. Three general guidelines will help you determine how much is enough.

• The larger the group you want your conclusion to cover, the greater the number of specific instances you should examine. If you wish to draw conclusions about members of an entire country or culture, you'll have to examine a considerable number of people before drawing even tentative conclusions.

"In the interest of streamlining the judicial process, we'll skip the evidence and go directly to sentencing."
J.B. Handelsman/The New Yorker Collection/The Cartoon Bank

- The greater the diversity of items in the class, the more specific instances you will have to examine. Pieces of pasta in boiling water are all about the same; thus, sampling one usually tells you something about all the others. On the other hand, college courses are probably very different from one another, so valid conclusions about the entire range of college courses will require a much larger sample.

- Beware of anecdotal evidence. Often you'll hear people use anecdotes to "prove" a point: "Women are like that; I have three sisters." "That's the way Japanese managers are; I've seen plenty of them." One reason this type of "evidence" is inadequate is that it overgeneralizes on the basis of too few observations. A second reason is that one person's observations may be unduly clouded by his or her own attitudes and beliefs.

REASONING FROM CAUSES AND EFFECTS   When **reasoning from causes and effects**, you may go in either of two directions: (1) You may reason from cause to effect—for example, *Smoking* (the cause) *contributes to lung cancer* (the effect)—or (2) you may reason from effect to cause: for example, *Low reading scores among elementary school children* (the effect) *are due to poverty* (the cause). In order to establish a cause–effect connection, you need to prove that possible causes other than the one you're postulating are not producing the effect. And so you'd need to determine whether causes other than smoking may contribute to lung cancer, or whether factors other than poverty contribute to low reading scores. Usually you won't be able to rule out *all* other factors, but it's important to demonstrate that the factors you are identifying are the main contributors. Scientific studies on the effects of smoking on cancer rates and the effects of poverty on reading scores would enable you to establish these cause–effect relationships.

You'd also want to demonstrate that the causation is in the direction you say it is. If two things occur together, it's often difficult to determine which is the cause and which is the effect. For example, a lack of interpersonal intimacy and a lack of self-confidence often occur in the same person but it's not clear which is the cause and which is the effect or even if a causal relationship exists.

REASONING FROM SIGN   When **reasoning from sign**, you may draw a conclusion on the basis of the presence of clues or symptoms that frequently occur together. Medical diagnosis is a good example of reasoning by sign. The general procedure is simple: If a sign and an object, event, or condition are frequently paired, the presence of the sign is taken as proof of the presence of the object, event, or condition. For example, fatigue, extreme thirst, and overeating serve as signs of hyperthyroidism, because they frequently accompany the condition.

You'd also want to show that other signs cannot logically point to the same conclusion. In the thyroid example, extreme thirst could be brought on by any number of factors. Similarly, the fatigue and the overeating could be attributed to other causes. Yet, taken together, the three signs seem to point to thyroid problems as a reasonable diagnosis. Generally, the more signs that point toward the conclusion, the more confidence you can have that it's valid.

LISTENING TO THE FALLACIES OF LOGICAL APPEALS   At the same time that you'll want to reason logically from specific instances, causes and effects, and sign, you'll want to avoid the fallacies of argument: persuasive tactics that have the feel of real arguments and seem to involve logical reasoning but are actually logically unsound and misleading. These fallacies appear to address the issues but really don't. Here are a few such fallacies that you'll want to avoid as a speaker and recognize as a listener (Lee & Lee 1972, 1995; Pratkanis & Aronson, 1991; Herrick, 2004).

- **Appealing to authority as proof** often takes the form of passing someone off as an authority when the person actually has little authority, expertise, or knowledge in the subject under discussion. Sometimes this fallacy takes the form of "experts say …" without telling you who the experts are. In still another form, it consists of using an authority's opinion instead of or as a substitute for facts and evidence. In listening to appeals to authority, ask yourself: Does the authority offer proof or reliable evidence? If so, then this is not fallacious reasoning. Is this pure opinion? If so, then ask: Is this person is a recognized authority in the pertinent field? If yes, then the argument is worth listening to. If not, then the argument may be logically suspect.

- **Appealing to numbers as truth** (in Latin *ad numerum*—literally, *to the numbers*—also referred to as *ad populum*, literally *to the people*), known as the bandwagon fallacy, argues that truth is determined by an idea's popularity. The best example is what was a near-universal belief before Columbus and at the time of Galileo, that the world was flat and that the sun revolved around the earth. A majority does not make a belief true. People (even all people) can be and have been wrong. In listening to argument by the numbers, ask yourself: Do these people have evidence for thinking as they do? If they have, then examine the evidence. If they have good reasons instead, then examine the logic of their reasoning and ask yourself if it makes sense.

- **Sliding down the slippery slope** involves the assumption that one event (i.e., the one the person is arguing against) will lead to another event that everyone agrees would be undesirable. In some cases, the connection between one event and another event is *assumed* to be direct (e.g., smoking pot will lead to smoking crack). In other cases, the connection between the original event and the unpleasant ultimate event is made through a series of linkages (e.g., smoking pot will lead to smoking crack, which will lead to more robberies, which will lead to general lawlessness). In listening to arguments implying a slippery slope, ask yourself: What evidence is there for the influence of one event on another event? How likely is it that the original event will cause the disastrous final event? As the chain of events gets longer, the connection becomes more suspect.

Emotional Appeals

Emotional appeals, often called **motivational appeals**, are appeals to your listeners' feelings, needs, desires, and wants, and are extremely powerful in persuasion. When you use emotional appeals, you appeal to those forces that motivate people to develop, change, or strengthen attitudes or ways of behaving. Developed more than 30 years ago, one of the most useful analyses of human motives remains Abraham Maslow's fivefold hierarchy of needs, reproduced in Figure 14.2 (Maslow, 1970; Benson & Dundis, 2003; Hanley & Abell, 2002; Kiel, 1999). If you can appeal to the needs the audience wants to fulfill, then you're likely to be persuasive.

- **Physiological needs** In many parts of the world, and even parts of the United States, people's basic physiological needs are not fully met, and thus are powerful motivating forces. In such circumstances the speaker who promises to meet fundamental physiological needs is the one the people will follow.

- **Safety needs** People who do not have their basic safety and freedom-from-fear needs met will be motivated by appeals to security, protection, and freedom from physical and psychological harm. You see this need addressed in advertisements for burglar protection devices for home and car and in political speeches promising greater police protection in schools.

- **Belonging and love needs** For most people, friendship and love relationships occupy a considerable amount of time and energy, especially, perhaps, among college students. If you can teach your audience how to be loved, how to find a partner, or how to be more popular, they'll be not only attentive but also grateful.

- **Self-esteem needs** We all want to see ourselves as self-confident, worthy, and contributing human beings. Speeches of the "you're the greatest" type, never seem to lack receptive and suggestible audiences. Self-esteem is raised by success (for example, a good grade or a promotion at work) and if your speech can tell people how to succeed in what they set out to do, you'll probably have an active and receptive audience.

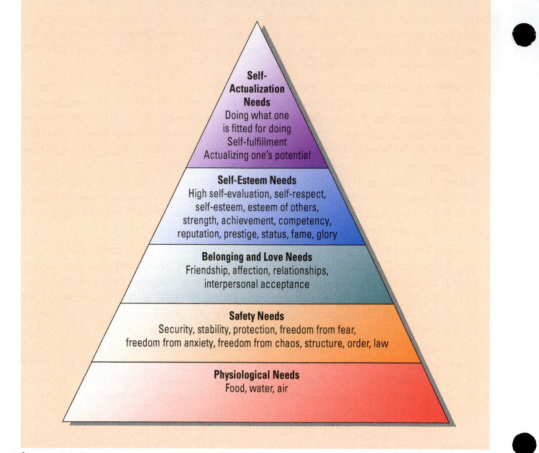

Figure 14.2 Maslow's Hierarchy of Needs

From which of these motives would your class members be convinced that campus violence is a real problem? Which might move them to donate their used books to students who can't afford them?

SOURCE: From Abraham Maslow, *Motivation and Personality*, 3rd ed., edited by Robert D. Frager and James Fadiman. Copyright © 1987. Printed and Electronically reproduced by permission of Pearson Education, Inc., Upper Saddle River, New Jersey.

- **Self-Actualization Needs** Each of us has a desire to self-actualize, to become what we feel we're fit for. If you see yourself as a poet, you must write poetry. If you see yourself as a teacher, you must teach. Appeals to self-actualization needs—to people's yearning "to be the best they can be"—encourage listeners to strive for their highest ideals and are welcomed by many audiences.

LISTENING TO THE FALLACIES OF EMOTIONAL APPEALS Emotional appeals are all around you, urging you to do all sorts of things—usually to buy a product or to support a position or cause. As you listen to these inevitable appeals, consider the following.

- **Emotions as proof** No matter how passionate the speaker's voice or bodily movement, no matter how compelling the language, passion does not prove the case a speaker is presenting.

- **Emotional appeals as diversion** If emotional appeals are being used as a diversion, to the exclusion of argument and evidence, or if you suspect that the speaker seeks to arouse your emotions so you forget that there's no evidence, ask yourself why.

- **Appeals to pity** Be especially on the lookout for the appeal to pity. This is what logicians call *argumentum ad misericordiam*, as in "I really need your help; I tried to do the work, but I've been having terrible depression and can't concentrate."

Communicating Ethically

APPEALS TO EMOTIONS

Emotional appeals are all around. People who want to censor the Internet may appeal to parents' fears about their children's accessing pornographic materials. Those who want to restrict media portrayals of violence may appeal to people's fear of increased violence in their own communities. Here are a few questions to consider as you develop your own ethical guidelines for the use of emotional appeals.

- Is the real estate broker ethical in appealing to your desire for status?
- Is the friend who wants a favor and appeals to your desire for social approval acting ethically?
- Is the car salesperson's appeal to your desire for sexual rewards ethical?
- Is it ethical for parents to use fear appeals to exaggerate the dangers of sex or smoking pot to prevent their children from engaging in these behaviors?
- Is it ethical for parents to use fear appeals to prevent their children from interacting with people of different races or nationalities or affectional orientation?

ETHICAL CHOICE POINT

You've been asked by the PTA to address the students at your old elementary school on the values of delaying sexual relationships. *Would it be ethical to use emotional appeals to scare them so that they'll avoid sexual relationships? Would it be ethical to use the same appeals to get them to avoid associating with teens of other races? What ethical obligations do you have in using emotional appeals in these situations? What would you do?*

Credibility Appeals

Your **credibility** is the degree to which your audience regards you as a believable spokesperson. Your credibility is in the minds of your audience; if your listeners see you as competent and knowledgeable, of good character, and charismatic or dynamic, they'll find you credible (i.e., believable). As a result, you'll be more effective in changing their attitudes or in moving them to do something.

What makes a speaker credible will vary from one culture to another. In some cultures people see competence as the most important factor in, say, their choice of a teacher for their preschool children. In other cultures the most important factor might be the goodness or moral tone of the teacher or perhaps the reputation of the teacher's family. At the same time, every culture may define each of the factors of credibility differently. For example, "character" may mean following the rules of a specific religion in some cultures, but following your individual conscience in others. The Quran, the Torah, and the New Testament will be ascribed very different levels of credibility depending on the religious beliefs of the audience. And this will be true even when all three books say essentially the same thing.

Before reading any more about the ways to establish your credibility, you may wish to take the self-test "How Credible Are You?"

COMPETENCE To demonstrate your **competence**, show your listeners that you are knowledgeable and thoroughly familiar with your topic. The more knowledge and expertise the audience attributes to you, the more likely the audience will believe you, just as you are more likely to believe a teacher or doctor if you think he or she is knowledgeable about the subject at hand.

VIEWPOINTS: The Persuasiveness Of Blogs

Visit a few blogs and analyze them in terms of their use of logical versus emotional support. *Which mode of support dominates? Or, do different types of blogs use different types of support? How are blogs like persuasive speeches? How are they different?*

Test Yourself

HOW CREDIBLE ARE YOU?

Respond to each of the following phrases to indicate how you think members of your class see you when you deliver a speech. Use the following scale.

5 = definitely true; **4** = probably true; **3** = neither true nor untrue; **2** = probably untrue; and **1** = definitely untrue

The audience/class generally sees me as someone who is:

____ 1. knowledgeable
____ 2. a thorough researcher
____ 3. informed about the subject matter
____ 4. fair in the presentation of material (i.e., evidence and argument)

____ 5. concerned with the audience's needs
____ 6. honest; unlikely to bend the truth
____ 7. assertive in personal style
____ 8. enthusiastic about the topic and in general
____ 9. active rather than passive

This test focuses on the three qualities of credibility—competence, character, and charisma—and is based on a large body of research (see McCroskey, 2006; Riggio, 1987). Items 1 to 3 refer to perceived competence: How capable do you seem to the audience? Items 4 to 6 refer to character: Does the audience see you as a good and moral person? Items 7 to 9 refer to charisma: Does the audience see you as dynamic and active? Total scores will range from a high of 45 to a low of 9. If you scored relatively high (around 32 or higher), then you feel your audience sees you as credible. If you scored relatively low (below 27), then you feel your audience sees you as lacking in credibility.

"I've never actually stormed a castle, but I've taken a bunch of siege-management courses."
Danny Shanahan/The New Yorker Collection/The Cartoon Bank

JOURNAL
COMMUNICATION CHOICE POINT
Establishing Credibility

You're planning a speech against free agency in professional sports. The problem is that you're a woman and you suspect that the men in your audience will not perceive you as credible, despite your knowing more about professional sports than any other person in the room. *What are some options you have to establishing your credibility? What are some of the things you might say?*

One way to demonstrate your competence is simply to tell listeners about it. Let the audience know of any special experience or training that qualifies you to speak on your topic. Another way is to cite a variety of research sources. Make it clear to your audience that you've thoroughly researched your topic. Do this by mentioning some of the books you've read, the people you've interviewed, and/or the articles you've consulted.

CHARACTER An audience will judge your credibility in terms of what they perceive is your **character**—whether they see you as someone who is honest and whom they can trust. One way to establish your moral character is to stress fairness. For example, stress that you've examined both sides of the issue (if indeed you have). Also, make it clear to the audience that you're interested in their welfare rather than seeking self-gain. If the audience feels that you're "out for yourself," they'll justifiably question your credibility. Tell your audience how the new legislation will reduce *their* taxes, how recycling will improve *their* community, how a knowledge of sexual harassment will make *their* workplace more comfortable. This display of high moral character has even been found to be financially profitable. For example, CEO's who are rated as "always" displaying integrity, responsibility, forgiveness, and compassion delivered better financial results than those who don't or do so only "about half the time" (Kiel, 2015).

CHARISMA Another quality that establishes credibility is **charisma**, a combination of your personality and dynamism as seen by the audience. An audience will perceive you as credible if they like you and see you as friendly and pleasant rather than aloof and reserved. Similarly, audiences favor the dynamic speaker over the hesitant, nonassertive speaker.

One way to stress charisma is to demonstrate a positive outlook. Show the audience that you have a positive orientation to the public speaking situation and to the entire speaker–audience encounter. Stress your pleasure at addressing the audience. Stress hope rather than despair, happiness rather than sadness. Demonstrate enthusiasm. Be emphatic. Use language that's vivid and concrete rather than colorless and vague. Use gestures that are clear and decisive rather than random and hesitant. Demonstrate a firm commitment to the position you're advocating.

LISTENING TO THE FALLACIES OF CREDIBILITY APPEALS AND CHARACTER ATTACKS As with logical or emotional appeals, become conscious of fallacious strategies that focus on attacking the person. Be alert for the following fallacies in the speeches of others, and eliminate them from your own reasoning.

- **Personal interest attacks** may attempt to disqualify someone from having a legitimate point of view because he or she isn't directly affected by an issue or proposal or doesn't have firsthand knowledge; for example, a speaker might dismiss an argument on abortion merely because it was made by a man. This type of fallacy may also attempt to disqualify someone because he or she will benefit in some way from a proposal. For example, arguing that someone is rich, middle class, or poor and thus will benefit greatly from a proposed tax cut does not mean that the argument for the tax cut is invalid. The legitimacy of an argument can be judged only on the basis of the evidence and reasoning presented.

- **Character attacks,** often referred to as *ad hominem* arguments, involve accusing another person (usually an opponent) of some wrongdoing or of some character flaw. The purpose is to discredit the person or to divert attention from the issue under discussion. Arguments such as "How can we support a candidate who has smoked pot [or avoided the military]?" or "Do you want to believe someone who has been unfaithful on more than one occasion?" are often heard in political discussions but probably have little to do with the logic of the argument.

- **Name-calling** occurs when the speaker gives an idea, a group of people, or a political philosophy a bad name ("bigoted," "soft on terrorism") to try to get listeners to condemn an idea without analyzing the argument and evidence. The opposite of name-calling is the use of "glittering generalities," in which the speaker tries to make you accept some idea by associating it with things you value highly ("democracy," "free speech," "academic freedom"). By using these "virtue words," the speaker tries to get you to ignore the evidence and simply approve of the idea.

Public Speaking Sample Assistant

AN EXCELLENT PERSUASIVE SPEECH

This excellent persuasive speech was constructed and delivered by Farrah Bara from the University of Texas at Austin. In explaining her interest in the topic, Farrah said "Growing up a Muslim in a post-9/11 American has certainly provided me with a very different outlook on the racism and hatred faced by many Muslims today. After reading a Human Rights Watch report on the FBI Entrapment Program, I felt that the issue was very important to talk about because awareness and activism are key to true justice for the millions of Muslims that live in this country." Farrah's biggest challenge was "convincing people that FBI Entrapment is more than just a conspiracy theory. I think people want to believe that the systems that are designed to protect us *are* protecting us. We want to believe that our law enforcement is good, that racial and religious injustice is something people do, not something a massive institution like the FBI engages in. So having to shatter that image of "justice" did create quite a challenge in the construction of this speech."

SPEECH	COMMENTS

The FBI Entrapment Program

What do you think of this title? Does it make you want to listen to this speech? What expectations does this title set up?

INTRODUCTION

As you'll see, this speech, like the informative speech presented earlier, has a fairly long introduction and a short conclusion.

On the tenth anniversary of 9/11, 26-year-old Rezwan Ferdaus aimed an explosive drone at the U.S. capitol. *The Guardian* of September 29, 2011, reports, moments before the attack, the FBI flooded the scene, arrested their culprit, and released a statement calling his capture a success. This, they said, is exactly how counterterrorism is supposed to work. This is what American taxpayers pay $3.3 billion for the FBI to do.

This speech deals with a pretty powerful and potentially explosive subject or topic and is sure to be one with which some will agree and some will disagree.
The speaker dives directly into the topic with a particularly effective attention getter—a single dramatic example.

But the April 23, 2013, *Florida Center for Investigative Reporting* reveals, Rezwan lives with his parents in Boston, has no source of income, and suffers from mental disabilities so severe, he couldn't have planned this crime; constructed a military-like drone; or even figured out how to buy a plane ticket to Washington. No, the real mastermind was a man named Khalil, who should be facing the 17-year prison sentence, except for one small technicality—Khalil works for the FBI.

Here the speaker builds her case for dismantling the entrapment program by detailing some major abuses committed under this program.
The information presented here is likely to be new to most listeners and some listeners are likely to take objection to this. But, the speaker effectively cites two powerful sources—and more later—to give what she's saying credibility.

The July 20, 2014, *New York Post* reveals Rezwan's story is part of the FBI Entrapment Program, which frames innocent Muslims, as terrorists. In fact, of the 500 US terrorism prosecutions since 9/11, the July 21, 2014, Human Rights Watch reports half were planned by the FBI, funded by the FBI, to be miraculously stopped by the FBI moments before the crime takes place. The FBI Entrapment Program—our leading counterterror strategy—is blatantly unconstitutional and terrorizes Americans, while we pay the FBI for what we think is security.

Here the speaker connects the specific example with the general issue of FBI entrapment. Often, beginning speakers fail to make the connection between the example and the idea the example is designed to support.

This program needs to end.

This is the thesis of the speech: The FBI entrapment program must be stopped. The specific purpose of the speech is also clear: to persuade listeners to actively support the ending of the FBI Entrapment program. The speaker offers specific suggestions later in the speech.

Let's first determine why it exists, next uncover the consequences, and finally develop solutions so that we can stop a program that willingly turns the law-abiding citizens into terrorists.

Here is a detailed orientation that identifies the three major parts of the speech (why it exists, the consequences of the program, and solutions to stop the program). The speech follows a problem solution pattern where the first main point explains the reasons for the program, the second establishes the problem, and the third point addresses the solutions.
In outline the speech would look something like this:
  I. Reasons for program
  II. Consequences of the program
  III. Solutions to the problem

BODY

Entrapment follows this routine: The FBI targets a person, sends an informant to befriend them, then watches as the informant pressures the target and orchestrates their arrest. This happens for two reasons: the illusion of counterterror and the presumption of guilt.

The FBI website notes, 67% of FBI agents are devoted to counterterror—it's literally their job—which is why the first reason entrapment happens is because the FBI wants to look like it's doing its job. Back in 2004, the 9/11 *Commission Report* detailed, after 9/11, we were thinking about dismantling the FBI completely. Instead, we gave them a second chance. And with it, as a June 2013 FBI report reveals, an 84% budget increase. So if the FBI needs anything, it's results. That's where entrapment comes in. A September 2013 report by the ACLU explains it's hard to tell the difference between a real terror plot and a fake one, which is the point—give the illusion that our counterterror program is fine. And for the FBI, entrapment becomes synonymous to a job well done.

It seems like entrapment should just be taken to court. And it has. In fact, in 1915, the federal judiciary recognized entrapment defense, which requires proof of FBI involvement and proof the defendant wouldn't naturally commit the crime.

The next reason entrapment happens is because we think Muslim Americans would naturally commit terrorism, failing the second criteria of entrapment defense. As the May 2014 *National Coalition to Protect Civil Freedoms* explains, 94% arbitrarily profile. And so to date, every person filing for entrapment, under terrorism, has failed. Additionally, entrapment is an affirmative defense, the 2014 *Washington University Law Review* explains this means if you're accused of terrorism, you are guilty, unless you can prove yourself innocent.

In 2007, the FBI approached Shahwar Siraj with a request—to place these bombs at the 34th Street Subway Station. The July 21, 2014, *Guardian* explains, Siraj, a middle-aged man with autism, replied "I need to ask my mom's permission first." He never got his mom's permission and never took the bombs, but the FBI arrested him anyway, embodying entrapment's effects: cyclical rights violations and unstable national security.

First, the FBI routinely abuses its power. The December 27, 2013, *Huffington Post* details in 2012, FBI informants committed 5,939 crimes, an increase of 5% from the year before. Former informant Craig Monteilh tells the March 4, 2015, *Daily Mail* as part of the entrapment program, Monteilh's "patriotic duty" included having sex with whatever Muslim woman he wanted, yet as Monteilh himself noted, "They were not espousing terrorist rhetoric, but I was still spying on them." We are so afraid of another 9/11, we continue to empower the very organization that abuses Americans. This past December, the ACLU reported, when President Obama approved guidelines to reduce racial profiling, he included a loophole that exempts the FBI.

Here the speaker clarifies how entrapment works as a preface to explaining why it exists.
This part of the speech in outline might look like this.
   I. Reasons for the program
      A. Illusion of counterterrorism
      B. Presumption of guilt

This is the speaker first main point and explains why the entrapment program is in effect. The first reason given here is that the FBI needs to make it seem they're effective and doing their job.

The speaker answers a question many listeners might be asking themselves.

Here is the second reason why this program continues in operation—people assume that Muslim Americans would normally commit acts of terrorism.

This is a particularly dramatic example of entrapment and especially of its injustice and ineffectiveness. It offers a specific example in support of the assumption the FBI makes about Muslims. In addition, the example leads directly into the second major point: the consequences of this program.
In outline the speech would look like this.
   II. Consequences of the program
      A. Abuse of power
      B. Unstable national security

Here the speaker addresses the first of the consequences: the abuse of power and of Americans.

Second, entrapment hurts national security because it disengages Muslim communities and wastes resources. The March 9, 2012, New York *Daily News* explains, since 2001, Muslims have become less cooperative with law enforcement. And so the people most capable of stopping terrorism, stopped trying. In a December 13, 2014, personal interview, investigative journalist Trevor Aaronson explained the idea of national security is a joke. Back in 2011, Russia warned Boston FBI agents of a man they thought was a terrorist. And Boston told them they were too busy. Too busy entrapping the mentally disabled Rezwan Ferdaus. Too busy and the FBI completely missed the lead up to the Boston Marathon bombing.

The FBI does not make stopping entrapment easy. Take Tarek Mehanna's 2012 trial. The previously cited *Human Rights Watch* explains, prosecutors showed 28 images of the World Trade Center burning, which had nothing to do with the trial. In an age where the FBI's words are taken for granted, we've got to take some precautions: legal aid and awareness.

First, we must fix a legal system that presumes Muslims guilty. Thankfully, the Constitutional Law Center for Muslims in America wants to do exactly that. When I asked Charles Swift, founder of the Center, on March 10, 2015 what we can do to help, he reminded me, the collegiate community is where revolutions ignite. As a mass group of people, we should help fund this Law Center, committed to legally combat the presumption of guilt. After the round, pick up a pledge card, fill it out, and hand it right back. Also, after talking to Muslim leaders in my community, they told me they'd double any amount of money we raise right now because as impossible as it seems to stop the FBI, our collective effort is the only thing standing in the FBI's way.

Second, the FBI wants to create the illusion of effective counterterror. To demystify that illusion, we've got to start spreading awareness. So pick up a folder. Think of it as your education toolbox, because it includes op-eds, case studies, articles, lists of books, and even a guide to write letters to the entrapped. Fifty years from now, those who remember 9/11 will remember it by the phrase "Never Forget." But those who remember entrapment will recall how a government replaced basic decency with fear. How thousands have been lashed out against for attacks they did not commit. How we forgot Muslims died on 9/11 too—victims who should not be forgotten because their skin is a different color or because their god has a different name.

CONCLUSION

The second consequence is that it hurts national security by disengaging the Muslim community and wastes resources that could be deployed elsewhere. The news article and the personal interview with an investigative journalist support the speaker's assertion that this discourages Muslims from stopping terrorism and that the FBI is in fact wasting resources.

Here the speaker introduces her third main point—the solution, which has two parts: legal aid and awareness. In outline this part of the speech would look like this.
III. Solutions to the problem
    A. Legal aid
    B. Awareness

Here the speaker details how the legal system must be fixed and offers the listeners a specific way to help. Notice too the speaker's personal involvement she talked with a key person.

Here is the second part of the solution—awareness—and again asks the listeners to do something specific. The folder offers substantial evidence that the speaker obviously prepared this speech very carefully.

This conclusion is rather short for a speech of this length. Though most contest speeches follow this pattern of long introductions and short conclusions, the general advice from public speaking theorists is to keep them about the same length. There are times, however, when the audience needs to be given background information—as in these two speeches—which justifies breaking the general rule of equal time for both introductions and conclusions.

The FBI built entrapment from desperation.

After looking at its causes, effects, and solutions, it's clear what they forgot is genuine security.

In 1908, President Roosevelt created the FBI to serve one purpose—law enforcement. It's about time the FBI fulfills its actual purpose.

WORKS CITED

Aaronson, Trevor. "How the FBI in Boston May Have Pursued the Wrong 'Terrorist'" *Florida Center for Investigative Reporting*. N.p., 23 Apr. 2013. Web. 10 Apr. 2015.

Ackerman, Spencer. "Shahawar Matin Siraj: 'impressionable' Young Man Caught in an NYPD Sting." *The Guardian*. The Guardian, 21 July 2014. Web. 12 Apr. 2015.

"Boston Marathon Bombing." Personal interview. 13 Dec. 2014.

"Cyber Security: Preparing for and Responding to the Enduring Threat." *FBI*. FBI, 12 June 2013. Web. 10 Apr. 2015.

Dailymail.com, Joel Christie For. "Former FBI Mole Who Was Paid to Go Undercover and Infiltrate California Mosques Says He Was 'encouraged' to Sleep with Muslim Women to Obtain Better Intel." *The Daily Mail Online*. Associated Newspapers, 05 Mar. 2015. Web. 10 Apr. 2015.

Downs, Stephen. "INVENTING TERRORISTS The Lawfare of Preemptive Prosecution." *Project SALAM*. National Coalition to Protect Civil Freedoms, May 2014. Web. 10 Apr. 2015.

"Ending Entrapment." Telephone interview. 10 Mar. 2015.

Harris, Paul. "FBI Faces Entrapment Questions over Rezwan Ferdaus Bomb Plot Arrest." *The Guardian*. N.p., 29 Sept. 2011. Web. 10 Apr. 2015.

"Illusion of Justice: Human Rights Abuses in U.S. Terrorism Prosecutions." *Human Rights Watch* (2014): N.p., 21 July 2014. Web. 10 Apr. 2015.

Murphy, Laura. "Time for Obama and Holder to Truly End Racial Profiling by Law Enforcement." *American Civil Liberties Union*. ACLU, 21 Dec. 2012. Web. 10 Apr. 2015.

Pagones, Stephanie. "'Newburgh Four' Terrorism Case Was FBI Entrapment: HBO Film." *New York Post*. N.p., 20 July 2014. Web. 10 Apr. 2015.

Reilly, Ryan J. "FBI Allowed Informants To Commit More Crimes In 2012 Than Year Before." The Huffington Post. TheHuffingtonPost.com, 27 Dec. 2013. Web. 12 Apr. 2015.

Roth, Jessica. "The Anomaly of Entrapment." *Washington University Law Review*. N.p., 22 Oct. 2014. Web. 10 Apr. 2015.

"UNLEASHED AND UNACCOUNTABLE The FBI's Unchecked Abuse of Authority." *ACLU* (N.D.): N.p., American Civil Liberties Union, Sept. 2013. Web. 10 Apr. 2015.

"The U.S. 9/11 Commission on Border Control." *Population and Development Review* 30.3 (2004): 569–74. 2004. Web. 10 Apr. 2015.

Summary of Concepts and Skills

This chapter looked at the persuasive speech, first covering guidelines and types of supporting materials for persuasion and then discussing three main types of persuasive speeches.

Goals of Persuasion

14.1 **Explain the goals of persuasive speaking.**

1. Persuasion has three main goals: (1) to strengthen or weaken attitudes, beliefs, or values; (2) to change attitudes, beliefs, or values; and (3) to motivate to action.

Guidelines for Persuasive Speaking

14.2 **Explain the guidelines for persuasive speaking.**

2. Among the important guidelines for persuasive speaking are (1) focus on your audience, (2) ask for reasonable amounts of change, (3) anticipate selective exposure, (4) adapt to the culture of your audience, and (5) follow a motivated sequence.

Three Types of Persuasive Speeches

14.3 Define and give examples of persuasive speeches on questions of fact, value, and policy.

3. Persuasive speeches on questions of fact focus on what is or is not true.
4. Persuasive speeches on questions of value focus on issues of good and bad, justice and injustice.
5. Persuasive speeches on questions of policy focus on what should or should not be done, what procedures should or should not be adopted.

Supporting Materials

14.4 Explain the types of and the fallacies of logical, emotional, and credibility appeals.

6. Three major types of support have special importance in speeches of persuasion: logical appeals, emotional appeals, and credibility appeals.

To be an effective public speaker, you need to master a variety of persuading skills. Place a check mark next to those skills you want to work on most.

_____ 1. In my persuasive speeches I apply (where relevant) the principles of persuasion: selective exposure, amounts of change, and identification.

_____ 2. In my persuasive speeches I critically analyze reasoning from specific instances to generalizations, causes and effects, and sign.

_____ 3. When listening to persuasive attempts, I detect fallacies such as personal attacks, appeals to authority, appeal to numbers, and the slippery slope.

_____ 4. To motivate my audience I use motivational appeals—for example, appeals to desires for power, control, and influence; self-esteem and approval; safety; achievement; and financial gain.

_____ 5. In my speeches I seek to establish my credibility by displaying competence, high moral character, and dynamism, as well as charisma.

Key Terms

character
charisma
commencement speech
competence
credibility
goodwill speech

logical appeals
motivated sequence
motivational appeals
persuasion
questions of policy
questions of fact

questions of value
reasoning from causes and effects
reasoning from sign
reasoning from specific instances
selective exposure

Skill Development Experiences
14.1 Developing Persuasive Speeches

Practicing the art of persuasion will prove useful in a wide variety of communication situations.

Select one of the following thesis statements and (1) identify the type of persuasive speech it is—fact, value, or policy; (2) from this thesis, generate two, three, or four main points for a persuasive speech; (3) identify a few forms of supporting material that might prove useful; and (4) select a suitable organizational pattern.

1. Condoms should be distributed to students in junior and senior high school.
2. Sports involving cruelty to animals, such as bullfighting, cockfighting, and fox-hunting, should be universally condemned and declared illegal.
3. All states should ban guns on college campuses.

14.2 Preparing a Persuasive Speech

Discussing rough outlines of speeches in small groups is an excellent way to see your speech from the perspective of your audience.

Consult an online topic generator such as WritingFix or McMaster eBusiness Research Center for persuasive speech topics. Select a topic and then create a rough outline in which you follow these guidelines.

1. Identify a specific purpose and thesis.
2. Analyze your classroom audience and note adaptations you'd make.
3. Generate at least two main points with persuasive supporting materials.
4. Construct a conclusion and an introduction.

Glossary

abstraction A general concept derived from a class of objects; a part representation of some whole. Also, the quality of being abstract.

active listening The process of putting together into some meaningful whole an understanding of a speaker's total message—the verbal and the nonverbal, the content and the feelings.

adaptors Nonverbal behaviors that satisfy some personal need and usually occur without awareness, such as scratching to relieve an itch or moistening your lips to relieve dryness. Three types of adaptors are often distinguished: **self-adaptors**, **alter-adaptors**, and **object-adaptors.**

affect displays Movements of the facial area that convey emotional meaning—for example, anger, fear, or surprise.

affinity-seeking strategies Behaviors designed to increase interpersonal attractiveness.

agapic love One of Lee's six types of love; compassionate and selfless love offered without concern for personal reward and without any expectation of reciprocation.

ageism Discrimination based on age.

allness The assumption that all can be known or is known about a given person, issue, object, or event.

alter-adaptors Body movements you make in response to your current interactions, such as crossing your arms over your chest when someone unpleasant approaches or moving closer to someone you like.

ambiguity The condition in which a message can be interpreted as having more than one meaning.

anonymous messages Messages that are unsigned; the author is unknown or hidden. *Contrast* **onymous messages.**

apology Expressions of regret or sorrow for having done what you did or for what happened.

argumentativeness A willingness to speak your mind, to argue for a point of view. *Contrast* **verbal aggressiveness.**

articulation The physiological movements of the speech organs as they modify and interrupt the air stream emitted from the lungs.

artifactual messages Messages conveyed through the wearing and arrangement of various artifacts—for example, clothing, jewelry, buttons, or the furniture in your house and its arrangement.

assertiveness A willingness to stand up for your rights while maintaining respect for the rights of others.

attraction The state or process by which one individual is drawn to another, forming a highly positive evaluation of that other person.

attraction theory A theory holding that we form relationships on the basis of our attraction for another person.

attractiveness A person's visual appeal and/or pleasantness in personality.

attribution of control A process by which you focus on explaining why someone behaved as he or she did.

audience The receivers of a public speech who witness it firsthand and also those who watch it or hear about it from others.

authoritarian leader A group leader who determines the group policies or makes decisions without consulting or securing agreement from group members.

avoidance An unproductive conflict strategy in which a person takes mental or physical flight from the actual conflict.

backchanneling cues Listener responses to a speaker that do not ask for the speaking role.

beltlining An unproductive conflict strategy in which one person hits at the emotional level at which the other person cannot withstand the blow.

blame An unproductive conflict strategy in which we attribute the cause of the conflict to the other person or devote our energies to discovering who is the cause and avoid talking about the issues causing the conflict.

boundary marker A marker that serves to divide your territory from that of others.

boundary markers A marker dividing one person's territory from another's—for example, a fence.

brainstorming A technique for generating ideas either alone or, more usually, in a small group.

bullying A pattern of abusive behavior (verbal or nonverbal) repeatedly committed by one person (or group) against another.

central marker An item that is placed in a territory to reserve it for a specific person—for example, a sweater thrown over a library chair to signal that the chair is taken.

certainty An attitude of closed-mindedness that creates a defensiveness among communication participants. *Contrast* **provisionalism.**

channel The vehicle or medium through which signals are sent.

character One of the qualities of credibility; the individual's honesty and basic nature; moral qualities.

charisma One of the qualities of credibility; the individual's dynamism or forcefulness.

chronemics The study of the communicative nature of time—the way we treat time and use it to communicate. Two general areas of chronemics are **psychological time, interpersonal time,** and **cultural time.**

civil inattention A polite ignoring of others so as not to invade their privacy.

closed-mindedness An unwillingness to receive certain communication messages.

collective orientation A cultural orientation that stresses the group's rather than the individual's goals and preferences. *Contrast* **individual orientation.**

collectivist culture A culture that emphasizes the group's rather than the individual's goals; a culture that values, for example, benevolence, tradition, and conformity. Contrast **individualistic culture.**

color communication The meanings that different cultures communicate via color.

commencement speech A special occasion speech designed to congratulate and inspire recent graduates.

communication apprehension Fear or anxiety over communicating; may be "trait apprehension" (i.e., fear of communication generally, regardless of the specific situation) or "state apprehension" (i.e., fear that is specific to a given communication situation).

communication competence Knowledge of the rules and skills of communication; the qualities that make for effectiveness in communication.

competence One of the dimensions of credibility; consists of a person's perceived levels of ability and knowledge.

complementarity A principle of attraction stating that we are attracted by qualities that we do not possess or that we wish to possess and to people who are opposite or different from ourselves. *Contrast* **similarity.**

compliment A message of praise, flattery, or congratulations.

computer-mediated communication A general term denoting all forms of communication between people that take place through some computer, electronic, or Internet connection.

confirmation A communication pattern that acknowledges another person's presence and also indicates an acceptance of this person and his or her definition of self, and the relationship as defined or viewed by this person. *Contrast* **disconfirmation.**

conformity-orientation The degree to which members of a family are free to express similar or dissimilar attitudes, values, and beliefs.

connotation The feeling or emotional aspect of meaning, generally viewed as consisting of evaluative (e.g., good/bad), potency (i.e., strong/weak), and activity (i.e., fast/slow) dimensions; the associations of a term. *Contrast* **denotation.**

consensus A process of reaching agreement (not necessarily unanimous) among group members.

contact The first stage of an interpersonal relationship, in which perceptual and interactional contact occurs.

content messages Messages that refer to matters external to the relationship between source and receiver.

context The physical, psychological, social, and temporal environment in which communication takes place.

contrast (principle of) Often-followed rule of perception: messages or people who are very different from each other probably don't belong together, and do not constitute a set or group.

conversational turns The process of exchanging speaking and listening turns during a conversation.

conversation-orientation The degree to which family members can speak their mind.

credibility The believability of a speaker; **competence, character,** and **charisma** (dynamism) are its major dimensions.

critical listening Listening that includes analyzing and evaluating the message rather than simply receiving it.

criticism The reasoned judgment of some work; although often equated with fault finding, criticism can involve both positive or negative evaluations.

cultural context The cultural beliefs and customs of those communicating.

cultural identifiers The terms used to talk about cultural identifications; for example, race or religion.

cultural time The meanings given to the ways time is treated in a particular culture.

culture The relatively specialized lifestyle of a group of people—consisting of values, beliefs, artifacts, ways of behaving, and ways of communicating—that is passed on from one generation to the next.

date An extensional device used to emphasize the notion of constant change and symbolized by a subscript; for example, John Smith$_{2008}$ is not John Smith$_{2011}$.

decoder Something that takes a message in one form (e.g., sound waves) and translates it into another form (e.g., nerve impulses) from which meaning can be formulated (e.g., in vocal–auditory communication). In human communication the decoder is the auditory mechanism; in electronic communication the decoder is, for example, the telephone earpiece. *See also* **encoder.**

decoding The process of extracting a message from a code—for example, translating speech sounds into nerve impulses. *See also* **encoding.**

defensiveness The self-protective attitude of an individual or an atmosphere in a group characterized by threats, fear, and domination. Messages evidencing evaluation, control, strategy, neutrality, superiority, and certainty are assumed to lead to defensiveness.

delivery outline A brief set of notes that is used while speaking, usually consisting of words and phrases rather than complete sentences.

Delphi group A type of group whose members are experts but there's no interaction among them; instead, they communicate by repeatedly responding to questionnaires.

democratic leader A group leader who stimulates self-direction and self-actualization of the group members.

denotation The objective or descriptive meaning of a word; its referential meaning.

deterioration A stage in an interpersonal relationship in which the bonds holding the individuals together are weakened and the partners begin drifting apart.

dialogue A form of communication in which each person is both speaker and listener; communication characterized by involvement, concern, and respect for the other person. *Contrast* **monologue.**

disconfirmation A communication pattern in which someone ignores a person or that person's messages, even denying the right of the individual to define himself or herself. *Contrast* **confirmation.**

disinhibition effect The tendency to disclose more in certain situations than in others; usually, used to refer to the tendency to be more uninhibited in online messaging.

dissolution The breaking of the bonds holding an interpersonal relationship together.

earmarker A marker that identifies an item as belonging to a specific person—for example, a nameplate on a desk or initials on an attaché case.

effect The outcome or consequence of an action or behavior; communication is assumed always to have some effect.

emblems Nonverbal behaviors that directly translate words or phrases—for example, the signs for "OK" and "peace."

emoticon Visual representation of emotion produced by a short sequence of keyboard characters.

empathy The ability to feel what another person feels; feeling or perceiving something from another person's point of view. A key component of interpersonal effectiveness.

encoder Something that takes a message in one form (for example, nerve impulses) and translates it into another form (for example, sound waves). In human communication, the encoder is the speaking mechanism; in electronic communication, the encoder is, for example, the telephone mouthpiece.

encoding The process of putting a message into a code—for example, translating nerve impulses into speech sounds. *See also* **decoding.**

equity theory A theory claiming that you experience relational satisfaction when there is an equal distribution of rewards and costs between the two persons in the relationship.

eros love One of Lee's six types of love; seeks beauty and sensuality and focuses on physical attractiveness.

ethics The branch of philosophy that deals with the rightness or wrongness of actions; the study of moral values.

ethnic identity Commitment to the beliefs and customs of a culture.

ethnocentrism The tendency to see others and their behaviors through our own cultural filters, often as distortions of our own behaviors; the tendency to evaluate the values and beliefs of our own culture more positively than those of another culture.

example   A relatively brief specific instance.

extemporaneous speech   A speech that is thoroughly prepared and organized in detail and in which certain aspects of style are predetermined.

extensional orientation   A tendency to give primary consideration to the world of experience and only secondary consideration to labels.

face-attacking conflict strategies   Strategies that attack a person's positive face or self-esteem or a person's negative face or need for autonomy and independence.

face-enhancing conflict strategies   Strategies that support and confirm a person's positive face or self-esteem or a person's negative face or need for autonomy.

facial feedback hypothesis   The theory that a person's facial expressions can produce physiological and emotional effects in the person.

facial management   Techniques used to mask certain emotions and to emphasize others: for example, intensifying your expression of happiness to make a friend feel good about a promotion.

fact–inference confusion   A misevaluation in which someone makes an inference, regards it as a fact, and acts on it as if it were a fact.

false memory syndrome   A condition in which memories are believed to be true but are actually incorrect.

feedback   Information that is given back to the source. Feedback may come from the source's own messages (as when we hear what we are saying) or from the receiver(s)—in forms such as applause, yawning, puzzled looks, questions, pokes, retweets, increased followers, and so forth. *See also* **negative feedback; positive feedback.**

feedforward   Information that is sent before a regular message telling the listener something about what is to follow.

focus group   A group designed to explore the feelings and attitudes of its members; usually follows a question-and-answer format.

force   An unproductive conflict strategy in which someone attempts to win an argument by physical force, threats of force, or some type of psychological bullying.

forum   A small-group format in which members of the group answer questions from the audience; often follows a **symposium.**

friendship   An interpersonal relationship between two people that is mutually productive, established and maintained through perceived mutual free choice, and characterized by mutual positive regard.

fundamental attribution error   The tendency to attribute a person's behavior to the kind of person he or she is (to internal factors such as the person's personality) and not to give sufficient importance to the situation the person is in.

general purpose   The major aim or objective of a public speech; usually identified as to inform and to persuade.

gossip   Communication about someone who is not present, usually about matters that are private to this third party.

group building and maintenance roles   Roles that serve the interpersonal needs of group members, rather than focus on the task to be accomplished.

group norm   Rules or expectations for appropriate behavior for a member of a group. Actively seek to discover the norms of a group, and take these norms into consideration when interacting in the group.

group task roles   Roles that focus on accomplishing the group's task.

groupthink   A tendency observed in some groups in which agreement among members becomes more important than the exploration of the issues at hand. Recognize and actively counter any groupthink tendencies evidenced in a group.

gunnysacking   An unproductive conflict strategy of storing up grievances—as if in a gunnysack—and holding them in readiness to dump on the other person in a conflict.

haptics   The study of touch communication.

heterosexism   Negative attitudes and beliefs about gay men and lesbians; the belief that all sexual behavior that is not heterosexual is unnatural and deserving of criticism and condemnation.

heterosexist language   Language that assumes all people are heterosexual and that thereby denigrates lesbians and gay men.

high and low context   The cultural dimension that refers to the degree to which the meaning of a message is encoded into speech.

high-context culture   A culture in which much of the information is in the context or in what each person already knows from previous experiences; the communication is often indirect.

high-power-distance cultures Cultures in which power is concentrated in the hands of a few, and there is a great difference between the power held by these people and the power held by the ordinary citizen. *Contrast* **low-power-distance cultures.**

home field advantage The increased power that comes from being in your own territory.

idioms Expressions that are unique to a specific language and whose meaning cannot be deduced from the individual words used.

illustration A relatively long and detailed example.

illustrators Nonverbal behaviors that accompany and literally illustrate verbal messages—for example, upward hand movements that accompany the verbalization "It's up there."

image-confirming strategies Techniques used to communicate or to confirm your self-image, the image you want others to see.

I-messages Messages in which the speaker accepts responsibility for personal thoughts and behaviors; messages in which the speaker's point of view is stated explicitly. *Contrast* **you-messages.**

immediacy A sense of contact and togetherness; a feeling of interest in and liking for the other person in an interchange. A quality of interpersonal effectiveness.

impostor phenomenon The tendency to disregard outward signs of success and to consider yourself an "impostor," a fake, a fraud, one who doesn't really deserve to be considered successful.

impression formation The processes you go through in forming an impression of another person.

impression management The processes you go through to create the impression you want the other person to have of you.

impromptu speech A speech delivered off-the-cuff, without preparation.

index An **extensional device** used to emphasize the notion of nonidentity (i.e., that no two things are the same) and symbolized by a subscript—for example, $politician_1$ is not $politician_2$.

indiscrimination A misevaluation caused when we categorize people, events, or objects into a particular class and respond to them only as members of the class; a failure to recognize that each individual is unique; a failure to apply the **index.**

individual orientation A cultural orientation that stresses the individual's rather than the group's goals and preferences. *Contrast* **collective orientation.**

individual roles Behavior in groups that is usually dysfunctional and works against a sense of groupness.

individualism–collectivism The cultural dimension that refers to the degree to which an individual's preferences or those of the group are given greater importance.

individualistic culture A culture that emphasizes the individual's rather than the group's goals and preferences. *Contrast* **collectivist culture.**

indulgence and restraint The cultural dimension that refers to the degree to which gratifications are enjoyed now or delayed.

inevitability In communication, the fact that communication cannot be avoided—that all behavior in an interactional setting is communication.

influencing strategies Strategies designed to influence the attitudes or behaviors of others.

information Knowledge that reduces uncertainty.

informative speech A public speech in which the speaker describes, demonstrates, or defines something.

intensional orientation A tendency to give primary consideration to the way things are labeled and only secondary consideration (if any) to the world of experience. *Contrast* **extensional orientation.**

internal summary A statement that summarizes what you have already discussed, usually some major subdivision of your speech.

interpersonal communication Communication between two persons or among a small group of persons, as distinguished from public or mass communication; communication of a personal nature, as distinguished from impersonal communication; communication between or among intimates or those involved in a close relationship; often, intrapersonal, dyadic, and small-group communication in general.

interpersonal conflict A conflict or disagreement between two persons.

interpersonal time A wide variety of time related elements that figure into interpersonal interaction.

interruptions In conversation, attempts to take over the role of the speaker.

interviewing A particular form of interpersonal communication in which two persons interact largely through questions and answers for the purpose of achieving specific goals.

intimacy The closest interpersonal relationship; usually involves a close primary relationship such as the relationship between spouses or partners.

intimate distance The closest proxemic distance, ranging from touching to 18 inches away.

involvement The stage in an interpersonal relationship that normally follows contact, in which the individuals get to know each other better and explore the potential for greater intimacy.

irreversibility The impossibility of reversing communication; a principle stating that once something has been communicated, it cannot be uncommunicated.

Johari window A diagram of the four selves (i.e., open, blind, hidden, and unknown) that illustrates the different kinds of information in each self.

just world hypothesis The belief that the world is just: Good things happen to good people (because they're good) and bad things happen to bad people (because they're bad).

kinesics The study of the communicative dimensions of facial and bodily movements.

laissez-faire leader A group leader who allows the group to develop and progress or make mistakes on its own.

leadership The quality by which one individual directs or influences the thoughts and/or the behaviors of others. *See also* **laissez-faire leader**, **democratic leader**, and **authoritarian leader**.

listening An active process of receiving messages sent orally; this process consists of five stages: receiving, understanding, remembering, evaluating, and responding.

long- and short-term orientation The cultural dimension that refers to the degree to which members enjoy immediate rewards or delay them for the future.

long-term memory Memory that is (theoretically) unlimited in storage capacity and that holds information for long periods of time. *Contrast* **short-term memory**.

looking-glass self The self-concept that results from the image of yourself that others reveal to you.

love "An interpersonal process in which one person feels a closeness, a caring, a warmth, and an excitement in relation to another person."

low-context culture A culture in which most of the information in communication is explicitly stated in the verbal messages. An **individualistic culture** is usually a low-context culture. *Contrast* **high-context culture.**

low-power-distance cultures Cultures in which power is more evenly distributed throughout the citizenry. *Contrast* **high-power-distance cultures.**

ludic love One of Lee's six types of love; based on entertainment and excitement, it is love as a game, not to be taken too seriously and with emotions held in check.

manic love One of Lee's six types of love; obsessive love, it is marked by a need for constant attention and affection, which when withheld leads to depression, jealousy, and self-doubt.

manipulation An unproductive conflict strategy in which a person avoids open conflict but attempts to divert the conflict by being especially charming and getting the other person into a noncombative frame of mind.

manner principle A principle of conversation that requires you to be clear, avoid ambiguities, be relatively brief, and organize your thoughts into a meaningful sequence.

manuscript speech A speech designed to be read verbatim from a script.

markers Devices that signify that a certain territory belongs to a particular person. *See also* **boundary marker**, **central marker**, and **earmarker.**

masculinity–femininity The cultural dimension that refers to the degree to which traditional masculine and traditionally feminine attitudes and beliefs are emphasized.

mass communication Communication that is addressed to an extremely large audience, mediated by audio and/or visual transmitters, and processed by gatekeepers before transmission.

maxim of agreement A maxim of conversation that refers to your seeking out areas of agreement and expressing them.

maxim of approbation A maxim of conversation that refers to praising someone or complimenting the person in some way.

maxim of generosity A maxim of conversation that helps to confirm the other person's importance—for example, the importance of the person's time, insight, or talent.

maxim of modesty A maxim of conversation that refers to your) minimizing any praise or compliments *you* might receive.

maxim of sympathy A conversational maxim that refers to the expression of understanding, sympathy, empathy, supportiveness, and the like for the other person.

maxim of tact   A maxim of conversation that helps to maintain the other person's autonomy or negative face.

mentoring   Guidance and support given by an experienced individual to a less-experienced person.

message   Any signal or combination of signals that serves as a stimulus for a receiver.

metacommunication   Communication about communication.

metamessage   A message that makes reference to another message—for example, remarks such as "Did I make myself clear?" or "That's a lie."

mindfulness   In a mindful state, we are aware of the logic and rationality of our behaviors and the logical connections existing among elements.

monochronic time orientation   A view of time in which things are done sequentially, with one thing being scheduled at a time. *Contrast* **polychronic time orientation.**

monologue   A form of communication in which one person speaks and the other listens; there is no real interaction among participants. *Contrast* **dialogue.**

motivated sequence   An organizational pattern in which a speaker arranges the information in a discourse to motivate an audience to respond positively to the speaker's purpose.

motivational appeals   Appeals to an audience's motives and emotions rather than to their logic.

narrative   A long example presented in the form of an anecdote, short story, or report, for example, Aesop's fables.

negative empathy   The condition in which you have such strong empathy for your own group that you feel a definite lack of empathy for other groups.

negative face   The need and desire to be autonomous, to have the right to do as one wishes.

netiquette   The rules for polite communication over the Internet.

networking   A broad process of enlisting the aid of other people to help you solve a problem or offer insight that bears on your problem.

neutrality   A response pattern lacking in personal involvement; encourages defensiveness. *Contrast* **empathy.**

noise   Anything that interferes with a person's receiving a message as the source intended the message to be received. Noise is present in a communication system to the extent that the message received is not the message sent.

nominal group   A collection of individuals who record their thoughts and opinions, which are then distributed to others. Without direct interaction, the thoughts and opinions are gradually pared down until a manageable list of solutions or decisions is produced. When this occurs, the nominal group (a group in name only) may restructure itself into a problem-solving group that analyzes the final list.

nonnegotiation   An unproductive conflict strategy in which an individual refuses to discuss the conflict or to listen to the other person in the encounter.

nonverbal communication   Communication without words; for example, communication by means of space, gestures, facial expressions, touching, vocal variation, or silence.

object-adaptors   Movements that involve manipulation of some object, such as punching holes in or drawing on a Styrofoam coffee cup, clicking a ballpoint pen, or chewing on a pencil.

oculesics   A technical term for the study of eye movements.

olfactory communication   Communication by smell.

online-only relationships   Relations that exist only online—for example, relationships between a Tweeter and a follower, a blogger and a reader, a friend or contact on Facebook or LinkedIn.

onymous messages   Messages that are signed; messages whose author is identified.

operational definition   A definition that describes how you would construct an object.

overattribution   The tendency to attribute a great deal of what a person does or believes to one or two obvious characteristics of the person.

panel   A small-group format in which "experts" meet to discuss a topic or solve a problem; participants often speak without any set pattern.

paralanguage   The vocal but nonverbal aspect of speech. Paralanguage consists of voice qualities (e.g., pitch range, resonance, tempo), vocal characterizers (e.g., laughing or crying, yelling or whispering), vocal qualifiers (e.g., intensity, pitch height), and vocal segregates (e.g., "uh-uh" meaning "no" or "sh" meaning "silence").

parasocial relationships   Relationship between a person and an imagined or fictional character; usually refers to a relationship between a viewer and a fictional character in a television show.

pauses   Silent periods in the normally fluent stream of speech. Pauses are of two major types: filled pauses (i.e., interruptions in speech that are filled with such vocalizations as "er" or "um") and unfilled pauses (i.e., silences of unusually long duration).

perception The process of becoming aware of objects and events via the senses. *See also* **interpersonal perception.**

perception checking The process of verifying your understanding of some message or situation or feeling to reduce uncertainty.

personal distance The second closest **proxemic distance,** ranging from 18 inches to four feet. See also **proxemics.**

persuasion The process of influencing attitudes, beliefs, values, and/or behavior.

persuasive speech In public speaking, a speech designed to change an audience's attitudes or behaviors. Apply (where relevant) the principles of persuasion: selective exposure, audience participation, identification, and amounts of change.

phatic communication Communication that is primarily social; "small talk" designed to open the channels of communication rather than to communicate something about the external world. "Hello" and "How are you?" in everyday interaction are examples.

physical context The tangible environment in which communication takes place.

physical noise Interference that is external to both speaker and listener and that interferes with the physical transmission of a signal or message.

physiological noise Interference within the sender or receiver of a message, such as visual impairments, hearing loss, articulation problems, and memory loss.

plagiarism The process of claiming authorship for the work of another and can apply to ideas as well as specific words.

polarization A form of fallacious reasoning by which only the two extremes are considered; also referred to as "black-and-white" or "either/or" thinking or as two-valued orientation.

politeness strategies Strategies that support another's face needs and may be used as a strategy to appear likeable.

polychronic time orientation A view of time in which several things may be scheduled or engaged in at the same time. *Contrast* **monochronic time orientation.**

positive face The need and desire to be viewed positively by others, to be thought of favorably.

power distance A cultural dimension referring to the degree of distance between those with power and those without power.

pragma love One of Lee's six types of love; traditional approach to love, valuing social qualifications and family background and emphasizing logic and practicality over feelings.

presentation aids Visual or auditory means for clarifying ideas.

primacy effect The condition by which what comes first exerts greater influence than what comes later. *Contrast* **recency effect.**

primacy–recency A principle of **perception** stating that we generally use early information to get a general impression of a person and use later information to add specificity to this impression.

primary relationship The relationship between two people who both consider it to be their most (or one of their most) important relationship; the relationship between spouses or domestic partners would be an example.

primary territory An area that you can consider your exclusive preserve—for example, your room or office.

principle of cooperation A principle of conversation that refers to the mutually agreed-upon assumption that two people will try to understand each other.

pronunciation The production of syllables or words according to some accepted standard—for example, as presented in a dictionary.

provisionalism An attitude of open-mindedness that leads to the creation of supportiveness. *Contrast* **certainty.**

proxemics The study of the communicative function of space and of how people unconsciously structure their space—the distances between people in their interactions, the organization of space in homes and offices, and even the design of cities.

proximity As a principle of **perception,** the tendency to perceive people or events that are physically close as belonging together or representing some kind of a unit. Also, physical closeness; one of the factors influencing interpersonal attraction.

psychological noise Mental interference in the speaker or listener, such as preconceived ideas, wandering thoughts, biases and prejudices, closed-mindedness, and extreme emotionalism.

psychological time The importance placed on past, present, or future time.

public communication Communication in which the source is one person and the receiver is an audience of many persons.

public distance   The longest **proxemic distance,** ranging from 12 to more than 25 feet.

public speaking   A form of communication in which a speaker addresses a relatively large audience with a relatively continuous discourse, usually in a face-to-face situation.

public territory   Area that is open to all people—for example, a restaurant or park.

punctuation of communication   The breaking up of continuous communication sequences into short sequences with identifiable beginnings and endings or stimuli and responses.

purr words   Highly positive words that express the speaker's feelings rather than any objective reality. *Contrast* **snarl words**.

Pygmalion effect   Condition in which we make a prediction of success, act as if it were true, and thereby make it come true; a type of **self-fulfilling prophecy.**

quality principle   A principle of conversation that states that you should say what you know or believe to be true and not say what you know to be false.

quantity principle   A principle of conversation that requires you to be only as informative as necessary to communicate your intended meaning.

questions of fact   Questions concerned with what is or is not true, what does or does not exist, what did or did not happen.

questions of policy   Questions concerning what should be or should not be done (or what policy should be adopted).

racism   Negative attitudes and beliefs that individuals or societies hold about specific ethnic groups.

racist language   Language that denigrates or is derogatory toward members of a race.

rate   The speed with which a person speaks, generally measured in words per minute.

recency effect   The condition in which what comes last (i.e., happened most recently) exerts greater influence than what comes first. *Contrast* **primacy effect.**

reciprocity of liking   A principle of attraction that claims you tend to be attracted to people you think are attracted to you; you come to like those who appear to like you.

regulators   Nonverbal behaviors that regulate, monitor, or control the communications of another person.

relation principle   A principle of conversation that asks that you talk about what is relevant to the conversation.

relationship development   The stages of relationships during which you move closer to intimacy; in the model of relationships presented here, relationship development includes the stages of contact and involvement.

relationship messages   Messages that comment on the relationship between the speakers rather than on matters external to them.

repair   Attempts to reverse the process of relationship deterioration.

research   A systematic search for information; an investigation of the relevant information on a topic.

role   The part an individual plays in a group; an individual's function or expected behavior.

roundtable   A small-group format in which group members arrange themselves in a circular or semicircular pattern; participants meet to share information or solve problems without any set pattern as to who speaks when.

rules theory   A theory that describes relationships as interactions governed by a series of rules that the members agree to follow. When the rules are followed, the relationship is maintained; when they are broken, the relationship experiences difficulty.

secondary territory   An area that does not belong to a particular person but that has been occupied by that person and is therefore associated with her or him—for example, the seat a person normally takes in class.

selective attention   The tendency to attend to those things that you want to see or that you expect to see.

selective exposure   The tendency of listeners to actively seek out information that supports their existing opinions, beliefs, attitudes, and values and to actively avoid information that contradicts them.

selective perception   The tendency to perceive certain things and not others; includes **selective attention** and **selective exposure**.

self-adaptors   Movements that satisfy a physical need, especially to make you more comfortable; for example, scratching your head to relieve an itch, moistening your lips because they feel dry, or pushing your hair out of your eyes.

self-awareness   The degree to which you know yourself.

self-concept An individual's self-evaluation or self-appraisal. Learn who you are: See yourself through the eyes of others; compare yourself to similar (and admired) others; examine the influences of culture; and observe, interpret, and evaluate your own message behaviors.

self-deprecating strategies Techniques used to signal your inability to do some task or your incompetence to encourage another to help you out.

self-destructive beliefs Beliefs that create problems; often beliefs that are unrealistic and set goals that are impossible to achieve.

self-disclosure The process of revealing something about yourself to another person. Usually refers to information that would normally be kept hidden.

self-esteem The value you place on yourself; your self-evaluation. Usually refers to a positive self-evaluation.

self-fulfilling prophecy The situation in which you make a prediction or prophecy that comes true because you act on it as if it were true.

self-handicapping strategies Techniques used to excuse possible failure—for example, setting up barriers or obstacles to make a task impossible so that when you fail, you won't be blamed or thought ineffective.

self-monitoring The manipulation of the image presented to others in interpersonal interactions so as to create a favorable impression

self-serving bias A bias in the self-attribution process that leads us to take credit for positive consequences and to deny responsibility for negative outcomes of our behaviors.

semantic noise Interference created when a speaker and listener have different meaning systems; such noise can include language or dialectical differences, the use of jargon or overly complex terms, or ambiguous or overly abstract terms whose meanings can be easily misinterpreted.

sexism Negative attitudes and beliefs about a particular gender; prejudicial attitudes and beliefs about men or women based on rigid beliefs about gender roles.

sexist language Language derogatory to one gender, usually women.

short-term memory Memory that is very limited in capacity; contains information that is quickly lost if it is not passed on to **long-term memory**.

signal-to-noise ratio In verbal interaction, the relationship between what is signal (i.e., meaningful) and what is noise (i.e., interference). This ratio also is relative to the communication analyst, the participants, and the context.

silence The absence of vocal communication; often misunderstood to refer to the absence of any and all communication. Silence often communicates feelings or prevents communication about certain topics.

similarity As a principle of **perception,** the tendency to see things that are physically similar as belonging together and/or constituting a unit. As a principle of **attraction,** your tendency to be attracted to people with qualities similar to your own and to people who are similar to you. *Contrast* **complementarity.**

simile A figure of speech in which two unlike objects are compared using the words *like* or *as.*

small group A collection of individuals who are connected to one another by some common purpose, are interdependent, have some degree of organization among them, and see themselves as a group.

small-group communication Communication among a collection of individuals small enough in number that all members may interact with relative ease as both senders and receivers, the members being related to one another by some common purpose and with some degree of organization or structure.

small talk Noncontroversial talk that is usually short in duration and often serves as a polite way of introducing oneself or a topic.

snarl words Highly negative words that express the feelings of the speaker rather than any objective reality. *Contrast* **purr words**.

social allergen A behavior of another that annoys you, much like an allergy.

social clock The cultural time table for the accomplishment of a variety of life's milestones.

social distance The third **proxemic distance,** ranging from 4 to 12 feet; the distance at which business is usually conducted.

social exchange theory A theory hypothesizing that people develop relationships in which their rewards, or profits, will be greater than their costs and that people avoid or terminate relationships in which the costs exceed the rewards.

social facilitation A theory holding that you exert more effort when you're a part of a group than when alone. Contrast **social loafing**.

social loafing A theory holding that you exert less effort when you're part of a group than when alone; people have a tendency to loaf.

social-psychological context The status relationships among speakers, the formality of the situation, the norms of a group or organization; you don't talk the same way in the cafeteria as you would at a formal dinner at your boss's house.

specific purpose   The information you want to communicate (in an informative speech) or the attitude or behavior you want to change (in a persuasive speech).

speech of demonstration   A speech devoted to showing how to do something or how something operates.

speech of description   A speech devoted to describing an object or person.

spontaneity   The communication pattern in which a person verbalizes what he or she is thinking without attempting to develop strategies for control; encourages **supportiveness**.

static evaluation   An orientation that fails to recognize that the world is characterized by constant change; an attitude that sees people and events as fixed rather than as constantly changing.

stereotype   In communication, a fixed impression of a group of people through which we then perceive specific individuals; stereotypes are most often negative but may also be positive.

storge love   One of Lee's six types of love; a gradually unfolding, peaceful and tranquil love marked by companionability and shared interests and activities, sometimes difficult to distinguish from friendship.

supporting materials   Usually used in reference to public speaking, enlarging a concept or principle through the use of examples, illustrations, and narratives; testimony; definitions; statistics; and visual aids.

supportiveness   An attitude of an individual or an atmosphere in a group that is characterized by openness, absence of fear, and a genuine feeling of equality.

symposium   A small-group format in which each member of the group delivers a relatively prepared talk on some aspect of the topic. Often combined with a **forum.**

taboo   Forbidden; culturally censored. Taboo language is language that is frowned on by "polite society." Topics and specific words may be considered taboo—for example, death, sex, certain forms of illness, and various words denoting sexual activities and excretory functions.

team   A particular kind of small group that is constructed for a specific task and whose members have clearly defined roles, are committed to achieving the same goal, and are content focused.

temporal communication   The messages communicated by a person's time orientation and treatment of time.

temporal context   A message's position within a sequence of events.

territoriality   A possessive or ownership reaction to an area of space or to particular objects.

testimony   A form of supporting material consisting of an experts' opinions or witnesses' accounts and may add an authoritative tone to your arguments.

thesis   The main assertion of a message—for example, the theme of a public speech.

tie signs   Nonverbal gestures or artifacts that communication your relationship status.

touch avoidance   The tendency to avoid touching and being touched by others.

touch communication   Communication through tactile means.

transitions   Words or statements that connect what was said to what will be said.

truth bias   The assumption that most people operate under (that the messages they hear are truthful).

turn-denying cues   Verbal or nonverbal cues indicating that the listener does not want to assume the role of speaker.

turn-maintaining cues   Verbal or nonverbal signals that communicate the wish to maintain the role of speaker.

turn-requesting cues   Verbal or nonverbal behaviors that let the speaker know that you would like to say something and take a turn as speaker.

turn-taking cues   Verbal or nonverbal signals that speakers and listeners use to comment on their roles in a conversation; behaviors that help regulate and structure conversation.

turn-yielding cues   Verbal or nonverbal signals indicating the speaker's desire to give up the speaker's role.

uncertainty avoidance   The degree to which a culture values predictability.

unrepeatability   A principle stating that a communication act can never be duplicated because everyone and everything is constantly changing.

verbal aggressiveness   A method of winning an argument by attacking the other person's **self-concept.** *Contrast* **argumentativeness.**

volume   The relative loudness of the voice.

you-messages   Messages in which the speaker denies responsibility for his or her own thoughts and behaviors; messages that attribute the speaker's perception to another person; messages of blame. *Contrast* **I-messages.**

References

Abel, G. G., & Harlow, N. (2001). *The stop child molestation book*. Philadelphia: Xlibris.

Acor, A. A. (2001). Employers' perceptions of persons with body art and an experimental test regarding eyebrow piercing. *Dissertation Abstracts International: Section B. The Sciences and Engineering, 61,* 3885.

Adams-Price, C. E., Dalton, W. T., & Sumrall, R. (2004, October). Victim blaming in young, middle-aged, and older adults: Variations on the severity effect. *Journal of Adult Development, 11,* 289–295.

Adrianson, L. (2001). Gender and computer-mediated communication: Group processes in problem solving. *Computers in Human Behavior, 17,* 71–94.

Afifi, W. A. (2007). Nonverbal communication. In B. B. Whaley & W. Samter (Eds.), *Explaining communication: Contemporary theories and exemplars* (pp. 39–60). Mahwah, NJ: Lawrence Erlbaum.

Afifi, W. A., & Johnson, M. L. (2005). The nature and function of tie-signs. In V. Manusov (Ed.), *The sourcebook of nonverbal measures: Going beyond words* (pp. 189–198). Mahwah, NJ: Lawrence Erlbaum.

Akinnaso, F. N. (1982). On the differences between spoken and written language. *Language and Speech, 25*(Part 2), 97–125.

Alessandra, T. (1986). How to listen effectively. *Speaking of success* [Videotape series]. San Diego, CA: Levitz Sommer Productions.

Altman, I. (1975). *The environment and social behavior.* Monterey, CA: Brooks/Cole.

Altman, I., & Taylor, D. (1973). *Social penetration: The development of interpersonal relationships.* New York: Holt, Rinehart & Winston.

Amato, P. R. (1994). The impact of divorce on men and women in India and the United States. *Journal of Comparative Family Studies, 25,* 207–221.

Andersen, J. F., Andersen, P. A., & Lustig, M. W. (1987). Opposite sex touch avoidance: A national replication and extension. *Journal of Nonverbal Behavior, 11,* 89–109.

Andersen, P. A., & Bowman, L. L. (1999). Positions of power: Nonverbal influence in organizational communication. In L. K. Guerrero, J. A. DeVito, & M. L. Hecht (Eds), *The nonverbal communication reader: Classic and contemporary readings* (2nd ed). Prospect Heights, IL: Waveland.

Andersen, P. A. (1991). Explaining intercultural differences in nonverbal communication. In L. A. Samovar & R. E. Porter (Eds.), *Intercultural communication: A reader* (6th ed., pp. 286–296). Belmont, CA: Wadsworth.

Andersen, P. A. (2004). *The complete idiot's guide to body language.* New York: Penguin Group.

Andersen, P. A., & Leibowitz, K. (1978). The development and nature of the construct of touch avoidance. *Environmental Psychology and Nonverbal Behavior, 3,* 89–106.

Anderson, K. J. et al. (1998, August). Meta-analysis of gender effects on conversational interruption: Who, what, when, where, and how. *Sex Roles, 39,* 225–252.

Angier, N. (1995, May 9). Scientists mull role of empathy in man and beast. *New York Times,* C1, C6.

Angier, N. (2010, August 29). Just don't call me .... *New York Times,* Weekend, p. 3.

Argyle, M. (1986). Rules for social relationships in four cultures. *Australian Journal of Psychology, 38,* 309–318.

Argyle, M. (1988). *Bodily communication* (2nd ed.). New York: Methuen.

Argyle, M., & Henderson, M. (1984). *The anatomy of relationships: And the rules and skills needed to manage them successfully.* London: Heinemann.

Argyle, M., & Ingham, R. (1972). Gaze, mutual gaze and distance. *Semiotica, 1,* 32–49.

Arnold, L. B. (2008). *Family communication: Theory and research.* Boston, MA: Allyn & Bacon.

Aronson, E., Wilson, T. D., & Akert, R. M. (2013). *Social psychology: The heart and the mind* (7th ed.). New York: Longman.

Aronson, J., Cohen, J., & Nail, P. (1998). Self-affirmation theory: An update and appraisal. In E. Harmon-Jones & J. S. Mills (Eds.), *Cognitive dissonance theory: Revival with revisions and controversies* (pp. 127–147). Washington, DC: American Psychological Association.

Asch, S. (1946). Forming impressions of personality. *Journal of Abnormal and Social Psychology, 41,* 258–290.

Ashcraft, M. H. (1998). *Fundamentals of cognition.* New York: Longman.

Atkinson, C. (2010). *The backchannel: How audiences are using Twitter and social media and changing presentations forever.* Berkeley, CA: New Riders.

Avtgis, T., & Rancer, A. S. (Eds.). (2010). *Arguments, aggression, and conflict: New directions in theory and research.* Clifton, NJ: Routledge.

Axtell, R. E. (1990). *Do's and taboos of hosting international visitors.* New York: Wiley.

Axtell, R. E. (1993). *Do's and taboos around the world* (3rd ed.). New York: Wiley.

Axtell, R. E. (2007). *Essential do's and taboos: The complete guide to international business and leisure travel.* Hoboken, NJ: Wiley.

Ayres, J. (1986). Perceptions of speaking ability: An explanation for stage fright. *Communication Education, 35,* 275–287.

Bach, G. R., & Wyden, P. (1968). *The intimate enemy.* New York: Avon.

Bacon, K. (2011). More deadly than sticks and stones. In Larry Schnoor (Ed.), *Winning Orations* (pp. 104–106). Mankato, MN: Interstate Oratorical Association.

Bains, G. (2015). *Cultural DNA: The psychological of globalization.* Hoboken, NJ: Wiley.

Balsam, K. F., Beauchaine, T. P., Rothblum, E. D., & Solomon, S. E. (2008). Three-year follow-up of same-sex couples who had civil unions in Vermont, same-sex couples not in civil unions, and heterosexual married couples. *Developmental Psychology, 44,* 102–116.

Barker, L. L. (1990). *Communication* (5th ed.). Englewood Cliffs, NJ: Prentice-Hall.

Barker, L., Edwards, R., Gaines, C., Gladney, K., & Holley, F. (1980). An investigation of proportional time spent in various communication activities by college students. *Journal of Applied Communication Research, 8,* 101–109.

Barnlund, D. C. (1970). A transactional model of communication. In J. Akin, A. Goldberg, G. Myers, & J. Stewart (Eds.), *Language behavior: A book of readings in communication.* The Hague: Mouton.

Barnlund, D. C. (1975). Communicative styles in two cultures: Japan and the United States. In A. Kendon, R. M. Harris, & M. R. Key (Eds.), *Organization of behavior in face-to-face interaction.* The Hague: Mouton.

Barnlund, D. C. (1989). *Communicative styles of Japanese and Americans: Images and realities.* Belmont, CA: Wadsworth.

Baron, R. A., & Byrne, D. (1984). *Social psychology: Understanding human interaction* (4th ed.). Boston: Allyn & Bacon.

Baron, R. A., Branscombe, N. R., & Byrne, D. R. (2009). *Social psychology,* 11th ed. Boston: Allyn & Bacon.

Barrett, L., & Godfrey, T. (1988). Listening. *Person Centered Review, 3,* 410–425.

Barry, D. T. (2003). Cultural and demographic correlates of self-reported guardedness among East Asian immigrants in the U.S. *International Journal of Psychology, 38,* 150–159.

Basso, K. H. (1972). To give up on words: Silence in Apache culture. In P. P. Giglioli (Ed.), *Language and social context.* New York: Penguin.

Bassellier, G., & Benbasat, I. (2004). Business competence of information technology professionals: Conceptual development and influence on IT-business partnerships. *MIS Quarterly* 28 (December), 673–694.

Baumeister, R. F., Bushman, B. J., & Campbell, W. K. (2000, February). Self-esteem, narcissism, and aggression: Does violence result from low self-esteem or from threatened egotism? *Current Directions in Psychological Science, 9,* 26–29.

Bavelas, J. B. (1990). Can one not communicate? Behaving and communicating: A reply to Motley. *Western Journal of Speech Communication, 54,* 593–602.

Baxter, L. A. (1983). Relationship disengagement: An examination of the reversal hypothesis. *Western Journal of Speech Communication, 47,* 85–98.

Baxter, L. A. (1984). An investigation of compliance-gaining as politeness. *Human Communication Research, 10,* 427–456.

Baxter, L. A. (1986). Gender differences in the heterosexual relationship rules embedded in break-up accounts. *Journal of Social and Personal Relationships, 3,* 289–306.

Beard, A. (2014). Mindfulness in the age of complexity: Interview with Ellen Langer. *Harvard Business Review, 94* (3), 68–73.

Beatty, M. J. (1988). Situational and predispositional correlates of public speaking anxiety. *Communication Education, 37,* 28–39.

Beatty, M. J., Rudd, J. E., & Valencic, K. M. (1999). A re-evaluation of the verbal aggressiveness scale: One factor or two? *Communication Research Reports, 16,* 10–17.

Bechler, C., & Johnson, S. D. (1995). Leadership and listening: A study of member perceptions. *Small Group Research, 26,* 77–85.

Beck, A. T. (1988). *Love is never enough.* New York: Harper & Row.

Bedford, V. H. (1996). Relationships between adult siblings. In A. E. Auhagen & M. von Salisch (Eds.), *The diversity of human relationships* (pp. 120–140). New York: Cambridge University Press.

Beebe, S. A., & Masterson, J. T. (2012). *Communicating in small groups: Principles and practices* (10th ed.). Boston, MA: Allyn & Bacon.

Bell, R. A., & Daly, J. A. (1984). The affinity-seeking function of communication. *Communication Monographs, 51,* 91–115.

Bellafiore, D. (2005). Interpersonal conflict and effective communication. Retrieved May 7, 2006, from www .drbalternatives.com/articles/cc2.html.

Benne, K. D., & Sheats, P. (1948). Functional roles of group members. *Journal of Social Issues, 4,* 41–49.

Bennis, W., & Nanus, B. (2003). *Leaders: The strategies for taking charge.* New York: Harper & Row.

Benoit, W. L., & Benoit, P. J. (1990). Memory for conversational behavior, *Southern Communication Journal, 55,* 17–23.

Benson, S. G., & Dundis, S. P. (2003). Understanding and motivating health care employees: Integrating Maslow's hierarchy of needs, training and technology. *Journal of Nursing Management, 11,* 315–320.

Berg, J. H., & Archer, R. L. (1983). The disclosure-liking relationship. *Human Communication Research, 10,* 269–281.

Berger, C. R., & Bradac, J. J. (1982). *Language and social knowledge: Uncertainty in interpersonal relations.* London: Edward Arnold.

Bernstein, W. M., Stephan, W. G., & Davis, M. H. (1979). Explaining attributions for achievement: A path analytic approach. *Journal of Personality and Social Psychology, 37,* 1810–1821.

Berry, J. N. III (2004). Can I quote you on that? *Library Journal, 129,* 10.

Berscheid, E., & Reis, H. T. (1998). Attraction and close relationships. In D. Gilbert, S. Fiske, & G. Lindzey (Eds.), *The Handbook of Social Psychology,* 4th ed. (Vol. 2, pp. 193–281).

Bersin, J. (2013). The 9 hottest trends in corporate recruiting. http://www.forbes.com/sites/joshbersin/2013/07/04/the-9-hottest-trends-in-corporate-recruiting/

Beshears, J., & Gino, F. (2015, May). Leaders as decision architects. *Harvard Business Review,* 52–62.

Blake, R. R., & Mouton, J. S. (1984). *The managerial grid III* (3rd ed.). Houston, TX: Gulf.

Blieszner, R., & Adams, R. G. (1992). *Adult friendship.* Newbury Park, CA: Sage.

Bochner, S., & Hesketh, B. (1994). Power distance, individualism/collectivism, and job-related attitudes in a culturally diverse work group. *Journal of Cross-Cultural Psychology, 25,* 233–257.

Bok, S. (1978). *Lying: Moral choice in public and private life.* New York: Pantheon.

Bok, S. (1983). *Secrets.* New York: Vintage.

Borden, G. A. (1991). *Cultural orientation: An approach to understanding intercultural communication.* Englewood Cliffs, NJ: Prentice-Hall.

Bower, B. (2001). Self-illusions come back to bite students. *Science News, 159,* 148.

Bower, S. A., & Bower, G. A. (2005). *Asserting yourself: A practical guide for positive change.* Cambridge, MA: DaCapo Press.

Brashers, D. E. (2007). A theory of communication and uncertainty management. In B. B. Whaley & W. Samter (Eds.), *Explaining communication: Contemporary theories and exemplars* (pp. 201–218). Mahwah, NJ: Lawrence Erlbaum.

Bridges, C. R. (1996). The characteristics of career achievement perceived by African American college administrators. *Journal of Black Studies, 26,* 748–767.

Brilhart, J., & Galanes, G. (1992). *Effective group discussion* (7th ed.). Dubuque, IA: Brown & Benchmark.

Brown, P. (1980). How and why are women more polite: Some evidence from a Mayan community. In S. McConnell-Ginet, R. Borker, & M. Furman (Eds.), *Women and language in literature and society* (pp. 111–136). New York: Praeger.

Brown, P., & Levinson, S. C. (1987). *Politeness: Some universals of language usage.* Cambridge, England: Cambridge University Press.

Brownell, J. (1987). Listening: The toughest management skill. *Cornell Hotel and Restaurant Administration Quarterly, 27,* 64–71.

Brownell, J. (2008). Exploring the strategic ground for listening and organizational effectiveness. *Scandinavian Journal of Hospitality and Tourism, 8,* 211–229.

Brownell, J. (2013). *Listening: Attitudes, principles, and skills* (5th ed.). New York: Routledge.

Brownell, J. (2010). *Listening: Attitudes, principles, and skills* (4th ed.). Boston, MA: Allyn & Bacon.

Bruneau, T. (1985). The time dimension in intercultural communication. In L. A. Samovar & R. E. Porter (Eds.), *Intercultural communication: A reader* (4th ed., pp. 280–289). Belmont, CA: Wadsworth.

Bruneau, T. (1990). Chronemics: The study of time in human interaction. In J. A. DeVito & M. L. Hecht (Eds.), *The nonverbal communication reader* (pp. 301–311). Prospect Heights, IL: Waveland Press.

Bruneau, T. (2009/2010). Chronemics: Time-binding and the construction of personal time. *General Semantics Bulletin, 76,* 82–94.

Buber, M. (1958). *I and thou* (2nd ed.). New York: Scribner's.

Buller, D. B., LePoire, B. A., Aune, K., & Eloy, S. (1992). Social perceptions as mediators of the effect of speech rate similarity on compliance. *Human Communication Research, 19,* 286–311.

Bullock, B. E., & Toribio, A. J. (2012). *The Cambridge handbook of linguistic code-switching.* Cambridge, UK: Cambridge University Press.

Burgoon, J. K., & Bacue, A. E. (2003). Nonverbal communication skills. In J. O. Greene & B. R. Burleson (Eds.), *Handbook of communication and social interaction skills* (pp. 179–220). Mahwah, NJ: Erlbaum.

Burgoon, J. K., & Hale, J. L. (1988). Nonverbal expectancy violations: Model elaboration and application to immediacy behaviors. *Communication Monographs, 55*, 58–79.

Burgoon, J. K., & Hoobler, G. D. (2002). Nonverbal signals. In M. L. Knapp & J. A. Daly (Eds.), *Handbook of interpersonal communication* (3rd ed., pp. 240–299). Thousand Oaks, CA: Sage.

Burgoon, J. K., Berger, C. R., & Waldron, V. R. (2000). Mindfulness and interpersonal communication. *Journal of Social Issues, 56*, 105–127.

Burgoon, J. K., Buller, D. B., & Woodall, W. G. (1996). *Nonverbal communication: The unspoken dialogue* (2nd ed.). New York: McGraw-Hill.

Burgoon, J. K., Guerrero, L. K., & Manusov, V. (2011). In Knapp, M. L., & Daly, J. A. (Eds.), *The sage handbook of interpersonal communication*, (4th ed., pp. 239–282). Los Angeles, CA: Sage.

Burgoon, J., Guerrero, L., & Floyd, K. (2010). *Nonverbal communication*. Boston, MA: Allyn & Bacon.

Burgoon, J. K. & Bacue, A. E. (2003). Nonverbal communication skills. In *Handbook of communication and social interaction skills*, J. O. Greene & B. R. Burleson (eds.). Mahwah, NJ: Lawrence Erlbaum, pp. 179–220.

Burgstahler, S. (2007, July). Managing an e-mentoring community to support students with disabilities: A case study. *Distance Education Report, 11*, 7–15.

Burleson, B. R., Holmstrom, A. J., & Gilstrap, C. M. (2005). "Guys can't say *that* to guys": Four experiments assessing the normative motivation account for deficiencies in the emotional support provided by men. *Communication Monographs, 72*, 468–501.

Burleson, B. R., Kunkel, A. W., & Birch, J. D. (1994). Thoughts about talk in romantic relationships: Similarity makes for attraction (and happiness, too). *Communication Quarterly, 42*, 259–273.

Burleson, B. R., Samter, W., & Luccetti, A. E. (1992). Similarity in communication values as a predictor of friendship choices: Studies of friends and best friends. *Southern Communication Journal, 57*, 260–276.

Burnard, P. (2003). Ordinary chat and therapeutic conversation: Phatic communication and mental health nursing. *Journal of Psychiatric and Mental Health Nursing, 10*, 678–682.

Butler, J., Pryor, B., & Grieder, M. (1998). Impression formation as a function of male baldness. *Perceptual and Motor Skills, 86*, 347–350.

Butler, P. E. (1981). *Talking to yourself: Learning the language of self-support*. New York: Harper & Row.

Byers, E. S., & Demmons, S. (1999). Sexual satisfaction and sexual self-disclosure within dating relationships. *Journal of Sex Research, 36*, 180–189.

Cahn, D. D., & Abigail, R. A. (2007). *Managing conflict through communication* (3rd ed.). Boston: Allyn & Bacon.

Cai, D. A., & Fink, E. L. (2002). Conflict style differences between individualists and collectivists. *Communication Monographs, 69*, 67–87.

Canary, D. J. (2003). Managing interpersonal conflict: A model of events related to strategic choices. In J. O. Greene & B. R. Burleson (Eds.), *Handbook of communication and social interaction skills* (pp. 515–550). Mahwah, NJ: Lawrence Erlbaum.

Canary, D. J., & Hause, K. (1993). Is there any reason to research sex differences in communication? *Communication Quarterly, 41*, 129–144.

Canary, D. J., Cupach, W. R., & Messman, S. J. (1995). *Relationship conflict: Conflict in parent-child, friendship, and romantic relationships*. Thousand Oaks, CA: Sage.

Cappella, J. N. (1993). The facial feedback hypothesis in human interaction: Review and speculation. *Journal of Language and Social Psychology, 12*, 13–29.

Caproni, P. J. (2012). *Management skills for everyday life* (3rd ed.). Boston, MA: Prentice-Hall.

Carroll, D. W. (1994). *Psychology of language* (2nd ed.). Pacific Grove, CA: Brooks/Cole.

Cate, R. J., Henton, J., Koval, R., Christopher, F., & Lloyd, S. (1982). Premarital abuse: A social psychological perspective. *Journal of Family Issues, 3*, 79–90.

Caughlin, J. P., Koerner, A. F., Schrodt, P., & Fitzpatrick, M. A. (2011). Interpersonal communication in family relationships. In Knapp, M. L., & Daly, J. A. (Eds.), *The Sage handbook of interpersonal communication*, 4th ed. (pp. 679–714). Los Angeles, CA: Sage.

Cawthon, S. W. (2001). Teaching strategies in inclusive classrooms with deaf students. *Journal of Deaf Studies and Deaf Education, 6*, 212–225.

Chadwick-Jones, J. K. (1976). *Social exchange theory: Its structure and influence in social psychology*. New York: Academic Press.

Chang, H., & Holt, G. R. (1996). The changing Chinese interpersonal world: Popular themes in interpersonal communication books in modern Taiwan. *Communication Quarterly, 44*, 85–106.

Chanowitz, B., & Langer, E. (1981). Premature cognitive commitment. *Journal of Personality and Social Psychology, 41*, 1051–1063.

Cheney, G., & Tompkins, P. K. (1987). Coming to terms with organizational identification and commitment. *Central States Speech Journal, 38*, 1–15.

Childress, H. (2004). Teenagers, territory and the appropriation of space. *Childhood: A Global Journal of Child Research, 11*, 195–205.

Chung, L. C., & Ting-Toomey, S. (1999). Ethnic identity and relational expectations among Asian Americans. *Communication Research Reports, 16,* 157–166.

Clance, P. R. (1985) *The impostor phenomenon: Overcoming the fear that haunts your success.* New York: Peachtree, 1985.

Clark, H. (1974). The power of positive speaking. *Psychology Today, 8,* 102, 108–111.

Clinton, H. (1995). Remarks to the U.N. 4th World Conference on Women Plenary Session. Retrieved May 9, 2012, from http://www.americanrhetoric.com/speeches/hillaryclint onbeijingspeech.htm.

Cody, M. J., & Dunn, D. (2007). Accounts. In B. B. Whaley and W. Samter (Eds.), *Explaining communication: Contemporary theories and exemplars* (pp. 237–256). Mahwah, NJ: Lawrence Erlbaum.

Coleman, P. (2002). *How to say it for couples: Communicating with tenderness, openness, and honesty.* Paramus, NJ: Prentice-Hall.

Collins, J. E., & Clark, L. F. (1989). Responsibility and rumination: The trouble with understanding the dissolution of a relationship. *Social Cognition, 7,* 152–173.

Comer, L. B., & Drollinger, T. (1999). Active emphatic listening and selling success: A conceptual framework. *Journal of Personal Selling and Sales Management, 19,* 15–29.

Cooley, C. H. (1922). *Human nature and the social order* (Rev. ed.). New York: Scribner's.

Cooper, A., & Sportolari, L. (1997). Romance in cyberspace: Understanding online attraction. *Journal of Sex Education and Therapy, 22,* 7–14.

Coover, G. E., & Murphy, S. T. (2000). The communicated self: Exploring the interaction between self and social context. *Human Communication Research, 26,* 125–147.

Cornwell, B., & Lundgren, D. C. (2001). Love on the Internet: Involvement and misrepresentation in romantic relationships in cyberspace vs. realspace. *Computers in Human Behavior, 17,* 197–211.

Crawford, M. (1994). Rethinking the romance: Teaching the content and function of gender stereotypes in the Psychology of Women course. *Teaching of Psychology, 21,* 151–153.

Crowley, A. (1999, August 30). Project leaders wanted. *PC Week,* 76.

Crown, C. L., & Cummins, D. A. (1998). Objective versus perceived vocal interruptions in the dialogues of unacquainted pairs, friends, and couples. *Journal of Language and Social Psychology, 17,* 372–389.

Cunningham, M. R. (2009). Social allergies. *Encyclopedia of human relationships,* H. T. Reis & S. Sprecher (Eds.). Thousand Oaks, Sage.

Dahle. C. (2004, July 25). Choosing a mentor? Cast a wide net. *New York Times,* BU 9.

Davis, F. (1973). *Inside intuition.* New York: New American Library.

Davitz, J. R. (Ed.). (1964). *The communication of emotional meaning.* New York: McGraw-Hill.

Deal, J. E., & Wampler, K. S. (1986). Dating violence: The primacy of previous experience. *Journal of Social and Personal Relationships, 3,* 457–471.

deBono, E. (1976). *Teaching thinking.* New York: Penguin.

Dell, K. (2005, February 14). Just for dudes. *Time,* B22.

Department of Health and Human Services. (2006, November). Gaining consensus among stakeholders through the nominal group technique. http://www.cdc.gov/healthyyouth/evaluation/pdf/brief7.pdf, acccessed February 17, 2015.

DePaulo, B. M., Lindsay, J. J., Malone, B. E., Muhlenbruck, L., Charlton, K., & Cooper, H. (2003). Cues to deception. *Psychological Bulletin, 129,* 74–118.

Derlega, V. J., Winstead, B. A., & Wong, P. T. P., & Greenspan, M. (1987). Self-disclosure and relationship development: An attributional analysis. In M. E. Roloff & G. R. Miller (Eds.), *Interpersonal processes: New directions in communication research* (pp. 172–187). Thousand Oaks, CA: Sage.

DeTurck, M. A. (1987). When communication fails: Physical aggression as a compliance-gaining strategy. *Communication Monographs, 54,* 106–112.

DeVito, J. A. (1965). Comprehension factors in oral and written discourse of skilled communicators. *Communication Monographs, 32,* 124–128.

DeVito, J. A. (1976). Relative ease in comprehending yes/no questions. In J. Blankenship & H. G. Stelzner (Eds.), *Rhetoric and communication* (pp. 143–154). Urbana: University of Illinois Press.

DeVito, J. A. (1981). *The psychology of speech and language: An introduction to psycholinguistics.* Washington, DC: University Press of America.

DeVito, J. A. (1996). *Brainstorms: How to think more creatively about communication (or about anything else).* New York: Longman.

DeVito, J. A. (2003). SCREAM before you scream. *ETC: A Review of General Semantics, 60* (Spring), 42–45.

DeVito, J. A. (2010). *The interviewing guidebook* (2nd ed.). Boston, MA: Pearson.

DeVito, J. A. (2012). *50 communication strategies.* Bloomington, IL: iUniverse.

DeVito, J. A. (2014). *The nonverbal communication book.* Dubuque, IA: Kendall-Hunt.

Dewey, J. (1910). *How we think.* Boston, MA: Heath.

Dillard, J. P., & Marshall, L. J. (2003). Persuasion as a social skill. In J. O. Greene & B. R. Burleson (Eds.),

Handbook of communication and social interaction skills (pp. 479–514). Mahwah, NJ: Erlbaum.

Dindia, K., & Canary, D. J. (2006). (Eds). *Sex differences and similarities in communication* (2nd ed.). Mahwah, NJ: Lawrence Erlbaum.

Donahue, W. A., with Kolt, R. (1992). *Managing interpersonal conflict.* Thousand Oaks, CA: Sage.

Donaldson, S. (1992). Gender and discourse: The case of interruptions. *Carleton Papers in Applied Language Studies, 9,* 47–66.

Donovan, J. (2014). *How to deliver a TED talk: Secrets of the world's most inspiring presentations.* New York: McGraw-Hill.

Dovidio, J. F., Gaertner, S. E., Kawakami, K., & Hodson, G. (2002). Why can't we just get along? Interpersonal biases and interracial distrust. *Cultural Diversity and Ethnic Minority Psychology, 8,* 88–102.

Drass, K. A. (1986). The effect of gender identity on conversation. *Social Psychology Quarterly, 49,* 294–301.

Dresser, N. (1996). *Multicultural manners: New rules of etiquette for a changing society.* New York: Wiley.

Dresser, N. (1999). *Multicultural celebrations: Today's rules of etiquette for life's special occasions.* New York: Three River Press.

Dresser, N. (2005). *Multicultural manners: Essential rules of etiquette for the 21st Century, rev. ed.* New York: Wiley.

Drews, D. R., Allison, C. K., & Probst, J. R. (2000). Behavioral and self-concept differences in tattooed and nontattooed college students. *Psychological Reports, 86,* 475–481.

Dreyfuss, H. (1971). *Symbol sourcebook.* New York: McGraw-Hill.

Drummond, K., & Hopper, R. (1993). Acknowledgment tokens in series. *Communication Reports, 6,* 47–53.

Dsilva, M., & Whyte, L. O. (1998). Cultural differences in conflict styles: Vietnamese refugees and established residents. *The Howard Journal of Communication, 9,* 57–68.

Dunbar, N. E., & Burgoon, J. K. (2005). Measuring nonverbal dominance. In V. Manusov (Ed.), *The sourcebook of nonverbal measures: Going beyond words* (pp. 361–374). Mahwah, NJ: Lawrence Erlbaum.

Dunbar, R. I. M. (2004). Gossip in evolutionary perspective. *Review of General Psychology 8,* 100–110.

Duncan, S. D., Jr. (1972). Some signals and rules for taking speaking turns in conversation. *Journal of Personality and Social Psychology, 23,* 283–292.

Dunn, D., & Cody, M. J. (2000). Account credibility and public image: Excuses, justifications, denials, and sexual harassment. *Communication Monographs, 67,* 372–391.

Duval, T. S., & Silva, P. J. (2002). Self-awareness, probability of improvement, and the self-serving bias. *Journal of Personality and Social Psychology, 82,* 49–61.

Eastwick, P. W., & Finkel, E. J. (2009). Reciprocity of Liking. In H. T. Reis & S. Sprecher (Eds.), *Encyclopedia of human relationships* (pp. 1333–1336). Thousand Oaks, CA: Sage.

Eccles, A. (2009). You're driving me crazy! *Psychology Today, 42,* 66–75.

Eden, D. (1992). Leadership and expectations: Pygmalion effects and other self-fulfilling prophecies in organizations. *Leadership Quarterly, 3,* 271–305.

Eder, D., & Enke, J. L. (1991). The structure of gossip: Opportunities and constraints on collective expression among adolescents. *American Sociological Review, 56,* 494–508.

Egan, K. G., & Moreno, M. A. (2011). Alcohol references on undergraduate male's Facebook profiles. *American Journal of Men's Health, 5,* 413–420.

Ehrenhaus, P. (1988). Silence and symbolic expression. *Communication Monographs, 55,* 41–57.

Einhorn, L. (2006). Using e-prime and English minus absolutisms to provide self-empathy. *ETC: A Review of General Semantics, 63,* 180–186.

Einstein, E. (1995). Success or sabotage: Which self-fulfilling prophecy will the stepfamily create? In D. K. Huntley (Ed.), *Understanding stepfamilies: Implications for assessment and treatment.* Alexandria, VA: American Counseling Association.

Ekman, P. (1985). *Telling lies: Clues to deceit in the marketplace, politics, and marriage.* New York, NY: Norton.

Ekman, P. (2003). *Emotions revealed.* New York: St. Martins.

Ekman, P. (2009). *Telling lies: Clues to deceit in the marketplace, politics, and marriage* (3rd ed.). New York: Norton.

Ekman, P., & Friesen, W. V. (1969). The repertoire of nonverbal behavior: Categories, origins, usage, and coding. *Semiotica, 1,* 49–98.

Ekman, P., Friesen, W. V., & Ellsworth, P. (1972). *Emotion in the human face: Guidelines for research and an integration of findings.* New York: Pergamon Press.

Elfenbein, H. A., & Ambady, N. (2002). Is there an in-group advantage in emotion recognition? *Psychological Bulletin, 128,* 243–249.

Ellis, A. (1988). *How to stubbornly refuse to make yourself miserable about anything, yes anything.* Secaucus, NJ: Lyle Stuart.

Ellis, A., & Dryden, W. (2007). *The practice of rational emotive therapy* (2nd ed.). New York: Springer.

Elmes, M. B., & Gemmill, G. (1990). The psychodynamics of mindlessness and dissent in small groups. *Small Group Research, 21,* 28–44.

Emmers-Sommer, T. M. (2004). The effect of communication quality and quantity indicators on intimacy and relational satisfaction. *Journal of Social and Personal Relationships, 21,* 99–411.

Exline, R. V., Ellyson, S. L., & Long, B. (1975). Visual behavior as an aspect of power role relationships. In P. Pliner, L. Krames, & T. Alloway (Eds.), *Nonverbal communication of aggression*. New York: Plenum Press.

Faigley, L. (2009). *The Penguin handbook* (3rd ed.). New York: Longman.

Fengler, A. P. (1974). Romantic love in courtship: Divergent paths of male and female students. *Journal of Comparative Family Studies*, 134–139.

Festinger, L. (1954). A theory of social comparison processes. *Human Relations, 7*, 117–140.

Fielder, F. E. (1967). *A theory of leadership effectiveness*. New York: McGraw-Hill.

Fitzpatrick, M. A. (1983). Predicting couples' communication from couples' self-reports. In R. N. Bostrom (Ed.), *Communication Yearbook 7* (pp. 49–82). Thousand Oaks, CA: Sage.

Fitzpatrick, M. A. (1988). *Between husbands and wives: Communication in marriage*. Thousand Oaks, CA: Sage.

Fitzpatrick, M. A. (1991). Sex differences in marital conflict: Social psychophysiological versus cognitive explanations. *Text, 11*, 341–364.

Fitzpatrick, M. A., Jandt, F. E., Myrick, F. L., & Edgar, T. (1994). Gay and lesbian couple relationships. In R. J. Ringer (Ed.), *Queer words, queer images: Communication and the construction of homosexuality* (pp. 265–285). New York: New York University Press.

Floyd, K., & Mikkelson, A. C. (2005). In V. Manusov (Ed.), *The sourcebook of nonverbal measures: Going beyond words* (pp. 47–56). Mahwah, NJ: Lawrence Erlbaum.

Folger, J. P., Poole, M. S., & Stutman, R. K. (2013). *Working through conflict: A communication perspective* (7th ed.). New York: Longman.

Folger, J. P., Poole, M. S., & Stutman, R. K. (2013). *Working through conflict: A communication perspective* (7th ed.). Boston, MA: Allyn & Bacon.

Forbes, G. B. (2001). College students with tattoos and piercings: Motives, family experiences, personality factors, and perception by others. *Psychological Reports, 89*, 774–786.

Freedman, J. (1978). *Happy people: What happiness is, who has it, and why*. New York: Ballantine.

French, J. R. P., Jr., & Raven, B. (1968). The bases of social power. In D. Cartwright & A. Zander (Eds.), *Group dynamics: Research and theory* (3rd ed., pp. 259–269). New York: Harper & Row.

Frentz, T. (1976). A general approach to episodic structure. Paper presented at the Western Speech Association Convention, San Francisco, CA. Cited in Reardon (1987).

Fridlund, A. J., & Russell, J. A. (2006). The functions of facial expressions. What's in a face? In V. Manusov & M. L. Patterson (Eds.), *The Sage handbook of nonverbal communication* (pp. 299–320). Newbury Park, CA: Sage.

Fried, M. (2013). Trending: Divorce rings. http://www.huffingtonpost.com/michael-fried/divorce-rings_b_4234373.html, accessed June 25, 2015.

Fukushima, S. (2004). *Requests and culture: Politeness in British English and Japanese*. New York: Peter Lang.

Fuller, D. (2004). Electronic manners and netiquette. *Athletic Therapy Today, 9*, 40–41.

Furlow, F. B. (1996). The smell of love. *Psychology Today*, 38–45.

Gallo, C. (2014). *Talk like TED: The 9 public-speaking secrets of the world's top minds*. New York: St. Martin's/Griffin.

Galvin, K. M., Braithwaite, D. O., & Bylund, C. L. (2015). *Family communication: Cohesion and change*, 9th ed. New York: Taylor & Francis.

Gamble, T. K., & Gamble, M. W. (2003). *The gender communication connection*. Boston: Houghton Mifflin.

Gamble, T. K., & Gamble, M. W. (2013), *Leading with communication*. Los Angeles, CA: Sage.

Gamson, J. (1998). Publicity traps: Television talk shows and lesbian, gay, bisexual, and transgender visibility. *Sexualities, 1* (February), 11–41.

Gao, G., & Gudykunst, W. B. (1995). Attributional confidence, perceived similarity, and network involvement in Chinese and American romantic relationships. *Communication Quarterly, 43*, 431–445.

Gelfand, M. J., Nishii, L. H., Holcombe, K. M., Dyer, N., Ohbuchi, K., & Fukuno, M. (2001). Cultural influences on cognitive representations of conflict: Interpretations of conflict episodes in the United States and Japan. *Journal of Applied Psychology, 86*, 1059–1074.

Georgas, J., et al. (2001). Functional relationships in the nuclear and extended family: A 16-culture study. *International Journal of Psychology, 36*, 289–300.

Gergen, K. J., Greenberg, M. S., & Willis, R. H. (1980). *Social exchange: Advances in theory and research*. New York: Plenum Press.

German, K., Gronbeck, B., Ehninger, D., & Monroe, A. H. (2013). *Principles of public speaking* (18th ed.). Boston, MA: Free Press.

Gibb, J. (1961). Defensive communication. *Journal of Communication, 11*, 141–148.

Giles, D. C. (2001). Parasocial interaction: A review of the literature and a model for future research. *Media Psychology, 4*, 279–305.

Giles, D. C., & Maltby, J. (2004, March). The role of media figures in adolescent development: Relations between autonomy, attachment, and interest in celebrities. *Personality and Individual Differences, 36*, 813–822.

Giles, H. (2008). Communication accommodation theory. In L. A. Baxter & D. O. Braithwaite (Eds.), *Engaging theories in interpersonal communication: Multiple perspectives* (pp. 161–173). Los Angeles, CA: Sage.

Giles, H., Mulac, A., Bradac, J. J., & Johnson, P. (1987). Speech accommodation theory: The first decade and beyond. In M. L. McLaughlin (Ed.), *Communication yearbook 10* (pp. 13–48). Thousand Oaks, CA: Sage.

Goffman, E. (1967). *Interaction ritual: Essays on face-to-face behavior.* New York: Pantheon.

Goffman, E. (1971). *Relations in public: Microstudies of the public order.* New York: HarperCollins.

Goldin-Meadow, S., Nusbaum, H., Kelly, S. D., & Wagner, S. (2001). Gesture—psychological aspects. *Psychological Science, 12,* 516–522.

Goldsmith, D. J. (2007). Brown and Levinson's politeness theory. In B. B. Whaley & W. Samter (Eds.), *Explaining communication: Contemporary theories and exemplars* (pp. 219–236). Mahwah, NJ: Lawrence Erlbaum.

Goldsmith, D. J., & Fulfs, P. A. (1999). "You just don't have the evidence": An analysis of claims and evidence. In M. E. Roloff (Ed.), *Communication yearbook 22* (pp. 1–49). Thousand Oaks, CA: Sage.

Goleman, D. (1995). *Emotional intelligence.* New York: Bantam.

Gonzalez, A., & Zimbardo, P. G. (1985). Time in perspective. *Psychology Today, 19,* 20–26.

Goodwin, R., & Lee, I. (1994). Taboo topics among Chinese and English friends: A cross-cultural comparison. *Journal of Cross-Cultural Psychology, 25,* 325–338.

Gorden, W. I., & Nevins, R. J. (1993). *We mean business: Building communication competence in business and professions.* New York: HarperCollins.

Gordon, T. (1975). *P.E.T.: Parent effectiveness training.* New York: New American Library.

Gottman, J. M., & Carrere, S. (1994). Why can't men and women get along? Developmental roots and marital inequities. In D. J. Canary and Laura Stafford (Eds.), *Communication and relational maintenance* (pp. 203–229). San Diego, CA: Academic Press.

Gottman, J. M., & Levenson, R. W. (1999). Dysfunctional marital conflict: Women are being unfairly blamed. *Journal of Divorce and Remarriage, 31,* 1–17.

Graham, J. A., & Argyle, M. (1975). The effects of different patterns of gaze combined with different facial expressions on impression formation. *Journal of Movement Studies, 1,* 178–182.

Graham, J. A., Bitti, P. R., & Argyle, M. (1975). A cross-cultural study of the communication of emotion by facial and gestural cues. *Journal of Human Movement Studies, 1,* 68–77.

Grant, A. (2013). Why some people have no boundaries online. http://www.huffingtonpost.com/adam-grant/why-some-people-have-no-b_b_3909799.html (accessed 8/28/15).

Greene, J. O. (2003). Models of adult communication skill acquisition: Practice and the course of performance improvement. In J. O. Greene & B. R. Burleson (Eds.), *Handbook of communication and social interaction skills* (pp. 51–92). Mahwah, NJ: Lawrence Erlbaum.

Greengard, S. (2001). Gossip poisons business. HR can stop it. *Workforce, 80,* 24–28.

Greene, K., Derlega, V., & Mathews, A. (2006). Self-disclosure in personal relationships. In: A. L. Vangelisti & D. Perlman (Eds.). *Cambridge Handbook of Personal Relationships* (pp. 409–427). Cambridge: Cambridge University Press.

Greif, E. B. (1980). Sex differences in parent-child conversations. *Women's Studies International Quarterly, 3,* 253–258.

Grice, H. P. (1975). Logic and conversation. In P. Cole & J. L. Morgan (Eds.), *Syntax and semantics,* Vol. 3, *Speech acts* (pp. 41–58). New York: Seminar Press.

Grierson, B. (2014, October, 22). The thought that counts. *New York Times Magazine, The Health Issue,* 52–56, 68–70.

Gross, L. (1991). The contested closet: The ethics and politics of outing. *Critical Studies in Mass Communication, 8,* 352–388.

Gross, T., Turner, E., & Cederholm, L. (1987, June). Building teams for global operation. *Management Review,* 32–36.

Gross, S. J. (2006). How to raise your self-esteem. *Psych Central.* Retrieved on December 28, 2013, from http://psychcentral.com/lib/how-to-raise-your-self-esteem/000737

Grossin, W. (1987). Monochronic time, polychronic time and policies for development. *Studi di Sociologia, 25,* 18–25.

Gu, Y. (1997). Polite phenomena in modern Chinese. *Journal of Pragmatics, 14,* 237–257.

Gudykunst, W. (1993). Toward a theory of effective interpersonal and intergroup communication: An anxiety/uncertainty management (AUM) perspective. In R. L. Wiseman (Ed.), *Intercultural communication competence.* Thousand Oaks, CA: Sage.

Gudykunst, W. B. (1994). *Bridging differences: Effective intergroup communication* (2nd ed.). Newbury Park, CA: Sage.

Gudykunst, W. B., & Kim, Y. Y. (Eds.). (1992). *Readings on communication with strangers: An approach to intercultural communication.* New York: McGraw-Hill.

Gudykunst, W. B. (1994). *Bridging differences: Effective intergroup communication*, 2nd ed. Thousand Oaks, CA: Sage.

Guerin, B. (2003). Combating prejudice and racism: New interventions from a functional analysis of racist language. *Journal of Community and Applied Social Psychology* 13 (January), 29–45.

Guerrero, L. K., & Andersen, P. A. (1991). The waxing and waning of relational intimacy: Touch as a function of relational stage, gender and touch avoidance. *Journal of Social and Personal Relationships, 8*, 147–165.

Guerrero, L. K., & Andersen, P. A. (1994). Patterns of matching and initiation: Touch behavior and touch avoidance across romantic relationship stages. *Journal of Nonverbal Behavior, 18*, 137–153.

Guerrero, L. K., & Hecht, M. L. (Eds.). (2006). *The nonverbal communication reader: Class and contemporary readings* (3rd ed.). Prospect Heights, IL: Waveland Press.

Guerrero, L. K., Andersen, P. A., & Afifi, W. A. (2007). *Close encounters: Communication in relationships* (2nd ed.). Thousand Oaks, CA: Sage.

Haar, B. F., & Krabe, B. (1999). Strategies for resolving interpersonal conflicts in adolescence: A German-Indonesian comparison. *Journal of Cross-Cultural Psychology, 30*, 667–683.

Hackman, M. Z., & Johnson, C. E. (1991). *Leadership: A communication perspective*. Prospect Heights, IL: Waveland Press.

Hafen, S. (2004). Organizational gossip: A revolving door of regulation and resistance, *Southern Communication Journal, 69* (Spring), 223–240.

Haga, Y. (1988). Traits de langage et caractère Japonais. *Cahiers de Sociologie Economique et Culturelle, 9*, 105–109.

Hall, E. T. (1959). *The silent language*. Garden City, NY: Doubleday.

Hall, E. T. (1963). A system for the notation of proxemic behavior. *American Anthropologist, 65*, 1003–1026.

Hall, E. T. (1966). *The hidden dimension*. Garden City, NY: Doubleday.

Hall, E. T. (1976). *Beyond culture*. Garden City, NY: Doubleday.

Hall, E. T. (1983). *The dance of life: The other dimension of time*. New York: Anchor Books/Doubleday.

Hall, E. T., & Hall, M. R. (1987). *Hidden differences: Doing business with the Japanese*. Garden City, NY: Doubleday.

Hall, J. A. (1998). How big are nonverbal sex differences? The case of smiling and sensitivity to nonverbal cues. In D. J. Canary & K. Dindia (Eds.), *Sex differences and similarities in communication: Critical essays and empirical investigations of sex and gender in interaction* (pp. 155–178). Mahwah, NJ: Erlbaum.

Haney, W. (1973). *Communication and organizational behavior: Text and cases* (3rd ed.). Homewood, IL: Irwin.

Hanley, S. J., & Abell, S. C. (2002, Fall). Maslow and relatedness: Creating an interpersonal model of self-actualization. *Journal of Humanistic Psychology, 42*, 37–56.

Harkins, S. (1987). Social facilitation and social loafing. *Journal of Experiemtnal Social Psychology, 23*, 1–18.

Hart, F. (1990). The construction of masculinity in men's friendships: Misogyny, heterosexuality, and homophobia. *Resources for Feminist Research, 19*, 60–67.

Harvey, J. C., & Katz, C. (1985). *If I'm so successful why do I feel like a fake: The impostor phenomenon*. New York: St. Martin's Press.

Hastings, S. O. (2000). "Egocasting" in the avoidance of disclosure: An intercultural perspective. In S. Petronio (Ed.), *Balancing the secrets of private disclosures* (pp. 235–248). Mahwah, NJ: Erlbaum.

Hatfield, E., & Rapson, R. L. (1996). *Love and sex: Cross-cultural perspectives*. Boston: Allyn & Bacon.

Hayakawa, S. I., & Hayakawa, A. R. (1989). *Language in thought and action* (5th ed.). New York: Harcourt Brace Jovanovich.

Hays, R. B. (1989). The day-to-day functioning of close versus casual friendships. *Journal of Social and Personal Relationships, 6*, 21–37.

Heap, J. L. (1992). Seeing snubs: An introduction to sequential analysis of classroom interaction. *Journal of Classroom Interaction, 27*, 23–28.

Heasley, J. B., Babbitt, C. E., & Burbach, H. J. (1995a). Gender differences in college students' perceptions of "fighting words." *Sociological Viewpoints, 11* (Fall), 30–40.

Heasley, J. B., Babbitt, C. E., & Burbach, H. J. (1995b). The role of social context in students' anticipatory reaction to a "fighting word." *Sociological Focus, 27*, 281–283.

Heath, W. P., Stone, J., Darley, J. M., & Grannemann, B. D. (2003). Yes, I did it, but don't blame me: Perceptions of excuse defenses. *Journal of Psychiatry and Law, 31*, 187–226.

Hecht, M. L. (1978). The conceptualization and measurement of interpersonal communication satisfaction. *Human Communication Research, 4*, 253–264.

Hecht, M. L., Jackson, R. L., & Ribeau, S. (2003). *African American communication: Exploing identify and culture* (2nd ed.). Mahwah, NJ: Erlbaum.

Helgeson, V. S. (2009). *Psychology of gender* (3rd ed.). Upper Saddle River, NJ: Prentice-Hall.

Helsper, E., & Whitty, M. (2010) Netiquette within married couples: Agreement about acceptable online behavior and surveillance between partners. *Computers in human behavior*, 26 (5). 916–926.

Hendrick, C., & Hendrick, S. (1990). A relationship-specific version of the love attitudes scale. In J. W. Heulip (Ed.), *Handbook of replication research in the behavioral and socialsciences* [Special issue]. *Journal of Social Behavior and Personality*, 5, 239–254.

Hendrick, C., Hendrick, S., Foote, F. H., & Slapion-Foote, M. J. (1984). Do men and women love differently? *Journal of Social and Personal Relationships, 1*, 177–195.

Herrick, J. A. (2004). *Argumentation: Understanding and shaping arguments*. State College, PA: Strata.

Hersey, P., Blanchard, K. H., & Johnson, D. E. (2001). *Management of organizational behavior: Leading human resources* (8th ed.). Upper Saddle River, NJ: Prentice-Hall.

Hesketh, B., & Neal, A. (2006). Using "war stories" to train for adaptive performance: Is it better to learn from error or success? *Applied Psychology: An International Review, 55*, 282–302.

Hewitt, J. P. (1998). *The myth of self-esteem: Finding happiness and solving problems in America*. New York: St. Martin's Press.

Hewitt, J., & Stokes, R. (1975). Disclaimers. *American Sociological Review, 40*, 1–11.

Himle, J. A., Abelson, J. L., & Haghightgou, H. (1999). Effect of alcohol on social phobic anxiety. *American Journal of Psychiatry, 156*, 1237–1243.

Hinduja, S., & Patchin, J. W. (2008). *Bullying: Beyond the schoolyard*. Thousand Oaks, CA: Corwin Press/Sage.

Hocker, J. L., & Wilmot, W. W. (1985). *Interpersonal conflict* (2nd ed.). Dubuque, IA: William C. Brown.

Hocker, J. L., & Wilmot, W. W. (2007). *Interpersonal conflict* (7th ed.). New York: McGraw Hill.

Hofstede, G. (1997). *Cultures and organizations: Software of the mind.* New York: McGraw-Hill.

Hofstede, G., Hofstede, G., & Minkov, M. (2010). *Cultures and organizations: Software of the mind* (3rd ed.). New York, NY: McGraw-Hill.

Hofstrand, D. (2006). Retrieved from http://www.extension.iastate.edu.

Hoft, N. L. (1995). *International technical communication: How to export information about high technology.* New York: Wiley.

Holmes, J. (1995). *Women, men and politeness.* New York: Longman.

Hollenbaugh, E. E., & Everett, M. K. (2013). The Effects of Anonymity on Self-Disclosure in Blogs: An Application of the Online Disinhibition Effect. *Journal of Computer-Mediated Communication*, 18, 283–302. DOI: 10.1111/jcc4.12008

Hsu, C-C., &. Sandford, B. A. (2007). The Delphi technique: Making sense of consensus. Practical assessment, research & evaluation. Retrieved from http://pareonline.net/pdf/v12n10.pdf, accessed March 12, 2015.

Hunt, M. O. (2000). Status, religion, and the "belief in a just world": Comparing African Americans, Latinos, and whites. *Social Science Quarterly, 81*, 325–343.

Huston, M., & Schwartz, P. (1995). The relationships of lesbians and gay men. In J. T. Wood, & S. Duck (Eds.), *Under-studied relationships: Off the beaten track* (pp. 89–121). Thousand Oaks, CA: Sage.

Iizuka, Y. (1993). Regulators in Japanese conversation. *Psychological Reports, 72*, 203–209.

In Knapp, M. L., & Daly, J. A. (Eds.), *The Sage handbook of interpersonal communication*, 4th ed. (pp. 679–714). Los Angeles, CA: Sage.

Infante, D. A. (1988). *Arguing constructively.* Prospect Heights, IL: Waveland Press.

Infante, D. A., & Rancer, A. (1982). A conceptualization and measure of argumentativeness. *Journal of Personality Assessment, 46*, 72–80.

Infante, D. A., & Rancer, A. S. (1995). Argumentativeness and verbal aggressiveness: A review of recent theory and research. In B. R. Burleson (Ed.), *Communication yearbook*, 19 (pp. 319–351). Thousand Oaks, CA: Sage.

Infante, D. A., & Wigley, C. J. (1986). Verbal aggressiveness: An interpersonal model and measure. *Communication Monographs*, 53, 61–69.

Infante, D. A., Rancer, A. S., & Womack, D. F. (2003). *Building communication theory* (4th ed.). Prospect Heights, IL: Waveland Press.

Iyengar, S. (2010). *The art of choosing.* New York: Hatchett Book Group.

Jacobson, D. (1999). Impression formation in cyberspace: Online expectations and offline experiences in text-based virtual communities. *Journal of Computer Mediated Communication*, 5.

Jambor, E., & Elliott, M. (2005, Winter). Self-esteem and coping strategies among deaf students. *Journal of Deaf Studies and Deaf Education, 10*, 63–81.

Jandt, F. E. (2010). *Intercultural communication* (6th ed.). Thousand Oaks, CA: Sage.

Janis, I. (1983). *Victims of group thinking: A psychological study of foreign policy decisions and fiascoes* (2nd ed.). Boston: Houghton Mifflin.

Jaworski, A. (1993). *The power of silence: Social and pragmatic perspectives.* Newbury Park, CA: Sage.

Jecker, J., & Landy, D. (1969). Liking a person as a function of doing him a favor. *Human Relations, 22*, 371–378.

Johannesen, R. L. (2001). *Ethics in human communication* (6th ed.). Prospect Heights, IL: Waveland Press.

Johannesen, R. L., Valde, K. S., & Whedbee, K. E. (2007). *Ethics in human communication* (6th ed.). Prospect Heights, IL: Waveland.

Johansson, W., & Percy, W. A. (1994). *Outing: Shattering the conspiracy of silence.* New York: Harrington Park Press.

Johnson, C. E. (1987). An introduction to powerful and powerless talk in the classroom. *Communication Education*, 36, 167–172.

Johnson, S. D., & Bechler, C. (1998). Examining the relationship between listening effectiveness and leadership emergence: Perceptions, behaviors, and recall. *Small Group Research*, 29, 452–471.

Johnson, S. M., & O'Connor, E. (2002). *The gay baby boom: The psychology of gay parenthood.* New York: New York University Press.

Joinson, A. N. (2001). Self-disclosure in computer-mediated communication: The role of self-awareness and visual anonymity. *European Journal of Social Psychology*, 31, 177–192.

Jones, B. C., DeBruine, L. M., Little, A. C., Burriss, R. P., & Feinberg, D. R. (2007). Social transmission of face preferences among humans. *Proceedings of the Royal Society, 274* (March 22): 899–903.

Jones, C., Berry, L., & Stevens, C. (2007). Synthesized speech intelligibility and persuasion: Speech rate and non-native listeners. *Computer Speech and Language, 21*, 641–651.

Jones, S. (2005). The touch-log record: A behavioral communication measure. In V. Manusov (Ed.), *The sourcebook of nonverbal measures: Going beyond words* (pp. 67–81). Mahwah, NJ: Lawrence Erlbaum.

Jones, S., & Yarbrough, A. E. (1985). A naturalistic study of the meanings of touch. *Communication Monographs, 52*, 19–56.

Jourard, S. M. (1968). *Disclosing man to himself.* New York: Van Nostrand Reinhold.

Jourard, S. M. (1971a). *Self-disclosure.* New York: Wiley.

Jourard, S. M. (1971b). *The transparent self* (Rev. ed.). New York: Van Nostrand Reinhold.

Judge, T. A., & Cable, D. M. (2004). The effect of physical height on workplace success and income. *Journal of Applied Psychology, 89*, 428–441.

Kallos, J. (2005). *Because netiquette matters! Your comprehensive reference guide to e-mail etiquette and proper technology use.* Philadelphia: Xlibris.

Kanner, B. (1989, April 3). Color schemes. *New York Magazine*, pp. 22–23.

Kapoor, S., Hughes, P. C., Baldwin, J. R., & Blue, J. (2003). The relationship of individualism-collectivism and self-construals to communication styles in India and the United States. *International Journal of Intercultural Relations, 27*, 683–700.

Katz, S. (2007). The importance of being beautiful. In *Down to earth sociology: Introductory readings* (14th ed., pp. 341–348). Henslin, J. W. (Ed.). New York: Free Press.

Kawasaki, G. (2015, May). Managing yourself: The art of evangelism. *Harvard Business Review*, 108–111.

Kelley, H. H., & Thibaut, J. W. (1978). *Interpersonal relations: A theory of interdependence.* New York: Wiley/Interscience.

Kelly, M. S. (2006). *Communication@work: Ethical, effective, and expressive communication in the workplace.* Boston, MA: Allyn & Bacon.

Kelly, P. K. (1994). *Team decision-making techniques.* Irvine, CA: Richard Chang Associates.

Kennedy, C. W., & Camden, C. T. (1988). A new look at interruptions. *Western Journal of Speech Communication, 47*, 45–58.

Kenrick, D. T., Neuberg, S. L., and Cialdini, R. B. (2007). *Social psychology: Goals in interaction* (4th ed.). Boston: Allyn & Bacon.

Ketcham, H. (1958). *Color planning for business and industry.* New York: Harper.

Keyes, R. (1980). *The height of your life.* New York: Warner.

Kiel, F. (2015). *Return on character.* Boston, MA: Harvard Business Review Press.

Kiel, J. M. (1999). Reshaping Maslow's hierarchy of needs to reflect today's education and managerial philosophies. *Journal of Instructional Psychology, 26*, 167–168.

Kindred, J., & Roper, S. L. (2004). Making connections via instant messenger (IM): Student use of IM to maintain personal relationships. *Qualitative Research Reports in Communication, 5*, 48–54.

Kleinfeld, N. R. (1992, October 25). The smell of money. *New York Times* (Section 9), pp. 1, 8.

Kleinke, C. L. (1986). *Meeting and understanding people.* New York: W. H. Freeman.

Knapp, M. L. (1984). *Interpersonal communication and human relationships.* Boston: Allyn & Bacon.

Knapp, M. L. (2008). *Lying and deception in human interaction.* Boston: Pearson.

Knapp, M. L., & Vangelisti, A. (2000). *Interpersonal communication and human relationships* (4th ed.). Boston: Allyn & Bacon.

Knapp, M. L., Hall, J. A., & Horgan, T. G. (2013). *Nonverbal communication in human interaction* (8th ed.). Thousand Oaks, CA: Wadsworth.

Knapp, M. L., Hart, R. P., Friedrich, G. W., & Shulman, G. M. (1973). The rhetoric of goodbye: Verbal and nonverbal correlates of human leave-taking. *Communication Monographs, 40*, 182–198.

Knobloch, L. K., & Solomon, D. H. (1999). Measuring the sources and content of relational uncertainty. *Communication Studies, 50,* 261–278.

Knobloch, L. K., Haunani, D., & Theiss, J. A. (2006). The role of intimacy in the production and perception of relationship talk within courtship. *Communication Research, 33,* 211–241.

Koerner, A. F., & Fitzpattrick, M. A. (1997). Family type and conflict: The impact of conversation orientation and conformity orientation on conflict in the family. *Communication Studies, 48,* 59–76.

Koerner, A. F., & Fitzpatrick, M. A. (2002, Fall). You never leave your family in a fight: The impact of family of origin of conflict behavior in romantic relationships. *Communication Studies, 53,* 234–252.

Koerner, A. F., & Fitzpatrick, M. A. (2004). Communication in intact families. In A. L. Vangelisti (Eds), *Handbook of family communication* (pp. 177–195). Mahwah, NJ: Erlbaum.

Komarovsky, M. (1964). *Blue collar marriage.* New York: Random House.

Koppelman, K. L., with Goodhart, R. L. (2005). *Understanding human differences: Multicultural education for a diverse America.* Boston: Allyn & Bacon.

Koscriski, K. (2007). Facial attractiveness: General patterns of facial preferences. *Anthropological Review, 70,* 45–79.

Krebs, G. L. (1989). *Organizational communication* (2nd ed.). Boston: Allyn & Bacon.

Krivonos, P. D., & Knapp, M. L. (1975). Initiating communication: What do you say when you say hello? *Central States Speech Journal, 26,* 115–125.

Kross, E., et al. (2014). Self-talk as a regulartory mechanism: How you do it matters. *Journal of Personality and Social Psychology, 196,* 304–324.

Kurdek, L. A. (1994). Areas of conflict for gay, lesbian, and heterosexual couples: What couples argue about influences relationship satisfaction. *Journal of Marriage and the Family, 56,* 923–934.

Lakoff, R. (1975). *Language and women's place.* New York: Harper & Row.

Lamm, K., & Lamm, K. (1999). *10,000 ideas for term papers, projects, reports, and speeches* (5th ed.). New York: Arco.

Lancer, D. (2013). Low self-esteem is learned. *Psych Central.* Retrieved on December 28, 2013, from http://psychcentral.com/lib/low-self-esteem-is-learned/00018092

Langer, E. J. (1989). *Mindfulness.* Reading, MA: Addison-Wesley.

Lanzetta, J. T., Cartwright-Smith, J., & Kleck, R. E. (1976). Effects of nonverbal dissimulations on emotional experience and autonomic arousal. *Journal of Personality and Social Psychology, 33,* 354–370.

Laroche, C., & deGrace, G. R. (1997). Factors of satisfaction associated with happiness in adults. *Canadian Journal of Counselling, 31,* 275–286.

Larsen, R. J., Kasimatis, M., & Frey, K. (1992). Facilitating the furrowed brow: An unobtrusive test of the facial feedback hypothesis applied to unpleasant affect. *Cognition and Emotion, 6,* 321–338.

Latané, B., Williams, K., & Harkins, S. (2006). Many hands make the light work: The causes and consequences of social loafing. In J. M. Levine & R. L. Moreland (Eds.), *Small groups* (pp. 297–308). New York: Psychology Press.

Lauer, C. S. (2003, February 10). Listen to this. *Modern Healthcare, 33,* 34.

Leathers, D., & Eaves, M. H. (2008). *Successful nonverbal communication: Principles and applications* (4th ed.). Boston: Allyn & Bacon.

Lederer, W. J. (1984). *Creating a good relationship.* New York: Norton.

Lee, A. M., & Lee, E. B. (1972). *The fine art of propaganda.* San Francisco: International Society for General Semantics.

Lee, A. M., & Lee, E. B. (1995). The iconography of propaganda analysis. *ETC: A Review of General Semantics, 52,* 13–17.

Lee, C. M., & Gudykunst, W. B. (2001). Attraction in initial interethnic interactions. *Journal of Intercultural Relations, 25,* 373–387.

Lee, H. O., & Boster, F. J. (1992). Collectivism–individualism in perceptions of speech rate: A cross-cultural comparison. *Journal of Cross-Cultural Psychology, 23,* 377–388.

Lee, J. A. (1976). *The colors of love.* New York: Bantam.

Lee, K., Cameron, C. A., Xu, F., Fu, G., & Board, J. (2011, June). Chinese and Canadian children's evaluations of lying and truth telling: Similarities and differences in the context of pro- and antisocial behaviors. Article published online: doi:10.1111/j.1467-8624.1997.tb01971.x.

Lee, R. L. M. (1984). Malaysian queue culture: An ethnography of urban public behavior. *Southeast Asian Journal of Social Science, 12,* 36–50.

Leech, G. (1983). *Principles of pragmatics.* London: Longman.

Lee, T. M. C., Liu, H. L., Tan, L. H., Chan, C. C. H., Mahankali, S., Feng, C. M., et al. (2002). Lie detection by functional magnetic resonance imaging. *Human Brain Mapping, 15,* 157–164.

Lenhart, A. (2009). Social networks grow: Friending Mom and Dad. Retrieved January 27, 2009, from http://www.Pewresearch.org/.../social-networks.

Lenhart, A., Madden, M., Smith, A., Purcell, K., Zickuhr, K., & Rainie, L. (2011). Teens, kindness and cruelty on social network sites. Retrieved from http://pewinterest.org/Reports/2011/Teens-and-social-media.aspx.

Leung, K. (1988, March). Some determinants of conflict avoidance. *Journal of Cross-Cultural Psychology, 19,* 125–136.

Leung, S. A. (2001). Editor's introduction. *Asian Journal of Counseling, 8,* 107–109.

Lever, J. (1995). The 1995 Advocate survey of sexuality and relationships: The women, lesbian sex survey. *The Advocate, 687/688,* 22–30.

Levine, D. (2000). Virtual attraction: What rocks your boat. *Cyber Psychology and Behavior, 3,* 565–573.

Levine, M. (2004, June 1). Tell the doctor all your problems, but keep it to less than a minute. *New York Times,* p. F6.

LeVine, R., & Bartlett, K. (1984). Pace of life, punctuality, and coronary heart disease in six countries. *Journal of Cross-Cultural Psychology, 15,* 233–255.

Lindeman, M., Harakka, T., & Keltikangas-Jarvinen, L. (1997). Age and gender differences in adolescents' reactions to conflict situations: Aggression, prosociality, and withdrawal. *Journal of Youth and Adolescence, 26,* 339–351.

Linstone, H. A., & Turoff, M. (1975/2002). The Delphi method: techniques and applications. Retrieved from http://is.njit.edu/pubs/delphibook/, accessed February 17, 2015.

Lu, L., & Shih, J. B. (1997). Sources of happiness: A qualitative approach. *Journal of Social Psychology, 137,* 181–188.

Luft, J. (1984). *Group process: An introduction of group dynamics* (3rd ed.). Palo Alto, CA: Mayfield.

Lukens, J. (1978). Ethnocentric speech. *Ethnic Groups, 2,* 35–53.

Lumsden, G., & Lumsden, D. (1996). *Communicating in groups and teams* (2nd ed.). Belmont, CA: Wadsworth.

Lustig, M. W., & Koester, J. (2013). *Intercultural competence: Interpersonal communication across cultures* (7th ed.). Boston, MA: Allyn & Bacon.

Ma, K. (1996). *The modern Madame Butterfly: Fantasy and reality in Japanese cross-cultural relationships.* Rutland, VT: Charles E. Tuttle.

Mackey, R. A., Diemer, M. A., & O'Brien, B. A. (2000). Psychological intimacy in the lasting relationships of heterosexual and same-gender couples. *Sex Roles, 43,* 201–227.

MacLachlan, J. (1979). What people really think of fast talkers. *Psychology Today, 13,* 113–117.

MacMillan, D., & Lehman, P. (2007, November 15). Social networking with the elite. *Business Week.* Retrieved from www.businessweek.com.

Madon, S., Guyll, M., & Spoth, R. L. (2004). The Self-fulfilling prophecy as an intrafamily dynamic. *Journal of Family Psychology, 18,* 459–469.

Mahaffey, A. L., Bryan, A., & Hutchison, K. E. (2005, March). Using startle eye blink to measure the affective component of antigay bias. *Basic and Applied Social Psychology, 27,* 37–45.

Malandro, L. A., Barker, L., & Barker, D. A. (1989). *Nonverbal communication* (2nd ed.). New York: Random House.

Marano, H. E. (2003). Procrastination: Ten things to know. *Psychology Today.* Retrieved from http://www.psychologytoday.com/articles/200308/procrastination-ten-things-know, accessed on September 12, 2009.

Marsh, P. (1988). *Eye to eye: How people interact.* Topside, MA: Salem House.

Marshall, L. L., & Rose, P. (1987). Gender, stress and violence in the adult relationships of a sample of college students. *Journal of Social and Personal Relationships, 4,* 299–316.

Martin, G. N. (1998). Human electroencephalographic (EEG) response to olfactory stimulation: Two experiments using the aroma of food. *International Journal of Psychophysiology, 30,* 287–302.

Martin, M. M., & Anderson, C. M. (1993). Psychological and biological differences in touch avoidance. *Communication Research Reports, 10,* 141–147.

Martin, M. M., & Anderson, C. M. (1995). Roommate similarity: Are roommates who are similar in their communication traits more satisfied? *Communication Research Reports, 12,* 46–52.

Martin, M. M., & Rubin, R. B. (1998). Affinity-seeking in initial interactions. *Southern Communication Journal, 63,* 131–143.

Maslow, A. (1970). *Motivation and personality.* New York: HarperCollins.

Matsumoto, D. (1991). Cultural influences on facial expressions of emotion. *Southern Communication Journal, 56,* 128–137.

Matsumoto, D., & Kudoh, T. (1993). American-Japanese cultural differences in attributions of personality based on smiles. *Journal of Nonverbal Behavior, 17,* 231–243.

McBroom, W. H., & Reed, F. W. (1992). Toward a reconceptualization of attitude-behavior consistency. Special Issue. Theoretical advances in social psychology. *Social Psychology Quarterly, 55,* 205–216.

McCarthy, M. (2003, January). Talking back: "Small" interactional response tokens in everyday conversation. *Research on Language and Social Interaction, 36,* 33–63.

McCroskey, J. C. (2006). *An introduction to rhetorical communication* (9th ed.). Boston, MA: Allyn & Bacon.

McCroskey, J. C., & Wheeless, L. (1976). *Introduction to human communication.* Boston: Allyn & Bacon.

McDevitt, M., Kiousis, S., & Wahl-Jorgensen, K. (2003). Spiral of moderation: Opinion expression in computer-mediated discussion. *International Journal of Public Opinion Research, 15,* 454–470.

McDonald, E. J., McCabe, K., Yeh, M., Lau, A., Garland, A., & Hough, R. L. (2005). Cultural affiliation and self-esteem as predictors of internalizing symptoms among Mexican American adolescents. *Journal of Clinical Child and Adolescent Psychology, 34,* 163–171.

McGill, M. E. (1985). *The McGill report on male intimacy.* New York: Harper & Row.

McGinley, S. (2000). Children and lying. Retrieved from http://www.ag.arizona.edu/pubs/general/resrpt2000/childrenlying.pdf.

McGlone, M. S., & Giles, H. (2011). Language and interpersonal communication. In M. L. Knapp & J. A. Daly (Eds.), *The Sage handbook of interpersonal communication,* 4th ed. (pp. 201–238). Los Angeles, CA: Sage.

McKerrow, R. E., Gronbeck, B. E., Ehninger, D., & Monroe, A. H. (2000). *Principles and types of speech communication* (14th ed.). Boston: Allyn & Bacon.

McCroskey, J. C. (1998). *Why we communicate the ways we do: A communibiological perspective.* Boston: Allyn & Bacon.

McLain, G. (2011). Deadlier than war: Combating military suicides. In Larry Schnoor (Ed.), *Winning Orations* (pp. 21–23). Mankato, MN: Interstate Oratorical Association.

McNamee, S., & Gergen, K. J. (Eds.). (1999). *Relational responsibility: Resources for sustainable dialogue.* Thousand Oaks, CA: Sage.

McNatt, D. B. (2001). Ancient Pygmalion joins contemporary management: A meta-analysis of the result. *Journal of Applied Psychology, 85,* 314–322.

Mealy, M., Stephan, W., & Urritia, C. (2007). The acceptability of lies: A comparison of Ecuadorians and Euro-Americans. *International Journal of Intercultural Relations, 31,* 689–702.

Mehl, M. R., Vazire, S., Ramirez-Esparza, N., Slatcher, R. B., & Pennebaker, J. W. (2007, July). Are women really more talkative than men? *Science, 6,* 82.

Merton, R. K. (1957). *Social theory and social structure.* New York: Free Press.

Messick, R. M., & Cook, K. S. (Eds.). (1983). *Equity theory: Psychological and sociological perspectives.* New York: Praeger.

Metts, S., & Planalp, S. (2002). Emotional communication. In M. L. Knapp & J. A. Daly (Eds.), *Handbook of interpersonal communication* (3rd ed., pp. 339–373). Thousand Oaks, CA: Sage.

Midooka, K. (1990). Characteristics of Japanese style communication. *Media Culture and Society, 12,* 47–49.

Miller, G. R. (1978). The current state of theory and research in interpersonal communication. *Human Communication Research, 4,* 164–178.

Miller, G. R. (1990). Interpersonal communication. In G. L. Dahnke & G. W. Clatterbuck (Eds.), *Human communication: Theory and research* (pp. 91–122). Belmont, CA: Wadsworth.

Miller, G. R., & Parks, M. R. (1982). Communication in dissolving relationships. In S. Duck (Ed.), *Personal relationships: Vol. 4. Dissolving personal relationships.* New York: Academic Press.

Miller, L. R. (1997, December). Better ways to think and communicate. *Association Management, 49,* 71–73.

Moghaddam, F. M., Taylor, D. M., & Wright, S. C. (1993). *Social psychology in cross-cultural perspective.* New York: W. H. Freeman.

Molloy, J. (1981). *Molloy's live for success.* New York: Bantam.

Monin, B. (2003, December). The warm glow heuristic: When liking leads to familiarity. *Journal of Personality and Social Psychology, 85,* 1035–1048.

Montagu, A. (1971). *Touching: The human significance of the skin.* New York: Harper & Row.

Moon, D. G. (1996). Concepts of "culture": Implications for intercultural communication research. *Communication Quarterly, 44,* 70–84.

Moran, R. T., Harris, P. R., & Moran, S. V. (2010). *Managing cultural differences: Global leadership strategies for cross-cultural business success* (8th ed.). Butterworth-Heinemann.

Morreale, S. P., & Pearson, J. C. (2008, April). Why communication education is important: The centrality of the discipline in the 21st century. *Communication Education, 57,* 224–240.

Morrill, C. (1992). Vengeance among executives. *Virginia Review of Sociology, 1,* 51–76.

Morris, D. (1977). *Manwatching: A field guide to human behavior.* New York: Abrams.

Motley, M. T. (1990a). On whether one can(not) not communicate: An examination via traditional communication postulates. *Western Journal of Speech Communication, 54,* 1–20.

Motley, M. T. (1990b). Communication as interaction: A reply to Beach and Bavelas. *Western Journal of Speech Communication, 54,* 613–623.

Mottet, T., & Richmond, V. P. (1998). Verbal approach and avoidance items. *Communication Quarterly, 46,* 25–40.

Mullen, B., Salas, E., & Driskell, J. (1989). Salience, motivation, and artifact as contributions to the relation between participation rate and leadership. *Journal of Experimental Social Psychology, 25,* 545–559.

Mullen, B., Tara, A., Salas, E., & Driskell, J. E. (1994). Group cohesiveness and quality of decision making: An interaction of tests of the groupthink hypothesis. *Small Group Research, 25,* 189–204.

Mullen, C. A. (2005). *Mentorship primer.* New York: Peter Lang.

Myers, K. K., Siebold, D. R., & Park, H. S. (2011). Interpersonal communication in the workplace. In Knapp, M. L., & Daly, J. A. (Eds.), *The Sage handbook of interpersonal communication* (4th ed., pp. 527–562). Los Angeles, CA: Sage.

Myers, S. A., & Zhong, M. (2004). Perceived Chinese instructor use of affinity-seeking strategies and Chinese college student motivation. *Journal of Intercultural Communication Research, 33* (September–December), 119–130.

Napier, R. W., & Gershenfeld, M. K. (1989). *Groups: Theory and experience* (4th ed.). Boston: Houghton Mifflin.

Neher, W. W., & Sandin, P. (2007). *Communicating ethically.* Boston: Allyn & Bacon.

Neher, W. W., & Sandin, P. (2007). *Communicating ethically.* Boston, MA: Allyn & Bacon.

Nelson, P. E., Pearson, J. C., & Kurylo, A. (2008). Developing an intellectual communication. In S. Morreale & P. Arneson (Eds.), *Getting the most from your graduate education in communication: A student's handbook.* Washington, DC: National Communication Association.

Neugarten, B. (1979). Time, age, and the life cycle. *American Journal of Psychiatry, 136,* 887–894.

Neuliep, J. W., & Grohskopf, E. L. (2000). Uncertainty reduction and communication satisfaction during initial interaction: An initial test and replication of a new axiom. *Communication Reports, 13,* 67–77.

Neuliep, J. W., Chaudoir, M., & McCroskey, J. C. (2001). A cross-cultural comparison of ethnocentrism among Japanese and United States college students. *Communication Research Reports, 18,* 137–146.

Newport, F. (2007). Black or African American. Retrieved from www.gallup.com/poll/28816/Black-African-American.aspx?, accessed on May 5, 2012.

Ng, S. H., Loong, C. S. F., He, A. P., Liu, J. H., & Weatherall, A. (2000). Communication correlates of individualism and collectivism: Talk directed at one or more addressees in family conversations. *Journal of Language and Social Psychology, 19,* 26–45.

Nie, J., & Sundar, S. S. (2013). Who would pay for Facebook? Self esteem as a predictor of user behavior, identity construction and valuation of virtual possessions. In P. Kotzé et al. (Eds.), Proceedings of INTERACT 2013, Part III, LNCS 8119, 726–743.

Noble, B. P. (1994, August 14). The gender wars: Talking peace. *New York Times,* p. 21.

Noelle-Neumann, E. (1973). Return to the concept of powerful mass media. In H. Eguchi & K. Sata (Eds.), *Studies in broadcasting: An international annual of broadcasting science* (pp. 67–112). Tokyo: Nippon Hoso Kyokai.

Noelle-Neumann, E. (1980). Mass media and social change in developed societies. In G. C. Wilhoit & H. de Bock (Eds.), *Mass communication review yearbook* (Vol. 1, pp. 657–678). Thousand Oaks, CA: Sage.

Noelle-Neumann, E. (1991). The theory of public opinion: The concept of the spiral of silence. In J. A. Anderson (Ed.), *Communication yearbook* 14 (pp. 256–287). Thousand Oaks, CA: Sage.

Noller, P. (1993). Gender and emotional communication in marriage: Different cultures or differential social power? [Special issue: Emotional Communication, Culture, and Power.] *Journal of Language and Social Psychology, 12,* 132–152.

Noller, P., & Fitzpatrick, M. A. (1993). *Communication in family relationships.* Englewood Cliffs, NJ: Prentice-Hall.

nonverbal measures: Going beyond words (pp. 67–81). Mahwah, NJ: Lawrence Erlbaum.

Northouse, P. G. (1997). *Leadership: Theory and practice.* Thousand Oaks, CA: Sage.

O'Hair, D., Cody, M. J., & McLaughlin, M. L. (1981). Prepared lies, spontaneous lies, Machiavellianism, and nonverbal communication. *Human Communication Research, 7,* 325–339.

Obama, B. (2009). www.obamaspeeches.com.

Oberg, K. (1960). Cultural shock: Adjustment to new cultural environments. Practical Anthropology 7, 177–182.

Olson, E. (2006, April 6). Better not miss the buss. *New York Times,* pp. G1–G2.

Osborn, A. (1957). *Applied imagination* (Rev. ed.). New York: Scribner's.

Park, H. S., Levine, T. R., McCornack, S. A., Morrison, K., & Ferrara, M. (2002). How people really detect lies. *Communication Monographs, 69,* 144–157.

Parks, M. R. (2011). Social networks and the life of relationships. In M. L. Knapp & J. A. Daly (Eds.), *The Sage handbook of interpersonal communication* (4th ed., pp. 355–388). Los Angeles, CA: Sage.

Paul, A. M. (2001). Self-help: Shattering the myths. *Psychology Today, 34,* 60ff.

Pearson, J. C. (1993). *Communication in the family* (2nd ed.). Boston: Allyn & Bacon.

Pearson, J. C., & Spitzberg, B. H. (1990). *Interpersonal communication: Concepts, components, and contexts* (2nd ed.). Dubuque, IA: William C. Brown.

Pearson, J. C., West, R., & Turner, L. H. (1995). *Gender and communication* (3rd ed.). Dubuque, IA: William C. Brown.

Pei, M. (1978). *Weasel words: the art of saying what you don't mean.* New York: Harper & Row.

Pelham, A. M., & Kravitz, P. (2008). An exploratory study of the influence of sales training content and salesperson evaluation on salesperson adaptive selling, customer orientation, listening and consulting behaviors. *Journal of Strategic Marketing, 16,* 413–435.

Penfield, J. (Ed.). (1987). *Women and language in transition.* Albany, NY: State University of New York Press.

Pennebacker, J. W. (1991). *Opening up: The healing power of confiding in others.* New York: Morrow.

Peterson, C. C. (1996). The ticking of the social clock: Adults' beliefs about the timing of transition events. *International Journal of Aging and Human Development, 42,* 189–203.

Petty, R. E., & Wegener, D. T. (1998). Attitude change: Multiple roles for persuasion variables. In D. T. Gilbert, S. T. Fiske, & G. Lindzey (Eds.), *The handbook of social psychology* (4th ed., Vol. 1, pp. 323–390). New York: McGraw-Hill.

Pittenger, R. E., Hockett, C. F., & Danehy, J. J. (1960). *The first five minutes.* Ithaca, NY: Paul Martineau.

Place, K. S., & Becker, J. A. (1991). The influence of pragmatic competence on the likeability of grade school children. *Discourse Processes, 14,* 227–241.

Placencia, M. E. (2004). The online disinhibition effect. *Journal of Sociolinguistics, 8,* 215–245.

Plaks, J. E., Grant, H., & Dweck, C. S. (2005). Violations of implicit theories and the sense of prediction and control: Implications for motivated person perception. *Journal of Personality and Social Psychology, 88,* 245–262.

Pornpitakpan, C. (2003). The effect of personality traits and perceived cultural similarity on attraction. *Journal of International Consumer Marketing, 15,* 5–30.

Porter, R. H., & Moore, J. D. (1981). Human kin recognition by olfactory cues. *Physiology and Behavior, 27,* 493–495.

Pratkanis, A., & Aronson, E. (1991). *Age of propaganda: The everyday use and abuse of persuasion.* New York: W. H. Freeman.

Psychometrics. (2010). Warring egos, toxic individuals, feeble leadership. Retrieved from http://www.psychometrics.com/docs/conflictstudy_09.pdf, accessed on May 11, 2012.

Rainie, L., Purcell, K., Goulet, L. S., & Hampton, K. N. (2011). Social networking sites in our lives. Pew Research Center Publications (www.pewresearch.org).

Rancer, A. S. (1998). Argumentativeness. In J. C. McCroskey, J. A. Daly, M. M. Martin, & M. J. Beatty (Eds.), *Communication and Personality: Trait Perspectives* (pp. 149–170). Cresskill, NJ: Hampton Press.

Rancer, A. S., & Avtgis, T. A. (2006). *Argumentative and aggressive communication: Theory, research, and application.* Thousand Oaks, CA: Sage.

Rapsa, R., & Cusack, J. (1990). Psychiatric implications of tattoos. *American Family Physician, 41,* 1481–1486.

Raven, R., Centers, C., & Rodrigues, A. (1975). The bases of conjugal power. In R. E. Cromwell & D. H. Olson (Eds.), *Power in families* (pp. 217–234). New York: Halsted Press.

Read, A. W. (2004). Language revision by deletion of absolutisms. *ETC: A Review of General Semantics, 61,* 456–462.

Reardon, K. K. (1987). *Where minds meet: Interpersonal communication.* Belmont, CA: Wadsworth.

Reisman, J. M. (1979). *Anatomy of friendship.* Lexington, MA: Lewis.

Reisman, J. M. (1981). Adult friendships. In S. Duck & R. Gilmour (Eds.), *Personal relationships. 2: Developing personal relationships* (pp. 205–230). New York: Academic Press.

Richards, I. A. (1951). Communication between men: The meaning of language. In Heinz von Foerster (Ed.), *Cybernetics: Transactions of the Eighth Conference.* New York: Josiah Macy, Jr. Foundation.

Richards, I. A. (1968). The secret of "feedforward." *Saturday Review, 51* (February 3), 14–17.

Richmond, V. P., Davis, L. M., Saylor, K., & McCroskey, J. C. (1984). Power strategies in organizations: Communication techniques and messages. *Human Communication Research, 11,* 85–108.

Richmond, V. P., McCroskey, J. C., & Hickson, M. L. (2012). *Nonverbal behavior in interpersonal relations* (7th ed.). Boston: Allyn & Bacon.

Richmond, V. P., McCroskey, J. C., & McCroskey, L. L. (2005). *Organizational communication for survival: Making work, work.* Boston: Allyn & Bacon.

Richmond, V. P., Smith, R., Heisel, A., & McCroskey, J. C. (2001). Nonverbal immediacy in the physician/patient relationship. *Communication Research Reports, 18,* 211–216.

Richmond, V. P., Wrench, J. S., & McCroskey, J. C. (2013). *Communication: Apprehension, avoidance, and effectiveness* (6th ed.). Boston, MA: Pearson.

Richmond, V., McCroskey, J. C., & Hickson, M. (2012). *Nonverbal behavior in interpersonal relations,* 7th ed. Boston, MA: Allyn & Bacon.

Riggio, R. E. (1987). *The charisma quotient.* New York: Dodd, Mead.

Riggio, R. E., & Feldman, R. S. (Eds.). (2005). *Applications of nonverbal communication.* Mahwah, NJ: Lawrence Erlbaum.

Robbins, S. P., & Hunsaker, P. L. (2009). *Training in interpersonal skills* (5th ed.). Boston: Allyn & Bacon.

Rogers, C. (1970). *Carl Rogers on encounter groups.* New York: Harrow Books.

Rogers, C., & Farson, R. (1981). Active listening. In J. DeVito (Ed.), *Communication: Concepts and processes* (3rd ed., pp. 137–147). Upper Saddle River, NJ: Prentice-Hall.

Roisman, G. I., Clausell, E., Holland, A., Fortuna, K., & Elieff, C. (2008). Adult romantic relationships as contexts of human development: A multimethod comparison of same-sex couples with opposite-sex dating, engaged, and married dyads. *Developmental Psychology, 44*, 91–101.

Rokach, A. (1998). The relation of cultural background to the causes of loneliness. *Journal of Social and Clinical Psychology, 17*, 75–88.

Rokach, A., & Brock, H. (1995). The effects of gender, marital status, and the chronicity and immediacy of loneliness. *Journal of Social Behavior and Personality, 19*, 833–848.

Rollman, J. B., Krug, K., & Parente, F. (2000, April). The chat room phenomenon: Reciprocal communication in cyberspace. *Cyber-Psychology and Behavior, 3*, 161–166.

Roloff, M. E., & Chiles, B. W. (2011). Interpersonal conflict: Recent trends. In M. L. Knapp & J. A. Daly (Eds.), *The Sage handbook of interpersonal communication*, 4th ed. (pp. 423–442). Los Angeles, CA: Sage.

Rose, A. J., & Asher, S. R. (1999, January). Children's goals and strategies in response to conflicts within a friendship. *Developmental Psychology, 35*, 69–79.

Rosen, E. (1998, October). Think like a shrink. *Psychology Today*, 54–69.

Rosengren, A., Orth-Gomér, K., Wedel, H., & Wilhelmsen, L. (1993). Stressful life events, social support, and mortality in men born in 1933. *British Medical Journal* (October 1993), 1102. doi:10.1136/bmj.307.6912.1102.

Rosengren, A., et al. (1993). Stressful life events, social support, and mortality in men born in 1933. *British Medical Journal.*

Rosenthal, R. (2002). Covert communication in classrooms, clinics, courtroom, and cubicles. *American Psychologist, 57*, 839–849.

Rosenthal, R. (2002). The Pygmalion effect and its mediating mechanism. In J. Aronson (Ed.), *Improving academic achievement: Impact of psychological factors on education* (pp. 25–36). San Diego, CA: Academic Press.

Rosenthal, R., & Jacobson, L. (1992). *Pygmalion in the classroom: Teacher expectations and pupils' intellectual development* (Rev. ed.). Norwalk, CT: Crown House.

Rosh, L., & Offermann, L. (2013, October). Be yourself, but carefully: How to be authentic without oversharing. *Harvard Business Review* 91, 135–139.

Roth, P. L., Schleifer, L. L. F., & Switzer, F. S. (1995). Nominal group technique—An aid in implementing TQM. *The CPA Journal, 65*, 68–69.

Rubin, R. B., & McHugh, M. (1987). Development of parasocial interaction relationships. *Journal of Broadcasting and Electronic Media, 31*, 279–292.

Rubin, R. B., Fernandez-Collado, C., & Hernandez-Sampieri, R. (1992). A cross-cultural examination of interpersonal communication motives in Mexico and the United States. *International Journal of Intercultural Relations, 16*, 145–157.

Rubin, Z. (1973). *Liking and loving: An invitation to social psychology.* New York: Holt, Rinehart & Winston.

Sagrestano, L. M., Heavey, C. L., & Christensen, A. (2006). Individual differences versus social structural approaches to explaining demand-withdrawal and social influence behaviors. In K. Dindia & D. J. Canary (Eds.), *Sex differences and similarities in communication* (2nd ed., pp. 379–395). Mahwah, NJ: Lawrence Erlbaum.

Samovar, L. A., & Porter, R. E. (Eds.). (1991). *Communication between cultures.* Belmont, CA: Wadsworth.

Samovar, L. A., Porter, R. E., & McDaniel, E. R. (2011). *Intercultural communication: A reader* (13th ed). Thousand Oaks, CA: Wadsworth.

Samter, W., & Cupach, W. R. (1998). Friendly fire: Topics variations in conflict among same- and cross-sex friends. *Communication Studies, 49*, 121–138.

Sanders, J. A., Wiseman, R. L., & Matz, S. I. (1991). Uncertainty reduction in acquaintance relationships in Ghana and the United States. In S. Ting-Toomey & F. Korzenny (Eds.), *Cross-cultural interpersonal communication* (pp. 79–98). Thousand Oaks, CA: Sage.

Satir, V. (1983). *Conjoint family therapy* (3rd ed.). Palo Alto, CA: Science and Behavior Books.

Scandura, T. (1992). Mentorship and career mobility: An empirical investigation. *Journal of Organizational Behavior, 13*, 169–174.

Schaap, C., Buunk, B., & Kerkstra, A. (1988). Marital conflict resolution. In P. Noller & M. A. Fitzpatrick (Eds.), *Perspectives on marital interaction* (pp. 203–244). Philadelphia: Multilingual Matters.

Schafer, M., & Crichlow, S. (1996). Antecedents of groupthink. *Journal of Conflict Resolution, 40*, 415–435.

Schegloff, E. (1982). Discourses as an interactional achievement: Some uses of "uh huh" and other things that come between sentences. In Deborah Tannen (Ed.), *Georgetown University roundtable on language and linguistics* (pp. 71–93). Washington, DC: Georgetown University Press.

Scherer, K. R. (1986). Vocal affect expression. *Psychological Bulletin, 99*, 143–165.

Scheufele, D. A., & Moy, P. (2000). Twenty-five years of the spiral of silence: A conceptual review and empirical outlook. *International Journal of Public Opinion Research, 12*, 3–28.

Schnoor, L. G. (Ed.). (1997). *Winning orations of the interstate oratorical association.* Mankato, MN: Interstate Oratorical Association.

Schnoor, L. G. (Ed.). (1999). *Winning orations of the interstate oratorical association.* Mankato, MN: Interstate Oratorical Association.

Schnoor, L. G. (Ed.). (2000). *Winning orations of the interstate oratorical association.* Mankato, MN: Interstate Oratorical Association.

Schultz, B. G. (1996). *Communicating in the small group: Theory and practice* (2nd ed.). New York: HarperCollins.

Schwartz, E. (2005, February 28). Watch what you say. *InfoWorld, 27*, 8.

Schwartz, M., & Task Force on Bias-Free Language of the Association of American University Presses. (1995). *Guidelines for bias-free writing.* Bloomington: Indiana University Press.

Scott, M. L., & Lyman, S. M. (1968). Accounts. *American Sociological Review, 33*, 46–62.

Seiter, J. S. (2007, March). Ingratiation and gratuity: The effect of complimenting customers on tipping behavior in restaurants. *Journal of Applied Social Psychology, 37*, 478–485.

Seiter, J. S., & Sandry, A. (2003). Pierced for success? The effects of ear and nose piercing on perceptions of job candidates' credibility, attractiveness, and hirability. *Communication Research Reports, 20*, 287–298.

Sethna, B., Barnes, C. C., Brust, M., & Kay, L. (1999). E-mail communications in colleges and universities: Are they private? *Journal of Education for Business, 74*, 347–350.

Severin, W. J. & Tankard, J. W., Jr. (2001). *Communication theories: Origins, methods, and uses in the mass media.* Boston: Allyn & Bacon.

Shaw, M. E., & Gouran, D. S. (1990). Group dynamics and communication. In G. Dahnke & G. W. Clatterbuck (Eds.), *Human communication: Theory and research.* Belmont, CA: Wadsworth.

Shechtman, Z., Hiradin, A., & Zina, S. (2003). The impact of culture on group behavior: A comparison of three ethnic groups. *Journal of Counseling and Development, 81*, 208–216.

Shimanoff, S. (1980). *Communication rules: Theory and research.* Thousand Oaks, CA: Sage.

Shuter, R. (1990). The centrality of culture. *Southern Communication Journal, 55*, 237–249.

Siavelis, R. L., & Lamke, L. K. (1992). Instrumentalness and expressiveness: Predictors of heterosexual relationship satisfaction. *Sex Roles, 26*, 149–159.

Signorile, M. (1993). *Queer in America: Sex, the media, and the closets of power.* New York: Random House.

Singelis, T. M. (1994). The measurement of independent and interdependent self-construals. *Personality and Social Psychology Bulletin, 20*, 580–591.

Singh, N., & Pereira, A. (2005). *The culturally customized web site.* Oxford, England: Elsevier Butterworth-Heinemann.

Slade, M. (1995, February 19). We forgot to write a headline. But it's not our fault. *New York Times,* p. 5.

Smith, A. (2011). Why Americans use social media. Pew Research Center Publications (www .pewresearch.org).

Smith, M. H. (2003). Body adornment: Know the limits. *Nursing Management, 34*, 22–23.

Smith-Lovin, L., & Brody, C. (1989). Interruptions in group discussions: The effects of gender and group composition. *American Sociological Review, 54*, 424–435.

Smoreda, Z., & Licoppe, C. (2000). Gender-specific use of the domestic telephone. *Social Psychology Quarterly, 63*, 238–252.

Snyder, C. R. (1984). Excuses, excuses. *Psychology Today, 18*, 50–55.

Snyder, C. R., Higgins, R. L., & Stucky, R. J. (1983). *Excuses: Masquerades in search of grace.* New York: Wiley.

Snyder, M. (1992). A gender-informed model of couple and family therapy: Relationship enhancement therapy. *Contemporary Family Therapy: An International Journal, 14*, 15–31.

Solomon, G. B., Striegel, D. A., Eliot, J. F., Heon, S. N., et al. (1996). The self-fulfilling prophecy in college basketball: Implications for effective coaching. *Journal of Applied Sport Psychology, 8*, 44–59.

Song, I, LaRose, R., Eastin, M. S., & Lin, C. A. (2004, August). Internet gratifications Internet addiction: On the uses and abuses of new media. *CyberPsychology & Behavior, 7*, 384–394.

Sorenson, P. S., Hawkins, K., & Sorenson, R. L. (1995). Gender, psychological type and conflict style preferences. *Management Communication Quarterly, 9*, 115–126.

Spence, C. (2008). Sensing the future. Retrieved from www.aqr.org.uk/inbrief/document.shtml?doc=charles.spence.28-02-2008.fut.

Spitzberg, B. H., & Cupach, W. R. (1989). *Handbook of interpersonal competence research.* New York: Springer.

Spitzberg, B. H., & Cupach, W. R. (2011). Interpersonal skills. In M. L. Knapp & J. A. Daly(Eds.), *The Sage handbook of interpersonal communication*, 4th ed. (pp. 481–526). Los Angeles, CA: Sage.

Spitzberg, B. H., & Hecht, M. L. (1984). A component model of relational competence. *Human Communication Research, 10*, 575–599.

Sprecher, S. (1987). The effects of self-disclosure given and received on affection for an intimate partner and stability of the relationship. *Journal of Social and Personal Relationships, 4*, 115–127.

Sprecher, S., & Metts, S. (1989). Development of the "romantic beliefs scale" and examination of the effects of gender and gender-role orientation. *Journal of Social and Personal Relationships, 6*, 387–411.

Srivastava, K., & More, A. T. (2010). Some aesthetic considerations for over-the-counter (OTC) pharmaceutical products. *International Journal of Biotechnology, 11* (3/4): 267. doi:10.1504/IJBT.2010.036600.

Stafford, L. (2008). Social exchange theories. In L. A. Baxter & D. O. Braithwaite (Eds.), *Engaging theories in interpersonal communication: Multiple perspectives* (pp. 377–389). Los Angeles, CA: Sage.

Steil, L. K., Barker, L. L., & Watson, K. W. (1983). *Effective listening: Key to your success.* Reading, MA: Addison-Wesley.

Stein, M. M., & Bowen, M. (2003). Building a customer satisfaction system: Effective listening when the customer speaks. *Journal of Organizational Excellence, 22* (Summer), 23–34.

Stern, L. (2007). *What every student should know about avoiding plagiarism.* Boston: Pearson Education.

Stern, R., & Divecha, D. (2015, May/June). The empathy trap. *Psychology Today, 48*, 31–34.

Stewart, L. P., Cooper, P. J., & Stewart, A. D., with Friedley, S. A. (2003). *Communication and gender* (4th ed.). Boston: Allyn & Bacon.

Stewart, S. (2006, October). A pilot study of email in an e-mentoring relationship. *Journal of Telemedicine and Telecare, 12*, 83–85.

Stratford, J. (1998). Women and men in conversation: A consideration of therapists' interruptions in therapeutic discourse. *Journal of Family Therapy, 20*, 383–394.

Strom, D. (2006, April 5). I.M. generation is changing the way business talks. *New York Times*, p. D4.

Suler, J. (2004). The online disinhibition effect. *CyberPsychology and Behavior, 7*, 321–326.

Sunnafrank, M., & Ramirez, A. (2004). At first sight: Persistent relational effects of get-acquainted conversations. *Journal of Social and Personal Relationships, 21*, 361–379.

Tang, T. L., & Butler, E. A. (1997). Attributions of quality circles' problem-solving failure: Differences among management, supporting staff, and quality circle members. *Public Personnel Management, 26*, 203–225.

Tannen, D. (1990). *You just don't understand: Women and men in conversation.* New York: Morrow.

Tannen, D. (1994a). *Gender and discourse.* New York: Oxford University Press.

Tannen, D. (1994b). *Talking from 9 to 5: How women's and men's conversational styles affect who gets heard, who gets credit, and what gets done at work.* New York: Morrow.

Tannen, D. (2006). *You're wearing that? Understanding mothers and daughters in conversation.* New York: Random House.

Tardiff, T. (2001). Learning to say "no" in Chinese. *Early Education and Development, 12*, 303–323.

Tata, J. (2000). Toward a theoretical framework of intercultural account-giving and account evaluation. *International Journal of Organizational Analysis, 8*, 155–178.

Tersine, R. J., & Riggs, W. E. (1980). The Delphi technique: A long-range planning tool. In S. Ferguson & S. D. Ferguson (Eds.), *Intercom: Readings in organizational communication* (pp. 366–373). Rochelle Park, NJ: Hayden Books.

Thibaut, J. W., & Kelley, H. H. (1986). *The social psychology of groups.* New Brunswick, NJ: Transaction.

Thompson, C. A., & Klopf, D. W. (1991). An analysis of social style among disparate cultures. *Communication Research Reports, 8*, 65–72.

Thompson, C. A., Klopf, D. W., & Ishii, S. (1991). A comparison of social style between Japanese and Americans. *Communication Research Reports, 8*, 165–172.

Thorne, B., Kramarae, C., & Henley, N. (eds.). (1983). *Language, gender and society.* Rowley, MA: Newbury House.

Tierney, P., & Farmer, S. M. (2004). The Pygmalion process and employee creativity. *Journal of Management, 30*, 413–432.

Timmerman, L. J. (2002). Comparing the production of power in language on the basis of sex. In M. Allen & R. W. Preiss (Eds.), *Interpersonal communication research: Advances through meta-analysis* (pp. 73–88). Mahwah, NJ: Lawrence Erlbaum.

Ting-Toomey, S. (1981). Ethnic identity and close friendship in Chinese-American college students. *International Journal of Intercultural Relations, 5*, 383–406.

Ting-Toomey, S. (1985). Toward a theory of conflict and culture. *International and Intercultural Communication Annual, 9*, 71–86.

Tolhuizen, J. H. (1989). Communication strategies for intensifying dating relationships: Identification, use, and structure. *Journal of Social and Personal Relationships, 6*, 413–434.

Trager, G. L. (1958). Paralanguage: A first approximation. *Studies in Linguistics, 13*, 1–12.

Trager, G. L. (1961). The typology of paralanguage. *Anthropological Linguistics, 3*, 17–21.

Trower, P. (1981). Social skill disorder. In S. Duck & R. Gilmour (Eds.), *Personal relationships, Vol. 3* (pp. 97–110). New York: Academic Press.

Tyler, J. J., Feldman, R. S., & Reichert, A. (2006). The price of deceptive behavior: Disliking and lying to people who lie to us. *Journal of Experimental Social Psychology, 42,* 69–77.

Vainiomaki, T. (2004). Silence as a cultural sign. *Semiotica, 150,* 347–361.

Vangelisti, A. L. (2011). Interpersonal processes in romantic relationships. In M. L.Knapp, & J. A. Daly (Eds.), *The Sage handbook of interpersonal communication,* 4th ed. (pp. 597–622). Los Angeles, CA: Sage.

Varma, A., Toh, S. M, Pichler, S. (2006). Ingratiation in job applications: Impact on selection decisions. *Journal of Managerial Psychology, 21,* 200–210.

Veenendall, T. L., & Feinstein, M. C. (1995). *Let's talk about relationships: Cases in study* (2nd ed.). Prospect Heights, IL: Waveland Press.

Velting, D. M. (1999). Personality and negative expectations: Trait structure of the Beck Hopelessness Scale. *Personality and Individual Differences, 26,* 913–921.

Victor, D. (1992). *International business communication.* New York: HarperCollins.

Vonk, R. (2002). Self-serving interpretations of flattery: Why ingratiation works. *Journal of Personality and Social Psychology, 82,* 515–526.

Wallace, K. (1955). An ethical basis of communication. *Communication Education, 4,* 1–9.

Walster, E., Walster, G. W., & Berscheid, E. (1978). *Equity: Theory and research.* Boston: Allyn & Bacon.

Walther, J. B. (2011). Theories of computer-mediated communication and interpersonal relations. In M. L. Knapp & J. A. Daly (Eds.), *The Sage handbook of interpersonal communication,* 4th ed. (pp. 443–480). Los Angeles, CA: Sage.

Watkins, K. (2007). How much time do you spend listening? Retrieved from http://articles/webraydian.com/article4793-How_much_time_do_you_spend_listening.html, accessed on August 9, 2009.

Watzlawick, P. (1977). *How real is real? Confusion, disinformation, communication: An anecdotal introduction to communications theory.* New York: Vintage.

Watzlawick, P. (1978). *The language of change: Elements of therapeutic communication.* New York: Basic Books.

Watzlawick, P., Beavin, J., & Jackson, D. D. (1967). *Pragmatics of human communication: A study of interactional patterns, pathologies, and paradoxes.* New York: Norton.

Weathers, M. D., Frank, E. M., & Spell, L. A. (2002). Differences in the communication of affect: Members of the same race versus members of a different race. *Journal of Black Psychology, 28,* 66–77.

Weinberg, H. L. (1959). *Levels of knowing and existence.* New York: Harper & Row.

Wennerstrom, A., & Siegel, A. F. (2003). Keeping the floor in multiparty conversation: Intonation, syntax, and pause. *Discourse Processes, 36,* 77–107.

Wert, S. R., & Salovey, P. (2004). Introduction to the special issue on gossip. *Review of General Psychology, 8,* 76–77.

Westwood, R. I., Tang, F. F., & Kirkbride, P. S. (1992). Chinese conflict behavior: Cultural antecedents and behavioral consequences. *Organizational Development Journal, 10,* 13–19.

Wetzel, P. J. (1988). Are "powerless" communication strategies the Japanese norm? *Language in Society, 17,* 555–564.

Wheeless, L. R., & Grotz, J. (1977). The measurement of trust and its relationship to self-disclosure. *Human Communication Research, 3,* 250–257.

Whitty, M., & Gavin, J. (2001). Age/sex/location: Uncovering the social cues in the development of online relationships. *Cyber-Psychology and Behavior, 4,* 623–630.

Wigley, C. J., III. (1998). Verbal aggressiveness. In J. C. McCroskey, J. A. Daly, M. M. Martin, & M. J. Beatty (Eds.), *Communication and personality: Trait perspectives* (pp. 191–214). Cresskill, NJ: Hampton Press.

Wilkins, B. M., & Andersen, P. A. (1991). Gender differences and similarities in management communication: A meta-analysis. *Management Communication Quarterly, 5,* 6–35.

Willis, J., & Todorov, A. (2006). First impressions: Making up your mind after a 100-Ms Exposure to a Face. *Psychological Science, 17,* 592–598.

Wilson, S. R., & Sabee, C. M. (2003). Explicating communicative competence as a theoretical term. In *Handbook of communication and social interaction skills* (pp. 3–50), J. O. Greene & B. R. Burleson (eds.). Mahwah, NJ: Erlbaum.

Windy, D., & Constantinou, D. (2005). *Assertiveness step by step.* London: Sheldon Press.

Winquist, L. A., Mohr, C. D., & Kenny, D. A. (1998). The female positivity effect in the perception of others. *Journal of Research in Personality, 32,* 370–388.

Winters, J. (2009). Olfactory communication and mate choice. Retrieved from www.replicatedtypo.wordpress.com/2009/09/01/olfaction.

Witcher, S. K. (1999, August 9–15). Chief executives in Asia find listening difficult. *Asian Wall Street Journal Weekly,* p. 11.

Won-Doornink, M. (1985). Self-disclosure and reciprocity in conversation: A cross-national study. *Social Psychology Quarterly, 48,* 97–107.

Won-Doornink, M. (1991). Self-disclosure and reciprocity in South Korean and U.S. male dyads.

In S. Ting-Toomey & F. Korzenny (Eds.), *Cross-cultural interpersonal communication* (pp. 116–131). Newbury Park, CA: Sage.

Wood, J. T. (1994). *Gendered lives: Communication, gender, and culture.* Belmont, CA: Wadsworth.

Worthington, D. L., & Fitch-Hauser, M. E. (2012). *Listening: Processes, functions, and competency.* Boston: Allyn & Bacon.

Wrench, J. S., & McCroskey, J. C. (2003). A communibiological examination of ethnocentrism and homophobia. *Communication Research Reports, 20,* 24–33.

Wrench, J. S., McCroskey, J. C., & Richmond, V. P. (2008). *Human communication in everyday life: Explanations and applications.* Boston, MA: Allyn & Bacon.

Yau-fair Ho, D., Chan, S. F., Peng, S., & Ng, A. K. (2001). The dialogical self: Converging East–West constructions. *Culture and Psychology, 7,* 393–408.

Yousuf, M. I. (2007). Using experts' opinions through Delphi technique. Practical Assessment, Research & Evaluation 12. Retrieved from http://pareonline.net/getvn.asp?v=12&n=4, accessed on February 17, 2015.

Zaleski, Z., Cycon, A., & Kurc, A. (2001). Future time perspective and subjective well-being in adolescent samples. In P. Schmuck & K. M. Sheldon (Eds.), *Life goals and well-being: Towards a positive psychology of human striving* (pp. 58–67). Cambridge, MA: Hogrefe & Huber.

Zornoza, A., Ripoll, P., & Peiró, J. M. (2002, October). Conflict management in groups that work in two different communication contexts: Face-to-face and computer-mediated communication. *Small Group Research, 33,* 481–508.

Zuckerman, M., Klorman, R., Larrance, D. T., & Spiegel, N. H. (1981). Facial, autonomic, and subjective components of emotion: The facial feedback hypothesis versus the externalizer–internalizer distinction. *Journal of Personality and Social Psychology, 41,* 929–944.

Zunin, L. M., & Zunin, N. B. (1972). *Contact: The first four minutes.* Los Angeles, CA: Nash.

Credits

Text Credits

Page 9: Source: Rubin, R. B., Fernandez-Collado, C., & Hernandez-Sampieri, R. (1992). A cross-cultural examination of interpersonal communication motives in Mexico and the United States. International Journal of Intercultural Relations, 16, 145–157.

Pages 9–10: Source: Based on Bersin, 2013.

Page 15: Source: From TICB14, CH 3, P. 72.

Page 16: Source: Hofstede, G., Hofstede, G., & Minkov, M. (2010). Cultures and organizations: Software of the mind (3rd ed.). New York, NY: McGraw-Hill.

Page 17: Gudykunst, W. B., & Kim, Y. Y. (Eds.). (1992). Readings on communication with strangers: An approach to intercultural communication. New York: McGraw-Hill. Gudykunst, 1991.

Page 27: Source: From TICB 14, CH 10, P. 257.

Page 28: Source: Joseph Luft, Group Process: An Introduction to Group Dynamics, 3rd ed. Copyright © 1984. New York: McGraw-Hill. Reprinted by permission.

Page 30: Source: Based on Reasoner, 2010.

Page 36: Source: Based on Rosh & Offermann, 2013.

Page 40: Sources: Based on Merton, R. K. (1957). Social theory and social structure. New York: Free Press. Madon, S., Guyll, M., & Spoth, R. L. (2004). The Self-fulfilling prophecy as an intrafamily dynamic. Journal of Family Psychology, 18, 459–469.Tierney, P., & Farmer, S. M. (2004). The Pygmalion process and employee creativity. Journal of Management, 30, 413–432.

Page 41: Source: Asch, S. (1946). Forming impressions of personality. Journal of Abnormal and Social Psychology, 41, 258–290.

Page 45: Source: Based on Berger, C. R., & Bradac, J. J. (1982). Language and social knowledge: Uncertainty in interpersonal relations. London: Edward Arnold.; Gudykunst, W. (1993). Toward a theory of effective interpersonal and intergroup communication: An anxiety/uncertainty management (AUM) perspective. In R. L. Wiseman, (Ed.), Intercultural communication competence. Thousand Oaks, CA: Sage.; Brashers, D. E. (2007). A theory of communication and uncertainty management. In B. B. Whaley & W. Samter (Eds.), Explaining communication: Contemporary theories and exemplars (pp. 201–218). Mahwah, NJ: Lawrence Erlbaum.

Page 46: Source: Based on Martin & Rubin, 1998; Myers, S. A., & Zhong, M. (2004). Perceived Chinese instructor use of affinity-seeking strategies and Chinese college student motivation. Journal of Intercultural Communication Research 33 (September-December), 119–130.; W rench, J. S., McCroskey, J. C., & Richmond, V. P. (2008). Human communication in everyday life: Explanations and applications. Boston: Allyn & Bacon.

Page 81: Sources: Based on Pearson, J. C. (1993). Communication in the family (2nd ed.). Boston: Allyn & Bacon; Braithwaite, & Bylund, 2015.

Page 84: Source: Based on Penfield, J. (Ed.). (1987). Women and language in transition. Albany, NY: State University of New York Press.

Page 85: Source: Newport, F. (2007). Black or African American. Retrieved May 5, 2012, from www.gallup.com/poll/28816/Black-African-American.aspx?

Page 98: Sources: Based on Andersen, P. A. (2004). The complete idiot's guide to body language. New York: Penguin Group. Riggio, R. E., & Feldman, R. S. (Eds.). (2005). Applications of nonverbal communication. Mahwah, NJ: Lawrence Erlbaum.

Page 103: Source: Based on Malandro, L. A., Barker, L., & Barker, D. A. (1989). Nonverbal communication (2nd ed.). New York: Random House; Metts, S., & Planalp, S. (2002). Emotional communication. In M. L. Knapp & J. A. Daly (Eds.), Handbook of interpersonal communication (3rd ed., pp. 339–373). Thousand Oaks, CA: Sage.

Page 106: Source: Based on Altman, I. (1975). The environment and social behavior. Monterey, CA: Brooks/Cole.

Page 109: Sources: Based on Jones, S. (2005). The touchlog record: A behavioral communication measure. In V. Manusov (Ed.), The sourcebook of nonverbal measures: Going beyond words (pp. 67–81). Mahwah, NJ: Lawrence Erlbaum.

Jones, S., & Yarbrough, A. E. (1985). A naturalistic study of the meanings of touch. Communication Monographs, 52, 19–56

Page 112: Sources: Based on Burgoon, J., Guerrero, L., & Floyd, K. (2010). Nonverbal communication. Boston, MA: Allyn & Bacon; Guerrero, L. K., & Hecht, M. L. (Eds.). (2006). The nonverbal communication reader: Class and contemporary readings (3rd ed.). Prospect Heights, IL: Waveland Press; Pearson, J. C., West, R., &

Turner, L. H. (1995). Gender and communication (3rd ed.). Dubuque, IA: William C. Brown.

Page 114: Source: Based on Gonzalez, A., & Zimbardo, P. G. (1985). Time in perspective. Psychology Today, 19, 20–26.

Page 115: Source: From TICB 14, CH 5, P. 138

Pages 115–116: Sources: Based on Burgoon, J., Guerrero, L., & Floyd, K. (2010). Nonverbal communication. Boston, MA: Allyn & Bacon; Andersen & Bowman, 1999; DeVito, 2014

Page 132: Sources: Based on Mottet, T., & Richmond, V. P. (1998). Verbal approach and avoidance items. Communication Quarterly, 46, 25–40: Richmond, McCroskey, & Hickson, 2008

Pages 146–147: Source: Based on Reisman, J. M. (1979). Anatomy of friendship. Lexington, MA: Lewis; Reisman, J. M. (1981). Adult friendships. In S. Duck & R. Gilmour (Eds.), Personal relationships. 2: Developing personal relationships (pp. 205–230). New York: Academic Press.

Page 147: Sources: Based on Lee, J. A. (1976). The colors of love. New York: Bantam.Hendrick, C., & Hendrick, S. (1990). A relationship-specific version of the love attitudes scale. In J. W. Heulip (Ed.), Handbook of replication research in the behavioral and social sciences [Special issue]. Journal of Social Behavior and Personality, 5, 239–254

Page 148: Sources: Based on Fitzpatrick, M. A. (1983). Predicting couples' communication from couples' self-reports. In R. N. Bostrom (Ed.), Communication Yearbook 7 (pp. 49–82). Thousand Oaks, CA: Sage; Fitzpatrick, M. A. (1988). Between husbands and wives: Communication in marriage. Thousand Oaks, CA: Sage; Fitzpatrick, M. A. (1991). Sex differences in marital conflict: Social psychophysiological versus cognitive explanations. Text, 11, 341–364.

Page 155: Source: Satir, V. (1983). Conjoint family therapy (3rd ed.). Palo Alto, CA: Science and Behavior Books

Page 156: Source: TICB,Table 9.3, page 240

Page 162: Source: Psychometrics (2010). Warring egos, toxic individuals, feeble leadership. Retrieved May 11, 2012 from http://www.psychometrics.com/docs/conflictstudy_09.pdf

Page 165: Source: TICB14, CH 11, page 291

Page 166: Source: Blake, R. R., & Mouton, J. S. (1984). The managerial grid III (3rd ed.). Houston, TX: Gulf.

Page 167: Source: Based on Koerner, A. F., & Fitzpatrick, M. A. (2002, Fall). You never leave your family in a fight: The impact of family of origin of conflict behavior in romantic relationships. Communication Studies 53, 234–252.

Page 174: Sources: Avtgis, T., & Rancer, A. S. (Eds.) (2010). Arguments, aggression, and conflict: New directions in theory and research. Clifton, NJ: Routledge. Rancer, A. S., & Avtgis, T. A. (2006). Argumentative and aggressive communication: Theory, research, and application.Thousand Oaks, CA: Sage.

Pages 174–175: Sources: Rancer, A. S., & Avtgis, T. A. (2006). Argumentative and aggressive communication: Theory, research, and application.Thousand Oaks, CA: Sage. Infante, D. A. (1988). Arguing constructively. Prospect Heights, IL: Waveland Press.

Page 179: Sources: Beebe, S. A., & Masterson, J. T. (2012). Communicating in small groups: Principles and practices (10th ed.). Boston, MA: Allyn & Bacon.

Hofstrand, D. (2006). Retrieved from http://www.extension.iastate.edu; Kelly, 2006

Page 184: Source: TICB14, CH 4, P. 86

Page 186: Source: Bok, S. (1983). Secrets. New York: Vintage.

Pages 188-189: Source: Department of Health and Human Services (2006)

Page 189: Source: Kelly, P. K. (1994). Team decision-making techniques. Irvine, CA: Richard Chang Associates.

Page 191: Source: From James C. McCroskey, An Introduction to Rhetorical Communication, 9/e. Copyright © 2005 by Allyn & Bacon. Printed and electronically reproduced by permission of Pearson Education, Inc., Englewood Cliffs, New Jersey.

Pages 191–192: Source: Rogers, C. (1970). Carl Rogers on encounter groups. New York: Harrow Books.

Page 197: Source: Kenrick, D. T., Neuberg, S. L., and Cialdini, R. B. (2007). Social psychology: Goals in interaction (4th ed.). Boston: Allyn & Bacon.

Pages 198: Source: Bennis, W., & Nanus, B. (2003). Leaders: The strategies for taking charge. New York: Harper & Row.

Page 205: Source: TICB, CH 12, P. 310 Power distance

Page 211: Source: From James C. McCroskey, An Introduction to Rhetorical Communication, 9/e. Copyright © 2005 by Routledge, ISBN 978-0205453511. Reprinted by permission of Linda McCroskey.

Page 217: Source: King, 2015

Page 222: Source: King, 2015

Page 224: Source: Stern, L. (2007). What every student should know about avoiding plagiarism. Boston: Pearson Education.

Page 239: King, 2015.

Page 240: Source: Based on Molloy, J. (1981). Molloy's live for success. New York: Bantam.; Kleinke, C. L. (1986). Meeting and understanding people. New York: W. H. Freeman.; Johnson, C. E. (1987). An introduction to powerful and powerless talk in the classroom. Communication Education, 36, 167–172.; Dillard, J. P., & Marshall, L. J. (2003). Persuasion as a social skill. In J. O. Greene & B. R. Burleson (Eds.), Handbook of communication and social interaction skills (pp. 479–514).

Mahwah, NJ: Erlbaum.; Lakoff, R. (1975). Language and women's place. New York: Harper & Row.; Timmerman, L. J. (2002). Comparing the production of power in language on the basis of sex. In M. Allen & R. W. Preiss (Eds.), Interpersonal communication research: Advances through meta-analysis (pp. 73–88). Mahwah, NJ: Lawrence Erlbaum.

Page 241: Sources: Burgoon, J., Guerrero, L., & Floyd, K. (2010). Nonverbal communication. Boston, MA: Allyn & Bacon. DeVito, 2014

Page 243: Source: Kevin King (2015)

Page 243: Source: Clinton, H. (1995). Remarks to the U.N. 4th World Conference on Women Plenary Session. Retrieved May 9, 2012, from http://www.american rhetoric.com/speeches/hillaryclintonbeijingspeech .htm.

Page 243: Source: Bacon, K. (2011). More deadly than sticks and stones. In Larry Schnoor (Ed.), Winning Orations (pp. 104–106). Mankato, MN: Interstate Oratorical Association.

Page 244: Source: King, 2015

Page 244: Source: King, 2015

Page 244: Source: Obama, B. (2009). www.obamaspeeches .com.

Page 254: Source: McCroskey, J. C. (2006). An introduction to rhetorical communication (9th ed.). Boston, MA: Allyn & Bacon.

Page 265: Sources: Wallace, K. (1955). An ethical basis of communication. Communication Education, 4, 1–9. Johannesen, R. L., Valde, K. S., & Whedbee, K. E. (2007). Ethics in human communication (6th ed.). Prospect Heights, IL: Waveland.

Page 271: Source: King, 2015.

Page 274: Source: Barker, L., Edwards, R., Gaines, C., Gladney, K., & Holley, F. (1980). An investigation of proportional time spent in various communication activities by college students. Journal of Applied Communication Research, 8, 101–109.

Pages 279–283: "A lot of heart," by Blake Bergeron.

Page 290: Source: German, K., Gronbeck, B., Ehninger, D., & Monroe, A. H. (2013). Principles of public speaking (18th ed.). Boston, MA: Free Press.

Pages 298–299: Source: Based on Lee, A. M., & Lee, E. B. (1972). The fine art of propaganda. San Francisco: International Society for General Semantics., Lee, A. M., & Lee, E. B. (1995). The iconography of propaganda analysis. ETC: A Review of General Semantics, 52, 13–17.; Pratkanis, A., & Aronson, E. (1991). Age of propaganda: The everyday use and abuse of persuasion. New York: W. H. Freeman.; Herrick, J. A. (2004). Argumentation: Understanding and shaping arguments. State College, PA: Strata.

Page 300: MASLOW, ABRAHAM H.; FRAGER, ROBERT D. .; FADIMAN, JAMES, MOTIVATION AND PERSONALITY, 3rd Ed., ©1987. Adapted and Electronically reproduced by permission of Pearson Education, Inc., New York, NY.

Page 302: Source: Kiel, 2015

Page 303: Source: An Excellent Persuasive Speech by Farrah Bara from the University of Texas at Austin

Photo Credits

Cover: Kenneth Munzlinger/Getty Images; Page 1: Todor Rusinov/Fotolia; 2, David Sipress/The New Yorker Collection/The Cartoon Bank; 4, David Malan/Getty Images; 6, racorn/Shutterstock; 10, Peathegee Inc/Getty Images; 11, Peter C. Vey/The New Yorker Collection/The Cartoon Bank; 16, Hill Street Studios/Getty Images; 19, Ramiro Olaciregui/Getty Images; 25, Hero Images/Getty Images; 32, JGI/Tom Grill/Getty Images; 33, William Haefeli/The New Yorker Collection/The Cartoon Bank; 34, Ezra Bailey/Getty Images; 36, image100 Business/Alamy; 41, Pixellover RM 9/Alamy; 42, Baloo-Rex May/CartoonStock.com; 44, Ampyang/Fotolia; 54, Tim Robberts/Getty Images; 55, William Haefeli/The New Yorker Collection/The Cartoon Bank; 56, Stephen Stickler/Getty Images; 57, Everett Collection; 61, Charles Barsotti/The New Yorker Collection/The Cartoon Bank; 63, Robert Morris/Alamy; 64, Chris Batson/Alamy; 69, Creatista/Shutterstock; 73, Shutter_M/Shutterstock; 74, Chris Wildt/CartoonStock.com; 77, Tetra Images/Getty Images; 83, Peter Steiner/New Yorker Cartoon Bank/The Cartoon Bank; 85, Steve Parkins/Demotix/Corbis; 87, Caiaimage/Sam Edwards/Getty Images; 91, Andrew Walters/Alamy; 95, Julian Stratenschulte/dpa/Corbis; 99, Heike Kampe/Getty Images; 102, Joson//Getty Images; 103, Chris Wildt/CartoonStock.com; 106, FancyVeerSet4/Alamy; 108, Tim PannellAlamy; 112, SeaJustice/Alamy; 116, Chris Wildt/CartoonStock.com; 124, Cultura RM/Natalie Faye/Getty Images; 128, David R. Frazier Photolibrary, Inc./Alamy; 131, Javier Larrea/AGE Fotostock; 135, Copyright 2004 by Randy Glasbergen www.glasbergen.com; 135, Flirt/Alamy; 136, ColorBlind Images/Getty Images; 140, scottchan/Fotolia; 142, oshepkov/Fotolia; 147, David Sipress/The New Yorker Collection/The Cartoon Bank; 146, Queerstock, Inc./Alamy; 149, John Morris/CartoonsStock.com; 151, Studiovespa/Fotolia; 153, PhotoInc/Getty Images; 160: Jamie Grill/JGI/Blend Images/Getty Images; 162: Hill Street Studios/Blend Images/Getty Images; 163: David Sipress/The New Yorker Collection/The Cartoon Bank; 164: Chris Rout/Bubbles Photolibrary/Alamy; 167: Stu's Views, www.stus.com; 172: SFM Stock 4/Alamy; 174: Tetra Images/Alamy; 177: Chris Batson/Alamy; 178: Jalapeno/Cultura Exclusive//Getty Images; 179: Peter C. Vey/The New Yorker Colection/The Cartoon Bank;

Index